Teacher's Edition

NEW SECOND EDITION

A·LM ®

SPANISH

LEVEL ONE

HARCOURT BRACE JOVANOVICH, INC.

New York   Chicago   San Francisco

Atlanta   Dallas

Introduction

1. Background Notes on the Second Edition

The past decade has brought significant changes in modern foreign language curriculum practice. But the roots of change go back even further. In the 1950's, scholarly groups, notably the Modern Foreign Language Association, pointed to the need for new materials and new methods, and engaged in pioneering efforts to develop them. Dr. James B. Conant, in his influential report on American schools (1957), helped clarify the problem by his statement on objectives. "The main purpose of studying a foreign language is to obtain something approaching a mastery of that language," he said. "And by a mastery is surely meant the ability to read the literature published in the language and, in the case of a modern language, to converse with considerable fluency and accuracy with an inhabitant of the country in question."

That broad objective implied the central concerns of the reform movement: (1) A redefinition of the objectives of foreign language study in high school, involving a commitment to the development of the four communication skills: listening, speaking, reading, and writing, in that order, and with particular emphasis on oral-aural competence. (2) The need for longer sequences of study; especially, the need for widespread availability of third- and fourth-year programs in the schools, with appropriate materials. (3) A new approach to methods of teaching and learning.

This, then, is the background of the First Edition of the A-LM program, Levels One through Four in French, German, Russian, and Spanish.[1] The program, published in 1965, has not only been widely used, but has also been widely influential.

2. Objectives of the Second Edition

Because the First Edition was, in a sense, experimental, unusual care was taken to note and consider the strengths and weaknesses of the program in actual classroom use. The Second Edition, of which Level One is published in 1969, reflects that concern. There are significant improvements in the program, explained in the following sections of this Teacher's Edition. Yet the spirit of the program and the main strands of its fabric have proven sound, and they remain. The long-range objectives of the Second Edition are the same as those of the First Edition. They are reflected in the level of proficiency which an A-LM student should have attained at the end of four levels of study.

[1] Levels One and Two in Italian were also developed and published at this time.

Listening Comprehension: He should understand an educated native speaking at normal speed, either in a relatively formal situation, as in a classroom or lecture hall, or under normal conditions of conversation.

Speaking: He should speak with a pronunciation and intonation acceptable to a native speaker, with grammatical accuracy, and with adequate fluency. He should be able to participate in a conversation or group discussion as well as speak at some length when a situation calls for it.

Reading: He should be able to read newspapers, magazines, and most non-technical contemporary writing with comprehension and be prepared to begin reading literature from periods other than his own.

Writing: He should be able to write correctly anything he can say. In addition, he should be aware of and observe the conventions which distinguish formal writing from informal spoken language. He should be able to write two or three pages on a topic within his experience in a style acceptable to a native speaker.

Culture: He should also have acquired a sensitivity to the value system and behavior patterns of the people whose language he is studying. If he ever has the opportunity to live among those people, he should be able to participate in their culture as a knowledgeable and sympathetic outsider.

3. Modifications

Experience in classrooms has shown that the audio-lingual approach to language teaching—the basis of A-LM—does indeed achieve effective results. Comments from teachers using the First Edition made clear, however, that modifying certain pedagogical approaches of the First Edition would strengthen the program and lead to even more effective language teaching. The Second Edition of Level One has been prepared in the light of both practical classroom experience and theoretical advances made in the fields of linguistics and the psychology of learning.

The most significant modifications in the Second Edition are outlined in the following pages.

PRE-READING PERIOD

In recent years, some educators have attached a great deal of importance to a lengthy pre-reading period of instruction. They have felt that the more this period was prolonged, the less the student's pronunciation would suffer from the interference of written symbols when the written language was finally introduced. There has, however, been no substantive evidence to support that theory. Many teachers have found that interference is not lessened by postponing the introduction of reading and that a *lengthy* pre-reading period is neither necessary nor desirable. In view of this, no provision has been made in the Second Edition for a lengthy pre-reading period. Although the basic material in all units is to be presented first audio-lingually, only Unit 1—which introduces the sounds of Spanish—is to be taught entirely audio-lingually before the students receive their books.

PRONUNCIATION

The treatment of pronunciation is more systematic and more complete than in the First Edition. Unit 1 is devoted almost entirely to phonology. It is designed to point out the most significant distinctions between the sound system of the foreign language and that of English. This unit consists of a large number of listening and pronunciation exercises, and a series of short dialogs which the students are required to memorize. Practice on pronunciation is continued in the Listening and Speaking Exercises of each subsequent unit.

MEMORIZATION Language learning cannot take place without a certain amount of memorization. However, if memorization is not supported by comprehension and the ability to manipulate, it is of little use. In the Second Edition, the emphasis has been placed more on the students' ability to *use* the new material than on their ability to recite it.

USE OF ENGLISH The problem of the use of English in the foreign language classroom has been debated for many years. Some teachers attempt to exclude it completely. Others, aware that it cannot be ignored, have learned how to use it to advantage. The authors of the Second Edition feel that if English is used judiciously and sparingly, it is a tool which can contribute to the language learning process.

English is used in the Level One textbook to help the students remember the meaning of the Basic Dialog and Supplement when they study the material at home. (In presenting these same sections in class, you may choose to minimize the use of English by using the Dialog and Supplement Posters which are available as part of the program.) English is also used in the Presentation and Generalization sections of the student textbook, which are intended exclusively for home study. In class, English is used in the Teacher Presentation of each new structure. It is also used in the English Cue Drills to contrast an idiom or construction in English and the foreign language.

PRESENTATION OF GRAMMAR As in the First Edition, Level One includes structure drills and generalizations which focus on particular points of grammar. Experience has shown that extensive drilling of structure plays an important part in the total language learning process and that no amount of explanation of a grammatical pattern can take the place of this practice. But it has also become clear that drilling grammar without any previous explanation can frustrate the students, and that it is more efficient to lead them to an understanding of the grammatical principle before beginning extensive drill practice.

The teacher will find suggestions on how to introduce each new structure in a section beginning on page T10. In these Teacher Presentations a series of questions guides the students to "discover" the grammatical principles which they are about to apply. After the presentation, the teacher proceeds immediately to the related structure drills. Only after a sufficient amount of drill in class are the Presentation and Generalization in the student textbook assigned for study at home.

LISTENING COMPREHENSION Understanding the spoken word is a basic objective in foreign language learning. The Listening and Speaking Program, a new feature in Level One of the Second Edition, includes listening comprehension exercises specifically designed to train the students in this skill. These exercises, which are to be used with each unit, take a variety of forms to both interest and challenge the students. For a complete description of the format and use of the Listening and Speaking program, see page T14.

SPEAKING The sequential development of the speaking skill is more controlled than in the First Edition. Each unit contains many activities intended to increase the students' speaking ability. Some are controlled in scope, for example, drill work on pronunciation, practice with the Basic Dialog and Supplement, and manipulation of structure in elementary drills. Others are designed to lead the students toward a more spontaneous and "personal" kind of communication. For example, a student is asked to respond to a personalized question (Free Response), to produce several new sentences based on an original one (Free Substitution), to react to remarks or questions from another student (Directed Drills), or to give a response to a remark made by the teacher (Rejoinders). In addition, the Recombination Material at the end of each unit is organized to prepare the students to participate in a short natural conversation (Conversation Stimulus). All of these activities take place, of course, within the framework of familiar structure and vocabulary.

READING   Reading is begun earlier than in the First Edition, and the development of the reading skill is more systematic.

The students first see the printed word after Unit 1 has been taught audio-lingually, after about five days. At that point, they read the dialogs and some of the exercises they have been working with in class.

Beginning with Unit 2, there is only a minimal time lag between the audio-lingual presentation and the reading of the same material. The students are expected to study at home everything that has been presented to them orally: Basic Dialog, Supplement, Structure Drills, and Recombination Material. In addition to their studying of "learned" material, they read Recombination Dialogs as early as Unit 2 and Recombination Narratives beginning with Unit 6.

Special reading lessons have also been provided to teach the students what sounds certain letters or letter combinations represent. These lessons appear in the Letter-Sound Correspondences section at the end of Units 2, 3, 4, 5, 6, 7, and 10.

WRITING   Writing practice has been considerably increased in the Second Edition. It ranges from copying in preparation for dictation to the rewriting of simple dialogs and paragraphs. For a more complete description of the writing exercises, see pp. T16–T17.

CULTURE   Culture is the sum total of the beliefs and behavior of a people, and culture, in this anthropological sense, is best reflected by language. Thus, a major emphasis has been placed on the appropriate use of language in culturally authentic situations.

Further insight into culture is provided by the many illustrations throughout the text and by an 18-page, full-color pictorial section. This section gives the students an idea of what the Spanish-speaking world looks like, what Spanish and Spanish-American homes are like, where Spanish-speaking people receive their education, how they make a living, and how they spend their leisure time. As the name of this section—*Glimpses of the Spanish World*—suggests, this "pictorial essay" is in no way a comprehensive study of the lives of Spanish-speaking people, but rather a modest attempt to introduce the students to the people whose language they are learning.

Note on Vocabulary and Usage. Because it is spoken in so many different countries, Spanish presents particular problems in terms of vocabulary and usage. Throughout this program, an effort has been made to include constructions and lexical items widely used and understood throughout the Spanish-speaking world. Special care has been taken to choose expressions which reflect current usage. (For example, the definite article is omitted before names of countries; **jugar fútbol** replaces the traditionally taught **jugar al fútbol**.) Extreme regionalisms have been avoided, and the language, in all cases, is that of educated speakers.

4. Components of the Program

The material in the Second Edition of A-LM Spanish Level One has been planned as the beginning of a sequential four-year program and may be used with any class in a junior or senior high school. Most classes which meet daily for a period of not less than 45 minutes should be able to complete this material in one academic year. A-LM Level One is a complete, teaching program. Following is a list of its components.

STUDENT TEXTBOOK

The Student Textbook consists of 15 two-week units illustrated throughout with full-color photographs. It also includes a full-color pictorial section on the Spanish-speaking world, an appendix with model Response Forms for Listening Exercises, a Spanish-English Vocabulary, and a Grammatical Index.

EXERCISE BOOK

Part I of the Exercise Book lists all the Listening and Speaking Exercises of the recorded program and contains the necessary Response Forms for the student (see also p. T15). Part II includes writing exercises to supplement those in the student textbook (see p. T16).

STUDENT PRACTICE RECORD SET

The Student Practice Record Set (also called "Take-Home Disks") contains the Basic Dialog and Supplement of each unit. It is designed for use by the individual student at home (see p. T20).

STUDENT TEST BOOKLET

The Student Test Booklet contains answer forms for the listening-reading-writing test to be administered after each unit beginning with Unit 2, a mid-term test (after Unit 7), and a final test (after Unit 15). It also includes score sheets for the speaking tests to be used by the teacher.

TEACHER MATERIALS

TEACHER'S EDITION

The Teacher's Edition, which correlates all the A-LM materials, serves as the keystone of the entire program. The first part describes the concepts of A-LM, the components of the Level One program, unit organization, and suggested procedures. It also contains an inventory of Pronunciation Exercises, the script of the Listening and Speaking Exercises, suggestions on how to teach Unit 1, and detailed suggested Teacher Presentations for every point of structure.

The second part reproduces the entire student textbook with annotations, which correlate—item by item—the visual materials, recorded materials, and extra written materials with the student textbook. Answers are given for those exercises without answers in the student textbook, and variations of structure drills are frequently suggested.

CUE CARDS

The Cue Cards reproduce the Dialogs, Supplements, and Structure Drills as they appear in the Teacher's Edition, i.e., with responses to drills, suggestions for drill variations, and references to visual materials.

DIALOG POSTERS

The Dialog Posters (13″ x 16″) illustrate the Basic Dialogs. They may be used to introduce and review the Basic Dialogs. (The annotated part of this book lists the identification number of each poster at the end of the line it illustrates.)

The Supplement Posters ($8\frac{1}{2}''$ x 11'') illustrate specific items in the Supplement of each unit, plus items from the Basic Dialogs of Unit 1. (Again, the annotated part of this book lists the identification number of each poster at the end of the line in which the item appears.) The posters are arranged by unit, but are also identified by category for the teacher who may want to review all the items relating to a particular topic. A symbol at the top of each poster identifies its category.

The Classroom/Laboratory Tape and Record Sets include (1) Basic Dialogs, (2) Supplements, (3) those Structure Drills that are marked in the text with a tape symbol, (4) a few additional Structure Drills, printed in the Teacher's Edition only, and (5) the Listening and Speaking Exercises. The Dialogs and Narratives of the Recombination Material have also been recorded and are included in each set. The recordings are available in three forms, each of which contains the same material: (1) a full-track tape set, (2) a two-track tape set, and (3) a 12-inch record set. For further details on the format and use of the recorded program, see p. T22.

The Teacher's Test Manual reproduces the Student Test Booklet and contains, in addition, the text of the recorded portions of each test, an answer key, and a guide to scoring. It also includes an explanation of the relationship of the tests to the entire program and suggests ways to conduct the tests in the language laboratory or the classroom. (The listening and speaking portions of each test have been recorded and are available in a separate Testing Tape Set.)

The Level One student textbook and Practice Record Set have been divided for sequential use in the seventh and eighth grades. The Set A Textbook includes Units 1–7, the pictorial section, Response Forms for the Listening and Speaking Exercises for Units 1–7, a Spanish-English Vocabulary, and a Grammatical Index. The Set A Practice Record Set includes seven 7-inch disks for the first seven units.

   The Set B Textbook includes Units 7–15, the pictorial section, Response Forms for the Listening and Speaking Exercises for Units 7–15, and the complete Level One Spanish-English Vocabulary and Grammatical Index. The Set B Practice Record Set includes nine 7-inch disks for Units 7–15.

See p. T215.

5. General Classroom Procedures

Achievement in a foreign language program depends on a number of factors, among which is the students' complete understanding of what you are attempting to do, and why and how you plan to do it. With this in mind, you may want to outline for your class the objectives of the course and the procedures you will follow. The following are some points you may want to make in your orientation.

1. Competence in a language involves four skills of communication: listening, speaking, reading, and writing. Learning a language means acquiring all four of them.
2. The first step in learning a foreign language is to become thoroughly familiar with the sounds of the language, i.e., to develop the listening and speaking skills. Perfecting these skills requires a great deal of practice and the kind of effort involved is different from the kind required in practically any other subject. Master-

ing a foreign language is something like learning to play a musical instrument: it is a matter of developing a new set of reflexes. Success will depend upon practice, correction, and more practice.

3. The students will learn short dialogs and sentences in the foreign language by imitating you or the recorded voices of native speakers. Through this imitation they will learn new words and new ways of putting words together to form sentences. The speech they will hear and will be expected to reproduce will always be spoken at the same speed as that of a native speaker. They will be expected to know the meaning of everything they learn.

4. The students will be taught the structure—or grammar—of the language, and each point of grammar will be practiced in special drills. Once they have learned a number of vocabulary items and structural patterns, they will be able to recombine them to fit new situations.

5. The students will also develop the skills of reading and writing. Just as they have to guard against producing English rather than Spanish sounds when speaking the foreign language, they will have to learn not to assign English values to the familiar letters of the alphabet when reading Spanish words.

INTRODUCING
NEW MATERIAL

When introducing new material, walk around the classroom so that all students can see and hear you. Model each new utterance several times at normal speed, remembering that gestures and facial expressions can often be of use in making meaning clear and in helping to recall a dialog line or to cue a response. If a sentence is too long for students to remember at first hearing, it is helpful to practice it in partials. If a word or phrase proves difficult, it should be practiced first in syllables. However, after the students have repeated the individual syllables or words, be sure to put the utterance together again and have them repeat it at normal speed.

ELICITING
STUDENT
RESPONSES

It is helpful to establish a signaling system with your class early in the course by which a particular gesture will always call for a particular kind of response. Some of the different kinds of responses are described below. They are usually most effective when used in combination.

Full-Choral Repetition. Give the utterance at normal speed, and indicate that the whole class is to repeat it. Train the class to speak in unison at a normal rhythm and to imitate you as closely as possible. It is best not to repeat with the class. Repeating with the students prevents you from hearing their mistakes and tends to make them dependent upon your participation.

Part-Choral Repetition. Divide the class into sections and have each section repeat the line. A section may consist of half the class, all the boys or all the girls, or individual rows of students. This technique is particularly useful when practicing the different roles in a new dialog.

Individual Repetition. During the practice with full-choral and part-choral repetition, ask individual students to repeat a single line. This helps to pinpoint difficulties and to maintain the students' attention.

Double Repetition. Occasionally, you may want to ask an individual student to repeat a full or partial utterance twice in quick succession. Some teachers feel that this double repetition establishes a firm acoustical image of the sequence of syllables and of the accent and melody of the utterance.

When a student makes a mistake, call on other students to supply the correct response and ask the original student to repeat it. If he continues to have difficulty, do not persist too long in the correction. Remember to work on it again with him, perhaps after class. If several students seem to be having difficulty with the same point, you may want to have the whole class repeat the correct answer.

6. Unit Organization and Teaching Suggestions

BASIC DIALOG
AND SUPPLEMENT

Format.   Except for Unit 1, all units begin with a Basic Dialog. Each dialog is eight to ten lines long and is divided into two parts. The language is standard, contemporary speech, and each dialog, while culturally authentic, depicts a situation with which American students can easily identify.

The Supplement introduces additional lexical items in sentences which are related to, and sometimes taken directly from, the dialog. It is divided into two parts, each of which corresponds to a section of the dialog.

Mastery of the Basic Dialog and Supplement is the first step in learning the material of a new unit. All lines should be introduced and drilled in class before the students are asked to study them at home. The English equivalent of each Dialog and Supplement line appears on the same page. Where further clarification is necessary, a literal translation is given in parentheses. This is not to encourage translation, but to make sure that the meaning of each line is clear to the students when they are studying by themselves.

Presentation.   During the initial classroom presentation of the Basic Dialog, students should not refer to their textbooks. They should devote their full attention to the material being presented and drilled orally—to its meaning, pronunciation, intonation, and rhythm.

The first step in introducing a new dialog is to establish context and meaning. This is probably best done by presenting the entire dialog first in English, then in Spanish. Visual aids can be very helpful at this stage; the Dialog Posters have been designed with this in mind. Meaning will be established more quickly if you use the same gestures and visual aids in presenting both the English and the Spanish.

Once you have "set the scene" with the initial presentation, begin intensive practice of the first part of the dialog. Work with this material one line at a time, breaking it down into partial utterances whenever necessary. Use all of the techniques previously described to elicit student responses. It is a good idea to move around the room during group recitation in order to hear individual students. Try to be sure that the entire class is involved and that all students are imitating you as accurately as possible. You may want to use the native voices on the tape or record as the model.

After sufficient practice with the first part of the dialog, introduce the corresponding part of the Supplement. The Supplement lines should not be taught in isolation as a random list of sentences. Give the dialog line that is most closely related to the one in the Supplement, and then introduce the new line. Meaning can be made clear either by giving the English equivalent of the new line or by using visual aids, such as the Supplement Posters. With some lines, a gesture may be enough to convey meaning.

The same techniques should be used in presenting and drilling the Supplement as for the Basic Dialog. It is suggested that no more than ten minutes at a time be spent on the presentation and repetition of new lines from the Basic Dialog and Supplement. Vary your class activities by using the appropriate material from the Vocabulary Exercises section (see p. T10). It will help to reinforce learning if you come back to the Basic Dialog and Supplement just before the end of the class period. Have the students repeat the lines after you, following along in their books. Then have them repeat the same material once again with books closed.

Assignment and Review.   Students should have had enough classroom practice to be able to complete the learning of the Basic Dialog and Supplement on their own.

Assign the first part of the dialog to be learned at home, along with the appropriate part of the Supplement. Impress upon your students the necessity of understanding the meaning of the lines they are learning, and make it very clear that they are expected to return to class the next day having mastered the new material.

The home learning process will be greatly facilitated for any student who has the Take-Home Disks. He should first work with the disk with his book closed, until he has mastered the pronunciation and rhythm of the new lines. At that point, he should open his book and read along as he listens.

The following day in class, some time should be spent reviewing the assigned material. You may want to begin by having the entire class repeat after you in chorus; then call for rapid part-choral and individual repetition of the lines. Or you may want to take one role in the dialog and have individual students take the other. But the most revealing check on whether the students have done their assignment will be the way they respond as you proceed to the Vocabulary Exercises.

The above suggestions refer to the first part of the Basic Dialog and Supplement. The second part can be introduced and taught in the same way on the following day.

READING NOTES   *Format.*   In Unit 1, Reading Notes follow each dialog. In Units 2 and 3, they follow the Supplement. These notes are intended to help the students without the Take-Home Disks remember how certain words in the Basic Dialog and Supplement were pronounced in class, or, occasionally, to point out a special feature of Spanish punctuation.

Presentation.   There should be no need to present the Reading Notes in class. However, since they do include the words and word combinations which are likely to give the students the most difficulty when they are studying alone, it might be a good idea to devote extra attention to those words in class. The first time the Reading Notes occur, explain to your students that the notes are for their reference. (A list of the phonetic symbols used in these notes appears on p. 356 of the student text.)

BASIC FORMS LIST   *Format.*   Beginning with Unit 3, the Supplement is followed by a Basic Forms list. This list identifies the new words from the Basic Dialog and Supplement that belong to a category that the students are familiar with. For example, after regular **a-**class verbs have been presented, the new verbs in each subsequent unit which belong to that class appear in the Basic Forms list. After gender has been treated, the new nouns (except those which end in a gender marker) in each subsequent unit are listed in this section with a gender indication. Once a new word has been identified as belonging to a familiar class, the students should be able to use it—and all its forms—as part of their active vocabulary. The Basic Forms list also includes new verbs, preceded by an asterisk, whose forms will be explained in the unit, and adjectives other than those ending in **o.**

T9

Presentation. The student will acquire basic information about many lexical items from the form in which they appear in the Basic Dialog or Supplement. However, it is still good teaching practice to systematically present and practice the gender of new nouns and the forms of new verbs and adjectives. Such presentation should be done after the Basic Dialog and Supplement have been learned, or as you do the Vocabulary Exercises.

If you have the Supplement Posters, you may use them to elicit gender, and, in some cases, even adjective and verb forms. Another way of checking gender is to supply only the noun, and have a student produce a sentence in which it occurs with an article. For practice with the forms of new verbs, a simple person-number substitution or a question-and-answer technique may be useful.

VOCABULARY EXERCISES

Format. Following the Basic Forms list is the Vocabulary Exercise section, which provides immediate practice on the material in the Basic Dialog and Supplement. The exercises in this section are varied and include questions on the dialog, personalized questions, antonym exercises, free completions, and Patterned Response Drills or English Cue Drills based on new idioms. All these exercises give students an opportunity to use the new vocabulary in different contexts, and help to verify comprehension.

Presentation. The Vocabulary Exercises are divided into two parts, corresponding to the parts of the Basic Dialog and Supplement. Once a given section of the Basic Dialog and Supplement has been introduced, the appropriate Vocabulary Exercises can be used as a check on comprehension. They can also be very profitably used when reviewing the Basic Dialog and Supplement, on the second or third day of each unit.

When working with the questions in this section and those in other parts of the unit, it is a good idea to accept both sentence fragments and complete sentences as correct answers. This gives the classroom give-and-take a naturalness which is missing if you always insist on full sentence answers.

Assignment and Review. Once you have worked with an exercise in class, assign it along with the appropriate parts of the Basic Dialog and Supplement for review at home. Many of the exercises may also be used for written practice, but it is suggested that they always be done orally in class first. As with the Basic Dialog and Supplement, you may find it useful to return to the exercises for review at some later time in the teaching of the unit.

GRAMMAR: PRESENTATION

Format. In the student text, the treatment of most points of grammar begins with a short Presentation. This usually consists of a series of sentences containing the new structure, followed by questions to the student designed to elicit an understanding of the grammatical principle involved.

Presentation. The Presentation in the student textbook is not intended for classroom use. Rather, it is the Teacher Presentation (included in pp. T138–T204) which is to be used for introducing every point of grammar. The Teacher Presentation is more detailed than the one in the student book and includes simple exercises for use as part of the presentation. After a new grammatical point has been presented, you can proceed immediately to the Structure Drills in the body of the book. Students should have a good deal of classroom practice with new forms and patterns before studying the same material at home.

Assignment and Review.   Once the Teacher Presentation and the related drills have been done in class, assign the Presentation in the student textbook for study at home.

Reading the Presentation should help the student "rediscover" the most significant points of grammar presented in class. (Students who were absent when a particular structure was presented can use the Presentation in their book to approximate the classroom learning process.)

(*Note:* A Teacher Presentation is provided for every point of grammar in the program. There are a few cases, however, where no Presentation is given in the student textbook. In such cases, the use of the structure is so subtle or so varied that the students would not gain by studying a Presentation at home before proceeding to the Generalization.)

GRAMMAR:
GENERALIZATION

Format.   For each new structure in Level One, a Teacher Presentation is used first to elicit an understanding of the grammatical point; then, the class practices the point in the Structure Drills. Later, when the student is studying at home, he may refer to the Generalization in his text, which summarizes the grammatical point presented and practiced in class. Since the student encounters these "rules" only after he has discovered the principles on his own and has had some practice in applying them, he learns them as principles *derived* from speech patterns rather than formulas which *lead* to speech patterns.

The Generalizations are worded simply and grammatical terms are explained whenever necessary. Grammatical patterns are often presented in chart form.

Assignment and Review.   Once the Teacher Presentation and related drills have been done in class, the Generalization may be assigned for study at home along with the student Presentation and the appropriate drills. In the following class period, students should be given an opportunity to discuss particular points in the Generalization, if necessary.

STRUCTURE
DRILLS

Format.   The Structure Drills provide practice in manipulating the new structure. Some of the initial drills are essentially habit-formation exercises. After doing drills of this type, the students progress to more challenging drills which incorporate the structure into previously learned patterns. In the most advanced exercises, the students use the new structure in a relatively spontaneous manner.

All structure drills are numbered consecutively within a unit. Most appear in a double column format, with the left side providing the stimuli and the right side the responses. Although all responses are included in the Teacher's Edition, the responses are not provided for all drills in the student textbook. Suggested drill variations, which may be useful in maintaining student interest, have been provided in the Teacher's Edition. (*Note:* There are also a few additional structure drills, which are recorded but are not printed in the student textbook. The point at which these occur in the recorded program is indicated in the annotated portion of this book, and the text of all such drills is printed in a section beginning on page T205.)

Presentation.   Structure drills should be conducted in class as soon as the new structure has been presented. Drills which involve only one aspect of a grammatical point are usually incorporated directly into the Teacher Presentation.

The various types of drills and the manner in which they should be conducted are described below. However, certain general procedures are appropriate for almost all drill types. It is always best to begin by modeling the initial stimulus and response. Have the entire class repeat the response once in chorus. When presenting a new drill type or a particularly difficult drill, you may want to repeat the initial stimulus two or three times, calling on individual students to respond. As you continue with the drill, it is best to call for individual rather than choral responses. It helps keep the students alert and discourages them from mumbling their answers. If an incorrect answer is given, give the stimulus again and call on another student. Then give the student who responded incorrectly an opportunity to repeat the correct response.

Since structure drills should proceed at a fairly rapid pace, it is best not to interrupt the rhythm to give extensive correction in pronunciation. Words which present particular difficulty may be practiced briefly after the drill is completed.

The Supplement Posters can be used to provide the cues for many drills.

Assignment and Review. Structure drills should be assigned for home study the same day they are done in class. If you do not have time to cover in class all the structure drills related to a particular grammatical presentation, you may want to assign for home study some that you did not cover as well as those you did. Related writing exercises may also be part of the same assignment. In reviewing this material the next day, the class should be able to do the same drills quite rapidly.

**STRUCTURE DRILLS:
INDIVIDUAL FORMATS**

The formats of the most common drill types are given below. (The reference in parentheses indicates the drill from which the example is taken.)

Substitution Drills. The initial stimulus consists of a model sentence plus an item to be substituted into the model sentence. Each subsequent stimulus is the substitution item alone.

**PERSON-NUMBER
SUBSTITUTION
(Drill 24.1, p. 121)**

Teacher	*Student*
Escribo una carta en inglés.	
(tú)	Escribes una carta en inglés.
(ellos)	Escriben una carta en inglés.

**ITEM SUBSTITUTION
(Drill 9.1, p. 52)**

Teacher	*Student*
Compramos una camisa.	
_____ regalo.	Compramos un regalo.
_____ corbata.	Compramos una corbata.

**DOUBLE ITEM SUBSTITUTION
(Drill 19, p. 188)**

Teacher	*Student*
Tengo poco dinero.	
_____ amigos.	Tengo pocos amigos.
_____ muchas____.	Tengo muchas amigas.

**PROGRESSIVE SUBSTITUTION
(Drill 27, p. 169)**

Teacher	*Student*
A los señores les encanta la idea.	
A nosotros _____.	A nosotros nos encanta la idea.
_____gusta_____.	A nosotros nos gusta la idea.
_____zapatos.	A nosotros nos gustan los zapatos.

The model sentence given in the book has one or more elements underlined. As you cue an element, the student is required to create a new sentence in which he replaces that element with a new word or words. His sentence then becomes the model, and the procedure continues.

The initial stimulus consists of the model sentence plus one of the underlined elements. (Since responses are free, two possible examples are shown for the same drill.)

Teacher	Student
La <u>fiesta</u> empieza <u>a las cinco</u>.	
fiesta	El desfile empieza a las cinco.
a las cinco	El desfile empieza ahora.
desfile	Las carreras empiezan ahora.

Teacher	Student
La <u>fiesta</u> empieza a las cinco.	
a las cinco	La fiesta empieza ahora.
ahora	La fiesta empieza a las dos.
fiesta	La película empieza a las dos.

Transformation Drills. The initial stimulus is the first sentence on the left. This class of drills encompasses the greatest variety of individual drill types. Shown below are a few representative samples.

NOUN → PRONOUN
(Drill 6.1, p. 228)

Teacher	Student
No veo el mapa.	No lo veo.
No veo al empleado.	No lo veo.

SINGULAR → PLURAL
(Drill 10, p. 205)

Teacher	Student
Nunca pido permiso.	Nunca pedimos permiso.
Repito el párrafo.	Repetimos el párrafo.

DIRECTED DIALOG
(Drill 31, p. 124)

Teacher	Student
Pregúntele a *Juan* qué dice esta carta.	¿Qué dice esta carta?
Juan, diga que usted no sabe, que está en alemán.	No sé, está en alemán.

Response Drills. The initial stimulus consists of the first sentence on the left plus the cue in parentheses, if any. (In the type of drill represented by the next example, repeat the initial stimulus each time.)

CUED RESPONSE
(Drill 16, p. 165)

Teacher	Student
¿A quién le escribes? (a mi mamá)	Le escribo a mi mamá.
¿A quién le escribes? (a Juana)	Le escribo a Juana.

PATTERNED RESPONSE
(Drill 20.2, p. 58)

Teacher	Student
Los chicos son franceses, ¿y la chica?	La chica es francesa también.
La blusa es nueva, ¿y los zapatos?	Los zapatos son nuevos también.

T13

Communication Drills. Each sentence is an independent stimulus; each student called upon should respond freely.

FREE RESPONSE
(Drill 18, p. 117)

Teacher	*Student*
¿Con quién estudia usted?	Con María.
	Estudio con mis amigos.
	Estudio con una chica española.

REJOINDERS
(Drill 22, p. 59)

Teacher	*Student*
¿Te gusta la chica alemana?	Sí, es muy simpática.
	No, es muy pretenciosa.
	¿Cuál chica alemana?

English Cue Drills. Model the Spanish sentence on the left and have the class repeat it. Then treat the first English line as the initial stimulus.

ENGLISH CUE DRILL
(Drill 5, p. 112)

Teacher	*Student*
¿Cómo es Enrique?	¿Cómo es Enrique? (*chorus*)
What is Conchita like?	¿Cómo es Conchita?
What is the station like?	¿Cómo es la estación?

LISTENING AND SPEAKING EXERCISES: GENERAL

Format. The Listening and Speaking Exercises are a new element in the A-LM program. They include listening exercises, pronunciation exercises, sound discrimination exercises, listening comprehension exercises, and dictations. These exercises are designed to train the students in four important skills: 1) to distinguish between Spanish sounds which are similar to each other, 2) to recognize certain aural cues as grammatical signals, 3) to understand spoken Spanish in a variety of contexts, and 4) to pronounce Spanish correctly.

These exercises are intended for audio-lingual presentation exclusively; therefore, they do not appear in the student textbook. They are presented most effectively by means of tapes or records. For the teacher who does not have the recordings, a complete script of the exercises appears in the front part of this book (pp. T24–T137).

The Listening and Speaking Exercises constitute an integral part of the A-LM program, and they are closely co-ordinated with the material in the textbook units. To facilitate your scheduling of these exercises, Units 2–15 of Level One are divided into four sections, and the sections are clearly marked—A, B, C, and D—in the annotated part of this book. (Unit 1 is divided into two sections.) Each section incorporates both textbook material (for example, Structure Drills) *and* Listening and Speaking Exercises to be done in conjunction with that material. The Listening and Speaking Exercises in a particular section should not be used until some of the structure in that section has been drilled in class.

LISTENING AND SPEAKING EXERCISES: PRONUNCIATION

Format. In Unit 1, only the most difficult sounds are introduced: those which are completely new to a speaker of English or similar enough to English sounds to cause interference. In subsequent units, there is a systematic presentation of other sounds and a review of some of the more difficult sounds which have previously been drilled. For example, the sound [r] is first introduced in Unit 1 and then reviewed in Units 4, 9, 11, 12, and 15.

There is at least one Pronunciation Exercise in each section of every unit. Each new sound is first introduced in a Listening Exercise. The students simply listen to a series of words containing the new sound. Then they practice saying the sound, with the aid of a brief phonological description, if necessary. Many contrastive pronunciation exercises (for example, [d] vs. [đ] and [r] vs. [rr]) have also been provided. These are sometimes preceded by a Sound Discrimination Exercise which trains the students to hear the difference in the sounds before they are asked to produce them.

Presentation and Review. Use the same repetition and correction techniques as described previously (p. T7). If you plan to use the recordings for pronunciation practice, it is usually better to present the sound yourself first in class. Pronunciation Exercises should be reviewed in class as often as seems necessary. It is suggested that you try to devote a few minutes of each day's lesson to pronunciation practice. A reference key on p. T209 will help you locate all the exercises that deal with any given sound.

LISTENING AND SPEAKING EXERCISES: LISTENING COMPREHENSION

Format. There is at least one Listening Comprehension Exercise in each section of every unit. The simplest exercises require the students to listen to a series of sentences and determine, for example, if the noun in each sentence is singular or plural. In some of the more challenging exercises, the students are asked to listen to a series of dialogs and choose the most appropriate of three possible comments on each dialog situation. All of the Listening Comprehension Exercises are divided into a problem-solving phase and a verification phase. *They are intended to be used for training rather than for testing.* The students should not be made to feel nervous about their performance, and should be encouraged to listen to each new exercise as carefully as possible.

Presentation. Since many of the Listening Comprehension Exercises include examples of the structure treated in a given section, they should always be conducted *after* you have done some oral work on the structure. If you have the tapes or records which accompany this program, it would be preferable to use them in presenting the exercises since they provide an appropriate variety of voices.

For every Listening Comprehension Exercise and Sound Discrimination Exercise, the students are required to make some notation of their answers on specially prepared Response Forms. These Response Forms comprise the first part of the student Exercise Book. Students without the Exercise Book can copy the appropriate Response Forms from the back of their textbook (pp. 311–337). To facilitate planning for the Listening Comprehension Exercises, each exercise that will require a written response from the students is marked with an asterisk in the annotated part of this book.

Verification. As soon as possible after a Listening Comprehension Exercise has been done, and students have verified their responses, you should get some indication of how well they performed. You might ask for a show of hands by students who got all the items right, more than two wrong, etc. Occasionally, you might want to collect the Exercise Books or answer papers. But do keep in mind—and make the students aware—that these exercises are not being used as tests. If performance is generally good, you may want to give individual attention after class to those students who did not do well. If there are many wrong answers, or if the majority of students answered a particular item incorrectly, it might be profitable to take time to conduct the exercise again. If you find that a particular structural point presents special difficulty, try to correct it with extra oral drill practice.

The last exercise in each unit is a Listening Comprehension Dialog with questions, to which the students are asked to write a few short answers. After this exercise is done, collect a large enough sampling of Response Forms to evaluate student performance.

LETTER-SOUND CORRESPONDENCE LESSONS

Format. The Letter-Sound Correspondence lessons are intended to teach the students the basic skills of reading and writing, to enable them to read words and sentences correctly and to write what they know how to say. These basic rules must be learned before the students can hope to master the long-range skills, rapid reading for comprehension and writing as free composition.

The final sections of Units 2, 3, 4, 5, 6, 7, and 10 provide lessons in Letter-Sound Correspondences. There are several lessons per unit, each of which deals with one or two specific problems. Each lesson begins with a brief rule which is followed by a reading exercise. The students are asked to read both familiar words and unfamiliar words. The unfamiliar words have been included to demonstrate the applicability of each rule and to require the students to actually "read" rather than pronounce words from memory. Each reading exercise ends with a series of sentences containing examples of the letter-sound correspondence just presented. No unfamiliar words have been included in the sentences.

The reading exercise is followed by a writing exercise, which requires the students to copy the sentences which they have practiced in class and to be prepared to write them from dictation. Whenever it is possible to give a concise rule for spelling a given sound, such a rule is provided in the Spelling Notes.

Presentation. Explain briefly to your students the particular letter-sound correspondence rule. Be sure to refer to the Spanish name of the letter (for example, the letter **ll** [eɥe] and to the Spanish sound it represents (for example, the sound [ɏ]). Then have the students open their books to the lesson you are teaching, and have individual students read the words and sentences.

Present one lesson every other day; an average lesson should only take between five and ten minutes of class time.

Assignment and Review. Once a lesson has been done in class, it can be assigned for review at home. Students should copy the sentences designated in the writing exercise. In the following class period, dictate one or two of these sentences, and correct any spelling mistakes immediately. (Dictation Exercises consisting of these sentences appear in the recorded program; for example, see p. T36.)

WRITING EXERCISES

Format. In the early units, there are writing exercises to be done in connection with the teaching of the Letter-Sound Correspondences (see preceding description). In addition, in the Grammar section of each unit of Level One, there are suggested Writing Exercises. These usually call for written responses to those drills that do not have a response printed in the student textbook. Beginning in Unit 6, there are special writing exercises which appear at the end of the Grammar section. These are usually more challenging than those within the Grammar section and often involve a combination of structures. They include such exercise types as Sentence Construction, Multiple Item Substitution, and Paragraph Rewrite.

The second half of the Exercise Book consists of supplementary writing exercises. The points within each unit at which these exercises may be assigned are indicated in the annotated section of this book.

Assignment and Review. The Writing Exercises on specific points of grammar (both the ones in the student book and those in the Exercise Book) should be assigned as homework after the structure has been drilled orally in class. Ideally, an exercise should be corrected the day it is due and returned to the students the next day. You may occasionally want to correct an exercise in class.

RECOMBINATION MATERIAL: GENERAL

Essentially, the Recombination Material in each unit contains, and is meant to elicit, only familiar vocabulary and structure. The Recombination Material of Units 2–5 includes three or four short dialogs; the remaining units include dialogs and a Narrative.

The Recombination Material is not intended as reading practice alone, but is designed to serve as the basis for speaking and writing as well. The dialogs are followed by questions, as well as Dialog Variations, Rejoinders, and a Conversation Stimulus. The Narratives are followed by questions.

Although the Recombination Material is printed at the end of the unit, it is suggested that the presentation of it be begun, whenever possible, while you are teaching the grammar in the unit. This will add to the variety of class activities.

RECOMBINATION MATERIAL: DIALOGS

Format. The Recombination Dialogs are four to twelve lines long, and are followed by questions which may be used to check student comprehension. The dialogs do not contain any new words; they represent a recombination of familiar vocabulary and structures in new situations.

Presentation. Present each dialog orally to give the students additional practice in listening comprehension. Check their understanding of the situation immediately by asking the questions. Then have them read the dialogs aloud. If there is a Dialog Variation, have students produce a new dialog by making the suggested changes. All these oral activities should prepare them to participate in the Conversation Stimulus.

Assignment and Review. The exercises following the dialogs can be used for a written assignment after oral work has been done in class. Dialog Variations are especially well suited for writing practice, since the student reviews the dialog while making grammatical and lexical changes.

RECOMBINATION MATERIAL: REJOINDERS AND CONVERSATION STIMULUS

Format. The Recombination Dialogs are often followed by a Rejoinders section which is related to the dialogs and which prepares the students for the Conversation Stimulus. The Rejoinders section includes a list of questions or statements to which the students are expected to provide natural responses. The Conversation Stimulus begins by briefly outlining a situation which will provide a context for a dialog between students. The situation is, of course, within the linguistic experience of the students.

Presentation. Elicit as many rejoinders as possible, keeping in mind that the response and the original sentence should always constitute a natural exchange. (Suggested Rejoinders have been listed in the annotated part of this book.)

In the initial presentation of the Conversation Stimulus, explain the situation to the students, and suggest a first line for a conversation. (A first line is always provided in the text.) Have a student give this first line, and elicit a response from any other student. Have a third student respond to the second, and so on, until the conversation seems exhausted. At this point, begin a new conversation, either with the same first line or another, and encourage the class to develop the situation differently. In some cases, you may want to ask two students to carry on an entire conversation.

RECOMBINATION MATERIAL: NARRATIVE

Format. Beginning in Unit 6, a Recombination Narrative appears at the end of every unit. The Narratives vary in length from half a page to four pages in later units. Cognates are introduced in every Narrative; each cognate is marked with an asterisk the first time it appears and is listed in the Spanish-English Vocabulary at the end of the book.

In the Narratives of Units 10–15, new lexical items are introduced. These words are clearly marked in the text, glossed in the margin, and included in the Spanish-English Vocabulary.

The Narrative is designed principally for reading practice. However, it may also provide an excellent opportunity for listening comprehension and speaking practice.

Presentation. The Narrative demands only a few minutes of presentation in class before it is assigned to be read at home. You may want to read the first paragraph of the Narrative for listening comprehension, before assigning it. Ask some of the questions on this material as a check on comprehension.

Assignment and Review. Assign the Narrative to be read at home, along with the questions that follow. Tell students that they are expected to understand the Narrative, to be able to answer the questions, and to learn the new words glossed in the margin (Units 10–15).

The review in class the next day should consist mainly of questions and answers. Before eliciting student responses to the questions, you can review the text of the Narrative in several ways. You may, for example, read a passage yourself, play a recording of a passage, or occasionally ask one or two students to read a few lines. Using a variety of methods will help maintain class interest.

The students are expected to learn the glossed words in the Narratives, since almost all of them will appear in later drills and exercises. Questions using these new words are printed in the margin of the annotated part of this book, and should be used as each paragraph is reviewed.

Once all of the questions on the Narrative have been treated in class, you may want to assign a certain number of them for written work at home.

GLIMPSES OF THE SPANISH WORLD

The pictorial section following page 133 is intended to give the students some insight into the lives of the people whose language they are learning.

Presentation. It is suggested that you assign certain parts of the section at various appropriate times. For example, you might assign the section on Education when you teach Unit 4, and the section on The Home and the Family when you teach Unit 6.

Have the students read the assigned section and look at the pictures. In the following class period, you may want to organize a brief discussion or question-and-answer period, and perhaps expand the topic on your own. It is not intended, however, that a great deal of class time be devoted to the pictorial section.

You can use the map to locate geographical points mentioned in the text, and thereby begin to make your students aware of the major geographical features of Spain and Spanish America.

7. Sample Lesson Plan

Although you will plan your daily lessons as you find most effective, the sample lesson plan on p. T210 may give you some ideas on how to balance the different components of each unit. Note that it provides variety and constant review of the material being taught. This plan has been organized with laboratory sessions in addition to regular class periods. This is the most effective arrangement, since it gives the students additional practice in manipulating structures, and allows more class time for activities leading to communication.

Each unit should be taught in two weeks. This plan shows how the material in Unit 11 may be distributed over ten days. Part of Day 11 should be devoted to the unit test.

8. Recorded Materials

STANDARDS   The tape recordings and records expose the students to authentic spoken Spanish in addition to that which can be provided by the teacher. The recordings provide uniform quality of performance and relieve the teacher of some of the burden of constant oral drill.

Any language is spoken with regional variations. The recorded materials include a variety of native speaker voices with a reasonable range of variations. Extreme regional differences have been avoided, however, and the variations are limited to those occurring in the speech of educated people.

STUDENT PRACTICE RECORD SET   The Student Practice Record Set (or "Take-Home Disks") includes fifteen 7-inch $33\frac{1}{3}$ rpm disks. Each disk contains the Basic Dialog and Supplement of one unit.[2] These disks are designed primarily for practice at home. They provide the student with an immediately accessible authentic model for imitation, and consequently speed the learning process while encouraging correct pronunciation and intonation. Listening to the disks should be part of a student's homework assignment. If it is not possible for each student to have a set, it is suggested that students take turns using the sets which are available, or that they work together in small groups. In some schools, it may be possible to set up listening stations, either with or without headphones, in a classroom or the library. The 7-inch disks can, of course, be used during the class period if neither the tapes nor the 12-inch disks are available.

TEACHER'S RECORDED MATERIALS   The teacher's recordings are available in three forms, each of which contains the same material:

(a) a 60–reel $7\frac{1}{2}$ ips full-track tape set
(b) a 30–reel $7\frac{1}{2}$ ips two-track tape set
(c) a 30–disk 12-inch $33\frac{1}{3}$ rpm record set

The recordings for each unit include material from the student textbook (Basic

---

[2] The disk for Unit 1 contains the short dialogs in that unit.

Dialog, Supplement, and Structure Drills) and the Listening and Speaking Exercises.[3] In some units, there are also additional structure drills. This material is divided into four 18–20 minute sections, A, B, C, and D. The following charts show the distribution of material in a typical unit.

<table>
<tr><td>

SECTION A

Basic Dialog (1st part)
Supplement (1st part)
Basic Dialog (2nd part)
Supplement (2nd part)
Listening & Speaking Exercises
Structure Drills (on idioms)*

</td><td>

SECTION B

Listening & Speaking Exercises
Structure Drills
(Additional Structure Drills)*

</td></tr>
<tr><td>

SECTION C

Listening & Speaking Exercises
Structure Drills
(Additional Structure Drills)*

</td><td>

SECTION D

Listening & Speaking Exercises
Structure Drills
(Additional Structure Drills)*
Listening & Speaking Exercise**

</td></tr>
</table>

*Included only in certain units.
**A final exercise requiring written answers to questions on a short dialog.

Indications in the annotated part of this book show where each recorded section begins, and what material is included in each section. For example, in Unit 11, "Section A" on page 199 indicates that all the recorded material which follows will be found in Section A. This includes the Basic Dialog, the Supplement, and Listening and Speaking Exercises 178, 179, 180*, and 181*, in that order.[4] On page 203, the material in Section B begins. This includes Listening and Speaking Exercises 182, 183, and 184*, and Structure Drills 6.1, 6.2, 7, 9, 10, and 11, in that order. Section C begins on page 208 and Section D on page 214. A complete inventory showing the distribution of sections in the tape and record sets appears on p. T206 and is included with every tape and record set.

USE OF THE RECORDED MATERIALS

THE LANGUAGE LABORATORY The most desirable arrangement is to have language laboratory sessions scheduled in addition to the usual class periods. The work done in the laboratory should always be a natural extension of work begun in class. Before taking your students to the laboratory to work with a given section, be sure that the vocabulary and structure contained in the section have been adequately presented and drilled in class. Since each lab session will require some written responses, students should go prepared with their Exercise Books, or with the appropriate Response Forms copied from the back of their texts.

---

[3]The Recombination Dialogs and Narratives have also been recorded to provide additional listening-comprehension practice and are included with each set of recorded materials on a separate tape reel or record.

[4]Remember that the asterisk next to an exercise number indicates that the students will need the Response Form in their Exercise Book or will have to have copied the appropriate form from the back of their textbook.

Laboratory sessions should be as frequent as possible, but it is recommended that a session not exceed twenty-five minutes in length. Whenever possible, students working with recorded materials should be monitored by a language teacher. This monitoring may be done by listening at the console through a monitoring system or simply by walking around the room. When several students make the same error, it may be profitable to stop the program, give the necessary explanations, and begin the exercise again. In the case of individual errors, correction should be as precise and brief as possible in order not to distract the student any longer than necessary. Once a section has been drilled in the laboratory, you should review it in class to be sure that the students have mastered the material.

(*Note:* Some language laboratories are equipped with facilities that allow each student to make his own recordings and play them back. These should be used judiciously. It has not yet been shown that students profit from listening to their own responses; they usually have difficulty hearing differences between their performance and that of the model, and even greater difficulty correcting their errors. If you do ask students to play back their own recordings, be sure to monitor them carefully.)

FORMAT OF THE RECORDED MATERIALS

The following is a description of the format used in most of the recorded materials. Every line has been recorded at normal speed and with natural intonation. Pauses for students' responses have been inserted through editing so that the naturalness of the native speaker's utterance is not affected. Each pause has been calculated in consideration of the time it would take a native speaker to respond *plus* the additional time a student needs to react.

BASIC DIALOG AND SUPPLEMENT
Basic Dialogs and Supplements are presented together in the following format.

1. The first half of the dialog for listening.
2. The first half of the dialog with each line broken into partials and recombined when necessary. Each partial and recombination is heard twice and followed by a pause for repetition.
3. The first half of the dialog, line by line, with pauses for repetition.
4. The first half of the supplement. Each item is heard twice and followed by a pause for repetition.
5. The second half of the dialog for listening.
6. The second half of the dialog in partials and recombinations with pauses for repetition.
7. The second half of the dialog, line by line, with pauses for repetition.
8. The second half of the supplement. Each item is heard twice and followed by a pause for repetition.
9. The entire dialog for listening.
10. The entire dialog, line by line, with pauses for repetition (only in some units).

STRUCTURE DRILLS
The Structure Drills have been recorded in a 6-phase format:

stimulus—pause for response—confirmation—
same stimulus—pause for response—confirmation.

This format allows the student to respond to the stimulus a second time instead of just echoing the correct response. The stimuli and responses are always spoken by different voices.

LISTENING AND SPEAKING EXERCISES

The Listening and Speaking Exercises include listening exercises, pronunciation exercises, sound discrimination exercises, listening comprehension exercises, and dictations. Each exercise in the program begins with instructions to the students. The formats of the different exercises are as follows:

LISTENING EXERCISES

The student listens to a series of words or sentences.

PRONUNCIATION EXERCISES

The student hears a word (twice) or contrastive word-pair (twice) and is then given time to repeat. In exercises consisting of dialogs, he first hears the entire dialog without interruption. Then he hears it line by line. Each item is heard twice, followed by a pause for repetition. (The short dialogs of Unit 1 appear in a slightly different format.)

SOUND DISCRIMINATION EXERCISES

The student hears a word and must determine whether it is a Spanish or an English word, or which of two similar Spanish sounds the word contains. He marks down his response as he hears each word. In the verification phase, he hears the word again, followed by the correct response.

LISTENING COMPREHENSION EXERCISES

Since many types of exercises are used, the variety of formats cannot be described here at length. All the exercises are divided into a problem-solving phase and a verification phase. For any one Listening Comprehension Exercise, the format is clearly indicated in the Listening and Speaking Exercises section of the Teacher's Edition (pp. T24–T137).

DICTATION

The student hears each sentence twice and is given time to write the sentence. In the verification phase he compares what he has written with the correct sentences printed in his Exercise Book or in the Response Form section of his textbook.

Listening and Speaking Exercises

Format. The first unit of Level One—which is to be taught entirely audio-lingually—is designed to teach the most difficult features of the Spanish sound system. Each sound (or sounds) is presented first in a Listening Exercise, which provides words containing examples of the sound or sounds being taught. When appropriate, this exercise is followed by a Sound Discrimination Exercise which trains the students to distinguish a given sound from a similar one. The Pronunciation Exercise which follows gives the students practice in saying the new sounds.

Unit 1 is divided into seven lessons. Teaching the entire unit should take from six to eight days. In general, each lesson includes the following material in the order indicated.

1. A Listening Exercise on a given sound or sounds
2. A Sound Discrimination Exercise, when appropriate
3. A Pronunciation Exercise
4. A short dialog, giving the student additional practice with the sound
5. Questions or exercises to check the students' comprehension of the dialog

Recordings. With the exception of the questions and exercises immediately following the four-line dialogs, all the material in this unit has been recorded and appears on the Classroom/Laboratory Sets. The student Take-Home Disks contain only the dialogs.

Presentation. In general, you should proceed through the exercises of each lesson in the order in which they appear in the book. You might present an entire lesson yourself first, and then play the recordings to reinforce what has been done in class; or you might intersperse your own presentation of the material with the playing of the disks or tapes. The recordings are especially appropriate, for example, when presenting the Sound Discrimination Exercises. It is usually better to model the Pronunciation Exercises yourself before you use the recordings. The students will benefit from watching you as you speak, and you will be able to correct immediately any mistake they may make.

If you find that it increases your students' motivation, you might have them listen to a dialog before doing the listening and pronunciation exercises that lead up to it. In presenting the dialogs, you may want to give first the English and then the Spanish. However, you may find that you can make meaning clear by means of visual aids or gestures. Numbers next to the dialogs refer to the Supplement Posters that may be used to illustrate the dialog lines.

The Basic Dialogs introduce vocabulary that is used in subsequent units. It is therefore essential that the students learn these dialogs. The questions and exercises following the Basic Dialogs provide immediate recombination practice and check student comprehension. Make certain the students understand what you are saying at all times, both in the dialogs and in the exercises on the dialogs.

When you have finished teaching Unit 1 audio-lingually, give the students the textbooks and have them practice reading the dialogs aloud.

Assignment. If your students have the Take-Home Disks, assign the dialogs for listening and repetition at home. It is probably best to begin each period with a review of the dialogs from the previous lesson.

UNIT 1—SECTION A

Lesson 1: Spanish Rhythm

EXERCISE 1. LISTENING

Spanish rhythm is different in important ways from English rhythm. This difference is most noticeable in two respects: First, Spanish syllables are all of about the same length, while in English some syllables are much longer than others. Second, Spanish vowels are all relatively clear and conspicuous, while some English vowel sounds are quite unclear.

To understand these differences, listen to these two English sentences:

> Could you <u>believe</u> it?
> I don't want to <u>leave</u> her.

You should have noticed in both sentences that the syllable [liv] was much longer than any of the others. Also, several of the vowels almost disappear, for example, the first vowel of *believe.* On the other hand, a person saying these sentences with a Spanish accent would not make these syllables longer than the others, nor would he pronounce any of the vowels less clearly than the others. This is precisely what you must learn to do in Spanish. Now listen to the same two sentences again, paying attention to the length of the syllables.

> Could you believe it?
> I don't want to leave her.

Listen to the following word in English: *banana.* The first and last syllables almost disappear. Now listen to the same word in Spanish: **banana**. All the syllables are of about the same length. Listen again: **banana**.

EXERCISE 2. PRONUNCIATION

Repeat each of the following phrases. Concentrate on making all vowels clear and sharp and all syllables the same length.

> bananas y papas / van a Panamá / casas y casos /
> unas señoras alemanas / francesas y franceses /
> en algunos casos cantan / en algunas casas cantan

```
                           BASIC  DIALOG  I
```

1–1 ELENA ¿Está Susana en casa?   Is Susana at home?
         MARÍA Sí, está con una amiga.   Yes, she's with a friend.
1–2 ELENA ¿Dónde están, en la sala?   Where are they, in the living
                                                room?
1–3 MARÍA No, en la cocina.   No, in the kitchen.

QUESTIONS

1. ¿Está Susana en casa?   Sí.
2. ¿Dónde está Susana?   Está en casa.
3. ¿Está con una amiga?   Sí, está con una amiga.
4. ¿Está Susana en la sala?   No.
5. ¿Está la amiga en la sala?   No.
6. ¿Dónde están Susana y (*and*) la   Están en la cocina.
   amiga?

DIRECTED DIALOG

Pregúntele a *María* si Susana está en la   ¿Está Susana en la cocina?
   cocina.
Dígale que no, que está en la sala.   No, está en la sala.

Lesson 2: [e]

Spanish [e]
vs.
English vowel

EXERCISE 3. LISTENING

In this exercise you will hear pairs of words. In each pair, the first word is English and the second word is Spanish. Listen carefully for the difference between the vowel sound in the English words and the vowel sound in the Spanish words.

day–de / say–sé / may–me / lay–le / pay–pe / bay–be

The English vowel sound is longer and has two parts. It sounds almost as if the words were "*day-ee*," "*say-ee*." The "ee" part at the end is called a glide. The Spanish vowel has no glide.

Spanish [e]
vs.
English vowel

EXERCISE 4. SOUND DISCRIMINATION

Be prepared to write your responses for Exercise 4. You will hear a series of words, some of which are Spanish, and some of which are English. For each word you hear, place a check mark in either the row labeled Spanish or the row labeled English. EXAMPLE   You hear: **me**   You place your check mark in column 1 of the row labeled Spanish because the word you heard was Spanish. It was pronounced without a glide. *We will begin now. Read each word once in the language indicated.*

1. day English   3. be Spanish   5. le Spanish   7. pe Spanish
2. sé   Spanish   4. pay English   6. me Spanish   8. say English

Now check your answers. *Repeat each of the preceding words once and confirm by naming the appropriate language.*

T25

EXERCISE 5. PRONUNCIATION

In this exercise you will say Spanish phrases which have the sound [e]. As you pronounce this sound be careful not to make a glide. Keep your mouth in the same
position throughout the vowel sound. Repeat each phrase once in the pause provided.

de / sé / le / me / ¡qué! / déme / empecemos /
en este mes / no sé qué es eso

Lesson 3: [o]

Spanish [o]
vs.
English vowel

EXERCISE 6. LISTENING

In this exercise you will hear pairs of words. In each pair, the first word is English,
and the second word is Spanish. Listen carefully for the difference between the vowel
sound in the English and Spanish words.

no–no / low–lo / dough–do / dose–dos / cone–con

The English vowel sound is longer and has a glide. It sounds almost like *"no-u."*
The Spanish vowel sound has no glide.

Spanish [o]
vs.
English vowel

EXERCISE 7. SOUND DISCRIMINATION

Be prepared to write your responses for Exercise 7. You will hear a series of words,
some of which are Spanish, and some of which are English. For each word you hear,
place a check mark in either the row labeled Spanish or the row labeled English.
EXAMPLE   You hear: *low*   You place your check mark in the row labeled English because the word you heard was English. We will begin now. *Read each word once in
the language indicated.*

1. dos	Spanish		6. dose	English
2. cone	English		7. con	Spanish
3. no	Spanish		8. low	English
4. lo	Spanish		9. dough	English
5. do	Spanish		10. no	English

Now check your answers. *Repeat each of the preceding words once and confirm by naming*
the appropriate language.

[o]

EXERCISE 8. PRONUNCIATION

In this exercise you will say phrases with the sound [o]. Keep your mouth in the
same rounded position throughout the vowel sound. Be careful to make the sound
short and to avoid the English glide. Repeat each phrase once.

no / lo / loco / como loco / yo no lo conozco /
los ocho tontos / cómo no

BASIC DIALOG II

ELENA	¡Hola, Susana! ¿Dónde está tu amiga?	Hi, Susana. Where's your friend?
1–4 SUSANA	En el teléfono.	On the telephone.

QUESTIONS

1. ¿Dónde está la amiga de Susana? — En el teléfono.
2. ¿Está la amiga con Susana en la cocina? — No.
3. ¿Está la amiga en el teléfono? — Sí, está en el teléfono.
4. ¿Está Susana en el teléfono? — No.

DIRECTED DIALOG

Pregúntele a *Susana* dónde está el teléfono. — ¿Dónde está el teléfono?

Dígale que está en la sala. — Está en la sala.

Lesson 4: [i], [u], and [a]

Spanish [i], and [u], and [a]
vs.
English vowel

EXERCISE 9. LISTENING

In this exercise you will hear pairs of words. In each pair, the first word is English and the second word is Spanish. Listen carefully for the difference between the vowel sounds in the English and Spanish words.

see–sí / me–mí / bee–vi / sue–su / two–tú / soup–supe / pot–pata / lot–lata / dot–dato

Note that the English [I] and [U] sounds are more relaxed than the Spanish ones. To produce the Spanish sounds correctly, the mouth should be held more tensely and the tongue should be held higher than for the corresponding English sounds. For the sound [i], the corners of the mouth should be drawn backward. For the sound [u], the lips should protrude in a whistling position.

Whether the Spanish [a] is easy for you—that is, how closely it resembles the [A] sound you use in English—depends on what part of the United States you are from. You must listen closely to see whether they are the same or not, and try to imitate the Spanish sound exactly.

[i], [u], and [a]

EXERCISE 10. PRONUNCIATION

In this exercise, you will say Spanish phrases with the sounds [i], [u], and [a]. Remember to make each vowel sound sharp and distinct. Repeat each phrase once.

¡sí, sí, sí, sí, sí! / tú, tú, tú, y tú / vas a Panamá / una linda chiquita / si tu tía llama . . . / dile que salimos / dime si tu usas . . . / pluma o lápiz

T27

```
┌─────────────────────────────────────────────────────────────────────────┐
│                     BASIC DIALOG III                                      │
│                                                                           │
│        ELENA    ¿Es Lili la tía de Susana?        Is Lili Susana's aunt (the │
│                                                      aunt of Susana)?     │
│                                                                           │
│        MARÍA    ¿Cómo? ¿Quién?                    What (how)? Who?        │
│   1-5  ELENA    Lili. Ésa que está en el sofá.    Lili. The one (that one │
│                                                      who's) on the sofa.  │
│                                                                           │
│        MARÍA    Ah, sí, es su tía.                Oh, yes, that's her aunt.│
└─────────────────────────────────────────────────────────────────────────┘
```

QUESTIONS
1. ¿Es Lili la amiga de Susana?   No.
2. ¿Quién es Lili?   Es la tía de Susana.
3. ¿Dónde está Lili?   En el sofá.
4. ¿Está Lili en la cocina?   No.
5. ¿Está en la sala?   Sí.

DIRECTED DIALOG
Dígale hola a *Susana*.   Hola, *Susana*.
Dígale hola, y pregúntele dónde está   Hola, ¿dónde está Lili?
  Lili.
Dígale que está en la sala.   Está en la sala.
Pregúntele con quién.   ¿Con quién?
Dígale que con su amiga.   Con su amiga.

NIT 1—SECTION B

Lesson 5: [r] *and* [rr]

Spanish [r]   **EXERCISE 11. LISTENING**
vs.
English consonant   The Spanish **r** is totally different from English *r*. No sound which you think of as
being an *r* in English will work at all in Spanish. But there is an English sound
which will work. Surprisingly, it's the one spelled *t* or *d* in words like *Betty, Teddy*.
In this exercise you will hear pairs of words. In each pair, the first word is an English
word with a *t* or a *d* in the middle. The **second** is a Spanish word with an **r** in the
same place. Listen carefully to each pair, comparing the English sound spelled *t* or
d with the Spanish [r] sound.

> petty–pero / Teddy–Tere / Eddie–ere / meter–mira /
> leader–lira / Peter–pira

[r]   **EXERCISE 12. PRONUNCIATION**

To say the Spanish **r**, concentrate on making a quick flip of the tongue, such as you

T28

make for the *t* or the *d* in *Betty* or *Teddy*. Remember that no American *r* sound will work. Now repeat each of the following Spanish phrases.

> pero / qué caro / ¡Pero qué caro! / la cera / es cara /
> La cera es cara. / por eso / te quiero / Por eso te quiero.

[rr]

EXERCISE 13. LISTENING

In this exercise you will hear a series of Spanish words containing the sound [rr]. The consonant [rr] is traditionally called "double **r**" because it is spelled with two **r**'s between vowels. The sound, however, should be called a "multiple **r**", because it is really a series of very rapid single **r**'s. Listen carefully to the sound [rr] in the following words.

> perro / carro / erre / rico / rápido

[rr]

EXERCISE 14. PRONUNCIATION

To say the sound [rr] correctly you must force the air out of your mouth with enough pressure to make the tip of your tongue flutter like a flag. Now repeat the following words and phrases.

> perro / corren / carro / erre / cigarro /
> rico / rápido / barril / ferrocarril

You will now hear a little jingle someone thought up to provide practice on the sound [rr]. If you can learn to say it, you won't have any trouble with this sound. Now listen to the following sentences.

> Erre con erre cigarro,
> Erre con erre barril,
> Rápido corren los carros
> Del ferrocarril.

Now repeat each sentence.

[r] *vs.* [rr]

EXERCISE 15. LISTENING

In this exercise you will hear pairs of words. The first word in each pair contains a single **r**. The second one contains a double **r**. The two words sound the same except for the **r**'s, but they have different meanings.

> caro–carro / pero–perro / cero–cerro /
> foro–forro / vara–barra / coro–corro

[r] *vs.* [rr]

EXERCISE 16. SOUND DISCRIMINATION

Be prepared to write your responses for Exercise 16. You will hear a series of words, some of which contain a single **r**, some of which contain a double **r**. For each word you hear, place a check mark in either the row labeled **r** or the row labeled **rr**. EXAMPLE You hear: **perro** You place your check mark in the row labeled **rr** because the word that you heard contained the double **r** sound. We will begin now. *Read each word once.*

1. vara	single **r**	5. cero	single **r**	9. coro	single **r**		
2. pero	single **r**	6. forro	double **r**	10. foro	single **r**		
3. carro	double **r**	7. caro	single **r**				
4. corro	double **r**	8. perro	double **r**				

Now check your answers. *Repeat each of the preceding words once and confirm by naming the sound as indicated.*

[r] *vs.* [rr]

EXERCISE 17. PRONUNCIATION

Repeat each of the following pairs of words once in the pause provided.

caro–carro / pero–perro / cero–cerro / foro–forro /
vara–barra / coro–corro

BASIC DIALOG IV

	ROBERTO	¿Pero adónde quiere ir Lili?	But where (to where) does Lili want to go?
	RAÚL	A las carreras.	To the races.
1–6	ROBERTO	¿A las carreras de perros?	To the dog races?
1–7	RAÚL	Sí, vamos en mi carro.	Yes, we'll go (we go) in my car.

QUESTIONS
1. ¿Adónde quiere ir Lili?   A las carreras.
2. ¿Quiere ir a la casa?   No.
3. ¿Quiere ir a las carreras?   Sí.
4. ¿A las carreras de perros?   Sí.
5. ¿Raúl quiere ir en su carro o (*or*) en   Quiere ir en su carro.
el carro de Lili?

DIRECTED DIALOG

Pregúntele a Raúl dónde está Susana.	¿Dónde está Susana?
Dígale que está en el carro.	Está en el carro.
Pregúntele adónde quiere ir.	¿Adónde quiere ir?
Dígale que a las carreras con su tía	A las carreras con su tía.

Lesson 6: [d] *and* [d̶], [b] *and* [b̶]

[d]

EXERCISE 18. LISTENING

Spanish has two different **d** sounds. One of these sounds is very much like the English *d* in *day, down, dead.* There is a difference, however. For the English *d*, the tongue touches the area above and behind the upper teeth; for the Spanish **d**, the tongue touches the back part of the upper teeth themselves. Listen to the following Spanish words.

de / do / caldo / el día / cuando

[d] **EXERCISE 19. PRONUNCIATION**

In this exercise you will say words with the sound [d]. Make sure the tip of your tongue touches the back of your upper teeth. Repeat each of the following words.

do / dónde / falda / caldo / el día / cuándo

[đ] **EXERCISE 20. LISTENING**

The other Spanish **d** sound is very much like the sound spelled *th* in English words like *mother*, *father*, *brother*. In this exercise you will hear pairs of words. The first word in each pair is an English word with *th* in the middle. The second is a Spanish word with the similar đ sound in the same place. Listen carefully to each pair, comparing the English sound spelled *th* with the Spanish [đ] sound.

neither–nido / lather–lado / bother–boda / mother–moda

[đ] **EXERCISE 21. PRONUNCIATION**

Repeat each of the following words.

nido / nudo / boda / mudo / lado / Adela / comido

[d] *vs.* [đ] **EXERCISE 22. LISTENING**

You must learn when to use the two Spanish **d** sounds. For the moment, remember this simple rule: If a **d** follows a vowel, it is like the English *th* in the word *mother*; if a **d** sound does not follow a vowel, it is like the English *d* except that the tip of the tongue touches the back part of the upper teeth. This rule holds even when more than one word is involved. Listen to the following pairs of words and phrases. Pay special attention to the difference between the **d** sounds.

el día–ese día / doy–no doy / da–le da / dama–una dama

[d] *vs.* [đ] **EXERCISE 23. PRONUNCIATION**

Repeat each of the following pairs of words and phrases once in the pause provided.

el día–ese día / doy–no doy / da–le da / dama–una dama /
dónde–adónde / dan–qué dan

[b] *and* [b̵] **EXERCISE 24. LISTENING**

Spanish has two different **b** sounds. One of these is like the English *b* of *boy*, *baby*, *bib*. The other has no English equivalent. It is produced like the familiar *b* but with this difference: for English *b* the lips close completely, stopping the flow of air out of the mouth; for the new Spanish sound the lips do not quite close—there is a

T31

narrow slit through which air continues to pass. Listen to the following Spanish words:

> hubo / uva / iba / a ver / una vez / me voy

[β]

EXERCISE 25. PRONUNCIATION

Repeat each of the following words and phrases.

> hubo / uva / iba / lava / a ver / una vez / me voy / se va

[b] *vs.* [β]

EXERCISE 26. LISTENING

You must learn when to use the two Spanish **b** sounds. The rule is like the one you learned for the two **d** sounds. If a **b** sound follows a vowel, it is pronounced without the lips closing completely; otherwise it is like English *b*. Listen to the following pairs of words and phrases. Pay special attention to the difference between the **b** sounds.

> voy–me voy / ver–a ver / va–se va / vez–una vez

[b] *vs.* [β]

EXERCISE 27. PRONUNCIATION

Repeat each of the following pairs.

> voy–me voy / ver–a ver / va–se va / vez–una vez /
> beca–una beca / vaca–una vaca

BASIC DIALOG V

LILI	¿Quién sabe cuándo llega Eva?	Who knows when Eva arrives?
1–8 ADELA	¿De los Estados Unidos? Yo sé.	From the United States? I know.
LILI	¿Cuándo, Adela?	When, Adela?
ADELA	El sábado.	(The) Saturday.

QUESTIONS
1. ¿Quién llega, Eva o Adela?   Eva.
2. ¿De dónde llega Eva?   Llega de los Estados Unidos.
3. ¿Quién sabe cuándo llega?   Adela sabe cuándo llega.
4. ¿Cuándo llega Eva?   Llega el sábado.

DIRECTED DIALOG

Dígale hola a Adela y pregúntele si Susana está en casa.   ¡Hola, Adela! ¿Está Susana en casa?

Dígale que no, que está en los Estados Unidos.   No, está en los Estados Unidos.

Pregúntele ¿Cómo? ¿Dónde?   ¿Cómo? ¿Dónde?

Dígale que en los Estados Unidos.   En los Estados Unidos.

Spanish [p], [t],
and [k] *vs.*
English consonants

EXERCISE 28. LISTENING

The sounds [p], [t], and [k] are similar in English and Spanish, but not identical. Listen carefully to the following English word: *tea*. Note that there is a puff of air between the consonant *t* and the vowel *e*. The same occurs with [p] and [k] sounds in English. In the corresponding Spanish sounds, however, there is no puff of air between the consonant and the following vowel. There is a further difference between the English and Spanish "t" sounds. In English, *t* is pronounced with the tip of the tongue touching the gums behind the upper teeth. In Spanish, the tongue does not touch the gums but the teeth themselves. You will now hear pairs of words. In each pair, the first word is English and the second is Spanish. Listen to each pair, noting carefully the difference between [p], [t], and [k] in English and Spanish.

two–tú, tea–ti, toss–tos, ten–ten, papa–papa, pour–por, kay–qué, cone–con

Spanish [p], [t],
and [k] *vs.*
English consonants

EXERCISE 29. SOUND DISCRIMINATION

Be prepared to write your responses for Exercise 29. You will hear a series of 12 words, some of which are Spanish, and some of which are English. You are to determine which are Spanish and which are English. For each word you hear, place a check mark in either the row labeled Spanish or the row labeled English. EXAMPLE You hear: **tan** You place your check mark in the row labeled Spanish because the word you heard was Spanish. We will begin now. *Read each word once in the language indicated.*

1. tone	English	5. pour	English	9. tos	Spanish
2. ti	Spanish	6. papa	Spanish	10. ten	English
3. tú	Spanish	7. cone	English	11. tea	English
4. toss	English	8. qué	Spanish	12. two	English

Now check your answers. *Repeat each of the preceding words and confirm by naming the appropriate language.*

[p], [t], [k]

EXERCISE 30. PRONUNCIATION

Repeat each of the following words.

tú, ti, tos, tan, tono, papa, por, pasa, qué, cana, con

EXERCISE 31. PRONUNCIATION

Listen to the following conversation. *Read the conversation once without interruption.*

¿Qué quieres, Arturo?
Quiero Coca-Cola.
¿Y tú, Pepe? ¿Quieres Coca-Cola?
Sí, tal vez.

Now repeat each of the following sentences. *Read each sentence separately, leaving a pause at the end.*

EXERCISE 32. LISTENING COMPREHENSION

Be prepared to write your responses for Exercise 32. You will hear a series of sentences. After each, you will hear two more sentences, A and B. Only one of these is a logical rejoinder to the first one. You are to determine which one it is.

EXAMPLE   You hear: Necesito practicar francés.
A. ¿Por qué no practicas conmigo?
B. ¿Escuchamos una canción, entonces?

You place your check mark in row A, because A is a logical rejoinder to the first sentence.

We will begin now. *Read each item once.*   Now check your answers. *Repeat each cue sentence and give correct answer as:*

1. ¿A quién llamas?
   A. En el teléfono.
   B. A la maestra.

   A la maestra.   B

2. Quiero practicar inglés.
   A. ¿Por qué no llamas a la chica americana?
   B. ¿Por qué no quieres?

   ¿Por qué no llamas a la chica americana?   A

3. ¿Qué pasa?
   A. No sé.
   B. Hablo con ella más tarde.

   No sé.   A

4. ¿Escuchamos unos discos ahora?
   A. No, tú y yo pronunciamos muy mal.
   B. No, quiero practicar inglés.

   No, quiero practicar inglés.   B

5. ¿Quieres practicar español?
   A. Si tú quieres.
   B. Sí, quiero practicar francés.

   Si tú quieres.   A

6. No contestan el teléfono.
   A. Tal vez no llega de la escuela todavía.
   B. Tal vez está en el sofá.

   Tal vez no llega de la escuela todavía.   A

7. ¿Quieres ir a las carreras?
   A. Sí, vamos a la casa.
   B. Sí, vamos en mi carro.

   Sí, vamos en mi carro.   B

8. Necesito practicar inglés.
   A. Está en la escuela.
   B. ¿Por qué?

   ¿Por qué?   B

9. Eva está en los Estados Unidos.
   A. ¿Cómo? ¿Dónde?
   B. No, está en California.

   ¿Cómo? ¿Dónde?   A

10. ¿Por qué no estudias conmigo?
    A. Muy bien, ¿cuándo?
    B. Porque tú y yo pronunciamos bastante bien.

    Muy bien, ¿cuándo?   A

11. Vamos a las carreras.
    A. ¿Cuándo? ¿Ahora?
    B. ¿Cómo? ¿Quién?

¿Cuándo? ¿Ahora?   A

12. ¿Está Adela en el teléfono?
    A. Sí, habla con la chica americana.
    B. No, está en el teléfono.

Sí, habla con la chica americana.   A

UNIT 2—SECTION B

Spanish [y]
vs.
English consonant

EXERCISE 33. LISTENING

Spanish has a consonant which is similar to the *y* of English *yes, yellow, year.* For the Spanish sound, however, the tongue is held more tensely, and comes closer to the roof of the mouth than for the English *y.* Because of this extra tightness, the Spanish [y] may sound almost like the *j* sound in the word *judge.* You will now hear pairs of words. In each pair, the first word is English and the second is Spanish. Compare the sound of the English *y* and Spanish [y] in each pair, noting the extra force of the Spanish sound.

yam–llama, yes–yeso, yen–lleno, you–lluvia

[y] at the
beginning of
a word

EXERCISE 34. PRONUNCIATION

Repeat each of the following words.

yo, yeso, llama, llega, ya, lluvia

[y] within
a word

EXERCISE 35. LISTENING

Listen to the following words. Note that the Spanish [y] always goes in the same syllable as the following vowel.

ella, silla, ellos, caballo

The syllable division for these words is as follows: [e–ya], [si–ya], [e–yos], [ka–ba–yo]. *English speakers tend to attach the* [y] *to the end of the preceding syllable, rather than to start the new syllable with* [y].

[y] within
a word

EXERCISE 36. PRONUNCIATION

Repeat each of the following words.

ella, oye, olla, silla, ellos, caballo

EXERCISE 37. LISTENING COMPREHENSION

Be prepared to write your responses for Exercise 37. You will hear six incomplete sentences. After each sentence you will hear three words or phrases, A, B, and C. You are to determine which word or phrase logically completes the sentence.

EXAMPLE   You hear: Habla muy
              A. quién.   B. bien.   C. inglés.

You circle the letter B, because **bien** logically completes the sentence.   *(continued)*

We will begin now. *Read each item once.*

Now check your answers. *Repeat each cue once, adding the appropriate completion.*

1. ¿Quieres escuchar
   A. las noticias?
   B. el teléfono?
   C. la escuela?

   ¿Quieres escuchar las noticias?   A

2. Vamos a la
   A. chica americana.
   B. canción.
   C. escuela.

   Vamos a la escuela.   C

3. ¿Escuchamos unos discos
   A. quién?
   B. más tarde?
   C. muy mal?

   ¿Escuchamos unos discos más tarde?   B

4. Hablo con ella
   A. ahora.
   B. americana.
   C. conmigo.

   Hablo con ella ahora.   A

5. Necesitas practicar español
   A. con la maestra.
   B. por la biblioteca.
   C. a Blanca.

   Necesitas practicar español con la maestra.   A

6. ¿Por qué no estudias
   A. entonces?
   B. bastante mal?
   C. cuándo?

   ¿Por qué no estudias entonces?   A

EXERCISE 38. DICTATION

Be prepared for a dictation. Cover the Spanish sentences which you have in front of you. Each sentence will be read twice. You are to write it as you hear it. We will begin now. *Read each sentence twice.*

1. ¿Qué escuchas? ¿Unos discos?
2. Quiero practicar con la chica americana.
3. ¿Por qué no practicas conmigo?

Uncover the Spanish sentences and compare them with the ones you have written. *Repeat each sentence once.*

UNIT 2—SECTION C

[ay], [ey], [oy], *and* [uy]

EXERCISE 39. LISTENING

Listen to the following Spanish sounds: [ay], [ey], [oy], [uy]. These sounds are produced by shifting rapidly from one vowel position to another. Now listen to the following English word: *boy.* The *-oy* in *boy* is also pronounced by shifting from one vowel to another. There is an important difference between this type of sound in English and Spanish: in Spanish the shifting, or gliding, is much faster and tenser. Now listen to the following pairs of words, noting the difference between the English and Spanish sounds.

I–ay, ray–rey, lay–ley, boy–voy

[ay], [ey], [oy], *and* [uy]

EXERCISE 40. PRONUNCIATION

Repeat each of the following words.

ay, baile, ley, seis, voy, soy, doy, hoy, uy, muy

EXERCISE 41. LISTENING COMPREHENSION

Be prepared to write your responses for Exercise 41. You will hear six sentences. You are to determine what subject pronoun corresponds to the verb in each sentence. EXAMPLE You hear: **Llamo a la maestra.** You circle the pronoun **yo** in the example column, because **yo** is the subject pronoun corresponding to the verb **llamo**.

We will begin now. *Read each sentence once.*

1. Escuchamos unos discos.
2. Llego después.
3. ¿Estudias con la chica americana?
4. No contestan el teléfono.
5. Pronuncia bastante bien.
6. Necesitas practicar español.

Now check your answers. *Repeat each sentence and give the correct answer as:*

nosotros
yo
tú
ellas
él
tú

EXERCISE 42. DICTATION

Be prepared for a dictation. Cover the Spanish sentences which you have in front of you. Each sentence will be read twice. You are to write it as you hear it. We will begin now. *Read each sentence twice.*

1. Tal vez escuchan una canción.
2. Susana pasa por la escuela.
3. Blanca pronuncia muy bien.

Uncover the Spanish sentences and compare them with the ones you have written. *Repeat each sentence once.*

UNIT 2—SECTION D

[a], [e], [i], [o], *and* [u]

EXERCISE 43. PRONUNCIATION

In this exercise you will say Spanish words with the sounds [a], [e], [i], [o], and [u]. Repeat each of the following words. Pay special attention to the vowel sounds.

Blanca, llama, habla, mal, está, bastante, alemán, chica, americana, practica, teléfono, escucha, disco

T37

EXERCISE 44. PRONUNCIATION

Repeat each of the following sentences.

Blanca está en el teléfono.
Llama a la chica americana.

Necesita practicar inglés.
Habla inglés bastante mal.

EXERCISE 45. LISTENING COMPREHENSION

Be prepared to write your responses for Exercise 45. You will hear a series of sentences. After each, you will hear two more sentences, A and B. Only one of these is a logical rejoinder to the first one. You are to determine which one it is.

EXAMPLE   You hear: ¿A quién llamas?
                      A. Llamo a la chica americana.
                      B. Llaman a la chica americana.

You place your check mark in row A, because A is the logical rejoinder to the first sentence.

We will begin now. *Read each item once.*

Now check your answers. *Repeat each cue sentence once and give the correct answer as:*

1. ¿Qué estudian ustedes?
   A. Estudian español.
   B. Estudiamos español.

   Estudiamos español.   B

2. ¿Pronuncia bien Blanca?
   A. Sí, pronuncia muy bien.
   B. Sí, pronuncio muy bien.

   Sí, pronuncia muy bien.   A

3. Necesitamos practicar inglés.
   A. ¿Por qué no estudian conmigo?
   B. ¿Por qué no estudia conmigo?

   ¿Por qué no estudian conmigo?   A

4. Eva no contesta.
   A. No llega de la escuela todavía.
   B. No llegas de la escuela todavía.

   No llega de la escuela todavía.   A

5. ¿Habla usted francés?
   A. No, pero hablo inglés y español.
   B. No, pero hablamos inglés y español.

   No, pero hablo inglés y español.   A

EXERCISE 46. DICTATION

Be prepared for a dictation. Cover the Spanish sentences which you have in front of you. Each sentence will be read twice. You are to write it as you hear it. We will begin now. *Read each item twice.*

1. ¿A quién llamas? ¿A ella?
2. ¿Llegan ahora Blanca y Arturo?
3. Yo no sé con quién habla.

Uncover the Spanish sentences and compare them with the ones you have written. *Repeat each item once.*

EXERCISE 47. LISTENING COMPREHENSION

Be prepared to write at the end of this exercise. You will hear a dialog between a boy, Pedro, and a girl, Blanca. You will then be asked to write answers to questions on the dialog. Your answers do not have to be complete sentences, but they should be grammatically correct. Now listen to the dialog.

PEDRO	Blanca, ¿quieres practicar inglés conmigo?
BLANCA	No, tú no pronuncias muy bien.
PEDRO	Entonces, ¿llamamos a la chica americana?
BLANCA	Sí, más tarde.

Now listen to the questions.

1. ¿Con quién habla Pedro?
2. ¿Por qué no quiere Blanca practicar con él?
3. ¿A quién quiere llamar Pedro entonces?
4. ¿Quiere Blanca llamar a la chica americana?

Now listen to the dialog again. *Repeat only the dialog and then give the students time to write their answers.*

UNIT 3—SECTION A

Spanish [l] after a vowel vs. English consonant

EXERCISE 48. LISTENING

A Spanish l after a vowel is very different from an English *l*. In both English and Spanish, the tip of the tongue touches the roof of the mouth. In English, however, the back part of the tongue is held low in the mouth; in Spanish, it is kept high throughout the [l] sound. You will now hear pairs of words. In each pair, the first word is English; the second is Spanish. Now listen to each pair, paying special attention to the contrast between the English and Spanish "l" sounds.

meal–mil, all–al, tall–tal, moll–mal, dell–del, "L"–el, hotel–hotel, coal–col

Spanish [l] after a vowel vs. English consonant

EXERCISE 49. SOUND DISCRIMINATION

Be prepared to write your responses for Exercise 49. You will hear a series of words, some of which are Spanish, and some of which are English. You are to determine which are Spanish and which are English. For each word you hear, place a check mark in either the row labeled Spanish or the row labeled English. EXAMPLE You hear: *all* You place your check mark in the row labeled English, because the word you heard was an English word. We will begin now. *Read each word once in the language indicated.*

1.	mil	Spanish	5.	hotel	Spanish
2.	al	Spanish	6.	coal	English
3.	tall	English	7.	meal	English
4.	mal	Spanish	8.	del	Spanish

Now check your answers. *Repeat each of the preceding words once and confirm by naming the appropriate language.*

EXERCISE 50. PRONUNCIATION

Repeat each of the following words.

mil, al, mal, del, hotel, col, el, Miguel, Manuel

EXERCISE 51. PRONUNCIATION

Listen to the following conversation. *Read the conversation once without interruption.*

¡Hola, Manuel!
¡Hola, Vidal! ¿Cómo estás?
Mal. ¿Dónde está Miguel?
En el hotel.

Now repeat each of the following sentences. *Read each item separately, leaving a pause at the end.*

EXERCISE 52. LISTENING COMPREHENSION

Be prepared to write your responses for Exercise 52. You will hear three sets of three sentences each. You are to match the time expressions in each sentence with the time expressions on your paper. EXAMPLE You hear: **Cierran a la una.** You place an A next to one o'clock on your paper.

We will begin now. *Read each sentence once.*

Now check your answers. *Repeat each sentence once and give the correct answer as:*

1. A. Cierran las tiendas a las cinco.
   B. La película empieza a las cuatro.
   C. La chica llega a la una.

   A. five o'clock
   B. four o'clock
   C. one o'clock

2. A. Las carreras empiezan a las dos.
   B. Vamos al desfile a las doce.
   C. El examen es a las nueve.

   A. two o'clock
   B. twelve o'clock
   C. nine o'clock

3. A. ¿Cuándo es la fiesta, a las ocho?
   B. Llaman a las tres.
   C. Cierran el mercado a las siete.

   A. eight o'clock
   B. three o'clock
   C. seven o'clock

UNIT 3—SECTION B

EXERCISE 53. LISTENING

In Spanish, an unstressed **i** followed by another vowel sounds like the *y* in *yes*, and forms one syllable with the following vowel. In this exercise you will hear sets of three words. In each set, the first word is an English word beginning with *y*; the second is the same English word with a consonant in front of it; and the third is a Spanish word with an unstressed **i** followed by another vowel. These Spanish words resemble the artificially created English words. Now listen to each set, paying attention to the sequence of similar sounds.

yes	d– yes	diez
yet	k– yet	quieto
yellow	s– yellow	cielo
yet	n– yet	nieto
yen	t– yen	tienda
yet	s– yet	siete

[y]

EXERCISE 54. PRONUNCIATION

Repeat each of the following words.

> diez, quieto, cielo, nieto, tienda, siete, pienso,
> pronuncio, noticias

EXERCISE 55. PRONUNCIATION

Listen to the following conversation. *Read the conversation once without interruption.*

> ¿A qué hora cierran las tiendas?
> A las siete. ¿Qué tienes que comprar?
> Algo para la chica italiana.

Now repeat each of the following sentences. *Read each item separately, leaving a pause at the end.*

EXERCISE 56. LISTENING COMPREHENSION

Be prepared to write your responses for Exercise 56. You will hear a series of sentences. After each, you will hear two more sentences or phrases, A and B. Only one of these is a logical rejoinder to the first one. You are to determine which one it is.

EXAMPLE   You hear: ¿Tienes que comprar algo?
    A. No, nada.   B. No, para mi mamá.

You place your check mark in row A, because A is a logical rejoinder to the first sentence.

We will begin now. *Read each item once.*   Now check your answers. *Repeat each cue sentence once and give the correct answer as:*

1. Me aprietan mucho los zapatos.   No vamos al centro, entonces.   A
   A. No vamos al centro, entonces.
   B. ¿Qué dan?

2. No puedo caminar más.   ¿Por qué no?   A
   A. ¿Por qué no?
   B. ¿Por qué no caminamos por el
      parque, entonces?

3. ¿Adónde van?   Al mercado.   B
   A. En el cine.
   B. Al mercado.

T41

4. Cierran a las seis.   ¡Apúrate, entonces!   B
   A. ¿En qué piensas?
   B. ¡Apúrate, entonces!

5. ¿Qué dan?   Una película americana.   B
   A. ¿Por qué? ¿Tienes que comprar
      algo?
   B. Una película americana.

6. ¿Cuándo es la fiesta?   No sé, ¿por qué?   B
   A. Vamos en mi carro.
   B. No sé, ¿por qué?

7. Vamos al cine.   ¿Por qué no estudiamos antes?   B
   A. Una película italiana.
   B. ¿Por qué no estudiamos antes?

8. No quiero practicar francés. Yo tampoco.   A
   A. Yo tampoco.
   B. Ya casi empieza.

9. ¿Vamos a las tiendas?   ¿Por qué? ¿Necesitas comprar algo?   B
   A. ¿Por qué? ¿Tienes que estudiar?
   B. ¿Por qué? ¿Necesitas comprar
      algo?

10. ¿Cuándo es la fiesta?   Mañana, a las ocho.   B
    A. En la escuela.
    B. Mañana, a las ocho.

11. ¿Dónde está Lili?   En el teléfono.   B
    A. Una chica italiana.
    B. En el teléfono.

12. ¿Es Adela de los Estados Unidos?   Sí, es americana.   B
    A. Sí, en la sala.
    B. Sí, es americana.

UNIT 3—SECTION C

*Spanish [h]
vs. English
consonant*

EXERCISE 57. LISTENING

In Spanish, the letter **g** before **e** or **i** and the letter **j** represent a sound similar—but not identical—to that of an English *h*. You will now hear pairs of words. In each pair, the first word is English and the second is Spanish. Now listen to each pair, comparing the sound of English *h* with the corresponding Spanish sound.

hen–gente, heel–Gil, here–gira, hose–José, home run–jonrón

[h]

EXERCISE 58. PRONUNCIATION

In this exercise you will say Spanish words with the letter **j** or the letter **g** before **e** or **i**. To say this sound, the back of your tongue should be held high in the mouth, to produce considerable friction noise. Now repeat each of the following words.

gente, Gil, justo, jugos, jonrón, jueves, mejor, hijo

EXERCISE 59. PRONUNCIATION

Listen to the following exchange. *Read the exchange once without interruption.*

> ¿Usted es Jorge o Jacinto?
> José, José Jiménez.
> ¿De Los Ángeles?
> No, de México.

Now repeat each of the following sentences. *Read each item separately, leaving a pause at the end.*

EXERCISE 60. LISTENING COMPREHENSION

Be prepared to write your responses for Exercise 60. In this exercise you will hear eight sentences. You are to determine whether the noun in each sentence is masculine or feminine. **EXAMPLE** You hear: **Los chicos llegan mañana.** You place your check mark in the row labeled Masculine, because **chicos** is a masculine noun.

We will begin now. *Read each sentence once.*

Now check your answers. *Repeat each cue sentence once and give the correct answer as:*

1. Las chicas estudian mucho. — chicas — feminine
2. Los señores llegan ahora. — señores — masculine
3. La maestra habla conmigo. — maestra — feminine
4. Las señoras compran algo. — señoras — feminine
5. El tío no habla mucho. — tío — masculine
6. Los maestros llegan tarde. — maestros — masculine
7. El chico pronuncia bien. — chico — masculine
8. Los amigos de Raúl no contestan. — amigos — masculine

EXERCISE 61. DICTATION

Be prepared for a dictation. Cover the Spanish sentences which you have in front of you. Each sentence will be read twice. You are to write it as you hear it. We will begin now. *Read each sentence twice.*

> 1. ¿Vamos a la biblioteca con Pedro?
> 2. El sábado vamos a un baile.
> 3. Blanca habla inglés bastante bien.

Uncover the Spanish sentences and compare them with the ones you have written. *Repeat each sentence once.*

UNIT 3—SECTION D

Spanish [ñ]
vs.
English consonant

EXERCISE 62. LISTENING

The sound represented by the Spanish consonant **eñe** is similar—but not identical—to the *ny* of English *canyon*. Listen to the English word *canyon*. In English, the *n* and the *y* are divided into two syllables: *can-yon*. The Spanish [ñ] sound is a single sound, occurring in the same syllable as the following vowel. Now listen to the following pairs of words, noting the difference between English *ny* or *ni* in the first word and Spanish **eñe** in the second.

canyon–caño, companion–acompaño, pinion–piña

[ñ]

EXERCISE 63. PRONUNCIATION

Repeat each of the following words.

señora, señor, señorita, mañana, español, caño, uña

EXERCISE 64. PRONUNCIATION

Listen to the following exchange. *Read the exchange once without interruption.*

¿Cuándo llegan los señores españoles?
Llegan mañana, señora.

Now repeat each of the following sentences. *Read each sentence separately, leaving a pause at the end.*

EXERCISE 65. LISTENING COMPREHENSION

Be prepared to write your answers for Exercise 65. You will hear a series of sentences, some of which are questions, some of which are statements. Place a check mark in either the row labeled Question or the row labeled Statement, according to whether the sentence you hear is a question or a statement.   EXAMPLE   You hear: **¿Manolo habla español?**   You place your check mark in the row labeled Question because the sentence you heard was a question.

We will begin now. *Read each sentence once.*

Now check your answers. *Repeat each sentence once and give the correct answer as:*

1. Cierra la puerta la maestra.	Statement
2. ¿Alguien pasa por la biblioteca?	Question
3. ¿Estudia Arturo en casa?	Question
4. Escuchan las noticias los chicos.	Statement
5. ¿Es mañana el Día de la Madre?	Question
6. Me aprietan los zapatos.	Statement
7. Ya empieza la película.	Statement
8. ¿Tú estudias español?	Question
9. Ella habla inglés.	Statement
10. ¿Quiere usted escuchar unos discos?	Question
11. ¿Pronuncio mal yo?	Question
12. Es americana ella.	Statement
13. ¿Las chicas están en la sala?	Question
14. Llegan más tarde ellos.	Statement
15. Necesitamos estudiar tú y yo.	Statement

EXERCISE 66. DICTATION

Be prepared for a dictation. Cover the Spanish sentences which you have in front of you. Each sentence will be read twice. You are to write it as you hear it. We will begin now. *Read each item twice.*

1. ¿Dónde estudia usted español, señorita?
2. ¿Qué día es mañana? Domingo.
3. Vamos al mercado y a las tiendas.

Uncover the Spanish sentences and compare them with the ones you have written. *Repeat each item once.*

EXERCISE 67. LISTENING COMPREHENSION

Be prepared to write at the end of this exercise. You will hear a dialog between a girl, Blanca, and a boy, Raúl. You will then be asked to write answers to questions on the dialog. Your answers do not have to be complete sentences, but they should be grammatically correct. Now listen to the dialog.

BLANCA   ¿En quién piensas, en la chica americana?
RAÚL   Sí, llega el jueves.
BLANCA   ¿Tú hablas inglés, Raúl?
RAÚL   No mucho, pero ella habla español muy bien.

Now listen to the questions.

1. ¿En quién piensa Raúl?
2. ¿Qué día llega la chica americana?
3. ¿Habla inglés Raúl?
4. ¿Cómo habla español la chica americana, bien o mal?

Now listen to the dialog again. *Repeat only the dialog and then give the students time to write their answers.*

UNIT 4—SECTION A

[g] *vs.* [ǧ]

EXERCISE 68. LISTENING

In Spanish the letter **g** before **a**, **o**, **u**, or a consonant may represent two different sounds. One of these is like the English *g* of *girl*. The other does not have an English equivalent. For the familiar [g] sound, the back part of the tongue touches the roof of the mouth, briefly stopping the flow of air. For the new [ǧ] sound, the back part of the tongue does not quite touch the roof of the mouth, so that air continues to flow while the sound is being produced. You will now hear pairs of words. In each pair, the first word is an English word with the [g] sound occurring between vowels. The second is a matching Spanish word with the new [ǧ] sound. Now listen to each pair, paying attention to the contrasting "g" sounds.

ragout–ragú, iguana–iguana, elegant–elegante

EXERCISE 69. PRONUNCIATION

In this exercise, you will say Spanish words with the new **g** sound. To produce this sound, the back part of your tongue should be raised toward the roof of the mouth, but should not actually touch it. Now repeat each of the following words.

amiga, luego, abrigo, regalo, hago, lago, contigo, conmigo

EXERCISE 70. LISTENING

You must learn when to use the two Spanish **g** sounds. The rule is the same one you learned for the two **d** and **b** sounds. If a **g** sound follows a vowel, it is pronounced with the back of the tongue close to—but not touching—the roof of the mouth; otherwise, it is like the English *g*. You will now hear pairs of words and phrases. In each pair, the first item is a Spanish word or phrase with a **g** at the beginning or following a consonant; the second item is a Spanish phrase with the **g** following a vowel. Listen carefully to each pair, noting the difference between the two **g** sounds.

gato–ese gato, gusto–mucho gusto, gusta–le gusta,
un guía–una guía

EXERCISE 71. PRONUNCIATION

Repeat each of the following pairs.

gato–ese gato, gusto–mucho gusto, gusta–le gusta,
un guía–una guía, gasta–no gasta, gota–una gota

EXERCISE 72. PRONUNCIATION

Listen to the following conversation. *Read the conversation once without interruption.*

Tengo que comprar un regalo.
¿Para un amigo?
No, para una amiga.

Now repeat each of the following sentences. *Read each sentence separately, leaving a pause at the end.*

EXERCISE 73. LISTENING COMPREHENSION

Be prepared to write your responses for Exercise 73. You will hear a series of sentences. After each, you will hear two more sentences or phrases, A and B. Only one of these is a logical rejoinder to the first one. You are to determine which one it is.

EXAMPLE You hear: Buenos días, Sr. Pérez.
A. Hola, Juan.
B. Ah, con razón.

You place your check mark in row A, because A is a logical rejoinder to the first phrase.

We will begin now. *Read each item once.*	Now check your answers. *Repeat each cue sentence once and give the correct answer as:*

1. Adiós, Susana.
  A. Hasta luego.
  B. Claro, don Pedro.
	Hasta luego. A

2. ¿Te gusta la nueva escuela?
  A. ¿Cuál de las dos es mayor?
  B. No mucho, ¿y a ti?
	No mucho, ¿y a ti? B

3. ¿Quién es esa chica?
  A. ¡Qué pretencioso!
  B. No sé.
	No sé. B

4. ¿Cuál de las dos es mayor?
  A. Ella.
  B. Somos amigos.
	Ella. A

5. Ustedes son hermanos, ¿verdad?
  A. Sí, somos alumnos.
  B. Sí, somos gemelos.
	Sí, somos gemelos. B

6. Ese chico no quiere hablar con nosotros.
  A. ¡Qué antipático!
  B. Es muy simpático.
	¡Qué antipático! A

7. Esta camisa es muy bonita.
  A. Sí, me gusta mucho.
  B. Sí, no me gusta.
	Sí, me gusta mucho. A

8. Ana y María son gemelas.
  A. Pero no son hermanas.
  B. Pero no son idénticas.
	Pero no son idénticas. B

9. ¿Te gusta esta corbata?
  A. Claro, es muy linda.
  B. Claro, es muy grande.
	Claro, es muy linda. A

10. Todos los compañeros son muy simpáticos.
  A. Excepto la chica americana.
  B. Excepto la maestra.
	Excepto la chica americana. A

11. ¿Quién es el chico rubio?
  A. Es un nuevo alumno.
  B. Es la hermana de Susana.
	Es un nuevo alumno. A

12. ¿Dónde están Susana y Cristina?
  A. Son gemelas.
  B. En la cocina.
	En la cocina. B

UNIT 4—SECTION B

[r] *vs.* [đ]   **EXERCISE 74. LISTENING**

In this exercise you will hear pairs of Spanish words. In each pair, the first word has an **r** between vowels; the second is a matching word with a **d** in the same place. Remember that a Spanish **r** between vowels is like the English *d* in *Eddy, Teddy,* and that a Spanish **d** between vowels is not like an English *d*, but like the English *th* in *either, neither.* Now listen to each pair. Note the difference between the **r** and **d** sounds.

cara–cada, cero–cedo, miro–mido, toro–todo

[r] *vs.* [d]

EXERCISE 75. SOUND DISCRIMINATION

Be prepared to write your responses for Exercise 75. You will hear a series of words, some of which contain an **r**, and some of which contain a **d**. For each word you hear, place a check mark in either the row labeled **r** or the row labeled **d**.   EXAMPLE You hear: **cada**   You place your check mark in the row labeled **d** because the word you heard contained the sound **d**. We will begin now. *Read each word once.*

1. miro **r**	3. cara **r**	5. todo **d**	7. puro **r**
2. pudo **d**	4. loro **r**	6. codo **d**	8. mido **d**

Now check your answers. *Repeat each of the preceding words once and confirm by naming the appropriate sound.*

[r] *vs.* [d]

EXERCISE 76. PRONUNCIATION

Repeat each of the following pairs of words. Make sure the **r** and **d** sound different.

cara–cada, cero–cedo, cera–ceda, toro–todo, coro–codo, loro–lodo,
miro–mido, puro–pudo

EXERCISE 77. LISTENING COMPREHENSION

Be prepared to write your responses for Exercise 77. You will hear a series of incomplete sentences followed by three possible completions, A, B, and C. You are to determine which one correctly completes the sentence.

EXAMPLE   You hear: Necesita un
                      A. vestido.
                      B. blusa.
                      C. zapatos.

You circle the letter A on your paper because **vestido** correctly completes the sentence.

We will begin now. *Read each item once.*

Now check your answers. *Repeat each cue once, adding the appropriate completion.*

1. Llega con unos
   A. amigo.   B. compañeros.
   C. maestra.

   Llega con unos compañeros.   B

2. ¿Tienes que comprar una
   A. falda?   B. corbatas?
   C. zapatos?

   ¿Tienes que comprar una falda?   A

3. Necesitamos un   Necesitamos un carro.   B
   A. discos.
   B. carro.
   C. corbatas.

4. ¿Por qué no compras una   ¿Por qué no compras una camisa?   B
   A. regalos?
   B. camisa?
   C. abrigo?

5. Estudiamos con unas   Estudiamos con unas amigas.   C
   A. maestro.
   B. compañeros.
   C. amigas.

6. Susana tiene un   Susana tiene un hermano.   A
   A. hermano.
   B. amiga.
   C. tías.

7. Quiero comprar un   Quiero comprar un sombrero.   C
   A. zapatos.
   B. camisa.
   C. sombrero.

8. ¿Por qué no vamos con unos   ¿Por qué no vamos con unos amigos?   A
   A. amigos?
   B. compañeras?
   C. chico?

9. ¿Quieres escuchar unas   ¿Quieres escuchar unas canciones?   B
   A. discos?
   B. canciones?
   C. canción?

10. Pienso en una   Pienso en una chica.   C
   A. examen.
   B. películas.
   C. chica.

EXERCISE 78. DICTATION

Be prepared for a dictation. Cover the Spanish sentences which you have in front of you. Each sentence will be read twice. You are to write it as you hear it. We will begin now. *Read each sentence twice.*

1. Las gemelas García son muy inteligentes.
2. ¿Cuál de las dos es mejor? Ninguna.
3. Miguel llega con alguien.
4. ¿Con Jorge? No, con Guillermo.

Uncover the Spanish sentences and compare them with the ones you have written. *Repeat each sentence once.*

[r] *before a*
consonant

EXERCISE 79. LISTENING

Be prepared for Exercise 79. Look at the words you have in front of you. The words in the left-hand and right-hand columns are artificially created English words. The words in the center column are Spanish words with a single **r** before a consonant. Remember that Spanish [r] is like the English *t* or *d* in *Betty* or *Teddy*. The made-up English words on the left, if rapidly pronounced, are similar to the Spanish words. The English words on the right do not sound at all like the Spanish words. Now listen to the Spanish words, noting the sound of Spanish [r] before a consonant.

totter they	tarde	tar day
sweater tay	suerte	swear tay
cotter taw	carta	car taw
cotter nay	carne	car nay
petter though nay	perdone	pear doh nay

[r] *before a*
consonant

EXERCISE 80. PRONUNCIATION

Repeat each of the Spanish words once.

tarde, suerte, carta, carne, perdone, martes, porque, Carlos, permiso

EXERCISE 81. PRONUNCIATION

Listen to the following conversation. *Read the conversation once without interruption.*

Buenas tardes, don Carlos.
Buenas tardes, Marta.
Yo soy Bárbara. Marta es mi hermana.
Ay, perdón.

Now repeat each of the following sentences. *Read each sentence separately, leaving a pause at the end.*

EXERCISE 82. LISTENING COMPREHENSION

Be prepared to write your responses for Exercise 82. You will hear a series of remarks. Each remark refers to a girl, a boy, two girls, or a mixed group. You are to decide to whom the remark refers.

EXAMPLE   You hear: ¡Qué alta es!

You place a check mark in the row labeled Girl, because the remark refers to a girl.

We will begin now. *Read each item once.*   Now check your answers. *Repeat each sentence once and give correct answer as:*

1. ¡Qué simpática!   girl
2. Es muy pretencioso.   boy

T50

3. Son muy bonitas.	two girls
4. No es alto, es bajo.	boy
5. No me gusta. Es muy antipática.	girl
6. Son casi idénticas.	two girls
7. Son americanos, ¿verdad?	mixed group
8. ¡Qué alto es!	boy
9. Son rubias y muy lindas.	two girls
10. No son tan pretenciosos.	mixed group

EXERCISE 83. DICTATION

Be prepared for a dictation. Cover the Spanish sentences which you have in front of you. Each sentence will be read twice. You are to write it as you hear it. We will begin now. *Read each sentence twice.*

1. Quiero comprar un regalo para don Pedro.
2. ¿A qué hora cierran el mercado?
3. La señorita americana no habla ruso.
4. ¡Ah, con razón!

Uncover the Spanish sentences and compare them with the ones you have written. *Repeat each sentence once.*

UNIT 4—SECTION D

[r] *after a consonant*

EXERCISE 84. LISTENING

Be prepared for Exercise 84. Look at the words you have in front of you. The words in the left-hand and right-hand columns are artificially created English words. The words in the center column are Spanish words with a single **r** after a consonant. Remember that Spanish [r] is like the English *t* or *d* in *Betty* or *Teddy*. The made-up English words on the left, if pronounced rapidly, are similar to the Spanish words. The English words on the right do not sound at all like the Spanish words. Now listen to the Spanish words, noting the sound of Spanish **r** after a consonant.

todáy say	trece	trace eh
put ówn toe	pronto	prone toe
could Émma	crema	cray ma
good écho	greco	Greco
fit éat oh	frito	free toe
git ón	gran	gran

[r] *after a consonant*

EXERCISE 85. PRONUNCIATION

Repeat each of the Spanish words.

trece, pronto, crema, greco, frito, gran

EXERCISE 86. PRONUNCIATION

Listen to the following conversation. *Read the conversation once without interruption.*

> ¿Quieres ir al centro conmigo, Cristina?
> ¡Claro! ¿Tienes que comprar algo para tu madre?
> No, para la maestra.

Now repeat each of the following sentences. *Read each sentence separately, leaving a pause at the end.*

EXERCISE 87. LISTENING COMPREHENSION

Be prepared to write your responses for Exercise 87. You will hear a series of short conversations. After each, you will hear an incomplete statement with two possible completions, A and B. You are to determine which one correctly completes the statement on the basis of the conversation.

EXAMPLE   You hear: ¿Lili es ésa que está en el sofá?
              Sí, ésa es Lili.

              El chico y la chica están
              A. en la sala.
              B. en el mercado.

You place your check mark in row A, because A completes the statement on the basis of the conversation.

We will begin now. *Read each item once.*

Now check your answers. Repeat each conversation and incomplete statement once, adding the appropriate completion.

1. Los compañeros son muy simpáticos.
   Sí, y los maestros también.
   El chico y la chica hablan de
   A. la escuela.
   B. un desfile.

   El chico y la chica hablan de la escuela. A

2. Necesito comprar un regalo.
   Yo también, para mi hermana.
   El chico y la chica necesitan ir
   A. a las tiendas.
   B. al cine.

   El chico y la chica necesitan ir a las tiendas. A

3. Yo soy Ana y ella es Juanita.
   ¡Pero son idénticas!
   Ana y Juanita son
   A. americanas.
   B. gemelas.

   Ana y Juanita son gemelas.   B

4. ¿Cuándo es el examen de inglés?
   Mañana a las diez.
   El chico y la chica necesitan
   A. ir al centro.
   B. estudiar inglés.

   El chico y la chica necesitan estudiar inglés. B

5. ¿Dónde está Adela?
   En la cocina.

   El chico y la chica están
   A. en el mercado.
   B. en una casa.

   El chico y la chica están en una casa.   B

6. ¿A qué hora empieza la película?
   A las dos. Apúrate.

   El chico y la chica quieren ir
   A. al cine.
   B. a la biblioteca.

   El chico y la chica quieren ir al cine.   A

7. Ese chico rubio es muy pretencioso.
   Es verdad. Casi no tiene amigos.

   El chico rubio es muy
   A. simpático.
   B. antipático.

   El chico rubio es muy antipático.   B

8. Yo necesito ir a las tiendas.
   Yo también. Quiero comprar unos
   zapatos.

   El chico y la chica necesitan ir
   A. al parque.
   B. al centro.

   El chico y la chica necesitan ir al centro.
   B

EXERCISE 88. LISTENING COMPREHENSION

Be prepared to write at the end of this exercise. You will hear a conversation between a teacher and two girls, Susana and Cristina. You will then be asked to write
answers to questions on the conversation. Your answers do not have to be complete
sentences, but they should be grammatically correct. Now listen to the conversation.

MAESTRO	Vamos a ver, ustedes son hermanas, ¿verdad?
SUSANA	Sí, señor. Somos gemelas.
MAESTRO	¿Ah, sí? Pero no son idénticas.
CRISTINA	No, Susana es mucho más alta que yo.

Now listen to the questions.

1. ¿Son hermanas las dos chicas?   3. ¿Son idénticas?
2. ¿Son gemelas?   4. ¿Cuál de las dos es más alta?

Now listen to the conversation again. *Repeat only the conversation and then give the
students time to write their answers.*

UNIT 5—SECTION A

Stress

EXERCISE 89. LISTENING

A stressed syllable is one which is more prominent than those around it. In a Spanish
word of several syllables, the stress may fall on any one of the last three. As you

learn each word, you must learn to stress the correct syllable. You will now hear pairs of words. The words in each pair are alike, except that a different syllable is stressed in each. Now listen to each pair, paying special attention to which syllable is stressed in each word.

papa–papá, tomas–Tomás, esta–está, llamo–llamó

Stress: words of two syllables

EXERCISE 90. STRESS DISCRIMINATION

Be prepared to write your responses to Exercise 90. You will hear a series of words. In some of the words the first syllable is stressed; in others, the second syllable is stressed. For each word you hear, place a check mark in either the row labeled First or the row labeled Second, according to whether the first or second syllable is stressed.

EXAMPLE   You hear: **llamo**   You place your check mark in the row labeled First because in the word you heard, the first syllable was stressed. We will begin now. *Read each word once.*

1. papá	second		6. esté	second
2. tomas	first		7. llego	first
3. compró	second		8. esta	first
4. habló	second		9. llamó	second
5. compro	first		10. cantó	second

Now check your answers. *Repeat each word and confirm by naming the appropriate syllable.*

Stress: words of two syllables

EXERCISE 91. PRONUNCIATION

In this exercise you will say pairs of Spanish words which are alike except for the stress. To say these pairs correctly, you should not make the stressed syllable too strong and the unstressed syllable too weak. Pronounce each pair with an even rhythm, making both syllables the same length, and giving a little more emphasis to the stressed syllable. Now repeat each of the following pairs.

papa–papá, tomas–Tomás, esta–está, llamo–llamó, este–esté, hablo–habló, llego–llegó, compro–compró

EXERCISE 92. LISTENING COMPREHENSION

Be prepared to write your responses for Exercise 92. You will hear a series of short conversations. After each, you will hear an incomplete statement followed by two possible completions, A and B. You are to select the correct completion on the basis of the conversation.

EXAMPLE   You hear: ¿Qué buscas, Luis?

Mis calcetines y mis zapatos. No encuentro nada en este dormitorio.

Luis está

A. en casa.

B. en la biblioteca.

You place your check mark in row A, because A logically completes the sentence on the basis of the conversation.

T54

We will begin now. *Read each item once.*

Now check your answers. *Repeat each conversation and incomplete statement once, adding the appropriate completion.*

1. ¡Apúrate! El partido empieza a las dos.

    Ay, caramba. No encuentro los boletos.

    Los dos chicos van
    A. a la biblioteca.
    B. al estadio.

    Los dos chicos van al estadio. B

2. Susana, ¿quieres ir a las tiendas conmigo?

    Sí, pero antes necesito ir al banco.

    Susana no tiene bastante
    A. dinero.
    B. comida.

    Susana no tiene bastante dinero. A

3. ¡Mamá! ¿Dónde están mis calcetines?

    Todo está en su lugar.

    El chico está
    A. en su cuarto.
    B. en la escuela.

    El chico está en su cuarto. A

4. ¡Los boletos son tan caros!

    Sí, pero es una película muy buena.

    Cuesta mucho dinero ir
    A. al estadio.
    B. al cine.

    Cuesta mucho dinero ir al cine. B

5. ¿Quién juega hoy?

    El Santos, campeón del mundo.

    Los dos chicos hablan de
    A. un desfile.
    B. un partido.

    Los dos chicos hablan de un partido. B

Note: In recorded program, exercise ends here ———→

6. Necesito comprar unos guantes, y también unas medias.

    Yo necesito comprar algo para mi mamá.

    Los dos chicos necesitan ir
    A. al café.
    B. a las tiendas.

    Los dos chicos necesitan ir a las tiendas. B

7. ¿Cuánto cuestan los boletos?

    Creo que cinco pesos.

    Los chicos van
    A. a las tiendas.
    B. a un partido.

    Los chicos van a un partido. B

    (continued)

8. ¡Juan! ¿Adónde vas con tanta
   prisa?
   Al aeropuerto. Mi mamá llega hoy
   de los Estados Unidos.

   La mamá de Juan llega   La mamá de Juan llega esta tarde.   A
   A. esta tarde.
   B. el martes o el miércoles.

9. ¿Quieres practicar inglés conmigo?
   Muy bien, si tú quieres.

   Los dos chicos   Los dos chicos estudian.   B
   A. escuchan discos. B. estudian.

10. ¿Qué día es hoy?
    Martes. Susana llega mañana de
    los Estados Unidos.

    Susana llega   Susana llega el miércoles.   B
    A. el martes. B. el miércoles.

11. ¿Qué necesitas comprar?
    Un regalo. El lunes es el Día de la
    Madre.

    La chica necesita comprar un regalo   La chica necesita comprar un regalo
    para   para su mamá. B
    A. su amiga. B. su mamá.

12. ¿Dónde están mis cosas?
    En tu dormitorio.

    Las cosas del chico están   Las cosas del chico están en la casa.   B
    A. en la escuela. B. en la casa.

EXERCISE 93. DICTATION

Be prepared for a dictation. Cover the Spanish sentences which you have in front of you. Each sentence will be read twice. You are to write it as you hear it. We will begin now. *Read each sentence twice.*

> A propósito, ¿Tomás está aquí?
> No, está en el café.
> Ah, con razón. Hoy es sábado.

Uncover the Spanish sentences and compare them with the ones you have written. *Repeat each sentence once.*

UNIT 5—SECTION B

*Stress: words
of three or more
syllables*

EXERCISE 94. LISTENING

In this exercise you will hear sets of three words each. The words in each set are similar, except that a different syllable is stressed in each.

ánimo	animo	animó
público	publico	publicó
práctico	practico	practicó
solícito	solicito	solicitó

EXERCISE 95. PRONUNCIATION

In this exercise you will say sets of three words each. Repeat each set, paying special attention to the stress.

ánimo	animo	animó
público	publico	publicó
práctico	practico	practicó
solícito	solicito	solicitó

EXERCISE 96. LISTENING COMPREHENSION

Be prepared to write your responses for Exercise 96. You will hear a series of sentences. After each you will hear the same speaker say two more sentences, A and B. Only one of these logically continues the thought of the first sentence. You are to determine which one it is.

EXAMPLE   You hear: Vamos al estadio.
            A. ¿Quieres ir con nosotros?
            B. Voy al parque.

You place your check mark in row A, because A logically continues the thought of the first sentence.

We will begin now. *Read each item once.*   Now check your answers. *Repeat each sentence once and give the correct answer as:*

1. El partido ya casi empieza.   ¡Apúrate!   A
   A. ¡Apúrate!
   B. Creo que el Santos.

2. ¡Cómo gritas!   No estoy sorda.   B
   A. Estamos sordas.
   B. No estoy sorda.

3. ¿Adónde vas con tanta prisa?   ¿A la escuela?   A
   A. ¿A la escuela?
   B. No sé.

4. Ustedes no buscan bien.   Todo está aquí.   B
   A. Nada está en su lugar.
   B. Todo está aquí.

5. Necesito ir al centro.   ¿Quieres ir conmigo?   B
   A. Tienes que comprar algo.
   B. ¿Quieres ir conmigo?

6. ¿Dónde están mis cosas?   ¿En la sala?   A
   A. ¿En la sala?
   B. Todo está en su lugar.

7. Los boletos son muy caros.   Cuestan ocho pesos.   A
   A. Cuestan ocho pesos.
   B. ¿Cuánto cuestan?

(continued)

8. ¿Cuándo limpian la casa?   ¿Esta tarde?   A
    A. ¿Esta tarde?
    B. Están en la cocina.

9. ¿Quién es esa chica?   ¿La hermana de Susana?   A
    A. ¿La hermana de Susana?
    B. ¿Tu hermano?

10. Todos los compañeros son tan   Los maestros también.   B
      simpáticos.
    A. No me gusta la escuela.
    B. Los maestros también.

EXERCISE 97. DICTATION

Be prepared for a dictation. Cover the Spanish sentences which you have in front of you. Each sentence will be read twice. You are to write it as you hear it. We will begin now. *Read each sentence twice.*

> ¿Estudias ruso, francés, alemán, o español?
> ¿Yo? Inglés.
> José y yo vamos al café.
> Después vamos al partido de fútbol.

Uncover the Spanish sentences and compare them with the ones you have written. *Repeat each sentence once.*

UNIT 5—SECTION C

[y]

EXERCISE 98. PRONUNCIATION

In this exercise you will say Spanish words with an unstressed **i** followed by another vowel. Be careful not to make the **i** into a separate syllable. Now repeat each of the following words.

> noticias, gracias, pronuncia, italiana, tienda, tienes, aprieta,
> empieza, diez, estudio, pronuncio, estadio, dormitorio, adiós

EXERCISE 99. PRONUNCIATION

Listen to the following conversation. *Read the conversation once without interruption.*

> ¿Quieres ir al estadio conmigo el viernes?
> Sí, gracias. ¿Cuándo empieza el partido?
> A las diez.

Now repeat each of the following sentences. *Read each sentence separately, leaving a pause at the end.*

EXERCISE 100. LISTENING COMPREHENSION

Be prepared to write your responses for Exercise 100. You will hear a series of sentences. After each, you will hear two more sentences, A and B. One of these is the opposite of the first sentence. You are to determine which one it is.

EXAMPLE   You hear: ¿Cuál de las dos es mayor?
              A. ¿Cuál de las dos es mejor?
              B. ¿Cuál de las dos es menor?

You place your check mark in row B, because B is the opposite of the first sentence.

We will begin now. *Read each item once.*   Now check your answers. *Repeat each sentence once and give the correct answer as:*

1. Ese vestido es muy caro.   Ese vestido es muy barato.   B
   A. Ese vestido es muy bonito.
   B. Ese vestido es muy barato.

2. Las gemelas son antipáticas.   Las gemelas son muy simpáticas.   B
   A. Las gemelas son pretenciosas.
   B. Las gemelas son muy simpáticas.

3. Todo está en su lugar.   Nada está en su lugar.   A
   A. Nada está en su lugar.
   B. Las cosas están en su lugar.

4. Esta cocina es muy pequeña.   Esta cocina es muy grande.   B
   A. Esta cocina es muy linda.
   B. Esta cocina es muy grande.

5. Hablan español muy bien.   Hablan español muy mal.   B
   A. Hablan español bastante bien.
   B. Hablan español muy mal.

6. Ese señor es bajo.   Ese señor es alto.   B
   A. Ese señor es sordo.
   B. Ese señor es alto.

EXERCISE 101. DICTATION

Be prepared for a dictation. Cover the Spanish sentences which you have in front of you. Each sentence will be read twice. You are to write it as you hear it. We will begin now. *Read each sentence twice.*

1. ¿Cuánto cuestan los boletos? No sé.
2. ¡Cómo gritas, hijo! ¿Qué quieres?
3. ¿Tú estás en tu cuarto?

Uncover the Spanish sentences and compare them with the ones you have written. *Repeat each sentence once.*

UNIT 5—SECTION D

[w]   ## EXERCISE 102. LISTENING

In Spanish, an unstressed **u** followed by another vowel sounds like the *w* in *west*, and forms one syllable with the following vowel. In this exercise you will hear sets of three words. In each set, the first word is an English word beginning with a *w*; the second is the same English word with a consonant in front of it; and the third is a Spanish word with an unstressed **u** followed by another vowel. These Spanish words resemble the artificially created English words. Now listen to each set, paying attention to the sequence of similar sounds.

west	p-west	puesto
wane	b-wane	bueno
wet	f-wet	fuete
we	f-we	fui
well	m-well	muela
well	n-well	Manuel
web	y-web	llueve

[w]

EXERCISE 103. PRONUNCIATION

Repeat each of the following words.

> puesto, bueno, fuete, fui, muela, Manuel, llueve, encuentro, juego, pañuelo, cuatro, cuánto, guante, Luisa

EXERCISE 104. PRONUNCIATION

Listen to the following conversation. *Read the conversation once without interruption.*

> ¿Cuándo juega el Santos?
> No recuerdo, Luis.
> ¿Sabes cuánto cuestan los boletos?
> ¡Son muy caros!

Now repeat each sentence once. *Read each sentence separately leaving a pause at the end.*

EXERCISE 105. LISTENING COMPREHENSION

Be prepared to write your responses for Exercise 105. You will hear a series of sentences. After each, you will hear two more sentences, A and B. Only one of these is a logical rejoinder to the first one. You are to determine which it is.

EXAMPLE   You hear: Los boletos son muy caros.
    A. ¿Cuánto cuestan?
    B. ¿Cuánto cuesta?

You place your check mark in row A, because A is a logical rejoinder to the first sentence.

We will begin now. *Read each item once.*

Now check your answers. *Repeat each sentence once and give the correct answer as:*

1. Hoy juega el Santos.
   A. ¿Ah, sí? ¿Dónde juega?
   B. ¿Ah, sí? ¿Dónde juego?

¿Ah, sí? ¿Dónde juega?   A

T60

2. No encuentro nada aquí.   Tú no buscas bien.   A
   A. Tú no buscas bien.
   B. Él no busca bien.

3. ¿Dónde están mis cosas?   Están en la sala.   A
   A. Están en la sala.
   B. Estamos en la sala.

4. Tía Luisa tiene que comprar algo.   ¿Qué tiene que comprar?   B
   A. ¿Qué tienes que comprar?
   B. ¿Qué tiene que comprar?

5. ¡Luisito! ¿Dónde estas?   ¡Estoy aquí!   B
   A. ¡Están aquí!
   B. ¡Estoy aquí!

6. ¿Sabe usted cuánto cuestan los boletos?   No, no recuerdo.   B
   A. No, no recuerdan.
   B. No, no recuerdo.

7. ¿Dónde juegan fútbol ustedes?   Jugamos en el parque.   B
   A. Juego en el parque.
   B. Jugamos en el parque.

8. ¿Encuentras tus cosas?   No, no encuentro nada.   A
   A. No, no encuentro nada.
   B. No, no encuentras nada.

EXERCISE 106. LISTENING COMPREHENSION

Be prepared to write at the end of this exercise. You will hear a dialog between a girl, Eva, and a boy, Roberto. You will then be asked to write answers to questions on the dialog. Your answers do not have to be complete sentences, but they should be grammatically correct. Now listen to the dialog.

EVA   Roberto, ¿adónde vas con tanta prisa?
ROBERTO   Al aeropuerto. Tío Arturo llega de los Estados Unidos esta tarde.
EVA   ¿A qué hora llega? ¿Puedo ir yo también?
ROBERTO   Claro. ¡Apúrate! Llega a las tres.

Now listen to the questions.

1. ¿Adónde va Roberto con tanta prisa?   3. ¿Quiere Eva ir con Roberto?
2. ¿De dónde llega tío Arturo?   4. ¿A qué hora llega tío Arturo?

Now listen to the dialog again. *Repeat only the dialog and then give the students time to write their answers.*

UNIT 6—SECTION A

Stressed vowels: contrasting pairs

EXERCISE 107. LISTENING

In this exercise you will hear pairs of words which sound alike, except for the vowel sound in the stressed syllables. Listen carefully for the difference between the contrasting vowel sounds.

mato–meto, caso–quiso, caro–coro, pelo–polo, mera–mira

EXERCISE 108. PRONUNCIATION

Repeat each of the following pairs. Pay special attention to the contrasting vowel sounds in the stressed syllables.

mato–meto, masa–mesa, caso–quiso, caro–coro, bata–bota, Ana–una, pelo–polo, mero–moro, mera–mira, pepa–pipa, Eva–uva, pilo–polo, Lima–loma, iba–uva

EXERCISE 109. LISTENING COMPREHENSION

Be prepared to write your responses for Exercise 109. You will hear a series of short conversations followed by an incomplete statement with three possible completions, A, B, and C. You are to select the correct completion on the basis of the conversation.

EXAMPLE You hear: ¡Qué graciosas son todas estas fotos!
                Sí, ¿verdad? Son fotos de una reunión de familia.
                Los chicos ven
                A. un álbum. B. una mesa. C. una silla.

You circle A in the example column, because A best completes the sentence on the basis of the conversation.

We will begin now. *Read each item once.*   Now check your answers. *Repeat each conversation and incomplete statement once, adding the appropriate completion.*

1. Hernán, ¿es doña Marta la mamá de
   tu mamá?
   No, es la mamá de mi padre.
   Doña Marta es   Doña Marta es la abuela de Hernán.
   A. la abuela de Hernán.   A
   B. la tía de Hernán.   (Es la mamá de su padre.)
   C. la mamá de Hernán.

2. ¿Cuándo es la cena?
   Es a las ocho, en la casa de mis tíos.
   Los chicos hablan   Los dos chicos hablan de una comida.
   A. de un examen.   B
   B. de una comida.   (Hablan de la cena.)
   C. de un desayuno.

3. ¡Qué guapa es esa chica!
   Sí, muy guapa. Es mi prima.
   La chica es   La chica es bonita.   C
   A. gorda.   (Es una chica muy guapa.)
   B. fea.
   C. bonita.

4. Esta chica es muy linda también.
   Ésa es Adela, mi hermana mayor. Está bonita en la foto, pero ella no es muy linda, francamente.

   El chico que habla es
   A. el primo de Adela.
   B. el hermano de Adela.
   C. un compañero de Adela.

   El chico que habla es el hermano de Adela. B
   (Ella es su hermana mayor.)

5. Carlos, ¿quién es ese señor que está en el sofá?
   ¿Ése que habla con Susana? Es mi tío Antonio.

   El tío de Carlos está
   A. enfermo.
   B. cansado.
   C. sentado.

   El tío de Carlos está sentado. C
   (Está en el sofá.)

6. ¿Quieres estudiar conmigo?
   Ahora, no. Quiero ver las noticias.

   El chico quiere ver
   A. un álbum.
   B. una foto.
   C. el periódico.

   El chico quiere ver el periódico. C
   (Quiere ver las noticias.)

7. ¿Cuánto cuesta esta camisa?
   Esta camisa cuesta quince pesos pero la otra es más barata.

   La otra camisa cuesta
   A. doce pesos.
   B. veinte pesos.
   C. dieciséis pesos.

   La otra camisa cuesta doce pesos. A
   (Es más barata.)

8. ¿Dónde están mis libros?
   Todas tus cosas están en la mesa.

   Las cosas del chico están
   A. en el sofá.
   B. en el comedor.
   C. en el suelo.

   Las cosas del chico están en el comedor. B
   (Están en la mesa.)

UNIT 6—SECTION B

Unstressed vowels: contrasting pairs

EXERCISE 110. LISTENING

You already know that in English, unstressed vowels are pronounced less clearly than stressed vowels. You also know that <u>all</u> Spanish vowels are pronounced distinctly, whether or not they are stressed. In this exercise you will hear pairs of words which sound alike, except for one unstressed vowel. Listen carefully for the difference between the contrasting vowel sounds.

mesas–meses, lunas–lunes, chicas–chicos, pases–pasos,
pesado–pisado, legado–ligado, hijito–ojito

EXERCISE 111. PRONUNCIATION

Repeat each of the following pairs. Make certain you pronounce all the vowels clearly, and pay special attention to the contrasting vowel sounds.

> mesas–meses, coman–comen, señoras–señores, chicas–chicos,
> primas–primos, hermanas–hermanos, grites–gritos, pases–pasos,
> pesado–pisado, hijito–ojito, imito–omito, izado–usado

EXERCISE 112. LISTENING COMPREHENSION

Be prepared to write your responses to Exercise 112. In this exercise you will hear two phrases which could be linked either by a form of **ser** or a form of **estar**. You are to circle the verb form which correctly links the two phrases. EXAMPLE You hear: **¿El señor? ¿de Colombia?** You circle the word **es** in the example column, because it correctly links the two phrases: **¿El señor es de Colombia?**

We will begin now. *Read each item once.*   Now check your answers. *Repeat each item once and give the correct answer as:*

1. ¿Usted? ¿de California?	es	¿Usted es de California?
2. ¿Nosotros? ¿en el aeropuerto?	estamos	¿Nosotros estamos en el aeropuerto?
3. ¿El periódico? ¿en el suelo?	está	¿El periódico está en el suelo?
4. ¿Esta comida? ¿para el perro?	es	¿Esta comida es para el perro?
5. ¿Susana? ¿La hermana de Cristina?	es	¿Susana es la hermana de Cristina?
6. ¿La reunión? ¿a las cinco?	es	¿La reunión es a las cinco?
7. ¿Yo? ¿un alumno?	soy	¿Yo soy un alumno?
8. ¿Tú? ¿un maestro?	eres	¿Tú eres un maestro?
9. ¿El Santos? ¿campeón del mundo?	es	¿El Santos es el campeón del mundo?
10. ¿Los gemelos? ¿en la sala?	están	¿Los gemelos están en la sala?
11. ¿La comida? ¿en la mesa?	está	¿La comida está en la mesa?
12. ¿El examen? ¿aquí, a las cuatro?	es	¿El examen es aquí a las cuatro?
13. ¿Todos los alumnos? ¿en la casa de la maestra?	están	¿Todos los alumnos están en la casa de la maestra?
14. ¿Todas mis cosas? ¿en el suelo?	están	¿Todas mis cosas están en el suelo?

UNIT 6—SECTION C

EXERCISE 113. LISTENING

Listen to the following sentence, paying particular attention to how each syllable begins and ends:

> Pe dri to lle ga ma ña na.

Every syllable begins with a consonant and ends with a vowel. This pattern is typical of Spanish syllables. When a word ending in a consonant is followed by one starting with a vowel, the consonant and the following vowel form the first syllable of the second word. Listen to the following sentence.

Va nal cine.

The final **n** of **van** is pronounced with a**l**. Listen again.

Va nal cine.

Syllabification

EXERCISE 114. PRONUNCIATION

Repeat each of the following sentences.

Va nal cine.	(Van al cine.)
¿Arre gla nel cuarto?	(¿Arreglan el cuarto?)
¿Habla nustede sespañol?	(¿Hablan ustedes español?)

EXERCISE 115. LISTENING COMPREHENSION

Be prepared to write your responses for Exercise 115. You will hear a series of sentences, each one followed by two more sentences, A and B. Only one of these is a logical rejoinder to the first one. Listen carefully, then place a check mark in either row A or B, depending on which of the two rejoinders is correct.

EXAMPLE   You hear: ¿Cómo es su mamá?
                        A. Bien, gracias.
                        B. Muy bonita.

You place your check mark in the example column of row B, because B is a logical rejoinder to the first sentence.

We will begin now. *Read each item once.*   Now check your answers. *Repeat each cue sentence once and give the correct answer as:*

1. ¿Cómo es tu novio?   Es muy guapo.   B
   A. Está enfermo hoy.
   B. Es muy guapo.

2. ¿De dónde son ustedes?   Somos de aquí.   B
   A. Estamos aquí.
   B. Somos de aquí.

3. ¿Dónde está la comida?   En la mesa.   B
   A. En el comedor, a las seis.
   B. En la mesa.

4. ¡Qué bonita está Adela en la foto!   Sí, pero ella no es muy linda francamente.   A
   A. Sí, pero ella no es linda francamente.
   B. Sí, pero ella no está muy linda francamente.

5. ¿Cómo son las gemelas?   Altas y rubias y muy lindas.   A
   A. Altas y rubias y muy lindas.
   B. Muy bien.

6. ¿Dónde es el examen?   Aquí, a las tres.   A
   A. Aquí, a las tres.
   B. Aquí, en la mesa de la maestra.

7. ¿Cómo estás?   ¿Yo? Muy cansada.   A
   A. ¿Yo? Muy cansada.
   B. ¿Yo? Gorda, pero muy simpática.

8. ¿De dónde eres?   De California.   B
   A. En California.
   B. De California.

EXERCISE 116. DICTATION

Be prepared for a dictation. Cover the Spanish sentences which you have in front of you. Each sentence will be read twice. You are to write it as you hear it. We will begin now. *Read each sentence twice.*

1. ¿Puedo ver la foto de la fiesta?
2. Claro, Felipe.
3. ¿Quién es esa chiquita?
4. Mi prima Beatricita. Es simpatiquísima.

Uncover the Spanish sentences and compare them with the ones you have written. *Repeat each sentence once.*

UNIT 6—SECTION D

Vowel sequences in more than one word

EXERCISE 117. LISTENING

Since Spanish has many words that end in a vowel, and many which begin with a vowel, it often happens that two vowels occur together. If the two, or sometimes even three, are the same vowel, they are pronounced in normal speech as if they were a single vowel. Listen to the following sentences.

¿Dónde está?   Es mi hijito.   Ese que está sentado.
Este estadio.

Vowel sequences in more than one word

EXERCISE 118. PRONUNCIATION

Repeat each of the following sentences.

¿Dónde está?   Es mi hijito.   Ese que está sentado.   Este estadio.
¿Pedro o Juan?   Son casi idénticas.   ¿Necesita algo?
Van a la fiesta antes.   Van a la tienda ahora.   Va a hablar.

EXERCISE 119. LISTENING COMPREHENSION

Be prepared to write your responses for Exercise 119. You will hear a series of incomplete sentences. After each, you will hear three possible completions, A, B, and C. You are to determine which one correctly completes the sentence.

EXAMPLE   You hear: ¿Cuándo es

A. la mesa?   B. la chica?   C. la reunión?

You circle the letter C in the example column, because C correctly completes the sentence.

We will begin now. *Read each item once.*   Now check your answers. *Repeat each item once and give the correct answer as:*

1. Luis está muy   Luis está muy cansado.   A
   A. cansado.
   B. hijo.
   C. barato.

2. Susana está muy   Susana está muy delgada.   B
   A. prima.
   B. delgada.
   C. tía.

3. Tus libros están en   Tus libros están en el suelo.   C
   A. aquí.
   B. el partido.
   C. el suelo.

4. ¿Ese señor? Es mi   ¿Ese señor? Es mi abuelo.   C
   A. libro.
   B. periódico.
   C. abuelo.

5. ¿Puedo ver   ¿Puedo ver el álbum?   A
   A. el álbum?
   B. muy caro?
   C. la idea?

6. Está sentado en   Está sentado en el sofá.   C
   Á. ahora.
   B. la canción.
   C. el sofá.

7. ¿Dónde es   ¿Dónde es la fiesta?   A
   A. la fiesta?
   B. la chica?
   C. el maestro?

8. ¿A qué hora es   ¿A qué hora es el desfile?   A
   A. el desfile?
   B. el álbum?
   C. la foto?

EXERCISE 120. LISTENING COMPREHENSION

Be prepared to write at the end of this exercise. You will hear a dialog between a girl, Adela, and her brother, Luis. You will then be asked to write answers to questions on the dialog. Your answers do not have to be complete sentences, but they should be grammatically correct.

Now listen to the dialog.

ADELA	¿Quieres ir al cine esta tarde?
SU HERMANO	Muy bien. ¿Qué dan?
ADELA	No sé. ¿Dónde está el periódico?
SU HERMANO	En la mesa. Vamos a ver qué dan en el cine California.

Now listen to the questions.

1. ¿Adónde quiere ir Adela?
2. ¿Quiere ir al cine su hermano?
3. ¿Sabe Adela qué dan?
4. ¿Qué busca ella?
5. ¿Dónde está el periódico?

Now listen to the dialog again. *Repeat only the dialog and then give the students time to write their answers.*

UNIT 7—SECTION A

Spanish nt *vs.*
English nt

EXERCISE 121. LISTENING

The pronunciation of *nt* in English words like *winter*, *banter*, varies considerably. Often, neither the *n* nor the *t* is pronounced clearly. For example, *winter* may be pronounced almost exactly like *winner*. In Spanish, however, both the **n** and the **t** are always clear and distinct. In this exercise you will hear pairs of words. In each pair, the first word is an English word with the consonants *nt*. The second is a similar Spanish word, also with **nt**. Listen carefully for the difference between the English and the Spanish "nt" sounds. Listen to the following English and Spanish words.

> quantity–cantidad, contented–contento, canter–canto,
> Santa Monica–Santa Mónica, identical–idéntico

nt

EXERCISE 122. PRONUNCIATION

Repeat each of the following words.

> cuánto, tanto, idéntico, contento, Santa Mónica, guantes,
> restaurante, antipático, delante, cuento, lento, cantan, inventa,
> constante

Note: In recorded program, exercise ends here

EXERCISE 123. LISTENING COMPREHENSION

Be prepared to write your responses for Exercise 123. In this exercise you will hear a short conversation and an incomplete statement with three possible completions, A, B, C. You are to select the correct completion on the basis of the conversation.

EXAMPLE You hear: ¡Pedrito! ¡Apúrate! ¿Tienes los boletos?

¿No tienes tú los boletos?

No. ¡Caramba! ¿Dónde están?

No recuerdo. En casa, tal vez.

Pedrito está

A. contento.   B. distraído.   C. enfermo.

You place your check mark in row B, because B best completes the sentence on the basis of the conversation.

We will begin now. *Read each item once.*   Now check your answers. *Repeat each conversation and incomplete statement once, adding the appropriate completion.*

1. ¿Tú sabes inglés?

Un poco. Pero necesito un diccionario. ¿Y tú?

Yo, no. Yo estudio francés.

El chico y la chica son   El chico y la chica son españoles.   C
A. ingleses.   (No saben mucho inglés.)
B. americanos.
C. españoles.

2. ¡Qué graciosa es esa foto! ¿Quién es esta chica de ojos verdes y pelo rubio?

Mi hermana mayor.

¡Qué bonita es!

La foto está   La foto está en colores.   B
A. en la mesa.   (La chica tiene los ojos azules y el pelo
B. en colores.   rubio.)
C. en blanco y negro.

3. Juanito, ¿quieres practicar inglés conmigo?

No, estoy muy cansado.

¿Qué quieres hacer, entonces?

Nada. Estoy cansadísimo.

Juanito es   Juanito es perezoso.   C
A. pelirrojo.   (No quiere hacer nada.)
B. listo.
C. perezoso.

4. Señorita, ¿puedo ver esos guantes grises?

Sí, señor. Aquí están. Son bonitos, ¿verdad?

Sí, muy bonitos. ¿Cuánto cuestan?

Mmm, a ver. Diez pesos.

El señor está   El señor está en una tienda.   C
A. en un mercado.   (Quiere comprar unos guantes.)
B. en la estación.
C. en una tienda.

Note: In recorded program, exercise ends here ⟶

T69

5. Tú sabes hablar francés, ¿verdad, Carlos?
Sí, hablo español, francés, y alemán.
¿Es verdad? ¡Qué inteligente eres!

Carlos es muy
A. perezoso.
B. guapo.
C. listo.

Carlos es muy listo.   C
(Habla español, francés, y alemán.)

6. Debes ver a mi prima. Es tan bonita.
¿Cómo es ella? ¿Alta y rubia como tú, Adela?
No, ella tiene pelo negro y ojos negros y es más baja que yo.

La prima de Adela es
A. muy linda.
B. muy perezosa.
C. idéntica a Adela.

La prima de Adela es muy linda.   A
(Adela dice que es tan bonita.)

EXERCISE 124. SPOT DICTATION

Be prepared to do the writing for Exercise 124. You have in front of you a reading selection from which certain words have been omitted. This selection will now be read to you. You are to write the words omitted from the text in the space provided. We will begin now. *The underlined words have been omitted from the students' copies. Pause at each slanted line to allow students time to write.*

Yo

Yo soy Francisco Castro, alumno de la Escuela Americana. Es una escuela muy bonita y moderna. / Me gusta mucho. Mis compañeros son todos muy buenos y simpáticos. / Aquí tengo dos fotos: una es de la escuela; bonita, ¿no? / La otra es de todos los chicos y chicas que están en mi clase, / y del maestro, don Pedro. Ése que está sentado con la chica rubia soy yo. /

Now listen to the reading selection once more. Later, when you have time, compare the words you have written with those in the Narrative at the end of Unit 6.

UNIT 7—SECTION B

[aw], [ew]

EXERCISE 125. LISTENING

Listen to the following Spanish words. Pay special attention to the sounds [aw] and [ew].

auto, autobús, causa, restaurante, Mauro, Mauricio, deuda, Europa, neutro, reunión, Eugenia

[aw], [ew]

EXERCISE 126. PRONUNCIATION

In this exercise you will say Spanish words with the sounds [aw] and [ew]. Spanish [aw] is similar to the English *ou* in words like *house*, *out*, but the last part should be pronounced more tensely, with the lips held in a rounded position. Spanish [ew] does not have an English equivalent, but you can imitate it easily by combining the *e* of *bet* with the *oo* of *boot*—*e-oo*. Now repeat each of the following words.

auto, autobús, causa, restaurante, Mauro, Mauricio,
deuda, Europa, neutro, reunión, Eugenia

[aw], [ew]

EXERCISE 127. PRONUNCIATION

Listen to the following conversation. *Read the conversation once without interruption.*

Mauro . . .
¿Sí, Eugenia?
¿Qué pasa con el auto?
¡Está en neutro!

Now repeat each of the following sentences. *Read each sentence separately, leaving a pause at the end.*

EXERCISE 128. LISTENING COMPREHENSION

Be prepared to write your responses for Exercise 128. In this exercise you will hear a series of short monologs. After each, you will hear three phrases, A, B, and C. You are to determine which phrase tells what the monolog is about.

EXAMPLE   You hear: Es rubia, de ojos azules. Creo que debe ser muy guapa.
A. una chica   B. un chico   C. dos señores.

You circle the A in the example column, because A tells what the monolog is about.

We will begin now. *Read each item once.*   Now check your answers. *Repeat each monolog once and give the correct answer as:*

1. Es francés, pero vive en los Estados   un señor   B
   Unidos. Es alto y trigueño y muy
   simpático.
   A. una maestra
   B. un señor
   C. unos chicos

2. Es muy bonita y muy lista, pero   una nueva alumna   A
   también es muy pretenciosa. Fran-
   camente, no me gusta mucho.
   A. una nueva alumna
   B. un nuevo maestro
   C. un compañero de clase

3. ¡Qué grande es! Es nueva, ¿sabes?   una estación   C
   Es mucho más bonita que la otra.
   A. un mercado
   B. unas tiendas
   C. una estación

T71

4. ¡Es tan linda! Es blanca y amarilla.   una falda   A
¿Quieres ver?
   A. una falda
   B. unos guantes
   C. un pañuelo

5. Son muy antipáticas, las dos. Una   las hermanas López   C
es alta y rubia y la otra es baja y
trigueña. Pero en una cosa son
idénticas: son muy antipáticas.
   A. los gemelos García
   B. el Sr. Pérez
   C. las hermanas López

6. Es que no estudian. Son inteligentes,   unos alumnos   A
pero son todos muy perezosos.
Francamente, yo no sé qué hacer
con ellos.
   A. unos alumnos
   B. una señora
   C. un chico

7. Sí, es nuevo. Es muy bonito,   un carro   B
¿verdad? ¿Te gusta el color?
   A. una camisa
   B. un carro
   C. unos pantalones

8. Qué graciosa, ¿verdad? Es muy   una película   B
buena. Me gusta mucho. ¿A ti te
gusta?
   A. unas fotos
   B. una película
   C. un álbum

Note: In recorded program, exercise ends here ⟶

9. Son muy altos y guapos. Están en   los gemelos García   A
mi clase de inglés. Los dos son muy
inteligentes.
   A. los gemelos García
   B. el chico americano
   C. las gemelas Pérez

10. Es pequeña, pero es bastante bonita,   una casa   B
¿verdad? El maestro de francés vive
allí.
   A. un mercado
   B. una casa
   C. unos cuartos

11. Las dos son alemanas. Una es alta   dos amigas   B
y trigueña y la otra es baja y rubia
y un poco gorda.
   A. dos primos
   B. dos amigas
   C. la maestra de alemán

(continued)

12. Es bonita y no muy difícil. Creo   una canción   C
    que es española.
    A. un periódico
    B. unos libros
    C. una canción

UNIT 7—SECTION C

Spanish [s] vs.
English consonant

EXERCISE 129. LISTENING

In this exercise you will hear pairs of words. In each pair, the first word is an English word with the sound [Z] and the second is a matching Spanish word with the sound [s]. In Spanish, the sound [s] is almost the same as the sound spelled *s* in English words like *see, sit, seven.* However, some Spanish words with the [s] sound are very similar to English words with the [Z] sound. You must be careful to distinguish English [Z] from Spanish [s] in these words. Now listen to each pair, paying close attention to the difference between the two sounds.

> president–presidente, present–presente, visit–visita,
> proposition–propósito, reason–razón

[s]

EXERCISE 130. PRONUNCIATION

Repeat each of the following words. Be careful not to substitute the English [Z] for the Spanish [s].

> presidente, presente, razón, visa, López, Pérez

EXERCISE 131. PRONUNCIATION

Listen to the following exchange. *Read the exchange once without interruption.*

> ¿Susana López?
> Presente.
> ¿José Jiménez?
> Presente.
> Hoy vamos a visitar el parque zoológico.

Now repeat each of the following sentences. *Read each sentence separately, leaving a pause at the end.*

EXERCISE 132. LISTENING COMPREHENSION

Be prepared to write your responses for Exercise 132. In this exercise you will hear a series of incomplete sentences. After each, you will hear three possible completions, A, B, and C. You are to determine which one correctly completes the sentence.

EXAMPLE   You hear: No hablan
          A. durante la clase.   B. sin la clase.   C. con la clase.

You circle the letter A in the example column, because A correctly completes the sentence.

We will begin now. *Read each item once.*

Now check your answers. *Repeat each incomplete sentence once, adding the appropriate completion.*

1. Es una carta
   A. para ella.   B. durante ella.
   C. sin ella.

Es una carta para ella.   A

2. Juan está
   A. de mí.
   B. conmigo.
   C. a mí.

Juan está conmigo.   B

3. Pasamos
   A. por la biblioteca.
   B. de la biblioteca.
   C. con la biblioteca.

Pasamos por la biblioteca.   A

4. Vamos a la tienda
   A. sin el recreo.
   B. durante el recreo.
   C. del recreo.

Vamos a la tienda durante el recreo.   B

5. Mamá está
   A. en la casa.
   B. a la casa.
   C. para la casa.

Mamá está en la casa.   A

6. ¿Quién es el señor que está sentado
   A. para ti?
   B. contigo?
   C. por ti?

¿Quién es el señor que está sentado contigo?   B

7. Son unos regalos
   A. sin usted.
   B. con usted.
   C. para usted.

Son unos regalos para usted.   C

8. Pensamos en el baile
   A. durante el examen.
   B. detrás del examen.
   C. delante del examen.

Pensamos en el baile durante el examen.   A

9. Escribo una carta
   A. sin la cena.
   B. delante de la cena.
   C. después de la cena.

Escribo una carta después de la cena.   C

10. Vamos al cine
    A. detrás de las clases.
    B. después de las clases.
    C. sin las clases.

Vamos al cine después de las clases.   B

EXERCISE 133. DICTATION

Be prepared for a dictation. Cover the Spanish sentences you have in front of you.

Each sentence will be read twice. You are to write it as you hear it. We will begin now. *Read each sentence twice.*

1. María todavía pronuncia muy mal.
2. ¿Qué día es la fiesta? El viernes.
3. ¿Vas al estadio con tu tío?
4. ¿Dónde está el diccionario? En tu cuarto.

Uncover the Spanish sentences and compare them with the ones you have written. *Repeat each sentence once.*

UNIT 7—SECTION D

Spanish palatals

EXERCISE 134. LISTENING

In this exercise you will hear pairs of words. In each pair, the first word is an English word with the letters *si, ti,* or *di* in the middle and the second is a matching Spanish word with these letters in the same position. Now listen to each pair. Note the difference between the sounds represented by *si, ti,* and *di* in English and Spanish.

mission–misión, vision–visión, question–cuestión, cordial–cordial

Spanish palatals

EXERCISE 135. PRONUNCIATION

Repeat each of the following words.

misión, loción, nacional, delicioso, civilización, visión, decisión, división, confusión, cuestión, cordial

EXERCISE 136. LISTENING COMPREHENSION

Be prepared to write your responses for Exercise 136. You will hear a series of sentences. After each, you will hear two more sentences, A and B. Only one of these is a logical rejoinder to the first one. You are to determine which one it is.

EXAMPLE   You hear: ¿A qué hora comes?
            A. Comes a las ocho.
            B. Como a las ocho.

You place a check mark in the row labeled B, because B is a logical rejoinder to the first sentence.

We will begin now. *Read each item once.*

Now check your answers. *Repeat each cue sentence once and give the correct answer as:*

1. Dice que tiene ojos azules.   Debe ser muy bonita.   A
   A. Debe ser muy bonita.
   B. Deben ser muy bonitas.
2. Tú sabes leer inglés, ¿verdad?   Leo un poco solamente.   A
   A. Leo un poco solamente.
   B. Leemos un poco solamente.

T75

3. ¿Dónde viven?   Vivimos en la esquina.   B
   A. Vives en la esquina.
   B. Vivimos en la esquina.

4. ¿Escribe una carta?   Sí, escribo una carta en francés.   B
   A. Sí, escribimos una carta en
      francés.
   B. Sí, escribo una carta en francés.

5. ¿Debo leer este libro?   No, debe leer el otro.   A
   A. No, debe leer el otro.
   B. No, debo leer el otro.

6. ¿Soy guapo, Susana? ¿Qué crees tú?   Creo que eres un gordito muy simpático.
   A. Creo que eres un gordito muy   A
      simpático.
   B. Creen que eres un gordito muy
      simpático.

7. ¡Deben estudiar más!   Pero nosotros estudiamos mucho.   A
   A. Pero nosotros estudiamos
      mucho.
   B. Pero tú estudias mucho.

8. ¿Viven en la esquina?   No, vivimos en esa casa blanca.   B
   A. No, vives en esa casa blanca.
   B. No, vivimos en esa casa blanca.

9. ¿Comes ahora?   No, como después.   A
   A. No, como después.
   B. No, comemos después.

10. ¿Qué escribe?   Escribo una carta en inglés.   A
    A. Escribo una carta en inglés.
    B. Escribimos una carta en inglés.

EXERCISE 137. LISTENING COMPREHENSION

Be prepared to write at the end of this exercise. You will hear a dialog between two
friends, Pedro and Susana. You will then be asked to write answers to questions on
the dialog. Your answers do not have to be complete sentences, but they should be
grammatically correct. Now listen to the dialog.

> PEDRO   ¿Qué quieres hacer esta tarde?
> SUSANA ¿Quieres practicar inglés?
> PEDRO   No, estoy muy cansado.
> SUSANA ¿Por qué no escuchamos unos discos, entonces?
> PEDRO   Buena idea. Yo tengo tres discos nuevos.

Now listen to the questions.

1. ¿Qué quiere hacer Susana esta tarde?   5. ¿Quiere Pedro escuchar discos
2. ¿Quiere Pedro practicar inglés?   también?
3. ¿Por qué no quiere?   6. ¿Qué tiene él?
4. ¿Qué quiere hacer Susana, entonces?

Now listen to the dialog again. *Repeat only the dialog and then give the students time
to write their answers.*

[b] *vs.* [ƀ]   **EXERCISE 138. PRONUNCIATION**

In this exercise you will be saying pairs of words and phrases containing the two **b** sounds. Remember, if the **b** sound follows a vowel, it is pronounced without the lips closing completely; otherwise, it is like the English *b*. Now repeat each of the following pairs.

vas–no vas / viernes–este viernes / baño–este baño /
banco–este banco / vestido–este vestido / blanco–este vestido blanco /
veinte–tengo veinte / boletos–Tengo veinte boletos. /
busca–no busca / bien–No busca bien.

EXERCISE 139. LISTENING COMPREHENSION

Be prepared to write your answers for Exercise 139. You will hear a series of short monologs. After each, you will hear two sentences, A and B. You are to determine which one best describes the situation in the monolog.

EXAMPLE   You hear: A ver, dice que se llama Sue, que es pelirroja, de ojos verdes. Dice que estudia español y quiere saber si yo estudio inglés. También quiere saber cómo soy yo.
A. El chico lee una carta.
B. El chico lee el periódico.

You place your check mark in row A of the example column, because A best describes the situation in the monolog.

We will begin now. *Read each item once.*   Now check your answers. *Repeat each monolog once and give the correct answer as:*

1. Vamos a ver. ¿Qué necesito comprar? Carne . . . huevos . . . leche . . . pan . . . no, tengo pan en la casa . . . café . . . mantequilla . . .

A. La señora está en el mercado.   La señora está en el mercado. A
B. La señora está en la biblioteca.   (Necesita comprar comida.)

2. ¡Hola, don Chico! ¿Tiene cartas para nosotros? ¿Sólo este periódico? ¿No hay más correo?

A. La señora habla con el cartero.   La señora habla con el cartero. A
B. La señora habla con su hijo.   (Habla del correo.)

3. ¡Ya son las doce y media! Tengo mucha hambre. ¿Qué hay de comer?

A. El señor quiere cenar.   Es la hora del almuerzo. B (Ya son
B. Es la hora del almuerzo.   las doce y media.)

4. ¿Qué hay de tomar? ¿No hay leche, o un poco de agua, tal vez?

A. El señor quiere comer.   El señor tiene sed. B (Quiere tomar
B. El señor tiene sed.   algo.)

5. Esa Susana López es tan antipática. Y es muy fea también.
   Está muy gorda ahora, ¿sabes?

A. La señora es muy amiga de Susana
   López.
B. A la señora no le gusta Susana
   López.

A la señora no le gusta Susana López.
B (Dice que es antipática.)

6. Mi hijo Luisito es tan inteligente. Y, ¿sabe usted, señora?
   es guapísimo. Es un chico tan bueno, tan simpático.

A. La señora que habla es la mamá
   de Luisito.
B. Es la maestra de Luisito.

La señora que habla es la mamá de
Luisito. A (Dice que su hijo es tan
inteligente.)

7. ¡Ay caramba! ¿Dónde está mi abrigo? Necesito mi abrigo.
   ¿Usted sabe dónde está?

A. La señora tiene mucho calor.
B. La señora tiene frío.

La señora tiene frío. B (Busca su
abrigo.)

8. ¡Qué graciosa es esa foto! Esta chica es lindísima.
   Es tu prima, ¿verdad? Y esta otra foto . . .
   ¿quién es ese señor que está sentado con tu hermano,
   tu abuelo o tu tío Ricardo?

A. El señor lee un periódico.
B. El señor ve un álbum.

El señor ve un álbum. B (Ve unas
fotos.)

EXERCISE 140. SPOT DICTATION

Be prepared to do the writing for Exercise 140. You have in front of you a reading
selection from which certain words have been omitted. This selection will now be
read to you. You are to write the words omitted from the text in the space provided.
We will begin now. *The underlined words have been omitted from the students' copies.*
Pause at each slanted line to allow students time to write.

El gordito contesta la carta de Sue

Estimada amiga:

   Muchas gracias por tu carta tan bonita. / Tú debes ser una chica muy inteligente. /
Y muy bonita también. ¿Cuántos años tienes? / ¿No tienes una foto? /
   Yo tengo casi quince años. / Soy pelirrojo, y tengo ojos castaños. / También soy
un poco gordo, no muy gordo, un poco solamente. /

Now listen to the reading selection once more. Later, when you have time, compare
the words you have written with those in the Narrative at the end of Unit 7.

UNIT 8—SECTION B

[d] *vs.* [d̪]

EXERCISE 141. PRONUNCIATION

In this exercise you will say pairs of words and phrases containing the letter **d**. Remember, if the **d** sound follows a vowel, it is pronounced like the *th* in the English

words *either*, *neither*. Otherwise, it is like the English *d*. Now repeat each of the following pairs.

> diez–la una y diez / dos–tengo dos / dice–¿Qué dice? /
> Diana–¿Qué dice Diana? / delante–está delante /
> de–Está delante de mí. / dan–¿Qué dan? /
> domingo–¿Qué dan este domingo?

[g] *vs.* [g]

EXERCISE 142. PRONUNCIATION

In this exercise you will be saying pairs of words and phrases containing the letter **g**. Remember, if the g sound follows a vowel, it is pronounced with the back of the tongue touching the roof of the mouth; otherwise it is like English *g*. Now repeat each of the following pairs.

> guante–este guante / gordo–Está gordo. / guapo–¡Qué guapo! /
> gusta–me gusta / Gonzalo–Me gusta Gonzalo.

EXERCISE 143. LISTENING COMPREHENSION

Be prepared to write your responses for Exercise 143. You will hear four sets of three sentences each. You are to match the time expressions in each sentence with the clocks on your paper.   EXAMPLE   You hear: **A La fiesta es a las ocho y media.** You place an A next to the clock which reads eight-thirty. Notice that the row labeled 1 on your paper has four clocks. You will hear three sentences, A, B, and C, after you hear the number 1 (**uno**). Be sure to fill in A, B, and C in row 1 before going on to row 2. Do not fill in any of the blanks in row 2 before you hear the number 2 (**dos**).

We will begin now. *Read each sentence once.*

Now check your answers. *Repeat each sentence and confirm with:*

1. A. Son las tres y media.
   A. three thirty
   B. Cierran las tiendas a las siete en punto.
   B. seven o'clock
   C. El desfile empieza a las dos y cuarto.
   C. two fifteen

2. A. ¿Quieres almorzar? Ya es la una y veinticinco.
   A. one twenty-five
   B. La clase empieza a las nueve menos cuarto.
   B. a quarter of nine
   C. Vamos a las cinco y veinte.
   C. five twenty

3. A. Ya son las ocho y diez. ¿Quieres cenar?
   A. eight ten
   B. ¡Apúrate! El partido es a las once y media.
   B. eleven thirty
   C. Son las cuatro menos veinte, según mi reloj.
   C. twenty of four

4. A. ¡Qué temprano viene el correo! Son las doce menos veinticinco.
   A. twenty-five of twelve
   B. Las carreras empiezan a las diez menos diez.
   B. ten of ten
   C. Llegan a las seis menos cinco.
   C. five of six

[b̶], [d̶], [g̶]   **EXERCISE 144. PRONUNCIATION**

In this exercise you will say sentences with the [b̶], [d̶], and [g̶] sounds occurring between vowels. Repeat each sentence once.

Eva llega el sábado, ¿verdad?   ¿Qué traes en esa bolsa, Miguel?
No, llega este viernes con Adela.   Helado para todos ustedes.

¿Ya son las diez?   ¿Qué hay de tomar?
Son las diez y media y Blanca no   Nada.
viene todavía.   ¿Agua?
                                                               El agua no está buena.

¿Es usted de Canadá?
No, de los Estados Unidos.
¿Y vive aquí ahora?
No, vivo en Chicago.

EXERCISE 145. LISTENING COMPREHENSION

Be prepared to write your responses for Exercise 145. You will hear a series of sentences followed by two more sentences, A and B. You are to determine which one logically continues the thought of the first sentence.

EXAMPLE   You hear: Tengo mucha hambre.
                            A. Quiero comer.
                            B. Quieres tomar algo.

You place your check mark in row A of the example column, because A logically continues the first sentence.

We will begin now. *Read each item once.*   Now check your answers. *Repeat each cue sentence once and give the correct answer as:*

1. Aquí viene el correo.   ¡Hola, don Chico! ¿Hay cartas?   A
   A. ¡Hola don Chico! ¿Hay cartas?
   B. No tengo la menor idea.

2. ¿Qué hay de tomar?   ¿Hay leche?   B
   A. ¿Hay carne?   B. ¿Hay leche?

3. Tengo mucho frío.   ¿Dónde está mi abrigo?   A
   A. ¿Dónde está mi abrigo?
   B. ¿Dónde están las cartas?

4. ¿Conoces a mi hijo?   Se llama Juan.   A
   A. Se llama Juan.
   B. ¿Cómo se llama?

5. Tengo una culebra en la bolsa.   ¿Por qué pones esa cara?   B
   A. Muchas gracias.
   B. ¿Por qué pones esa cara?

6. ¿Qué hay de comer?   ¿Huevos con papas fritas?   A
   A. ¿Huevos con papas fritas?
   B. ¿Té con leche?

7. Hasta luego, señores.
    A. Con permiso.
    B. ¡Hola! ¿Cómo están?

Con permiso.   A

8. ¿Cómo? ¿Ya son las doce?
    A. ¡Ya es hora del desayuno!
    B. ¡Ya es hora de almuerzo!

¡Ya es hora de almuerzo!   B

UNIT 8—SECTION D

Vowel clusters:
[a], [e], [o]

EXERCISE 146. LISTENING

You already know that in Spanish an unstressed **i** or **u** before another vowel forms a single syllable with the following vowel. In contrast, in combinations of **a**, **e**, or **o**, each vowel is pronounced as a separate syllable. Listen to the following words.

maestro, trae, ahora, correo, leo, geografía, preocupado

Vowel clusters:
[a], [e], [o]

EXERCISE 147. PRONUNCIATION

Repeat each of the following words.

maestro, trae, cae, distrae, ahora, lea, crea, lee, cree, correo, leo, creo, geografía, peor, preocupado

EXERCISE 148. LISTENING COMPREHENSION

Be prepared to write your responses for Exercise 148. You will hear a series of sentences followed by two more sentences, A and B. Only one of these is a logical rejoinder to the first one. You are to determine which one it is.

EXAMPLE   You hear: ¿Cuándo salen?
                          A. Salgo ahora.
                          B. Salimos ahora.

You place a check mark in row B of the example column, because B is a logical rejoinder to the first sentence.

We will begin now. *Read each item once.*

Now check your answers. *Repeat each cue sentence once and give the correct answer as:*

1. ¿Oyes eso?
    A. ¿Qué? No oigo nada.
    B. ¿Qué? No oye nada.

¿Qué? No oigo nada.   A

2. ¿Conoce a Juan?
    A. No, pero conoces a su hermano.
    B. No, pero conozco a su hermano.

No, pero conozco a su hermano.   B

3. Tenemos mucha hambre.
    A. ¿Quieres comer ahora?
    B. ¿Quieren comer ahora?

¿Quieren comer ahora?   B

4. ¿Qué trae a clase?
   A. ¡Traigo una culebra en una bolsa!
   B. ¡Traen una culebra en una bolsa!

¡Traigo una culebra en una bolsa!   A

5. Tengo sed.
   A. ¿Tienen sed? ¿Qué quieren tomar?
   B. ¿Tienes sed? ¿Qué quieres tomar?

¿Tienes sed? ¿Qué quieres tomar?   B

6. Pone las cartas en la mesa.
   A. ¿Pone todas las cartas allí?
   B. ¿Ponen todas las cartas allí?

¿Pone todas las cartas allí?   A

7. ¿Qué traen en la bolsa?
   A. Traigo algo para ti.
   B. Traemos algo para ti.

Traemos algo para ti.   B

8. ¿Cuándo vienen?
   A. Vienen mañana.
   B. Vengo mañana.

Vienen mañana.   A

9. ¿Reconocen este lugar?
   A. No, no reconocemos nada.
   B. No, no reconozco nada.

No, no reconocemos nada.   A

10. Salimos ahora.
    A. ¿Salen ahora? ¿Adónde van?
    B. ¿Sales ahora? ¿Adónde vas?

¿Salen ahora? ¿Adónde van?   A

EXERCISE 149. LISTENING COMPREHENSION

Be prepared to write at the end of this exercise. You will hear a dialog between a boy and his mother. You will then be asked to write answers to questions on the dialog. Your answers do not have to be complete sentences, but they should be grammatically correct. Now listen to the dialog.

EL HIJO	¿Qué hay de comer, mamá?
LA MADRE	¿Ya tienes hambre?
EL HIJO	Claro. Son casi las doce y cuarto.
LA MADRE	¿Quieres unos huevos con papas fritas?
EL HIJO	Sí, y leche.

Now listen to the questions.

1. ¿Tiene hambre el hijo?
2. ¿Qué hora es?
3. ¿Qué hay de comer?
4. ¿Qué quiere tomar el hijo?

Now listen to the dialog again. *Repeat only the dialog and then give the students time to write their answers.*

T82

[r]

EXERCISE 150. PRONUNCIATION

In this exercise you will say words with a Spanish single **r** between vowels. Repeat each word.

> cara, claro, hora, para, pero, eres, de veras, enero, señora, ahora, dinero, Perú

EXERCISE 151. PRONUNCIATION

Listen to the following conversation. *Read the conversation once without interruption.*

> ¡Qué perezoso eres!
> Pero no quiero ir al cine ahora.
> ¿Qué te parece si estudiamos entonces?
> ¡Caramba! Eso no. ¿A qué hora empieza la película?

Now repeat each of the following sentences. *Read each sentence separately, leaving a pause at the end.*

EXERCISE 152. LISTENING COMPREHENSION

Be prepared to write your responses for Exercise 152. You will hear a series of numbers. You are to write the Arabic numeral which corresponds to each number you hear. EXAMPLE You hear: **setenta y cuatro.** You write the number 74 on your paper. We will begin now. *Read each number once.*

1. veintiocho *twenty-eight* 28   2. ciento doce *one hundred twelve* 112   3. treinta y tres *thirty-three* 33   4. noventa y siete *ninety-seven* 97   5. cuarenta *forty* 40   6. ochenta y nueve *eighty-nine* 89   7. sesenta y uno *sixty-one* 61   8. cincuenta y cuatro *fifty-four* 54   9. setenta y seis *seventy-six* 76   10. ciento diecinueve *one hundred nineteen* 119   11. ciento noventa y nueve *one hundred ninety-nine* 199   12. sesenta y tres *sixty-three* 63   13. veintiuno *twenty one* 21   14. cuarenta y ocho *forty eight* 48   15. cien *one hundred* 100   16. setenta y dos *seventy-two* 72   17. cincuenta y siete *fifty seven* 57   18. ciento treinta y cuatro *one hundred thirty-four* 134   19. ciento trece *one hundred thirteen* 113   20. sesenta y cinco *sixty-five* 65

Now check your answers. *Repeat each number and confirm by naming the appropriate English equivalent.*

EXERCISE 153. SPOT DICTATION

Be prepared to do the writing for Exercise 153. You have in front of you a reading selection from which certain words have been omitted. This selection will now be read to you. You are to write the words omitted from the text in the space provided.

We will begin now. *The underlined words have been omitted from the students' copies. Pause at each slanted line to allow students time to write.*

Lunes-día feo

¡Imposible! ¡Qué tarde! ¡Lunes! ¡Las siete de la <u>mañana</u>! / ¡Escuela! ¡Examen de <u>geografía</u>! / ¡Qué <u>horrible</u>! / ¡Y no sé nada, absolutamente nada! ¡Examen con don Pedro, el maestro más <u>estricto</u> del mundo! / No, imposible, no puedo ir a la escuela hoy, estoy enfermo, tengo <u>temperatura</u>. / Yo sé que no sé nada . . . a ver: ¿la capital de <u>Brasil</u>? / Este . . . Este . . . Río de Janeiro. . . . No no no, no es Río de Janeiro, ahora tienen otra nueva, ¿cómo se <u>llama</u>? . . . no recuerdo. / ¿Los productos <u>principales</u> de Colombia? / No tengo la menor idea.

Now listen to the reading selection once more. Later, when you have time, compare the words you have written with those in the Narrative at the end of Unit 8.

UNIT 9—SECTION B

[rr]

EXERCISE 154. PRONUNCIATION

In this exercise you will say words with the Spanish sound [rr]. Repeat each of the following words.

> carro, perro, forro, corro, arreglo, torre, pelirrojo, correo, Ramos, rubio, rojo, ruso

EXERCISE 155. PRONUNCIATION

Listen to the following conversation. *Read the conversation once without interruption.*

> ¿Quién es ese chico pelirrojo?
> ¿El de la camisa roja? Es Roberto Ramos.
> ¿Y ese rubio?
> Ése se llama Raúl. Es de Costa Rica.

Now repeat each of the following sentences. *Read each sentence separately, leaving a pause at the end.*

EXERCISE 156. LISTENING COMPREHENSION

Be prepared to write your responses for Exercise 156. You will hear a series of short monologs. After each, you will hear two sentences, A and B. You are to determine which one best describes the situation in the monolog.

EXAMPLE   You hear: Durante las vacaciones voy a ir a España. Voy primero a Buenos Aires y allí tomo el avión para Madrid.
A. Durante las vacaciones la señorita va a hacer un viaje.
B. Durante el mes de julio la señorita va a ir a México.

You place your check mark in row A, because A best describes the situation in the monolog.

T84

We will begin now. *Read each item once.*

Now check your answers. *Repeat each monolog once and give correct answer as:*

1. ¡Ay, caramba! Yo no voy a salir ahora. ¿No ves cómo llueve? ¡Y hace tanto frío!
   A. La señorita no va a salir porque hace mal tiempo.
   B. La señorita no quiere salir porque hace calor.

La señorita no va a salir porque hace mal tiempo.   A (Llueve y hace frío.)

2. Este mes vamos a hacer un viaje a Lima. Vamos a pasar quince días allí.
   A. La señorita va a pasar quince días en Perú.
   B. La señorita no quiere hacer un viaje este mes.

La señorita va a pasar quince días en Perú.   A (Va a ir a Lima.)

3. ¿Sabe que en Lima nunca llueve? Y nunca hace ni frío ni calor. Hace muy buen tiempo allí.
   A. El clima de Lima es muy bueno.
   B. En Lima llueve mucho.

El clima de Lima es muy bueno.   A (No hace ni frío ni calor.)

4. Estimada Anita: Ahora estoy en Nueva York, donde voy a pasar tres días más. Todo es muy bonito aquí; todo me encanta. El problema es que hace un calor horrible.
   A. La señorita escribe esta carta durante el mes de diciembre.
   B. La señorita está en Nueva York en agosto.

La señorita está en Nueva York en agosto.   B (Hace un calor horrible.)

5. ¡Mi mamá llega de Lima esta tarde! Voy a ir al aeropuerto ahora. ¿Quieres ir conmigo?
   A. La mamá de la señorita llega en avión.
   B. La mamá de la señorita llega en tren.

La mamá de la señorita llega en avión.   A (La señorita va a ir al aeropuerto.)

6. ¡Ay, qué cansada estoy! Es horrible trabajar aquí. Primero viene una señora que dice que quiere comprar un vestido; después dice que no quiere comprar un vestido, que quiere un abrigo. Después llega otra que quiere una blusa amarilla. Y yo no tengo ninguna blusa amarilla. ¡Ay, caramba! ¡Qué día!
   A. La señorita trabaja en un mercado.
   B. La señorita trabaja en una tienda.

La señorita trabaja en una tienda.   B (Viene una señora a comprar un vestido.)

[r] *vs.* [rr]   **EXERCISE 157. PRONUNCIATION**

In this exercise you will say pairs of words with the single **r** and the double **rr** sounds. Be careful to make the single **r** different from the double **rr**. Now repeat each of the following pairs.

> caro–carro, pero–perro, cero–cerro, foro–forro, vara–barra,
> coro–corro, para–parra, ahora–ahorra

EXERCISE 158. LISTENING COMPREHENSION

Be prepared to write your responses for Exercise 158. You will hear a series of sentences. After each, you will hear two more sentences, A and B. Only one of these is a logical rejoinder to the first one. You are to determine which one it is.

EXAMPLE   You hear: ¿Me das cinco pesos?
                 A. Te puedo dar dos, solamente.
                 B. Les puedo dar dos, solamente.

You place your check mark in row A, because A is a logical rejoinder to the first sentence.

We will begin now. *Read each item once.*   Now check your answers. *Repeat each cue sentence once and give the correct answer as:*

1. Te traigo un regalo.   ¿De veras? ¿Me traes un regalo?   A
     A. ¿De veras? ¿Me traes un regalo?
     B. ¿De veras? ¿Le traes un regalo?

2. ¿Qué nos preguntan?   Les preguntan cuál es la fecha.   A
     A. Les preguntan cuál es 1a fecha.
     B. Te preguntan cuál es la fecha.

3. No le quiero hablar.   ¿No le quiere hablar?   B
     A. ¿No nos quiere hablar?
     B. ¿No le quiere hablar?

4. Te voy a contar una cosa.   ¿Qué me vas a contar?   A
     A. ¿Qué me vas a contar?
     B. ¿Qué les vas a contar?

5. Les compro unos discos.   ¿Nos compras unos discos? ¡Gracias!   B
     A. ¿Me compras unos discos?
         ¡Gracias!
     B. ¿Nos compras unos discos?
         ¡Gracias!

6. A ellos no les doy nada.   ¿No les da nada?   A
     A. ¿No les da nada?
     B. ¿No me da nada?

7. ¿Me van a contestar mañana?   Sí, le contestamos mañana.   A
     A. Sí, le contestamos mañana.
     B. Sí, les contestamos mañana.

8. ¿Cuándo le escribe?   Le escribo esta tarde.   A
   A. Le escribo esta tarde.
   B. Te escribo esta tarde.

9. ¿Me trae unas cartas?   No, no le traigo ninguna.   B
   A. No, no les traigo ninguna.
   B. No, no le traigo ninguna.

10. ¿Nos da dinero para los boletos?   Sí, les doy diez pesos.   B
    A. Sí, te doy diez pesos.
    B. Sí, les doy diez pesos.

UNIT 9—SECTION D

[r] *after a*
consonant

EXERCISE 159. PRONUNCIATION

In this exercise you will say words with the Spanish single **r** immediately following another consonant. Pay special attention to the sound of the single **r** <u>after</u> a consonant. Now repeat each of the following words.

> tren, trae, creo, negro, trabaja, detrás, libro, culebra, primero,
> pregunto

[r] *before a*
consonant

EXERCISE 160. PRONUNCIATION

In this exercise you will say words with the Spanish single **r** immediately preceding another consonant. Pay special attention to the sound of the single **r** <u>before</u> a consonant. Now repeat each of the following words.

> marzo, duerme, carta, tarde, permiso, almuerzo

EXERCISE 161. LISTENING COMPREHENSION

Be prepared to write your responses for Exercise 161. You will hear a series of sentences. After each, you will hear three words, A, B, and C. You are to determine which one is the subject of the sentence.

EXAMPLE   You hear: A Carlos no le gusta el carro.
                         A. Carlos
                         B. le
                         C. carro

You circle the letter C in the example because C is the subject of the sentence.

We will begin now. *Read each item once.*   Now check your answers. *Repeat each
                                                   cue sentence once and give the correct
                                                   answer as:*

1. A mí me encanta la idea.   idea   B
   A. me
   B. idea
   C. yo

2. ¿A ti te gusta esta escuela?   escuela A
   - A. escuela
   - B. tú
   - C. te

3. El maestro nos parece simpático.   maestro C
   - A. nosotros
   - B. nos
   - C. maestro

4. A Juan le aprietan los zapatos.   zapatos C
   - A. Juan
   - B. le
   - C. zapatos

5. A los chicos les encanta el disco.   disco B
   - A. chicos
   - B. disco
   - C. les

6. A nosotros no nos gusta eso.   eso C
   - A. nosotros B. nos C. eso

7. Eso no nos gusta a nosotros.   eso C
   - A. nosotros B. nos C. eso

8. A Miguel le parece bonita Susana.   Susana C
   - A. Miguel
   - B. le
   - C. Susana

9. ¿A usted le gustan las canciones?   canciones A
   - A. canciones
   - B. le
   - C. usted

10. El chico les parece pretencioso a las gemelas.   chico A
    - A. chico
    - B. les
    - C. gemelas

EXERCISE 162. LISTENING COMPREHENSION

Be prepared to write at the end of this exercise. You will hear a dialog between a father and his daughter. You will then be asked to write answers to questions on the dialog. Your answers do not have to be complete sentences, but they should be grammatically correct.

Now listen to the dialog.

PADRE	¿Qué te pasa? ¿Te aprietan los zapatos?
HIJA	Sí, papi. No puedo caminar más.
PADRE	¿Qué quieres hacer, entonces?
HIJA	¿Por qué no tomamos algo en ese café?
PADRE	Buena idea. Tengo mucha sed.

Now listen to the questions.

1. ¿Qué le pasa a la hija?
2. ¿Puede caminar más ella?
3. ¿Adónde quiere ir la hija?
4. ¿Quiere el padre ir al café también?

Now listen to the dialog again. *Repeat only the dialog and then give the students time to write their answers.*

UNIT 10—SECTION A

[y]

EXERCISE 163. PRONUNCIATION

In this exercise you will say words with the Spanish double l and the Spanish y between vowels. Remember that these letters represent a sound similar to the English *y* of *yes*, *yellow*, but that they are produced by holding the tongue more tensely and closer to the roof of the mouth than for the similar English sound. The Spanish sound, in fact, may sound quite similar to the English *j* in *jello*. Now repeat each of the following words.

allá, allí, calle, silla, playa, suyo, llega, llora

EXERCISE 164. PRONUNCIATION

Listen to the following conversation. *Read the conversation once without interruption.*

¿Dónde hay un salón de belleza?
En la calle Medellín.

Now repeat each of the following sentences. *Read each sentence separately, leaving a pause at the end.*

EXERCISE 165. LISTENING COMPREHENSION

Be prepared to write your responses for Exercise 165. You will hear a series of short monologs, followed by two sentences, A and B. You are to determine which one describes the situation in the monolog.

EXAMPLE   You hear: No, señora. No le puedo arreglar estos zapatos para mañana.
Para el sábado, tal vez.
A. El señor nunca le va a arreglar los zapatos a la señora.
B. El señor es zapatero.

You place your check mark in row B, because B describes the situation in the monolog.

We will begin now. *Read each item once.*

Now check your answers. *Repeat each monolog once and give correct answer as:*

1. Perdón, señorita. ¿Tiene usted la nueva edición de este diccionario? Y también quiero ver un nuevo libro que acaba de salir. A ver . . . ¿cómo se llama?
A. El señor está en la peluquería.
B. El señor está en una librería.

El señor está en una librería.   B (Quiere comprar un diccionario y otro libro.)

T89

2. ¿Aló? ¿Aló? ¿Está el Sr. Gómez? Habla el Sr. García. ¿Cómo? ¿Acaba de salir? ¿Y sabe usted cuándo vuelve?
   A. El Sr. García está en la casa del Sr. Gómez.
   B. El Sr. García habla por teléfono.

El Sr. García habla por teléfono. B (Dice ¿aló? ¿aló? y pregunta si está el Sr. Gómez.)

3. ¡Ay, caramba! Mamá, ¿sabes dónde está Luisito? El partido va a empezar en una hora y él tiene los boletos.
   A. El chico no quiere ir al partido.
   B. El chico está preocupado porque Luisito tiene los boletos.

El chico está preocupado porque Luisito tiene los boletos. B (El partido va a empezar en una hora y él tiene los boletos.)

4. Buenas tardes, señorita. ¿Me puede arreglar el pelo ahora? ¿Tiene ese nuevo producto para el pelo rubio?
   A. La señora está en una peluquería.
   B. La señora está en la oficina de un médico.

La señora está en una peluquería. A (Pregunta si le pueden arreglar el pelo ahora.)

5. ¡Lunes! ¡Examen de geografía! Y yo no sé nada. Y con don Pedro, el maestro más estricto de la escuela. ¡Qué horrible! ¡Yo no sé nada!
   A. El chico es muy amigo de don Pedro.
   B. El chico está asustado.

El chico está asustado. B (Porque hay un examen de geografía y él no sabe nada.)

6. Muy bien, señorita. Voy a limpiar la mesa y le traigo un café inmediatamente. ¿No desea usted otra cosa? ¿Un helado, tal vez?
   A. El chico que habla trabaja en un banco.
   B. El chico es un camarero.

El chico es un camarero. B (Le va a traer un café a la señorita.)

EXERCISE 166. SPOT DICTATION

Be prepared to do the writing for Exercise 166. You have in front of you a reading selection from which certain words have been omitted. This selection will now be read to you. You are to write the words omitted from the text in the space provided. We will begin now. *The underlined words have been omitted from the students' copies. Pause at each slanted line to allow students time to write.*

Jeem, Beel, y Beector

Salen de Washington el día 25 de junio y calculan llegar a Laredo, Tejas, cinco días más tarde. El jueves salen de Laredo, pasan el Río Grande y entran a México por Nuevo Laredo, / donde pasan la noche, para luego continuar su viaje hasta llegar al Distrito Federal, / la capital, que también se llama México, D. F. /

En México van a pasar unos diez días, más o menos, porque quieren visitar muchos lugares. / Quieren ver, por ejemplo, / las famosas pirámides de San Juan Teotihuacán, / los museos que tienen las reliquias de las grandes civilizaciones indias de México, / los puertos de Acapulco en el Pacífico y Veracruz en el Atlántico. Y muchas cosas más. /

Now listen to the reading selection once more. Later, when you have time, compare the words you have written with those in the Narrative at the end of Unit 9.

UNIT 10—SECTION B

Spanish [u]
vs. English vowel

EXERCISE 167. LISTENING

English has a number of different *u* sounds. One of the most common is the complex *yuw,* as in *pure, cube.* In Spanish, however, the letter **u** always represents the simple vowel [u]. Listen to the following pairs of words, comparing the English *yuw* with the Spanish [u]. The first word in each pair is English; the second word is Spanish.

> pure–puro, Cuba–Cuba, accuse–acusa, excuse–excusa,
> figure–figura, future–futuro, mute–mudo, music–música,
> monument–monumento

[u]

EXERCISE 168. PRONUNCIATION

Repeat each of the following words.

> puro, Cuba, acusa, excusa, figura, futuro, mudo, música,
> monumento

EXERCISE 169. LISTENING COMPREHENSION

Be prepared to write your answers for Exercise 169. You will hear a series of sentences. After each, you will hear three more sentences, A, B, and C. You are to determine which one logically continues the thought of the first sentence.

EXAMPLE   You hear: ¡Tres veces he llamado!
   A. Y la línea sigue ocupada.
   B. A sus órdenes.
   C. No hay servicio telefónico aquí.

You circle the A in the example column because A logically continues the first sentence.

We will begin now. *Read each item once.*   Now check your answers. *Repeat each cue sentence once and give the correct answer as:*

1. Todavía no han recibido la segunda   ¡Qué mala suerte!   A
   edición.
   A. ¡Qué mala suerte!
   B. ¿No es el veinte-trece-cero cero?
   C. ¿Desea dejar algún recado?

T91

2. No están aquí.   Ya todos han salido a comer.   B
   A. ¿Está el Sr. Campos, por favor?
   B. Ya todos han salido a comer.
   C. Todos están aquí.

3. ¿Cómo? ¿No están en la tienda?   ¿Me puede dar el número de la casa?
   A. Librería Campos, a sus órdenes.   C
   B. ¿Cómo se llama?
   C. ¿Me puede dar el número de
      la casa?

4. Lo siento, pero el Sr. Pérez acaba   ¿Desea usted dejar algún recado?   B
   de salir.
   A. Yo no sé.
   B. ¿Desea usted dejar algún recado?
   C. No tengo la menor idea.

5. No hay ningún Sr. Campos aquí,   Usted está equivocada.   B
   señorita.
   A. Usted está aburrida.
   B. Usted está equivocada.
   C. Usted está preocupada.

6. ¿Aló? Zapatería García.   A sus órdenes.   A
   A. A sus órdenes.
   B. Tres veces he marcado.
   C. ¿Cuál es la dirección?

7. ¿El médico?   No está en su oficina.   C
   A. No está en su librería.
   B. No está en su peluquería.
   C. No está en su oficina.

8. ¡Qué calor!   ¿Por qué no tomamos algo frío?   C
   A. ¿Quieres tu abrigo?
   B. ¿Por qué no tomamos un café
      caliente?
   C. ¿Por qué no tomamos algo frío?

9. Tengo mucha sed.   ¿Me das un poco de agua?   C
   A. ¿Tenemos carne?
   B. Quiero comer algo.
   C. ¿Me das un poco de agua?

10. ¿Cuánto cuestan los boletos?   ¿Son muy caros?   A
   A. ¿Son muy caros?
   B. No me gusta el fútbol.
   C. Es el campeón del mundo.

EXERCISE 170. DICTATION

Be prepared for a dictation. Cover the Spanish sentences which you have in front of you. Each sentence will be read twice. You are to write it as you hear it. We will begin now. *Read each sentence twice.*

1. Luis, ¿cuántas veces has leído este libro? ¡Seis!
2. ¿Qué te han traído? Veinte pesos.
3. Yo no oigo nada. ¿Tú has oído algo?

Uncover the Spanish sentences and compare them with the ones you have written. *Repeat each sentence once.*

UNIT 10—SECTION C

Spanish [p], [t], and [k] vs. English consonants

EXERCISE 171. LISTENING

In this exercise you will hear pairs of words. In each pair, the first word is an English word with the sounds represented by the letters *p, t,* or *k* followed by a vowel. The second is a Spanish word with a similar sound. Listen to each pair, comparing the sounds of *p, t,* and *k* in English with the corresponding Spanish sounds.

two–tú, tea–ti, toss–tos, pour–por, kay–qué

[p], [t], and [k]

EXERCISE 172. PRONUNCIATION

In this exercise you will say words with the Spanish sounds you have just been studying. Remember that in Spanish the vowel follows the consonant immediately, leaving no room for a puff of air between consonant and vowel. Now repeat each of the following words.

tú, ti, tos, tienes, tiendas, todo, tanta, por, papa, para, partido, qué, quién, cómo, cuarto, quinto

EXERCISE 173. LISTENING COMPREHENSION

Be prepared to write your responses for Exercise 173. You will hear a series of sentences, each one with a past participle. After each sentence you will hear a noun which could be substituted for the subject of the sentence. You are to determine whether the past participle will change or not if this noun is substituted for the subject of the sentence. EXAMPLE You hear: **El cliente ha salido. (clienta)** You place your check mark in the column labeled No change, because **salido** does not change if **clienta** becomes the subject of the sentence.

We will begin now. *Read each item once.*

Now check your answers. *Repeat each item once and give the correct answer as:*

1. El señor no ha llegado todavía. (señora)

La señora no ha llegado todavía. *no change*

2. El chico está resfriado. (chica)

La chica está resfriada. *change*

3. El peluquero ha cerrado la puerta. (peluquera)

La peluquera ha cerrado la puerta. *no change*

4. El médico está preocupado. (secretaria)

La secretaria está preocupada. *change*

T93

5. El camarero ha limpiado la mesa. (camarera)

La camarera ha limpiado la mesa. *no change*

6. El jefe está enojado. (jefa)

La jefa está enojada. *change*

7. El alumno está asustado. (alumna)

La alumna está asustada. *change*

8. El maestro no ha venido todavía. (maestra)

La maestra no ha venido todavía. *no change*

9. El criado ya ha comido. (criada)

La criada ya ha comido. *no change*

10. El chico está aburrido. (chica)

La chica está aburrida. *change*

11. El cliente está equivocado. (clienta)

La clienta está equivocada. *change*

12. El abuelo ha llamado tres veces. (abuela)

La abuela ha llamado tres veces. *no change*

13. El dentista ya ha salido. (señorita)

La señorita ya ha salido. *no change*

14. El zapatero está ocupado. (señora)

La señora está ocupada. *change*

15. El padre está preocupado. (madre)

La madre está preocupada. *change*

UNIT 10—SECTION D

[ñ]

EXERCISE 174. PRONUNCIATION

Repeat each of the following words.

> año, mañana, pañuelo, castaño, español, señora, señor, trigueño, uña, cañón, moño, Toño

EXERCISE 175. PRONUNCIATION

Listen to the following conversation. *Read the conversation once without interruption.*

> ¿Quién es el Sr. de pelo castaño?
> Creo que es el señor Muñoz.
> ¿Es español?
> No, es puertorriqueño.

Now repeat each of the following sentences. *Read each sentence separately, leaving a pause at the end.*

EXERCISE 176. LISTENING COMPREHENSION

Be prepared to write your responses for Exercise 176. You will hear a series of short dialogs. After each dialog, you will hear two sentences, A and B. You are to determine which one is more likely to be the next line of the dialog.

EXAMPLE   You hear: Zapatería Venus, a sus órdenes.
¿No es el veinte-treinta- dieciocho?
A. No, señor. Está equivocado.
B. No, señor. Acaba de salir.

You place your check mark in row A, because A is more likely to be the next line of the dialog.

We will begin now. *Read each item once.*

Now check your answers. Repeat each dialog once and give the correct answer as:

1. Estoy muy resfriado.
   ¿Por qué no vas al médico?
   A. Ésta es la segunda vez.
   B. No está en su oficina hoy.

No está en su oficina hoy.   B

2. ¿Por qué estás tan preocupado?
   Tengo un examen de geografía hoy.
   A. El maestro de inglés es muy estricto.
   B. ¿Y no has estudiado?

¿Y no has estudiado?   B

3. ¿Quieres ir a las carreras?
   No, estoy muy cansado.
   A. ¡Qué perezoso eres!
   B. ¿Vas a jugar fútbol entonces?

¡Qué perezoso eres!   A

4. ¿Aló? ¿Está el Sr. Campos?
   No, señorita, acaba de salir.
   A. ¿Adónde quiere ir?
   B. ¿Sabe usted cuándo va a volver?

¿Sabe usted cuándo va a volver?   B

5. El médico no ha venido hoy a la oficina.
   ¡Qué mala suerte!
   A. Acaba de salir a almorzar.
   B. ¿Está usted muy enfermo?

¿Está usted muy enfermo?   B

6. ¿Hay un recado para mí?
   Sí, Juan Gómez ha llamado tres veces hoy.
   A. ¿De veras? ¿Sabe usted qué quiere?
   B. ¿Está ocupada la línea?

¿De veras? ¿Sabe usted qué quiere?   A

7. Estoy tan aburrido.
   ¿Por qué? ¿No tienes nada que hacer?
   A. Sí, pero no quiero estudiar más. Estoy cansado.
   B. Sí, pero todos los maestros son muy antipáticos.

Sí, pero no quiero estudiar más. Estoy cansado.   A

8. Éste es el quinto cliente americano que ha venido hoy.
   ¿El quinto o el sexto?
   A. El quinto. Ese señor rubio no es americano; es inglés.
   B. ¿Cuántas veces han venido? ¿Recuerdas?

El quinto. Ese señor rubio no es americano; es inglés.   A

EXERCISE 177. LISTENING COMPREHENSION

Be prepared to write at the end of this exercise. You will hear a dialog between

Mr. Pérez and a maid. You will then be asked to write answers to questions on the dialog. Your answers do not have to be complete sentences, but they should be grammatically correct. Now listen to the dialog.

EL SEÑOR	¿Aló? ¿Está la Srta. López?
LA CRIADA	No, señor, acaba de salir.
EL SEÑOR	¿Y cuándo vuelve, sabe usted?
LA CRIADA	La verdad es que no sé. ¿Quiere dejar algún recado?
EL SEÑOR	No, gracias.

Now listen to the questions.

1. ¿Con quién quiere hablar el señor?
2. ¿Por qué no puede hablar con ella?
3. ¿Sabe la criada cuándo vuelve la señorita?
4. ¿Quiere dejar un recado el señor?

Now listen to the dialog again. *Repeat only the dialog and then give the students time to write their answers.*

UNIT 11—SECTION A

Vowel sequences in more than one word

EXERCISE 178. LISTENING

Listen to the following sentences. Notice that when two or more of the same vowel occur together, they are pronounced as a single vowel.

La chica̸ americana.   ¿Dónde̸ está?   Lil̸y y Susana.
Habl̸o o estudio.   S̸u uniforme.

Vowel sequences in more than one word

EXERCISE 179. PRONUNCIATION

Repeat each of the following sentences.

La chica̸ americana̸ habla̸ alemán.   Llega̸ ahora.
¿Dónde̸ está ese̸ examen?   Parece̸ enojado.   Debe̸ estudiar.
Es casi̸ imposible.   Es mi̸ idea.   Habl̸o o estudio.
Pedr̸o o Juan.   S̸u uniforme.   Va̸ a̸ hablar.   Llega̸ a̸ almorzar.

EXERCISE 180. LISTENING COMPREHENSION

Be prepared to write your responses for Exercise 180. You will hear a series of incomplete sentences. After each, you will hear four possible completions, A, B, C, and D. You are to determine which one correctly completes the sentence.

EXAMPLE   You hear: Voy a ir con
          A. mi tío.   C. mi escritorio.
          B. mi libro.   D. mi pupitre.

You circle the letter A, because A correctly completes the sentence.

We will begin now. *Read each item once.*

Now check your answers. *Repeat each sentence once, adding the appropriate completion.*

1. ¿Puede repetir
   A. la frase?   C. el lápiz?
   B. la cara?   D. la bolsa?

¿Puede repetir la frase?   A

2. ¡Qué difícil es
   A. este escritorio!   C. este
                          cuaderno!
   B. esta comida!   D. esta tarea!

¡Qué difícil es esta tarea!   D

3. ¿Me prestas
   A. tu frase?   C. tus palabras?
   B. tu pluma?   D. tu dirección?

¿Me prestas tu pluma?   B

4. Ella habla
   A. muy difícil.   C. muy
                          pequeño.
   B. muy despacio.   D. muy listo.

Ella habla muy despacio.   B

5. ¿Qué signo pongo aquí?
   A. ¿Un lápiz?   C. ¿Un signo
                         de interro-
                         gación?
   B. ¿Una pluma?   D. ¿Un papel?

¿Qué signo pongo aquí? ¿Un signo de interrogación?   C

6. Los chicos vienen
   A. pronto.   C. mal.
   B. bien.   D. nada.

Los chicos vienen pronto.   A

7. ¿Puedo ver
   A. la idea?   C. la mentira?
   B. este punto?   D. tus apuntes?

¿Puedo ver tus apuntes?   D

8. ¿Cómo? ¿Todavía no estás
   A. listo?   C. bajo?
   B. alto?   D. pequeño?

¿Cómo? ¿Todavía no estás listo?   A

9. Siempre tomamos
   A. té.   C. ensalada.
   B. carne.   D. papas fritas.

Siempre tomamos té.   A

10. ¿La foto? Está en
    A. mi tío.   C. la pared.
    B. mi prima.   D. unos compañeros.

¿La foto? Está en la pared.   C

EXERCISE 181. SPOT DICTATION

Be prepared to do the writing for Exercise 181. You have in front of you a reading selection from which certain words have been omitted. This selection will now be read to you. You are to write the words omitted from the text in the space provided. We will begin now. *The underlined words have been omitted from the students' copies. Pause at each slanted line to allow students time to write.*

El teléfono

Ese aparato feo y de color negro, de figura poco artística, / frío de personalidad, / ese instrumento que un señor con uniforme de la Compañía Nacional de Electricidad colgó en una pared de la cocina de mi casa, / ése es neustro indispensable y sincero amigo, el teléfono.

Si de todos los aparatos eléctricos que la técnica moderna ha creado, / alguien me dice que solamente uno puedo tener en mi casa, y me ordena eliminar todos los otros, yo inmediatamente selecciono el teléfono y elimino el refrigerador, / el radio, y todos los otros que tenemos en la casa, inclusive la televisión en colores que es tan bonita. /

Now listen to the reading selection once more. Later, when you have time, compare the words you have written with those in the Narrative at the end of Unit 10.

UNIT 11—SECTION B

Spanish rhythm

EXERCISE 182. LISTENING

Listen to each of the following sentences, paying particular attention to the rhythm. Remember, in Spanish sentences, all of the syllables are of about the same length, and all the vowels are pronounced clearly.

¿Están listos? ¿Dónde está Salgado? Anda tomando agua.
¡Qué barbaridad! ¿Me prestas tu pluma? Esta cosa no sirve.

Spanish rhythm

EXERCISE 183. PRONUNCIATION

Repeat each of the following sentences.

¿Están listos? ¿Dónde está Salgado? Anda tomando agua.
¡Qué barbaridad! ¿Me prestas tu pluma? Esta cosa no sirve.
¿Estás loco? ¿Y con qué escribo yo? García está molestando.
¡Qué mentira!

EXERCISE 184. LISTENING COMPREHENSION

Be prepared to write your responses for Exercise 184. You will hear a series of short dialogs. After each, you will hear two more sentences, A and B. You are to determine which one is more likely to be the next line of the dialog.

EXAMPLE   You hear: ¿Quieres jugar tenis conmigo?
                              No, yo siempre pierdo cuando juego contigo.
                              A. No es verdad. Tú siempre pierdes.
                              B. No es verdad. Tú juegas muy bien.

You place your check mark in row B, because B is more likely to be the next line of the dialog.

We will begin now. *Read each item once.*

Now check your answers. *Repeat each dialog once and give correct answer as:*

1. ¿Me prestas tu pluma, por favor?
   No tengo pluma. ¿Quieres un lápiz?
   A. ¿Y con qué escribo yo?
   B. Sí, muchas gracias.

   Sí, muchas gracias.   B

2. García está molestando.
   ¡Qué mentira!
   A. No es mentira. Tú siempre molestas.
   B. No es mentira. Tú siempre pones atención.

   No es mentira. Tú siempre molestas.   A

3. ¿Estás listo para el examen?
   No, yo no sé nada.
   A. Tú siempre dices eso.
   B. No sé qué pasa.

   Tú siempre dices eso.   A

4. Mamá, ¿dónde está mi cuaderno?
   Creo que está en tu escritorio.
   A. No, ya he buscado allí.
   B. No, está en mi cuaderno.

   No, ya he buscado allí.   A

5. ¿Por qué no vamos al centro esta tarde?
   No. Tengo un dictado mañana y necesito estudiar.
   A. Tú siempre tienes tanta tarea.
   B. ¿Por qué no vamos al cine, entonces?

   Tú siempre tienes tanta tarea.   A

6. Este carro no va muy rápido.
   No. Está muy viejo. Anda muy despacio.
   A. Sí, pero no tan pronto.
   B. ¿Vas a comprar uno nuevo?

   ¿Vas a comprar uno nuevo?   B

7. ¿Qué pongo aquí? ¿Un punto o un signo de exclamación?
   No sé. ¿Por qué no le preguntas a la maestra?
   A. Ella nunca me presta nada.
   B. Ella está ocupada ahora.

   Ella está ocupada ahora.   B

8. ¿Qué pasa?
   Esta pluma no sirve.
   A. ¿Quieres mi lápiz?
   B. Tal vez está en tu pupitre.

   ¿Quieres mi lápiz?   A

9. ¿Puede repetir la frase, por favor?
   ¿Por qué no ponen Uds. atención?
   A. Es que Ud. lee muy rápido.
   B. Pero yo siempre entiendo todo lo que Ud. dice.

   Es que Ud. lee muy rápido.   A

10. ¿Tú estudias todos los días?
    Claro. Tenemos muchísimo trabajo.
    A. Es verdad. Yo creo que esos
       maestros nunca han sido alum-
       nos.
    B. No es verdad. Tenemos muchí-
       sima tarea.

Es verdad. Yo creo que esos maestros nunca han sido alumnos.   A

UNIT 11—SECTION C

[h]

EXERCISE 185. PRONUNCIATION

In this exercise you will say words with the Spanish [h] sound. Repeat each of the following words.

> jefe, junio, julio, gemela, hijo, mejor, relojes, trabajo, mojado, enojado, inteligente

EXERCISE 186. PRONUNCIATION

Listen to the following conversation. *Read the conversation once without interruption.*

> El jefe está enojado.
> ¿Por qué? ¿No trabajamos bien?
> Sí, pero tenemos que trabajar mejor.

Now repeat the following sentences. *Read each sentence separately, leaving a pause at the end.*

EXERCISE 187. LISTENING COMPREHENSION

Be prepared to write your responses for Exercise 187. You will hear a series of sentences. After each you will hear two more sentences, A and B. One of these is the negative of the first sentence. You are to determine which one it is.

EXAMPLE   You hear: Habla con alguno de los chicos.
          A. No habla con ninguno de los chicos.
          B. No habla nunca con los chicos.

You place your check mark in row A, because A is the negative of the first sentence.

We will begin now. *Read each item once.*

Now check your answers. *Repeat each cue sentence once and give the correct answer as:*

1. ¿Hay algo aquí?
   A. ¿No hay nada aquí?
   B. ¿No hay nadie aquí?

¿No hay nada aquí?   A

2. Vamos a la tienda también.
   A. No vamos a la tienda nunca.
   B. No vamos a la tienda tampoco.

No vamos a la tienda tampoco.   B

3. Algunas veces estudiamos con ellos.   Nunca estudiamos con ellos.   A
   A. Nunca estudiamos con ellos.
   B. Ni siquiera estudiamos con ellos.

4. ¿Buscas a alguien?   ¿No buscas a nadie?   A
   A. ¿No buscas a nadie?
   B. ¿No buscas nada?

5. Algunos de los alumnos ponen aten-   Ninguno de los alumnos pone atención.
   ción.   A
   A. Ninguno de los alumnos pone
      atención.
   B. Ni siquiera los alumnos ponen
      atención.

6. ¿Quieres comer algo?   ¿No quieres comer nada?   B
   A. ¿No quieres comer nunca?
   B. ¿No quieres comer nada?

7. Ella necesita papel también.   Ella no necesita papel tampoco.   A
   A. Ella no necesita papel tampoco.
   B. Ella no necesita nada.

8. Algunas veces hago la tarea.   Nunca hago la tarea.   A
   A. Tampoco hago la tarea.
   B. Nunca hago la tarea.

UNIT 11—SECTION D

Final [r]   **EXERCISE 188.** LISTENING

In this exercise you will hear Spanish words with a single **r** at the end. Now listen to each word, noting the sound of the final **r**.

> hablar, llegar, comer, hacer, ir

Final [r]   **EXERCISE 189.** PRONUNCIATION

Repeat each of the following words.

> hablar, llegar, estar, comer, hacer, poner

EXERCISE 190. LISTENING COMPREHENSION

Be prepared to write your responses for Exercise 190. You will hear a story which has been broken up into a series of short paragraphs. After each paragraph you will hear two incomplete sentences followed by two possible completions, A and B. You are to select the correct completion on the basis of the paragraph. EXAMPLE You hear: Hoy es el Día de la Madre y Juan todavía no le ha comprado nada a su mamá. Juan está muy preocupado, porque ya son las seis y cierran las tiendas a las ocho.

Juan está preocupado porque
A. no tiene un regalo para su mamá.   B. las tiendas están todas cerradas.

You place your check mark in row A, because A correctly completes the sentence on the basis of the paragraph.

We will begin now. *Read each item once.*

Now check your answers. *Repeat each incomplete sentence once, adding the appropriate completion.*

Now listen to the first paragraph.

Todos los alumnos están listos. La maestra empieza el dictado. Sólo Eugenio no está en su lugar.

1. Hoy hay
   A. un examen.
   B. un dictado.

Hoy hay un dictado. B (La maestra empieza el dictado.)

2. Eugenio
   A. empieza a escribir.
   B. no está en clase hoy.

Eugenio no está en clase hoy. B (Sólo Eugenio no está en su lugar.)

Now listen to the second paragraph.

La maestra pregunta dónde está Eugenio. Nadie contesta. Tal vez está enfermo. Tal vez está en casa. Ninguno de los alumnos sabe dónde está Eugenio.

3. Cuando la maestra pregunta dónde está Eugenio,
   A. García dice que anda tomando agua.
   B. nadie dice nada.

Cuando la maestra pregunta dónde está Eugenio, nadie dice nada. B (La maestra pregunta dónde está Eugenio, pero nadie contesta.)

4. Tal vez Eugenio
   A. está en clase.
   B. está en casa.

Tal vez Eugenio está en casa. B (No está en clase.)

Now listen to the third paragraph.

La maestra empieza a leer otra vez. Todos los alumnos escriben. Uno de los alumnos no oye una palabra, pero la maestra no quiere repetir nada. El dictado es muy difícil.

5. La maestra
   A. no empieza el dictado porque Eugenio no está.
   B. lee el dictado una vez y no repite nada.

La maestra lee el dictado una vez y no repite nada. B (Uno de los alumnos no oye una palabra, pero la maestra no quiere repetir nada.)

6. Todos los alumnos
   A. entienden perfectamente lo que dice la maestra.
   B. escriben el dictado.

Todos los alumnos escriben el dictado. B (Todos los alumnos escriben cuando la maestra empieza a leer otra vez.)

Now listen to the fourth paragraph.

¿Qué es esto? Eugenio entra a la clase. A la maestra no le dice nada. Eugenio parece asustado. La maestra está muy enojada. ¡Eugenio!, grita ella. ¡Usted siempre llega tarde cuando hay un dictado! ¡Pero esta vez no voy a repetir la primera parte para usted! Eugenio no contesta. Está con la cara roja. Empieza a escribir.

7. La maestra
   A. no le dice nada a Eugenio.
   B. no está muy contenta.

La maestra no está muy contenta. B (Está muy enojada y le grita a Eugenio.)

8. Eugenio
   A. escribe la primera parte del dictado.
   B. no dice nada pero empieza a escribir.

Eugenio no dice nada pero empieza a escribir.   B (Eugenio no contesta cuando la maestra dice que no va a repetir la primera parte para él. Empieza a escribir.)

EXERCISE 191. LISTENING COMPREHENSION

Be prepared to write at the end of this exercise. You will hear a dialog between a boy, Pedro, and a girl, Luisa. You will then be asked to write answers to questions on the dialog. Your answers do not have to be complete sentences, but they should be grammatically correct. Now listen to the dialog.

PEDRO   ¿Estás lista para el dictado de inglés?
LUISA   ¿Estás loco? Ni siquiera he estudiado.
PEDRO   Pero tú siempre sales bien en inglés.
LUISA   No sé. Es que la maestra habla muy rápido y nunca repite nada.
PEDRO   Sí, tú siempre dices eso, pero siempre entiendes todo.

Now listen to the questions.

1. ¿En qué clase tienen un dictado Pedro y Luisa?
2. ¿Ha estudiado Luisa?
3. ¿Ella siempre sale bien o mal en inglés, según Pedro?
4. ¿Cómo habla la maestra, según Luisa?
5. ¿Qué le contesta Pedro?

Now listen to the dialog again. *Repeat only the dialog and then give the students time to write their answers.*

UNIT 12—SECTION A

[ɣ] *vs. vowel cluster*

EXERCISE 192. LISTENING

You already know that the Spanish sound [ɣ] is similar to the *y* of English words like *yes* or *yellow*, except that for the Spanish sound the tongue is held more tensely. Now listen to the following pairs of words. The first word in each pair does not have the sound [ɣ]. The second one does.

mía–milla, pío–pillo, lees–leyes, vea–bella, sea–sella

[ɣ] *vs. vowel cluster*

EXERCISE 193. SOUND DISCRIMINATION

Be prepared to write your responses for Exercise 193. You will hear a series of words, some of which have the sound [ɣ] between vowels, some of which do not. For each word you hear, place a check mark in either the row labeled [ɣ] or the row labeled No [ɣ].   EXAMPLE   You hear: **bella**   You place your check mark in the row labeled [ɣ], because the word you heard has the sound [ɣ] between vowels. We will begin now. *Read each item once.*

1. milla [y]	6. pío no [y]
2. calle [y]	7. sea no [y]
3. veo no [y]	8. sella [y]
4. mía no [y]	9. lees no [y]
5. leyes [y]	10. bello [y]

Now check your answers. *Repeat each word once, and confirm by naming the appropriate sound.*

[y] *vs. vowel cluster*

EXERCISE 194. PRONUNCIATION

Repeat each of the following pairs.

mía–milla, cae–calle, lees–leyes, vea–bella, sea–sella

EXERCISE 195. PRONUNCIATION

Listen to the following conversation. *Read the conversation once without interruption.*

¿Tú vives en esta calle?
Sí, esa casa amarilla es la mía.

Now repeat each of the following sentences. *Read each sentence separately, leaving a pause at the end.*

EXERCISE 196. LISTENING COMPREHENSION

Be prepared to write your responses for Exercise 196. You will hear a series of sentences. After each, you will hear three more sentences, A, B, and C. You are to determine which one logically continues the thought of the first sentence.

EXAMPLE   You hear: No puedo ir contigo.
             A. Mi marido me mata si le hablo de ir de compras.
             B. Además, no tengo que arreglar la sala.
             C. En todo caso, vamos.

You circle the A, because A logically continues the first sentence.

We will begin now. *Read each item once.*

Now check your answers. *Repeat each cue sentence once and give the correct answer as:*

1. Siempre gasta tanto.
   A. Mis padres me matan.
   B. Esa chica no sabe lo que cuesta el dinero.
   C. Pero nunca gasta nada.

Esa chica no sabe lo que cuesta el dinero.
B

2. Venden trajes muy bonitos aquí.
   A. Yo me voy a comprar uno.
   B. Pero no tienen ropa muy linda.
   C. Además, no venden nada.

Yo me voy a comprar uno.   A

3. Hay una liquidación hoy.   Tal vez hay unas gangas. **B**
   A. No compran nada.
   B. Tal vez hay unas gangas.
   C. Todo está más caro hoy.

4. Tengo tres sobrinos y cuatro nietos.   Ya ves que tengo muchos parientes. **C**
   A. Pero no tengo parientes.
   B. Mi abuelo está viejo.
   C. Ya ves que tengo muchos parientes.

5. Tengo dos exámenes mañana.   Además, tengo un dictado en la clase de inglés. **B**
   A. Por consiguiente, no tengo que estudiar.
   B. Además, tengo un dictado en la clase de inglés.
   C. Pero no tengo exámenes.

Note: In recorded program, exercise ends here ⟶

6. Si salgo ahora, . . .   mis padres me matan. **A**
   A. mis padres me matan.
   B. estoy en la casa.
   C. nunca pasa nada.

7. ¡Sólo diez pesos por este swéater!   Es una ganga. **A**
   A. Es una ganga.
   B. ¿Te gustan los guantes?
   C. Los trajes no son bonitos tampoco.

8. Es un almacén grandísimo.   Y tienen ropa muy linda allí. **C**
   A. Pero no es una tienda muy grande.
   B. Pero es muy pequeño, francamente.
   C. Y tienen ropa muy linda allí.

EXERCISE 197. SPOT DICTATION

Be prepared to do the writing for Exercise 197. You have in front of you a reading selection from which certain words and punctuation marks have been omitted. This selection will now be read to you. You are to write the words and punctuation marks omitted from the text in the space provided. We will begin now. *The underlined words and punctuation marks have been omitted from the students' copies. Pause at each slanted line to allow the students time to write.*

América y los americanos

"(*Signo de exclamación*) Todos los habitantes de este Hemisferio somos americanos, / no sólo la población de los Estados Unidos! / ¡Porque América es Canadá, es Argentina, / es todo el Hemisferio Occidental (*signo de exclamación*)" /

Ésta es la eterna protesta de unos pocos extremistas, quienes no están contentos porque los americanos han monopolizado esta palabra y han limitado su aplicación a la nacionalidad de los Estados Unidos. / Es una protesta sin mucha importancia. / Técnicamente es verdad que todos nosotros somos americanos, pero la realidad de las cosas es que cuando hablamos de "nacionalidad americana" o de "productos americanos", sabemos muy bien que esa nacionalidad y esos productos no corresponden a ningún otro país del hemisferio sino a los Estados Unidos. / Es simplemente una convencia, / un término que ha sido adaptado por los Estados Unidos y aceptado en todo el mundo, inclusive en el resto de América (*punto*) /

Note: In recorded program, selection is not repeated ⟶ Now listen to the reading selection once more. Later, when you have time, compare the words and punctuation marks you have written with those in the Narrative at the end of Unit 11.

UNIT 12—SECTION B

[r] *vs.* [t]

EXERCISE 198. LISTENING

You already know that a Spanish **r** between vowels is like the English *t* in *Betty*. Recall that the Spanish **t** is <u>not</u> like this English *t*. For Spanish **t**, the tongue touches the back of the upper teeth. In this exercise you will hear pairs of Spanish words. In each pair, the first word has a **t** between the vowels; the second is a matching word with an **r** in the same place. Now listen to each pair, noting the difference between the Spanish **r** and the Spanish **t**.

bata–vara, pata–para, mita–mira, zeta–cera, moto–moro

[r] *vs.* [t]

EXERCISE 199. SOUND DISCRIMINATION

Be prepared to write your responses for Exercise 199. You will hear a series of words, some of which have an **r** between vowels, and some of which have a **t**. For each word you hear, place a check mark in either the row labeled **r** or the row labeled **t**. EXAMPLE You hear: **mira** You place your check mark in the row labeled **r**, because the word you heard had an **r** between vowels. We will begin now. *Read each item once.*

1. bata   t
2. cera   r
3. moro   r
4. pata   t
5. paro   r

6. zeta   t
7. mera   r
8. mira   r
9. dote   t
10. pato   t

Now check your answers. *Repeat each word once and confirm by naming the appropriate sound.*

[r] *vs.* [t]

EXERCISE 200. PRONUNCIATION

Repeat each of the following pairs.

bata–vara, pata–para, mita–mira, meta–mera, zeta–cera, moto–moro

EXERCISE 201. LISTENING COMPREHENSION

Be prepared to write your responses for Exercise 201. You will hear a series of short monologs. In each one, some object or person is referred to, but not named. After each monolog you will hear three noun phrases, A, B, and C. You are to determine which one of these names the object or person that was being talked about.

T106

You hear: No, no la conozco. Nunca la he visto antes.

A. una señora   B. dos chicos   C. un maestro

You circle the A, because **una señora** is the only feminine singular noun in the list, and therefore the only one to which **la** could refer.

We will begin now. *Read each item once.*   Now check your answers. *Repeat each cue sentence once and give correct answer as:*

1. ¿Por qué no los abres ahora? ¿No los quieres abrir ahora, Juanito?   los regalos   C
   A. las ventanas
   B. la puerta
   C. los regalos

2. No, yo no los tengo. No sé dónde están. Tal vez Roberto los tiene.   los libros de español   A
   A. los libros de español
   B. el periódico
   C. la pluma

3. La busco pero no la encuentro. ¿La has visto tú?   la bolsa   C
   A. los apuntes
   B. el lápiz
   C. la bolsa

4. Lo he llamado tres veces y no contesta. Ya no lo llamo más.   el médico   A
   A. el médico
   B. los gemelos
   C. la secretaria

5. ¿No lo has leído todavía? ¡Apúrate, porque lo quiero ver yo antes de salir!   el periódico   C
   A. los libros
   B. la carta de papá
   C. el periódico

6. ¡Siempre las molestas! ¿Por qué no las dejas estudiar?   las chicas   A
   A. las chicas
   B. Susana
   C. Juan y Pedro

7. ¿Cómo? ¿La van a vender? Pero la acaban de comprar. ¿Estás seguro?   la casa   C
   A. los discos
   B. el carro
   C. la casa

8. No la sé, pero la voy a buscar ahora.   la dirección del Sr. García   C
   A. el número de teléfono del jefe
   B. el nombre del libro
   C. la dirección del Sr. García

(continued)

9. No lo puedo arreglar ahora. Lo   el cuarto de Juanito   C
   limpio más tarde, si quieres.
   A. la casa
   B. el dormitorio y la sala
   C. el cuarto de Juanito

10. Las voy a llamar ahora. Tal vez las   las gemelas López   A
    visito mañana.
    A. las gemelas López
    B. Juan y María
    C. los abuelos

UNIT 12—SECTION C

Spanish nt   **EXERCISE 202. LISTENING**

Listen to each of the following words. Recall that when **n** and **t** occur together in Spanish, both are pronounced clearly and distinctly.

> cuánto, tanto, idéntico, mantequilla, punto, caliente, cuento

Spanish nt   **EXERCISE 203. PRONUNCIATION**

Repeat each of the following words.

> cuánto, tanto, idéntico, mantequilla, punto, caliente, cuento

EXERCISE 204. PRONUNCIATION

Listen to the following conversation. *Read the conversation once without interruption.*

> ¿Cuánto cuestan estos guantes?
> Treinta y dos, noventa y cinco.

Now repeat each of the following phrases. *Read each sentence separately, leaving a pause at the end.*

EXERCISE 205. LISTENING COMPREHENSION

Be prepared to write your answers for Exercise 205. You will hear a monolog which has been broken into a series of short paragraphs. After each paragraph you will hear two incomplete sentences followed by two possible completions, A and B. You are to select the correct completion on the basis of the paragraph.   EXAMPLE You hear:

Sólo cincuenta pesos por este saco. Está de liquidación. ¡Qué ganga! ¡Y estos pantalones! Son muy bonitos y están tan baratos hoy.

> El chico está
> A. en un almacén.
> B. en la escuela.

You place your check mark in row A, because A correctly completes the sentence on the basis of the paragraph.

We will begin the monolog now. *Read each item once.*

Now check your answers. *Repeat each incomplete sentence, adding the appropriate completion.*

Now listen to the first paragraph.

¡Viera la liquidación de ropa que tienen en esa tienda! ¡Trajes de baño por sólo doce pesos! ¡Faldas por seis cincuenta y blusas por cinco noventa y cinco! Sí, es verdad. Lo acabo de ver en el periódico.

1. Hay una liquidación en
   A. la Zapatería García.
   B. un gran almacén.

Hay una liquidación en un gran almacén.   B (Venden trajes de baño y faldas y blusas allí.)

2. La señora sabe que hay una liquidación porque
   A. acaba de ir a la tienda.
   B. lo ha leído.

La señora sabe que hay una liquidación porque lo ha leído.   B (Lo acaba de ver en el periódico.)

Now listen to the second paragraph.

Yo no sé si mi marido me deja ir. Creo que me mata si le hablo de ir de compras. Pero yo quiero ir a esa liquidación porque estoy segura que tienen muchas gangas.

3. El marido de la señora
   A. quiere ir con ella.
   B. tal vez no le permite ir.

El marido de la señora tal vez no le permite ir.   B (Ella no sabe si él la deja ir.)

4. Pero ella quiere ir a esa liquidación porque
   A. está segura que todas sus amigas van a ir.
   B. cree que va a encontrar cosas buenas y baratas.

Pero ella quiere ir a esa liquidación porque cree que va a encontrar cosas buenas y baratas.   B (Está segura que tienen muchas gangas.)

Now listen to the third paragraph.

El problema es que siempre le prometo a mi marido no gastar mucho. Pero cuando veo tantas cosas bonitas . . . y tan baratas . . . no sé . . . compro y compro. En todo caso, le voy a preguntar si puedo ir.

5. Cuando la señora va a una liquidación
   A. siempre gasta mucho dinero.
   B. nunca gasta mucho.

Cuando la señora va a una liquidación siempre gasta mucho dinero.   A (Cuando ve tantas cosas bonitas y tan baratas, compra y compra.)

6. De todos modos la señora va a ver
   A. si su marido la deja ir.
   B. si puede hacer algunas cosas.

De todos modos la señora va a ver si su marido la deja ir.   A (Le va a preguntar si puedo ir.)

Now listen to the fourth paragraph.

Mis amigas dicen que hay unos vestidos lindísimos allí, y también unos zapatos muy bonitos . . . y también unos sacos sport . . . mmm . . . buena idea . . . tal vez si le prometo comprar algo para él . . .

7. Las amigas de la señora dicen que
   A. todo es caro en ese almacén.
   B. hay muchas cosas bonitas en ese almacén.

Las amigas de la señora dicen que hay muchas cosas bonitas en ese almacén.   B (Dicen que hay unos vestidos lindísimos allí, y también unos zapatos muy bonitos.)

(continued)

8. Tal vez el marido de la señora la deja ir si ella
   A. le dice que le va a comprar un regalo.
   B. promete no gastar mucho dinero.

Tal vez el marido de la señora la deja ir si ella le dice que le va a comprar un·regalo.   A (Tal vez la deja ir si le promete comprar algo para él.)

UNIT 12—SECTION D

Spanish [s] vs. English consonant

EXERCISE 206. LISTENING

Listen to the following pairs of words. The English word in each pair has the sound [Z], the Spanish word has the sound [s].

president–presidente, present–presente, visit–visita, proposition–propósito, reason–razón

[s]

EXERCISE 207. PRONUNCIATION

Repeat each of the following words. Be careful not to substitute the English [Z] for the Spanish [s].

presente, Susana, visitar, rosa, Venezuela, razón, propósito, presidente, visa

EXERCISE 208. PRONUNCIATION

Listen to the following conversation. *Read the conversation once without interruption.*

A propósito, ¿tú conoces a José Pérez?
¿Ese chico de Venezuela?
No, creo que es de Brasil.
¿De veras? Con razón. Por eso sabe portugués.

Now repeat each of the following sentences. *Read each sentence separately, leaving a pause at the end.*

EXERCISE 209. LISTENING COMPREHENSION

Be prepared to write your responses for Exercise 209. You will hear a series of short dialogs. After each, you will hear two sentences, A and B. You are to determine which one is more likely to be the next line of the dialog.

EXAMPLE   You hear: ¡Qué bonita es esa bicicleta!
Sí, ¿verdad? ¿Es de Juan?
A. Sí, creo que es suya.
B. Sí, creo que es mía.

You place your check mark in the row labeled A, because A is more likely to be the next line of the dialog.

T110

We will begin now. *Read each item once.*

Now check your answers. *Repeat each cue sentence once and give the correct answer as:*

1. ¿Te gusta esta pluma?
   Sí, es linda. ¿Es tuya?
   A. Sí, es mía.
   B. Sí, es suya.

   Sí, es mía.   A

2. ¿Quién es esa chica?
   Es una prima mía.
   A. ¿De veras? ¿Es una prima mía?
   B. ¿De veras? ¿Es una prima suya?

   ¿De veras? ¿Es una prima suya?   B

3. ¿Puedo ir a la liquidación? Marta dice que . . .
   ¡Esas amigas tuyas no saben lo que cuesta el dinero!
   A. ¿Cómo? ¡Las amigas mías!
   B. ¿Cómo? ¡Las amigas nuestras!

   ¿Cómo? ¡Las amigas mías!   A

4. ¿De quién son estos guantes?
   No sé. No son míos. Tal vez son de Juan.
   A. No, no son suyos.
   B. No, no son tuyos.

   No, no son suyos.   A

5. ¡Qué grande es esta casa!
   Sí, ¿verdad? ¿No es de las gemelas García?
   A. Sí, creo que es suya.
   B. Sí, creo que es tuya.

   Sí, creo que es suya.   A

6. Esa bicicleta es nuestra.
   ¿Y este carro?
   A. También es nuestro.
   B. También es suyo.

   También es nuestro.   A

7. ¿Usted sabe hablar inglés?
   Sí, todos estos libros en inglés son míos.
   A. ¿De veras? ¿Son todos suyos?
   B. ¿De veras? ¿Son todos míos?

   ¿De veras? ¿Son todos suyos?   A

8. ¿De quién es ese disco?
   Creo que es de la maestra.
   A. No, no es nuestro.
   B. No, no es suyo.

   No, no es suyo.   B

EXERCISE 210. LISTENING COMPREHENSION

Be prepared to write at the end of this exercise. You will hear a dialog between a boy, Roberto, and his cousin, Cristina. You will then be asked to write answers to questions on the dialog. Your answers do not have to be complete sentences, but they should be grammatically correct. Now listen to the dialog.

CRISTINA	¿Vas a ir al partido de fútbol, Roberto?
ROBERTO	¿Para qué? Estoy seguro que vamos a perder.
CRISTINA	¿Por qué dices eso?
ROBERTO	Porque nosotros nunca ganamos.
CRISTINA	Eso no es verdad. Además, todo el mundo va a ir.
ROBERTO	No sé, tal vez. De todos modos, yo te llamo.

Now listen to the questions.

1. ¿De qué están hablando Roberto y Cristina?
2. ¿Por qué no quiere ir al partido Roberto?
3. ¿Por qué dice eso?
4. ¿Quién va a ir al partido, según Cristina?
5. ¿Qué va a hacer Roberto, de todos modos?

Now listen to the dialog again. *Repeat only the dialog and then give the students time to write their answers.*

UNIT 13—SECTION A

Stress: words of two syllables

EXERCISE 211. LISTENING

Listen to the following pairs of words. In the first word in each pair, the first syllable is stressed. In the second, the second is stressed.

papa–papá, tomas–Tomás, esta–está, hablo–habló, llego–llegó, bailo–bailó

Stress: words of two syllables

EXERCISE 212. PRONUNCIATION

Repeat each of the following pairs.

papa–papá, tomas–Tomás, esta–está, hablo–habló, llego–llegó, bailo–bailó, canto–cantó, paso–pasó

EXERCISE 213. LISTENING COMPREHENSION

Be prepared to write your responses for Exercise 213. You will hear a series of incomplete sentences. After each you will hear four possible completions, A, B, C, and D. You are to determine which one correctly completes the sentence.

EXAMPLE   You hear: ¿Cuándo es
          A. el país? B. la reunión? C. el tamaño? D. la tierra?

You circle the letter B, because B correctly completes the sentence.

We will begin now. *Read each item once.*   Now check your answers. *Repeat each incomplete sentence once, adding the appropriate completion.*

1. Me voy a lavar
  A. la cara. C. el verano.
  B. la lista. D. el invierno.

                Me voy a lavar la cara.   A

2. Ella cumple quince
   A. en la estación.
   B. en el verano.
   C. en la casa.
   D. en la sala.

Ella cumple quince en el verano.   B

3. ¿Cuándo es
   A. su abrigo?
   B. su santo?
   C. su regalo?
   D. su vestido?

¿Cuándo es su santo?   B

4. ¿Me pongo
   A. el mapa?
   B. la estación?
   C. el cuaderno?
   D. los guantes?

¿Me pongo los guantes?   D

5. ¿Por qué no te quedas
   A. unos países más?
   B. un número más?
   C. una cosa más?
   D. una hora más?

¿Por qué no te quedas una hora más?
D

6. No sé
   A. su nombre.
   B. su tía.
   C. su mamá.
   D. su hijo.

No sé su nombre.   A

7. Nunca he visitado
   A. esa coma.
   B. ese lugar.
   C. esa lengua.
   D. ese tamaño.

Nunca he visitado ese lugar.   B

8. Pienso invitar a diez
   A. hombres.
   B. direcciones.
   C. números.
   D. nombres.

Pienso invitar a diez hombres.   A

9. Siempre me levanto
   A. hoy.
   B. bastante tarde.
   C. mañana.
   D. muy libre.

Siempre me levanto bastante tarde.   B

10. Todavía no ha hecho
    A. el papel.
    B. la tarea.
    C. el lápiz.
    D. la pluma.

Todavía no ha hecho la tarea.   B

EXERCISE 214. SPOT DICTATION

Be prepared to do the writing for Exercise 214. You have in front of you a reading selection from which certain words and punctuation marks have been omitted. This selection will now be read to you. You are to write the words and punctuation marks omitted from the text in the space provided. We will begin now. *The underlined words and punctuation marks have been omitted from the students' copies. Pause at each slanted line to allow students time to write.*

El Nuevo Mundo

Si <u>miramos</u> un mapa del Hemisferio Occidental (*coma*) / podemos observar que el Nuevo Mundo tiene la forma de dos triángulos unidos por una delgada faja de <u>tierra</u>. / El triángulo superior contiene tres grandes países (*dos puntos*) / Canadá, Estados Unidos, y México, y llamamos esta parte del continente "<u>Norteamérica</u>". / Por esta razón también les decimos "norteamericanos" a los americanos. <u>Sin embargo</u>, / nadie les aplica esta término a los habitantes de Canadá y México, que por su <u>posición</u> geográfica también son norteamericanos. / La <u>nacionalidad</u> de cada una de estas dos <u>repúblicas</u> es una palabra tan claramente derivada del nombre del país / – canadiense y mexicano – que para no hacer <u>confusión</u> preferimos reservar "norteamericanos" para los habitantes de los Estados Unidos. /

Now listen to the reading selection once more. Later, when you have time, compare the words and punctuation marks you have written with those in the narrative at the end of Unit 12.

UNIT 13—SECTION B

Stress: words of three or more syllables

EXERCISE 215. LISTENING

In this exercise you will hear sets of three words each. The words in each set are similar except that in the first word, the third from the last syllable is stressed; in the second, the next-to-the-last syllable is stressed; and in the third, the last syllable is stressed.

ánimo	animo	animó
público	publico	publicó
práctico	practico	practicó
solícito	solicito	solicitó

Stress: words of three or more syllables

EXERCISE 216. STRESS DISCRIMINATION

Be prepared to write your responses for Exercise 216. You will hear a series of words. Some of the words are stressed on the third-from-the-last syllable, some are stressed on the next-to-the-last syllable, and some are stressed on the last syllable. For each word you hear, place a check mark in the row labeled Third-from-last, Next-to-last, or Last, according to which syllable is stressed.   EXAMPLE You hear: **solícito** You place your check mark in the row labeled Third-from-last, because in the word you heard, the third-from-last syllable was stressed.

We will begin now. *Read each word once.*   Now check your answers. *Repeat each word once and confirm with:*

1. publico   next-to-last
2. práctico   third-from-last
3. magnificó   last
4. ánimo   third-from-last
5. público   third-from-last
6. especifico   next-to-last
7. practico   next-to-last
8. magnífico   third-from-last

Stress: words of three or more syllables

EXERCISE 217. PRONUNCIATION

In this exercise you will say sets of three words each. Repeat each set once, paying special attention to the stress.

ánimo	animo	animó
público	publico	publicó
práctico	practico	practicó
solícito	solicito	solicitó

EXERCISE 218. LISTENING COMPREHENSION

Be prepared to write your responses for Exercise 218. You will hear a series of short conversations. After each, you will hear a question followed by two possible answers, A and B. You are to select the correct answer on the basis of the conversation.

EXAMPLE   You hear: ¡Qué calor!

¿Por qué no tomamos un helado en ese café?

Buena idea. Hace mucho calor para ir de compras.

¿En qué estación estamos?

A. En el verano.

B. En el invierno.

You place your check mark in row A, because A is the correct answer on the basis of the conversation.

We will begin now. *Read each item once.*   Now check your answers. *Repeat each conversation and question once and give the correct answer as:*

BÁRBARA   Tú vas a cumplir quince años muy pronto, ¿verdad, Cecilia?

CECILIA   Sí, en dos meses más cumplo las quince primaveras.

BÁRBARA   ¿Vas a dar una fiesta?

1. ¿Cuántos años tiene Cecilia ahora?   Tiene catorce años.   A (Va a cumplir
   A. Tiene catorce años.   quince muy pronto.)
   B. Tiene casi dieciséis.

CECILIA   No voy a hacer una fiesta muy grande.

BÁRBARA   ¿A quiénes piensas invitar?

CECILIA   A diez muchachas y al doble de hombres.

T115

2. ¿A cuántos hombres va a invitar Cecilia?
   A. A veinte hombres.
   B. A diez hombres.

   A veinte hombres.   A (Piensa invitar a diez muchachas y al doble de hombres.)

> BÁRBARA   ¿Ya has hecho la lista, Cecilia?
> CECILIA   No, ni siquiera la he empezado.
> BÁRBARA   La tienes que hacer muy pronto, entonces. Ya es el quince de mayo.

3. ¿Ya ha hecho la lista Cecilia?
   A. No, la va a hacer el quince de mayo.
   B. No, no la ha hecho todavía.

   No, no la ha hecho todavía.   B. (Ni siquiera la ha empezado.)

> CECILIA   Ya he recibido unos regalos, ¿sabes?
> BÁRBARA   ¿De veras? ¿De quiénes?
> CECILIA   Uno de mi tía Susana, uno de mis abuelos, y dos de mis padres.

4. ¿De quiénes ha recibido regalos Cecilia?
   A. De unos amigos y compañeros de clase.
   B. De algunos de sus parientes.

   De algunos de sus parientes.   B (De su tía Susana, de sus abuelos, y de sus padres.)

> BÁRBARA   ¿Ya has abierto todos los regalos?
> CECILIA   No, los voy a abrir el día de mi cumpleaños.
> BÁRBARA   ¡Qué paciencia! ¿Cómo los puedes dejar sin abrir?

5. ¿Ya ha abierto todos los regalos Cecilia?
   A. No, no los va a abrir antes de su cumpleaños.
   B. No, solamente ha abierto algunos.

   No, no los va a abrir antes de su cumpleaños.   A (Los va a abrir el día de su cumpleaños.)

> CECILIA   No sé si voy a invitar a esa Ana Pérez.
> BÁRBARA   ¿Por qué no? Me parece muy simpática.
> CECILIA   Pero nunca me invita a las fiestas suyas.

6. ¿Por qué no quiere Cecilia invitar a Ana Pérez?
   A. Ana no parece muy simpática.
   B. Ana no invita a Cecilia a sus fiestas.

   Ana no invita a Cecilia a sus fiestas.   B (Nunca invita a Cecilia a las fiestas suyas.)

> BÁRBARA   Tal vez es que eres nueva y Ana todavía no te conoce bien.
> CECILIA   Sí, tal vez. De todos modos, ella es muy pretenciosa.
> BÁRBARA   No me parece. ¿Por qué no la invitas?

7. Según Cecilia, ¿cómo es Ana?
   A. Cecilia no la conoce.
   B. Es antipática.

   Es antipática.   B (Cecilia dice que Ana es muy pretenciosa.)

CECILIA	No sé. Primero voy a hacer la lista.
BÁRBARA	Ella tiene un hermano muy guapo y simpático, ¿sabes?
CECILIA	¿De veras? Mmm... Tal vez la invito. Bien pensado, esa Ana no me parece tan mala persona.

8. ¿Qué piensa hacer Cecilia por fin?

A. Piensa no invitar a Ana, porque no le gusta su hermano.

B. Piensa invitar a Ana.

Piensa invitar a Ana.   B (Bien pensado, no le parece mala persona, y además, tiene un hermano guapo y simpático.)

UNIT 13—SECTION C

[y]

EXERCISE 219. PRONUNCIATION

Recall that an unstressed **i** followed by another vowel forms one syllable with the following vowel. Now repeat each of the following words.

pienso, empiezo, quiero, entiendo, italiano, noticia, diccionario, adiós, ciudad

EXERCISE 220. LISTENING COMPREHENSION

Be prepared to write your responses for Exercise 220. You will hear a series of short monologs. You are to determine which of these occur in the morning, which in the afternoon, and which in the evening. Place your check mark in the appropriate row.

EXAMPLE   You hear: ¡Ya son las nueve y media! Usted siempre llega tarde a la escuela.

You place your check mark in the row labeled Morning, because the monolog takes place in the morning.

We will begin now. *Read each monolog once.*

Now check your answers. *Repeat each monolog once and give the correct answer as:*

1. ¿Me puedo lavar las manos? Ya vamos a cenar.

evening

2. No me levanto todavía. Es muy temprano y tengo mucho sueño.

morning

3. ¿Cómo? ¿Ya te vas a la escuela? Pero todavía no has desayunado.

morning

4. ¿Por qué no te sientas aquí? Vamos a almorzar ahora.

afternoon

5. Me pongo el abrigo y me voy. Ya son las once y me tengo que levantar temprano mañana.　　evening

6. No me acuesto todavía. Es tarde pero todavía no he hecho toda mi tarea.　　evening

7. ¡Apúrate! Ya son las tres y va a empezar el desfile.　　afternoon

8. ¿Cómo? Son las diez y media y todavía no han abierto esa tienda. ¿Pero cuándo la van a abrir?　　morning

UNIT 13—SECTION D

[w]

EXERCISE 221. PRONUNCIATION

Recall that an unstressed **u** followed by another vowel forms one syllable with the following vowel. Now repeat each of the following words.

escuela, juego, recuerdo, suerte, bueno, cuatro, cuanto, guante, cuota, continuo, Luisa, suizo

EXERCISE 222. LISTENING COMPREHENSION

Be prepared to write your responses for Exercise 222. You will hear a series of sentences. After each, you will hear two more sentences, A and B. Only one of these is a logical rejoinder to the first one. You are to determine which one it is.

EXAMPLE　You hear: ¿Por qué no se queda un rato más?
　　　　　　　A. No, gracias. Me tengo que ir ahora.
　　　　　　　B. No, gracias. Te tienes que ir ahora.

You place a check mark in row A, because A is a logical rejoinder to the first sentence.

We will begin now. *Read each item once.*

Now check your answers. *Repeat each cue sentence once and give the correct answer as:*

1. ¿Se sienta aquí?
   A. Aquí, no. Me siento en el sofá.
   B. Aquí, no. Nos sentamos en el sofá.

   Aquí, no. Me siento en el sofá.　A

2. ¡Siempre te enojas!
   A. No es verdad. No me enojo mucho.
   B. No es verdad. No se enoja mucho.

   No es verdad. No me enojo mucho.　A

3. ¡Cómo nos aburrimos!
   A. ¿Te aburres mucho?
   B. ¿Se aburren mucho?

   ¿Se aburren mucho?　B

T118

4. Me voy a acostar ahora.   ¿Ya se acuesta? ¿Por qué tan temprano?
   - A. ¿Ya se acuesta? ¿Por qué tan   A
   temprano?
   - B. ¿Ya se acuestan? ¿Por qué tan
   temprano?

5. Me tengo que levantar mañana a   ¿De veras? ¿Te levantas a las siete?   B
   las siete.
   - A. ¿De veras? ¿Se levantan a las
   siete?
   - B. ¿De veras? ¿Te levantas a las
   siete?

6. Tengo un examen mañana.   ¿Por qué te preocupas? Has estudiado
   - A. ¿Por qué te preocupas? Has es-   mucho. A
   tudiado mucho.
   - B. ¿Por qué se preocupan? Han estudiado mucho.

7. Se compra un carro nuevo.   ¿Qué dices? ¿Se compra un carro nuevo?
   - A. ¿Qué dices? ¿Se compra un carro   A
   nuevo?
   - B. ¿Qué dices? ¿Se compran un
   carro nuevo?

8. ¿Por qué no se ponen los guantes?   No tenemos frío. A
   - A. No tenemos frío.
   - B. No tienes frío.

EXERCISE 223. LISTENING COMPREHENSION

Be prepared to write at the end of this exercise. You will hear a dialog between a boy, Carlos, and a girl, María. You will then be asked to write answers to questions on the dialog. Your answers do not have to be complete sentences, but they should be grammatically correct. Now listen to the dialog.

MARÍA	El viernes es el cumpleaños de Cecilia, ¿verdad?
CARLOS	Sí, ¿tú le vas a comprar un regalo?
MARÍA	Claro. ¿Tú, no?
CARLOS	Sí, pero no sé qué les gusta a las chicas.
MARÍA	¿Por qué no le compras unos guantes bonitos o una blusita?
CARLOS	¿Estás loca? Le compro un disco, mejor.

Now listen to the questions.

1. ¿Por qué le van a comprar un regalo a Cecilia los dos chicos?
2. ¿Por qué no sabe Carlos qué comprar para Cecilia?
3. Según María, ¿qué le debe comprar Carlos a Cecilia?
4. ¿Carlos le quiere comprar eso?
5. ¿Qué le va a comprar, mejor?

Now listen to the dialog again. *Repeat only the dialog and then give the students time to write their answers.*

Spanish palatals

EXERCISE 224. LISTENING

Listen to the following pairs of words. The first word in each pair is English; the second is Spanish.

lotion–loción, national–nacional, question–cuestión

Spanish palatals

EXERCISE 225. PRONUNCIATION

Repeat each of the following words.

!oción, nación, acción, gracioso, celestial, cordial

EXERCISE 226. PRONUNCIATION

Listen to the following conversation. *Read the conversation once without interruption.*

Hoy vamos al museo nacional.
Tienen muchas reliquias allí.
De civilizaciones indias, ¿verdad?
Sí, tienen una colección excepcional.

Now repeat each of the following sentences. *Read each sentence separately, leaving a pause at the end.*

EXERCISE 227. LISTENING COMPREHENSION

Be prepared to write your responses for Exercise 227. You will hear a series of statements with the last word missing. In front of you is the first letter of the missing word and spaces for the remaining letters. You are to complete the word by placing a letter in each of the spaces.

EXAMPLE   You hear: ¡Apúrate, Juan! Ya van a cerrar las tiendas y tengo mucha ———— .

You see the letter **p** followed by four spaces for letters. You fill in the spaces to form the word **prisa**, the correct completion.

We will begin now. *Read each statement once.*

Now check your answers. *Repeat each statement once, adding the correct completion.*

1. ¡Lavar la ropa! ¡Limpiar la casa! ¡Arreglar la sala! No puedo hacer tantas cosas. No tengo mil ———— .

   ¡Lavar la ropa! ¡Limpiar la casa! ¡Arreglar la sala! No puedo hacer tantas cosas. No tengo mil manos.

2. Los muchachos no están allí arriba. Están aquí ——— .

   Los muchachos no están allí arriba. Están aquí abajo.

3. Está lloviendo. Necesito mi impermeable y mi ——— .

   Está lloviendo. Necesito mi impermeable y mi paraguas.

4. Mañana, muy temprano, vamos a tomar el tren para Lima. Ahora tengo que hacer las _____ .

5. Se van el primero de mayo y no sé cuándo van a _____ .

6. No vivimos en una casa. Vivimos en un _____ .

7. Tenemos tres maletas y un baúl. Siempre viajamos con mucho _____ .

8. Mi abuelo tiene ochenta años. Ya es muy _____ .

9. ¿Cómo? ¿Vamos a hacer un viaje a Venezuela? ¿Y vamos a viajar en avión? ¡Qué _____ !

10. Estoy perdido. No sé si debo ir a la derecha o a la _____ .

Mañana, muy temprano, vamos a tomar el tren para Lima. Ahora tengo que hacer las maletas.

Se van el primero de mayo y no sé cuándo van a regresar.

No vivimos en una casa. Vivimos en un departamento.

Tenemos tres maletas y un baúl. Siempre viajamos con mucho equipaje.

Mi abuelo tiene ochenta años. Ya es muy viejo.

¿Cómo? ¿Vamos a hacer un viaje a Venezuela? ¿Y vamos a viajar en avión? ¡Qué brutal!

Estoy perdido. Ne sé si debo ir a la derecha o a la izquierda.

EXERCISE 228. DICTATION

Be prepared for a dictation. A passage from a reading selection will be read to you twice. The first time, just listen to it. The second time, it will be broken up into segments. Each segment will be read twice. You are to write it as you hear it. We will begin now. *Read the selection once, and then repeat each segment twice, pausing at the slanted line to allow students time to write.*

A mí me encanta ver la televisión (*coma*) / pero desgraciadamente (*coma*) / a mi hermanito también le gusta mucho (*punto*) / Él siempre quiere ver esos programas para niños (*coma*) / esos programas aburridos de cowboys (*punto*) / Me cansa tener que pelear con él / cada vez que quiero ver algo interesante (*punto*) /

Note: In recorded program, passage is not repeated ——→ Now listen to the reading selection once more. Later, when you have time, compare what you have written with the first paragraph of the Narrative at the end of Unit 13.

UNIT 14—SECTION B

[ay], [ey], [oy], *and* [uy]

EXERCISE 229. PRONUNCIATION

In this exercise you will say words with the Spanish sounds [ay], [ey], [oy], and [uy]. Repeat each of the following words.

ay, baile, seis, ley, doy, hoy, voy, uy, muy

EXERCISE 230. LISTENING COMPREHENSION

Be prepared to write your responses for Exercise 230. You will hear a series of sentences. After each, you will hear two more sentences, A and B. You are to determine which one of these describes what was said in the first sentence.

You hear: Me llamo Claudia.
  A. La chica dice que se llama Claudia.
  B. La chica dice que te llamas Claudia.

You place your check mark in row A, because A describes what the speaker said in the first sentence.

We will begin now. *Read each item once.*

Now check your answers. *Repeat each cue sentence once and give the correct answer as:*

1. ¡Ay, ese hombre no nos oye!
   A. La chica dice que ese hombre no las oye.
   B. La chica dice que ese hombre no te oye.

   La chica dice que ese hombre no las oye. A

2. Él tiene mi maleta y no me la da.
   A. Dice que él tiene su maleta y no se la da.
   B. Dice que él tiene tu maleta y no te la da.

   Dice que él tiene su maleta y no se la da. A

3. ¡Caramba!, me van a abrir el baúl.
   A. Dice que les van a abrir el baúl.
   B. Dice que le van a abrir el baúl.

   Dice que le van a abrir el baúl. B

4. Si me lo abren, ¿cómo lo voy a cerrar otra vez?
   A. Pregunta que si nos lo abren, ¿cómo lo vamos a cerrar otra vez?
   B. Pregunta que si se lo abren, ¿cómo lo va a cerrar otra vez?

   Pregunta que si se lo abren, ¿cómo lo va a cerrar otra vez? B

5. Allí están nuestros padres. Nos están llamando.
   A. Dice que sus padres las están llamando.
   B. Dice que mis padres me están llamando.

   Dice que sus padres las están llamando. A

6. Mi hermano me está gritando.
   A. Dice que nuestro hermano nos está gritando.
   B. Dice que su hermano le está gritando.

   Dice que su hermano le está gritando. B

7. ¡Qué grande está! Casi no lo reconozco.
   A. Dice que casi no me reconoce.
   B. Dice que casi no lo reconoce.

   Dice que casi no lo reconoce. B

8. Le traigo un regalo. Se lo doy ahora.
   A. Dice que nos trae un regalo y que nos lo da ahora.
   B. Dice que le trae un regalo y que se lo da ahora.

Dice que le trae un regalo y que se lo da ahora.   B

9. ¡Por fin me van a dar mi equipaje!
   A. Dice que por fin nos van a dar nuestro equipaje.
   B. Dice que por fin le van a dar su equipaje.

Dice que por fin le van a dar su equipaje.   B

10. ¡Qué emoción! Me encanta estar de vuelta en Colombia.
    A. Dice que le encanta estar de vuelta en Colombia.
    B. Dice que me encanta estar de vuelta en Colombia.

Dice que le encanta estar de vuelta en Colombia.   A

UNIT 14—SECTION C

[aw] *and* [ew]

EXERCISE 231. PRONUNCIATION

In this exercise you will say words with the sounds [aw] and [ew]. Repeat each of the following words.

auto, autobús, causa, restaurante, Europa, reunión

EXERCISE 232. LISTENING COMPREHENSION

Be prepared to write your answers for Exercise 232. You will hear a series of sentences in which one or more pronouns occur before a verb with a person-number ending. After each sentence, you will hear an incomplete sentence, which you are to complete by writing the infinitive or present participle plus the pronouns which occur in the first sentence.

EXAMPLE   You hear: Me voy a sentar. Voy a _____.

You write **sentarme** in the space provided.

We will begin now. *Read each item once.*

Now check your answers. *Repeat each item once, adding the appropriate completion.*

1. Te estoy hablando. Estoy _____.

Estoy hablándote.

2. No la debemos invitar. No debemos _____.

No debemos invitarla.

3. El niño no se quiere acostar. El niño no quiere _____.

El niño no quiere acostarse.

4. ¿Le estás escribiendo? ¿Estás _____?

¿Estás escribiéndole?

5. Nos acaban de llamar. Acaban de _____.

Acaban de llamarnos.

T123

6. Se lo tengo que comprar. Tengo que _____ .

Tengo que comprárselo.

7. Te lo acabo de decir. Acabo de _____ .

Acabo de decírtelo.

8. ¿No me lo puede traer? ¿No puede _____ ?

¿No puede traérmelo?

9. Se lo estoy trayendo. Estoy _____ .

Estoy trayéndoselo.

Later, when you have time, compare the words you have written with those in Drill 15 of Unit 14.

UNIT 14—SECTION D

Vowel clusters:
[a], [e], [o]

EXERCISE 233. PRONUNCIATION

Repeat each of the following words. Pay particular attention to the vowel clusters. Remember, vowel clusters composed of combinations of **a**, **e**, or **o** are pronounced as two different syllables.

> maestro, trae, tarea, cumpleaños, preocupado, geografía, creo, cree, lee

EXERCISE 234. PRONUNCIATION

Listen to the following conversation. *Read the conversation once without interruption.*

> El maestro de geografía es el peor.
> Yo no creo. Debe ser el de geometría.

Now repeat each of the following sentences. *Read each sentence separately, leaving a pause at the end.*

EXERCISE 235. LISTENING COMPREHENSION

Be prepared to write your responses for Exercise 235. You will hear a narrative which has been broken up into short paragraphs. After each paragraph, you will hear two incomplete sentences followed by three possible completions, A, B, and C. You are to determine which one correctly completes the sentence on the basis of the paragraph.

EXAMPLE   You hear:

La familia García vive en Bogotá, la capital y ciudad más importante de Colombia. Esta tarde, el Sr. y la Sra. García y su hijo Alberto están en el aeropuerto de Bogotá, porque llegan de vuelta Gloria y Claudia, las dos hijas mayores, quienes han estado estudiando en Nueva York.

La familia García
A. está en el aeropuerto de Bogotá.
B. es de los Estados Unidos.
C. estudia en Nueva York.

You circle the letter A, because A correctly completes the sentence.

We will begin now. *Read each item once.*   Now check your answers. *Repeat each incomplete sentence once, adding the appropriate completion.*

Now listen to the first paragraph.

Gloria y Claudia acaban de regresar de los Estados Unidos, donde han estado estudiando en una escuela para señoritas. Las dos han aprendido a hablar inglés bastante bien, pero están contentas de estar de vuelta en Colombia, y no de tener que hablar inglés todos los días.

1. Gloria y Claudia han estado estudiando
   A. en una escuela para señoritas en los Estados Unidos.
   B. en una escuela para alumnos latinoamericanos.
   C. en Canadá.

Gloria y Claudia han estado estudiando en una escuela para señoritas en los Estados Unidos. A (Regresan de los Estados Unidos, donde han estado estudiando en una escuela para señoritas.)

2. Las dos chicas saben
   A. hablar español, pero no muy bien.
   B. leer en inglés y en francés.
   C. hablar inglés bastante bien.

Las dos chicas saben hablar inglés bastante bien. C (Han aprendido a hablar inglés bastante bien.)

Now listen to the second paragraph.

Gloria tiene dieciséis años y Claudia tiene dieciocho. Las dos chicas tienen un hermanito, Alberto, de trece años, que escucha con la boca abierta todo lo que le cuentan de su viaje a los Estados Unidos. Alberto también quiere ir a estudiar allá.

3. Gloria y Claudia tienen
   A. un hermano mayor.
   B. una hermana menor.
   C. un hermano menor.

Gloria y Claudia tienen un hermano menor. C (Gloria tiene dieciséis años y Claudia tiene dieciocho. Alberto tiene trece.)

4. A Alberto
   A. no le interesa escuchar a sus hermanas.
   B. le encanta escuchar a sus hermanas hablar de los Estados Unidos.
   C. no le gustan los Estados Unidos.

A Alberto le encanta escuchar a sus hermanas hablar de los Estados Unidos. B (Él escucha con la boca abierta todo lo que le cuentan.)

Now listen to the third paragraph.

Gloria y Claudia cuentan que allá en Nueva York tienen muchas amigas norteamericanas y también algunas latinoamericanas. Dicen que todas las compañeras son muy simpáticas. Algunas de las americanas hablan español muy bien, observa Gloria, porque enseñan español en casi todas las escuelas—es decir, en casi todos los "high schools"—de los Estados Unidos.

5. En Nueva York las chicas
   A. sólo conocen a latinoamericanos.
   B. nunca hablan español.
   C. conocen a muchas muchachas norteamericanas.

En Nueva York las chicas conocen a muchas muchachas norteamericanas. C (Tienen muchas amigas norteamericanas y también algunas latinoamericanas.)

6. Algunas de la americanas
   A. hablan español muy bien.
   B. han estudiado en todas las escuelas de los Estados Unidos.
   C. No hablan inglés.

Algunas de las americanas hablan español muy bien. A (Hablan bien porque enseñan español en casi todos los "high schools" de los Estados Unidos.)

Now listen to the fourth paragraph.

Claudia dice que el clima de Nueva York es muy malo. En el invierno hace un frío horrible y en el verano hace mucho calor. No es como Bogotá, donde casi siempre hace buen tiempo. No hace ni mucho frío, como en las regiones muy altas de Colombia, ni mucho calor, como en la costa.

7. En Bogotá
   A. hace más calor que en Nueva York.
   B. no hace ni mucho frío ni mucho calor.
   C. hace un frío espantoso en el invierno.

En Bogotá no hace ni mucho frío ni mucho calor. B (Allá casi siempre hace buen tiempo.)

8. En Colombia
   A. cada región tiene un clima diferente.
   B. hace calor en todas las regiones del país.
   C. no hay costa.

En Colombia cada región tiene un clima diferente. A (Hace frío en las regiones altas y hace calor en la costa. En Bogotá, no hace ni frío ni calor.)

Note: In recorded program, exercise ends here ———➤

Now listen to the fifth paragraph.

Nueva York les encanta a Gloria y a Claudia, pero las dos hermanas están contentas de estar de vuelta. Les gustan los edificios altos, los museos, y los almacenes de Nueva York, pero Bogotá también tiene grandes edificios, museos y tiendas, y además, tiene plazas lindísimas y muchos parques y jardines. Es bonito viajar, dicen Gloria y Claudia, pero también es bonito regresar a casa.

9. A las dos muchachas
   A. no les gusta Nueva York.
   B. no les gusta estar vuelta en Colombia.
   C. les gusta mucho Nueva York.

A las dos muchachas les gusta mucho Nueva York. C (Nueva York les encanta a Gloria y Claudia.)

10. Claudia y Gloria piensan que
   A. los almacenes de Bogotá son mejores que los de Nueva York.
   B. es bonito viajar.
   C. no hay museos en Colombia.

Claudia y Gloria piensan que es bonito viajar. B (Es bonito viajar, pero también es bonito regresar a casa.)

EXERCISE 236. LISTENING COMPREHENSION

Be prepared to write at the end of this exercise. You will hear a dialog between a man, Sr. Ramos, and his wife, Sra. Ramos. You will then be asked to write answers to questions on the dialog. Your answers do not have to be complete sentences, but they should be grammatically correct. Now listen to the dialog.

SR. RAMOS	¿Estás haciendo las maletas?
SRA. RAMOS	Sí, ¿dónde está mi cepillo?
SR. RAMOS	En el baño. ¿Ya has puesto toda la ropa?
SRA. RAMOS	Sí, casi. ¿Cuántas camisas tuyas pongo?
SR. RAMOS	Unas diez. ¡Apúrate! El tren sale a las cuatro en punto.

Now listen to the questions.

1. ¿Qué está haciendo la Sra. Ramos?
2. ¿Qué busca ella?
3. ¿Ya ha puesto toda la ropa en la maleta?
4. ¿Qué no ha puesto todavía?
5. ¿La familia Ramos, va a viajar en tren o en avión?

Note: In recorded program, dialog is not repeated → Now listen to the dialog again. *Repeat only the dialog and then give the students time to write their answers.*

UNIT 15—SECTION A

Intervocalic [rr] vs. initial [rr]

EXERCISE 237. LISTENING

Listen to the following pairs of words. The first word in each pair has a [rr] between vowels. The second starts with [rr].

cerro–rezo, tarro–rato, barrio–rabio, mirra–rima

Intervocalic [rr] vs. initial [rr]

EXERCISE 238. PRONUNCIATION

Repeat each of the following pairs of words.

cerro–rezo, tarro–rato, borro–robo, corra–roca, zorro–rozo

EXERCISE 239. PRONUNCIATION

Listen to the following conversation. *Read the conversation once without interruption.*

¿Puede repetir el párrafo, por favor?
Pero, Raúl, ya he repetido dos veces.

Now repeat each of the following sentences. *Read each sentence separately, leaving a pause at the end.*

EXERCISE 240. LISTENING COMPREHENSION

Be prepared to write your responses for Exercise 240. You will hear a series of statements with the last word missing. In front of you is the first letter of the missing word and spaces for the remaining letters. You are to complete the word by placing a letter in each of the spaces.

EXAMPLE   You hear: Hemos estado caminando todo el día. Usted no sabe como nos duelen las _____.

You see the letter **p**, followed by six spaces for letters. You fill in the spaces to form the word **piernas**, the correct completion.

We will begin now. *Read each statement once.*

Now check your answers. *Repeat each statement once, adding the correct completion.*

1. Me encanta el campo. Este año voy a pasar el verano en una _____ .

   Me encanta el campo. Este año voy a pasar el verano en una hacienda.

2. Hace mucho calor. Yo no quiero estudiar más. ¿Por qué no vamos a la _____ ?

   Hace mucho calor. Yo no quiero estudiar más. ¿Por qué no vamos a la playa?

3. Yo no recuerdo ni las fechas ni los nombres. Estudio mucho, pero siempre paso raspando en _____ .

   Yo no recuerdo ni las fechas ni los nombres. Estudio mucho, pero siempre paso raspando en historia.

4. A mi hermano le encanta todo lo que es matemáticas. Siempre saca un diez en _____ .

   A mi hermano le encanta todo lo que es matemáticas. Siempre saca un diez en álgebra.

5. Mi hermana menor es muy artística. Ella saca muy buenas notas en música y en _____ .

   Mi hermana menor es muy artística. Ella saca muy buenas notas en música y en dibujo.

6. A mí me gusta leer. Ahora estoy leyendo un libro muy interesante; es una _____ .

   A mí me gusta leer. Ahora estoy leyendo un libro muy interesante; es una novela.

7. ¿Estás resfriado? ¿Te duele mucho la _____ ?

   ¿Estás resfriado? ¿Te duele mucho la garganta?

8. No me gusta mucho la ciudad. Prefiero vivir en el _____ .

   No me gusta mucho la ciudad. Prefiero vivir en el campo.

9. Todo el mundo se ha ido. Sólo yo me tengo que quedar aquí. Estoy sola y muy _____ .

   Todo el mundo se ha ido. Sólo yo me tengo que quedar aquí. Estoy sola y muy triste.

10. ¿Cómo? ¿Tú vas a pasar las vacaciones en Argentina? ¡Qué suerte! ¿Me mandas una _____ ?

    ¿Cómo? ¿Tú vas a pasar las vacaciones en Argentina? ¡Qué suerte! ¿Me mandas una tarjeta?

UNIT 15—SECTION B

[d], [r], [t]

EXERCISE 241. LISTENING

Listen to the following sets of words. The words in each set sound the same except for the following differences: the first word in each set has a **d** between vowels; the second has an **r**; and the third a **t**.

mido	miro	mito
seda	cera	zeta
modo	moro	moto
cada	cara	cata
hado	aro	ato

EXERCISE 242. SOUND DISCRIMINATION

Be prepared to write your responses for Exercise 242. You will hear a series of words, some of which contain a **d** between vowels, some of which contain an **r**, and some of which contain a **t**. For each word you hear, write the letter **d**, **r**, or **t** in the space provided.   EXAMPLE   You hear: **cara**   You write the letter **r**, because the word you heard contained an **r** between vowels.

1.	mido	d	5.	zeta	t	9.	miro	r
2.	ato	t	6.	cera	r	10.	modo	d
3.	cara	r	7.	moro	r	11.	cata	t
4.	aro	r	8.	seda	d	12.	hado	d

Now check your answers. *Repeat each word once and confirm by naming the appropriate letter.*

[d], [r], [t]

EXERCISE 243. PRONUNCIATION

Repeat each of the following sets of words.

mido	miro	mito
seda	cera	zeta
modo	moro	moto
cada	cara	cata

EXERCISE 244. LISTENING COMPREHENSION

Be prepared to write your responses for Exercise 244. In this exercise you will hear a series of short paragraphs. After each, you will hear three incomplete sentences. Each incomplete sentence will be followed by three possible completions, A, B, and C. You are to determine which one correctly completes the sentence on the basis of the paragraph.

EXAMPLE   You hear: El Nuevo Mundo tiene la forma de dos triángulos unidos por una delgada faja de tierra. El triángulo de arriba es el continente de Norteamérica; el de abajo es el de Suramérica. La faja de tierra que los une se llama Centroamérica.

> El Nuevo Mundo tiene la forma de
> A. tres continentes diferentes.
> B. dos triángulos unidos por una faja de tierra.
> C. una delgada faja de tierra.

You circle the letter B because B correctly completes the sentence.

We will begin now. *Read each item once.*   Now check your answers. *Repeat each incomplete sentence once, adding the appropriate completion.*

Now listen to the first paragraph.

Yo soy Pedro Fernández. Este verano voy a pasar las vacaciones con mis tíos en Argentina. Me voy el veintiuno de diciembre, que es el primer día del verano aquí, y no regreso hasta mediados de marzo, cuando empiezan las clases. ¡Va a ser un verano fantástico!

1. El muchacho va a Argentina por   El muchacho va a Argentina por el
   A. el invierno.   verano. B
   B. el verano.
   C. la primavera.

2. En Argentina el verano empieza
   A. en junio.
   B. en marzo.
   C. en diciembre.

En Argentina el verano empieza en diciembre.   C

3. Las clases empiezan
   A. en septiembre.
   B. en octubre.
   C. en marzo.

Las clases empiezan en marzo.   C

Now listen to the second paragraph.

Mis tíos viven en Buenos Aires, capital de Argentina. Yo nunca he estado allí, pero sé que es una ciudad muy grande y muy moderna, con calles lindísimas y edificios altos. He visto muchas fotos de Buenos Aires, y siempre he querido visitar esa lindísima ciudad.

4. Buenos Aires es
   A. un pueblo chico.
   B. una ciudad grande y moderna.
   C. la capital de Chile.

Buenos Aires es una ciudad grande y moderna.   B

5. Buenos Aires tiene
   A. pocos edificios modernos.
   B. calles bonitas y edificios grandes.
   C. una población pequeña.

Buenos Aires tiene calles bonitas y edificios grandes.   B

6. El muchacho que está hablando
   A. no quiere ir a Buenos Aires.
   B. cree que Buenos Aires no es muy lindo.
   C. ha visto muchas fotos de Buenos Aires.

El muchacho que está hablando ha visto muchas fotos de Buenos Aires.   C

Now listen to the third paragraph.

En Buenos Aires hay muchos almacenes y tiendas, donde uno puede comprar muchas cosas bonitas que no tenemos aquí, en el campo. Mi familia ya me ha dado una lista de cosas que comprar. ¡Cada uno quiere algo diferente! Un swéater para mi hermana menor, una cartera para mi hermana mayor, camisas para mis hermanos y una televisión nueva para mis padres.

7. En Buenos Aires hay
   A. muy pocas tiendas bonitas.
   B. muchos almacenes y tiendas.
   C. un almacén que se llama Macy's.

En Buenos Aires hay muchos almacenes y tiendas.   B

8. La familia del muchacho le ha dado
   A. una lista de cosas que ver en Buenos Aires.
   B. una nueva televisión.
   C. una lista de cosas que comprar.

La familia del muchacho le ha dado una lista de cosas que comprar.   C

9. Cada uno quiere
   A. algo diferente de la ciudad.
   B. unas camisas.
   C. una cartera bonita.

Cada uno quiere algo diferente de la ciudad.   A

Note: In recorded program, exercise ends here ⟶

Now listen to the fourth paragraph.

Además, Buenos Aires tiene playas lindísimas, estadios enormes donde juegan fútbol y otras cosas, museos interesantes, y cafés donde uno puede pasar la tarde conversando o simplemente mirando a la gente en la calle. Allí tienen todas las cosas que uno encuentra siempre en una gran ciudad. ¡Éste va a ser el mejor verano de mi vida!

10. En los cafés de Buenos Aires
     A. uno tiene que irse inmediata-mente cuando termina de tomar su café.
     B. uno puede pasar la tarde con-versando.
     C. no hay nada que tomar.

En los cafés de Buenos Aires uno puede pasar la tarde conversando.   B

11. Buenos Aires es
     A. una gran ciudad.
     B. una pequeña ciudad que sin embargo tiene un museo.
     C. una ciudad sin playas ni esta-dios.

Buenos Aires es una gran ciudad.   A

12. El chico piensa que
     A. éste va a ser un verano fantás-tico.
     B. éste va a ser un verano muy aburrido.
     C. no le va a gustar Buenos Aires.

El chico piensa que éste va a ser un verano fantástico.   A

EXERCISE 245. DICTATION

Be prepared for a dictation. A passage from a reading selection will be read to you twice. The first time, just listen to it. The second time, it will be broken up into seg-ments. Each segment will be read twice. You are to write it as you hear it. In this dictation, punctuation marks will not be read. We will begin now. *Read the selection once, and then repeat each segment twice, pausing at the slanted line to allow students time to write.*

Folklore de pueblo chico /

Mi abuelo es uno de los hombres / más viejos del pueblo, / y conoce todas las leyendas de la región. / Cuenta la historia de un marinero / —figura importante de nuestro folklore— / que, ya viejo, / abandona su barco / y viene a vivir a nuestro pueblo / a la casa de su hija Consuelo / y del marido de ella. / Vive y trabaja en el pueblo, / pero piensa constantemente en el mar, / su gran amor. /

Note: In recorded program, passage is not repeated ⟶ Now listen to the reading selection once more. Later, when you have time, compare what you have written with the first paragraph of the Narrative at the end of Unit 14.

UNIT 15—SECTION C

[a], [e], [i], [o], and [u] in unstressed syllables

EXERCISE 246. LISTENING

Listen to the following groups of words. In each group, one particular vowel sound occurs in the unstressed syllable of each word. The unstressed vowel sound will be identified before the group is read.

[a]
mesas, jefas, llaman, gritas, casas, chicas, niñas, hijas, primas

[e]
meses, jefes, comes, vives, haces, lunes, piden

[i]
tesis, casi, cursis, iris, fácil, difícil

[o]
gritos, casos, chicos, niños, hijos, primos, versos

[u]
tifus, tribus, espíritus

[a], [e], [i], [o], and [u] in unstressed syllables

EXERCISE 247. SOUND DISCRIMINATION

Be prepared to write your responses for Exercise 247. In this exercise you will hear a series of words. Each word contains an unstressed vowel. You are to determine what the unstressed vowel is and circle the corresponding letter on your paper.   EXAMPLE You hear: **mesas**   You circle the letter **a**, because the unstressed vowel in **mesas** is **a**.

We will begin now. *Read each word once.*

Now check your answers. *Repeat each word once and give the correct answer as:*

1.	meses	letter e
2.	casos	letter o
3.	niños	letter o
4.	llaman	letter a
5.	primos	letter o
6.	jefes	letter e
7.	tesis	letter i
8.	tribus	letter u
9.	versos	letter o
10.	chicas	letter a

[a], [e], [i], and [o] in unstressed syllables

EXERCISE 248. PRONUNCIATION

Repeat each of the following pairs of words.

mesas–meses, jefas–jefes, lunas–lunes, gritas–gritos, chicas–chicos, niñas–niños, primas–primos

EXERCISE 249. LISTENING COMPREHENSION

Be prepared to write your answers for Exercise 249. In this exercise, you will hear a series of sentences. After each, you will hear three more sentences or phrases, A, B, and C. Only one of these is a logical rejoinder to the first one. You are to determine which it is.

T132

EXAMPLE   You hear: ¿Me devuelve este libro dentro de una semana?

    A. Sí, se lo traigo en tres semanas.

    B. Sí, se lo traigo de hoy en quince.

    C. Sí, se lo traigo de hoy en ocho.

You circle the letter C in the example column, because C is a logical rejoinder to the first sentence.

We will begin now. *Read each item once.*	Now check your answers. *Repeat each cue sentence and give correct answer as:*
1. Vamos a pasar las vacaciones en Venezuela. A. ¿De veras? ¿En Lima? B. ¿De veras? ¿Acaban de volver de Venezuela? C. ¿De veras? ¿Me mandan una tarjeta?	¿De veras? ¿Me mandan una tarjeta? C
2. He estado jugando tenis todo el día. A. Te debe doler la garganta. B. ¿Nunca juegas tenis? C. ¿Te duelen los brazos?	¿Te duele el brazo. C
3. Yo siempre saco un diez en historia. A. Tú siempre sacas buenas notas en matemáticas. B. ¿Cómo puedes recordar tantos nombres y fechas? C. Tú vas a pasar raspando.	¿Cómo puedes recordar tantos nombres y fechas? B
4. Me duelen los pies. A. ¿Te aprietan los zapatos? B. ¿Por qué no seguimos caminando, entonces? C. ¿Te duele todo el brazo?	¿Te aprietan los zapatos? A
5. Nosotros tenemos una hacienda en Colombia. A. ¿Tienen muchos animales allí? B. Porque nunca has estado en el campo. C. En la ciudad.	¿Tienen muchos animales allí? A
6. Muchas gracias, señorita. A. ¡Hola, Juan! B. De nada, Juan. C. Ah, con razón.	De nada, Juan. B
7. ¿Qué estás leyendo? A. Una revista española. ¿Quieres ver? B. Una máquina de escribir. C. Leo y escribo un poco, solamente.	Una revista española. ¿Quieres ver? A

8. ¿Qué te pasa? Pareces tan triste.   Me duele la cabeza.   B
   A. ¡Qué emoción!
   B. Me duele la cabeza.
   C. Tú siempre pones esa cara.

9. ¿Me escribes una carta?   No, pero te mando una tarjeta, sin falta.
   A. No, pero te mando una tarjeta,   A
      sin falta.
   B. Sí, pero te mando una nota.
   C. Ya me han escrito.

10. Siempre pasas raspando en álgebra.   Sí, porque no me gustan las matemá-
    A. Sí, porque me encanta.   ticas.   B
    B. Sí, porque no me gustan las
       matemáticas.
    C. Sí, pero mañana por la ma-
       ñana.

UNIT 15—SECTION D

Final [l]

EXERCISE 250. PRONUNCIATION

Repeat each of the following words, paying particular attention to the l sound.

mal, tal, Manuel, hotel, gol, sol, mil, Gil

EXERCISE 251. LISTENING COMPREHENSION

In this exercise you will hear a series of monologs and dialogs. After each monolog or dialog, you will hear three phrases, A, B, and C. You are to determine which one describes where the speakers are.

EXAMPLE   You hear: ¡Qué lindo el cuarto!
                      Sí, ¿verdad? ¿Ya han traído las maletas?
                      Todavía no. ¿Cuánto tiempo vàmos a estar
                      en esta ciudad?
                      Tres días. Después vamos a Lima.
                      A. una estación   B. un hotel   C. una tienda

You circle the letter B, because B describes where the speakers are.

We will begin now. *Read each item once.*   Now check your answers. *Repeat each*
                                                  dialog or monolog once and give the cor-
                                                  rect answer as:

1. Señorita, ¿nos va a dar las notas   una escuela   A
   hoy?
   No, mañana por la mañana.
   ¿Pero no me puede dar la mía
   ahora?
   Lo siento, José Luis. No puedo.
   A. una escuela   B. una casa
   C. una playa

T134

2. Yo voy a pedir carne con papas fritas.

    Yo no sé qué pedir. Una ensalada, tal vez.

    ¿Dónde está el camarero? No lo veo. Aquí viene.

    A. un mercado   B. una cocina
    C. un restaurante

                                  un restaurante C

3. Primero me dicen que no tienen mi tamaño. Después me dicen que sí lo tienen, pero que no tienen el vestido en el color que yo quiero. He perdido toda una mañana aquí y no he comprado nada.

    A. una peluquería
    B. un almacén   C. una sala

                                  un almacén B

4. ¡Qué bonito tu traje de baño!
    ¿Te gusta? Es nuevo.
    Me encanta el mar.
    A mí también. ¿Nos bañamos ahora?
    A. una piscina
    B. un almacén   C. la playa

                                  la playa C

5. ¡Qué grande! Nunca he visto tantos animales.

    Sí, tenemos miles de caballos. ¿Te gusta montar?

    Nunca he montado, ¿sabes? Ésta es la primera vez que vengo al campo.

    A. un jardín   B. una hacienda
    C. una ciudad

                                  una hacienda B

6. ¿Cómo? ¿No ha llegado todavía la nueva edición de esa novela? Bueno, de todos modos quiero comprar ese diccionario inglés-español y un libro de viajes.

    A. una biblioteca   B. una escuela
    C. una librería

                                  una librería C

Note: In recorded program, exercise ends here ⟶

7. A ver, ¿qué le duele?
    Me duele la cabeza y tengo temperatura.
    ¿Y la garganta?
    No, no me molesta mucho.
    Muy bien, le voy a dar algo para la cabeza, y creo que debe quedarse en casa por algunos días.
    A. la oficina de un médico
    B. la oficina de un dentista
    C. la oficina del jefe de una compañía

                              la oficina de un médico A

8. ¡Qué rápido corre ese caballo!   las carreras C
   Parece que ése es el que va a ganar.
   No . . el otro . . . el blanco lo está
   pasando.
   A ver . . . no lo ha pasado todavía
   . . . el negro todavía está delante . . .
   A. un estadio de fútbol
   B. el campo
   C. las carreras

9. Sí, señor. Éste es un lugar lindí-   Costa Rica   B
   simo. Esta hacienda ha estado en
   mi familia por cuatro generaciones.
   Hay ríos y playas y miles de animales. Yo he visto muchas culebras,
   cantidades de iguanas, y hasta cocodrilos. Ustedes deben creer que
   estoy exagerando, pero no. Es verdad.
   A. Canadá
   B. Costa Rica
   C. Nueva York

10. ¿Qué le parece este vestido, señora?   una tienda   B
    Ay, no. Mi marido me mata si com-
    pro ese vestido.
    Pero las minifaldas están de última
    moda.
    Puede ser, pero yo prefiero una
    falda más larga.
    Muy bien, señora. Y este vestido
    azul, ¿qué le parece?
    A. un museo
    B. una tienda
    C. una plaza

EXERCISE 252. SPOT DICTATION

Be prepared to do the writing for Exercise 252. You have in front of you a reading
selection from which certain words have been omitted. This selection will now be
read to you. You are to write the words omitted from the text in the space provided.
We will begin now. *The underlined words have been omitted from the students' copies.*
Pause at each slanted line to allow students time to write.

Carta de un alumno costarricense

   Bueno, voy a hablar de otra cosa porque si no, no termino nunca esta carta, /
pero quiero decirles antes / que me alegra muchísimo la noticia / de que este año
vamos a pasar todas las vacaciones en la hacienda. Ya tengo hechas las dos maletas
y solamente estoy esperando pasar el último examen, / el de álgebra, que es de hoy
en ocho, para salir corriendo directamente para el aeropuerto. /

A propósito, quiero pedirles permiso / para llevar a a dos amigos míos a pasar las vacaciones con nosotros. Son Jack Parducci y Bob O'Brien, de quienes ya les he hablado a ustedes. Son muy buenos muchachos, muy decentes y simpáticos. Mis dos hermanitas probablemente se van a alegrar mucho de esta noticia. / Ya ellos tienen el permiso de la casa y están completamente listos. No hablan de otra cosa que de montar a caballo / y de entrar a la cueva / para ver si encuentran el famoso tesoro.

Note: In recorded program, passage is not repeated ——→ Now listen to the reading selection once more. Later, when you have time, compare the words you have written with those in the narrative at the end of Unit 15.

EXERCISE 253. LISTENING COMPREHENSION

Be prepared to write at the end of this exercise. You will hear a dialog between a student, Carlos, and his teacher. You will then be asked to write answers to questions on the dialog. Your answers do not have to be complete sentences, but they should be grammatically correct. Now listen to the dialog.

MAESTRA   Carlos, ¿cuál es la capital de Brasil?
CARLOS   Mmm, ¿de dónde?
MAESTRA   De Brasil.
CARLOS   Este . . . Es que no puedo pensar. García me está molestando.
MAESTRA   Es que usted no está poniendo atención.
CARLOS   ¿Los Ángeles?
MAESTRA   ¡Qué barbaridad! ¡Cero!
CARLOS   Mmm . . . ¡qué mala suerte! Otro cero en geografía. No voy a pasar ni siquiera raspando este año.

Now listen to the questions.

1. ¿Qué le pregunta la maestra a Carlos?
2. ¿Contesta bien él?
3. ¿Por qué no puede contestar, según él?
4. ¿Y según la maestra?
5. ¿Cuál nota saca Carlos en geografía?
6. ¿Va a pasar este año él?

Note: In recorded program, dialog is not repeated ——→ Now listen to the dialog again. *Repeat only the dialog and then give the students time to write their answers.*

Teacher Presentations of Structure

This section contains suggested presentations for the introduction of each new structure. The procedure used in each presentation is as follows:

1. Sentences containing examples of the structure are presented to the students.
2. Questions based on these sentences lead the students to discover the grammatical point involved.
3. Simple exercises are provided to check the students' comprehension of the point before the Structure Drills are introduced.

All presentations should move fairly rapidly; questions should be answered quickly (acceptable answers appear in brackets). Occasionally, you may find it useful to write the relevant part of some sentences on the board as you proceed through a presentation. A few suggestions have been made for writing on the board in specific presentations. In general, however, it is preferable to keep writing to a minimum while doing the presentations.

As each new point is established, the Structure Drills which might be done at that moment are indicated in the presentation. After covering an adequate number of drills in class, you will probably want to assign the Presentation, Generalization, and Structure Drills in the student text for study at home. Tell your students that this material is a review of what they have done in class. They should try to answer the questions in the Presentation before going on to the Generalization and the Drills. Be sure that they understand that learning the spelling of all new words and forms is part of their homework assignment.

Note: The symbol Ⓡ precedes sentences which should be repeated (chorally and/or individually) by the students. In the suggested exercises, use the name of a student in your class to replace any name which appears in italics.

Regular a–Class Verbs

*In this presentation you want the students to discover the concept of verb stem, theme vowel, and ending. You want them to see that the subject of the sentence is reflected in the ending, even if no subject pronoun is present. Write each form of **practicar** on the board after it has been presented for the first time.*

First person singular

ℝ Hablo con ella más tarde.

What does the sentence mean in English? [*I'll talk with her later.*] What is the subject of the English sentence? [*I*] Which word is the verb in the Spanish sentence? [**hablo**] What is the final vowel of the verb? [**o**]

ℝ Practico con ella más tarde.

Can you guess what the sentence means in English? [*I'll practice with her later.*] What is the subject of the English sentence? [*I*] Which word is the verb in the Spanish sentence? [**practico**] What is the final vowel of the verb? [**o**]

Second person singular

ℝ ¿Por qué no estudias conmigo?   ℝ ¿Por qué no practicas conmigo?

What do these sentences mean in English? [*Why don't you study with me? Why don't you practice with me?*] What is the subject of the English sentences? [*you*] Which words are the verbs in the Spanish sentences? [**estudias, practicas**] What are the final vowel and consonant of the verbs? [**as**] On the basis of the sentences you just heard, what part of a Spanish sentence indicates what the subject is? [the verb] What is the final vowel of verbs whose subject is *I*, that is, first person singular? [**o**] What are the final vowel and consonant of verbs in sentences whose subject is *you*, that is, second person singular? [**as**]

SUGGESTED EXERCISE

Juan ¿estudias francés o español?	Estudio español.
Luisa, ¿hablas inglés o español en casa?	Hablo inglés.
Susana, ¿pronuncias bastante bien o muy mal?	Pronuncio bastante bien (*or* muy mal).
Pepe, ¿necesitas practicar español or ruso?	Necesito practicar español.
Raúl, ¿practicas español o ruso ahora?	Practico español.

Third person singular

ℝ Tal vez no llega.   ℝ Tal vez no practica.

What do the sentences mean in English? [*Maybe she doesn't arrive. Maybe she doesn't practice.*] What is the subject of the English sentences? [*she*] If the subject of a Spanish sentence is *he* or *she*, that is, third person singular, what is the final vowel of the verb? [**a**]

SUGGESTED EXERCISE

¿Habla Arturo con Blanca o con la chica americana?	Habla con la chica americana.
¿Llama Arturo a la chica americana o a la maestra?	Llama a la chica americana.
¿Pronuncia Blanca bastante bien o muy mal?	Pronuncia muy mal.

Juan, pregúntele a *Luisa* si estudia francés o español.

Luisa, ¿estudias francés o español?

Luisa, contéstele (*answer him*).

Estudio español.

Juan, ¿estudia *Luisa* francés o español?

Estudia español.

Raúl, pregúntele a *Pepe* si habla inglés o español en casa.

Pepe, ¿hablas inglés o español en casa?

Pepe, contéstele.

Hablo inglés.

Raúl, ¿habla *Pepe* inglés o español en casa?

Habla inglés.

Susana, pregúntele a *Pedro* si pronuncia bastante bien o muy mal.

Pedro, ¿pronuncias bastante bien o muy mal?

Pedro, contéstele.

Pronuncio bastante bien (*or* muy mal).

Susana, ¿pronuncia *Pedro* bastante bien o muy mal?

Pronuncia bastante bien (*or* muy mal).

María, pregúntele a *Arturo* si necesita practicar español o ruso.

Arturo ¿necesitas practicar español o ruso?

Arturo, contéstele.

Necesito practicar español.

María, ¿necesita *Arturo* practicar español o ruso?

Necesita practicar español.

First person plural

Ⓡ **Tú y yo pronunciamos.**   Ⓡ **Tú y yo practicamos.**

What does each sentence mean? [*You and I pronounce. You and I practice.*] What is the subject? [*you and I*] What English pronoun could be substituted for *you and I*? [*we*] If the subject of the sentence is *we* or *you and I*, that is, first person plural, how does the verb end in the Spanish sentence? [**amos**]

SUGGESTED EXERCISE

¿Hablamos inglés o español ahora?

Hablamos español.

¿Practicamos español o ruso?

Practicamos español.

¿Pronunciamos bien o mal?

Pronunciamos bien (*or* mal).

¿Escuchamos discos ahora o practicamos español?

Practicamos español.

¿Estudiamos inglés o español ahora?

Estudiamos español.

Third person plural

Ⓡ **No contestan.**   Ⓡ **No practican.**

What does each sentence mean? [*They don't answer. They don't practice.*] What is the subject? [*they*] How does the Spanish verb end if the subject of the sentence is *they*, that is, third person plural? [**an**]

SUGGESTED EXERCISE

¿Estudian francés o inglés Arturo y Blanca?

Estudian inglés.

¿Necesitan practicar inglés o alemán?

Necesitan practicar inglés.

¿Pronuncian bien o mal?

Pronuncian mal.

¿Escuchan unos discos o las noticias?

Escuchan unos discos.

¿Estudian ahora o más tarde?

Estudian más tarde.

Stem, theme vowel, ending   Ⓡ **Más tarde practico con ella.**   Ⓡ **Tú y yo practicamos.**
Ⓡ **¿Por qué no practicas conmigo?**   Ⓡ **No practican.**
Ⓡ **Tal vez no practica.**

What part of the verb stays the same in all the forms? [the front part, the first part, **practic**] *Tell students that the part that doesn't change is called the stem.* Except when the subject is *I*, what vowel sound occurs after the stem in all these verb forms? [**a**] *Tell students that **a** is called the theme vowel.* What part of the verb changes according to the subject? [the last part, the end] *Tell students that this part is called the ending.*

Verb classes   *Explain that every Spanish verb belongs to one of three classes, and that a verb is classified according to whether its theme vowel is **a**, **e**, or **i**.* Are the verbs we have been studying **a**–class, **e**–class, or **i**–class verbs? [**a**–class verbs]

Ⓡ Necesito practicar inglés.

Infinitive   Which word tells what the subject is? [**necesito**] What is the subject? [*I*] How do we know the subject is *I*? [**Necesito** ends in **o**.] Which word means *practice* in this sentence? [**practicar**] Does **practicar** have an ending that refers to a particular subject? [no] What consonant does **practicar** end in? [**r**] What is this ending attached to? [stem + **a**] *Explain that the verb form composed of stem + theme vowel + **r** is called the infinitive. This form does not correspond to any particular subject, but is simply used as the name form.*

SUGGESTED EXERCISE

Blanca estudia inglés ahora.	Quiero estudiar con ella.
Susana practica español ahora.	Quiero practicar con ella.
María escucha discos ahora.	Quiero escuchar con ella.
Lili habla inglés ahora.	Quiero hablar con ella.
Ana estudia español ahora.	Quiero estudiar con ella.

Necesito hablar inglés.

English equivalents of the Spanish present tense   What does the sentence mean in English? [*I need to practice English.*] Does **necesito** correspond to the simple present tense in the English sentence? [yes]

¿A quién llamas?

What English equivalent have you learned for this sentence? [*Who are you calling?*] *Tell students that this form of the English verb is called the present progressive.* Does the verb **llamas** correspond to the simple present tense or to the present progressive in this sentence? [the present progressive]

Hablo con ella más tarde.

What English equivalent have you learned for this sentence? [*I'll talk with her later.*] In this sentence, does the verb **hablo** correspond to the simple present tense or to the future tense in English? [the future]

▶ DRILLS 7–11, pp. 12–13

T141

Negation

*In this presentation you want the student to become aware of the most simple form of negation: placing the word **no** before the verb.*

Ⓡ **Contestan el teléfono.** Ⓡ **Sé qué pasa.**

Are these sentences affirmative or negative? [affirmative]

Ⓡ **No contestan el teléfono.** Ⓡ **No sé qué pasa.**

Are these sentences affirmative or negative? [negative] Which word tells us they're negative? [**no**] What is the position of **no** in relation to the verb? [immediately before]

no occurring twice in a row

¿Quieres practicar inglés? Ⓡ **No, no quiero practicar inglés.**

Which word tells us the sentence is negative, the first **no** or the second? [the second] What English word does the first **no** correspond to? [*no*] Explain that **no** can occur twice in a Spanish sentence: the first **no** simply answers the question; the second makes the sentence negative.

SUGGESTED EXERCISE

¿Hablamos inglés ahora?	No, no hablamos inglés ahora.
¿Practicamos ruso ahora?	No, no practicamos . . .
¿Llamamos a Susana hoy?	No, no llamamos . . .
¿Pronunciamos muy mal?	No, no pronunciamos . . .
¿Estudiamos francés ahora?	No, no estudiamos . . .
¿Vamos a las carreras hoy?	No, no vamos . . .
¿Pasamos por la biblioteca hoy?	No, no pasamos . . .

▶ DRILL 13, p. 14

Subject Pronouns and Subject-Verb Agreement

*In this presentation you want the students to learn the Spanish subject pronouns, the difference between **tú** and **usted**, and which form of the verb is required by each of the Spanish subject pronouns.*

Although Subject Pronouns and Subject-Verb Agreement are treated as separate sections in the textbook in order to provide the students with easily handled units for home study, it will be more efficient to teach them together in class. It is suggested that these two sections not be assigned for home study until the entire presentation has been completed in class.

Since the students have already been exposed to sentences without subject pronouns, questions may arise about when and when not to use them. In such cases, tell students that Spanish sentences are complete and correct both with and without subject pronouns, and that their use will be explained in class shortly.

yo *and* tú

Ⓡ Yo hablo con ella más tarde.

Which word corresponds to *I*? [**yo**] If the subject of the sentence is **yo**, what is the verb ending? [**o**]

Ⓡ ¿Por qué no estudias tú conmigo?

Which word corresponds to *you*? [**tú**] If the subject of the sentence is **tú**, what is the verb ending? [**s**]

Arturo no llega todavía.   **Ⓡ Él no llega todavía.**

él, ella

Which word replaces **Arturo**? [**él**] If the subject of the sentence is **él**, how does the verb end? [in **a**, in the theme vowel **a**]

Blanca no llega todavía.   **Ⓡ Ella no llega todavía.**

Which word replaces **Blanca**? [**ella**] If the subject of the sentence is **ella**, how does the verb end? [in **a**, in the theme vowel **a**]

SUGGESTED EXERCISE

¿Tú hablas bien?	¿Yo? Sí.
¿Raúl habla bien?	¿Él? Sí.
¿Susana habla bien?	¿Ella? Sí.
¿Arturo habla bien?	¿Él? Sí.
¿Tú hablas bien?	¿Yo? Sí.

SUGGESTED EXERCISE

¿Tú estudias francés?

1ST STUD.   No, yo estudio español.
2ND STUD.   Él (*or* ella) estudia español.

¿Tú practicas francés? — No, yo practico . . . / Él (ella) practica . . .
¿Tú hablas francés? — No, yo hablo . . . / Él (ella) habla . . .
¿Tú necesitas practicar francés? — No, yo necesito . . . / Él (ella) necesita . . .
¿Tú necesitas estudiar francés? — No, yo necesito . . . / Él (ella) necesita . . .

tú *vs.* usted

These two sentences have the same English equivalent.

¿Por qué no estudias tú conmigo?
¿Por qué no estudia usted conmigo?

Which word means *you* in the first sentence? [**tú**] Can you guess which word means *you* in the second? [**usted**] *Explain that both **tú** and **usted** mean* you *in Spanish.*

In the following sentences, I'm speaking to just one person. First, to a friend:

¿A quién llamas tú?

Which word did I use for *you*? [**tú**]

Now to the principal:

¿A quién llama usted, Sr. García?

Which word did I use for *you*? [**usted**]   (*continued*)

T143

Now, to a lady I just met:

¿A quién llama usted, Sra. López?

Which word did I use for *you*? [**usted**]

Which word meaning *you* do you use when you're talking to a friend? [**tú**] Which should you use when you're talking to one of your classmates? [**tú**] Which should you use when you're talking to a person of authority or to someone you just met? [**usted**] *Tell students that it is important for them to learn when to use **tú** and when to use **usted**. Tell them **tú** is used for close friends, classmates, and, in most Spanish-speaking countries, members of one's family. They will use **usted** when talking to a teacher, a stranger, or someone they address as **Señor** (Mr.), **Señora** (Mrs., Ma'am) or **Señorita** (Miss).*

SUGGESTED EXERCISE

Tell whether you would use **tú** or **usted** to address each of the following people.

Your best friend	tú
A gentleman you just met	usted
Your sister	tú
A saleswoman	usted
Me	usted

Now listen to the following two sentences once again.

¿Por qué no estudia usted conmigo?
¿A quién llama usted?

If the subject of a sentence is **usted**, how does the verb end? [in the theme vowel **a**] Is **usted** a second person or a third person pronoun? [second] Does it take the second or the third person form of the verb? [third] *Here you might mention that **usted** was once used to address aristocratic individuals, like your highness or your grace in English, and, like those terms, takes the third person form of the verb: Is your highness in good health? rather than Are you all right?*

SUGGESTED EXERCISE

Ask the following question of the persons indicated by the English cue.

¿Cuándo llega usted?

(Ask your friend.)	¿Cuándo llegas tú?
(Ask your brother.)	¿Cuándo llegas tú?
(Ask the mailman.)	¿Cuándo llega usted?
(Ask the boy (girl) next to you.)	¿Cuándo llegas tú?

SUGGESTED EXERCISE

Él pronuncia bien. tú	Tú pronuncias bien.
yo	Yo pronuncio bien.
ella	Ella pronuncia bien.
usted	Usted pronuncia bien.
tú	Tú pronuncias bien.
él	Él pronuncia bien.

In the dialog, Arturo says to Blanca:

Tú y yo pronunciamos muy mal.

He could also say:

® **Nosotros pronunciamos muy mal.**

Which word replaces **tú y yo**? [**nosotros**] If the subject of the sentence is **nosotros**, what is the verb ending? [**mos**]

Let's suppose Arturo is talking to Roberto. He says:

® **Nosotros pronunciamos muy mal.**

Which word replaces **tú y yo**? [**nosotros**]

Let's suppose Blanca is talking to Susana. She says:

® **Nosotras pronunciamos muy mal.**

Which word replaces **tú y yo**? [**nosotras**] If the subject of the sentence is **nosotras**, what is the verb ending? [**mos**] What two words mean *we* in Spanish? [**nosotros, nosotras**] If the speaker includes himself in a group made up of boys and girls (for example, when Arturo is talking to Blanca), which word does he use? [**nosotros**] If the speaker includes himself in a group made up entirely of boys, which word does he use? [**nosotros**] If the speaker is a girl, and includes herself in a group made up entirely of girls, which word does she use? [**nosotras**]

ellos, ellas

Arturo y Pedro no contestan.   ® **Ellos no contestan.**

Which word replaces Arturo y Pedro? [**ellos**] If the subject of the sentence is **ellos**, what is the verb ending? [**n**]

Arturo y Blanca no contestan.   ® **Ellos no contestan.**

Which word replaces Arturo y Blanca? [**ellos**]

Blanca y Susana no contestan.   ® **Ellas no contestan.**

Which word replaces Blanca y Susana? [**ellas**] What two words mean *they* in Spanish? [**ellos, ellas**] Which word is used to refer to two boys? [**ellos**] to a mixed group? [**ellos**] to two girls? [**ellas**]

ustedes

Arturo is talking to Susana:

¿A quién llamas tú?

Which word does he use for *you*? [**tú**]

Now he is talking to Susana and María:

® **¿A quién llaman ustedes?**

Which word does he use now? [**ustedes**]   *(continued)*

Which word meaning *you* is used to address two or more people, each of whom you address individually as **tú**? [**ustedes**]

Arturo is talking to Mr. García:

¿A quién llama usted?

Which word does he use for *you*? [**usted**]

Now he's talking to Mr. and Mrs. García.

Ⓡ **¿A quién llaman ustedes?**

Which word meaning *you* is used to address two or more people, each of whom you address individually as **usted**? [**ustedes**] *Mention to students that in Spain (and occasionally in Spanish America) vosotros is used as the plural of tú, but point out that in most Spanish-speaking countries, ustedes is generally used as the plural of both usted and tú.*

Now listen to this sentence again:

¿A quién llaman ustedes?

If the subject of the sentence is **ustedes**, what is the verb ending? [**n**] Is **ustedes** a second or a third person pronoun? [second] Does it take a second or a third person verb ending? [third]

SUGGESTED EXERCISE

Ask the following question of the persons indicated by the cue.

¿Escucha usted las noticias?
    (Ask Susana and María.)   ¿Escuchan ustedes las noticias?
    (Ask Mr. García.)   ¿Escucha usted . . . ?
    (Ask Mr. and Mrs. López.)   ¿Escuchan ustedes . . . ?
    (Ask the boy (*or* girl) next to you.)   ¿Escuchas tú . . . ?
    (Ask the boys (*or* girls) behind you.)   ¿Escuchan ustedes . . . ?

SUGGESTED EXERCISE

¿Hablan ustedes con Blanca?	1ST STUD. No, nosotros (*or* nosotras) hablamos con Arturo.
(*Point to two students to cue nosotros, nosotras, and ellos, ellas.*)	2ND STUD. Ellos (*or* ellas) hablan con Arturo.
¿Practican ustedes con Blanca?	No, nosotros practicamos . . . / Ellos practican . . .
¿Estudian ustedes con Blanca?	No, nosotros estudiamos . . . / Ellos estudian . . .
¿Llegan ustedes con Blanca?	No, nosotros llegamos . . . / Ellos llegan . . .

▶ DRILLS 16, p. 17; 18.1–18.2, p. 18

Verb agreement with compound subjects

Before presenting Verb Agreement with Compound Subjects, *do drills 15.1 and 15.2, p. 16. If students have difficulty with these exercises, remind them that in Spanish, as in English, a compound subject which includes the pronoun* **yo** *(I) corresponds to* **nosotros** *(we). Remind them also that* **ustedes** *is the plural of both* **tú** *and* **usted**, *so that a compound subject which includes either* **tú** *or* **usted**, *but does not include the pronoun* **yo**, *corresponds to* **ustedes**.

Nosotros pronunciamos muy mal.   R Tú y yo pronunciamos muy mal.

Do **nosotros** and **tú y yo** require the same verb ending? [yes] *Explain that any compound subject which includes the pronoun* **yo** *requires the first person plural form of the verb.*

R Blanca y ella hablan muy mal.   R Usted y ella hablan muy mal.
R Juan y él hablan muy mal.   R Tú y ellos hablan muy mal.

Which form of the verb do all these compound subjects require? [the third person plural, the form that corresponds to **ellos** and **ustedes**, the form that ends in **n**] *Explain that any compound subject that does not include the pronoun* **yo**, *requires the third person plural form of the verb.*

▶ DRILLS 18.3–23, pp. 18–19

Use of Subject Pronouns

R Hablo con ella más tarde.

What does this sentence mean? [*I'll talk with her later.*] Does any word in this sentence correspond to *I*? [no] Is a Spanish sentence complete and correct without a subject pronoun? [yes]

R Yo hablo con ella más tarde.

Is the subject pronoun stated in this sentence? [yes] Which word is the subject pronoun? [**yo**] This sentence means *I'll talk with her later. Explain that the subject pronoun is used in Spanish when it is necessary to emphasize the subject.*

R Necesita practicar inglés.

Can you tell what the subject of this sentence is? [no] What are the three subject pronouns which could be used in this sentence? [**él, ella, usted**] If the subject is unclear to the listener, might it be necessary for the speaker to use a subject pronoun? [yes] Why? [to clarify the subject, to tell who the subject is] *Tell the students that subject pronouns are sometimes used in Spanish to clarify the subject.*

▶ DRILLS 25–27, pp. 20–21

Stem Alternation: e–ie
a–Class Verbs

Write the verb forms on the board as you do this presentation.

Ⓡ **¿En qué piensas?**   Ⓡ **Pienso en el Día de la Madre.**

Is the stem stressed or unstressed in each verb form? [stressed] What is the vowel sound in the stem when stressed? [**ye**] How is the sound written? [**ie**]

Ⓡ **Pensamos en el regalo.**   Ⓡ **Necesitamos pensar en el regalo.**

Is the stem stressed or unstressed in the forms of **pensar**? [unstressed] What is the vowel sound in the stem when unstressed? [**e**] How is the sound written? [**e**]

*Explain to students that in certain verb stems the vowel **e** alternates with **ie**; **ie** occurs when the stem is stressed, as in **pienso**, **piensas**, **piensa**, and **piensan**; **e** occurs when the stem is unstressed, as in **pensamos**, and **pensar**. The a–class verbs they have had so far which have this stem alternation are **apretar**, **cerrar**, **empezar**, and **pensar**.*

SUGGESTED EXERCISE

Pienso en el regalo.	Pensamos en el regalo.
Cierro la puerta.	Cerramos la puerta.
Empiezo el examen.	Empezamos el examen.
Pienso en la fiesta.	Pensamos en la fiesta.
Cierro la ventana.	Cerramos la ventana.

SUGGESTED EXERCISE

Empezamos ahora.	Empiezo ahora.
Pensamos en el Día de la Madre.	Pienso en el Día de la Madre.
Cerramos la tienda.	Cierro la tienda.
Empezamos más tarde.	Empiezo más tarde.
Pensamos en las carreras.	Pienso en las carreras.

▶ DRILLS 6–9, pp. 32–33

Gender

Gender and the Definite Article

Write the nouns and the corresponding definite articles on the board as you do this presentation.

Ⓡ **Esa que está en el carro es Lili.**   Ⓡ **Caminamos por el centro.**
Ⓡ **Pensamos en el regalo después.**   Ⓡ **Está en el teléfono.**

What is the final vowel sound of each of the nouns? [**o**] Which Spanish word corresponds to *the* in these sentences? [**el**]

Ⓡ **Cierran la puerta.**   Ⓡ **Pensamos en la fiesta.**
Ⓡ **Están en la cocina.**   Ⓡ **Pasa por la biblioteca.**

What is the final vowel sound of each of the nouns? [**a**] Which Spanish word corresponds to *the* in these sentences? [**la**]

T148

¿Dónde está el carro?	chica	¿Dónde está la chica?
	regalo	¿Dónde está el regalo?
	tienda	¿Dónde está la tienda?
	perro	¿Dónde está el perro?
	biblioteca	¿Dónde está la biblioteca?
	teléfono	¿Dónde está el teléfono?

Tell students that all Spanish nouns belong to one of two gender classes: masculine or feminine. Explain that these are merely grammatical terms. They are used to classify a noun, not to indicate a quality or characteristic. Nonetheless, most nouns which refer to male persons are masculine; most nouns which refer to female persons are feminine.

Is the noun **señor** masculine or feminine? [masculine] How do you know? [It refers to a male person.] Is the noun **madre** masculine or feminine? [feminine] How do you know? [It refers to a female person.] *Tell students that most nouns which end in **o** are masculine and most nouns which end in **a** are feminine.* Are the nouns **carro**, **regalo**, **centro** and **teléfono** masculine or feminine? [masculine] How do you know? [They end in o.] Are the nouns **puerta**, **cocina**, **fiesta**, and **biblioteca** masculine or feminine? [feminine] How do you know? [They end in a.] *Point out that the form of the definite article used with a noun depends on the gender of the noun.* Which form of the definite article is used with masculine singular nouns? [**el**] Which form of the definite article is used with feminine singular nouns? [**la**]

*Use the following Supplement posters to elicit nouns and their definite articles: **la casa** 1–1, **la sala** 1–2, **la cocina** 1–3, **el teléfono** 1–4, **el perro** 1–6 (Cover one of the dogs.), **el carro** 1–7, **la maestra** 2–1, **la señora** 2–2, **la señorita** 2–3, **el disco** 2–5 (Cover all but one record.), **la escuela** 2–6, **la biblioteca** 2–7, **el señor** 2–8, **la tienda** 3–1, **la puerta** 3–2, **la ventana** 3–3, **el mercado** 3–6, **el centro** 3–7, **la película** 3–9, **la comida** 3–12, **la fiesta** 3–13, **el zapato** 3–16 (Point to one shoe.). If you do not have Supplement posters, say the noun and have the student supply the definite article: **casa** [**la casa**].*

*Tell students that many nouns do not end in **o** or **a** and do not refer to males or females. In addition, there are some exceptions to the rule that nouns which end in **o** are masculine and nouns which end in **a** are feminine. One hint that will help them remember the gender of some of these nouns is that the names of days of the week are masculine, while most nouns that end in **ción** (like **canción**) are feminine. On page 34 there is a list of nouns whose gender must simply be memorized.*

*Use the following Supplement posters to teach the gender of these nouns: **el sofá** 1–5, **el parque** 3–4, **el cine** 3–5, **el examen** 3–11, **el desfile** 3–14, **el baile** 3–15.*

Ⓡ **La chica estudia inglés.**

Nouns with masculine and feminine forms

Is **chica** a masculine or a feminine noun? [feminine] What does **chica** mean in English? [*girl*]

Ⓡ **El chico estudia inglés.**

Is **chico** a masculine or a feminine noun? [masculine] Can you guess what **chico** means in English? [*boy*]

® **Lili es la tía de Susana.**

Is **tía** a masculine or a feminine noun? [*feminine*] What does **tía** mean in English? [*aunt*]

® **Roberto es el tío de Susana.**

Is **tío** a masculine or a feminine noun? [*masculine*] Can you guess what **tío** means in English? [*uncle*]

*Point out that some nouns which refer to people have both a masculine and a feminine form which are identical except for final **o** or **a**. The form which ends in **o** refers to a male person; the form which ends in **a** refers to a female person.*

If **maestra** refers to a lady teacher, what word refers to a man teacher? [**maestro**] If **amiga** refers to a friend who's a girl, what word refers to a friend who's a boy? [**amigo**]

▶ DRILLS 11.1–11.2, p. 35

Plural of nouns

Plural of Nouns and of the Definite Article

Write the nouns but not the definite article on the board as you do this part of the presentation.

® **Pensamos en el regalo.**   ® **Pensamos en la fiesta.**

Which words are the nouns? [**regalo, fiesta**] Are the nouns singular or plural? [*singular*] Do they end in a consonant or in a vowel? [*in a vowel*]

® **Pensamos en los regalos.**   ® **Pensamos en las fiestas.**

Which words are the nouns? [**regalos, fiestas**] Are they singular or plural? [*plural*] How is the plural formed for nouns whose singular ends in a vowel? [*by adding* **s**]

® **Hablo con el señor.**   ® **Hablo con los señores.**

Which word is the noun in the first sentence? [**señor**] Is **señor** singular or plural? [*singular*] Does it end in a vowel or a consonant? [*a consonant*] Which word is the noun in the second sentence? [**señores**] Is **señores** singular or plural? [*plural*] How is the plural formed for nouns whose singular ends in a consonant? [*by adding* **es**]

® **Estudio el lunes.**   ® **Estudio los lunes.**

The first sentence means *I study on Monday.* The second one means *I study on Mondays.* Is **lunes** singular or plural in the first sentence? [*singular*] And in the second? [*plural*] What consonant does **lunes** end in? [**s**] Is the last syllable stressed or unstressed? [*unstressed*] If a singular noun ends in **s** and the last syllable is unstressed how is the plural formed? [*By not adding anything; the singular and plural are the same.*]

T150

Write the nouns and the corresponding definite articles on the board as you do this part of the presentation.

ℝ **Pensamos en el regalo.**   ℝ **Pensamos en los regalos.**
ℝ **Hablo con el señor.**   ℝ **Hablo con los señores.**

Are the nouns in these sentences masculine or feminine? [masculine] How does the noun in the second sentence in each pair differ from the noun in the first? [It's plural.] What definite article is used with plural masculine nouns? [**los**]

ℝ **Pensamos en la fiesta.**   ℝ **Pensamos en las fiestas.**

Are the nouns in these sentences masculine or feminine? [feminine] How does the noun in the second sentence differ from the noun in the first? [It's plural.] What definite article is used with plural feminine nouns? [**las**]

Masculine nouns to refer to mixed groups

Juana, Roberto, y yo estudiamos mucho.
Nosotros estudiamos mucho.

In this sentence, does **nosotros** refer to a group consisting entirely of boys or to a mixed group? [a mixed group]

Juana, Roberto, y Susana estudian mucho.
Los chicos estudian mucho.

In this sentence, does **chicos** refer to a group consisting entirely of boys or to a mixed group? [a mixed group]

Explain that masculine plural nouns are often used to refer to mixed groups, when there is no special reason to point out that girls or women are included. Thus, the equivalent of boys and girls may be either **chicos y chicas** or **chicos**.

▶ DRILLS 13–16, p. 37

Some Uses of the Definite Article

Definite article with days of the week

Tell the students that there are some cases in which the definite article is used in Spanish, where it is not used in English.

ℝ **El desfile es el sábado.**   ℝ **Estudio los lunes.**
ℝ **El martes es el Día de la Madre.**

Do these sentences tell when an activity or event takes place? [yes] Is the definite article used with days of the week to tell when an activity or event takes place? [yes] Is it used in the English equivalents of these sentences? [no]

ℝ **Hoy es sábado.**   ℝ **Mañana es miércoles.**

Is the definite article used with days of the week to identify **hoy** and **mañana**? [no]

(sábado)

1ST STUD. Mañana es sábado.
2ND STUD. El sábado es el Día de la Madre.

(domingo)

Mañana es domingo. / El domingo es . . .

Repeat drill using the rest of the days of the week.

Definite article with titles

® **El Sr. Vargas habla ruso.** ® **La Sra. Pérez llega hoy.**
® **La Sra. García pronuncia bien.**

Is the definite article used with titles such as **Sr., Sra.** and **Srta.** when people with these titles are spoken of? [yes] Is it used in the English equivalents of these sentences? [no]

® **Sr. Vargas, ¿habla usted ruso?** ® **¿Llega usted hoy, Sra. Pérez?**
® **Usted pronuncia bien, Srta. García.**

Is the definite article used with these titles when a person is spoken to? [no]

SUGGESTED EXERCISE

Sr. Vargas, usted pronuncia bien.
Srta. Pérez, usted no estudia bastante.
Sra. García, usted llega tarde.
Sr. López, usted necesita estudiar.
Sra. Vargas, usted habla mucho por teléfono.

El Sr. Vargas pronuncia bien.
La Srta. Pérez no estudia bastante.
La Sra. García llega tarde.
El Sr. López necesita estudiar.
La Sra. Vargas habla mucho por teléfono.

▶ DRILLS 18–19, pp. 38–39

Word Order in Statements and Yes/No Questions

Before starting this presentation you may want to explain the difference between subject *and* predicate. *Tell the students that the subject is the part of the sentence (almost always a noun phrase) about which something is stated or asked, and that the predicate is the part which expresses what is stated or asked about the subject.*

Blanca habla inglés.

Is the sentence a question or a statement? [a statement] Which word is the subject? [**Blanca**] Which part is the predicate? [**habla inglés**]

® **¿Blanca habla inglés?**

Is the sentence a statement or a question? [a question] Is the word order the same or different from the statement? [the same]

Habla inglés Blanca.

Is the sentence a question or a statement? [a statement] Which word is the subject? [**Blanca**] Which part is the predicate? [**habla inglés**]

ⓡ **¿Habla inglés Blanca?**

Is the sentence a statement or a question? [a question] Is the word order the same or different from the statement you just heard? [the same]

Habla Blanca inglés.

Is the sentence a question or a statement? [a statement] Which word is the subject? [**Blanca**] Which part is the predicate? [**habla inglés**]

ⓡ **¿Habla Blanca inglés?**

Is the sentence a statement or a question? [a question] Is the word order the same of different from the statement you just heard? [the same] How many word orders are possible for a statement like **Blanca habla inglés.**? [three] And for the corresponding question? [three] *Explain that Spanish permits exactly the same order of words in statements as in questions.*

ⓡ **Blanca habla inglés.**   ⓡ **¿Blanca habla inglés?**

Which sentence is a statement? [the first one] Which is a question? [the second one] How can you tell? [The melody (pitch) is different; the intonation changes.] What is the difference? [The voice goes up; the pitch (melody) rises at the end of a question.] *Explain that the same word order is possible for both questions and statements in Spanish; it is only the intonation (melody) that tells if a sentence is a statement or a question. The pitch of the voice normally falls at the end of a statement, but rises at the end of a yes/no question.*

▶ DRILLS 20–22, pp. 40–41

ser, *Present Tense*

Singular forms

ⓡ **Yo soy Cristina.**

Which form of the verb corresponds to **yo**? [**soy**]

ⓡ **¿Por qué eres tan amiga de él?**

Which form of the verb corresponds to **tú**? [**eres**]

ⓡ **Usted es Susana, ¿no?**

Which form of the verb corresponds to **él, ella,** and **usted**? [**es**]

SUGGESTED EXERCISE

¿Usted es *José*?   No, yo soy *Juan.* Él es *José.*

Repeat exercise several times, calling on different students.

SUGGESTED EXERCISE: CHAIN DRILL

¿De dónde es usted?   1ST STUD.   Yo soy de California, ¿y tú *Juan,* de dónde eres?

                              2ND STUD.   Yo soy de California también, ¿y tú *María,* de dónde eres?

Plural forms

Ⓡ **Somos gemelas.**

Which form of the verb corresponds to **nosotros**? [**somos**]

Ⓡ **Los compañeros son tan simpáticos.**

Which form of the verb corresponds to **ellos, ellas,** and **ustedes**? [**son**]

SUGGESTED EXERCISE

¿Son alumnos ustedes dos?	Sí, somos alumnos.
¿Son de los Estados Unidos?	Sí, somos de los Estados Unidos.
¿Son hermanos?	No, no somos hermanos.
¿Son gemelos?	No, no somos gemelos.
¿Son compañeros?	Sí, somos compañeros.

SUGGESTED EXERCISE

Pregúnteles a *Juan* y a *Pepe* si son hermanos.	¿Son hermanos?
Pepe, contéstele.	No, no somos hermanos.
. . . a *María* y a *Ana* si son hermanas.	¿Son hermanas?
Ana, contéstele.	No, no somos hermanas.
. . . a *José* y a *Arturo* si son amigos.	¿Son amigos?
Arturo, contéstele.	Sí, somos amigos.
. . . a *Eva* y a *Lili* si son gemelas.	¿Son gemelas?
Lili, contéstele.	No, no somos gemelas.
. . . a *Lupe* y a *Luisa* si son compañeras.	¿Son compañeras?
Luisa, contéstele.	Sí, somos compañeras.
. . . a *Marta* y a *Pedro* si son alumnos.	¿Son alumnos?
Pedro, contéstele.	Sí, somos alumnos.

Infinitive

Ⓡ **Cristina y Susana quieren ser maestras.**

What is the infinitive of the verb we have been studying? [**ser**]

▶ DRILLS 5–7, pp. 50–51

The Indefinite Article

Write the nouns and the corresponding indefinite articles on the board as you do this presentation.

Singular forms

Ⓡ **¿Tienes que comprar un regalo?**   Ⓡ **Escuchan un disco.**

Are the nouns in these sentences masculine or feminine? [masculine] Are they singular or plural? [singular] Which form of the indefinite article (the word which means *a, an*) is used with masculine singular nouns? [**un**]

Ⓡ **Dan una película italiana.**   Ⓡ **Escuchan una canción.**

Are the nouns in these sentences masculine or feminine? [feminine] Are they singular or plural? [singular] Which form of the indefinite article is used with feminine singular nouns? [**una**]

T154

¿Qué es esto (*this*)?   *Show Supplement*   (Es) un vestido.
Poster 4–8 or point to a dress.

Using this model, show Supplement Posters to cue the following items: **una casa** *1–1,* **una sala** *1–2,* **una cocina** *1–3,* **un teléfono** *1–4,* **un sofá** *1–5,* **un carro** *1–7,* **una escuela** *2–6,* **una biblioteca** *2–7,* **un señor** *2–8,* **una tienda** *3–1 (Point to* one *store.),* **una puerta** *3–2,* **una ventana** *3–3,* **un parque** *3–4,* **un cine** *3–5,* **un mercado** *3–6,* **una película** *3–9,* **un regalo** *3–10,* **un examen** *3–11,* **una fiesta** *3–13,* **un desfile** *3–14,* **un baile** *3–15,* **una blusa** *4–4,* **una falda** *4–5,* **una corbata** *4–6,* **una camisa** *4–7,* **un vestido** *4–8,* **un abrigo** *4–9,* **un sombrero** *4–10. If you do not have posters, say the noun and have the student say the response supplying the correct form of the definite article:* ¿Qué es esto?   (**blusa**) [**Es una blusa.**]

Plural forms

Ⓡ **Compro unos regalos.**   Ⓡ **Escuchan unos discos.**

Are the nouns in these sentences masculine or feminine? [masculine] Are they singular or plural? [plural] Which form of the indefinite article is used with masculine plural nouns? [**unos**]

Ⓡ **Compro unas corbatas.**   Ⓡ **Escuchan unas canciones.**

Are the nouns in these sentences masculine or feminine? [feminine] Are they singular or plural? [plural] Which form of the indefinite article is used with feminine plural nouns? [**unas**]

Compro un regalo.   Compro unos regalos.
Necesito una camisa.   Necesito unas camisas.
Quiero un disco.   Quiero unos discos.
Estudio con una chica.   Estudio con unas chicas.
Hablo con un señor.   Hablo con unos señores.
Compro una falda y un vestido.   Compro unas faldas y unos vestidos.
Necesito una corbata y un sombrero. Necesito unas corbatas y unos sombreros.

▶ DRILLS 9–12, pp. 52–53

Adjective Agreement

Write the nouns and adjectives on the board as you do this presentation.

Ⓡ **El chico es muy pretencioso.**

Masculine singular
Ⓡ **Don Pedro es simpático.**   Ⓡ **El abrigo es muy bonito.**

Are the nouns in these sentences masculine or feminine? [masculine] Are they singular or plural? [singular] In each sentence, which word is an adjective? [**pretencioso, simpático, bonito.**] What is the final vowel of the adjective if the noun it modifies is masculine singular? [**o**]

Ⓡ **La película es italiana.**   Ⓡ **La escuela es pequeña.**

Are the nouns in these sentences masculine or feminine? [feminine] Are they singular or plural? [singular] In each sentence, which word is an adjective? [**italiana, pequeña**] What is the final vowel of the adjective if the noun it modifies is feminine singular? [**a**]

SUGGESTED EXERCISE

¿Es Pedro alto o bajo?	Es alto.
¿Y Susana?	Es alta también.
¿Es Juan americano o italiano?	Es americano.
¿Y María?	Es americana también.
¿Es Cristina alta or baja?	Es alta.
¿Y Julio?	Es alto también.
¿Es Blanca americana o rusa?	Es americana.
¿Y Pedro?	Es americano también.

▶ DRILL 14.1, p. 55

Masculine and feminine plural

Ⓡ **El compañero es tan simpático.**   Ⓡ **Los compañeros son tan simpáticos.**
Ⓡ **¿La chica? Es americana.**   Ⓡ **¿Las chicas? Son americanas.**

In each pair, how does the noun in the second sentence differ from the noun in the first? [It's plural.] How does the adjective differ? [It's plural; it ends in s.] How is the plural formed for adjectives whose singular ends in a vowel? [by adding **s**]

SUGGESTED EXERCISE

El chico es pretencioso.	Los chicos son pretenciosos.
La maestra es simpática.	Las maestras son simpáticas.
El alumno es bueno.	Los alumnos son buenos.
La película es americana.	Las películas son americanas.
El regalo es bonito.	Los regalos son bonitos.

▶ DRILL 14.2, p. 55

Adjectives used to modify two or more nouns

Ⓡ **Juan y Pedro son simpáticos.**

Which word is an adjective? [**simpáticos**] What two nouns does **simpáticos** modify? [**Juan, Pedro**] What is the gender of these nouns? [masculine] Which form of the adjective is used to modify two masculine nouns? [masculine plural]

Ⓡ **Susana y María son simpáticas.**

What two nouns does the adjective modify? [**Susana, María**] What is the gender of these nouns? [feminine] Which form of the adjective is used to modify two feminine nouns? [feminine plural]

Ⓡ **Susana y Pedro son simpáticos.**

What two nouns does the adjective modify? [**Susana, Pedro**] What is the gender of each of these nouns? [**Susana** is feminine; **Pedro** is masculine.] Which form of the adjective is used to modify nouns of different genders? [masculine plural]

Ana es pretenciosa. Pedro también.	Ana y Pedro son pretenciosos.
El señor es antipático. La señora también.	El señor y la señora son antipáticos.
La escuela es nueva. El parque también.	La escuela y el parque son nuevos.
María es americana. Susana también.	María y Susana son americanas.
Roberto es italiano. El maestro también.	Roberto y el maestro son italianos.
El abrigo es bonito. La falda también.	El abrigo y la falda son bonitos.

▶ DRILL 14.3, p. 55

Other Types of Adjectives

Write the nouns and adjectives on the board as you do this presentation.

Adjectives which end in a consonant: gender agreement

Ⓡ **El chico es mayor.** Ⓡ **La chica es mayor.**
Ⓡ **El examen es difícil.** Ⓡ **La canción es difícil.**

In each pair, is the noun in the first sentence masculine or feminine? [masculine] And in the second? [feminine] Do the adjectives in each pair end in a vowel or in a consonant? [in a consonant] Do adjectives which end in a consonant show gender agreement? [no]

Adjectives which end in a consonant: number agreement

Ⓡ **El chico es mayor.** Ⓡ **Los chicos son mayores.**
Ⓡ **La canción es difícil.** Ⓡ **Las canciones son difíciles.**

In each pair, how does the noun in the second sentence differ from the noun in the first? [It's plural.] Do adjectives which end in a consonant show number agreement? [yes]

Adjectives which end in e: gender agreement

Ⓡ **El mercado es grande.** Ⓡ **La biblioteca es grande.**

Is the noun in the first sentence masculine or feminine? [masculine] Is the noun in the second sentence masculine or feminine? [feminine] Do adjectives which end in **e** show gender agreement? [no]

Adjectives which end in e: number agreement

Ⓡ **Los mercados son grandes.** Ⓡ **Las bibliotecas son grandes.**

Are the nouns in these sentences singular or plural? [plural] Do adjectives which end in **e** show number agreement? [yes] What generalization can you make about adjectives which end in **e** or a consonant? [They show number agreement, but not gender agreement.]

▶ DRILLS 16–18, p. 57

Adjectives of Nationality

Write the nouns and adjectives on the board as you do this presentation.

Masculine singular

Ⓡ El maestro es francés.

Is the noun in this sentence masculine or feminine? [masculine] Does the adjective end in a vowel or a consonant? [a consonant] What does the adjective **francés** tell us about the noun it modifies: **maestro**? [that he's French, his nationality]

Feminine singular

Ⓡ La maestra es francesa.

Is the noun masculine or feminine? [feminine] Does the adjective show gender agreement? [yes] What vowel is added to the final consonant of the masculine singular of the adjective to form the feminine singular? [**a**]

Explain that adjectives of nationality whose masculine form ends in a consonant show both number and gender agreement. These adjectives are different from other adjectives which end in a consonant, like **difícil** *and* **fácil**, *which do not show gender agreement.*

Masculine plural

Ⓡ Los maestros son franceses.

Is the noun masculine or feminine? [masculine] Is the noun singular or plural? [plural] Does the adjective show number agreement? [yes] How is the masculine plural of the adjective formed? [by adding **es** to the masculine singular form]

Feminine plural

Ⓡ Las maestras son francesas.

Is the noun masculine or feminine? [feminine] Is the noun singular or plural? [plural] Does the adjective show number agreement? [yes] How is the feminine plural of the adjective formed? [by adding **s** to the feminine singular form, by adding **as** to the masculine singular form.]

Tell students that if the masculine singular ends in **és** *(or* **án**)*, the other forms do not require a written accent.*

SUGGESTED EXERCISE

El chico es alemán. ¿Y la chica?	La chica es alemana también.
¿Y los señores?	Los señores son alemanes también.
¿Y las señoras?	Las señoras son alemanas también.

Repeat the same pattern, substituting **español**, **inglés**, *and* **francés**.

▶ DRILLS 20–27, pp. 58–60

Information Questions

Write the interrogative words on the board as you do this presentation.

qué

Ⓡ ¿Qué canción escucha usted?   Ⓡ ¿Qué canciones escucha usted?

Which is the word that asks the question in each sentence? [**qué**] Does **qué** change form to show number agreement? [no]

quién | ℝ **¿Quién es don Pedro?** | ℝ **¿Quiénes son las gemelas?**

Which is the word that asks the question in each sentence? [**quién, quiénes**] Does **quién** show number agreement? [yes]

cuál | ℝ **¿Cuál maestro es mejor?** | ℝ **¿Cuáles maestros son mejores?**

Which is the word that asks the question in each sentence? [**cuál, cuáles**] Does **cuál** show number agreement? [yes] *Explain that these words are called interrogative words. Point out that when these words are used to introduce a question they are written with an accent mark.*

SUGGESTED EXERCISE

¿Quién es la chica? (las chicas)   ¿Quiénes son las chicas?
¿Cuál vestido compra? (vestidos)   ¿Cuáles vestidos compra?
¿Qué disco escucha? (discos)   ¿Qué discos escucha?
¿Quién es el maestro? (maestros)   ¿Quiénes son los maestros?
¿Cuál corbata quiere? (corbatas)   ¿Cuáles corbatas quiere?

Word order | ℝ **¿Qué canción escucha usted?** | ℝ **¿Cuál vestido compra Blanca?**

In the first sentence, what word is the subject? [**usted**] And in the second? [**Blanca**] In both cases, does the subject occur before or after the predicate? [after] If a sentence begins with an interrogative phrase like **¿Qué canción . . .** or **¿Cuál vestido . . .** , what is the word order following the interrogative phrase? [predicate / subject]

SUGGESTED EXERCISE

Juan estudia.   ¿Qué estudia Juan?
Blanca escucha.   ¿Qué escucha Blanca?
María practica.   ¿Qué practica María?
Las gemelas contestan.   ¿Qué contestan las gemelas?
Los alumnos necesitan estudiar. ¿Qué necesitan estudiar los alumnos?

▶ DRILL 29, p. 62

Prepositions with interrogative words | ¿Estudias con ella? ¿Piensas en la fiesta? | ℝ **¿Con quién estudias?** ℝ **¿En qué piensas?**

What is the position of the preposition in relation to the interrogative word? [immediately before] *Tell students that the Spanish equivalent of* whose *is* **de quién**: *¿De quién es el sombrero?* Whose hat is it?

SUGGESTED EXERCISE

¿Practicas con ellas?   ¿Con quiénes practicas?
¿Piensas en el baile?   ¿En qué piensas?
¿Llamas a la chica americana?   ¿A quién llamas?
¿Hablas de ese chico rubio?   ¿De quién hablas?
¿Estudias con Arturo?   ¿Con quién estudias?

▶ DRILLS 30–31, pp. 62–63

T159

estar, *Present Tense*

Ⓡ **Aquí estoy.**

Which form of the verb corresponds to **yo**? [**estoy**]

Ⓡ **¿Dónde estás?**

Which form of the verb corresponds to **tú**? [**estás**]

Ⓡ **Todo está en su lugar.**

Which form of the verb corresponds to **él, ella, usted**? [**está**]

Ⓡ **No estamos sordas.**

Which form of the verb corresponds to **nosotros**? [**estamos**]

Ⓡ **¿Dónde están mis cosas?**

Which form of the verb corresponds to **ellos, ellas, ustedes**? [**están**]

Ⓡ **Tienes que estar en casa a las ocho.**

What is the infinitive of the verb you have been studying? [**estar**] Which form of the present tense of **estar** has an ending that differs from those of regular **a**–class verbs like **practicar**? [**estoy**] Is the theme vowel stressed or unstressed in the other forms? [stressed] How do the other forms (except **estamos**) differ from those of regular **a**–class verbs? [The stress is on the theme vowel, rather than on the next-to-the last syllable, as for regular verbs.]

SUGGESTED EXERCISE

Dígale hola a *Pepe*, y pregúntele cómo está.	1ST STUD. Hola, *Pepe*. ¿Cómo estás?
Pepe, contéstele	2ND STUD. Estoy bien, gracias, ¿y tú?
	1ST STUD. Estoy bien, gracias.

Repeat the same model with different pairs of students.

SUGGESTED EXERCISE

Ask the following question of the persons indicated by the cue.

¿Cómo está usted?

Pregúntele al Sr. Pérez.	¿Cómo está usted?
Pregúntele a su amiga Juana.	¿Cómo estás?
Pregúnteles a sus amigos María y Pedro.	¿Cómo están ustedes?
Pregúnteme a mí.	¿Cómo está usted?
Pregúnteles a dos señores.	¿Cómo están ustedes?

▶ DRILLS 6–8, pp. 72–73

Information Questions

Write the interrogative words on the board as you do this presentation.

dónde, adónde

Ⓡ **¿Dónde están mis cosas?**

Which is the word that asks the question in this sentence? [**dónde**]

Ⓡ **¿Adónde vas con tanta prisa?**

Which is the word that asks the question in this sentence? [**adónde**] Does **dónde** question the location of something (that is, where something is) or does it question direction of movement (where something is going)? [location, where something is] Does **adónde** question location or direction of movement? [direction of movement] *Explain that* **adónde** *is really a phrase consisting of the preposition* **a**, *(to) +* **dónde**, *(where), which has come to be written as one word.*

SUGGESTED EXERCISE

¿Adónde va Pedro?	¿——— está Pedro?	¿Dónde está Pedro?
¿——— vamos nosotros?		¿Adónde vamos nosotros?
¿——— estamos nosotros?		¿Dónde estamos nosotros?
¿——— estás tú?		¿Dónde estás tú?
¿——— vas tú?		¿Adónde vas tú?
¿——— va María?		¿Adónde va María?
¿——— está María?		¿Dónde está María?

cuándo

Ⓡ **¿Cuándo limpian la casa?**

Which is the word that asks the question in this sentence? [**cuándo**]

cómo

Ⓡ **¿Cómo vas al partido?**

Which is the word that asks the question in this sentence? [**cómo**]

por qué

Ⓡ **¿Por qué arreglan la sala?**

Which are the words that ask the question in this sentence? [**por qué**]

cuánto

Ⓡ **¿Cuánto dinero necesitas?**

Which is the word that asks the question in this sentence? [**cuánto**]

Ⓡ **¿Cuánto dinero necesitas?**   Ⓡ **¿Cuántos pesos tienes?**

Ⓡ **¿Cuánta comida compramos?**   Ⓡ **¿Cuántas cosas buscas?**

Does **cuánto** agree in gender and number with the noun it modifies? [yes] What is the English equivalent of the singular form **cuánto**? [*how much*] and of the plural form **cuántos**? [*how many*] *Point out that when these words are used to introduce a question, they are written with an accent mark.*

▶ DRILLS 10–11, p. 75

T161

Contraction of the Definite Article

> Vamos a la biblioteca.
> ¿Vas a las carreras?
> No quiero ir a los partidos.
> ℝ Vamos al centro.

What happens when **a** and **el** come together in a sentence? [They contract to **al**; they are replaced by **al**.] Do the other forms contract? [no]

> ¿A qué hora llegan de la escuela?
> ¿Vas a la fiesta de las gemelas García?
> Es el campeón de los Estados Unidos.
> ℝ ¡Qué linda es la casa del maestro!

What happens when **de** and **el** come together in a sentence? [They contract to **del**; they are replaced by **del**.] Do the other forms contract? [no]

▶ DRILLS 13.1–13.4, pp. 76–77

Possession with de

> ℝ ¿Es Lili la tía de Susana?

Which part of this sentence means *Susana's aunt*? [**la tía de Susana**]

> ℝ Son los problemas de Pedrito.

Which part of this sentence means *Pedrito's problems*? [**los problemas de Pedrito**]

Write on the board: **la tía de Susana**   *Susana's aunt*
                       los problemas de Pedrito   *Pedrito's problems*

How is possession indicated in the English examples? [by apostrophe *s*] Does Spanish use the apostrophe to indicate possession? [no] What Spanish construction is used instead of apostrophe *s*? [definite article + noun + **de** + possessor]

▶ DRILLS 14–15, pp. 77–78

Personal a

> ℝ Escuchan el disco.   ℝ Escuchan al maestro.

What are the direct object nouns in these two sentences? [**disco, maestro**]

> ℝ ¿Buscas los boletos?   ℝ ¿Buscas a los chicos?

What are the direct object nouns in these two sentences? [**boletos, chicos**]

> ℝ No encuentro mis cosas.   ℝ No encuentro a mis hijas.

What are the direct object nouns in these two sentences? [**cosas, hijas**] In each of these three pairs of sentences, does the noun in the first sentence refer to an object or to a person? [to an object] And in the second? [to a person] *Before proceeding to the next question, you may wish to explain that a* noun phrase *is a noun or a pronoun plus any modifiers it may have.* If the direct object noun refers to a person, what word normally precedes the noun phrase? [a] *Explain that this* a, *usually called the* personal a, *has no English equivalent and simply marks the direct object as referring to a person. Point out that the* personal a *is often omitted with the verb* tener, have: **Tengo dos hermanos.**

▶ DRILLS 17–18, p. 79

Stem Alternation: o–ue
a–*Class Verbs*

Write the verb forms on the board as you do this presentation.

Ⓡ **No encuentro nada.**   Ⓡ **¿Cómo? ¿No encuentras nada?**

Is the stem stressed or unstressed in each verb form? [stressed] What is the vowel sound in the stem when stressed? [we] How is the sound written? [ue]

Ⓡ **No encontramos nada.**   Ⓡ **Tengo que encontrar los boletos.**

Is the stem stressed or unstressed in these forms of **encontrar**? [unstressed] What is the vowel sound in the stem when unstressed? [o] How is the sound written? [o] *Explain to the students that in certain verb stems the vowel* o *alternates with* ue; ue *occurs when the stem is stressed, as in* **encuentro, encuentras, encuentra, encuentran;** o *occurs when the stem is unstressed, as in* **encontramos** *and* **encontrar.** *The* a–*class verbs they have had so far which have this stem alternation are* **costar, encontrar,** *and* **recordar.**

Ⓡ **El Santos juega hoy.**   Ⓡ **Nosotros jugamos hoy.**

Which vowel alternates with [we] in **jugar**? [u] *Explain to the students that* **jugar** *is the only Spanish verb which has a* u-ue *stem alternation.*

SUGGESTED EXERCISE

Recuerda el examen.	Tiene que recordar el examen.
Cuesta mucho.	Tiene que costar mucho.
Juega hoy.	Tiene que jugar hoy.
Encuentra los boletos.	Tiene que encontrar los boletos.
Recuerda al señor.	Tiene que recordar al señor.

SUGGESTED EXERCISE

No encuentro las cosas.	No encontramos las cosas.
Juego fútbol mañana.	Jugamos fútbol mañana.
No recuerdo quién es Pedro.	No recordamos quién es Pedro.
No encuentro nada.	No encontramos nada.
¿Juego ahora?	¿Jugamos ahora?

T163

No recordamos qué día es hoy.　　　No recuerdo qué día es hoy.
Jugamos los sábados.　　　　　　　Juego los sábados.
Recordamos la fiesta.　　　　　　　Recuerdo la fiesta.
Encontramos muchas cosas.　　　　Encuentro muchas cosas.
No jugamos con ellos.　　　　　　　No juego con ellos.

▶ DRILLS 20–24, pp. 80–82

UNIT 6

ser *and* estar *with Predicate Nouns and Adverbs*

In this presentation you want the student to learn that there are two Spanish verbs, ser *and* estar, *which correspond to the English verb* be. *You want him to discover those situations in which the choice between* ser *and* estar *is not free; that is, in which he must choose one verb or the other, depending on the other elements in the sentence.*

Two words meaning be 　　　　　Ⓡ **Juan está aquí.**　　　Ⓡ **Juan es mi primo.**

Which word means *is* in each sentence? [**está, es**] What is the infinitive of **está**? [**estar**] What is the infinitive of **es**? [**ser**] Which two Spanish verbs correspond to *be*? [**ser** and **estar**]

estar *for location*　　　　　　　Ⓡ **Todo está en su lugar.**
　　　Ⓡ **Mis cosas están en la cocina.**　　　Ⓡ **Estoy aquí.**

What do all of these sentences tell about the subject? [where it is, its location] Which verb, **ser** or **estar**, is used to refer to the location of something of someone? [**estar**]

SUGGESTED EXERCISE

¿Dónde está María, aquí o en casa?　　Está aquí.
¿Y Pedro y Juan?　　　　　　　　　　Están aquí.
¿Y Pepe?　　　　　　　　　　　　　　Está aquí.
¿Y usted?　　　　　　　　　　　　　　Estoy aquí.
¿Y las hermanas García?　　　　　　　Están aquí.
¿Y Juan y su amigo?　　　　　　　　　Están aquí.

ser *to link*
noun phrases　　　*This might be a good moment to remind the students that a* noun phrase *is a noun or a pronoun plus any modifiers it may have.*

Ⓡ **Esa chica es mi prima.**

What are the two noun phrases in this sentence? [**esa chica, mi prima**]

Ⓡ **Yo soy Cristina.**

What are the two noun phrases in this sentence? [**yo, Cristina**]

Ⓡ **El señor alto es don Pedro.**

What are the two noun phrases in this sentence? [**el señor alto, don Pedro**] Which

T164

verb, **ser** or **estar**, is used to link two noun phrases? [**ser**]

SUGGESTED EXERCISE

¿Quién es ese chico?   Ese chico es (*Pedro*).
¿Quién es esa chica?   Esa chica es (*Ana*).
¿Quién es usted?   Yo soy (*Arturo*).
¿Quién soy yo?   Usted es (el maestro, la maestra).

SUGGESTED EXERCISE

¿Qué es esto? (*Show a book or Supplement*   Es un libro.
   Poster 6–3).
¿Dónde está? (*Put book on a table.*)   Está en la mesa.

Repeat drill using items found in the classroom or the following Supplement Posters:
discos *2–5,* **regalo** *3–10,* **abrigo** *4–9,* **sombrero** *4–10,* **guantes** *5–7,* **pañuelos** *5–8,* **álbum**
6–1, **periódico** *6–2,* **foto** *6–7.*

ser to link
expressions with de
and para

☐ **María es de los Estados Unidos.**

What does the expression **de los Estados Unidos** tell us about the subject, **María**?
[where she's from] Which verb, **ser** or **estar**, is used to link a noun phrase and expressions with **de**, that indicate source (where something or someone comes from)?
[**ser**]

☐ **Los regalos son para mi mamá.**

What does the expression **para mi mamá** tell us about the subject, **los regalos**? [who
they're for] Which verb, **ser** or **estar**, is used to link a noun phrase and expressions
with **para**, that indicate destination (what or whom something is intended for)?
[**ser**]

SUGGESTED EXERCISE

¿Dónde está su mamá?   Está en (casa).
¿De dónde es su mamá?   Es de (California).
¿Dónde está su hermano?   Está en (la escuela).
¿De dónde es su hermano?   Es de (Nueva York).
¿Dónde está usted?   Estoy aquí.
¿De dónde es usted?   Soy de (Los Ángeles).
¿Dónde están sus abuelos?   Están en (casa).
¿Son de aquí sus abuelos?   Sí, son de aquí. (No, no son de aquí.)

SUGGESTED EXERCISE

El regalo es para Susana. de María   El regalo es de María.
   aquí   El regalo está aquí.
   en la mesa   El regalo está en la mesa.   (*continued*)

para mi mamá	El regalo es para mi mamá.
de Juan	El regalo es de Juan.
en el suelo	El regalo está en el suelo.
de mi tío	El regalo es de mi tío.

▶ DRILLS 8–10, p. 94

ser *for time and place of events*

Ⓡ **La reunión es a las ocho.**   Ⓡ **La fiesta es ahora.**

Which verb is used to tell the time of an event? [**ser**]

Ⓡ **¿Dónde es la fiesta?**   Ⓡ **El examen es aquí.**

Which verb is used to tell the place of an event? [**ser**] Tell the students that in sentences like these, **ser** means *take place, occur, be held.* Remind students that **estar** *is used to tell the location of a person or object, while* **ser** *is used for an event.*

SUGGESTED EXERCISE   (*Suggested responses are given in parentheses.*)

¿Cuándo es la fiesta?	1st stud. Es (a las siete, ahora).
¿Y dónde es?	2nd stud. Es (en mi casa, la sala).
¿Cuándo es la reunión?	Es (a las cuatro).
¿Y dónde es?	Es (en la escuela, el comedor, mi casa).
¿Cuándo es el baile?	Es (a las ocho).
¿Y dónde es?	Es (en la sala, la escuela).
¿Cuándo es el partido?	Es (a las dos).
¿Y dónde es?	Es (en el estadio, el parque).
¿Cuándo es la carrera?	Es (a la una, a las tres).
¿Y dónde es?	Es (en el estadio, aquí, en la escuela).

SUGGESTED EXERCISE

¿Dónde es la reunión? (el libro)?	¿Dónde está el libro?
(la fiesta)	¿Dónde es la fiesta?
(la carrera)	¿Dónde es la carrera?
(la foto)	¿Dónde está la foto?
(el carro)	¿Dónde está el carro?
(el baile)	¿Dónde es el baile?
(el disco)	¿Dónde está el disco?
(el perro)	¿Dónde está el perro?

Nouns that refer to either objects or events

Ⓡ **La comida está en la mesa.**   Ⓡ **La comida es en mi casa.**

In the first sentence, does **comida** mean *food* (the actual things eaten) or *meal* (the event of eating that food)? [*food*] And in the second sentence? [*meal*] Tell students that some Spanish nouns can refer to either objects or events. For example, **película** may mean film (the object that goes into a camera or projector) or movie (the event of showing a film). **Almuerzo** may mean either the food one eats at noon or the event of eating that food. If the speaker refers to an object, he uses **estar** to tell its location; if he refers to an event, he uses **ser.**

▶ DRILLS 11–15, pp. 94–96

ser *and* estar *with Predicate Adjectives*

In this presentation you want the students to become aware that the choice of **ser** *or* **estar** *to link a noun phrase and a predicate adjective depends on the intention of the speaker. There is no easily discovered grammatical principle; the choice is subjective. It will therefore be most effective to define predicate adjective and then simply to explain the generalization on pages 96–97. Then do the following suggested exercises.*

SUGGESTED EXERCISE

Tell whether each of the following sentences expresses a norm (how the subject normally is), or an attribute of the subject at a particular time.

María es linda.	(norm)
María está linda.	(attribute at a particular time)
Pedro está gordo.	(attribute . . .)
No estamos sordos.	(attribute . . .)
Está bonita en la foto.	(attribute . . .)
Tú eres muy simpático.	(norm)
¡Qué delgado estoy!	(attribute . . .)
Estamos cansados.	(attribute . . .)
Es muy alto.	(norm)
Está muy alto.	(attribute . . .)

SUGGESTED EXERCISE

Give the Spanish equivalent of each of the following English sentences:

Roberto is thin. (He's a thin boy.)	Roberto es delgado.
Roberto is thin. (He has lost a lot of weight.)	Roberto está delgado.
Juan is tall. (He has grown a lot during the summer.)	Juan está alto.
Juan is tall. (He's a tall boy.)	Juan es alto.
These shoes are ugly. (They're ugly shoes.)	Estos zapatos son feos.
These shoes are ugly. (They're all worn out.)	Estos zapatos están feos.

▶ DRILLS 17–21, pp. 97–99

The Suffix -ito

Es un regalo muy lindo.   Ⓡ Es un regalito muy lindo.

Which word in the second sentence is different from the corresponding word in the first? [**regalito**] How is it different? [It has a suffix; it has a special ending.] What is the ending? [**-ito**] What is the ending attached to? [to the **l**, to the final consonant, to the noun minus the last vowel] *Explain that Spanish has a number of suffixes, called diminutive suffixes, which are used to indicate smallness, cuteness, or a feeling of affection on the part of the speaker. The most common of these is* **-ito** (**-ita**, *feminine*), *which* can be added to the stem of most nouns and many adjectives. (The stem is the noun or adjective minus the final vowel, if there is one.) The gender of a noun is never changed by the addition of the diminutive suffix. The plural of the diminutive is formed by adding **s**.

SUGGESTED EXERCISE

Give the diminutive of the following nouns.

casa	casita
perro	perrito
abuelo	abuelito
Juan	Juanito
hermanos	hermanitos
chica	chiquita
primas	primitas

▶ DRILL 23, p. 100

The Suffix -ísimo

Juan es alto.   R **Juan es altísimo.**

Which word in the second sentence is different from the corresponding word in the first? [**altísimo**] How is it different? [It has a suffix; it has a special ending.] What is the ending? [**-ísimo**] What is the ending attached to? [to the stem] What part of speech is **alto**? [an adjective] *Explain that the suffix* **-ísimo**, *which has the meaning* extremely, *can be affixed to the stem of most adjectives. The* **-ísimo** *form of the adjective is usually called the* superlative form. *The* **-ísimo** *form agrees in gender and number with the noun it modifies.*

SUGGESTED EXERCISE

Give the superlative of the following adjectives.

lindo	lindísimo
grande	grandísimo
fácil	facilísimo
gorda	gordísima
pequeños	pequeñísimos
delgada	delgadísima
guapo	guapísimo

▶ DRILLS 24–25, pp. 100–101

ir

ir *and* dar, *Present Tense*

R **¿Adónde voy yo?**   R **¿Adónde vas tú?**
R **¿Adónde va él?**

Which form of the verb corresponds to **yo**? [**voy**] to **tú**? [**vas**] to **él, ella,** and **usted**? [**va**]

R ¿Adónde vamos? R ¿Adónde van?

Which form of the verb corresponds to **nosotros**? [**vamos**] to **ellos, ellas,** and **ustedes**? [**van**]

R ¿Adónde quiere ir?

What is the infinitive of the verb we have been studying? [**ir**] What is the English equivalent of **ir**? [*go*] What is the theme vowel of the infinitive **ir**? [**i**] What is the theme vowel in the present tense forms? [**a**] What is the stem? [**v**] Which present tense form has an irregular ending? [**voy**]

▶ DRILLS 27.1–27.2, p. 102

dar

R ¿Qué dan?

Which word is the verb? [**dan**] What is the literal equivalent of **dar**? [*give*]

R **Doy una fiesta.**
R **Das una fiesta.**
↓ R **Da una fiesta.**

R **Damos una fiesta.**
R **Dan una fiesta.**
↓ R **Quiero dar una fiesta.**

Which form of dar is irregular? [**doy**]

▶ DRILLS 28–29, pp. 102–103

Position of Descriptive Adjectives

R **Llamo a la chica americana.**

Which word is the noun? [**chica**] Which word is the adjective? [**americana**]

R **Excepto ese chico rubio.**

Which word is the noun? [**chico**] Which word is the adjective? [**rubio**]

R **Tiene ojos azules.**

Which word is the noun? [**ojos**] Which word is the adjective? [**azules**]

In each of these sentences, what is the position of the adjective in relation to the noun? [after] *Explain that adjectives which specify some quality or characteristic of the noun they modify are called descriptive adjectives. Descriptive adjectives often occur inside a noun phrase after the noun they modify.*

SUGGESTED EXERCISE

La chica es linda.
El señor es simpático.
El gordito es muy perezoso.
La señora es trigueña.
Los guantes son blancos.
Los zapatos son grises.
Las medias son caras.

Es una chica linda.
Es un señor simpático.
Es un gordito muy perezoso.
Es una señora trigueña.
Son unos guantes blancos.
Son unos zapatos grises.
Son unas medias caras.

▶ DRILLS 6–15, pp. 113–115

Prepositions

Ⓡ **Vamos a las carreras.**

Which word is a preposition? [**a**]

Ⓡ **Más tarde hablo con ella.**

Which word is a preposition? [**con**]

Ⓡ **No llega de la escuela todavía.**

Which word is a preposition? [**de**]

Do these prepositions consist of one or of more than one word? [one word] *Tell students that prepositions consisting of one word are called simple prepositions.*

SUGGESTED EXERCISE

Hacemos el almuerzo para mamá.
  (sin)   Hacemos el almuerzo sin mamá.
  (con)   Hacemos el almuerzo con mamá.
  (para)   Hacemos el almuerzo para mamá.

Caminamos por el parque.
  (en)   Caminamos en el parque.
  (por)   Caminamos por el parque.

No llega de la fiesta.
  (a)   No llega a la fiesta.
  (durante)   No llega durante la fiesta.
  (de)   No llega de la fiesta.

Ⓡ **Está delante de Conchita.**   Ⓡ **Está detrás de Conchita.**

Which words are the prepositions in these sentences? [**delante de, detrás de**] Do these prepositions consist of one or of more than one word? [more than one] *Tell students that prepositions which consist of more than one word are called compound prepositions.* What is the second word in each compound preposition? [**de**] *Tell students that compound prepositions consist of an adverb plus the simple preposition* **de**.

SUGGESTED EXERCISE

Pedro está delante. (Ana)	Pedro está delante de Ana.
Estudiamos después. (la película)	Estudiamos después de la película.
Pensamos en el regalo antes. (el Diá de la Madre)	Pensamos en el regalo antes del Día de la Madre.
Elena está detrás. (María)	Elena está detrás de María.
La maestra está delante. (la clase)	La maestra está delante de la clase.

▶ **DRILLS 17–18, pp. 116–117**

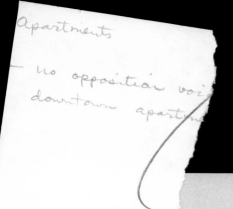

apartments

— no opposition voi...
downtown apart...

Pronouns as Objects of Prepositions

® Usted pronuncia bien.

...n word is the subject pronoun? [usted]

® Quiero estudiar con usted.

Which word is the object of the preposition? [usted] In these sentences, is the pronoun used as the object of the preposition the same as or different from the subject pronoun? [the same]

El pronuncia bien.	® Quiero estudiar con él.
Ella pronuncia bien.	® Quiero estudiar con ella.
Nosotros pronunciamos bien.	® ¿Quieres estudiar con nosotros?
Ustedes pronuncian bien.	® Quiero estudiar con ustedes.
Ellos pronuncian bien.	® Quiero estudiar con ellos.
Ellas pronuncian bien.	® Quiero estudiar con ellas.

In these examples, are the pronouns used as the objects of prepositions the same as or different from the corresponding subject pronouns? [the same]

SUGGESTED EXERCISE

Ella es muy simpática.	Este regalo es para ella.
Él es muy simpático.	Este regalo es para él.
Ellas son muy simpáticas.	Este regalo es para ellas.
Usted es muy simpático.	Este regalo es para usted.
Ellos son muy simpáticos.	Este regalo es para ellos.

mí, ti

® Yo estoy aquí, y Ana está delante de mí.
® Tú estás aquí, y Ana está delante de ti.

In these examples, are the pronouns used as the objects of prepositions the same as or different from the subject pronouns? [different] Which Spanish word corresponds to the word *me* after a preposition? [mí] Which word corresponds to *you* (familiar)? [ti] *Write on the board:* **mí, ti.** *Point out that unlike the possessive adjective* **mi** (**mi libro**), *the prepositional pronoun* **mí** *has a written accent over the i* (**para mí**).

conmigo
contigo

Yo voy al centro.   ® ¿Quieres ir conmigo?
¿Tú vas al centro?   ® ¿Puedo ir contigo?

What special form of **mí** is used after the preposition **con**? [migo] What special form of **ti** is used? [tigo] *Write on the board:* **conmigo, contigo,** *and point out that the preposition and the special form of the pronoun are written as a single word.*

SUGGESTED EXERCISE

Pregúntele a *Susana* quién está delante   ¿Quién está delante de ti?
de ella.

Susana, contéstele.   (*Juan Gómez*) está delante de mí.

T171

Pregúntele a *Pepe* quién está detrás de él.

Pepe, contéstele.

Pregúntele a *María* quién estudia con ella.

María, contéstele.

Pregúntele a *Roberto* si este libro es para él.

Roberto, contéstele.

▶ DRILLS 19–20, pp. 118–119

¿Quién está detrás de ti?

(*María López*) está detrás de mí.

¿Quién estudia contigo?

(*Marcos Pérez*) estudia conmigo.

¿Este libro es para ti?

Sí (no), este libro es (no es) para mí.

Regular e–*Class Verbs*

Write each verb form on the board as you do this presentation.

® ¿Qué quieres comer?	® ¿Qué come?
® ¿Qué como?	® ¿Qué comemos?
↓ ® ¿Qué comes?	↓ ® ¿Qué comen?

What is the stem of the verb **comer**? [**com**] What is the theme vowel? [**e**] What ending attached to the stem indicates the subject is **yo**? [**o**] What ending attached to the stem + theme vowel indicates the subject is **tú**? [**s**] él, ella, usted? [none] **nosotros**? [**mos**] ellos, ellas, ustedes? [**n**] Are these endings the same as those added to the stem or stem + theme vowel of regular **a**-class verbs? [yes] *Tell the students that there is a large class of verbs whose theme vowel is* **e**. *The regular verbs of this class which they have encountered so far are* **comer, creer, deber,** *and* **leer.**

SUGGESTED EXERCISE

¿Come usted ahora o más tarde?

¿Cree usted que soy americano o español?

¿Debe usted estudiar más o menos?

¿Lee usted español bien o un poco solamente?

¿Come usted antes o después de esta clase?

Como más tarde.

Creo que usted es americano (español).

Debo estudiar más.

Leo un poco solamente (bien).

Como después (antes) de esta clase.

SUGGESTED EXERCISE

Have the students ask each of the above questions to each other. Start like this:

Pregúntele a *Juana* si come ahora.

Juana, contéstele.

¿Comes ahora?

No, como más tarde.

SUGGESTED EXERCISE

The following questions refer to the Basic Dialog. Have students answer with a complete sentence.

T172

¿Debe ser bonita Sue?	Sí, debe ser muy bonita.
¿Lee inglés Conchita?	Sí, lee inglés.
¿Debe buscar un diccionario Conchita?	Sí, debe buscar un diccionario.
¿Cree Conchita que Enrique es simpático?	Sí, cree que es simpático.

SUGGESTED EXERCISE

¿Deben ustedes estudiar ahora? (*Point to two students*)	1ST STUD. Sí, debemos estudiar ahora.
	2ND STUD. Ellos deben estudiar ahora.
¿Comen en casa esta noche?	Sí, comemos en . . . / Ellos comen . . .
¿Creen todas esas cosas?	Sí, creemos . . . / Ellos creen . . .
¿Leen muchos libros?	Sí, leemos . . . / Ellos leen . . .
¿Deben practicar español?	Sí, debemos . . . / Ellos deben . . .

▶ DRILLS 22.1–22.3, p. 120

Regular i–Class Verbs

Write each verb form on the board as you do this presentation.

↓	® Sé escribir un poco solamente.	↓	® Escribe un poco solamente.
	® Escribo un poco solamente.		® Escribimos un poco solamente.
	® Escribes un poco solamente.		® Escriben un poco solamente.

What is the stem of the verb **escribir**? [**escrib**] What is the theme vowel? [**i**] In which present tense forms does the theme vowel differ? [in **escribes, escribe,** and **escriben**] How does it differ? [It's **e** instead of **i**.] What difference do you notice between the present tense forms of **escribir** and those of **e**–class verbs like **comer**? [The theme vowel for the first person plural (the form that corresponds to **nosotros**) is **i** for **escribir** and **e** for **e**–class verbs.] *Tell the students that there is a third class of verbs, called i–class verbs, whose theme vowel is i when stressed (as in* **escribimos***) and e when unstressed (as in* **escribes, escribe, escriben***). The present tense forms of this class of verbs are like those of e–class verbs except for the first person plural. The regular i–class verbs they have encountered so far are* **escribir** *and* **vivir***.*

▶ DRILLS 24.1–24.2, p. 121

SUGGESTED EXERCISE

Soy de Canadá pero . . .	Soy de Canadá pero vivo aquí.
Es de Canadá pero . . .	Es de Canadá pero vive aquí.
Eres de Canadá pero . . .	Eres de Canadá pero vives aquí.
Son de Canadá pero . . .	Son de Canadá pero viven aquí.
Somos de Canadá pero . . .	Somos de Canadá pero vivimos aquí.

▶ DRILLS 25–27, p. 122

saber, ver, hacer, *Present Tense*

R No sé qué pasa.	R No sabemos qué pasa.
R No sabes qué pasa.	R No saben qué pasa.
R No sabe qué pasa.	

Which form of the verb **saber** is irregular? [**sé**] Which subject pronoun corresponds to **sé**? [**yo**]

R No veo nada.	R No vemos nada.
R No ves nada.	R No ven nada.
R No ve nada.	

Which form of the verb **ver** is irregular? [**veo**] Which subject pronoun corresponds to **veo**? [**yo**]

R ¿Qué hago aquí?	R ¿Qué hacemos aquí?
R ¿Qué haces aquí?	R ¿Qué hacen aquí?
R ¿Qué hace aquí?	

Which form of the verb **hacer** is irregular? [**hago**] Which subject pronoun corresponds to **hago**? [**yo**]

▶ DRILLS 29–32, pp. 124–125

Stem Alternation: e-ie
e–*Class and* i–*Class Verbs*

Write the verb forms on the board as you do this presentation.

R Quiero unos discos.	R ¿Cuántos discos quieres?
R Prefiero eso.	R ¿Sí?, ¿prefieres eso?

Is the stem stressed or unstressed in the forms of **querer** and **preferir**? [stressed] What is the vowel sound in the stem when stressed? [**ye**] How is the sound written? [**ie**]

R Queremos unos discos.	R Deben querer unos discos.
R Preferimos eso.	R Deben preferir eso.

Is the stem stressed or unstressed in the forms of **querer** and **preferir**? [unstressed] What is the vowel sound in the stem when unstressed? [**e**] How is the sound written? [**e**] What verb class does **querer** belong to? [**e**-class] What verb class does **preferir** belong to? [**i**-class] Do **e**-class and **i**–class verbs with **e-ie** stem alternation follow the same pattern as **a**–class verbs like **pensar**? [yes] *Tell students that the e-class and i-class verbs they have had so far which have this stem alternation are **querer**, **preferir**, **entender**, and **sentir**.*

T174

Pregúnteles a *Juana* y a *Pepe* si prefieren escuchar discos o estudiar ahora.
Juana, contéstele.
(*Continue the drill, calling on different groups of students.*)

¿Prefieren escuchar discos o estudiar ahora?
Preferimos escuchar discos.

. . . si quieren comer ahora o más tarde. / . . . , contéstele.
. . . si entienden mejor inglés o español. / . . . , contéstele.
. . . si piensan en el examen o en una fiesta. / . . . , contéstele.
. . . si prefieren leer en inglés o en español. / . . . , contéstele.

¿Quieren comer ahora o más tarde? / Queremos comer (ahora).
¿Entienden mejor inglés o español? / Entendemos mejor inglés.
¿Piensan en el examen o en una fiesta? Pensamos en una (fiesta).
¿Prefieren leer en inglés o en español? / Preferimos leer en (inglés).

▶ DRILLS 6–10, pp. 136–137

allí *and* haber

Ⓡ **La comida está allí.**   Ⓡ **Hay más comida.**

Which sentence tells where the food is, that is, the location of the food? [the first] Does the second sentence tell us where the food is, or simply that more food exists? [that more food exists] What does each sentence mean in English? [*The food is there. There is more food.*] Explain that the English word <u>there</u> is used in two ways: 1) to express the location of something 2) to express the existence of something. Spanish has separate equivalents for these two uses of <u>there</u>. If <u>there</u> indicates location, **allí** is used. If <u>there</u> + a form of <u>be</u> indicates the existence of something (There is more food.), *it is expressed by* the irregular verb **haber**. One present tense form of **haber**, **hay**, corresponds to both <u>there is</u> and <u>there are</u>.

¿Qué hay en la mesa?
(*Put a book on the table or use Supplement Poster 6–3.*)
¿Dónde está el libro?

Hay un libro.

Está allí.

Repeat the exercise using objects in the classroom or the following Supplement Posters:
álbum *6–1,* **periódico** *6–2,* **foto** *6–7,* **diccionario** *7–3,* **carta** *7–4,* **reloj** *8–1,* **bolsa** *8–18,* **culebra** *8–19.*

▶ DRILLS 12–13, p. 138

Demonstrative Adjectives

Masculine singular Ⓡ **¿Puedo ver este periódico?** Ⓡ **¿Puedo ver este libro?**

Which words are the nouns in these sentences? [**periódico, libro**] What are the gender and number of **periódico** and **libro**? [masculine singular] What word meaning *this* is used with masculine singular nouns? [**este**]

Ⓡ **¿Puedo ver ese periódico?** Ⓡ **¿Puedo ver ese libro?**

What word meaning *that* is used with masculine singular nouns? [**ese**]

Masculine plural Ⓡ **¿Puedo ver estos periódicos?** Ⓡ **¿Puedo ver estos libros?**

What are the gender and number of the nouns in these sentences? [masculine plural] What word meaning *these* is used with masculine plural nouns? [**estos**] Can you guess which word meaning *those* is used? [**esos**]

SUGGESTED EXERCISE

Necesito este disco. (libro 6–3)   1ST STUD. Necesito este libro.
     2ND STUD. Necesito estos libros.

Repeat the exercise, using the following Supplement Posters (or say the noun and have the students supply the demonstrative adjectives): dinero 5–15, reloj 8–1, boleto 5–16, diccionario 7–3, periódico 6–2.

Feminine singular Ⓡ **Esta blusa es muy linda.** Ⓡ **Esta falda es muy linda.**

Which words are the nouns in these sentences? [**blusa, falda**] What are the gender and number of **blusa** and **falda**? [feminine singular] What word meaning *this* is used with feminine singular nouns? [**esta**]

Feminine plural Ⓡ **Esa blusa es muy linda.** Ⓡ **Esa falda es muy linda.**

What word meaning *that* is used with feminine singular nouns? [**esa**]

Ⓡ **Estas blusas son muy lindas.** Ⓡ **Estas faldas son muy lindas.**

What is the gender and number of the nouns in these sentences? [feminine plural] What word meaning *these* is used with feminine plural nouns? [**estas**] Can you guess which word meaning *those* is used? [**esas**]

SUGGESTED EXERCISE

¿Compramos esa camisa? (corbata 4–6)   1ST STUD. ¿Compramos esa corbata?
   2ND STUD. ¿Compramos esas corbatas?

Repeat the exercise, using the following Supplement Posters (or say the noun and have the student supply the demonstrative adjective): mesa 6–9, silla 6–11, blusa 4–4, falda 4–5.

▶ DRILLS 15–19, pp. 140–141

The Neuter Demonstratives esto and eso

Ⓡ ¿Qué es esto?   Ⓡ ¿Eso? No sé.

Are there any nouns in these sentences? [no] Do **esto** and **eso** modify any particular noun? [no] *Explain that* **esto** *and* **eso** *never modify a noun, and thus never show gender agreement. They are called neuter demonstratives because they belong to no gender class. Neuter demonstratives are used in the following situations: when the speaker does not know what a particular thing is (¿Qué es esto?); to identify a previously unidentified object (Eso es un huevo.); and to refer to situations, ideas, and actions when these are not associated with any particular noun (Eso no es verdad.).*

SUGGESTED EXERCISE

¿Qué es esto?   (bolsa 8-18)   Eso es una bolsa.

Repeat, using classroom objects and/or Supplement Posters. The following posters are suggested: **reloj** 8-1, **carne** 8-8, **pan y mantequilla** 8-12, **helado** 8-13, **leche** 8-14, **café** 8-15, **agua** 8-16, **bolsa** 8-18, **culebra** 8-19.

SUGGESTED EXERCISE

California está en los Estados Unidos.	Eso es verdad.
Yo soy un alumno.	Eso no es verdad.
Usted es un maestro.	Eso no es verdad.
Estudiamos francés aquí.	Eso no es verdad.
Hay una culebra en esta bolsa.	Eso es (no es) verdad.
Ustedes son muy inteligentes.	Eso es verdad.

▶ DRILLS 21-23, pp. 142-143

Verbs with Stem Irregularities: conocer, poner, salir

As you do each section of this presentation, write the irregular verb forms on the board.

conocer

Ⓡ Conozco a Toni.   Ⓡ Conocemos a Toni.
Ⓡ Conoces a Toni.   Ⓡ Conocen a Toni.
Ⓡ Conoce a Toni.

Which form of **conocer** is irregular? [**conozco**] What subject pronoun corresponds to **conozco**? [yo] What sound is added to the stem of the first person singular? [k] How is the spelling affected by this? [The **c** is replaced by **z** and the letter **c** is added to the stem.] *Point out that the letter* **z** *in* **conozco** *is simply a spelling convention; the sound remains* [s]. **Reconocer** *follows the same pattern as* **conocer**.

poner

Ⓡ Pongo las cosas allí.   Ⓡ Ponemos las cosas allí.
Ⓡ Pones las cosas allí.   Ⓡ Ponen las cosas allí.
Ⓡ Pone las cosas allí.

Which form of **poner** is irregular? [**pongo**] What subject pronoun corresponds to **pongo**? [yo] What sound is added to the stem of the first person singular? [g] *Tell students that* **salir** *also adds the sound* [g] *to its stem in the first person singular.*

¿Conoce usted al maestro de inglés?	Sí, conozco al maestro de inglés.
¿Sale usted más tarde?	Sí, salgo más tarde.
¿Pone sus libros aquí?	Sí, pongo mis libros aquí.
¿Reconoce usted este libro?	Sí, reconozco ese libro.
¿Conoce usted a *María*?	Sí, conozco a *María*.

▶ DRILLS 25.1, 25.2, and 25.3, pp. 144–145

Verbs with Stem Irregularities: traer, oír

As you do each section of this presentation, write the irregular verb forms on the board.

traer

R Traigo el correo.	R Traemos el correo.
R Traes el correo.	R Traen el correo.
R Trae el correo.	

Which form of **traer** is irregular? [**traigo**] What subject pronoun corresponds to **traigo**? [**yo**] Which two letters are added to the stem of the first person singular? [**ig**] *Point out that* **traigo** *has two syllables:* **trai-go**.

▶ DRILL 27.1, p. 146

oír

R Quiero oír a mi hijo.   R Ya oigo a mi hijo.

In the first sentence, which word is an infinitive? [**oír**] Is **oigo** regular or irregular? [**irregular**] What subject pronoun corresponds to **oigo**? [**yo**] Which two letters are added to the stem of the first person singular? [**ig**] *Point out that* **oigo** *has two syllables:* **oi-go**.

R Oyes a Luis.   R Oye a Luis.   R Oyen a Luis.

Which form of the verb corresponds to **tú**? [**oyes**] Which form corresponds to **él, ella, usted**? [**oye**] Which form corresponds to **ellos, ellas, ustedes**? [**oyen**] What letter is added to the stem in these verb forms? [**y**]

R Oímos a Luis.

Which form of the verb corresponds to **nosotros**? [**oímos**] Is **oímos** regular or irregular? [**regular**] *Point out that the stressed theme vowel* i *requires a written accent, since it is pronounced as a separate, stressed syllable.*

▶ DRILLS 27.2–30, p. 146

Verbs with Stem Irregularities: tener, venir

R Debo tener cinco pesos.   R Debo venir a las ocho.

Which word is the infinitive in each sentence? [**tener, venir**]

® **Tengo cinco pesos.**   ® **Vengo a las ocho.**

What sound is added to the stem of the first person singular? [**g**]

® **Tienes cinco pesos.**   ® **Vienes a las ocho.**

Is the stem stressed or unstressed in each verb form? [stressed] What is the vowel sound in the stem? [**ye**] How is the sound written? [**ie**]

® **Tenemos cinco pesos.**   ® **Venimos a las ocho.**

Is the stem stressed or unstressed in each verb form? [unstressed] What is the vowel sound in the stem when unstressed? [**e**] How is the sound written? [**e**] What two irregularities do **tener** and **venir** have? [They add **g** to the stem of the first person singular, and the stem vowel alternates between unstressed **e** and stressed **ie**, except in the first person singular.]

▶ DRILLS 32–36, pp. 147–148

Stem Alternation: o-ue
e–*Class and* i–*Class Verbs*

Write the verb forms on the board as you do this presentation.

® **Vuelvo en septiembre.**   ® **Duermo mucho.**

Is the stem stressed or unstressed in each verb form? [stressed] What is the vowel sound in the stem when stressed? [**we**] How is the sound written? [**ue**]

® **Volvemos en septiembre.**   ® **Tenemos que volver en septiembre.**
® **Dormimos mucho.**   ® **Tenemos que dormir mucho.**

Is the stem stressed or unstressed in the forms of **volver** and **dormir**? [unstressed] What is the vowel sound in the stem when unstressed? [**o**] How is the sound written? [**o**] What verb class does **volver** belong to? [**e**–class] What verb class does **dormir** belong to? [**i**–class] Do **e**–class and **i**–class verbs with an **o-ue** stem alternation follow the same pattern as **a**–class verbs like **encontrar**? [yes] *Tell students that the **e**–class and **i**–class verbs they have had so far which have this stem alternation are **llover**, **poder**, **volver**, and **dormir**.*

SUGGESTED EXERCISE

Pregúnteles a *Juana* y a *Pepe* si vuelven aquí mañana.

Juana, contéstele.

(*Call on different groups of students.*)

. . . si pueden ir al cine hoy. / . . . contéstele.

. . . si duermen en clase. / . . . contéstele.

¿Vuelven aquí mañana?

Sí, volvemos aquí mañana.

¿Pueden ir . . . ? / Sí, podemos ir. . . .

¿Duermen en . . . ? / No, no dormimos en . . .

UNIT 9

T179

... si juegan tenis esta tarde. / ... contéstele.

¿Juegan tenis ...? / Sí, jugamos tenis ...

... si recuerdan cuándo es el examen. / ... contéstele.

¿Recuerdan cuándo ...? / Sí, recordamos cuándo ...

... si vuelven a casa ahora. / ... contéstele.

¿Vuelven a ...? / Sí, volvemos a ...

... si pueden salir esta noche. / ... contéstele.

¿Pueden salir ...? / Sí, podemos salir ...

▶ DRILLS 5–8, pp. 160–161

ir + a + *Infinitive*

Ⓡ **Voy a viajar en tren.**

What three parts make up the verb in this sentence? [**voy** + **a** + **viajar**]

Ⓡ **¿Vas a pasar las vacaciones en España?**

What three parts make up the verb? [**vas** + **a** + **pasar**]

Ⓡ **Vamos a hacer un viaje allá.**

What three parts make up the verb? [**vamos** + **a** + **hacer**] What is the infinitive form of **voy**, **vas**, and **vamos**? [**ir**] In each sentence, what word follows a form of **ir**? [**a**] In each sentence, what verb form follows the word **a**? (That is, what form of the verb are **viajar**, **pasar** and **hacer**?) [infinitive] *Explain to the students that in English we often use a form of be + going to + an infinitive when referring to an event that will take place in the future:* I'm going to travel by train. *The equivalent construction in Spanish consists of a form of the verb* **ir** + **a** + *an infinitive.*

SUGGESTED EXERCISE

Yo voy a estudiar esta noche.	(tú)	Tú vas a estudiar esta noche.
	(leer)	Tú vas a leer esta noche.
	(Juan)	Juan va a leer esta noche.
	(llegar)	Juan va a llegar esta noche.
	(los chicos)	Los chicos van a llegar esta noche.
	(venir)	Los chicos van a venir esta noche.
	(ustedes)	Ustedes van a venir esta noche.
	(salir)	Ustedes van a salir esta noche.
	(nosotros)	Nosotros vamos a salir esta noche.

▶ DRILLS 10–11, pp. 161–162

Indirect Object Pronouns

In this presentation, you want the students to learn the forms and meanings of the Spanish indirect object pronouns. Since in normal spoken Spanish the indirect object pronoun *does not replace the indirect object noun, but simply repeats it (**Le doy el libro a Juan**.), no attempt has been made to relate Spanish sentences with indirect object pronouns and English sentences in which the indirect object pronoun replaces a noun (I give Juan the book; I give him the book.).*

me

® **Juan me escribe una carta.**

Which word means to me? [**me**] *Tell students that* **me** *is called an indirect object pronoun. Explain that in English, the indirect object pronoun may occur before the direct object* (Juan writes me a letter.) *or after the direct object, following the preposition* to *or* for (Juan writes a letter to me. Juan buys a present for me.). What is the position of the indirect object pronoun in Spanish? [immediately before the verb]

te

® **Juan te escribe una carta.**

Which word means *to you*? [**te**] Which word is the indirect object pronoun? [**te**]

SUGGESTED EXERCISE

Me escriben una carta.	1st stud.	Me escriben una carta.
	2nd stud.	¿De veras? ¿Te escriben una carta?
Me traen un regalo.		Me traen . . . / ¿De veras? ¿Te traen un . . . ?
Me dicen muchas cosas.		Me dicen . . . / ¿De veras? ¿Te dicen . . . ?
Me dan diez pesos.		Me dan . . . / ¿De veras? ¿Te dan . . . ?
Me hablan en español.		Me hablan . . . / ¿De veras? ¿Te hablan . . . ?

le

Juan tiene diez pesos.   ® **Su papá le da mucho dinero.**

Which word is the indirect object pronoun? [**le**] Who does **le** refer to; that is, who does the father give the money to? [**Juan**]

Susana tiene diez pesos.   ® **Su papá le da mucho dinero.**

Which word is the indirect object pronoun? [**le**] Who does **le** refer to? [**Susana**] If you hear the sentence **Le da mucho dinero.**, can you tell whether **le** refers to a boy or a girl? [no]

Usted tiene diez pesos.   ® **Su papá le da mucho dinero.**

Which word is the indirect object pronoun? [**le**] Which word does **le** refer to? [**usted**]

SUGGESTED EXERCISE

Yo necesito un libro.	Yo le voy a dar uno.
Ana necesita un periódico.	Yo le voy a dar uno.
Juan necesita un peso.	Yo le voy a dar uno.
Yo necesito un disco.	Yo le voy a dar uno.
María necesita un boleto.	Yo le voy a dar uno.

T181

® **Juan nos escribe una carta.**

Which word means *to us*? [**nos**] Which word is the indirect object pronoun? [**nos**]

les

Juan y Pedro tienen diez pesos. ® **Su papá les da mucho dinero.**

Which word is the indirect object pronoun? [**les**] Who does **les** refer to? [**Juan y Pedro**]

María y Juana tienen diez pesos. ® **Su papá les da mucho dinero.**

Which word is the indirect object pronoun? [**les**] Who does **les** refer to? [**María y Juana**] If you hear the sentence **Les da mucho dinero.**, can you tell whether **les** refers to boys or girls? [no]

Ustedes tienen diez pesos. ® **Su papá les da mucho dinero.**

Which word does **les** refer to? [**ustedes**]

SUGGESTED EXERCISE

¿Sus amigos les cuentan muchas cosas?

1ST STUD. Sí, nos cuentan muchas cosas.

Point to two students. Note that 2nd response refers to first: (**A ellos**) **les cuentan muchas cosas.**

2ND STUD. Les cuentan muchas cosas.

¿Les hablan de sus vacaciones?
¿Les dicen adónde quieren ir?
¿Les traen fotos de esos lugares?
¿Les escriben durante las vacaciones?

Sí, nos hablan de . . . / Les hablan de . . .
Sí, nos dicen . . . / Les dicen . . .
Sí, nos traen . . . / Les traen . . .
Sí, nos escriben . . . / Les escriben . . .

▶ DRILLS 13–14, p. 164

Indirect object noun and pronoun in the same sentence

® **Le escribo una carta a María.**

Who am I writing a letter to? [**María**] What is the indirect object noun in this sentence? [**María**] If an indirect object noun is present in a sentence, is the indirect object pronoun also present? [yes]

SUGGESTED EXERCISE

María necesita un disco. Juan le da uno.
Las chicas necesitan un periódico. Juan les da uno.
Pepe necesita un boleto. Juan le da uno.
Susana necesita un libro. Juan le da uno.
Los gemelos necesitan un mapa. Juan les da uno.

Juan le da un disco a María.
Juan les da un periódico a las chicas.

Juan le da un boleto a Pepe.
Juan le da un libro a Susana.
Juan les da un mapa a los gemelos.

a + prepositional pronoun for clarity or emphasis

® **Le escribo.** ® **Les escribo.**

Can you tell from the first sentence whether I'm writing to a boy or a girl? [no] Can you tell from the second whether I'm writing to boys or girls? [no]

R **Le escribo a él.**   R **Les escribo a ellas.**

In the first sentence, am I writing to a boy or a girl? [a boy] And in the second? [to girls] These sentences mean *I'm writing to him*, *I'm writing to them* (feminine). *Explain that in order to emphasize an indirect object pronoun or to clarify the gender of* **le**, **les**, *or* **nos**, *a* + *a prepositional pronoun is used.* What is the English equivalent of **Me escribo a mí**? [*He's writing to me.*]

▶ DRILLS 15–19, pp. 164–166

More Indirect Object Constructions

Indirect objects for service–disservice verbs

¿Arregla mamá la casa?
R **No, Juan le arregla la casa a mamá.**

Who is cleaning the house? [**Juan**] For whom? [**mamá**] *Tell students that in Spanish, the indirect object is often used to indicate persons for whom a service or disservice is performed.*

Juanito está enfermo.
R **Mamá le toma la temperatura a Juanito.**

Who is taking the temperature? [**mamá**] Whose temperature is she taking? [**Juanito's**] What is the English equivalent of this sentence? [*Mom is taking Juanito's temperature.*] *Point out that in English a possessive construction is used, while in Spanish the indirect object construction is used. A definite article is used before the direct object in the Spanish sentence.*

▶ DRILLS 21, 22, and 23.1, p. 167

Meanings of sentences with indirect objects

Mi hermano Juan quiere esa bicicleta.
R **Le compro la bicicleta a Juan.**

What am I going to buy? [*a bicycle*] Am I going to buy it <u>from</u> **Juan** or <u>for</u> **Juan**? [for **Juan**]

Juan tiene dos bicicletas.
Yo necesito una bicicleta.
R **Le compro la bicicleta a Juan.**

And now, am I going to buy the bicycle <u>from</u> **Juan** or <u>for</u> **Juan**? [from **Juan**] How can you tell? [from the situation, from the explanation, from the context] *Explain that indirect objects in Spanish are used to indicate persons or things involved in the action of the verb. The kinds of involvement expressed by indirect objects are more varied in Spanish than in English. In fact, with some verbs, such as* **comprar**, *an indirect object construction may have more than one English equivalent.* **Le compro la bicicleta a Juan.** *may mean either* <u>I buy the bicycle for Juan.</u> *or* <u>I buy the bicycle from Juan.</u> *The way in which* **Juan** *is involved in the purchase is understood only from the context of the conversation.*

▶ DRILL 23.2, p. 167

Indirect Objects: Further Details

Ⓡ **Le traigo un regalo a María.**

What is the indirect object noun? [**María**] And the direct object noun? [**regalo**]

Ⓡ **Les compro un disco a los chicos.**

What is the indirect object noun? [**chicos**] And the direct object noun? [**disco**]

Ⓡ **Le arreglamos la casa a mamá.**

What is the indirect object noun? [**mamá**] And the direct object noun? [**casa**] *Tell
students that most verbs can take both direct and indirect objects. Some verbs, however,
can take only indirect objects.* **Encantar**, **gustar**, **parecer**, *and* **pasar** *take only indirect
objects when used with the meanings given on page 168.*

SUGGESTED EXERCISE

No me gusta esa escuela. (a ella)	No le gusta esa escuela.
(a ellos)	No les gusta esa escuela.
(a ti)	No te gusta esa escuela.
(a nosotros)	No nos gusta esa escuela.
(a mí)	No me gusta esa escuela.

SUGGESTED EXERCISE

Me encanta la idea (a nosotros)	Nos encanta la idea.
(a usted)	Le encanta la idea.
(a ellas)	Les encanta la idea.
(a ella)	Le encanta la idea.

SUGGESTED EXERCISE

¿Qué te pasa? (a él)	¿Qué le pasa?
(a ellos)	¿Qué les pasa?
(a usted)	¿Qué le pasa?
(a ti)	¿Qué te pasa?
(a nosotros)	¿Qué nos pasa?

Ⓡ **Me gusta esta escuela.**

What does this sentence mean in natural English? [*I like this school.*] What is the subject of the English sentence? [*I*] What is the subject of the Spanish sentence? [**escuela**]
*Point out that in sentences of this type the subject and object are the reverse of what
they are in the corresponding English sentences.*

Me gusta esta escuela.   Ⓡ **Me gustan estas escuelas.**

What is the subject of the second sentence? [**escuelas**] Is **escuelas** singular or plural?
[**plural**] What is the verb? [**gustan**] Which word does the verb agree with? [**escuela,
the subject**]

▶ DRILLS 25–29, pp. 168–170

T184

The Present Perfect

Write the verb forms on the board as you do this presentation.

Ⓡ **Tres veces he llamado.**   Ⓡ **Ya he marcado el número.**

Which two words make up the verb in the first sentence? [**he llamado**] And in the second? [**he marcado**] In both sentences, which word is the first part of the verb? [**he**] In each sentence, which word is the second part of the verb? [**llamado, marcado**] *Tell students that the present perfect is a compound tense in both Spanish and English. It consists of two parts: an auxiliary verb (**haber** in Spanish, <u>have</u> in English), and a form of the main verb called the past participle (**llamado**/<u>called</u>, **marcado**/<u>dialed</u>).*

Forms of haber

Ⓡ **Yo he llamado tres veces.**

Which form of **haber** corresponds to **yo**? [**he**]

Ⓡ **Tú has llamado tres veces.**

Which form of **haber** corresponds to **tú**? [**has**]

Ⓡ **Juan ha llamado tres veces.**

Which form of **haber** corresponds to **él, ella, usted**? [**ha**]

Ⓡ **Nosotros hemos llamado tres veces.**

Which form of **haber** corresponds to **nosotros**? [**hemos**]

Ⓡ **Los chicos han llamado tres veces.**

Which form of **haber** corresponds to **ellos, ellas, ustedes**? [**han**] Does the past participle change form to agree with the subject? [no]

SUGGESTED EXERCISE

Ya he marcado el número. (ella)	Ya ha marcado el número.
(tú)	Ya has marcado el número.
(ustedes)	Ya han marcado el número.
(nosotros)	Ya hemos marcado el número.
(la chica)	Ya ha marcado el número.
(yo)	Ya he marcado el número.

Formation of the past participle

Ⓡ **¿Ya ha llamado?**   Ⓡ **¿Ya ha salido?**

What is the ending of the past participle? [**do**] What is the ending attached to? [stem + theme vowel]

Ⓡ **No ha comido todavía.**

What verb class does **comer** belong to? [**e**–class] What is the theme vowel for the past participle of **e**–class verbs? [**i**] *Tell students that in the past participle the theme*

T185

vowel is *i* for both *e*–class and *i*–class verbs. *Point out that the auxiliary* **haber** *and the past participle are not usually separated in Spanish, although they frequently are in English:* **Ya he llamado tres veces.** / I've already called three times. *Do Letter-Sound Correspondences, p. 196.*

▶ DRILLS 6–11, pp. 183–184

acabar de + *Infinitive*

Ⓡ **Acaba de salir.**   Ⓡ **Acaba de empezar.**

Is the Spanish present perfect used to express (*he*) *has just* + past participle (for example, *He has just left. He has just begun.*)? [no] What special construction is used? [**acabar de** + infinitive] *Tell the students that* **acabar de** + *infinitive is used to express constructions like* He just began *as well as like* He has just begun.

▶ DRILL 12, p. 184

Past Participles as Adjectives

No he comido todavía.   **Los chicos ya han llegado.**

Does the past participle change form to agree with the subject in these sentences? [no]

Ⓡ **El cliente está equivocado.**   Ⓡ **Los alumnos están aburridos.**
Ⓡ **Las chicas están asustadas.**   Ⓡ **La línea sigue ocupada.**

Does the past participle show number and gender agreement with the noun it modifies in these sentences? [yes] Does the past participle function as an adjective or as part of the verb in these sentences? [as an adjective] *Point out that the past participle used as an adjective can occur with other verbs besides* **estar: parece enojado, sigue ocupada.**

▶ DRILLS 14–18, pp. 186–187

Adjective Position

Ⓡ **Tiene ojos azules.**

What is the position of the adjective in relation to the noun in this sentence? [immediately after] *Remind the students that descriptive adjectives, that is, adjectives which specify some quality or characteristic, normally occur after the noun in Spanish.*

Ⓡ **Hay muchas corbatas aquí.**   Ⓡ **¡Tiene tanto dinero!**

Tell students that there is another class of adjectives called limiting adjectives. Which word is the limiting adjective in each of these sentences? [**muchas, tanto**] What is the position of limiting adjectives in relation to the noun they modify? [before] *Tell students that limiting adjectives include cardinal and ordinal numbers, adjectives which* indicate quantity (*mucho*, *poco*, etc.) and possessive adjectives like *mi*, *tu*, *su*. Point out that some adjectives, like *bueno* and *malo*, occur freely before or after the noun they modify.

▶ DRILLS 19–20, pp. 188–189

¿Ha dejado algunos recados?	Ⓡ ¿Ha dejado algún recado?
És la primera señora que ha venido.	Ⓡ Es el primer señor que ha venido.

What is the number and gender of the noun in the second sentence in each pair? [masculine singular] What happens when adjectives like **alguno** and **primero** occur before a masculine singular noun? [They occur without the final **o**.] *Explain that certain adjectives drop the final o before a masculine singular noun. Those they have learned so far are* **alguno**, **bueno**, **malo**, **primero**, **tercero**, *and* **ninguno**. *Point out that* **grande** *has a shortened form,* **gran**, *which is used before any singular noun:* **un gran señor**; **una gran señora**. **Grande** *means* <u>great</u> *when used before a noun,* <u>large</u> *or* <u>big</u> *when used after a noun.*

▶ DRILLS 21–23, p. 189

conocer *and* saber

Ⓡ No sé cuál es la capital de Perú.	Ⓡ Conozco a ese señor.

Which word means *know* in the first sentence? [**sé**] Which word means *know* in the second sentence? [**conozco**] What is the infinitive form of **sé**? [**saber**] And of **conozco**? [**conocer**] *Tell the students that both* **saber** *and* **conocer** *correspond to the English verb* <u>know</u>. *Explain the difference in meaning between* **conocer** *and* **saber**. *See page 190.*

▶ DRILLS 25–26, pp. 190–191

Stem Alternation: e-i
i–*Class Verbs*

Write the forms of **pedir** *on the board as you do this presentation.*

Ⓡ Ni siquiera voy a pedir permiso.
Ⓡ Ni siquiera pedimos permiso.
Ⓡ Ni siquiera hemos pedido permiso.

In each of these sentences, which vowel occurs in the stem of the forms of **pedir**? [**e**] Is the syllable which follows the stem stressed or unstressed? [stressed] What vowel occurs in the stressed syllable that follows the stem? [**i**] Which vowel occurs in the stem when there is a stressed **i** in the next syllable? [**e**]

Ⓡ Ni siquiera pido permiso.
Ⓡ Ni siquiera pides permiso.
Ⓡ Ni siquiera pide permiso.

In each of these sentences, which vowel occurs in the stem of the forms of **pedir**? [**i**] Does the syllable which follows the stem have a stressed **i**? [no] Which vowel occurs in the stem when there is no stressed **i** in the next syllable? [**i**] *Point out that some i–class verbs have a type of stem alternation not found in a–class and e–class verbs: the last stem vowel is* **e** *if a stressed* **i** *occurs in the next syllable; otherwise, the last stem vowel is* **i**. *Tell students that the verbs they have studied so far which have this stem alternation are* **pedir**, **seguir**, **repetir**, *and* **servir**.

SUGGESTED EXERCISE

¿Pide usted permiso antes de salir?	1ST STUD. Sí, pido permiso, ¿y ustedes?
(*Have 1st stud. point to two others.*)	2ND STUD. Sí, nosotros pedimos permiso también.
¿Sigue usted resfriado?	Sí, sigo . . . ¿ . . . ? / Sí, nosotros seguimos . . .
¿Repite usted la lección?	Sí, repito . . . , ¿ . . . ? / Sí, nosotros repetimos . . .
¿Sirve usted la cena a las seis?	Sí, sirvo . . . , ¿ . . . ? / Sí nosotros servimos . . .
¿Le pido usted los apuntes al maestro?	Sí, le pido . . . al . . . , ¿ . . . ? / Sí, nosotros le pedimos . . .

▶ DRILLS 6–7, pp. 203–204

The Irregular Verb decir

®	No digo nada.	®	No decimos nada.
®	No dices nada.	®	No dicen nada.
®	No dice nada.	®	No voy a decir nada.

To what verb class does **decir** belong? [**i**–class] Does it have an **e-i** stem alternation? [yes] What other irregularity do you notice in the present tense forms of **decir**? [The first person singular (**digo**) is irregular.]

▶ DRILLS 9–12, p. 205

The Present Progressive

Write the verbs on the board as you do this presentation.

a-class verbs   ® **Está tomando agua.**   ® **García está molestando.**

Which two words make up the verb in the first sentence? [**está tomando**] And in the second? [**está molestando**] In both sentences, which word is the first part of the verb? [**está**] In each sentence, which word is the second part of the verb? [**tomando, molestando**] What is the theme vowel of **tomar** and **molestar**? [**a**] What ending is added to the stem + theme vowel of **tomar** and **molestar**? [**-ndo**] *Tell the students that the verbs in these sentences are examples of the present progressive. Point out that the present progressive is a compound tense in both English and Spanish. It consists of an auxiliary verb (*estar *in Spanish,* be *in English), followed by a form of the main verb called the present participle (*tomando */ *drinking). The present participle is formed by attaching* *the ending* **-ndo** *to the stem + theme vowel of the main verb. Only* **estar**, *never the present participle, changes form to show agreement with the subject.*

SUGGESTED EXERCISE

Estoy hablando por teléfono.　(él)　　　Está hablando por teléfono.
　(nosotros)　　　　　　　　　　　　　Estamos hablando por teléfono.
　(tú)　　　　　　　　　　　　　　　　Estás hablando por teléfono.
　(ellos)　　　　　　　　　　　　　　　Están hablando por teléfono.
　(él)　　　　　　　　　　　　　　　　Está hablando por teléfono.
　(yo)　　　　　　　　　　　　　　　　Estoy hablando por teléfono.

SUGGESTED EXERCISE

¿Va a llamar?　　　　　　　　Estoy llamando ahora.
¿Va a cenar?　　　　　　　　　Estoy cenando ahora.
¿Va a estudiar?　　　　　　　　Estoy estudiando ahora.
¿Va a practicar?　　　　　　　　Estoy practicando ahora.
¿Va a bailar?　　　　　　　　　Estoy bailando ahora.

e-class verbs and   Ⓡ **Usted no está poniendo atención.**   Ⓡ **Yo no estoy haciendo nada.**
i-class verbs

Which verb class do the present participles in these sentences belong to? [e–class]

i-class verbs   Ⓡ **¿Está escribiendo una carta?**   Ⓡ **¿Dónde está viviendo?**

Which verb class do the present participles in these sentences belong to? [i–class]
What is the theme vowel in the present participle of both **e**–class and **i**–class verbs?
[**ie**]

Ⓡ **Estoy leyendo el periódico.**

What is the present participle in this sentence? [**leyendo**] What is the infinitive form
of **leyendo**? [**leer**] What is the stem? [**le**] Does the stem end in a vowel or a consonant? [a vowel] How is the theme vowel written in the present participle? [**ye**]
Point out that in **e**-class *and* **i**-class *verbs whose stem ends in a vowel, like* **leer** *and*
creer, *and in the verb* **ir**, *the theme vowel of the present participle is spelled* **ye**.

SUGGESTED EXERCISE

¿Qué está haciendo?　(comer)　　　　¿Qué está comiendo?
　(leer)　　　　　　　　　　　　　　　¿Qué está leyendo?
　(escribir)　　　　　　　　　　　　　¿Qué está escribiendo?
　(traer)　　　　　　　　　　　　　　¿Qué está trayendo?
　(hacer)　　　　　　　　　　　　　　¿Qué está haciendo?

Verbs with e-i stem   **¿Cuándo van a servir?**   Ⓡ **Ya están sirviendo.**
alternation

What kind of stem alternation does **servir** have? [**e-i**] In the present participle, is
there a stressed **i** in the syllable which follows the stem? [no] What is the stem vowel
in the present participle of verbs with an **e-i** stem alternation? [**i**]

T189

¿Qué dicen?	¿Qué están diciendo?
¿Qué piden?	¿Qué están pidiendo?
¿Qué repiten?	¿Qué están repitiendo?
¿Qué sirven?	¿Qué están sirviendo?
¿Qué siguen?	¿Qué están siguiendo?

Explain the difference between the present progressive and the simple present tense in Spanish. See page 207. Point out that several verbs besides **estar** *may occur as auxiliaries before a present participle. See pages 207–208.*

▶ DRILLS 14–15, p. 208

Negative words

More about Negation

Algo le pasa.	Ⓡ **Nada le pasa.**

What is the negative counterpart of **algo**? [nada]

Alguien pone atención.	Ⓡ **Nadie pone atención.**

What is the negative counterpart of **alguien**? [nadie]

Alguno de los dos es mayor.	Ⓡ **Ninguno de los dos es mayor.**

What is the negative counterpart of **alguno**? [ninguno]

Algunas veces llueve.	Ⓡ **Nunca llueve.**

What is the negative counterpart of **algunas veces** (*sometimes*)? [nunca]

Eugenio también pide permiso.	Ⓡ **Eugenio tampoco pide permiso.**

What is the negative counterpart of **también**? [tampoco]

O el indio o el español . . .	Ⓡ **Ni el indio ni el español . . .**

What is the negative counterpart of **o . . . o . . .** (*either . . . or . . .*)? [ni . . . ni . . .]

SUGGESTED EXERCISE

Alguien viene.	Nadie viene.
También habla español.	Tampoco habla español.
Algunas veces llega tarde.	Nunca llega tarde.
Algo le parece mal.	Nada le parece mal.
Alguno de los dos es mejor.	Ninguno de los dos es mejor.

Position of negative words

Ⓡ **Nadie pone atención.**

What is the position of the negative word in relation to the verb? [before]

T190

Ⓡ **No pone atención nadie.**

What is the position of **nadie** in relation to the verb in this sentence? [after] What negative word precedes the verb? [**no**] *Point out that sentences using any of these negative words may occur in two forms, both with the same meaning. A negative word may precede the verb; it may also follow it. If it does, ho or another negative word must precede the verb. Tell the students that in Spanish, negation is marked at every opportunity:* **Yo no le doy nada a nadie nunca.**

▶ DRILLS 17–22, pp. 211–212

Possessive Adjectives

mi, tu

Ⓡ **Mi pluma y mi cuaderno.**   Ⓡ **Mis plumas y mis cuadernos.**

Which words express possession in these phrases? [**mi, mis**] Does **mi** show gender agreement? [no] Does it show number agreement? [yes]

Ⓡ **¿Me prestas tu pluma y tu libro?**   Ⓡ **¿Me prestas tus plumas y tus libros?**

Which words express possession in these sentences? [**tu, tus**] Does **tu** show gender agreement? [no] Does it show number agreement? [yes] *Tell students that this is just another case of grammatical agreement. The possessive adjectives agree with what is possessed, not with the possessor.*

SUGGESTED EXERCISE

(libro)   1ST STUD.   ¿Me prestas tu libro?
                           2ND STUD.   ¿Mi libro? Sí, aquí tienes.
(pluma)   ¿Me prestas tu . . . ? / ¿Mi . . . ? Sí,
                             aquí . . .
(apuntes)   ¿Me prestas tus . . . ? / ¿Mis . . . ? Sí,
                             aquí . . .
(lápiz)   ¿Me prestas tu . . . ? / ¿Mi . . . ? Sí,
                             aquí . . .
(cuaderno)   ¿Me prestas tu . . . ? / ¿Mi . . . ? Sí,
                             aquí . . .

▶ DRILLS 24.1–24.2, pp. 214–215

nuestro

Ⓡ **Vamos con nuestro abuelo y nuestra tía.**

Which words express possession in this sentence? [**nuestro, nuestra**]

Ⓡ **Vamos con nuestros abuelos y nuestras tías.**

Which words express possession in this sentence? [**nuestros, nuestras**] Does **nuestro** show gender agreement? [yes] Does it show number agreement? [yes]

▶ DRILL 24.4, p. 215

T191

® **Van con su tía y su tío.**   ® **Van con sus tías y sus tíos.**

Which words express possession in these sentences? [**su, sus**] Does **su** show number agreement? [yes] Does it show gender agreement? [no]

▶ DRILL 24.3, p. 215

® **Juan tiene un carro.**   **Su carro es azul.**
® **Susana tiene un carro.**   **Su carro es azul.**
® **Usted tiene un carro.**   **Su carro es azul.**

Which word names the possessor in the first pair of sentences? [**Juan**] And in the second? [**Susana**] And in the third? [**usted**] If you hear the sentence **Su carro es azul.**, can you tell if the possessor is a girl or a boy? [no] Can you tell if **su** refers to **él, ella,** or **usted**? [no]

® **Los chicos tienen un carro.**   **Su carro está aquí.**
® **Las chicas tienen un carro.**   **Su carro está aquí.**
® **Ustedes tienen un carro.**   **Su carro está aquí.**

Which word names the possessor in the first pair of sentences? [**los chicos**] And in the second? [**las chicas**] And in the third? [**ustedes**] If you hear the sentence **Su carro está aquí.**, can you tell if the possessor is one or more than one person? [no] *Tell students that when it is not clear from context which of the possible meanings of **su** or **sus** is intended, **su** or **sus** can be replaced by the appropriate form of the definite article before the noun, and **de** + **ustedes, él, ella, ellos,** or **ellas** after the noun.*

SUGGESTED EXERCISE

Juana tiene un carro.	1ST STUD. Su carro es muy bonito. 2ND STUD. El carro de ella es muy bonito.
Roberto tiene una bicicleta.	Su . . . es muy bonita / La . . . de él es . . .
Los gemelos tienen un álbum.	Su . . . es muy bonito. / El . . . de ellos es . . .
Las chicas tienen un carro.	Su . . . es muy bonito. / El . . . de ellas es . . .
Las hermanas García tienen unas primas.	Sus . . . son muy bonitas. / Las . . . de ellas son . . .
Los hermanos Pérez tienen unos regalos.	Sus . . . son muy bonitos. / Los . . . de ellos son . . .
María tiene una hermana.	Su . . . es muy bonita. / La . . . de ella es . . .
Ellos tienen una amiga.	Su . . . es muy bonita. / La . . . de ellos es . . .

▶ DRILLS 25–27, p. 215

*Point out that unlike English, Spanish often uses the definite article rather than a possessive adjective when it is obvious who the possessor is. Typical instances are with parts of the body and articles of clothing: **Tengo algo en el ojo.** Point out to the students that the possessive adjectives **mi** and **tu** do not have a written accent (as distinct from the pronouns **mí** and **tú**.)*

▶ DRILL 28, pp. 215–216

Direct Object Pronouns

lo, la

Digo el número.	Ⓡ Lo digo.
Encuentro el dinero.	Ⓡ Lo encuentro.
Busco al médico.	Ⓡ Lo busco.

Are the nouns in the first sentence in each pair masculine or feminine? [masculine] Are they singular or plural? [singular] Do they function as subjects or objects? [objects] Direct or indirect? [direct] (*If the personal* **a** *in the third pair causes difficulty, remind the students that the word* **a** *marks the direct object noun as referring to a person. It does not indicate an indirect object.*) Which direct object pronoun replaces a masculine singular noun phrase? [**lo**] *Point out that direct object pronouns make no distinctions between persons and things.* **Lo** *replaces both* **el número** *and* **al médico.** What is the position of the direct object pronoun in relation to the verb? [immediately before]

Repito la palabra.	Ⓡ La repito.
Veo la casa.	Ⓡ La veo.
Llamo a la chica americana.	Ⓡ La llamo.

What is the gender and number of the direct object noun in the first sentence in each pair? [feminine singular] Which direct object pronoun replaces a feminine singular noun phrase? [**la**]

SUGGESTED EXERCISE

¿Encuentra el boleto?	Sí, lo encuentro.
¿Encuentra el dinero?	Sí, lo encuentro.
¿Encuentra la pluma?	Sí, la encuentro.
¿Encuentra el cuaderno?	Sí, lo encuentro.
¿Encuentra la casa?	Sí, la encuentro.
¿Encuentra el disco?	Sí, lo encuentro.

SUGGESTED EXERCISE

¿Llama a la chica?	Sí, la llamo ahora.
¿Llama al señor?	Sí, lo llamo ahora.
¿Llama al médico?	Sí, lo llamo ahora.
¿Llama a la empleada?	Sí, la llamo ahora.
¿Llama a la secretaria?	Sí, la llamo ahora.

Hasta luego, Sr. García.	Ⓡ Lo veo mañana.
Hasta luego, Sra. Pérez.	Ⓡ La veo mañana.

In the first pair, am I speaking to a man or to a woman? [a man] Would I address **Sr. García** as **tú** or **usted**? [**usted**] Which direct object means *you*, referring to a male person one addresses as **usted**? [**lo**] In the second pair, am I speaking to a man or a woman? [a woman] Which direct object pronoun means *you*, referring to a female person one addresses as **usted**? [**la**]

La llamo mañana. (Dígale eso al Sr. López.)	Lo llamo mañana.
. . . al Sr. García.	Lo llamo mañana.
. . . a la Sra. Pérez.	La llamo mañana.
. . . a la Srta. Ruiz.	La llamo mañana.
. . . al médico.	Lo llamo mañana.
Dígame eso a mí.	Lo (la) llamo mañana.

los, las

No encuentro los apuntes.	Ⓡ **No los encuentro.**
No encuentro a los señores.	Ⓡ **No los encuentro.**

What is the number and gender of the direct object noun in the first sentence in each pair? [masculine plural] What direct object pronoun replaces a masculine plural noun phrase? [los]

No encuentro las cosas.	Ⓡ **No las encuentro.**
No encuentro a las chicas.	Ⓡ **No las encuentro.**

What is the gender and number of the direct object noun in the first sentence in each pair? [feminine plural] What direct object pronoun replaces a feminine plural noun phrase? [las]

Llamo a los chicos y a las chicas.   Ⓡ **Los llamo.**

What direct object pronoun replaces nouns of mixed gender? [los]

▶ DRILLS 6.1–6.2, pp. 228–229

Hasta luego, Juan y Pablo.	Ⓡ **Los veo mañana.**
Hasta luego, Susana y Cristina.	Ⓡ **Las veo mañana.**
Hasta luego, Susana y Pablo.	Ⓡ **Los veo mañana.**

In the first pair, am I speaking to boys or girls? [boys] Which direct object pronoun means *you*, referring to a group of boys or men? [los] In the second pair, am I speaking to boys or girls? [girls] Which direct object pronoun means *you*, referring to a group of girls or women? [las] In the last pair, am I speaking to boys, to girls, or to a mixed group? [mixed group] Which direct object pronoun means *you*, referring to a mixed group? [los]

me, te, nos

Tú no me quieres.   Claro que te quiero.   Él no nos quiere.

Are the direct object pronouns **me**, **te**, and **nos** the same as the corresponding indirect object pronouns? [yes]

▶ DRILLS 7–8, p. 229

Lo llamo.   Ⓡ **Lo llamo a él.**   **Te llamo.**   Ⓡ **Te llamo a ti.**

What words are added after the verb to emphasize or clarify a direct object pronoun? [a + a prepositional pronoun]

▶ DRILL 9, pp. 229–230

Direct vs. Indirect Objects

Lo dejo ir.   **Le permito ir.**

In the first sentence, does the verb take a direct or an indirect object? [direct] And in the second? [indirect] *Tell the students that they must learn the kinds of objects a Spanish verb may take as they learn the verb. Most verbs may take both direct and indirect objects. Verbs that have to do with some form of communication are typical.*

Ⓡ **Escribo la carta. La escribo.**
Ⓡ **Le escribo a Juan. Le escribo.**

In the first sentence, is the object direct or indirect? [direct] Does the direct object refer to what is written or to whom it is written? [what is written] In the second pair, is the object direct or indirect? [indirect] Does it refer to what is written or to whom it is written? [to whom it is written] *Explain that for verbs of this type (for example,* **preguntar, gritar, decir, escribir, contestar**) *the person communicated with is the indirect object; what is communicated is the direct object.* **Llamar***, though it seems like a verb of communication, takes a direct object for the person called:* **Llamo a Juan. Lo llamo.**

▶ DRILLS 11–13, pp. 231–232

The Infinitive as the Object of a Preposition

Ⓡ **Me mata si le hablo de ir de compras.**   Ⓡ **Nunca viene sin llamar.**
Ⓡ **¿Siempre pides permiso antes de salir?**

Which words are the prepositions in these sentences? [**de, sin, antes de**] Which form of the verb immediately follows the preposition? [the infinitive]

▶ DRILLS 15–17, pp. 233–234

Possessive Adjectives: Long Forms

Ⓡ **Una amiga mía dice eso.**   Ⓡ **Esas amigas tuyas no saben nada.**
Ⓡ **¿Es un amigo suyo?**   Ⓡ **Son unos amigos nuestros.**

Which is the word that expresses possession in each of these sentences? [**mía, tuyas, suyo, nuestros**] What is its position in relation to the noun? [after] Does it agree in gender and number with the noun it modifies? [yes]

Juan tiene un carro.	Las chicas tienen un carro.
Este carro es suyo.	Este carro es suyo.
↓ Ⓡ Este carro es de él.	↓ Ⓡ Este carro es de ellas.

Tell students that **suyo**, like **su**, can refer to any third person possessor. Which words can replace **suyo** to clarify the meaning? [**de** + a prepositional pronoun] *Explain to the students in which situations long form possessive adjectives are used. See page 234.*

▶ DRILLS 19–22, pp. 236–237

T195

Generic Use of the Definite Article

Ⓡ **Los carros son caros.**

This sentence means, *"Cars are expensive"*. When I say *"Cars are expensive."*, am I referring to cars in general or to specific cars? [cars in general] The word *generic* means *"referring to a class of things as a whole, rather than to any particular member of the class"*.

Los carros son caros.   **Las mujeres hablan mucho.**
La geografía es fácil.

When the subject noun is used in a generic sense in Spanish, what part of speech is the word that precedes it? [the definite article]

▶ DRILLS 24–25, pp. 237–238

Irregular Past Participles

The purpose of this presentation is to elicit the irregular past participles that the students have already learned. First, tell the students that some Spanish verbs have an irregular past participle, then elicit each past participle through questions on familiar material and personalized questions. The students should answer with complete sentences. In some responses object pronouns can be used, but it may be preferable not to insist on them since you are focusing on another point.

¿Están abiertas las tiendas a las diez de la mañana?	Sí, están abiertas.
Y el mercado, ¿está abierto también?	Sí, está abierto también.
¿He abierto la puerta?	Sí, usted ha abierto la puerta.

What is the past participle of **abrir**? [**abierto**]

¿He dicho cuál es la lección para mañana?	No, usted no ha dicho cuál es . . .
¿He dicho que todos aquí pronuncian bien?	No, usted no ha dicho que . . .
¿He dicho quién es el mejor alumno de la clase?	No, usted no ha dicho quién es . . .

What is the past participle of **decir**? [**dicho**]

¿Ustedes ya han escrito la tarea para esta clase?	No, nosotros no hemos escrito la . . .
¿Hay un trabajo escrito para mañana?	Sí, hay un trabajo escrito . . .

What is the past participle of **escribir**? [**escrito**]

Según Cecilia, ¿Ana ya ha hecho la lista?	No, no la ha hecho todavía. (*or* No, no ha hecho la lista todavía.)

T196

¿Ya ha hecho usted todo su trabajo para mañana?	No, no lo he hecho todavía.

What is the past participle of **hacer**? [**hecho**]

¿Dónde ha puesto usted sus libros?	Los he puesto en el pupitre (la mesa, el suelo).
¿Los ha puesto en el pupitre?	Sí, los he puesto en . . .

What is the past participle of **poner**? [**puesto**]

¿Alguien ha visto al maestro de inglés?	Sí, yo he visto al . . .
¿Han visto ustedes todos los partidos de fútbol este año?	Sí, hemos visto todos . . .

What is the past participle of **ver**? [**visto**]

A fines de agosto, ¿ya han vuelto ustedes de las vacaciones?	No, no hemos vuelto todavía.
En el diálogo **Un dictado** (*Unit 11*), ¿ya ha vuelto Eugenio cuando la maestra empieza el dictado?	No, no ha vuelto todavía.

What is the past participle of **volver**? [**vuelto**]

▶ DRILLS 5–9, pp. 249–250

Reflexive Pronouns

® **Sólo yo me presento.**	® **Sólo nosotros nos presentamos.**
® **Sólo tú te presentas.**	® **Sólo ellos se presentan.**
® **Sólo él se presenta.**	

Which word means *myself*? [**me**] *yourself* (familiar)? [**te**] *himself*? [**se**] *ourselves*? [**nos**] *themselves*? [**se**] What is the position of these words in relation to the verb? [immediately before] *Tell students that reflexive pronouns are object pronouns which are the same in reference as the subject. In English they end in -self or -selves (He cut himself.).* Which of the reflexive pronouns is different from the corresponding direct and indirect object pronouns? [**se**]

® **Juan se presenta tarde.**	® **Susana se presenta tarde.**
	® **Usted se presenta tarde.**

Does **se** show gender agreement, like **lo** and **la**? [no]

® **Los chicos se presentan tarde.**	® **Las chicas se presentan tarde.**
	® **Ustedes se presentan tarde.**

Does **se** show number agreement, like **le** and **les**? [no]

▶ DRILLS 11–12. p. 252

Reflexive Pronouns with Service-Disservice Verbs

Mamá le lava las manos a Juanito.   Ⓡ **Mamá se lava las manos.**

In the first sentence, whose hands is Mom washing? [**Juanito's**] In the second sentence, is she washing someone else's hands or her own hands? [her own hands] What is the equivalent of the second sentence in natural English? [*Mom is washing her hands.*] *Point out that in English the direct object is preceded by the possessive adjective* (her). Is the direct object preceded by the definite article or by the possessive adjective in Spanish? [the definite article]

▶ DRILLS 14–17, pp. 253–254

More about Reflexive Pronouns

Juan asusta a las chicas.   Ⓡ **Juan se asusta.**

What is the subject of both sentences? [**Juan**] What is the direct object of the first sentence? [**las chicas**] In the second sentence, who receives the action—that is, who gets frightened, **Juan** or the girls? [**Juan**] What then is the direct object in the second sentence? [**se**] In the second sentence, is the direct object the same or different in reference as the subject? [the same] What is the equivalent of the second sentence in natural English? [*Juan gets frightened.*] *Tell students that some Spanish verbs always have a direct object. Explain that if the direct object is the same in reference as the subject, a reflexive direct object pronoun is used in the Spanish sentence, while the English equivalent may show no object at all (**Me preocupo.** I worry.), use get + an adjective, (**Se asusta.** He gets frightened.), or use words like up or down (**Se sienta.** He sits down.). There is a list of verbs of this type on page 255.*

SUGGESTED EXERCISE

Mamá viste a los chiquitos.	Mamá se viste.
José moja las ventanas.	José se moja.
El señor aburre a los muchachos.	El señor se aburre.
El maestro asusta a los alumnos.	El maestro se asusta.
Yo levanto al chiquito.	Yo me levanto.
Tú preocupas a tu mamá.	Tú te preocupas.
Yo presento a mis amigos.	Yo me presento.

Point out that certain verbs are always reflexive when they are used with particular meanings. See pages 254–256.

▶ DRILLS 19–30, pp. 256–259

Object Pronouns in Sequence

Write the second sentence in each pair on the board as you do this presentation.

¿Me da la maleta, por favor?	Ⓡ ¿Me la da, por favor?
Te presto los apuntes.	Ⓡ Te los presto.
Nos dice el nombre.	Ⓡ Nos lo dice.
Se pone los guantes.	Ⓡ Se los pone.

In each pair, is there a direct object noun in the first sentence? [yes] How does the second sentence in each pair differ from the first? [The noun is replaced by a pronoun.] Which word is the direct object pronoun in each second sentence? [the second word: **la, los, lo, los**] Which word is the indirect object pronoun? [the first word; **me, te, nos, se**] What is the position of the direct object pronoun in relation to the indirect object pronoun? [immediately after]

▶ DRILL 7.1, p. 270

Ya le doy la maleta.	Ⓡ Ya se la doy.
¿Les prestas el carro?	Ⓡ ¿Se lo prestas?

What single object pronoun replaces both **le** and **les** immediately preceding another object pronoun beginning with the letter **l**? [**se**]

▶ DRILLS 7.2–14, pp. 270–272

Position of Object Pronouns

After a present participle

Ⓡ **García nos está molestando.**

Which word is the object pronoun in this sentence? [**nos**] What word does it precede? [**está**]

(Write the next sentence on the board.)

Ⓡ **García está molestándonos.**

Which word does **nos** follow in this sentence? [**molestando**] What form of the verb is **molestando**? [present participle]

(Write the second sentence of the next pair on the board when you say it.)

Ⓡ ¿Me estás poniendo atención?   Ⓡ ¿Estás poniéndome atención?

Which word does the object pronoun precede in the first sentence? [**estás**] Which word does it follow in the second? [**poniendo**] What form of the verb is **poniendo**? [present participle] In these sentences, are the forms of **estar** verb forms with a person-number ending? [yes] *Remind students that object pronouns may precede a verb with a person-number ending; point out that they may also follow a present participle. If they do, the present participle and the object pronouns are written as one word. The present participle requires a written accent on the stressed syllable when one or more object pronouns are attached to the end.*

T199

As you do this presentation, write the second sentence in each pair on the board.

Ⓡ **¿Me puedo lavar las manos?**   Ⓡ **¿Puedo lavarme las manos?**

Which word does the object pronoun precede in the first sentence? [**puedo**] Which word does it follow in the second? [**lavar**]

Ⓡ **Mi papá me lo va a comprar.**   Ⓡ **Mi papá va a comprármelo.**

Which word do the object pronouns precede in the first sentence? [**va**] Which word do they follow in the second? [**comprar**] In these two pairs, are the words **puedo** and **va** verbs with a person-number ending? [yes] What form of the verb are **lavar** and **comprar**? [infinitive] *Point out that object pronouns may follow an infinitive. If they do, the infinitive and the object pronouns are written as one word. The infinitive requires a written accent on the stressed syllable when more than one object pronoun is attached to the end.*

▶ DRILLS 15–16.2, pp. 274–275

Nominalization

La maleta negra.   Ⓡ **La negra.**

What is the English equivalent of these two phrases? [*The black suitcase. The black one.*]

Esa maleta no.   Ⓡ **Ésa no.**

What is the English equivalent of these two phrases? [*Not that suitcase. Not that one.*] In both of these pairs, what word occurs in the English equivalent of the second phrase? [*one*] In the examples in Spanish, how does the second phrase in each pair differ from the first? [The noun is omitted.] *Tell students that the deletion of **maleta** from the noun phrase in these sentences is called* nominalization*; the adjective now functions as a noun.*

SUGGESTED EXERCISE

¡Por favor, la maleta mía!	¡Por favor, la mía!
Y la maleta mía también.	Y la mía también.
¿Cuál maleta is la maleta suya?	¿Cuál es la suya?
¿La maleta roja?	¿La roja?
No, la maleta negra.	No, la negra.
La maleta que acaba de tocar.	La que acaba de tocar.
Esa maleta.	Ésa.

Tell students that nominalized demonstrative adjectives have a written accent on the stressed syllable: **ese baúl → ése.**

▶ DRILLS 18–20, pp. 276–278

Comparatives: más/menos . . . que

Ⓡ **Esta escuela es más bonita que la otra.**
Ⓡ **Juan es menos alto que Pepe.**

Which words mean *more . . . than* in the first sentence? [**más . . . que**] Which words mean *less . . . than* in the second sentence? [**menos . . . que**] *Tell students that sentences of this type are called comparative sentences. In English, we use* -er *or* more/less *. . .* than *in comparative sentences.*

SUGGESTED EXERCISE

Pedro es alto. Juan es más alto.	Juan es más alto que Pedro.
Olga es linda. Ana es más linda.	Ana es más linda que Olga.
Pedro es listo. Luis es más listo.	Luis es más listo que Pedro.
José es simpático. Juan es más simpático.	Juan es más simpático que José.
Lupe es baja. Ella es menos baja.	Ella es menos baja que Lupe.
Ellos son perezosos. Ella es menos perezosa.	Ella es menos perezosa que ellos.
Toni es pretencioso. Chucho es menos pretencioso.	Chucho es menos pretencioso que Toni.

Ⓡ **Yo soy más perezoso que tú.**   Ⓡ **Él es más alto que yo.**

If a pronoun follows **que**, is it the subject pronoun or the prepositional pronoun? [the subject pronoun]

SUGGESTED EXERCISE

(Make certain that students use adjectives in the appropriate gender.)

alto	1ST STUD. Yo soy más alto que tú.
	2ND STUD. No, yo soy más alto que tú.
perezoso	Yo soy más perezoso . . . / No, yo soy . . .
listo	Yo soy más listo . . . / No, yo soy . . .
delgado	Yo soy más delgado . . . / No, yo soy . . .
alto	Yo soy más alto . . . / No, yo soy . . .

Irregular comparative adjectives

Este libro es bueno.   Ⓡ **El otro es mejor.**
Este programa es malo.   Ⓡ **El otro es peor.**

Which word is used instead of **más bueno**? [**mejor**] Which is used instead of **más malo**? [**peor**]

Mi papá es joven.   Ⓡ **Mi mamá es menor.**
Mi abuela es vieja.   Ⓡ **Mi abuelo es mayor.**

Which word is used instead of **más joven**? [**menor**] Which is used instead of **más viejo**? [**mayor**] *Point out that* **más bueno**, **más malo**, *and* **más joven** *are used interchangeably with* **mejor**, **peor**, *and* **menor**. **Más viejo**, *however, is not completely interchangeable with* **mayor**. **Más viejo** *classifies the person or object as old:* **Mi abuelo es más viejo que mi abuela**. **Mayor** *simply describes an age relationship; it does not imply that the persons* or objects described are old: **Ana es mayor que María**; or, if I wish simply to describe an age relationship between my grandfather and my grandmother: **Mi abuelo es mayor que mi abuela.**

▶ DRILLS 22.1–22.2, pp. 279–280

▶ DRILLS 22.1–22.2, pp. 279–280

de instead of que *before numbers*

Yo tengo más dinero que tú.
Ⓡ Yo tengo más de cien pesos.

Ana tiene más equipaje que yo.
Ⓡ Ana tiene más de tres maletas.

Is there a number in the first sentence in each pair? [no] And in the second? [yes] In the second sentence in each pair, which word is used to mean *than*? [**de**]

▶ DRILL 26, p. 281

▶ DRILL 26, p. 281

Superlative construction

Yo soy alto; Juan es más alto.
Ⓡ Pero Pedro es el más alto de todos.

María es una buena alumna; Ana es mejor.
Ⓡ Pero Juana es la mejor alumna de la escuela.

Paco es perezoso; Jorge es menos perezoso.
Ⓡ Pero Juan es el menos perezoso de todos.

To express the ideas *most, least,* what kind of word is placed before **más** or **menos** or an irregular comparative adjective? [a definite article] In sentences like these, which word is the equivalent of *in*? [**de**]

▶ DRILLS 23–27, pp. 280–281

▶ DRILLS 23–27, pp. 280–281

UNIT 15

Infinitives as Verb Complements

Ⓡ ¿No me puede dar la mía ahora?   Ⓡ Prometo no gastar mucho.
Ⓡ ¿Desea dejar algún recado?   Ⓡ ¿Quieres escuchar unos discos?
Ⓡ Debe ser muy bonita.

Does the first verb in each sentence have a person-number ending? [yes] Does the second? [no] What is the form of the second verb? [infinitive] *Tell students that many Spanish verbs may be followed by an infinitive or an infinitive phrase.*

▶ DRILLS 5–7, p. 294

▶ DRILLS 5–7, p. 294

More about Infinitives as Verb Complements

Verbs which require a *before an infinitive*

Ⓡ Vamos a estar en vacaciones.   Ⓡ ¿Aprenden a hablar español?

What word precedes the infinitive in each of these sentences? [**a**] *Tell students that some Spanish verbs require the preposition **a** before an infinitive. The ones they have encountered so far are listed in the chart on p. 295.*

T202

Students should answer with complete sentences.

¿Aprenden a hablar español aquí?	Sí, aprendemos a hablar . . .
¿Ya comienzan a hablar bien?	Sí, ya comenzamos a hablar . . .
¿Quién les enseña a hablar español?	Usted nos enseña a hablar . . .
¿Usted sale a bailar esta noche? *(Call on a girl.)*	Sí (No), yo (no) salgo a . . .
¿Quién la invita a bailar?	(Mi novio) me invita a bailar.
¿A qué hora empieza a hacer su tarea?	Empiezo a hacer mi tarea a . . .
¿A qué hora lo llama a cenar su mamá?	Me llama a cenar a las . . .
¿Viene a la escuela a jugar o a estudiar?	Vengo a estudiar.
¿Aprende a escribir francés aquí?	No, aprendo a escribir español.

Verbs which require de before an infinitive

Ⓡ **Acaba de salir.**   Ⓡ **¿Cuándo terminas de escribir la tarea?**

What word precedes the infinitive in these sentences? [**de**] *Tell students that some Spanish verbs require the preposition* **de** *before an infinitive. The ones they have encountered so far are* **acabar** *and* **terminar.**

Ⓡ **Tengo que estudiar.**

tener que

What word precedes the infinitive in this sentence? [**que**] *Tell the students that in the expression "have to",* **tener** *requires* **que** *before the infinitive.*

▶ DRILLS 9–12, pp. 297–298

Adverbs with -mente

Here you may wish to explain that an adverb is a word which may be used to modify a verb, an adjective, or another adverb.

Ⓡ **Ella no es muy bonita, francamente.**   Ⓡ **¡Es absolutamente imposible!**
Ⓡ **Voy a hablar con su jefe inmediatamente.**

Which words are the adverbs in these sentences? [**francamente, absolutamente, inmediatamente**, the ones which end in **-mente**] What suffix do they end in? [**-mente**] What part of speech is the word to which the suffix is attached? [an adjective] Is it attached to the masculine or to the feminine form? [feminine]

▶ DRILLS 14–16, p. 298

Comparatives: tan/tanto . . . como

tan

Ⓡ **Ellos no están tan tristes como yo.**
Ⓡ **Cristina no aprende tan fácilmente como tú.**

Which words mean *as . . . as* in these sentences? [**tan . . . como**] What part of speech is the word that follows **tan** in the first sentence? [an adjective] And in the second sentence? [an adverb] *Tell students that **tan** can be followed by either an adjective or an adverb. **Tan** never changes form.* If a pronoun follows **como**, is it the subject pronoun or the prepositional pronoun? [the subject pronoun]

SUGGESTED EXERCISE

¿Es usted tan alto como yo?	No, yo no soy tan alto como usted.
¿Es Ana tan alta como María?	No, Ana no es tan alta como María.
¿Habla usted tan rápido como yo?	No, yo no hablo tan rápido como usted.
¿Habla español tan bien como inglés?	No, no hablo español tan bien como inglés.
¿Es el inglés tan fácil como el español?	No, el inglés no es tan fácil como el español.

▶ DRILLS 17.1, 18.1, and 19, pp. 300–301

The adjective tanto

Ⓡ **Él no tiene tanto dinero como ella.**
Ⓡ **Ellos no tienen tantos problemas como yo.**
Ⓡ **Yo no tengo tanta prisa como ella.**

Which words mean *as much . . . as* or *as many . . . as*? [**tanto, tantos, tanta . . . como**] Do the forms of **tanto** modify a noun in these sentences? [yes] Do they show gender and number agreement? [yes] What part of speech does **tanto** function as in these sentences? [an adjective]

The adverb tanto

Ⓡ **Los otros no sufren tanto como yo.**

Does **tanto** modify a noun in this sentence? [no] Does it modify a verb? [yes] Does **tanto** function as an adverb or as an adjective in this sentence? [as an adverb]

SUGGESTED EXERCISE

¿Hay tantos muchachos como muchachas aquí?	Sí, hay tantos muchachos como muchachas.
¿Hay tantos maestros como alumnos aquí?	No, no hay tantos maestros como alumnos.
¿Hay tantos alumnos de francés como alumnos de español?	Sí (No), (no) hay tantos alumnos de francés como alumnos de español.
¿Hablan los chicos tanto como las chicas?	Sí (No), los chicos (no) hablan tanto como las chicas.
¿Molestan las chicas tanto como los chicos?	Sí (No), las chicas (no) molestan tanto como los chicos.

▶ DRILLS 17.2, 18.2, 18.3, and 20, pp. 300–301

Additional Structure Drills

Unit 3

Section B

SINGULAR → PLURAL

Pienso en el Día de la Madre.   Pensamos en el Día de la Madre.
Cierro la ventana.   Cerramos la ventana.
Empiezo el examen   Empezamos el examen.
Pienso en la fiesta.   Pensamos en la fiesta.
Cierro la puerta.   Cerramos la puerta.
Empiezo más tarde.   Empezamos más tarde.

Unit 3

Section D

DIRECT → INDIRECT ADDRESS

Usted pronuncia bien, Srta. Pérez.   La Srta. Pérez pronuncia bien.
¿Dónde está usted, Sr. Vargas?   ¿Dónde está el Sr. Vargas?
Usted habla muy bien, Sra. López.   La Sra. López habla muy bien.
¿Cómo está usted, Srta. Pérez?   ¿Cómo está la Srta. Pérez?
Usted llega tarde, Sr. Vargas.   El Sr. Vargas llega tarde.
Usted tiene que practicar más, Sra. López.   La Sra. López tiene que practicar más.

INDIRECT → DIRECT ADDRESS

El Sr. García pronuncia bien.   Usted pronuncia bien, Sr. García.
La Srta. Pérez llega tarde.   Usted llega tarde, Srta. Pérez.
La Sra. González habla muy bien.   Usted habla muy bien, Sra. González.
El Sr. Castro tiene que estudiar.   Usted tiene que estudiar, Sr. Castro.
La Srta. Díaz necesita practicar.   Usted necesita practicar, Srta. Díaz.

Unit 6

Section D

PATTERNED RESPONSE

Nosotros vamos al partido, y tú?   Yo voy también.
Ana va al centro, ¿y su hermana?   Su hermana va también.
Yo voy a la biblioteca, ¿y ustedes?   Nosotros vamos también.
Ustedes van a la fiesta, ¿y nosotros?   Ustedes van también.
Los chicos van al cine, ¿y las chicas?   Las chicas van también.
Pedro va al estadio, ¿y usted?   Yo voy también.

Unit 10

Section C

PERSON-NUMBER SUBSTITUTION

La maestra parece enojada.   La maestra parece enojada.
Tú _____.   Tú pareces enojado.
El médico _____.   El médico parece enojado.
La criada _____.   La criada parece enojada.
Ustedes _____.   Ustedes parecen enojados.
El jefe _____.   El jefe parece enojado.
Las señoras _____.   Las señoras parecen enojadas.

AUDIO INDEX

Unit		Full-Track Tape	Two-Track Tape	12″ Records
1	Section A	Reel 1	Reel 1 Track 1	Record 1 Side 1
	Section B	Reel 2	Reel 1 Track 2	Record 1 Side 2
2	Section A	Reel 3	Reel 2 Track 1	Record 2 Side 1
	Section B	Reel 4	Reel 2 Track 2	Record 2 Side 2
	Section C	Reel 5	Reel 3 Track 1	Record 3 Side 1
	Section D	Reel 6	Reel 3 Track 2	Record 3 Side 2
3	Section A	Reel 7	Reel 4 Track 1	Record 4 Side 1
	Section B	Reel 8	Reel 4 Track 2	Record 4 Side 2
	Section C	Reel 9	Reel 5 Track 1	Record 5 Side 1
	Section D	Reel 10	Reel 5 Track 2	Record 5 Side 2
4	Section A	Reel 11	Reel 6 Track 1	Record 6 Side 1
	Section B	Reel 12	Reel 6 Track 2	Record 6 Side 2
	Section C	Reel 13	Reel 7 Track 1	Record 7 Side 1
	Section D	Reel 14	Reel 7 Track 2	Record 7 Side 2
5	Section A	Reel 15	Reel 8 Track 1	Record 8 Side 1
	Section B	Reel 16	Reel 8 Track 2	Record 8 Side 2
	Section C	Reel 17	Reel 9 Track 1	Record 9 Side 1
	Section D	Reel 18	Reel 9 Track 2	Record 9 Side 2
6	Section A	Reel 19	Reel 10 Track 1	Record 10 Side 1
	Section B	Reel 20	Reel 10 Track 2	Record 10 Side 2
	Section C	Reel 21	Reel 11 Track 1	Record 11 Side 1
	Section D	Reel 22	Reel 11 Track 2	Record 11 Side 2
7	Section A	Reel 23	Reel 12 Track 1	Record 12 Side 1
	Section B	Reel 24	Reel 12 Track 2	Record 12 Side 2
	Section C	Reel 25	Reel 13 Track 1	Record 13 Side 1
	Section D	Reel 26	Reel 13 Track 2	Record 13 Side 2
8	Section A	Reel 27	Reel 14 Track 1	Record 14 Side 1
	Section B	Reel 28	Reel 14 Track 2	Record 14 Side 2
	Section C	Reel 29	Reel 15 Track 1	Record 15 Side 1
	Section D	Reel 30	Reel 15 Track 2	Record 15 Side 2
9	Section A	Reel 31	Reel 16 Track 1	Record 16 Side 1
	Section B	Reel 32	Reel 16 Track 2	Record 16 Side 2
	Section C	Reel 33	Reel 17 Track 1	Record 17 Side 1
	Section D	Reel 34	Reel 17 Track 2	Record 17 Side 2
10	Section A	Reel 35	Reel 18 Track 1	Record 18 Side 1
	Section B	Reel 36	Reel 18 Track 2	Record 18 Side 2
	Section C	Reel 37	Reel 19 Track 1	Record 19 Side 1
	Section D	Reel 38	Reel 19 Track 2	Record 19 Side 2

Unit		Full-Track Tape	Two-Track Tape	12" Records
11	Section A	Reel 39	Reel 20 Track 1	Record 20 Side 1
	Section B	Reel 40	Reel 20 Track 2	Record 20 Side 2
	Section C	Reel 41	Reel 21 Track 1	Record 21 Side 1
	Section D	Reel 42	Reel 21 Track 2	Record 21 Side 2
12	Section A	Reel 43	Reel 22 Track 1	Record 22 Side 1
	Section B	Reel 44	Reel 22 Track 2	Record 22 Side 2
	Section C	Reel 45	Reel 23 Track 1	Record 23 Side 1
	Section D	Reel 46	Reel 23 Track 2	Record 23 Side 2
13	Section A	Reel 47	Reel 24 Track 1	Record 24 Side 1
	Section B	Reel 48	Reel 24 Track 2	Record 24 Side 2
	Section C	Reel 49	Reel 25 Track 1	Record 25 Side 1
	Section D	Reel 50	Reel 25 Track 2	Record 25 Side 2
14	Section A	Reel 51	Reel 26 Track 1	Record 26 Side 1
	Section B	Reel 52	Reel 26 Track 2	Record 26 Side 2
	Section C	Reel 53	Reel 27 Track 1	Record 27 Side 1
	Section D	Reel 54	Reel 27 Track 2	Record 27 Side 2
15	Section A	Reel 55	Reel 28 Track 1	Record 28 Side 1
	Section B	Reel 56	Reel 28 Track 2	Record 28 Side 2
	Section C	Reel 57	Reel 29 Track 1	Record 29 Side 1
	Section D	Reel 58	Reel 29 Track 2	Record 29 Side 2
R.M.*	Section A	Reel 59	Reel 30 Track 1	Record 30 Side 1
	Section B	Reel 60	Reel 30 Track 2	Record 30 Side 2

*Recombination Material

Key to Pronunciation Exercises

[a]

UNIT 1   p. T27
UNIT 2   p. T37
UNIT 15 p. T131 (unstressed position)

[e]

UNIT 1   p. T25
UNIT 2   p. T37
UNIT 15 p. T131 (unstressed position)

[i]

UNIT 1   p. T27
UNIT 2   p. T37
UNIT 3   p. T40   (i + vowel)
UNIT 5   p. T59   (i + vowel)
UNIT 13 p. T117 (i + vowel)
UNIT 15 p. T131 (unstressed position)

[o]

UNIT 1   p. T26
UNIT 2   p. T37
UNIT 15 p. T131 (unstressed position)

[u]

UNIT 1   p. T27
UNIT 2   p. T37
UNIT 5   p. T58   (u + vowel)
UNIT 10 p. T91   (u vs. Eng. *yuw*)
UNIT 13 p. T118 (u + vowel)
UNIT 15 p. T131 (unstressed position)

VOWELS: CONTRASTING PAIRS

UNIT 6   p. T61   (stressed position)
UNIT 6   p. T63   (unstressed position)

DIPHTHONGS
[ay], [ey], [oy], [uy]

UNIT 2   p. T36
UNIT 14 p. T121

[aw], [ew]

UNIT 7   p. T70
UNIT 14 p. T123

VOWEL COMBINATIONS

UNIT 3   p. T40   (i + vowel)
UNIT 5   p. T59   (i + vowel)
            p. T59   (u + vowel)
UNIT 13 p. T117 (i + vowel)
            p. T118 (u + vowel)

VOWEL SEQUENCES
IN MORE THAN ONE WORD

UNIT 6   p. T66
UNIT 11 p. T96

VOWEL CLUSTERS: [a], [e], [o]

UNIT 8   p. T81
UNIT 14 p. T124

[r]

UNIT 1   p. T28
            p. T29   (r vs. rr)
UNIT 4   p. T47   (r vs. đ)
            p. T50   (before consonant)
            p. T51   (after consonant)
UNIT 9   p. T83
            p. T86   (r vs. rr)
            p. T87   (after consonant)
            p. T87   (before consonant)
UNIT 11 p. T101 (final r)
UNIT 12 p. T106 (r vs. t)
UNIT 15 p. T128 (đ, r, t)

[rr]

UNIT 1   p. T29
            p. T29   (r vs. rr)
UNIT 9   p. T84
            p. T86   (r vs. rr)
UNIT 15 p. T127 (intervocalic rr
                     vs. initial rr)

[d] *and* [đ]

UNIT 1   p. T30
            p. T31   (đ)
            p. T31   (d vs. đ)
UNIT 4   p. T47   (r vs. đ)
UNIT 8   p. T78   (d vs. đ)
            p. T80   (b̶, đ, g̶)
UNIT 15 p. T128 (đ, r, t)

T208

Sample Lesson Plan (Unit 11)

	REVIEW	PRESENT	ASSIGN FOR HOME STUDY	LABORATORY
DAY 1	• Test from previous unit	• 1st half of Basic Dialog • 1st half of Supplement • Vocabulary Exercises 1 and 2	• 1st half of Basic Dialog and Supplement (Use take-home disk)	
DAY 2	• 1st half of Basic Dialog and Supplement • Selected items from Vocabulary Exercises 1–2	• 2nd half of Basic Dialog • 2nd half of Supplement • Basic Forms • Vocabulary Exercises 3–5 • Listening Exercise 178 • Pronunciation Exercise 179	• 2nd half of Basic Dialog and Supplement (Use take-home disk)	
DAY 3	• Entire Basic Dialog and Supplement • Basic Forms • Selected items from Vocabulary Exercises 3–5.	• Stem Alternation: **e–i, i–** Class Verbs Use Teacher Presentation • Drills 6–7	• Stem Alternation: **e–i, i–** Class Verbs Student Presentation Generalization • Drill 8: Writing Exercise • Ex. 1 (*Exercise Book*)	• Section A
DAY 4	• Basic Dialog and Supplement briefly • Drills 6–7	• The Irregular Verb **decir** Use Teacher Presentation • Drills 9–12 • Listening Exercise 182 • Pronunciation Exercise 183	• The Irregular Verb **decir** Generalization • Drill 13: Writing Exercise • Ex. 2–3 (*Exercise Book*)	
DAY 5	• Stem Alternation: **e–i,** including **decir** • Drills 9–12	• The Present Progressive • Use Teacher Presentation • Drills 14–15	• The Present Progressive Student Presentation Generalization • Drill 16: Writing Exercise • Ex. 4–6 (*Exercise Book*)	• Section B
DAY 6	• Basic Dialog and Supplement • Drills 14–15	• More about Negation Use Teacher Presentation • Drills 17–19 • Recombination Dialog I • Pronunciation Ex. 185–186	• More about Negation Student Presentation Generalization • Drill 23: Writing Exercise • Ex. 7–8 (*Exercise Book*)	
DAY 7	• Basic Dialog and Supplement • More about Negation • Drills 17–19	• Drills 20–22 • Recombination Dialog II • Recombination Dialog III	• Drills 20–21 (oral) • Ex. 9–10 (*Exercise book*)	• Section C
DAY 8	• Drills 20–22	• Possessive Adjectives Use Teacher Presentation • Drills 24–28 • Recombination Dialog IV	• Possessive Adjectives Student Presentation Generalization • Drill 29: Writing Exercise • Ex. 11–12 (*Exercise Book*)	
DAY 9	• Drills 24–28	• Narrative • Listening Exercise 188 • Pronunciation Exercise 189	• Narrative and Questions (oral) • Multiple Item Substitution, page 216	
DAY 10	• Recombination Dialogs • Narrative (Ask questions) • Any material necessary to prepare students for test	• Rejoinders	• Review of Unit 11 for test • Dialog Rewrite, p. 217	• Section D

Teaching Culture by Dr. Nelson Brooks

Culture, for the foreign language teacher, is something more than the way to hold a fork and something more than listening to a string quartet. The social amenities are a valid part of culture, and so are all kinds of esthetic experience. But the core of culture is, first of all, what distinguishes a man from his dog; it is also what distinguishes a man living to the east of the Rhine from one living to the west. Put another way, the first question of culture is: What makes this animal human? And the second: What makes this human animal French (or German or Japanese)? The language teacher has an easy time with the first question, for our man can talk whereas his dog can't. (And culture began, of course, with the invention of language.) But the second question is much harder, and involves not only how people talk but what their talk refers to—which, upon reflection, turns out to be no less than their entire way of thinking and living, including their use of table silver and their enjoyment of music. The first task of the teacher is to become aware of the character and scope of the field of culture, then to narrow his perspective to that view of it which is appropriate to foreign language instruction.

The study of culture as a supplement or complement to learning words and sentences permits the student to arrive at a better grasp of meaning in the target language, a meaning that is less in terms of his own experience and more in terms of those whose native language it is. Simply stated, teaching culture means bringing into awareness, making explicit and significant, that which is already inherent in the language being learned. The *full* meaning of a language is found only in the culture to which it belongs. When a foreign word stands for something more or other than its mere lexical equivalent in the student's mother tongue, the difference is an index of the "otherness" that characterizes a life-way similar to, yet unlike, his own. The totality of this life-way is the culture to which every segment of language directly leads.

The foreign equivalent of such common American words as *school, home, breakfast, lunch hour, price, football, vacation* and a multitude of others often represents something notably different from what our students are acquainted with. Very different also may be the general attitude toward those who are engaged in formal study, whether as teacher or students. At the same time the teenager who is not in school may be quite free from the appearance of failure suggested by our word *drop-out.*

Cultural differences often come even closer to grammar itself. For example, with whom may one use the various equivalents of the word *you* and the related forms of verb, pronoun, and adjective? What is implied in addressing a person whose name is James as "Jim"? Is an overtone of friendliness or deprecation suggested by the use of an ending as in the change from *dear* to *dearie* or from *lad* to *laddie*. The student needs to know that nicknames and suffixes in the foreign language may bear a surprising measure of familiarity, affection, or disparagement.

But together with difference there is also its counterpart, sameness. The ties that bind mother and child, members of the same family, fraternity brothers, all the speakers of a common language, are universal and are likely to be deep and strong. The appreciation of beauty, the power of taboo, the precedence established by the facts of age or wealth, of brains or physical strength, are to be found everywhere. A surface difference may hide a fundamental sameness, and this discovery is not the least of the rewards that come with the awakened perception of how another nation lives.

If culture is to be more than an occasional interlude in the language course, an ornament to be inserted when time permits, if instead it is to be a central part of daily work, answers must be found to a number of pertinent questions:

How are we to define culture?

How is our concept of culture to be related to the teaching of grammar and the skills?

How are students to be briefed on this element of their learning task?

Where are we to begin?

How is the notion of culture to evolve as the learner advances?

How are we to envision the total perspective of a culture?

What is Culture?

Several different meanings are packaged together in the word *culture*. Two of them merit the special attention of the language learner. One refers to the expression and appreciation of esthetic talent in the various fine arts: music, literature, painting, dancing, and the like. The other refers to the ways in which the members of a language community live, believe, speak, and act in relation to each other, to themselves, to their surroundings, and to the community which they form. These two concepts are equally important but they differ widely in nature and in the role they may play in the language course. The first concept, culture as artistic expression, has long been popular with teachers, who need little encouragement toward its inclusion in their classes—provided the learning of the skills is not made to suffer as a result. The second concept, the life-way of an entire language community, is so comprehensive in nature and is to such an extent participated in by everyone, old and young and in all circumstances, that its inclusion in the language class, from a beginner's course to the most advanced studies, is entirely possible and fully appropriate.

Culture, Grammar, and the Skills

In themselves, grammar and the skills are vehicles of expression, and they can be examined and even mastered as such. But if the cargo they bear is to have psychological meaning, we are led directly to the culture in which they are rooted. Intonations, agreements, verb forms, pronouns, and the like should be modeled for the learner in ways not only linguistically correct but also culturally valid. The difference between *thanks* and *thank you* is both a matter of grammar (noun vs. verb, etc.) and of appropriate use. The drills for learning grammar and the skills have the right and the need to be enlivened with the magic of cultural meaning.

Briefing the Student

At the start, students are likely to think that culture means theater, concerts, museums, and literary works rather than information like that found in the texts and pictures presented by the National Geographic Society. He needs to know that culture means both, and that nothing is more typical of a foreign people than the language they use, whether it be while eating with one another or while composing a poem in solitude. The workings of a foreign language can be modeled, imitated, and learned in one's own country. But for meaning, the student must go, in imagination if not in fact, to the foreign country and observe language in action in its own territory. This realization will help him appreciate the value of that part of class time in which English is put aside by everyone. For nothing is more characteristic of a foreign people, wherever we may observe them, than the use of their own language without reference to any other. Once the student has perceived that culture can mean both art and life, he will realize that it may be studied in a systematic way with different emphases, at times upon the individual and his relation to society and at times upon the appreciation of the arts. How is he to distinguish readily between culture as art and culture as life? A useful way of marking the distinction will be to call one meaning *Culture MLA* (music, literature, arts) and the other *Culture BBV* (belief, behavior, values). When the word is encountered in general reading, both student and teacher will do well to pause and each ask himself: "Which meaning is intended here, Culture MLA or Culture BBV?" Although the learner will observe culture of both types bit by bit as he goes along, he should bear in mind that each segment of culture has its full significance only as part of a totality.

Where to Begin?

The study of culture rightly begins in the language the student is learning—which implies that this language bears or could bear a cultural meaning. The grammar of "Where is my aunt's pen?" is impeccable, but the expression is culturally empty. Questions such as "Where is your friend's house?" or "Where is your dog's collar?" display the same grammar and are also something one person might be likely to say to another in a meaningful situation. The dialogue form that has become popular in the initial phase of language learning provides ample scope both for linguistic forms that are being methodically learned and for situations that are culturally alive.

Culture in Succeeding Levels

As the language course progresses through one year after another, the cultural complement achieves a better balance between daily living and artistic expression. In passages that are studied, in books that are read, in pictures that are presented, in descriptions that are given of the organization of society in the foreign country, the two types of culture we have distinguished emerge more and more clearly as the learner continues to gain the language competence that is his essential aim.

The Total Perspective

While encountering culture in a programmatic way as it makes its presence felt in the language being learned, the student is entitled to a comprehensive overview of what he is studying, just as he needs a comprehensive review of grammar. Like language itself, culture is a double-ended structure with the individual at one end and the social group at the other. Our present interest is to concentrate upon culture as it appears in the individual; eventually we shall observe how the individual relates to the institutions of society. We do not actually see culture, any more than we see the wind. What we see are its effects. Where are we to look for the totality of these effects? This may be done by seeking out salient points in personal thought and behavior at which the effects of interest to us become discernible. The features they present will differ from one country to another, yet the fact of their presence everywhere will soon become apparent.

Without attempting at this point to enter upon a systematic and detailed scrutiny of all the facets of culture, we may consider a selective list of topics of immediate interest that can provide a useful and representative overview for the beginning student, whose first concern is to observe and understand culture from the point of view of the individual.

Ties That Bind
Learning
Language and Life
In the Family
Fun and Games
Diplomas and
  Hard Knocks
Mine and Thine
Walls and Clocks
Formal Worship
Art and Chic

Land, Wind, and
  Weather
Sick or Injured
Poise and Charm
Vive la Difference!
Heroes and Taboos
Pecking Order
Gifts, Honors,
  and Awards
Food and Drink
Keeping Fit

Golden Rule
Special Days
Time Off
Wit and Humor
Pomp and Circumstance
The True, the Good,
  and the Beautiful
Earning a Living
Rights and Duties
Society and Self

Interrelation and overlapping in these salient points will at once be apparent. This is all to the good, for it reminds the learner that each segment of a culture is fully meaningful only as it plays its part in a totality. A list like the one above can be of value to anyone who wishes to arrive at an estimate of a culture, of any individual member of it, or (and this is by no means the least important) of his own personal relationship to the culture in which he lives.

How can these topics be put to use in foreign language study when culture is being taught and learned? Viewed in the light of this list, any dialogue or passage, any story or character in a story, any situation or individual or group, any proverb or idiom will take on added dimensions. Revealed will be unsuspected connotations and associations, habits of thought, and taken-for-granted assumptions, insights, values, and depths of meaning. These are characteristic effects upon the individual that the field of culture in which he exists has. These effects, in turn, are reflected back from him upon the culture as a whole. At first glance the list may seem too long. Further thought may suggest that it is too short. At all events, one can hardly say that a just impression or estimate of any culture or any member of it can be reached without taking into account what is referred to here.

Culture Components of the New Second Edition

1. At the end of the student textbook, a 32-page full-color *Culture Supplement* with information in Spanish.
   The insert is composed of eight sections:

   Educación
   Recreación y deportes
   La familia
   Hablando de comidas
   Donde vive la gente
   La electricidad y los bananos
   No tenemos "teenagers"
   Hispanoamericanos en Estados Unidos

2. In this *Teacher's Edition*, a special section with the following material:
   ▶ "Teaching Culture," an essay by Dr. Nelson Brooks.
   ▶ Background notes on the full-color culture supplement.
   ▶ An essay in English on each of the above cultural topics giving additional background information on the supplement.
3. An *Activity Book* with exercises on the culture supplement.
4. *Culture Filmstrips* containing the same pictures as the culture supplement.
5. *Recordings* of the information and captions in the supplement and of separate picture descriptions that are printed in the Activity Book.

Notes on the Full-Color Culture Supplement

Introduction

The culture supplement is divided into 8 sections: *Educación, Recreación y deportes, La familia, Hablando de comidas, Donde vive la gente, La electricidad y los bananos, No tenemos "teenagers,"* and *Hispanoamericanos en Estados Unidos.* In the teacher's pages, you will find for each of these culture sections a corresponding essay in English designed to give additional background information. The Activity Book provides the student with the basic background information, items of vocabulary necessary to discuss each topic, and culture and vocabulary exercises. You may want to present *Educación* after Unit 4, *Recreación y deportes* after Unit 5, *La familia* after Unit 6, *Hablando de comidas* after Unit 8, *Donde vive la gente* after Unit 9, *La electricidad y los bananos* after Unit 10, *No tenemos "teenagers"* after Unit 13, and *Hispanoamericanos en Estados Unidos* after Unit 14 or 15. However, this order of presentation may be modified to fit any individual situation.

How to Use the Culture Supplement

Give the students, in English, any background information on the topic you may deem necessary. If the students have the Activity Book, you may ask them merely to follow the instructions given in the book.

The procedure followed in the Activity Book for most pictures requires the student to:

1. read the brief text in English stating the culture points illustrated by the picture.
2. look at the picture and read the corresponding information in Spanish.
3. do the exercises based on the culture content of the picture. (In these exercises, the students will have to use new words and phrases from the Spanish text, but they will not have to manipulate new structures.)
4. read the Spanish descriptions of the picture, provided in the Activity Book. (As they read, the students may listen to the recording of this text or look at the black and white picture reproduced in the Activity Book with additional vocabulary, to identify what is mentioned in this text. At this point it may be useful for the student to listen to the recording of the text a second time, while looking at the color picture in the textbook or the filmstrip.)
5. do the exercises based on the above-mentioned text.
6. read the concluding comments in English.

Background Essays

Education *by H. Ernest Lewald*

Schools everywhere seem much the same. Students are required to go to class, prepare homework, and pass exams. And everywhere they are told what to do, and especially what not to do, by teachers and administrators.

Yet, from one part of the world to another, there are differences. A classroom is part of a special system that is shaped by cultural traditions and local circumstances. Thus, schools south of the Río Bravo (which we in the United States call the Rio Grande) do differ in significant ways from those we are acquainted with in our own country.

Throughout Latin America students enter secondary school following five or six years of grade school. But different nations organize secondary education in different ways.

Mexico, for instance, has a five-year secondary program, after which the student has to complete two further years of "preparatory" school before entering the university.

In Argentina and Uruguay there are three different kinds of schools in secondary education: normal school, commercial school, and the *liceo*. The first type combines high school with elementary-teacher training; the second is basically a business school where bookkeeping, secretarial skills, and English are emphasized; the *liceo* has a traditional slant and offers general academic subjects (ancient history and Latin, for instance, in addition to such standard courses as geography, literature, physics, mathematics, and a modern language). The *liceo* is the only one of the three types that leads to admission to a university.

In general, secondary school programs throughout Latin America run for five or six years, but seldom offer any electives to the student.

In addition to these differences in the way they organize secondary education, Latin American schools also differ from those in the United States in other ways. For instance, if we ask who goes to high school in Latin America, we will find what is perhaps the most important difference.

Statistics are far from accurate, but it is a certainty that not every boy or girl goes to high school. In the large towns of even the richest Latin American countries, such as Venezuela or Argentina, the answer might be at best one out of five children of high school age. In the mountains or jungles of the poorer nations, maybe one in a hundred.

Why so few? The lack of a large middle class in underdeveloped regions means that most people there are either very rich or very poor. Children in very poor families usually must work; if not that, then their parents don't have the money to send them to school. And even if they could afford it, the free public schools are usually so crowded that many children would have to be turned away.

This brings up the matter of private versus public secondary schools. The public ones are free but overcrowded. Parents are often told that their child may have to wait several years before being admitted. Thus, families that can afford it will put their children in private schools.

These private schools are mostly parochial, since Catholicism is the dominant religion in all of Latin America. Other private schools are usually French, English, or German high schools that were originally founded for the children of foreign residents but which soon found favor with the local inhabitants, who sent their children to learn a second language there.

In some countries, notably in Mexico, the rigorous class divisions reflected in this system are lessened somewhat by laws requiring every private school to offer a certain number of scholarships to poor students.

What do Latin American high schools look like? With the exception of a few foreign or modern showcase schools, nothing like the average complex in the United States. The typical secondary school in Lima, Santiago, or Montevideo is located in an old town house on some crowded street, with only a plaque or emblem at the door to indicate what is inside. Usually a huge double door opens past the street-front rooms into a sunlit patio, Spanish style. Stairs lead to a second story, around which there is a balcony. On both floors, rooms are built around the walk that looks out onto the patio. Some classrooms have no windows, but in general all are furnished with a blackboard, desk for the teacher, and rows of chairs or benches holding up to thirty students.

At noon there is a recess, and everybody goes home. There are no lunch rooms or cafeterias. There are also no such entertaining things as gymnasiums, stadiums, workshops, or libraries—nor, naturally, intramurals, newspapers, or bands. They are all too expensive and would take up space that the two-story house could not possibly provide, in addition to requiring costly equipment and technical supervision.

Allowing for lunch at home, school resumes for another three-hour session beginning at two or three in the afternoon. In some regions, however, when students go home for lunch they are through for the day, and a new group of students comes in for the afternoon session, in order for the school to take care of more students.

Teachers in the secondary school system seldom stay at any one school for more than a couple of hours a day, since most are part-time and have to teach in two or more schools in order to make a decent living. Most of them are women and well qualified in their fields, holding the equivalent of a master's degree.

Public school teachers are paid by the national government (rather than by the municipal government as in the United States); and all teachers, including those in private schools, have to be approved or certified by a national ministry of education and culture that is based on European models. Textbooks and examinations too are standardized nationally. Theoretically this is intended to insure the same level of achievement for schools in the rural areas as for those in the capital or big cities, but it doesn't often work out that way.

The grading system is usually based on numbers, most frequently running from zero to ten, with six as the passing grade. Ten amounts to an "A-plus" but is seldom seen.

Summer vacations start in December and end in February or March in South American countries, since their seasons are the reverse of those in the Northern Hemisphere. Mexico used to share that schedule with its Latin American sister republics, but recently changed its school year to coincide with that of the United States.

Teachers in out-of-the-way country schools sometimes have to wait months for their pay checks; nevertheless, teachers and students alike share a feeling of being socially an elite, way above the average person in their country, since they know they represent a small and highly select group that, through education, is united both to the universal achievements of the past and to a worldwide community of educated people.

Leisure and Sports *by H. Ernest Lewald*

Many of the activities with which we are all familiar have existed as long as mankind itself. Take spectator sports, for example. The Ancient Romans had their circuses in which gladiators dueled to the death in the arena, and amphitheaters in which comedies had the audience rolling in the aisles. Spain was a Roman colony for centuries; thus every major town had its arena.

The bullring—offering blood, sand, and final death by the horns or the sword—is a direct descendant of the Roman arena or coliseum; And today some Latin American countries—among them Mexico, Peru, Colombia, and Venezuela—carry on this most Spanish of all spectator sports, which some of its defenders say is not a sport at all but a quasi-religious ceremony with deep pagan roots. Nowadays, however, the most popular spectator sport in much of the Spanish-speaking world, as well as in Europe and Africa, is the game called *fútbol* or soccer.*

Like the words *sport, esport,* and *deporte, fútbol* is an English term that invaded Latin America around 1900, largely through British influence. Having little in common with American-type football, it is a very fast game in which the players use their feet to dribble a spherical ball and try to kick it into a net defended by a goalie. (A version of American football is played in Latin America but either goes under its original English name, *rugby,* or is called *fútbol americano.*)

Madrid today has its bullring that seats some 80,000 people, but it also has a soccer stadium with a capacity of way over 100,000. The Latin Americans naturally had to outdo their former colonizers and have built even larger stadiums, which are filled every weekend.

Latin American crowds are quite excitable and at times violent. Thus, fights frequently break out, and mounted police and even a tear-gas squad are often on hand for the big games. In the summer of 1969 Honduras and El Salvador actually had a "football war," triggered by a match in Mexico City between the teams of these two Central American neighbors. That war took thousands of lives.

Fútbol stars are of course national heroes. The Brazilian player Pelé has become an international figure, and streets the world over have been named after him. *Béisbol's* popularity is evident from the number of players from these countries who have made the big leagues in the United States. Most of the Spanish terms in this game are adaptations from English: for example, *pitcher, estraik,* and *jonrón.*

Other spectator sports, such as polo and tennis, draw small and highly select groups of upper-class fans. None of these sports can come close to *fútbol* in popularity.

What about women as sports fans? Of course, a lot depends on country and social class, but in most Hispanic countries women are expected to stay home and listen to the soap operas (in general even more tasteless than similar fare in the United States) endlessly offered on the radio and on TV.

Most families do not have a TV set as yet, but they can usually visit a neighbor who has a set and doesn't mind sharing it, or they can go to the movies. In fact,

*Baseball, however, has become the top-ranking spectator sport in Panama, Nicaragua, Venezuela, and the Caribbean countries.

Latin Americans are movie-goers, and whole families often crowd into theaters showing double or triple features. Babies are also included in these theater parties, since poor families do not have maids and the custom of "baby-sitting" is not yet established in Latin America.

Taking an active part in sports is not common among the lower classes. Most of these people use up all their energy just to survive. The *campesino* labors in the field, from dawn to dusk, and millions of the very poor in the mountains of Andean countries or the desert areas of Mexico or northeast Brazil are constantly underfed. Even if they had the energy, they could not afford to buy equipment to hunt, play golf, or go scuba diving.

Sports were an invention of the European nobility. Since a gentleman could not do physical labor, yet needed to stay trim, the landed gentry found ways of getting exercise while having fun doing so. Upper-class Latin Americans continue this tradition, and quite a few of them play polo. But a polo pony costs about 20,000 dollars, and a player needs several ponies to be effective.

One thing that less fortuante families can do is have outings. On Sundays, groups ranging from grandparents to babies have picnics in such places as the famous Chapultepec Park inside Mexico City. Young people kick an old soccer ball around; older ones put a hook and line on a bamboo stick and head for a river. (In Latin America any stream, even the tiniest creek, is called *rio*.)

Perhaps the best and cheapest outdoor entertainment is going to the beaches. Since most Latin Americans now live in urban zones near the Atlantic or Pacific Ocean, they can take a city bus and spend the day at any one of the endless sandy beaches. They are mostly free and open.

If the average Latin American family should ever get to own a car—and the VW factories in Mexico and Brazil are turning out more and more each year—a revolution in leisure habits would surely change the sports activities too.

In Mexico this revolution is already in progress. On Sundays, for a hundred miles around Mexico City, all the recreational facilities are crowded and the roadsides are jammed with picnicking facilities, with the older folks clustered around their parked cars and the children scattered in the woods and fields.

The Family *by H. Ernest Lewald*

Family and home naturally go together, in Latin America as well as everywhere else.

The moderately well-to-do Latin American family might rent or own a house built in the traditional Spanish or colonial shape. The house borders directly on the sidewalk and stands wall-to-wall with neighboring houses. One or two rooms, called *salas,* have heavily grilled windows opening onto the street. A hallway connects the front door with the patio. The traditional patio is always the physical and social center of the house, is usually full of flowers and vines, with maybe a tree or two, and has a number of windowless rooms opening either directly onto it or onto a porchlike corridor along its edges. The kitchen, bath, and servants' quarters are in the rear.

Few such houses have a heating system or air-conditioning. Luckily, winters are mild throughout most of Latin America, and in summer the patio with the coolness of its tiled floor and shady plants and trees is a good place to sit.

Now, who lives in such a house? Naturally the head of the family with his wife, and they will be in one of the nice *salas*. Next come the children, sometimes a son with his wife and sometimes an unmarried daughter, no matter if she is 15 or 50. Spanish and Latin American children usually don't try to leave home until they are married and have a good job, something that might take twenty years of looking. Then we often find a grandmother, an aunt, a sister-in-law, and grandchildren. All of them would share the smaller rooms. A servant girl may sleep in a little room on the roof. Thus it is social importance that determines living arrangements in the house; and if a grandfather owns it, he would sleep in the nicest *sala*.

With so many people around, the house is never empty, privacy is limited, and baby-sitting is unknown. Everybody meets constantly in the patio and talks about what is going on in the world, in the neighborhood, and in the family.

The way of talking to each other is still fairly traditional too. Older people are listened to politely because age means experience and knowledge.

Another sign of this politeness is that older people are given the title of *don* or *doña* coupled with their first name. This is similar to being called "sir" or "ma'am," and may be used by children even with young adults in their twenties. The principle is that *don* or *doña* may be used in addressing anybody who is obviously a generation or so older than the speaker. Thus as one grows older, one becomes "*don* Pedro" or "*doña* Maria" to more and more people.

In some countries children use the *usted* form when talking with grown-ups in the family, often including their parents, because it sounds more respectful. Adults use *tú* with children except when they become angry, at which point they switch to *usted* and the child quickly switches to another room.

Family spirit in Latin America is not only strong but far-reaching. Second and third cousins are considered part of the family and may show up to stay for months while looking for a job in the city. Weddings and funerals bring together the whole clan down to third cousins, and there are endless meals at which everybody catches up on family news and gossip.

Family loyalty is practically a social law. It demands that one put the family name and needs above the interests of the outside world, even if at times it might be necessary to ignore or even break the law in order to save a relative in distress.

The family also serves as a kind of mutual aid society. If *don* José needs a lawyer or a dentist, he will look first of all for a relative, believing that he would get better service and be charged less, for the sake of the family spirit. If *doña* Emilia wants to buy a couch or a stove, she will try a relative first and expect to find a specially low price tag. And if young Dorotea or Luis just graduated from the *Instituto Comercial* and needs an office job, *tío* Paco, who just happens to be a bank manager, will be invited for a big family dinner to discuss the chances of "giving the kid a break."

An extension of the family is *compadrazgo,* which is a socially established form of kinship. This results from the practice of choosing a godfather or godmother for the newborn child. The terms *comadre* and *compadre* refer to the relation of the godparents to the child's actual parents; they become co-parents. Since godparents accept the obligation to look out for the child later on in life, they are chosen with great care—if possible, from among the rich and powerful. *Compadrazgo* is especially popular with the poor, who want to give their children a chance to go to school or live with a well-to-do family some day. Needless to say, a large landowner or a wealthy widow will be very much in demand, and some of them have numerous godchildren, sometimes twenty or more.

Maids, usually country girls or Indian women who charge less, who probably never saw the inside of a schoolhouse, might earn 15 to 30 dollars a month and sleep in a six-by-four room. But if they stay long enough with one family, they have the same rights and privileges as poor distant relatives. Then they can expect hand-me-downs for themselves, medicine for their sick father, or a phone call to City Hall if their brother is in trouble with the police. It is a system that sometimes works almost as well as *compadrazgo*.

One further link to family interests is *personalismo*. It is this oldest form of human relations that in Latin America has become an art. Basically *personalismo* refers to the practice of making as many friends and contacts as possible because you never know when you might need one of them to do you a little favor. Without using *personalismo* you can sit from 9 o'clock to 4 in the office of the *Registro Civil* waiting for a birth certificate, and be told at 4:05 to come back *mañana*. Nobody in his right mind would head for a municipal, state, or federal office without first calling a friend who has a friend who works there. But, on the other hand, perfect strangers will suddenly try to help you in every way they can if they should find out that your friend who probably never saw the inside of a schoolhouse is also their friend, or if they should, for no apparent reason, decide to befriend you.

Even high school and college students stand to benefit from *personalismo*. If their teacher is an old friend of anyone in the family, he cannot very well hand out a failing grade, or even a barely passing grade, without offending the whole family.

Human relations are complicated, but Latin Americans generally know how to make the best of them—and also the most of them.

Talking about Food *by H. Ernest Lewald*

The old saw "Tell me what you eat and I will tell you who you are" is not so far-fetched. Only when close to starvation will most human beings stop being fussy about the source, mode of preparation, and the taste of the food they are willing to eat.

At other times food and drink are closely tied to the way of life of a given region anywhere in the world. Many Indian communities in the Americas live on corn; most Asian ones, on rice. Arabs and Jews refuse pork; Hindus don't eat beef. Americans have sandwiches for lunch, and the French are known to spend up to fifty percent of their income on meals.

Once again we have to remember that the Hispanic world includes Spain as well as the whole of one continent and a third of another—and that this world contains many regions, from the tropical islands in the Caribbean to the Argentine pampas. Each region produces its own kind of food and has its own ways of cooking it. But still, we could not know what any particular family eats until we had found out not only what region it was from, but also whether that family was rich or poor, black or Indian, *mestizo* or *criollo*.

Let us look first at the Indian and his land. From the upper Rio Bravo (or Rio Grande) to Panama, the Pueblo, Toltec, Aztec, and Mayan civilizations lived principally on corn. Each community worked the *milpas* (or corn fields) as one big family. Just as in Longfellow's *Hiawatha*, the corn and rain gods had to be kind to their Indian children because nature was not. The land that stretches from Oklahoma down to Guatemala has little enough good soil, few trees, and hardly any water. Today, almost as if time had stood still for 500 years, all over the parched *meseta* of Mexico and in the border areas of Texas and Arizona, Indian women rise at daybreak, start a fire, grind the corn into flour, then make a thick dough by adding water, pat the dough flat and bake a few *tortillas,* after having heated some *frijoles* (beans) and a pot of water for some thin coffee. Wealthier *campesinos* might raise *chinacates* (a type of chicken) or *guajalotes* (small turkeys) and eat *huevos rancheros* (eggs on top of a *tortilla* with a hotly spiced sauce) before going to work in the fields. Dishes like *tacos* (*tortillas* wrapped around a filling of cheese, meat, or beans), *enchiladas* (*tacos* made with *tortillas* that have been spread first with a hotly spiced sauce), and *guacamole* (a salad made of cut-up or mashed avocados, tomatoes, and onions, sometimes with *chiles*) are very little known in other Latin American countries and not at all in Spain. Only the Mexican *tomatl* spread throughout the world as the *tomate* or tomato.

In Central America vegetation is more tropical and food more abundant. A few miles out of Guatemala City, Indian women carry baskets and trays with pineapples, avocados, or *plátanos* (bananas), which they sell for pennies. There are over fifty varieties of *plátanos,* some of which have to be stewed, fried, or baked before being eaten. Central America gave the Western world *chocolatl* or *cacaohuatl,* which the Spaniards called *cacao* and we call "cocoa bean." Among the Mayans during classical times, only the nobles and priests could freely enjoy a cup of hot chocolate. According to their religion, the common people had to wait for their chocolate delights in the next world.

On the barren mountainsides of the former Incan empire along the Pacific coast of South America, food is hard to come by. The Indians in what now remains of the *ayllu* or village community live on something like a thousand calories a day, eating mainly potatoes, corn and dried fish. Many of them chew the leaves of the *coca* tree, from which cocaine is derived, in order to appease their hunger and to forget their miserable condition. *Papa,* the Quechua word for the common potato, was the gift of the Indian peoples to the Spaniards, who took the word, the plant, and its fruit back to Europe, probably in 1524. Earlier the *batata* had arrived from the Caribbean islands, and the confusion of names led to the use of *patata* as the common name for both, which still holds in Spain, though *papa* is ordinarily used throughout Latin America.

In the tropical Caribbean, on the coasts of Venezuela and Brazil, and, to a lesser extent, around the Gulf of Mexico, African cooking and names for foods are common. For instance, *quimbombó* or *quingombó* (gumbo soup), *ñame* (yam), *gandinga* (tripe stew), and *calalú* (a leafy vegetable). The list of tropical fuits is almost endless, as there are *guayabas, papayas, chirimoyas,* and *mangos,* which may be eaten raw or made into juices, jams, or used in hot dishes. And there is always *cocada,* a sweet made mainly of dried shredded coconut.

Whereas people near the ocean live off the sea, eating *atún* (tuna) as well as *camarones* (shrimp), the Gauchos drive their big herds of cattle across the endless pasturelands of the pampas in Argentina, Uruguay, and southern Brazil and believe that the only thing that makes a meal is a hunk of meat. In the good old days the Gaucho down in chilly Patagonia made a campfire, roasted a young steer or a sheep, and ate four or five pounds of fresh meat, washing it down with an endless supply of *mate,* an Indian tea from Paraguay that is drunk from a special gourd cup, also called *mate.* There were no vegetable gardens or grocery stores in the pampas in the old days, and no women there to spend hours beside the fire preparing *tortillas.* Today the

Gaucho eats a little less meat, since his government now feels the need to sell much of it abroad.

In the towns and cities of Latin America, a meal will be as lean or as fancy as the shopper's pocketbook. Restaurants from Guadalajara to Santiago de Chile feature menus with Spanish dishes; elegant ones use French names, while ordinary ones offer *comida corrida* ("quick lunch"), a type of meal which nevertheless consists of several courses, each quite skimpy and with little choice of entreés.

What do people in cities and towns eat at home? Again, it depends on social position. A "typical" middle-class family will have a light and hurried breakfast made up of *café con leche* (hot milk mixed with strong coffee, usually served in a tall heavy glass) and French bread or rolls with butter. Around noon the children come home from school for the midday meal, and their father will usually be there too, presiding at the table as a true Latin *padre de familia* should. Here the Spanish heritage is still quite strong. The midday dinner and the evening supper are social occasions, to be taken leisurely and with a great show of good manners.

Such meals always take a good hour or more. As the servant brings out cold cuts, appetizers, or soup, the mother begins to cut the long loaf of crisp white bread. In some countries like Argentina and Chile, it is common to drink wine with meals, and the father pours out a glass for all but the very small children. Everybody starts talking at once until the father tells everyone to be quiet because he wants to ask Pepe or Rosita why they got only a six on their last math test. The next course could be a *guiso de carne* (a meat stew) or a *cazuela de pescado* (a fish casserole). There is no end to the specialties from the different provinces of Spain alone: smoked or spicy *longaniza* or *morcilla* (types of sausages), the famous *paella a la Valenciana,* (a rice casserole with a variety of vegetables, chicken, lobster, crabmeat, mussels, shrimp, and spices), or cheeses and meat pies from Pamplona to Cadiz. And there are always the old standbys: the Spanish *tortilla* (which, unlike the Mexican one, is a thick and juicy omelette made with eggs, potatoes, onions, and bacon) and the *puchero* (a heavy stew made with boiled pork or beef, potatoes, and cabbage doused in olive oil). *Ganarse el puchero* is the old Spanish saying for "bringing home the bacon" and is still in use all over Latin America.

Desserts in most countries are rare at meal times, and fruit or custard pies fairly unknown. The servant usually serves cheese and fruit to end the meal—except in Mexico, where a small piece of *jalea* (a solid fruit paste) is a common dessert. After dinner adults like a small cup of strong black coffee—it is never served with the meal—and men might light up cheroots.

At this point a *siesta* begins to look pretty good, but in these harried times that is a luxury which city dwellers can hardly afford. *Hay que ganarse el puchero.*

Where the People Live *by H. Ernest Lewald*

The person who really knows how to read a physical map can quickly discover that Latin America is much more in the grip of the forces of nature than, for instance, the United States. The map will show that huge mountain ranges, deserts, and jungles make living and communications very difficult. Let's look at two countries for now: Chile and Brazil. Chile looks like a sausage that is squeezed between the highest mountains of the Americas and the deep Pacific ocean; for the Chileans it means that they have no place to go and must fish a lot in the ocean and farm a little in the few central valleys. Brazil is larger than the United States (without Alaska) but only 4 to 5% of its land is usable. Imagine that a thousand miles east and west of the Mississippi River are only rain forests and swamplands with no roads anywhere, that the only transportation is steamboats connecting a few settlements on the big waterways. Life is far from easy in the jungle: metal objects rust within days and clothes get moldy, mosquitoes swarm around by the millions, trees rain ticks, and the water hides many unfriendly creatures, from piranha fish that can strip a horse of its flesh in a minute to blood-sucking leeches. The powerful Ford Motor Company is said to have lost one hundred million dollars when it tried to fight the jungle and harvest latex from the rubber trees near the Amazon delta. But the rain forest is also a big zoo without cages: spider monkeys swing on giant trees that filter out the sun; swarms of large parrots in brightest reds, greens, yellows, and blues fly by; groups of white or pink flamingoes stand in ponds; and armadilloes and anteaters roam between mangrove bushes. For the jungle-farmer, life is a never-ending struggle that he cannot win. He has to cut down trees and shrubs, burn trunks and roots, and try to sow corn, squash, or beans, hoping that the rodents will not eat the seeds and the insects will not devour the plants. His farming methods are as primitive as the jungle itself, and the jungle always drives him back.

On the West Coast the Andes Mountains cut off the lowlands from the interior. Here the highest peak in all of the Americas, the Aconcagua, stands almost 23,000 feet above sea level. Few roads cross the Andes, and to get to Iquitos in Peru, one would have to take a ship from the Atlantic ocean and travel up the Amazon River. The mountaineers or *serranos* (from *sierra*) are Indians whose life has changed little since the Spaniards came 450 years ago. Most live in their native communities called *ayllus*. Here they try to survive on 1,000 calories a day or even fewer, battling an arid soil, icy winds, and the *soroche,* the high-altitude sickness caused by too little oxygen. There are no jobs in those high *sierras.* Women make woolen ponchos and pottery; the men take these goods down to the cities and exchange them for food. Here the llama is man's best friend, giving wool, milk, and free transportation; but these animals have a mind of their own and refuse to budge if the load is too heavy or if they are yelled at. Roads are a nightmare, and dangling rope-bridges still sway over ravines thousands of feet below. Jeeps and buses loaded with Indians, goats, and chickens, plus a pile of boxes and bags on the roof, rattle around curves on a road that is carved out of the rock and that may be only ten feet wide, the open side dropping off thousands of feet. British engineers long ago built the world's highest railroad leading to Lake Titicaca, where the world's highest steamship takes passengers from Bolivia to Peru. For those who feel the need for adventure and have a frontier spirit, there is a bus that goes from Bogotá, past Quito, Lima, and La Paz, to Buenos Aires on the Rio de la Plata. If you look at the route on the map, you will probably be surprised to learn that the trip costs only fifty dollars or so. Unfortunately, however, the Andes region is plagued by earthquakes. Southern Chile was completely destroyed some twenty years ago, and in 1970 entire cities in Peru collapsed, burying thousands of victims.

To the North, much of Mexico is geographically an extension of Arizona or Texas: deserts where the lack of water makes agriculture next to impossible. No wonder the Aztecs' most important god was Tlaloc, maker of rain. The many islands in the Caribbean (e.g., Cuba, the Dominican Republic, and Puerto Rico) have a tropical climate and at times too much rain as part of the seasonal hurricanes.

Where, then, is nature friendly in Latin America? Maybe in the coastal zones and on the rolling prairies of Argentina, Uruguay, and Southern Brazil. Here millions of cattle graze and multiply, and the corn or wheat fields remind American visitors of the countryside in Iowa. Food is cheap and almost everybody insists on eating a pound of beef a day.

The Southern continent narrows as we move to Patagonia and Fire Land, where giant Indians were supposed to have lived. Here we find no real cities, but millions of sheep, owned in many instances by Scottish and Welsh farmers who don't mind the icy winds blowing from Antarctica. Below the equator the seasons are reversed, July being the coldest month, and the farther south we get, the colder it becomes. The last vegetation disappears as we near Cape Horn at land's end, the graveyard of countless ships that have tried to cross from one ocean to the other during the last centuries. Some years ago an Argentine warship sank there without leaving a trace.

Unlike the North Pole region that consists of a frozen sea, Antarctica is a large mass of land covered by a thick layer of permanent ice. Some geographers call it a continent, and scientists have found that under the ice lie very rich deposits of coal, oil, and even gold. Looking ahead, Chile and Argentina, along with other nations, have claimed large parts of the last unexplored continent on this Earth and set up a naval base. So maybe here is where Latin America ends.

Electricity and Bananas *by H. Ernest Lewald*

It is very hard to imagine what we have not experienced, especially problems that we are not familiar with. Try to imagine, for instance, what the future holds in store for the typical teenager in a country like Nicaragua or Ecuador. Neither country has many factories or office buildings, and most jobs are connected with the growing of bananas, coffee, and cocoa beans. Unfortunately, harvesting crops and taking them to the ports where they are shipped overseas pays but pennies an hour, and such work lasts only a few months each year. Where then will Rosita, who is seventeen, and Pepe, who just turned eighteen, find a job? Most likely, they will stay on the small farm owned by their family and work without pay. If they belong to the lucky few who have high school diplomas, they might try the big city—Managua, or Guayaquil—looking for an office job with the government, a small bank, or an export business. Yet, there will be many applicants for each job, and our Pepe might have to wait years until he is finally hired as a bookkeeper or inspector's helper; only then would he consider leaving home and marrying the girl of his dreams, who has been waiting just as patiently. Once hired, Pepe will hardly ever change jobs again, even if his present one has little future.

As a married couple, Pepe and Rosita have certain ambitions. Outside of locally made furniture, they would like to buy an electric fan for the hot summers, a radio, brass lamps, and some day, an electric refrigerator. In the meantime they do need such things as silverware, ball-point pens, and watches. However, their country produces none of these goods, and so they all must be brought by ship from faraway countries like Japan, Germany, or the United States. The big question now is how can Nicaragua, Ecuador, or similar countries pay for all these imported goods? Only by selling their bananas or coffee beans. But bananas and coffee beans cannot buy all the products needed by modern people, from safety pins to spark plugs; and besides, the price of manufactured goods keeps going up while that of bananas and coffee does not. As a result Nicaragua or Ecuador cannot import too many goods; and as a result most people there enjoy no plumbing, electricity, or modern transportation, and maybe one family in three hundred has a telephone. To live off one product, whether coffee, bananas, tin, or copper, is called *monocomercio,* a bad word in Latin America today because almost everybody's job depends on selling that one item; and if the price of bananas or copper drops, even one cent a pound, it means more hardships for the already underprivileged.

Even the largest and most advanced Latin American nations—Argentina, Brazil, and Mexico—still live largely on *monocomercio.* Argentina sells meat and wool; Brazil, coffee and rubber; and Mexico, minerals. All three, however, have huge, modern cities with skyscrapers, factories, subways, and traffic jams. Yet, a closer look reveals that the car assembly plants belong to VW, Fiat, or Ford, and the shiny office buildings to General Electric or Kodak. The Argentine railroads were built by the British, and the new elegant subway system in Mexico City by the French. Over half of the movies and television programs are American, dubbed in Spanish or Portuguese, from *Mis tres hijos* to *Yo amo a Lucy.* The modern way of life is imposed by the superindustrialized countries and, not surprisingly then, many Latin American young people don't think much of their bananas or wool anymore and instead dream of a life led by the middle classes in the United States or Germany. In fact, the lucky ones who work in an IBM branch in Buenos Aires or for the Standard Oil Company in Caracas feel a special pride of belonging to the modern world that has come to parts of Latin America. The VW mechanics in São Paulo, Brazil, enjoy the envy and admiration of their neighbors because they are working on what every Brazilian wants and so few can afford to buy.

But for many Latin American university students and writers, material progress is not necessarily a good thing, especially when it is controlled by powerful countries abroad; and they bitterly ask American visitors: "How would you feel if your home state produced only copper, the mines belonged to the French, and the copper prices were fixed in England? And would you like it if your banks were controlled by the Japanese, the factories or warehouses owned by the Germans, and all high company officials were foreigners?" For the Latin American who insists on absolute independence, his country must get rid of "cocacolonization." People must throw the Coca-Cola bottles into the ocean and start drinking their native papaya juice or grape wine, as their proud forebears did. And, of course, all industry, utilities, and transportation should be locally owned and run.

As an ideal, to be self-sufficient is attractive to people anywhere; but unless the students and writers of today's Latin America want to be without books or newspapers, they will need papermills, typewriters, printing presses, and telephones, all manufactured abroad up till now. Behind the showcase of elegant avenues and shops, of skyscrapers, of the IBM or Olivetti building in the largest cities, Latin America, from Mexico to Chile, still belongs to the unfortunate "Third World." Made up of the so-called "have-not" countries, "Third-World" nations still depend on the good will of the rich industrial powers that might buy Cuba's sugar, Bolivia's tin, or Uruguay's wool. These powers risk their money and know-how to build, for example, a dam in Peru or a steel mill in Brazil, hoping that the next local government will not decide next year that all foreign property belongs to the state. Even with foreign companies operating in Latin America today, it takes easily five years to get a telephone installed in a city like Buenos Aires or Montevideo, because no new lines are available and dialing a number in Lima or Santiago can be an adventure in wrong connections.

It has been figured out that to bring the "Third World" up to the standard of living enjoyed by the United States, the world's industries would have to use seventy times more metal, wood, oil, and other materials. At such a rate the world's oil reserves alone would be gone in a couple of years, and pollution would choke everybody to death. This industrialization will not happen, and this means that the masses in Latin America, now close to three hundred million, will not participate in our "jet age," now or in the year 2000. The population of Latin America still doubles every twenty-some years. How these added hundreds of millions will live off the same old banana or coffee *monocomercio* is anybody's guess.

We Don't Have Teenagers *by H. Ernest Lewald*

The word "teenager" cannot really be translated into Spanish since the Spaniard or Latin American never set aside such an age group; so the word has been brought over into Spanish together with terms like "blue jeans" or "drug store." Why the word "teenager" is missing in the Spanish dictionary is another matter. To be a "teenager" is not just to fall between the ages of 13 and 19. Rather it means to move in a special world that has been placed off limits to other age groups; it has its own heroes, villains, language, fashions, magazines, and music. However, in Latin America most young people between 13 and 19 cannot be considered "teenagers" in the American sense; and if we try to examine their way of life, we would come up with three or four patterns.

The first one would be traditional youths in any one of the big cities. As children of upright citizens, they are expected to go through assigned stages, always carefully controlled by their elders. Certain magical numbers are important here, especially 7 and any multiple of 7. One's elementary education starts around age 7 and ends around 14; 21 is the age to become legally independent, and at 35 one supposedly reaches maturity. Around 14 the boys begin to wear men's suits and ties and most start to work as apprentices or office boys. As such they join the adult world, imitate the ways of the older people at work, and behave like underaged adults when joining in the talk about women, sports, or politics. By the same token a woman's world awaits the girl of 15 who becomes a shopworker or seamstress.

In some countries 13 to 14 is also the age for a very important initiation into the Catholic religion—the first communion—although in other countries this takes place at a much earlier age. This is a highlight in a girl's or boy's life and one must prepare for it by memorizing the catechism. This is a booklet with questions and answers based on Catholic faith and the Ten Commandments, meant as a guideline for life. Once again, the multiple of 7 is at work, since 14 is roughly the age at which a person is considered old enough to separate right from wrong. At the communion itself the girls must wear fancy white dresses and the boys a black suit.

In some countries girls have a "coming-out" party not long after turning 14 or 15. Back in 1900 many a girl was married at such an age, in Europe as well as in the Americas. Up to that time there were almost no public schools or jobs for middle-class girls, and marriage was the only way to get out of the house. Today the girls from good families might spend as many as 16 years in different schools before "facing" life. Still, the function of a "coming-out" party goes back to one of the oldest family practices: to advertise that here is a young girl from a fine family, now old enough to begin looking for a suitable bachelor for marriage in the not too far-distant future. For girls from wealthy families, the "coming-out" party is usually an elegant affair where debutantes dance with carefully chosen boys under the watchful eyes of smiling mothers and fathers.

But in the big cities there are many forces at work that are changing traditions. A son or daughter in the middle or upper class watches *Mod Squad* and the *Partridge Family* on the family TV; he or she most likely also listens to the latest rock records at a friend's house, takes English in high school, and is proud of using American slang picked up at the local movie theater.

From this social group in cities like Mexico, Rio de Janeiro, or Caracas, quite a few "teenagers" are sent to an American campus after finishing high school or prep school. When they return with an American college diploma in their pocket, the prestige alone helps them to find jobs with companies doing business with the United States.

Before leaving the city, we should at least cast a glance at the *pícaro,* the orphan who had to beg for a piece of bread and cow's hoof in the streets of Seville or Toledo when Columbus sailed for the Indies, and whose lot has improved little today. He might sleep in a doorway, steal hubcaps, snatch purses, and ride away on the rear bumper of a pickup truck. He is not rebelling against anybody; he is as tough as nails because he could not survive otherwise in a society that ignores him and where a laborer has to feed and house his family on maybe thirty dollars a month. He would not understand the meaning of the word "teens."

In the small towns, life is slow and manners downright old-fashioned. On weekends rows of girls and boys walk along the main streets to the Courthouse and back, exchanging jokes and flirting a little. Movies are still very popular since television often has not arrived yet. After dark, girls are seldom allowed to go out without a chaperon; boys cannot just drop in on a girl either; and most homes don't have phones. Any girl staying out alone with a boy till midnight would quickly get a bad name. Jobs are quite scarce because there is little industry or office work. Thus the boys leave for the big city, and the girls stay to do the daily household chores, stopping every so often to dream about getting married some day. Like the traditional group in the cities, the young people in the provinces do not belong to a "teenage" culture at all, since they are constantly sharing the family activities with two other generations.

Spanish Americans in the United States *by Arturo Madrid*

There are at present over 10 million people of Spanish-speaking descent in the United States. They have come from every Spanish-speaking country in the world, but the majority are of Mexican, Puerto Rican, and Cuban descent. These people make up the second largest minority in the United States.

Several years before the Pilgrims landed at Plymouth Rock, in the year 1598, Spanish settlers were establishing a colony in the northern part of what is today the state of New Mexico. These settlers, having moved north from Mexico, are the ancestors of the Mexican-American population of the United States. In the period between 1598 and the conquest of the Southwest by the United States in 1847, other settlements were established in Arizona, California, Colorado, and Texas.

At the time of the signing of the Treaty of Guadalupe Hidalgo, which ended the war with Mexico, the Mexican population of the Southwest was approximately 75,000. It increased substantially during the following century. Many Mexicans came to work in the mines during the gold rush of 1849, to build the railroads of the West, to herd cattle and sheep, and to plant and harvest cotton, vegetables, and fruit. Today there are approximately 7.5 million Mexican-Americans in the United States, mostly in the states of California, Texas, New Mexico, Arizona, Colorado, Utah, and Nevada. In addition, there are also large colonies in the states of the Northwest as well as in the Midwestern states of Illinois, Minnesota, and Michigan. Many Mexican-Americans prefer to refer to themselves as Chicanos; the term is derived from an archaic pronunciation of the word *Mexicano,* in which the "x" represented a sound similar to the "ch" in modern Spanish.

The Spanish-Mexican heritage is very evident in the West and the Southwest. Many cities still have their original Spanish names (San Francisco, San Antonio, Santa Fe, Las Vegas), as do rivers (Rio Grande, Sacramento, Gila) and mountain ranges (Sierra Nevada, Sangre de Cristo, San Gabriel).

The social contributions of these people are varied and of profound significance for the development of the West. Most of the techniques of raising horses, cattle, and sheep are of Spanish-Mexican origin, and many English terms associated with the care of livestock are derived from Spanish words: for example, *rodeo, lasso, bronco, mustang, stampede.* Mining techniques and laws were also strongly influenced by the Spanish-Mexicans, as were irrigation techniques and laws concerning water usage. The Spanish-Mexican heritage is still evident in the kinds of food, music, art, and architecture predominant in the Southwest.

Life in the United States has not been easy for the Mexican-Americans. Principal hindrances to full participation in American society have been the language and cultural barriers. These barriers have resulted in low educational attainment and corresponding economic disadvantages. Mexican-Americans have a higher unemployment rate and a lower income level than the majority of other Americans. They are not well represented in either the professions (law, medicine, education) or in the financial or political world.

Most of the population is young (under 25 years of age) and urban. Today, many Chicanos are giving considerable emphasis to improving their educational, economic, and political situation through developing bilingual education programs in the elementary schools; increasing higher educational opportunities; instituting Chicano Studies programs in high schools, colleges, and universities; and by forming Mexican-American political organizations such as the Raza Unida Party.

Perhaps the most prominent Chicano leader today is Cesar Chavez, who heads the farmworkers of California. Mr. Chavez has been organizing farmworkers throughout the West in order to increase their income and better their living and working conditions. Most of the farmworkers in California are Mexican-Americans. Other popular Chicano figures are Reies Lopez Tijerina, the fiery leader of the Land Grant movement in the Southwest; "Corky" Gonzales, the director of the Crusade for Justice, based in Denver, Colorado; and José Angel Gutiérrez, the founder of the Raza Unida party.

Chicanos are also beginning to penetrate the political system of the United States, including representation in the Congress of the United States. Their elected leaders include U.S. Senator Joseph Montoya (New Mexico) and U.S. Representatives Eligio de la Garza (Texas), Henry Gonzales (Texas), Manuel Lujan, Jr. (New Mexico), and Edward Roybal (California).

Many Chicanos have also achieved prominence in entertainment and sports. Pancho Gonzalez, the tennis star; Lee Trevino, the outstanding golfer; and football stars Joe Kapp and Jim Plunkett are Mexican-Americans. The leader of the rock group *Santana* is Mexican-American as are also popular singers Vicki Carr, Trini Lopez, and Joan Baez.

The second largest Spanish-speaking group in the United States is the Puerto Ricans, who number over 1.5 million. Most of them, about 1 million, live in New York City and its environs, but there are also large colonies in New Jersey, Connecticut, and Massachusetts as well as in such large Midwestern cities as Chicago and Detroit.

Puerto Rico was settled by Spain in the sixteenth century and remained a Spanish colony until it became a dependency of the United States as a result of the Spanish American War of 1898. The Boricuas, as they call themselves (the name derives from the pre-Spanish name for the island, Borinquen), are the products of three races and three cultures: the Spanish, the Indian natives, and the African blacks who were brought over as slaves. Their music, art, architecture, and life style are a reflection of the intermingling of these three peoples.

Puerto Ricans were made American citizens in 1917, and Puerto Rico today has a commonwealth status with the United States. They first started migrating to the mainland after the first World War, and what was a trickle in the 1920's and 1930's became a large and steady flow in the 1940's and continues into the 1970's.

The migration to the mainland has taken place for economic reasons: Puerto Rico has a very high population density (11 times more than the U.S.), a very high level of unemployment (a constant 13% rate), and very low per capita income (only about $1000 per year). In the 1940's and the 1950's, during the second World War and the Korean War, Puerto Ricans found work in war-related factories, but thereafter they were faced with unemployment caused by economic recessions and increasing automation.

Like the Chicanos in the West, the Puerto Ricans are also victims of the linguistic barrier, deficient education, and quite often a lack of educational opportunities. As a result, Puerto Ricans have a high unemployment rate (10%) and low incomes (30% are below the poverty level). But the Puerto Ricans have also begun to address themselves to their socio-economic conditions. Since the majority of Puerto Ricans are quite young (the median age is 19 years), educational programs and opportunities to meet their needs are being developed in many East Coast universities. Like the Chicanos they are also developing bilingual education programs so that having to learn English does not deter their educational development.

Puerto Ricans are also beginning to receive national recognition. One of their most prominent political leaders is Herman Badillo, formerly a Councilman of the City of New York, later a candidate for the Mayorship, and at present a Representative in the Congress of the United States. Puerto Ricans have long been prominent in sports, particularly in baseball. Among the many excellent baseball players are Orlando Cepeda and the late Roberto Clemente. Young Americans are also acquainted with the blind rock singer, José Feliciano, who is Puerto Rican.

The Cubans are a third large group of Spanish speakers living in the United States, primarily in Florida, although there are small colonies of Cubans throughout the large cities. Florida was the site of one of the earliest Spanish colonies in North America, and its parent colony was Cuba, less than 100 miles away. Cuba came under American influence after the Spanish American War of 1898, but Cubans had lived in Florida for many years previously, often as a result of voluntary or forced exile from their homeland. Others came to work in the cigar and tobacco factories of Florida.

Large numbers of Cubans emigrated to the United States before and after the Cuban Revolution of 1958 as a result of the political instability and turmoil in Cuba. The majority settled in Florida, which not only has a climate similar to that of their homeland but also a large Cuban population, which has given some of Florida's cities a Latin atmosphere.

The Cubans number approximately 750,000. Despite the recent arrival of most of them and the turbulent conditions of their departure from Cuba, they have adapted rapidly and well to living in America. Many of the exiled Cubans were professionals or merchants in their native country and have entered into similar activity in the United States.

NEW SECOND EDITION

A·LM®

SPANISH

LEVEL ONE

HARCOURT BRACE JOVANOVICH, INC.

New York   Chicago   San Francisco
Atlanta   Dallas

The first edition of this work was produced pursuant to a contract between the Glastonbury Public Schools and the United States Office of Education, Department of Health, Education, and Welfare.

PRINTED IN THE UNITED STATES OF AMERICA

ISBN 0-15-388635-8

TEXT PHOTOS: opp. p. 1, Carmelo Guadagno, courtesy Museum of the American Indian; 6 Sergio Larrain, Magnum; 16, 26 Harbrace; 30, 42, 46, 55 Monkmeyer; 64 Photo Researchers; 68 Cornell Capa, Magnum; 81 Shostal; 88 Foto Cine Colón, Vernis, S. A.; 108 Pix; 118 Photo Researchers; 131 Rapho-Guillumette; 134 Black Star; 152 FPG; 154 Mauro Mujica; 158 Black Star; 172 Museum of the American Indian; 176 Rapho-Guillumette; 180 Harbrace; 198 Magnum; 214, DPI; 217 Photo Researchers; 222 Harbrace; 232 Monkmeyer; 238 Rapho-Guillumette; 244 Foto Cine Colón Vernis, S. A.; 250 Harbrace; 264, 274 Photo Researchers; 283 Harbrace; 286 Magnum; 288 Rapho-Guillumette; 292, 306, 308 Photo Researchers.

PICTORIAL SECTION PHOTOGRAPHS: Positions are shown in abbreviated form as follows: *t*–top, *b*–bottom, *l*–left, *r*–right, *c*–center.

G1 Haas, Magnum; G5 *t* Fredric A. Bakunin; *tl* Bernard Wolf; *tr* Katherine Young; *c* Black Star; *bl* Katherine Young; *br* Photo Researchers. G6 *tl* Photo Researchers; *bl* Susan McCartney; *br* Photo Researchers. G7 *tl* Alpha Photo Associates; *tr* Photo Researchers; *bl* Mauro Mujica; *br* Photo Researchers. G8 *t* Pix; *bl* Photo Researchers; *br* James Romeo. G9 *l* Photo Researchers; *tr* Susan McCartney; *br* Pix. G10 *t* Photo Researchers; *br* Photo Researchers. G11 *tl* Thomas Gilbert; *tr* Elliott Erwitt, Magnum; *bl* Elliott Erwitt, Magnum; *br* Monkmeyer. G12 *l* Pix; *tr* Bernard Wolf; *bl* Photo Researchers; *br* Harbrace. G13 *tl* Rapho-Guillumette; *tr* Photo Researchers; *bl* Photo Researchers; *br* Harbrace. G14 *tl* D.P.I.; *tr* Photo Researchers; *br* Susan McCartney. G15 *tl* Photo Researchers; *tr* Photo Researchers; *b* Susan McCartney. G16 Photo Researchers. G17 Photo Researchers

MAPS: PG2-3 Harbrace Map incorporating "Base Map © 1956, Jeppesen and Co.; Denver, Colo., U.S.A. All rights reserved." PG4 Harbrace Map incorporating "Base Map © 1958, Jeppesen and Co.; Denver, Colo., U.S.A. All rights reserved."

TEXT CREDITS: The contrastive word lists which appear in this book on pp. 316–17 are taken from *The Sounds of English and Spanish* by Robert P. Stockwell and J. Donald Bowen, Univ. of Chicago Press, 1965, pp. 124–125. Used with the authors' permission.

WRITING AND CONSULTING STAFF

WRITERS: **Barbara Kaminar de Mujica**

Guillermo Segreda, *Manhattanville College*

CONSULTING LINGUISTS: **Robert P. Stockwell,** *University of California, Los Angeles*

James W. Harris, *Massachusetts Institute of Technology*

TEACHER CONSULTANT: **Russell Webster,** *formerly Hackensack Public Schools and River Dell Regional Schools, New Jersey*

RECORDING SPECIALIST: **Pierre J. Capretz,** *Yale University*

GENERAL CONSULTANT: **Nelson Brooks,** *Yale University*

Level One Program: *New Second Edition*

Student Materials:

STUDENT TEXTBOOK

EXERCISE BOOK*

SPANISH CULTURE: ACTIVITY BOOK

PRACTICE RECORD SET*

STUDENT TEST ANSWER FORM BOOKLET*

Teacher Materials:

TEACHER'S EDITION

CUE CARDS*

TEACHER'S TEST MANUAL*

Visual Materials:

DIALOG POSTERS*

SUPPLEMENT POSTERS*

SOUND FILMSTRIPS*

SPANISH CULTURE: FILMSTRIPS WITH CASSETTES

Classroom/Laboratory Recorded Materials:

$7\frac{1}{2}$ ips FULL-TRACK TAPE SET*

$7\frac{1}{2}$ ips TWO-TRACK TAPE SET*

$7\frac{1}{2}$ ips FULL-TRACK TESTING TAPE SET*

$33\frac{1}{3}$ rpm RECORD SET*

TWO-TRACK CASSETTES, BASIC DIALOGS AND SUPPLEMENTS

TWO-TRACK CASSETTES, LISTENING AND SPEAKING EXERCISES

TWO-TRACK CASSETTES, STRUCTURE DRILLS

"Half Sets"

SPANISH 7 TEXTBOOK (*Units* 1–7)*

SPANISH 7 PRACTICE RECORD SET*

SPANISH 8 TEXTBOOK (*Units* 8–15)*

SPANISH 8 PRACTICE RECORD SET*

*Materials identical with Second Edition

CONTENTS

vii

This entire unit is to be taught audio-lingually.
You should not distribute the textbooks to the students
until you have finished teaching the unit.

UNIT 1

FOR COMPLETE TEACHING SUGGESTIONS, SEE PAGE T23.

BASIC DIALOGS

From now on you will be reading and writing Spanish as well as speaking it. You must avoid the tendency to pronounce a written word the way it would be pronounced if it were English. Spanish spelling is simple to learn, but some letters are used differently from the way they are used in English. Reading Notes will call your attention to those features of Spanish spelling which might otherwise be troublesome. The details of how sounds are represented in writing will be explained in the Letter ↔ Sound Correspondences section at the end of each unit.

Read each dialog, remembering how it sounded in class. Note what each line means. Study all the Reading Notes carefully.

I

ELENA	¿Está Susana en casa?
MARÍA	Sí, está con una amiga.
ELENA	¿Dónde están, en la sala?
MARÍA	No, en la cocina.

ELENA	Is Susana at home?
MARÍA	Yes, she's with a friend.
ELENA	Where are they, in the living room?
MARÍA	No, in the kitchen.

READING NOTES

Questions in Spanish are preceded by an inverted question mark: **¿Está Susana en casa?**

◀ *A community of pre-Columbian dolls from Jalisco, Nayarit, and Colima, Mexico.*

QUESTIONS

1. ¿Está Susana en casa?
2. ¿Dónde está Susana?
3. ¿Está con una amiga?
4. ¿Está Susana en la sala?
5. ¿Está la amiga en la sala?
6. ¿Dónde están Susana y (*and*) la amiga?

DIRECTED DIALOG

A directed dialog is a conversation in which each speaker is told what to say. You will hear the words **pregúntele si . . .** *ask him* (or *her*) *if . . .* when you are to direct a question to another student, and the words **dígale que . . .** *tell him* (*her*) *that . . .* when you are to direct a remark to another student.

For example:

Pregúntele a *Elena* si Susana está en casa.	¿Está Susana en casa?
Ask Elena if Susana is at home.	*Is Susana at home?*
Dígale que sí, que está en la sala.	Sí, está en la sala.
Tell her yes, she's in the living room.	*Yes, she's in the living room.*

Do the following Directed Dialog.

Pregúntele a *María* si Susana está en la cocina.	¿Está Susana en la cocina?
Dígale que no, que está en la sala.	No, está en la sala.

II

ELENA	¡Hola*, Susana! ¿Dónde está tu amiga?
SUSANA	En el teléfono.

ELENA	Hi, Susana. Where's your friend?
SUSANA	On the telephone.

READING NOTES

<u>H</u>ola: **h** represents no sound.

Exclamations in Spanish are preceded by an inverted exclamation mark: **¡Hola, Susana!**

QUESTIONS

1. ¿Dónde está la amiga de Susana?
2. ¿Está la amiga con Susana en la cocina?
3. ¿Está la amiga en el teléfono?
4. ¿Está Susana en el teléfono?

DIRECTED DIALOG

Pregúntele a *Susana* dónde está el teléfono.   ¿Dónde está el teléfono?
Dígale que está en la sala.   Está en la sala.

III

ELENA	¿Es Lili la tía de Susana?
MARÍA	¿Cómo?* ¿Quién?*
ELENA	Lili. Ésa que* está en el sofá.
MARÍA	Ah, sí, es su tía.

ELENA	Is Lili Susana's aunt (the aunt of Susana)?
MARÍA	What (how)? Who?
ELENA	Lili. The one (that one who's) on the sofa.
MARÍA	Oh, yes, that's her aunt.

READING NOTES

¿Cómo?, literally *how,* is used to mean *what* when asking a person to repeat something.

Q̲uién, q̲ue: qu represents the sound [k][1], as in *key.*

QUESTIONS

1. ¿Es Lili la amiga de Susana?
2. ¿Quién es Lili?
3. ¿Dónde está Lili?
4. ¿Está Lili en la cocina?
5. ¿Está en la sala?

---

[1] Throughout this book it will be necessary to distinguish letters from sounds. A symbol in brackets will be used to indicate a sound. You will not be required to write these symbols, but you should learn to recognize them. There is a complete reference list on page 356.

DIRECTED DIALOG

Dígale hola a *Susana.*	Hola, *Susana.*
Dígale hola, y pregúntele dónde está Lili.	Hola, ¿dónde está Lili?
Dígale que está en la sala.	Está en la sala.
Pregúntele con quién.	¿Con quién?
Dígale que con su amiga.	Con su amiga.

IV

ROBERTO*	¿Pero adónde quiere* ir Lili?
RAÚL*	A las carreras.
ROBERTO	¿A las carreras de perros?
RAÚL	Sí, vamos* en mi carro.

ROBERTO	But where (to where) does Lili want to go?
RAÚL	To the races.
ROBERTO	To the dog races?
RAÚL	Yes, we'll go (we go) in my car.

> **READING NOTES**
>
> **R**oberto, **R**aúl: **r** represents the sound [rr].
> **qu**iere: **qu** represents the sound [k].
> **v**amos: **v** represents the sound [b].

QUESTIONS

1. ¿Adónde quiere ir Lili?
2. ¿Quiere ir a la casa?
3. ¿Quiere ir a las carreras?
4. ¿A las carreras de perros?
5. ¿Raúl quiere ir en su carro o (*or*) en el carro de Lili?

DIRECTED DIALOG

Pregúntele a *Raúl* dónde está Susana.	¿Dónde está Susana?
Dígale que está en el carro.	Está en el carro.
Pregúntele adónde quiere ir.	¿Adónde quiere ir?
Dígale que a las carreras con su tía.	A las carreras con su tía.

V

LILI	¿Quién sabe cuándo llega* Eva?
ADELA	¿De los Estados Unidos? Yo sé.
LILI	¿Cuándo, Adela?
ADELA	El sábado.

LILI	Who knows when Eva arrives?
ADELA	From the United States? I know.
LILI	When, Adela?
ADELA	(The) Saturday.

READING NOTES

Llega: ll represents the sound [ɣ], similar to the y in _yes_.

QUESTIONS

1. ¿Quién llega, Eva o Adela?
2. ¿De dónde llega Eva?
3. ¿Quién sabe cuándo llega?
4. ¿Cuándo llega Eva?

DIRECTED DIALOG

Dígale hola a _Adela_ y pregúntele si Susana está en casa.

¡Hola, _Adela!_ ¿Está Susana en casa?

Dígale que no, que está en los Estados Unidos.

No, está en los Estados Unidos.

Pregúntele ¿Cómo? ¿Dónde?

¿Cómo? ¿Dónde?

Dígale que en los Estados Unidos.

En los Estados Unidos.

| *Note:* For teaching suggestions see p. T8

BASIC DIALOG

Necesito practicar inglés

BLANCA	¿A quién llamas? ¿A la chica americana?[1] 2-1
ARTURO	Sí, quiero practicar inglés.
BLANCA	¿Por qué no estudias conmigo? 2-2
ARTURO	Porque tú y yo pronunciamos muy mal. 2-3
ARTURO	No sé qué pasa, no contestan. 2-4
BLANCA	Tal vez no llega de la escuela todavía.
ARTURO	Bien, hablo con ella más tarde.
BLANCA	Entonces, ¿escuchamos unos discos ahora? 2-5
ARTURO	Si tú quieres. 2-6

I Need to Practice English

BLANCA	Who(m) are you calling? The American girl?
ARTURO	Yes, I want to practice English.
BLANCA	Why don't you study with me?
ARTURO	Because you and I pronounce very badly.
ARTURO	I don't know what's wrong (what passes), they don't answer.
BLANCA	Maybe she's not home (doesn't arrive) from school yet.
ARTURO	Well, I'll talk with her later (more late).
BLANCA	Then shall we listen to some records now?
ARTURO	If you want to.

---

[1] The word **a** has no English equivalent in these two sentences.

◄ *Modern architecture and traditional Spanish furnishings are features of this home in Chile.*

7

Supplement

¿A quién llamas? ¿A la maestra? 2-1   Who are you calling? The teacher?
señora 2-2   lady
señorita 2-3   young lady
chica 2-4

Quiero practicar español.   I want to practice Spanish.
francés   French
alemán   German
ruso   Russian

Tú y yo pronunciamos muy bien.   You and I pronounce very well.
bastante bien   quite (enough) well

Hablo con ella hoy.   I'll talk with her today.
mañana   tomorrow
unos discos 2-5
¿Quieres escuchar una canción?   Do you want to listen to a song?
las noticias   the news
escuela 2-6
El señor pasa por la biblioteca. 2-7   The gentleman stops by the library.
Alguien   Someone
El señor 2-8

Listening and Speaking Exercises 28, 29*, 30, 31, 32*, p. T33 ⊗

Note: The asterisk after 29 indicates that these exercises call for a written response from the student. Response forms are provided in the Exercise Book. Students without the Exercise Book can copy the appropriate forms from the section Response Forms for Listening Exercises, which begins on page 311 of the student text.

Note: Point out that *pasar por* may mean either *pass by* or *stop by*.

Note: For suggestions on Reading Notes see p. T9

READING NOTES

The following notes are to help you pronounce some of the new words in the Basic Dialog and Supplement.

Dialog

quiero, porque, quieres   qu represents the sound [k].
llamas, ella   ll represents the sound [y].
tal vez   v represents the sound [b].
tal vez   z represents the sound [s].
hablo, ahora   h represents no sound.

Supplement

señora, señorita, español, mañana, señor   ñ represents approximately the sound of *ny* in *canyon*.
ruso   r represents the sound [rr].
hoy   h represents no sound.
alguien   gu represents the sound [g], as in *again*.

| *Note:* For teaching suggestions see p. T10

Vocabulary Exercises

1. DIALOG RECALL

Use each of the following words in a sentence from the Basic Dialog.

inglés	Necesito practicar inglés.
español	Necesito practicar español.
chica	*¿A la chica americana?*
practicar	*Sí, quiero practicar inglés.*
por qué	*¿Por qué no estudias conmigo?*
pronunciamos	*Tú y yo pronunciamos muy mal.*
alemán	Necesito practicar alemán.
señorita	*¿A quién llamas? ¿a la señorita?*

2. FREE COMPLETION | *Note:* Responses given for "free" exercises are suggestions. In most cases, there are other possible answers.

Complete the following sentences with any appropriate word or phrase.

1. Quiero practicar _____. *inglés, español, francés*
2. ¿A quién llamas? ¿A la _____? *chica americana, maestra, señora, señorita*
3. ¿Por qué no estudias _____? *conmigo, con Blanca, con Arturo*
4. Tú y yo pronunciamos muy _____. *mal, bien*

---

3. DIALOG RECALL

contestan
tal vez
más tarde
discos
la biblioteca
ahora
las noticias

4. FREE COMPLETION

1. No llega de la _____.
2. Más tarde hablo con _____.
3. ¿Quieres escuchar _____?
4. Alguien pasa por _____.

1. escuela, biblioteca

2. ella, Blanca, la maestra

3. las noticias, una canción

4. la biblioteca, la escuela, la casa

5. QUESTIONS

1. ¿Quieres practicar inglés o español?
2. ¿Quieres practicar ruso?
3. ¿Quién no llega de la escuela todavía, Blanca o la chica americana? *La chica americana.*
4. ¿Tú quieres escuchar unos discos?
5. ¿Qué quieres escuchar, una canción o las noticias? | *Note:* Accept one-word answers.

6. BASIC DIALOG VARIATION

Repeat the Basic Dialog, making whatever changes are necessary to adapt it to the following situation:

Arturo calls up the teacher to practice Spanish, but she is probably still at the library.

The following lines require changes: *¿A quién llamas? ¿A la maestra?*
Sí, quiero practicar español.
Tal vez no llega de la biblioteca todavía.

GRAMMAR

| *Note:* For teaching suggestions see p. T10

Regular a-Class Verbs

PRESENTATION *TEACHER PRESENTATION, p. T138*

Habl<u>o</u> con ella más tarde.
Practic<u>o</u> con ella más tarde.

If the subject of the sentence is *I*, what is the final vowel of the verb?

¿Por qué no **estudi<u>as</u>** conmigo?
¿Por qué no **practic<u>as</u>** conmigo?

If the subject of the sentence is *you*, what are the final vowel and consonant of the verb?

Tal vez no **lleg<u>a</u>**.
Tal vez no **practic<u>a</u>**.

If the subject of the sentence is *he* or *she*, what is the final vowel of the verb?

Tú y yo **pronunci<u>amos</u>**.
Tú y yo **practic<u>amos</u>**.

Which English pronoun could be substituted for *you and I?* If the subject of the sentence is *we* or *you and I*, how does the verb end?

No **contest<u>an</u>**.
No **practic<u>an</u>**.

How does the verb end if the subject of the sentence is *they?*

Más tarde **practic<u>o</u>** con ella.
¿Por qué no **practic<u>as</u>** conmigo?
Tal vez no **practic<u>a</u>**.
Tú y yo **practic<u>amos</u>**.
No **practic<u>an</u>**.

What base or stem do all the forms of the verb have in common? Except when the subject is *I*, what vowel sound occurs after the stem in all these verb forms? What part of the verb changes according to the subject?

GENERALIZATION

| *Note:* **For teaching suggestions see p. T11**

1. Spanish verbs, as you have seen, have different forms. The above forms are those of the present tense. These forms are composed of the verb stem, followed by a theme vowel and an ending, as shown in the following chart:

practicar, PRESENT TENSE	Stem	Theme vowel	Ending
SINGULAR			
1st person	practic	–	o
2nd person	practic	a	s
3rd person	practic	a	–
PLURAL			
1st person	practic	a	mos
3rd person	practic	a	n

Observe the following details:

a. The theme vowel does not appear in the first person singular: **practico**.
b. There is no ending for the third person singular.
c. No second person plural is shown, since that form is normally used only in Spain.
d. Stress always falls on the next-to-the-last syllable, regardless of whether this is the stem or the theme vowel: **prac<u>ti</u>co, prac<u>ti</u>cas, prac<u>ti</u>ca, practic<u>a</u>mos, prac<u>ti</u>can.**

2. There are three classes of Spanish verbs. A verb is classified according to whether its theme vowel is **a, e,** or **i.** Verbs which follow the above chart in every detail are called regular **a**-class verbs.

3. One form of the verb, called the infinitive, is used as the name form. The infinitive of every Spanish verb consists of the stem + the theme vowel + the ending **r.** The infinitives of the regular **a**-class verbs you have learned so far are these.

contestar	*answer*	**llamar**	*call*	**pasar**	*pass, happen*
escuchar	*listen*	**llegar**	*arrive*	**practicar**	*practice*
estudiar	*study*	**necesitar**	*need*	**pronunciar**	*pronounce*
hablar	*talk, speak*				

4. The simple present tense in Spanish often corresponds precisely to the simple present tense in English.

Necesito practicar inglés.
I need to practice English.

Often, however, the simple present tense is used in Spanish where English uses a progressive construction (a form of the verb *be* followed by the main verb + *-ing*).

¿A quién llamas?
Whom are you calling?

Spanish also uses the simple present tense to refer to an event planned for the future.

Hablo con ella más tarde.
I'll talk with her later.

Listening and Speaking Exercises 33, 34, 35, 36, 37*, 38*, p. T35 ⊗

SECTION B

STRUCTURE DRILLS

7. ENGLISH CUE DRILLS | *Note:* For teaching suggestions on Structure Drills see p. T11

1. Quiero estudiar. ⊗   Quiero estudiar.
   (practice)   Quiero practicar.
   (answer)   Quiero contestar.
   (pass)   Quiero pasar.
   (talk)   Quiero hablar.
   (listen)   Quiero escuchar.

2. ¿Quieres hablar conmigo? ⊗
   (study–practice–listen–arrive–pronounce) *estudiar–practicar–escuchar*
                                        llegar–pronunciar

8. ITEM SUBSTITUTION

1. Más tarde hablo con ella. ⊗   Más tarde hablo con ella.
   (llegar)   Más tarde llego con ella.
   (estudiar)   Más tarde estudio con ella.
   (practicar)   Más tarde practico con ella.

2. ¿Por qué no estudias conmigo? ⊗
   (hablar–pronunciar–practicar)   *hablas–pronuncias–practicas*

3. Arturo no contesta. ⊗
   (estudiar–escuchar–llegar–llamar)   *estudia–escucha–llega–llama*

4. Mañana llegamos con la chica americana. ⊗
   (practicar–estudiar–hablar)   *practicamos–estudiamos–hablamos*

9. PERSON-NUMBER SUBSTITUTION

1. Escuchan una canción. ⊗   Escuchan una canción.
   (she)   *Note:* English cues will be used   Escucha una canción.
   (you)   only until Spanish subject   Escuchas una canción.
            pronouns are introduced.
   (we)   Escuchamos una canción.
   (they)   Escuchan una canción.
   (he)   Escucha una canción.

2. Llega mañana. ⊗
   (you–I–they–he–we)   *llegas–llego–llegan–llega–llegamos*

3. Pronunciamos bastante bien. ⊗
   (I–we–he–you–they)   *pronuncio–pronunciamos–pronuncia–pro-*
                                             nuncias–pronuncian

10. FREE RESPONSE

¿Con quién habla Arturo, con Blanca o con la chica americana? *Habla con Blanca.*
¿A quién llama Arturo?   *Llama a la chica americana.*
¿Por qué no contesta la chica americana?   *Tal vez no llega de la escuela todavía.*
¿Cómo pronuncian Blanca y Arturo?   *Pronuncian muy mal.*
¿Necesita Arturo practicar inglés o español?   *Necesita practicar inglés.*
¿Qué escuchan Blanca y Arturo, unos discos o las noticias?   *Escuchan unos discos.*
¿Estudias tú español o ruso?
¿Dónde estudias, en casa o en la biblioteca?
¿Hablas inglés muy bien o bastante mal? ¿y español?
¿Hablas mucho por teléfono?
¿Con quién hablas ahora, con la maestra o con una amiga?
¿Quieres escuchar unos discos o estudiar?

11. FREE SUBSTITUTION

Make as many new sentences as you can by substituting one word at a time for the under-lined words.

Arturo llea mañana. *estudia, llama, pasa, habla / ahora, más tarde, hoy*

12. WRITING EXERCISE

Write the responses to Drills 9.2 and 9.3. *EXERCISE BOOK: EXERCISE 1 MAY BE ASSIGNED AT THIS POINT.*

Negation

TEACHER PRESENTATION, p. T142
GENERALIZATION

1. A Spanish sentence is made negative by placing the word **no** before the verb.

> **Quiero practicar inglés.**
> *I want to practice English.*
> **No quiero practicar inglés.**
> *I don't want to practice English.*

2. Spanish **no** can also have the same meaning as English *no*. Thus, the word **no** can occur twice in a row in a Spanish sentence.

> **No, no quiero practicar inglés.**
> *No, I don't want to practice English.*

Listening and Speaking Exercises 39, 40, 41*, 42*, p. T36 ⊗
            SECTION C

STRUCTURE DRILLS

13. AFFIRMATIVE → NEGATIVE ⊗

Hablamos alemán.	No hablamos alemán.
La chica americana pronuncia bien.	*La chica americana no pronuncia bien.*
¿Estudias conmigo?	*¿No estudias conmigo?*
Juan y María llegan hoy.	*Juan y María no llegan hoy.*
Llamo a Susana.	*No llamo a Susana.*
Pasan por la biblioteca.	*No pasan por la biblioteca.*
Contestan el teléfono.	*No contestan el teléfono.*
Vamos a las carreras.	*No vamos a las carreras.*

14. WRITING EXERCISE

Write the responses to Drill 13.

EXERCISE BOOK: EXERCISE 2

Subject Pronouns

→ *TEACHER PRESENTATION, p. T142*
GENERALIZATION

Note: Throughout this book, *usted* is used to address students in Free Response drills except in those which precede this generalization. Both *tú* and *usted* are used in other Structure Drills.

1. The English subject pronouns have the following Spanish equivalents:

	Singular		*Plural*	
1ST PERSON	**yo**	*I*	**nosotros**	*we*
			nosotras	*we* (*f.*)
2ND PERSON	**tú**	*you* (familiar)	**ustedes**	*you* {(formal *or* familiar)
	usted	*you* (formal)		
3RD PERSON	**él**	*he*	**ellos**	*they*
	ella	*she*	**ellas**	*they* (*f.*)

2. There are three ways to say *you* in Spanish: **tú, usted** (often abbreviated as **Ud.**), and **ustedes** (often abbreviated as **Uds.**).

   In most Spanish-speaking countries, **tú** is used to address a close friend, a member of one's family, or a young child. It is called the familiar form of address. You will use **tú** with your classmates.

   Usted is used primarily among strangers and people who address each other as **señor, señora,** or **señorita;** it is used when a student addresses a teacher, when a patient addresses a doctor, and in other similar situations, and is often called the formal, or polite form of address. Your teacher may address you as either **tú** or **usted.**

   Ustedes is the plural of both **tú** and **usted.** That is, **ustedes** is used to address two or more people, each of whom you would address individually either as **usted** or as **tú.** (In Spain, **vosotros** is used as the plural of **tú.** See paragraph 1c, page 11.)

3. In two other cases Spanish makes more distinctions than English: in the first person plural **(nosotros)** and in the third person plural **(ellos).**

   Nosotros is used when the speaker includes himself in a group of boys or men, or in a mixed group. **Nosotras** is used in just one situation: when a girl or a woman includes herself in a group consisting entirely of girls or women. Thus, a woman may say either **noso-**

tros (when referring to a mixed group) or **nosotras** (when referring to a group of women); a man will use only **nosotros**.

Ellos is used to refer to either a group of boys or men or to a mixed group. **Ellas** is used to refer to a group of girls or women.

STRUCTURE DRILLS

15. PRONOUN DRILL

Give the pronoun that corresponds to each of the following subjects.

1. Blanca y usted ⊗   ustedes
   usted y yo   nosotros
   Blanca   ella
   Eva y Blanca   ellas
   Adela y Arturo   ellos
   Arturo y yo   nosotros

2. Blanca y yo ⊗   *nosotros*
   Arturo   *él*
   usted y Blanca   *ustedes*
   tú y ella   *ustedes*
   tú, tú, y tú   *ustedes*
   usted, él y yo   *nosotros*

American music as well as Latin rhythms are popular with these Mexican youngsters.

16. PATTERNED RESPONSE

¿Llama usted? ⊗

¿Hablo francés yo?

¿Practica ella?

¿Llegan ellos?

¿Pronuncias mal tú?

¿Escucha discos él?

¿Necesitan practicar ellas?

¿Yo? No.

¿Usted? No.

¿Ella? No.

¿Ellos? No.

¿Yo? No.

¿Él? No.

¿Ellas? No.

17. WRITING EXERCISE

Write the responses to Drill 16.

Subject-Verb Agreement

TEACHER PRESENTATION, p. T142

GENERALIZATION

1. Spanish subjects and verbs agree in person and number. That is, if a subject is first person plural, the verb must have the first person plural ending.

yo practico	nosotros practicamos
tú practicas	nosotras practicamos
usted practica	ustedes practican
él practica	ellos practican
ella practica	ellas practican

Usted and **ustedes** require a third person verb ending in spite of their second person meaning. The ancestor of the modern word **usted** was once used to address aristocratic individuals, royalty in particular (like *your highness* or *your grace* in English) and like *your highness,* **usted** takes a third person verb form: *Is your highness in good health?*

2. A compound subject requires a plural verb ending. If the compound subject includes the pronoun **yo,** the first person plural form of the verb is used.

Tú y yo pronunciamos muy mal.

La maestra y yo hablamos inglés.

If the compound subject does not include the pronoun **yo,** the third person plural form is used.

Juan y ella llegan hoy.

Tú y María escuchan discos.

STRUCTURE DRILLS

18. PERSON-NUMBER SUBSTITUTION

1. Yo no contesto. ⊗
   Ellos _____.
   Usted _____.
   Tú _____.
   Nosotros _____.

   Yo no contesto.
   Ellos no contestan.
   Usted no contesta.
   Tú no contestas.
   Nosotros no contestamos.

2. ¿Cuándo llegan ellos? ⊗
   (tú–ella–ustedes–él–usted)

   llegas–llega–llegan–llega–llega

3. Usted y yo escuchamos unos discos. ⊗
   (Blanca y usted–Arturo y la maestra–Susana y yo–tú y ella–Arturo y yo)

   escuchan–escuchan–escuchamos–escuchan–
   escuchamos

Listening and Speaking Exercises 43, 44, 45*, 46, p. T37 ⊗   SECTION D

19. PATTERNED RESPONSE

¿Hablan francés Arturo y usted? ⊗   No, nosotros no hablamos francés.
¿Contesta el teléfono Raúl?   No, él no contesta el teléfono.
¿Llegan tarde Blanca y Elena?   *No, ellas no llegan tarde.*
¿Estudia inglés Cristina?   *No, ella no estudia inglés.*
¿Necesito practicar inglés yo?   *No, usted no necesita practicar inglés.*
¿Llaman Miguel y usted?   *No, nosotros no llamamos.*
¿Pronuncia muy mal usted?   *No, yo no pronuncio muy mal.*

Note: Substitute the names of students in your class for the names in italics.

20. DIRECTED DRILL

Diga que usted estudia con *Arturo*. ⊗   Yo estudio con *Arturo*.
Diga que *Juan* y usted estudian con *Arturo*.   *Juan* y yo estudiamos con *Arturo*.
Diga que yo hablo español.   Usted habla español.
Diga que *Susana* y yo hablamos español. *Susana* y usted hablan español.

21. FREE SUBSTITUTION

Carlos y yo hablamos mucho. *La chica americana y yo, tú y ella, Blanca y él /*
                            estudiar, practicar.

22. FREE RESPONSE

¿Necesitan practicar alemán Arturo y Blanca?   *No, no necesitan practicar alemán.*
¿Qué necesitan practicar ellos?   *Necesitan practicar inglés.*
¿Necesitan practicar alemán *Roberto* y usted?
¿Quiere usted escuchar unos discos o las noticias?

Y usted, ¿quiere escuchar una canción?

¿Qué pasa? ¿Usted no quiere escuchar unos discos?

¿Hablo yo inglés o español ahora?

Y usted, ¿qué habla?

23. DIRECTED DRILL

Dígale a *Lili* que ella pronuncia bien. ⊗	Tú pronuncias bien.
Dígales a *Eva* y a *Arturo* que ellos pronuncian bien.	Ustedes pronuncian bien.
Dígame que yo pronuncio bien.	Usted pronuncia bien.
Dígale a *Raúl* que él pronuncia bien.	Tú pronuncias bien.
Pregúnteme si yo hablo alemán.	¿Usted habla alemán?
Pregúnteles a *Rosita* y a *Pedro* si ellos hablan alemán.	¿Ustedes hablan alemán?
Pregúntele a *Juan* si él habla alemán.	¿Tú hablas alemán?

VARIATION: Do the entire drill again using the phrase *estudiar mucho.* Start like this: *Dígale a* Lili *que ella estudia mucho.* *Dígales a* Eva y a Arturo *que ellos estudian mucho.*

24. WRITING EXERCISE

Write the responses to Drills 18.2, 18.3, and 19.

EXERCISE BOOK: EXERCISE 3

Use of Subject Pronouns

TEACHER PRESENTATION, p. T147

GENERALIZATION

Since person and number are already indicated by verb endings, a Spanish sentence is complete and correct without subject pronouns. Subject pronouns are used in Spanish, however, when necessary for clarity or emphasis.

Necesito practicar inglés.
I need to practice English.

Yo necesito practicar inglés.
I (not you or John) *need to practice English.*

Hablamos español bien.
We speak Spanish well.

Nosotros hablamos español bien, pero él habla mal.
We speak Spanish well, but he speaks badly.

STRUCTURE DRILLS

25. PAIRED SENTENCES

Tal vez escuchan las noticias. ⊗
Maybe they're listening to the news.
Maybe they're listening to the news.

Tal vez escuchan las noticias.
Tal vez ellos escuchan las noticias.
Tal vez escuchan las noticias.

No contesta el teléfono.
She doesn't answer the telephone.
She doesn't answer the telephone.

No contesta el teléfono.
Ella no contesta el teléfono.
No contesta el teléfono.

¿A quién llamas tú?
Who are you calling?
Who are you calling?

¿A quién llamas tú?
¿A quién llamas?
¿A quién llamas tú?

Nosotros estudiamos con Blanca.
We study with Blanca.
We study with Blanca.

Nosotros estudiamos con Blanca.
Estudiamos con Blanca.
Nosotros estudiamos con Blanca.

26. FREE RESPONSE

¿Arturo y Blanca estudian ruso o inglés?   *Estudian inglés.*
¿Qué necesita practicar Arturo?   *Necesita practicar inglés.*
¿Con quién estudia él?   *Estudia con la chica americana.*
¿Por qué no estudia con Blanca?   *Blanca y él pronuncian muy mal.*
¿Contestan el teléfono en la casa de la chica americana?   *No, no contestan.*
¿Sabe Arturo qué pasa con el teléfono?   *No, no sabe.*
¿Por qué no contestan?   *Tal vez ella no llega de la escuela todavía.*
¿Estudia usted español o francés?
¿Necesita usted estudiar ahora?
¿Cómo habla usted español, bien, bastante bien, o mal?
¿Cómo pronuncia usted inglés?
¿Habla usted con alguien ahora?
¿Hablan ustedes conmigo hoy?
¿Dónde estudian ustedes, en casa o en la biblioteca?
¿Con quién hablan ustedes ahora?

27. DIRECTED ADDRESS

Ask the following questions of the persons indicated by the English cue.

1. ¿Escucha las noticias? ⊗
   (your brother)

¿Escuchas las noticias?

(your friends)	¿Escuchan las noticias?
(your friend's mother)	¿Escucha las noticias?
(your sister)	¿Escuchas las noticias?
(your teacher)	¿Escucha las noticias?

2. ¿Pasa por la escuela ahora? ⊗

(your cousin)	*¿Pasas por la escuela ahora?*
(your friend's parents)	*¿Pasan por la escuela ahora?*
(a little girl)	*¿Pasas por la escuela ahora?*
(some classmates)	*¿Pasan por la escuela ahora?*
(the mailman)	*¿Pasa por la escuela ahora?*

28. WRITING EXERCISE

Write the responses to Drill 27.2.
EXERCISE BOOK: EXERCISES 4, 5, 6, 7, 8

Listening and Speaking Exercise 47*, p. T39 ⊗

RECOMBINATION MATERIAL | *Note:* For teaching suggestions see p. T17

Dialogs

I

MARÍA	¿Qué pasa? ¿Por qué no contestan?
ARTURO	¿A quién llamas? *¿A quién llama?* ←
MARÍA	A Susana.
ARTURO	Tal vez está en la biblioteca.

QUESTIONS

VARIATION: The two speakers address each other as *usted.* —

1. ¿A quién llama María?
2. ¿Contesta alguien el teléfono?
3. ¿Por qué no contesta Susana?

II

RAÚL	¿Dónde está Elena?
MARÍA	Está en el teléfono.
RAÚL	¿Con quién habla?
MARÍA	Con la chica americana.

QUESTIONS

1. ¿Habla Raúl con María o con Elena?
2. ¿Estudia Elena o habla por teléfono?
3. ¿Con quién habla Elena?

III

PEPE	¿Hablas inglés bien? ¿Habla inglés bien?
MANOLO	No, muy mal, ¿y tú? No, muy mal, ¿y usted?
PEPE	Bastante bien, ¿y Blanca?
MANOLO	Blanca habla muy bien.

QUESTIONS

VARIATION: The conversation is between two adults who address each other as *usted*.

1. ¿Manolo habla inglés bien?
2. Y Pepe, ¿habla bien?
3. Y Blanca, ¿cómo habla inglés?
4. Y usted, ¿habla español bien, bastante bien, o bastante mal?

IV

FLORA	¿Quiere usted hablar con alguien?
RICARDO	Sí, con María.
FLORA	No llega de la escuela todavía.
RICARDO	Muy bien, llamo mañana.

QUESTIONS

1. ¿Con quién habla Ricardo ahora, con María o con Flora?
2. ¿Con quién quiere hablar?
3. ¿Por qué no habla Ricardo con María?

Directed Dialogs

Pregúntele a *Ana* si llama a Susana.
Ana, diga que no, que llama a la chica americana.

¿Llamas a Susana?
No, llamo a la chica americana.

Pregúntele a *Fernando* si llama a Susana.
Fernando, diga que sí, que necesita hablar con ella.

¿Llamas a Susana?
Sí, necesito hablar con ella.

Pregúntele a *María* si llama a Susana.
María, diga que sí, que necesita practicar español.

¿Llamas a Susana?
Sí, necesito practicar español.

Rejoinders

Give as many responses as you can to each of the following sentences. Your responses may be questions, statements, exclamations, or phrases. Use only the words and forms you have learned so far.

Possible Rejoinders

1. Quiero practicar inglés.

¿Por qué no llamas a la chica americana?
¿Por qué no estudias conmigo?
Tú y yo pronunciamos muy mal.
Yo no hablo bien.
¿Por qué?

2. ¿Llamas a la chica americana?

Sí, pero no contesta. / Sí, quiero practicar inglés. / No, llamo a Blanca. / No, llamo a la maestra. / Sí, quiero estudiar con ella. / Sí, quiero hablar inglés con ella.

LETTER ↔ SOUND CORRESPONDENCES

| *Note:* For teaching suggestions see p. T16

Lesson 1

Note: Teach the Spanish alphabet before beginning these exercises, so that you can always refer to the letters by their Spanish names.

READING: ch

The **ch** is a separate letter in the Spanish alphabet and represents the sound [ch], which is similar to the *ch* in the English word *chalk.*

FAMILIAR WORDS chica, escuchamos

UNFAMILIAR WORDS echa, leche, muchacho

READING: c = [k]

The letter **c** before **a, o, u,** or a consonant represents the sound [k].

FAMILIAR WORDS con, americana, conmigo, practicar, contestan, escuela, discos, biblioteca, carro

UNFAMILIAR WORDS casi, cuna, compra, comida, claro

READING: qu = [k]

The letters **qu,** which occur only before **e** and **i,** represent the sound [k].

FAMILIAR WORDS qué, quién, quiero, quieres

UNFAMILIAR WORDS parque, queso, esquina

SENTENCES

1. ¿Qué escuchas? ¿Unos discos?
2. Quiero practicar con la chica americana.
3. ¿Por qué no practicas conmigo?

WRITING

Copy the above sentences and be prepared to write them from dictation.

Spelling Note: The sound [k] is represented by **c** before **a, o, u,** or a consonant, by **qu** before **e** and **i.**

Lesson 2

READING: s, z = [s]

The letters **s** and **z** both represent the sound [s].

FAMILIAR WORDS   pasa, inglés, Susana, están, sala, tal vez

UNFAMILIAR WORDS   blusa, presente, presidente, plaza, perezoso, zapatos, diez

Note: In some parts of Spain, the letter *z* represents the sound [s̪], similar to the *th* in *thought.* Throughout the student text, only Spanish-American pronunciation is given.

READING: c = [s]

The letter **c** before **e** or **i** represents the sound [s].

FAMILIAR WORDS   francés, necesito, canción, cocina, pronunciamos

UNFAMILIAR WORDS   cine, cinco, gracias, estación, nación, edición

Note: In some parts of Spain, the letter *c* before *e* or *i* represents the sound [s̪].

SENTENCES

1. Tal vez escuchan una canción.
2. Susana pasa por la escuela.
3. Blanca pronuncia muy bien.

WRITING

Copy the above sentences and be prepared to write them from dictation.

Spelling Notes:

The sound [s] may be represented by **s** or **z**, or by **c** before **e** or **i**. There is no way to predict which letter will be used. You must memorize the spelling of each new word as you learn it, but the following hints may be helpful:

a. The letter **z** does not normally occur before **e** or **i**.

b. Most cognates, that is, words which are almost the same in form and meaning in English and Spanish, are spelled with the same letter in both languages: **pronuncio,** *pronounce.*

Lesson 3

READING: h

The letter **h** represents no sound.

    FAMILIAR WORDS   hablo, ahora, hoy

    UNFAMILIAR WORDS   hora, hombre, hambre, hermano

READING: ll, y = [y̶]

The letters **ll** and **y** both represent the sound [y̶].

    FAMILIAR WORDS   yo, ella, llamas, llega

    UNFAMILIAR WORDS   ya, oye, silla, olla, llanto, ellos

Note: In some parts of Spain and of Spanish America, the letter *ll* represents the sound [l̶y̶].

READING: y = [i]

The letter **y** represents the sound [i] in the word **y** (*and*).

SENTENCES

1. ¿A quién llamas? ¿A ella?
2. ¿Llegan ahora Blanca y Arturo?
3. Yo no sé con quién habla.

WRITING

Copy the above sentences and be prepared to write them from dictation.

Spelling Note: There is no way to predict which words will be written with **ll** and which with **y.** You must memorize the spelling of each new word as you learn it.

BASIC DIALOG

El Día de la Madre[1]

MANUEL   ¿En qué piensas?
MIGUEL   En nada. ¿A qué hora cierran las tiendas?   `3-1`
MANUEL   No sé. ¿Por qué? ¿Tienes que comprar algo?
MIGUEL   Sí, y tú también. Para tu mamá. El lunes es el Día de la Madre.   `3-2`

MIGUEL   Me aprietan mucho los zapatos. No puedo caminar más.   `3-3`
MANUEL   Yo tampoco. ¿Vamos al cine, mejor?
MIGUEL   Vamos. Pensamos en el regalo después. ¿Qué dan?⎤
MANUEL   Una película italiana. ¡Apúrate! Ya casi empieza. ⎦   `3-4`

Mother's Day

MANUEL   What are you thinking about? (In what are you thinking?)
MIGUEL   (In) nothing. What time (At what hour) do they close the stores?
MANUEL   I don't know. Why? Do you have to buy something?
MIGUEL   Yes, and you too. For your mom. Monday is Mother's Day (the day of the mother).

MIGUEL   My shoes are too tight. (To me squeeze much the shoes.) I can't walk any more.
MANUEL   Neither can I. (I, neither.) Shall we go to the movies instead (better)?
MIGUEL   Let's go. We'll think about the gift later. What's playing? (What are they giving?)
MANUEL   An Italian movie (film). Hurry up! It's about to begin. (Already almost it begins.)

---

[1] Mother's Day is celebrated in most Spanish-speaking countries on the Feast of the Immaculate Conception, the eighth of December.

◀ *Movie-going is a popular form of entertainment in many Spanish-speaking cities.*

◀ *Note:* The motion picture industry is of growing importance in Spanish America. Buenos Aires and Mexico City are the principal movie-making centers.

Supplement

uno, dos, tres, cuatro, cinco, seis, siete, ocho, nueve, diez, once, doce	1, 2, 3, 4, 5, 6, 7, 8, 9, 10, 11, 12

Note: Use the chalkboard to cue numbers.

Cierran las tiendas a la una.   They close the stores at one o'clock.
          las dos   two o'clock
          las tres   three o'clock
     las tiendas   3-1
Cierran la puerta.   3-2   They close the door.
      la ventana   3-3   the window

Miguel tiene que comprar algo.   Miguel has to buy something.

El lunes es el Día de la Madre.   Monday is Mother's Day.
El martes   Tuesday
El miércoles   Wednesday
El jueves   Thursday
El viernes   Friday
El sábado   Saturday
El domingo   Sunday

Note: Point out that the days of the week are not capitalized.

Caminamos por el parque.   3-4   We're walking through the park.
     al cine   3-5
Vamos al mercado.   3-6   Let's go to the market.
      al centro   3-7   downtown (to the center)

Pensamos en el regalo antes.   We'll think about the gift first
        el Día de la Madre   3-8   (beforehand).
        la película   3-9
        el regalo   3-10
Pensamos en el examen.   3-11   We're thinking about the exam.
       la comida   3-12   the dinner, food, meal
       la fiesta   3-13   the party
       el desfile   3-14   the parade
       el baile   3-15   the dance
Me aprietan mucho los zapatos.   3-16 ·

Listening and Speaking Exercises 48, 49*, 50, 51, 52*, p. T39 ⊗

BASIC FORMS

The verbs in the following list are taken from the Basic Dialog and Supplement. They include the infinitives of verbs that follow a grammatical pattern you already know, and those of new verbs (preceded by an asterisk) whose forms will be explained in this unit.

Note: For suggestions on how to teach new vocabulary, see p. T9

Verbs

*apretar	comprar
caminar	*empezar
*cerrar	*pensar

READING NOTES

Dialog

<u>v</u>amos	**v** represents the sound [b].
me<u>j</u>or	**j** represents the sound [h].
<u>r</u>egalo	**r** represents the sound [rr].

Supplement

nue<u>v</u>e, la <u>v</u>entana, jue<u>v</u>es	**v** represents the sound [ƀ].
<u>j</u>ueves	**j** represents the sound [h].

Vocabulary Exercises

1. QUESTIONS

1. ¿Con quién habla Manuel?   *Habla con Miguel.*
2. ¿Tiene que comprar algo Miguel?   *Sí, tiene que comprar algo.*
3. ¿Manuel también tiene que comprar algo? *Sí, también.*
4. ¿Qué día es el Día de la Madre?   *El lunes es el Día de la Madre.*

(*continued*)

(*continued*)

5. ¿En los Estados Unidos, cierran las tiendas a las seis o a las siete?
6. ¿En los Estados Unidos, es el Día de la Madre el domingo o el lunes?

2. ENGLISH CUE DRILL

¿Tienes que comprar algo? ⊗	¿Tienes que comprar algo?
Do you have to talk with her?	¿Tienes que hablar con ella?
Do you have to go to the races?	¿Tienes que ir a las carreras?
Do you have to practice Spanish?	¿Tienes que practicar español?
Do you have to listen to some records?	¿Tienes que escuchar unos discos?
Do you have to buy something?	¿Tienes que comprar algo?

3. DIALOG RECALL

piensas	*¿En qué piensas?*
las tiendas	*¿A qué hora cierran las tiendas?*
algo	*¿Tienes que comprar algo?*
el Día de la Madre	*El lunes es el Día de la Madre.*
la puerta	*¿A qué hora cierran la puerta?*
el jueves	*El jueves es el Día de la Madre.*

Large crowds of shoppers spill over into the street in a commercial section of Lima.

4. QUESTIONS

1. ¿Quiere ir Manuel a las tiendas o al cine? *Quiere ir al cine.*
2. ¿Y Miguel también quiere ir al cine? *Sí, también.*
3. ¿Compran o no compran el regalo? *No compran el regalo.*
4. ¿Qué película dan? *Una película italiana.*
5. ¿Usted quiere ir al cine el sábado? ¿Qué película dan?
6. ¿A qué hora empieza?

5. DIALOG RECALL

zapatos	*Me aprietan mucho los zapatos.*
caminar	*No puedo caminar más.*
mejor	*¿Vamos al cine, mejor?*
el regalo	*Pensamos en el regalo después.*
casi	*Ya casi empieza.*
centro	*¿Vamos al centro, mejor?*
antes	*Pensamos en el regalo antes.*

GRAMMAR

Stem Alternation: e–ie
a–*Class Verbs*

PRESENTATION *TEACHER PRESENTATION: p. T147*

¿En qué **pie**nsas?
Pensamos en el regalo.

Is the stem stressed or unstressed in each verb form? What is the vowel sound in the stem when stressed? How is the sound written? What is the vowel sound in the stem when unstressed? How is the sound written?

GENERALIZATION

1. In certain verb stems the vowel **e** alternates with **ie** (pronounced [ye]); **ie** occurs when the stem is stressed; **e** occurs when the stem is unstressed.

	Stressed Stem	*Unstressed Stem*
	p<u>ie</u>nso	p<u>e</u>nsar
	p<u>ie</u>nsas	p<u>e</u>nsamos
	p<u>ie</u>nsa	
	p<u>ie</u>nsan	

2. There is no way to know in advance whether a verb will have this alternation in its stem. You must learn this for each new verb as you encounter it. The **a**-class verbs you have learned so far which have this stem alternation are **apretar, cerrar, empezar,** and **pensar.**

Listening and Speaking Exercises 53, 54, 55, 56*, p. T40 ⊗   SECTION B

STRUCTURE DRILLS

6. PATTERNED RESPONSE

¿Empieza ahora? ⊗	Sí, tiene que empezar.
¿Cierra ahora?	Sí, tiene que cerrar.
¿Piensa ahora?	Sí, tiene que pensar.
¿Empieza ahora?	Sí, tiene que empezar.

7. PERSON-NUMBER SUBSTITUTION

1. Empiezo el examen. ⊗	Empiezo el examen.
(tú)	Empiezas el examen.
(él)	Empieza el examen.
(Manolo y yo)	Empezamos el examen.
(ellos)	Empiezan el examen.
(ustedes)	Empiezan el examen.

2. Pensamos en el Día de la Madre. ⊗   *pienso–piensan–piensa–*
   (yo–Manolo y usted–él–nosotros–tú)   *pensamos–piensas*

3. No cierran la ventana. ⊗   *cerramos–cierro–cierras–*
   (nosotros–yo–tú–ella–usted)   *cierra–cierra*

8. PAIRED SENTENCES

Piensa en la fiesta. ⊗	Piensa en la fiesta.
(nosotros)	Pensamos en la fiesta.
(ella)	Piensa en la fiesta.

¿Por qué no cierras la puerta?   *¿Por qué no cierras la puerta?*
   (nosotros)   *¿Por qué no cerramos la puerta?*
   (tú)   *¿Por qué no cierras la puerta?*

Empiezo mañana.   *Empiezo mañana.*
   (nosotros)   *Empezamos mañana.*
   (yo)   *Empiezo mañana.*

ADDITIONAL STRUCTURE DRILL, p. T205 ⊗

9. FREE RESPONSE

¿Piensan ustedes en inglés o en español?
¿Cierran las tiendas a las cinco o a las seis?
¿A qué hora cierran el mercado? ¿y la escuela?
¿Cierran ustedes las ventanas ahora?
¿Quiere usted cerrar la puerta, *Juan?*
¿Cuándo empieza la película el sábado, a las dos o más tarde?
¿En qué piensa usted, en el examen?

10. WRITING EXERCISE

Write the responses to Drills 7.2, 7.3, and 8.

EXERCISE BOOK: EXERCISES 1 AND 2

Gender and the Definite Article

PRESENTATION *TEACHER PRESENTATION, p. T148*

Ésa que está en **el carro** es Lili.
Pensamos en **el regalo** después.
Caminamos por **el centro**.
Está en **el teléfono**.

What is the final vowel sound of each of the nouns in heavy type? Which Spanish word corresponds to *the* in these sentences?

Cierran **la puerta**.
Están en **la cocina**.
Pensamos en **la fiesta**.
Pasa por **la biblioteca**.

What is the final vowel sound of each of the nouns in heavy type? Which Spanish word corresponds to *the* in these sentences?

GENERALIZATION

1. All Spanish nouns belong to one of two gender classes: <u>masculine</u> or <u>feminine</u>. Note that these are purely grammatical terms. They are used to classify a word, not to indicate a quality or characteristic.

2. The Spanish form of the definite article *the* is determined by the gender of the noun it is used with: **el** is used with masculine singular nouns; **la** is used with feminine singular nouns.

Note: Use the following Supplement posters to elicit nouns and the corresponding definite article.

Masculine		Feminine					
el carro	1-7	**la puerta**	3-2	la casa	1-1	el disco	2-5
el regalo	3-10	**la cocina**	1-3	la comida	3-12	el mercado	3-6
el centro	3-7	**la fiesta**	3-13	la escuela	2-6	el señor	2-8
el teléfono	1-4	**la biblioteca**	2-7	la maestra	2-1		
el perro	1-6	**la tienda**	3-1	la sala	1-2		
el zapato	3-16	**la película**	3-9	la señora	2-2		
				la señorita	2-3		
				la ventana	3-3		

3. In general, you will have to memorize the gender of a noun when you first learn the noun. The following hints, however, will be useful in helping you remember the gender of most Spanish nouns:

Masculine	*Feminine*
a. Most nouns that refer to males are masculine: **el chico, el tío, el señor.**	a. Most nouns that refer to females are feminine: **la chica, la tía, la señora.**
b. Most nouns that end in **o** are masculine: **el regalo, el zapato.**	b. Most nouns that end in **a** are feminine: **la puerta, la película.**
c. The names of all the days of the week are masculine: **el lunes, el martes.**	c. Most nouns that end in **-ción** are feminine: **la canción.**

4. The following are the nouns you have learned so far for which none of these hints is helpful.

el baile	3-15	**el examen**	3-11
el cine	3-5	**el parque**	3-4
el desfile	3-14	**el sofá**	1-5
el día			

5. Some nouns which refer to people have both a masculine and a feminine form which are identical except for final **o** or **a**. For example, corresponding to the feminine noun **tía** (*aunt*), there is the masculine noun **tío** (*uncle*).

Male person	*Female person*
el amigo	**la amiga**
el chico	**la chica**
el maestro	**la maestra**

Listening and Speaking Exercises 57, 58, 59, 60*, 61*, p. T42 ⊗   SECTION C

STRUCTURE DRILLS

11. ITEM SUBSTITUTION

1. El señor pronuncia muy bien. ⊗
   — señorita _____.
   — chica _____.
   — maestro _____.
   — tía _____.
   — chico _____.

   El señor pronuncia muy bien.
   La señorita pronuncia muy bien.
   La chica pronuncia muy bien.
   El maestro pronuncia muy bien.
   La tía pronuncia muy bien.
   El chico pronuncia muy bien.

2. La película empieza a las siete. ⊗
   (desfile–comida–examen–baile–carrera)

   el desfile–la comida–el examen–
   el baile–la carrera

12. WRITING EXERCISE

Write the responses to Drill 11.2.

EXERCISE BOOK: EXERCISE 3

Plural of Nouns and of the Definite Article

PRESENTATION *TEACHER PRESENTATION, p. T150*

Pensamos en **el rega<u>l</u>o.**
Pensamos en **los rega<u>l</u>os.**
<u>La</u> **ma<u>dre</u>** no llega todavía.
<u>Las</u> **ma<u>dres</u>** no llegan todavía.
Hablo con **el seño<u>r</u>.**
Hablo con <u>los</u> **seño<u>re</u>s.**

In each pair of sentences, which noun is singular? Which is plural? If a singular noun ends in a vowel, how is its plural formed? If a singular noun ends in a consonant, how is its plural formed? What definite article is used with plural masculine nouns? What definite article is used with plural feminine nouns?

GENERALIZATION

1. Nouns whose singular ends in a vowel add **s** to form the plural.

	Singular	*Plural*
	regalo	**regalos**
	puerta	**puertas**
	madre	**madres**

2. Most nouns whose singular ends in a consonant add **es** to form the plural.

	señor	**señores**

3. If, however, a noun ends in **s,** and the last syllable is unstressed, nothing is added to form the plural. The most common examples are the first five days of the week.

lunes	*Monday*	**lunes**	*Mondays*
martes	*Tuesday*	**martes**	*Tuesdays*
miércoles	*Wednesday*	**miércoles**	*Wednesdays*
jueves	*Thursday*	**jueves**	*Thursdays*
viernes	*Friday*	**viernes**	*Fridays*

4. Recall that the masculine plural pronouns **nosotros** and **ellos** refer to mixed groups as well as to groups consisting of men or boys. Similarly, masculine plural nouns are often used to refer to mixed groups, when there is no special reason to point out that girls or women are included.

boys and girls	**chicos y chicas**	or	**chicos**
aunts and uncles	**tías y tíos**	or	**tíos**
men and women teachers	**maestros y maestras**	or	**maestros**

5. The definite article **los** is used with masculine plural nouns; the definite article **las** is used with feminine plural nouns.

6. The following are the forms of the definite article in Spanish:

	Singular	*Plural*
MASCULINE	**el (maestro)**	**los (maestros)**
FEMININE	**la (maestra)**	**las (maestras)**

STRUCTURE DRILLS

Note: Use the Supplement posters extensively in this section to elicit gender and number.

13. SINGULAR → PLURAL

El chico pronuncia bien. ⊗	Los chicos pronuncian bien.
La señorita estudia mucho.	Las señoritas estudian mucho.
El señor habla francés.	Los señores hablan francés.
La maestra piensa en algo.	Las maestras piensan en algo.
El maestro no contesta.	Los maestros no contestan.
La chica llega ahora.	Las chicas llegan ahora.

VARIATION: Use right-hand column as stimulus, and have student give singular forms.

14. ITEM SUBSTITUTION

1. Pienso en los regalos. ⊗   Pienso en los regalos.   *VARIATION:* Do the
   _____ canción.   Pienso en la canción.   drill again, substituting
   _____ disco.   Pienso en el disco.   the nouns in Drill 14.2.
   _____ exámenes.   Pienso en los exámenes.
   _____ noticias.   Pienso en las noticias.
   _____ chico.   Pienso en el chico.

2. Juan llega con los discos. ⊗   *el regalo–las chicas–la señorita–*
   (regalo–chicas–señorita–maestro–comida–carro)   *el maestro–la comida–el carro*

3. ¿A qué hora cierran las tiendas? ⊗   *la biblioteca–los mercados–el parque–*
   (biblioteca–mercados–parque–tienda)   *la tienda*

15. PROGRESSIVE SUBSTITUTION

VARIATION

La maestra compra los discos. ⊗	La maestra compra los discos.	
__ señoras _____.	Las señoras compran los discos.	chicas
_____ escuchan _____.	Las señoras escuchan los discos.	necesitan
_____ noticias.	Las señoras escuchan las noticias.	carro
__ maestro _____.	El maestro escucha las noticias.	señor

16. FREE SUBSTITUTION

La fiesta empieza a las cinco. *el desfile, las carreras, la película / (empiezan) / ahora,*
a las dos, más tarde

17. WRITING EXERCISE

Write the responses to Drills 14.2 and 14.3.
EXERCISE BOOK: EXERCISES 4 AND 5.

Some Uses of the Definite Article

TEACHER PRESENTATION, p. T151

GENERALIZATION

In general, the definite article is used in Spanish much as it is in English. There are, however, some cases where it is used in Spanish where it would not be in English.

a. With days of the week used to tell when an activity or event takes place:

El desfile es el sábado.
The parade is on Saturday.
Estudio los lunes.
I study on Mondays.

But if the name of a day is used to answer the question *"What day is it?"* with **hoy, mañana** or **ahora,** the article is not used:

Hoy es sábado.
Today is Saturday.

b. With titles such as **Sr., Sra., Srta.**[2], when people with these titles are spoken of:

El Sr. Vargas habla ruso.
Mr. Vargas speaks Russian.

But if the person is directly addressed, the definite article is not used:

Sr. Vargas, ¿habla usted ruso?
Mr. Vargas, do you speak Russian?

Listening and Speaking Exercises 62, 63, 64, 65*, 66*, p. T43 ⊗   SECTION D

STRUCTURE DRILLS

18. PAIRED SENTENCES

La fiesta es el viernes. ⊗	La fiesta es el viernes.
Today is Friday.	Hoy es viernes.
The party is Friday.	La fiesta es el viernes.
Mañana es lunes.	*Mañana es lunes.*
Monday is Mother's Day.	*El lunes es el Día de la Madre.*
Tomorrow is Monday.	*Mañana es lunes.*

---

[2] **Señor, señora,** and **señorita,** when followed by a proper name, may be abbreviated **Sr.** (*Mr.*), **Sra.** (*Mrs.*), and **Srta.** (*Miss*).

El Sr. Vargas habla bastante bien.
You speak pretty well, Mr. Vargas.
Mr. Vargas speaks pretty well.

El Sr. Vargas habla bastante bien.
Usted habla bastante bien, Sr. Vargas.
El Sr. Vargas habla bastante bien.

La Srta. García piensa en el Sr. Pérez.
Miss García, you're thinking about Mr. Pérez.
Miss García is thinking about Mr. Pérez.

La Srta. García piensa en el Sr. Pérez.
Srta. García, usted piensa en el Sr. Pérez.
La Srta. García piensa en el Sr. Pérez.

ADDITIONAL STRUCTURE DRILLS, p. T205 🗙

19. FREE RESPONSE

¿Es la fiesta de la escuela el sábado o el domingo?
¿Cuándo es el baile de la escuela?
¿Qué día es hoy?
¿Qué día es mañana?
Sr. *García,* ¿pronuncia bien la Srta. *Pérez?*
¿En qué piensan las chicas, en los exámenes o en los chicos?
¿Quién cierra las ventanas?
¿Quiere usted ir a la escuela los sábados y los domingos?
¿Qué días estudia usted?
¿Cierran las tiendas los domingos o los lunes?

EXERCISE BOOK: EXERCISE 6

Word Order in Statements and Yes/No Questions

GENERALIZATION   *TEACHER PRESENTATION, p. T152*

1. The order in which words may occur in sentences is much freer in Spanish than in English. Also, Spanish permits exactly the same order of words in statements as in questions. The three most common patterns in simple sentences are the following:

	Subject	+	*Predicate*		
STATEMENT	**Blanca**		**habla inglés.**		
QUESTION	**¿Blanca**		**habla inglés?**		

	Predicate	+	*Subject*		
STATEMENT	**Habla inglés**		**Blanca.**		
QUESTION	**¿Habla inglés**		**Blanca?**		

	Verb	+	*Subject*	+	*Remainder*
STATEMENT	**Habla**		**Blanca**		**inglés.**
QUESTION	**¿Habla**		**Blanca**		**inglés?**

2. Some Spanish speakers consider the order Subject + Predicate to be more typical of statements, and the other two orders to be more typical of questions. However, all three orders are used for both types of sentences.

3. Since the same patterns of word order occur in both statements and questions, one can tell only by the intonation, or melody, of a sentence whether it is a statement or a question. At the end of a statement the pitch of the voice falls, but at the end of a question the pitch of the voice rises.

STRUCTURE DRILLS

20. QUESTION FORMATION

Change each of the following statements to a question by raising the pitch of your voice.

Miguel necesita zapatos. ⊗	¿Miguel necesita zapatos?
Caminan por el parque Juan y Pablo.	*¿Caminan por el parque Juan y Pablo?*
Cierra la puerta la maestra.	*¿Cierra la puerta la maestra?*
Arturo estudia en la biblioteca.	*¿Arturo estudia en la biblioteca?*
El Sr. García pasa por el mercado.	*¿El Sr. García pasa por el mercado?*
Los exámenes empiezan el miércoles.	*¿Los exámenes empiezan el miércoles?*
Estudias español tú.	*¿Estudias español tú?*

21. ANSWER → QUESTION

Ask two appropriate questions for each of the following answers.

No, el lunes no es el Día de la Madre.	¿Es el lunes el Día de la Madre?
	¿El lunes es el Día de la Madre?

Sí, Arturo piensa en Blanca.	*¿Piensa Arturo en Blanca? / ¿Piensa en Blanca Arturo?*
Sí, la película empieza a la una.	*¿La película empieza a la una? / ¿Empieza la película a la una?*
No, los chicos no pronuncian mal.	*¿Pronuncian mal los chicos? / ¿Los chicos pronuncian mal?*
No, la señora no habla español.	*¿Habla español la señora? / ¿Habla la señora español?*
Sí, Raúl estudia inglés.	*¿Estudia inglés Raúl? / ¿Estudia Raúl inglés?*

22. DIRECTED DRILL

Pregúntele a *Juan* si Blanca habla inglés.	¿Blanca habla inglés?
	¿Habla inglés Blanca?
Pregúntele a *María* si Susana y Teresa llegan a la una.	*¿Llegan a la una Susana y Teresa?*
	¿Llegan Susana y Teresa a la una?
Pregúntele a *Manuel* si los tres chicos estudian ruso.	*¿Los tres chicos estudian ruso?*
	¿Estudian ruso los tres chicos?

Note: There is a third possible question for each of the cues in Drills 21 and 22.

Pregúntele a *Juanita* si el baile empieza a las nueve.

Pregúntele a *Lupe* si Miguel pasa por el parque.

Pregúntele a la maestra si *Camilo* y usted pronuncian bien.

¿Empieza el baile a las nueve?
¿Empieza a las nueve el baile?
¿Miguel pasa por el parque?
¿Pasa Miguel por el parque?
¿Camilo y yo pronunciamos bien?
¿Pronunciamos bien Camilo y yo?

23. WRITING EXERCISE

Write the responses to Drills 21 and 22. Write two different questions for each sentence in Drill 22.

EXERCISE BOOK: EXERCISES 7 AND 8

Listening and Speaking Exercise 67*, p. T45 ⊗

RECOMBINATION MATERIAL

Dialogs

I

MIGUEL	Paquito, ¿qué día es hoy?
PAQUITO	Hoy es sábado.
MIGUEL	¿Es hoy el Día de la Madre?
PAQUITO	No, es mañana.

QUESTIONS

1. ¿Sabe Paquito qué día es?
2. ¿Qué día es?
3. ¿Es el Día de la Madre?
4. ¿Qué día es el Día de la Madre?

II

SUSANA	Vamos al centro.
LUCINDA	No, mejor mañana, hoy no puedo caminar más.
SUSANA	¿Por qué? ¿Qué pasa?
LUCINDA	Me aprietan mucho los zapatos.

REJOINDERS

Vamos al centro.

No, no quiero. / No, mañana mejor. / No, no puedo caminar más. / Muy bien, si tú quieres. / ¿Por qué? / Muy bien, yo necesito comprar un regalo. / Muy bien, ¿cuándo? / Más tarde.

Outdoor markets, like this one in Mexico City, are common in most Spanish-speaking countries.

III

FERNANDO	El miércoles empiezan los exámenes.
RICARDO	¿Tienes que estudiar mucho?
FERNANDO	Sí, ¿y tú?
RICARDO	Yo también.
FERNANDO	Vamos a la biblioteca entonces.

QUESTIONS

1. ¿Qué día empiezan los exámenes?
2. ¿Tiene que estudiar Fernando?
3. ¿Y Ricardo?
4. ¿Para qué quiere Fernando ir a la biblioteca?

IV

CAROLINA	¿Qué película dan?
FLORA	Una película italiana.
CAROLINA	¿A qué hora empieza?
FLORA	A las cuatro. Apúrate.

QUESTIONS

1. ¿De qué hablan Carolina y Flora?
2. ¿Quiere ir Flora al cine?
3. ¿Dan una película italiana o americana?
4. ¿A qué hora empieza la película?

Rejoinders

1. Vamos al cine, mejor.

No, me aprietan mucho los zapatos.
¿Qué dan?
No, quiero estudiar.
No, no puedo caminar más.
¿A qué hora empieza la película?

2. No puedo estudiar más.   *¿Quieres escuchar unos discos, entonces? / Yo tampoco. / ¿Por qué no?*
3. ¿Ya empieza el desfile?   *Sí, ¡apúrate! / No, empieza a la una. / No, empieza más tarde.*
4. ¿Cierran a las cinco?   *Sí, ¡apúrate! Ya son las cuatro. / No, cierran a las seis hoy. /*
No sé a qué hora cierran. / ¿Por qué? ¿Tú necesitas comprar algo?

LETTER ↔ SOUND CORRESPONDENCES

Lesson 1

READING: b, v = [b]

The letters **b** and **v** both represent the sound [b] after a pause and after the sound [m].

FAMILIAR WORDS   bastante, bien, vamos, ventana, viernes,
baile, también

UNFAMILIAR WORDS   vaso, base, voy, bote, vote, bonita, hombre,
hambre, caramba

READING: b, v = [ƀ]

The letters **b** and **v** both represent the sound [ƀ] in any position except after a pause or after the sound [m].

FAMILIAR WORDS   Eva, sabe, la biblioteca, la ventana, nueve,
jueves, sábado

UNFAMILIAR WORDS   uva, novio, a ver, autobús

READING: b AND v

The letters **b** and **v** represent exactly the same two sounds. Whether they represent [b] or [b̷] depends only on their position in the word or phrase, never on which letter is used. There is no sound [v] in normal Spanish.

Note: Although some Spanish speakers have consciously taught themselves to produce the sound [v], this sound does not occur in normal spoken Spanish.

PAIRS	[b]	[b̷]
	bien	muy bien
	vamos	no vamos
	ventana	la ventana
	viernes	ese viernes
	baile	ese baile

READING: n = [m]

The letter **n** represents the sound [m] when it occurs before the sounds [b] and [p].

FAMILIAR WORDS   con Blanca, un viernes, un baile, con Pepe

UNFAMILIAR WORDS   don Pedro, con permiso, un vaso, un vestido

SENTENCES

1. ¿Vamos a la biblioteca con Pedro?
2. El sábado vamos a un baile.
3. Blanca habla inglés bastante bien.

WRITING

Copy the above sentences and be prepared to write them from dictation.

Spelling Notes:

There is no way to predict which words will be written with **b** and which with **v.** You will have to memorize the spelling of each new word as you learn it. However, the following hints may be helpful:
a. Most cognates are spelled with the same letter in both languages: **verbo,** *verb;* **victoria,** *victory;* **bomba,** *bomb;* **verso,** *verse.*
b. Only the letter **b** may follow an **m: ta<u>mb</u>ién.**

Lesson 2

READING: d = [d]

The letter **d** represents the sound [d] after a pause and after the sounds [n] and [l].

FAMILIAR WORDS   dan, dos, día, disco, desfile, doce, domingo, después, dónde, cuándo, tienda

UNFAMILIAR WORDS   dulce, dinero, anda, blando, lindo, grande, falda, caldo.

READING: d = [đ]

The letter **d** represents the sound [đ] when it occurs in any position except after a pause or after the sounds [n] and [l].

FAMILIAR WORDS   nada, puedo, Adela, mercado, estudia, sábado, tarde, madre, usted

UNFAMILIAR WORDS   lado, cada, seda, sido, medias, espada, padre, adiós, verdad, sed

FAMILIAR PAIRS	[d]	[đ]
	dan	¿qué dan?
	día	¿qué día?
	dos	uno y dos
	dónde	adónde
	después	y después
	discos	y discos

READING: ñ

The letter **ñ** represents the sound [ñ], similar to the _ny_ in _canyon_.

FAMILIAR WORDS   señora, señor, señorita, mañana, español

UNFAMILIAR WORDS   uña, año, baño, castaño, España

SENTENCES

1. ¿Dónde estudia usted español, señorita?
2. ¿Qué día es mañana? Domingo.
3. Vamos al mercado y a las tiendas.

WRITING

Copy the above sentences and be prepared to write them from dictation.

BASIC DIALOG

La nueva escuela

Note: At this time, you may wish to assign the section on Education in *Glimpses of the Spanish World.*

EL MAESTRO	Vamos a ver, usted es Susana, ¿no? **4-1**
CRISTINA	No, don[1] Pedro. Ella es Susana; yo soy Cristina.
EL MAESTRO	¡Pero son idénticas! ¿Cuál de las dos es mayor? **4-2**
SUSANA	Ninguna. Somos gemelas.
EL MAESTRO	Ah, con razón. Muy bien, hasta mañana. **4-3**
SUSANA	Esta escuela es muy bonita. Me gusta mucho. ¿A ti te gusta? **4-4**
CRISTINA	¡Claro! Es mucho más linda que la otra.
SUSANA	Sí, y los compañeros son tan simpáticos, ¿verdad?
CRISTINA	Excepto ese chico rubio. ¡Qué pretencioso! **4-5**
SUSANA	¿Y por qué eres tan amiga de él entonces? **4-6**

The New School

THE TEACHER	Let's see, you're Susana, aren't you (no)?
CRISTINA	No, don Pedro. She's Susana; I'm Cristina.
THE TEACHER	But you're identical! Which one (of the two) is older?
SUSANA	Neither one (none). We're twins.
THE TEACHER	Oh, no wonder (with reason). All right, see you (until) tomorrow.
SUSANA	This school is very nice (pretty). I like it a lot. (To me it pleases much.) Do you like it? (To you it pleases?)
CRISTINA	Of course! It is much nicer (more pretty) than the other one.
SUSANA	Yes, and the kids (companions) are so nice, aren't they (truth)?
CRISTINA	Except that blond boy. What a showoff! (How pretentious!)
SUSANA	And why are you so friendly with him (friend of his) then?

---

[1] **Don** is a title of respect used with first names. **Doña** is the corresponding title for women.

◀ *Note:* In many countries, public as well as private schools require uniforms. The type of uniform varies from country to country, and often from school to school.

◀ *A school in Ecuador. Most school children wear uniforms in Spanish-speaking countries.*

47

Supplement

Buenos días.	Good morning.
Buenas tardes.	Good afternoon.
Buenas noches².	Good evening, good night.
Hasta luego.	See you later. (Until then.)
Adiós.	Good-bye.

¿Cuál de las dos es menor?   mayor   4-1   4-2

    gemelos

Which one is younger?

Somos alumnos.
    hermanos

We are students.
    brothers (brothers and sisters)

Esta escuela es pequeña.
    grande   4-3

This school is small.
    big

Esta blusa es muy bonita.   4-4
    falda   4-5
    corbata   4-6
    camisa   4-7

This blouse is very pretty.
    skirt
    tie
    shirt

A usted le gusta mucho.
A él le gusta mucho.
A ella le gusta mucho.

You like it a lot.
He likes it a lot.
She likes it a lot.

Excepto ese vestido.   4-8
    abrigo   4-9
    sombrero   4-10

Except that dress.
    coat
    hat

Ese examen es fácil.
    difícil

That exam is easy.
    difficult

¡Qué antipático!
    inteligente
    alto
    bajo   4-11
    pretencioso   4-12

How unpleasant!
    intelligent
    tall
    short

Listening and Speaking Exercises 68, 69, 70, 71, 72, 73*, p. T45 ⊗

---

² **Buenas noches** means both *good evening* when meeting someone in the evening, and *good night* when departing.

BASIC FORMS

The new nouns included in the Basic Forms list are only those which do not end in **o** or **a.** The letter *m.* or *f.* following each noun indicates its gender.

Verb

*ser

Nouns

noche *f.*   razón *f.*   tarde *f.*

Vocabulary Exercises

1. QUESTIONS

1. ¿Con quién hablan las gemelas? *Con don Pedro.*
2. ¿Hablan en español o en inglés? *En español.*
3. ¿Quién es don Pedro? *El maestro.*
4. ¿Es don Pedro un alumno? *No.*
5. ¿Son hermanas Susana y Cristina? *Sí.*
6. ¿Son gemelas? *Sí.*
7. ¿Son idénticas Susana y Cristina? *Sí.*
8. ¿Cuál de las dos hermanas es mayor? *Ninguna.*
9. ¿Cuál es menor? *Ninguna.*

2. DIALOG RECALL

vamos	*Vamos a ver, usted es Susana, ¿no?*
pero	*¡Pero son idénticas!*
cuál	*¿Cuál de las dos es mayor?*
gemelas	*Somos gemelas.*
hasta	*Muy bien, hasta mañana.*
menor	*¿Cuál de las dos es menor?*
hermanos	*Somos hermanos.*

3. QUESTIONS

1. ¿Es bonita la nueva escuela? *Sí, muy bonita.*
2. ¿Le gusta a Susana? *Sí, mucho.*
3. ¿A Cristina también le gusta? *Sí, también.*
4. ¿Son simpáticos los compañeros? *Sí, excepto el chico rubio.*
5. El chico rubio, ¿es simpático o antipático? *Antipático.*
6. ¿Por qué? *Es pretencioso.*
7. ¿Le gusta a usted esta escuela?
8. ¿Es grande o pequeña?
9. ¿Es bonita esta escuela?

4. DIALOG RECALL

bonita	*Esta escuela es muy bonita.*
linda	*Es mucho más linda que la otra.*
verdad	*Sí, y los compañeros son tan simpáticos, ¿verdad?*
excepto	*Excepto ese chico rubio.*
pretencioso	*¡Qué pretencioso!*
pequeña	*Esta escuela es muy pequeña.*

GRAMMAR

ser, *Present Tense*

PRESENTATION *TEACHER PRESENTATION, p. T153*

Yo **soy** Cristina.
¿Por qué **eres** tan amiga de él?
Usted **es** Susana, ¿no?
Ella **es** Susana.
Somos gemelas.
Los compañeros **son** tan simpáticos.

Which form of the verb corresponds to **yo**? to **tú**? to **él, ella** and **usted**? Which form corresponds to **nosotros**? to **ellos, ellas, ustedes**?

GENERALIZATION

The verb **ser** is highly irregular. The forms of the present tense must be memorized.

ser, PRESENT TENSE		
	Singular	*Plural*
1	soy	somos
2	eres	son
3	es	

Listening and Speaking Exercises 74, 75*, 76, 77*, 78*, p. T47 ⊗ **SECTION B**

STRUCTURE DRILLS

5. PERSON-NUMBER SUBSTITUTION

1. ¿De dónde eres? ⊗   ¿De dónde eres?
    (ustedes)   ¿De dónde son?
    (usted)   ¿De dónde es?
    (nosotros)   ¿De dónde somos?
    (él)   ¿De dónde es?
    (yo)   ¿De dónde soy?

2. Son de los Estados Unidos. ⊗   *es–somos–eres–soy–son*
    (ella–Pedro y yo–tú–yo–ellos)

6. FREE RESPONSE

¿Quiénes son Susana y Cristina?   *Son gemelas. (Son alumnas, hermanas.)*
¿Quién es don Pedro?   *Es el maestro.*
¿Son Susana y Cristina hermanas?   *Sí, son hermanas.*
¿Es Cristina menor que Susana? ¿Por qué?   *No, son gemelas.*
¿Es Susana mayor que Cristina? ¿Por qué?   *No, son gemelas.*
¿Es usted hermana gemela?
¿Son hermanas ustedes dos?
¿De dónde es usted?
¿Son ustedes de los Estados Unidos?
¿Quién es ese chico?
¿Quién es usted?
¿Quién soy yo?
¿Es usted un alumno o el maestro?
¿Y yo?

7. DIRECTED DIALOG

Pregúntele a *Susana* de dónde es.   ¿De dónde eres?
Dígale que usted es de los Estados Unidos.   Soy de los Estados Unidos.
Pregúntele si *María* y ella son amigas.   ¿*María* y tú son amigas?
Dígale que sí, que *María* también es de   Sí, *María* también es de los Estados Unidos.
   los Estados Unidos.

8. WRITING EXERCISE

Write the responses to Drill 5.2.

EXERCISE BOOK: EXERCISES 1 AND 2

The Indefinite Article

PRESENTATION *TEACHER PRESENTATION, p. T154*

¿Tienes que comprar **un** regalo?
Escuchan **un** disco.

Dan **una** película italiana.
Escuchan **una** canción.   *(continued)*

(*continued*)

Which form of the indefinite article (the word which means *a, an*) is used with singular masculine nouns? with singular feminine nouns?

Compro <u>unos</u> regalos.
Escuchan <u>unos</u> discos.

Compro <u>unas</u> corbatas.
Escuchan <u>unas</u> canciones.

Which form of the indefinite article is used with plural masculine nouns? with plural feminine nouns?

GENERALIZATION

	Singular	*Plural*
MASCULINE	un (compañer<u>o</u>)	un<u>os</u> (compañer<u>os</u>)
FEMININE	un<u>a</u> (compañer<u>a</u>)	un<u>as</u> (compañer<u>as</u>)

Like the definite article, the indefinite article agrees in number (singular or plural) and gender (masculine or feminine) with the noun it modifies.

In English, the singular form of the indefinite article is *a* or *an;* the plural form is *some.*

STRUCTURE DRILLS

Note: Use Supplement posters extensively in this section to elicit gender and number.

9. ITEM SUBSTITUTION

1. Compramos una camisa. ⊗
   _____ regalo.
   _____ corbata.
   _____ abrigo.
   _____ falda.
   _____ vestido.
   _____ blusa.
   _____ perro.

   Compramos una camisa.
   Compramos un regalo.
   Compramos una corbata.
   Compramos un abrigo.
   Compramos una falda.
   Compramos un vestido.
   Compramos una blusa.
   Compramos un perro.

2. ¿Llega con unos compañeros? ⊗
   (amigas–señores–amigos–chicos–señoritas–alumnos)

   unas amigas–unos señores–unos amigos–
   unos chicos–unas señoritas–
   unos alumnos

3. Quiero un sombrero. ⊗
   (camisas–discos–falda–vestidos–abrigo–blusas–carro)

   *unas camisas–unos discos–una falda–
   unos vestidos–un abrigo–
   unas blusas–un carro*

4. ¿Por qué no compras unos discos? ⊗
   (blusas–corbata–abrigo–zapatos–perro)

   *unas blusas–una corbata–un abrigo–
   unos zapatos–un perro*

10. FREE COMPLETION

1. Necesito una _____.   *blusa, falda, corbata, camisa*
   Necesito un _____.   *carro, perro, vestido, abrigo, sombrero, disco*
   Necesito unas _____.   *blusas, faldas, corbatas, camisas*
   Necesito unos _____.   *vestidos, sombreros, discos*

2. Llegan con un _____.   *amigo, hermano, maestro, chico, tío, compañero, señor*
   Llegan con unas _____.   *amigas, hermanas, maestras, chicas, tías, compañeras, señoras*
   Llegan con unos _____.   *amigos, hermanos, maestros, chicos, tíos, compañeros, señores*
   Llegan con una _____.   *amiga, hermana, maestra, chica, tía, compañera, señora, señorita*

11. FREE RESPONSE

¿Necesita usted comprar un regalo?
¿Quiere usted comprar algo? ¿Qué quiere comprar?
Y usted, ¿qué quiere comprar?
¿Necesita usted unos discos?
¿Qué necesita usted?

12. FREE SUBSTITUTION

Estudia con unos amigos.   *habla, llega, practica, camina / unos compañeros, una amiga,
un maestro, unos señores, unas chicas*

13. WRITING EXERCISE

Write the responses to Drills 9.2, 9.3, and 9.4.

EXERCISE BOOK: EXERCISE 3

Adjective Agreement

PRESENTATION *TEACHER PRESENTATION, p. T155*

El chico es muy **pretencioso**.
Don Pedro es **simpático**.
El abrigo es muy **bonito**.

(continued)

(*continued*)

What is the gender and number of the noun in each sentence? What is the final vowel of the adjective if the noun it modifies is masculine singular?

La película es italiana.
La escuela es pequeña.

What is the gender and number of the noun in each sentence? What is the final vowel of the adjective if the noun it modifies is feminine singular?

El compañero es tan simpático.
Los compañeros son tan simpáticos.

¿La chica? Es americana.
¿Las chicas? Son americanas.

In each pair, how does the noun in the second sentence differ from the noun in the first? How does the adjective differ? How is the plural formed for adjectives whose singular ends in a vowel?

GENERALIZATION

1. An adjective agrees in gender and number with the noun it modifies.

El señor es pretencioso.
Los señores son pretenciosos.
La señora es pretenciosa.
Las señoras son pretenciosas.

Adjectives like **pretencioso, pretenciosa** consist of a stem (**pretencios-**) + a gender marker (**o** for masculine, **a** for feminine). The stem + the gender marker (**pretencioso, pretenciosa**) is pluralized by adding **s,** just like nouns which end in a vowel.

2. The masculine plural form of an adjective is used to modify two or more masculine nouns.

Juan y Pedro son rubios.

The feminine plural form is used to modify two or more feminine nouns.

María y las otras chicas son simpáticas.

The masculine plural form is used to modify two or more nouns of different genders.

El señor y la señora son antipáticos.
María, Paco, y Elena son americanos.

Listening and Speaking Exercises 79*, 80, 81, 82*, 83*, p. T50 ⊗ SECTION C

STRUCTURE DRILLS

14. ITEM SUBSTITUTION

1. El maestro no es nuevo. ⊗   El maestro no es nuevo.
   La maestra _____.   La maestra no es nueva.
   El vestido _____.   El vestido no es nuevo.
   El abrigo _____.   El abrigo no es nuevo.
   La película _____.   La película no es nueva.
   El carro _____.   El carro no es nuevo.

2. Los hermanos son casi idénticos. ⊗   *idénticas–idénticos–idénticos–idénticas–*
   (las gemelas–los sombreros–los vestidos–las faldas–las chicas) *idénticas*

3. Las gemelas son bastante altas. ⊗   *es bastante alto–son bastante altos–son*
   (el señor–los chicos–Juan y María–las hermanas–la señorita) *bastante altos–son*
   bastante altas–es bastante alta

15. WRITING EXERCISE

Write the responses to Drills 14.2 and 14.3.

EXERCISE BOOK: EXERCISES 4 AND 5

A home economics class in Peru.

Other Types of Adjectives

PRESENTATION *TEACHER PRESENTATION, p. T157*

<u>El chico</u> es **mayor**.
<u>La chica</u> es **mayor**.

<u>El examen</u> es **difícil**.
<u>La canción</u> es **difícil**.

Do adjectives which end in a consonant show gender agreement?

<u>El chico</u> es **mayor**.
<u>Los chicos</u> son **mayores**.

<u>La canción</u> es **difícil**.
<u>Las canciones</u> son **difíciles**.

Do adjectives which end in a consonant show number agreement?

<u>El mercado</u> es **grande**.
<u>La biblioteca</u> es **grande**.
<u>Los mercados</u> son **grandes**.
<u>Las bibliotecas</u> son **grandes**.

Do adjectives which end in <u>e</u> show gender agreement? Do they show number agreement? What generalization can you make about adjectives which end in <u>e</u> or a consonant?

GENERALIZATION

Many adjectives whose singular form ends in <u>e</u> or a consonant, rather than in the gender markers <u>o</u> and <u>a</u>, do not show gender agreement with the noun they modify.

El chico
La chica } es inteligente.   El chico
La chica } es mayor.

These adjectives, however, do agree in number. Their plurals are formed in the usual way— by adding <u>s</u> after <u>e</u>, or <u>es</u> after a consonant.

Los chicos
Las chicas } son inteligentes.   Los chicos
Las chicas } son mayores.

STRUCTURE DRILLS

16. ITEM SUBSTITUTION

1. ¿Es grande la biblioteca? ⊗   ¿Es grande la biblioteca?
   ¿——————— el cine?   ¿Es grande el cine?
   ¿——————— los parques?   ¿Son grandes los parques?
   ¿——————— las tiendas?   ¿Son grandes las tiendas?
   ¿——————— la escuela?   ¿Es grande la escuela?
   ¿——————— los mercados?   ¿Son grandes los mercados?
   ¿——————— el desfile?   ¿Es grande el desfile?

2. El chico es inteligente y simpático. ⊗   *es inteligente y simpática–son inteligentes y simpáticos–*
   (la chica–los maestros–las maestras–la alumna–los alumnos) *son inteligentes y simpáticas–*
         es inteligente y simpática–son inteligentes y simpáticos

3. El baile es muy fácil. ⊗
   (los bailes–la canción–el examen–las canciones) *son fáciles–es fácil–es fácil–son fáciles*

4. La chica es mayor. *son mayores–es mayor–es mayor–son mayores*
   (los gemelos–la tía–el señor–los dos chicos)

17. PAIRED SUBSTITUTIONS

¿Los compañeros? ¡Qué simpáticos!   ¿Los compañeros? ¡Qué simpáticos!
¿La maestra? ¡———————————!   ¿La maestra? ¡Qué simpática!
¿Los gemelos? ¡Qué pretenciosos!   *¿Los gemelos? ¡Qué pretenciosos!*
¿La chica rubia? ¡———————!   *¿La chica rubia? ¡Qué pretenciosa!*
¿La cocina? ¡Qué pequeña!   *¿La cocina? ¡Qué pequeña!*
¿El carro? ¡———————!   *¿El carro? ¡Qué pequeño!*
¿El baile? ¡Qué difícil!   *¿El baile? ¡Qué difícil!*
¿Las canciones? ¡————!   *¿Las canciones? ¡Qué difíciles!*
¿Las chicas? ¡Qué inteligentes!   *¿Las chicas? ¡Qué inteligentes!*
¿El Sr. Pérez? ¡———————!   *¿El Sr. Perez? ¡Qué inteligente!*

18. FREE SUBSTITUTION

¿Las corbatas? ¡Qué lindas! *la falda, el carro, los sombreros, las casas / bonito, grande, pequeño*

19. WRITING EXERCISE

Write the responses to Drills 16.2 and 16.3.

Adjectives of Nationality

TEACHER PRESENTATION, p. T157
GENERALIZATION

1. Many adjectives which refer to nationality have the gender markers <u>o</u>, <u>a</u>. There are also nationality adjectives whose masculine singular form ends in a consonant. These show both gender and number agreement. The feminine singular is formed by adding <u>a</u> to the final consonant. The plurals are formed by adding <u>es</u> to the masculine singular and s to the feminine singular.

<u>El maestro</u> es francé<u>s</u>.
<u>La maestra</u> es frances<u>a</u>.

<u>Los maestros</u> son frances<u>es</u>.
<u>Las maestras</u> son frances<u>as</u>.

If the masculine singular ends in <u>és</u>, the other forms do not require a written accent (**francés, francesa**).

2. Here are the adjectives of nationality you have learned so far which do not end in <u>o</u> or <u>a</u>.

alemán, alemana   **francés, francesa**
español, española   **inglés, inglesa**

STRUCTURE DRILLS

20. PATTERNED RESPONSE

1. La película es italiana, ¿verdad?   No, es española.
   Los zapatos son italianos, ¿verdad?   *No, son españoles.*
   El carro es italiano, ¿verdad?   *No, es español.*
   Las canciones son italianas, ¿verdad?   *No, son españolas.*
   El abrigo es italiano, ¿verdad?   *No, es español.*
   Los gemelos son italianos, ¿verdad?   *No, son españoles.*

VARIATION: La película es americana, ¿verdad?   *No, es francesa.*

2. Los chicos son franceses, ¿y la chica?   La chica es francesa también.
   La blusa es nueva, ¿y los zapatos?   *Los zapatos son nuevos también.*
   El Sr. Pérez es rubio, ¿y la Sra. Pérez?   *La Sra. Pérez es rubia también.*
   Los compañeros son inteligentes, ¿y las   *Las compañeras son inteligentes también.*
      compañeras?
   El parque es grande, ¿y la escuela?   *La escuela es grande también.*

Las gemelas son bajas, ¿y la madre?   *La madre es baja también.*
La maestra es muy buena, ¿y los alumnos?   *Los alumnos son muy buenos también.*

Listening and Speaking Exercises 84, 85, 86, 87*, p. T51 ⊗

SECTION D

21. FREE COMPLETION

Me gusta esta escuela. Es muy _____.   *bonita, linda, grande, buena*
Los vestidos son tan _____.   *bonitos, lindos*
Juan y María son bastante _____.   *simpáticos, antipáticos, pretenciosos*
No me gusta ese chico. Es _____.   *antipático, pretencioso*
¿Las gemelas? Son muy _____.   *inteligentes, altas, simpáticas*

22. REJOINDERS

¿Te gusta la chica alemana?   *Sí, es simpática. / Sí, me gusta mucho.*
Sí, habla español muy bien. / No, es anti-
pática. / No, es muy pretenciosa. / ¿Cuál
chica alemana?

Esta escuela es muy buena, ¿verdad?   *Sí, me gusta mucho. / Sí, es más grande que*
la otra. / Sí, los compañeros son tan sim-
| **Note:** Male teachers should   *páticos. / Sí, los maestros son muy buenos. /*
| substitute *ingleses.* _____   *No, me gusta más la otra.*

23. PROGRESSIVE SUBSTITUTION

Lupita y yo somos inglesas. ⊗ ←   Lupita y yo somos inglesas. *VARIATION*
El señor _____.   El señor es inglés.   *el chico*
_____ son _____.   Los señores son ingleses.
_____ antipático.   El señor es antipático.   *simpático*
Las chicas _____.   Las chicas son antipáticas.   *las maestras*
_____ es _____.   La chica es antipática.
_____ idénticos.   Los chicos son idénticos.   *buenos*

24. FREE SUBSTITUTION

El maestro es inteligente y simpático.   *el chico, la chica, los gemelos, las alumnas /*
alto y rubio, antipático y pretencioso, inteli-
gente y bueno

25. FREE RESPONSE

¿Son Susana y Cristina idénticas?   *Sí, son idénticas*
¿Es bonita la escuela?   *Sí, es bonita.*
¿Son los compañeros simpáticos o antipáticos?   *Son simpáticos.*
¿Cuál de los compañeros no es tan simpático?   *El chico rubio.*
¿Por qué no es simpático?   *Es pretencioso.*
¿Es nueva esta falda? ¿y ese vestido? ¿y esta corbata?
¿Es *Camilo* alto o bajo? ¿y usted? ¿y ella?
¿Es *Mauricio* mayor o menor que la maestra? ¿y ustedes? ¿y él?
¿Son ustedes españoles?

26. DIRECTED ADDRESS

1. Make the following remark to the persons indicated.

¡Es tan inteligente! ⊗
    (a un amigo)
    (a dos chicas)
    (a un chico y a una chica)
    (al Sr. García)
    (a su hermana)

¡Es tan inteligente!
¡Eres tan inteligente!
¡Son tan inteligentes!
¡Son tan inteligentes!
¡Es tan inteligente!
¡Eres tan inteligente!

2. Ask the following question of the persons indicated.

¿Es americano o alemán? ⊗
    (a dos chicas)
    (a un chico)
    (a una chica y a un chico)
    (a unos alumnos)
    (a un maestro)

¿Son americanas o alemanas?
¿Eres americano o alemán?
¿Son americanos o alemanes?
¿Son americanos o alemanes?
¿Es americano o alemán?

27. BASIC DIALOG VARIATION

Repeat the Basic Dialog, this time making the twins boys named Arturo and Camilo.

The following lines require changes:

28. WRITING EXERCISE

Write the responses to Drills 20.1 and 20.2.

EXERCISE BOOK: EXERCISE 6 AND 7

Vamos a ver, usted es Arturo, ¿no?
No, don Pedro. Él es Arturo; yo soy Camilo.
¡Pero son idénticos! ¿Cuál de los dos es mayor?
Ninguno. Somos gemelos.
Excepto esa chica rubia. ¡Qué pretenciosa!
¿Y por qué eres tan amigo de ella entonces?

Information Questions

PRESENTATION *TEACHER PRESENTATION, p. T158*

¿**Qué** canción escuchas?
¿**Qué** canciones escuchas?

¿**Quién** es don Pedro?
¿**Quiénes** son **las gemelas**?

¿**Cuál** maestro es mejor?
¿**Cuáles maestros** son mejores?

Which is the word that asks the question in each sentence? Which of the above interrogative words show number agreement?

GENERALIZATION

1. Spanish **qué** generally corresponds to English *what.*

¿Qué estudia Juan?
What is John studying?

¿Qué canción escucha Juan?
What song is John listening to?

2. Spanish **quién** corresponds to English *who.*

¿Quién estudia español?
Who is studying Spanish?

Unlike English, Spanish has a plural *who,* **quiénes,** which is used to refer to a plural noun.

¿Quiénes van? ¿Todos ustedes?
Who is going? All of you?

Note that the verb that goes with **quiénes** is also plural.

3. Spanish **cuál** generally corresponds to English *which.*

¿Cuál corbata compra?
Which tie is he buying?

¿Cuál de las corbatas compras?
Which of the ties are you buying?

Note: The *qué/cuál* contrast will be explained in Level III.

Like **quién, cuál** has a plural form: **cuáles.**

¿Cuáles chicos estudian?
Which boys are studying?

¿Cuáles de los chicos estudian?
Which of the boys are studying?

4. In questions which use the interrogatives **qué, quién(es),** or **cuál(es)** the word order is (1) interrogative phrase, (2) predicate, (3) subject.

¿Qué estudia Juan?
1   2   3

¿Qué canción escucha María?
1   2   3

¿Cuál de las corbatas compra el chico rubio?
1   2   3

5. In English sentences such as *Who(m) are you studying with?* (*With whom are you studying?*), the preposition can be placed either at the beginning or at the end of the sentence. In Spanish the preposition always occurs at the beginning of the sentence, preceding the interrogative word.

¿Con quién estudias?
Who(m) are you studying with?

¿En qué piensas?
What are you thinking about?

The Spanish equivalent of *whose* is **de quién** (*of whom*).

¿De quién es este libro?
Whose book is this?

STRUCTURE DRILLS

29. ANSWER → QUESTION

Make a question for each answer by replacing the underlined words with an interrogative word.

Manolo estudia español. ⊗	¿Quién estudia español?
Camilo estudia inglés.	*¿Qué estudia Camilo?*
Cristina y Susana estudian inglés también.	*¿Quiénes estudian inglés también?*
Manolo y Camilo son alumnos.	*¿Quiénes son alumnos?*
Esta escuela es más bonita que la otra.	*¿Cuál escuela es más bonita que la otra?*
Las películas italianas son mejores que las otras.	*¿Cuáles películas son mejores que las otras?*

30. ENGLISH CUE DRILLS

1. ¿En qué piensas? ⊗   ¿En qué piensas?
   Who are you thinking about?   ¿En quién piensas?
   Who (*pl.*) are you thinking about?   ¿En quiénes piensas?
   Which girl are you thinking about?   ¿En cuál chica piensas?
   Which girls are you thinking about? ¿En cuáles chicas piensas?
   What are you thinking about?   ¿En qué piensas?

2. ¿De quién es el sombrero? ⊗   *¿De quién es el sombrero?*
   Whose coat is it?   *¿De quién es el abrigo?*
   Whose shirt is it?   *¿De quién es la camisa?*

Whose records are they?	*¿De quién son los discos?*
Whose presents are they?	*¿De quién son los regalos?*
Whose car is it?	*¿De quién es el carro?*
Whose hat is it?	*¿De quién es el sombrero?*

31. ANSWER → QUESTION

Los zapatos son de mi hermano.	¿De quién son los zapatos?
El carro es de unos amigos.	*¿De quién es el carro?*
Ese perro es de doña Marta.	*¿De quién es ese perro?*
Esta corbata es de mi tío.	*¿De quién es esta corbata?*
Los regalos son de mi madre.	*¿De quién son los regalos?*
El disco es de las gemelas.	*¿De quién es el disco?*
Las canciones son de la maestra.	*¿De quién son las canciones?*

32. WRITING EXERCISE

Write the responses to Drills 29, 30.2, and 31.

EXERCISE BOOK: EXERCISE 8

Listening and Speaking Exercise 88*, p. T53 ⊗

RECOMBINATION MATERIAL

Dialogs

I

JUAN	¿Te gusta esta escuela?
JOSÉ	Sí, pero me gusta más la otra.
JUAN	¿Por qué? ¿Es más grande?
JOSÉ	No, pero los compañeros son más simpáticos.

QUESTIONS

1. ¿A Juan le gusta esta escuela?
2. ¿Le gusta más esta escuela o la otra?
3. ¿Es más grande la otra escuela?
4. ¿Por qué le gusta más, entonces?

Girls play in a courtyard in Argentina.

II

OLGA ¿Quieres ir a las carreras conmigo? ¿Quieres ir al cine conmigo?

ANA No puedo. Tengo que ir a la tienda.

OLGA ¿Qué necesitas comprar?

ANA Un regalo para mi tío. Un regalo para mi mamá.

QUESTIONS

VARIATION: Olga wants Ana to go to the movies, but Ana has to buy a present for her mother.

1. ¿Adónde quiere ir Olga?
2. ¿Adónde tiene que ir Ana?
3. ¿Qué necesita comprar ella?
4. ¿Para quién necesita comprar un regalo?

III

LILI ¿Quién es ese chico?

ROSA ¿Cuál?

LILI Ése que pasa por la biblioteca.

ROSA No sé quién es.

REJOINDER

¿Quién es ese chico?

¿Cuál? / No sé. / Es mi hermano. / Es Juan. / Es mi amigo. / Es un chico americano. / Es el amigo de Cristina. / Es un nuevo alumno.

IV

LUISA	¡Qué linda es tu blusa!
EVA	¿Te gusta?
LUISA	Sí, me gusta mucho. ¿Es nueva?
EVA	Sí, es un regalo de mi mamá.

¡Qué lindo es tu vestido! ←

...¿Es nuevo?

Sí, es un regalo de mi tía.

VARIATION: The two girls are talking about a dress Eva received from her aunt.

QUESTIONS

1. ¿De qué hablan Luisa y Eva?
2. ¿Es bonita la blusa de Eva?
3. ¿Es nueva?
4. ¿Es un regalo de quién?

Rejoinders

1. Buenas noches, doña Marta.   *Hasta luego. / Hasta mañana. / Buenas noches. / Adiós.*
2. Ana y María son casi idénticas.   *Sí, son gemelas. / No, Ana es más alta. / No, Ana es más baja. / Sí, es verdad.*
3. Necesitamos comprar algo.   *¿Qué necesitan comprar? / Yo también. / ¿Para quién? / ¿Un regalo? / Cierran las tiendas a las ocho.*

LETTER ⟷ SOUND CORRESPONDENCES

Lesson 1

READING: g = [g] OR [g̸]

Note: Remind students that if *g* occurs immediately after a vowel, the sound is [g̸]. Otherwise the sound is [g]. See p. T46.

The letter **g** before **a, o, u** or a consonant represents either the sound [g] or [g̸].

FAMILIAR WORDS   llega, conmigo, algo, amigo, abrigo, gusta, ninguna, inglés

UNFAMILIAR WORDS   gato, liga, gordo, contigo, segundo, gracias, grita

READING: gu = [g] OR [g̸]

The letter combination **gu** before **e** or **i** represents either the sound [g] or [g̸].

FAMILIAR WORDS   Miguel, alguien

UNFAMILIAR WORDS   sigue, llegue, guerra, guía, en seguida

READING: g = [h]

The letter **g** before **e** or **i** represents the sound [h].

(continued)

(continued)

FAMILIAR WORDS gemelas, inteligente

UNFAMILIAR WORDS gente, ligero, álgebra, gira, gigante, biología, geología

READING: j = [h]

The letter **j** always represents the sound [h].

FAMILIAR WORDS mejor, jueves, bajo

UNFAMILIAR WORDS hijo, ojo, rojo, jefe, viaje, viejo, mojado, Jiménez

SENTENCES

1. Las gemelas García son muy inteligentes.
2. ¿Cuál de las dos es mejor? Ninguna.
3. Miguel llega con alguien.
4. ¿Con Jorge? No, con Guillermo.

WRITING

Copy the above sentences and be prepared to write them from dictation.

Spelling Notes:

1. The sounds [g] and [ǥ] before **a, o, u** or a consonant are represented by the letter **g.**

2. The sounds [g] and [ǥ] before **e** and **i** are represented by the letters **gu.**

3. The sound [h] before **e** or **i** is represented by either the letter **g** or the letter **j.** There is no way to predict which words will be spelled with **g** and which with **j.** You will have to memorize the spelling of each new word as you learn it, but it may help you to remember that most cognates are spelled with the same letter in both languages: **inteligente,** *intelligent;* **Jerusalén,** *Jerusalem.*

Lesson 2

READING: r = [r]

The letter **r** represents the sound [r], except after **n, l, s,** and at the beginning of a word.

FAMILIAR WORDS americana, quiero, hora, para, claro, madre, otra, practica, martes, tarde, llamar, pensar, comprar, mayor, menor

UNFAMILIAR WORDS toro, loro, mira, sorda, prisa, buscar, lugar

READING: r, rr = [rr]

The letter **r** represents the sound [rr] at the beginning of a word or after **n, l,** and **s.** The letter **rr** always represents the sound [rr].

FAMILIAR WORDS ruso, regalo, razón, rubio, cierran, perro

UNFAMILIAR WORDS rojo, roto, rana, Puerto Rico, Costa Rica, Enrique, enredo, alrededor, Israel, arregla, correo

The letter **r** at the beginning of a word represents the sound [rr] even when the preceding word ends in a vowel.

FAMILIAR AND UNFAMILIAR PAIRS

[rr]	[r]
habla ruso	hablar uno
busca razones	buscar algo
canta Rosa	cantar óperas
llega rápido	llegar aquí
come rápido	comer algo
hace ropa	hacer obras

SENTENCES

1. Quiero comprar un regalo para don Pedro.
2. ¿A qué hora cierran el mercado?
3. La señorita americana no habla ruso.
4. ¡Ah, con razón!

WRITING

Copy the above sentences and be prepared to write them from dictation.

Spelling Notes:

1. The sound [rr] is represented by:
   a. the letter **r** at the beginning of a word;
   b. the letter **r** within a word after **n, l,** or **s;**
   c. the letter **rr** (**rr** occurs only between vowels within a word).

2. The sound [r] within a word is represented by the letter **r,** except after **n, l,** or **s.** The sound [r] does not occur at the beginning of a word.

Vocabulary Exercises

1. QUESTIONS

1. ¿Quién grita?   *Pedrito.*
2. ¿Gritan mucho ustedes?
3. ¿Grito mucho yo?
4. ¿A quiénes llama Pedrito?   *A su mamá y a su tía.*
5. ¿Quién contesta, la mamá o la tía?   *La mamá.*
6. ¿Qué busca Pedrito?   *Sus cosas.*
7. ¿Busca él bien o busca mal?   *Busca mal.*
8. ¿Dónde están las cosas que Pedrito busca?   *Todo está en su lugar.*

2. DIALOG RECALL

arreglan *Cuando arreglan mi cuarto, no encuentro nada.*
sordas   *¡No estamos sordas!*
aquí   *Aquí estoy.*
lugar   *Todo está en su lugar.*
limpian   *Cuando limpian mi cuarto, no encuentro nada.*
dormitorio *Cuando limpian mi dormitorio, no encuentro nada.*
pantalones *¿Dónde están mis pantalones?*

---

3. QUESTIONS

1. ¿Adónde quiere ir Pedrito?   *Al partido de fútbol.*
2. ¿Adónde va usted hoy?
3. ¿Tiene dinero Pedro?   *No, no tiene dinero.*
4. ¿Quién limpia su dormitorio, usted o su mamá?
5. ¿Quién arregla la sala de su casa?
6. ¿Quién limpia la cocina? ¿y el baño?

4. DIALOG RECALL

prisa   *¿Adónde vas con tanta prisa?*
campeón   *Sí, juega El Santos, campeón del mundo.*
dinero   *No tienes dinero.*
restaurante *¿Adónde vas con tanta prisa? ¿Al restaurante?*

5. ANTONYM DRILL

Repeat each of the following sentences, replacing the underlined word with a word that has the opposite meaning.

Luisa es <u>mayor</u> que Pedro.   Luisa es menor que Pedro.
Los boletos son <u>caros</u>.   *Los boletos son baratos.*
Mi tía es <u>simpática</u>.   *Mi tía es antipática.*
El comedor es <u>grande</u>.   *El comedor es pequeño.*
¿Cómo está usted? Muy <u>bien</u>.   *¿Cómo está usted? Muy mal.*
Pedrito es bastante <u>alto</u>.   *Pedro es bastante bajo.*
La ventana es <u>pequeña</u>.   *La ventana es grande.*

GRAMMAR

estar, *Present Tense*

PRESENTATION *TEACHER PRESENTATION, p. T160*

Aquí **estoy.**
¿Dónde **estás?**
Todo **está** en su lugar.
No **estamos** sordas.
¿Dónde **están** mis cosas?

Which form of the present tense of **estar** has an ending that differs from those of regular **a**-class verbs like **practicar?** How do the other forms (except **estamos**) differ from those of regular **a**-class verbs?

GENERALIZATION

estar,	PRESENT TENSE	
	Singular	*Plural*
1	est – oy	est a mos
2	est á s	est á n
3	est á –	

This verb has two peculiarities: (1) the first person singular ending is **oy** rather than **o**; (2) the stress is on the **o** of **estoy** and on the theme vowel of all other forms, rather than on the next-to-last syllable as for regular verbs.

Listening and Speaking Exercises 94, 95, 96*, 97*, p. T56 ⊗   SECTION B

STRUCTURE DRILLS

6. PERSON-NUMBER SUBSTITUTION

Estamos en la sala. ⊗   Estamos en la sala.
   (yo)   Estoy en la sala.
   (tú)   Estás en la sala.

(ella)   Está en la sala.
(ustedes)   Están en la sala.
(ellos)   Están en la sala.
(usted)   Está en la sala.

7. PATTERNED RESPONSE

¿Dónde están mis cosas? ⊗   Están aquí.
¿Dónde están ustedes?   *Estamos aquí.*
¿Dónde están mis calcetines?   *Están aquí.*
¿Dónde está el dinero?   *Está aquí.*
¿Dónde estás tú?   *Estoy aquí.*
¿Dónde estoy yo?   *Está aquí.*
¿Dónde está mi mamá?   *Está aquí.*
¿Dónde está usted?   *Estoy aquí.*

8. FREE RESPONSE

¿Dónde está Pedrito?   *Está en su cuarto.*
Y sus cosas, ¿dónde están?   *Todo está en su lugar. (Están en su lugar.)*
¿Dónde está usted, en casa?
¿Cómo está su mamá?
¿Dónde estamos ahora?

9. WRITING EXERCISE

Write the responses to Drill 7. *EXERCISE BOOK: EXERCISE 1*

Information Questions

PRESENTATION *TEACHER PRESENTATION, p. T161*

¿**Dónde** están mis cosas?
¿**Adónde** vas con tanta prisa?
¿**Cuándo** limpian la casa?
¿**Cómo** vas al partido?
¿**Cuánto** cuestan los boletos?
¿**Por qué** arreglan la sala?

Which is the word that asks the question in each of the above sentences?

¿**Cuánto** dinero necesitas?

¿**Cuánta** comida compramos?

¿**Cuántos** pesos tienes?

¿**Cuántas** cosas buscas?

Does **cuánto** agree in gender and number with the noun it modifies? What is the English equivalent of the singular form **cuánto?** of the plural form **cuántos?**

GENERALIZATION

1. Spanish **cómo, cuándo,** and **por qué** generally correspond to English *how, when,* and *why.*

2. Spanish **dónde** corresponds to English *where* when the location of something is being questioned.

¿**Dónde** están mis cosas?

Where are my things?

Spanish has another word for *where,* **adónde,** which is used to question direction of movement rather than location.

¿**Adónde** vas con tanta prisa?

Where are you going in such a hurry?

Adónde is really a phrase consisting of the preposition **a,** *to,* + **dónde,** *where,* which has come to be written as one word.

3. Spanish **cuánto** corresponds to English *how much.*

¿**Cuánto** cuestan los boletos?

How much do the tickets cost?

Cuánto may modify a noun; if it does, it agrees in number and gender with the noun it modifies.

¿**Cuánta** comida compramos?

How much food shall we buy?

¿**Cuántos** boletos necesitan?

How many tickets do they need?

English makes a distinction between *how much* with singular nouns and *how many,* with plural nouns. In Spanish the distinction is made merely by using the singular or the plural form of **cuánto.**

STRUCTURE DRILLS

10. ENGLISH CUE DRILLS

1. ¿Adónde vas? ⊗   ¿Adónde vas?
   When are you going?   ¿Cuándo vas?
   How are you going?   ¿Cómo vas?
   Why are you going?   ¿Por qué vas?
   Where are you going?   ¿Adónde vas?

2. ¿Cómo hablas español? ⊗   *¿Cómo hablas español?*
   Where do you speak Spanish?   *¿Dónde hablas español?*
   When do you speak Spanish?   *¿Cuándo hablas español?*
   Why do you speak Spanish?   *¿Por qué hablas español?*
   How do you speak Spanish?   *¿Cómo hablas español?*

11. ANSWER → QUESTION

Make a question for each of the following statements by replacing the underlined words with the appropriate interrogative word.

1. Pedro y Pablo están <u>en el dormitorio</u>. ⊗   ¿Dónde están Pedro y Pablo?
   Van <u>al estadio</u>.   *¿Adónde van?*
   <u>Hoy</u> juega El Santos.   *¿Cuándo juega El Santos?*
   El Santos juega <u>muy bien</u>.   *¿Cómo juega El Santos?*
   Van al partido con <u>Roberto</u>.   *¿Con quién van al partido?*
   Necesitan comprar <u>boletos</u>.   *¿Qué necesitan comprar?*
   Cuestan <u>cuatro pesos</u>.   *¿Cuánto cuestan?*
   Compran <u>tres</u> boletos.   *¿Cuántos boletos compran?*

2. Tía Luisa quiere ir <u>a las tiendas</u>.   ¿Adónde quiere ir tía Luisa?
   Las tiendas están <u>en el centro</u>.   *¿Dónde están las tiendas?*
   Ella necesita comprar <u>un regalo</u>.   *¿Qué necesita comprar ella?*
   El regalo es para <u>Pedrito</u>.   *¿Para quién es el regalo?*
   Tía Luisa tiene <u>diez</u> pesos.   *¿Cuántos pesos tiene tía Luisa?*
   Necesita más dinero <u>porque el regalo   *¿Por qué necesita más dinero?*
   cuesta mucho</u>.
   Tía Luisa tiene <u>problemas</u>.   *¿Qué tiene tía Luisa?*
   <u>Mañana</u> va al banco.   *¿Cuándo va al banco?*
   Va <u>a las tiendas</u> después.   *¿Adónde va después?*

12. WRITING EXERCISE

Write the responses to Drills 10.2 and 11.2.

EXERCISE BOOK: EXERCISE 2

Contraction of the Definite Article

PRESENTATION *TEACHER PRESENTATION, p. T162*

Vamos **a la** biblioteca.
¿Vas **a las** carreras?
No quiero ir **a los** partidos.
Vamos <u>**al**</u> centro.

What happens when **a** and **el** come together in a sentence?

¿A qué hora llegan **de la** escuela?
¿Vas a la fiesta **de las** gemelas García?
Es el campeón **de los** Estados Unidos.
¡Qué linda es la casa <u>**del**</u> maestro!

What happens when **de** and **el** come together in a sentence?

GENERALIZATION

The masculine singular form of the definite article contracts with **a** and **de:**

$$a \ + \ el \ \rightarrow \ al$$
$$de \ + \ el \ \rightarrow \ del$$

The other forms do not contract.

STRUCTURE DRILLS

|*Note:* Use Supplement posters extensively in this section.

13. ITEM SUBSTITUTION

1. ¿Adónde vas? ¿Al estadio? ⊗   ¿Adónde vas? ¿Al estadio? *VARIATION:* Do
_____ banco?   ¿Adónde vas? ¿Al banco? the drill again,
_____ sala?   ¿Adónde vas? ¿A la sala? substituting the
_____ comedor?   ¿Adónde vas? ¿Al comedor? nouns in Drill 13.4.
_____ aeropuerto?   ¿Adónde vas? ¿Al aeropuerto?
_____ cocina?   ¿Adónde vas? ¿A la cocina?
_____ tiendas?   ¿Adónde vas? ¿A las tiendas?

2. Llegan tarde a la escuela. ⊗   *al baile–a las fiestas–a la biblioteca–*
(baile–fiestas–biblioteca–centro–partidos) *al centro–a los partidos*

3. ¿Tienes el disco de la señora? ⊗   ¿Tienes el disco de la señora?   *VARIATION*
_____ señor?   ¿Tienes el disco del señor?   *chico*
_____ alumnos?   ¿Tienes el disco de los alumnos?   *gemelos*
_____ chicas?   ¿Tienes el disco de las chicas?   *gemelas*
_____ maestro?   ¿Tienes el disco del maestro?   *Sr. Pérez*
_____ maestra?   ¿Tienes el disco de la maestra?   *Sra. García*

4. Tal vez no llega de la escuela todavía.   *del centro–de las tiendas–del banco–*
(centro–tiendas–banco–fiesta–café–aeropuerto–carreras)   *de la fiesta–del café–del aeropuerto–de las carreras*

Possession with de

TEACHER PRESENTATION, p. T162
GENERALIZATION

In English, *'s* after a noun is often used to indicate possession. Spanish does not have an equivalent for the English *'s*. Instead, the following construction is used: definite article + noun + **de** + possessor.

¿Dónde está el abrigo de Juan?
Where is John's coat?

Listening and Speaking Exercises 98, 99, 100*, 101*, p. T58 ⊗   **SECTION C**

STRUCTURE DRILLS

14. TRANSFORMATION DRILL

Make new sentences using the possessive construction. Follow the pattern given.

María compra un pañuelo muy bonito. ⊗   El pañuelo de María es muy bonito.

Juan compra unos pantalones muy caros.   *Los pantalones de Juan son muy caros.*
Lupe compra unos guantes nuevos.   *Los guantes de Lupe son nuevos.*
Cristina compra unas medias lindas.   *Las medias de Cristina son lindas.*
Manolo compra una corbata francesa.   *La corbata de Manolo es francesa.*
Pedro compra unos boletos muy baratos.   *Los boletos de Pedro son muy baratos.*

15. ENGLISH CUE DRILL

No es la tía de María. ⊗   *No es la tía de María.*
He's not María's brother.   *No es el hermano de María.*
They're not María's friends.   *No son los amigos de María.*
She's not María's daughter.   *No es la hija de María.*   *(continued)*

(continued)

They're not María's problems.	*No son los problemas de María.*
It's not María's car.	*No es el carro de María.*
They're not María's things.	*No son las cosas de María.*
She's not María's aunt.	*No es la tía de María.*

16. WRITING EXERCISE

Write the responses to Drills 13.2, 13.4, and 14.

EXERCISE BOOK: EXERCISES 3 AND 4

Personal a

PRESENTATION *TEACHER PRESENTATION, p. T162*

Escuchan **el disco.**
Escuchan **al maestro.**

¿Buscas **los boletos**?
¿Buscas **a los chicos**?

No encuentro **mis cosas.**
No encuentro **a mis hijas.**

When the direct object is a noun which refers to a person, which word precedes the noun and its modifiers?

GENERALIZATION

When the direct object of a verb is a noun or an indefinite pronoun which refers to a person, it is normally preceded by **a.**

Llamo <u>a</u> la chica americana.
Busco <u>a</u> alguien.
¿<u>A</u> quién llamas?

This **a,** usually called the personal **a,** has no equivalent in English; it simply marks the direct object as referring to a person.
　　The personal **a** is often omitted with the verb **tener,** *have.*

Tiene dos hermanos.

STRUCTURE DRILLS

17. ITEM SUBSTITUTION

1. Buscamos al chico. ⊗
    _____ campeones.
    _____ banco.
    _____ gemelas.
    _____ baño.
    _____ Sr. González.
    _____ Susana.
    _____ puerta.
    _____ alguien.

Buscamos al chico.
Buscamos a los campeones.
Buscamos el banco.
Buscamos a las gemelas.
Buscamos el baño.
Buscamos al Sr. González.
Buscamos a Susana.
Buscamos la puerta.
Buscamos a alguien.

VARIATION
Use the nouns
in Drill 17.2.

2. No encuentro los guantes. ⊗ *a los señores–a Pedro–el restaurante–las cosas–*
    (señores–Pedro–restaurante–cosas–alumnas–chico–café–Roberto) *a las alumnas–al chico–*
    VARIATION: Use the nouns in Drill 17.1. *el café–a Roberto*

18. QUESTION FORMATION ⊗

Escuchan al <u>maestro</u>.
Llamas a <u>Cristina</u>.
Busca los <u>guantes</u>.
Llaman después a <u>Arturo y a Pedro</u>.
Arregla el <u>dormitorio</u>.

¿A quién escuchan?
¿A quién llamas?
¿Qué busca?
¿A quiénes llaman después?
¿Qué arregla?

19. WRITING EXERCISE

Write the responses to Drills 17.2 and 18.
EXERCISE BOOK: EXERCISE 5

Stem Alternation: o-ue
a-*Class Verbs*

PRESENTATION *TEACHER PRESENTATION, p. T163*

No **encuentro** nada.
No **encontramos** nada.

Is the stem stressed or unstressed in each verb form? What is the vowel sound in the stem when stressed? How is the sound written? What is the vowel sound in the stem when unstressed? How is the sound written?

GENERALIZATION

1. In certain verb stems the vowel **o** alternates with **ue** (pronounced [we]); **ue** occurs when the stem is stressed; **o** occurs when the stem is unstressed.

Stressed Stem	*Unstressed Stem*
enc**ue**ntro	enc**o**ntrar
enc**ue**ntras	enc**o**ntramos
enc**ue**ntra	
enc**ue**ntran	

2. Notice that the **o-ue** stem alternation is like the **e-ie** stem alternation in that it occurs only in stressed syllables.

3. In the verb **jugar**, **u** rather than **o** alternates with **ue. Jugar** is the only Spanish verb which has a **u-ue** alternation.

4. The **a**-class verbs you have learned so far which have this stem alternation are **costar, encontrar, jugar,** and **recordar.**

Listening and Speaking Exercises 102, 103, 104, 105*, p. T59 ⊗   SECTION D

STRUCTURE DRILLS

20. PERSON-NUMBER SUBSTITUTION

1. No recuerdo qué día es hoy. ⊗   No recuerdo qué día es hoy.
   (el maestro)   No recuerda qué día es hoy.
   (los alumnos)   No recuerdan qué día es hoy.
   (nosotros)   No recordamos qué día es hoy.
   (tú)   No recuerdas qué día es hoy.
   (ustedes)   No recuerdan qué día es hoy.
   (mis amigos y yo)   No recordamos qué día es hoy.
   (yo)   No recuerdo qué día es hoy.

2. Juegan fútbol el sábado. ⊗   *juego–juega–jugamos–juegas–juegan–jugamos–juega*
   (yo–Juan–nosotros–tú–ustedes–mi hermano y yo–usted)

21. PAIRED SENTENCES

No encuentra los boletos.
    (nosotros)
    (él)

    No encuentra los boletos.
    No encontramos los boletos.
    No encuentra los boletos.

¿Por qué no juegan ahora?
    (nosotros)
    (ellos)

    ¿Por qué no juegan ahora?
    ¿Por qué no jugamos ahora?
    ¿Por qué no juegan ahora?

¡Qué bien recuerdo ese partido!
    (nosotros)
    (yo)

    ¡Qué bien recuerdo ese partido!
    ¡Qué bien recordamos ese partido!
    ¡Qué bien recuerdo ese partido!

22. PROGRESSIVE SUBSTITUTION

Yo no encuentro el café.
Mi amiga y yo _____.
_____ buscamos _____.
_____ cosas.
Pedrito _____.
_____ recuerda _____.
_____ baile.
Nosotros _____.
_____ vamos _____.
_____ cocina.

Yo no encuentro el café.
Mi amiga y yo no encontramos el café.
Mi amiga y yo no buscamos el café.
Mi amiga y yo no buscamos las cosas.
Pedrito no busca las cosas.
Pedrito no recuerda las cosas.
Pedrito no recuerda el baile.
Nosotros no recordamos el baile.
Nosotros no vamos al baile.
Nosotros no vamos a la cocina.

A professional soccer match in Madrid. Soccer is played throughout the Spanish-speaking world.

23. FREE SUBSTITUTION

<u>Yo</u> no <u>recuerdo</u> <u>al Sr. García.</u> . . . / *buscar, llamar, encontrar* / *al maestro, a la chica americana, a los gemelos*

24. FREE RESPONSE

¿Le gusta jugar fútbol a usted?
¿Cuándo juegan ustedes fútbol?
¿Recuerda usted adónde quiere ir Pedrito?
¿Recuerda cuánto cuestan los boletos para el partido?
A propósito, ¿cuánto cuesta ir al cine aquí?
¿Cuánto cuesta ir a un partido de fútbol?
¿Juega usted fútbol? ¿Con quiénes?
¿Juegan fútbol las chicas?

25. WRITING EXERCISE

Write the responses to Drills 20.2, 21, and 22.
EXERCISE BOOK: EXERCISES 5 and 6

Listening and Speaking Exercise 106*, p. T61 ⊗

RECOMBINATION MATERIAL

Dialogs

I

PEDRITO	Tía Luisa, ¿dónde está mamá? ¿Ah, tía Luisa? ¡tía Luisa! ¡tía Luisa!
TÍA LUISA	¿Por qué gritas, Pedrito? No estoy sorda. ¿Qué quieres?
PEDRITO	Busco mis pantalones.
TÍA LUISA	¿Tus calcetines?
PEDRITO	¡Mis PAN-TA-LO-NES!

QUESTIONS

1. ¿A quién llama Pedrito?
2. ¿Con quién quiere hablar?
3. ¿Quién grita?
4. ¿Qué cosa busca él?
5. ¿Sabe tía Luisa si Pedrito busca sus pantalones?

II

EL CHICO	Buenos días. ¡Qué bonita esta corbata! ¿Cuánto cuesta?
EL SEÑOR	Muy barata, mi amigo, muy barata: diez pesos.
EL CHICO	¡Diez pesos! Adiós.
EL SEÑOR	¿Le gusta la corbata? Ocho pesos.
EL CHICO	No, gracias. Muy cara todavía.
EL SEÑOR	¡Siete!
EL CHICO	Muy cara. Cinco, tal vez.
EL SEÑOR	¡No no no no no no y no! No puedo. ¡Seis pesos! Un regalo.
EL CHICO	Cinco.
EL SEÑOR	¡Ay caramba! Está bien: cinco.

REJOINDERS

1. ¡Qué bonitos los guantes! *Muy baratos, mi amigo, muy baratos. / Cuestan cinco pesos. / Sí, pero son muy caros.*
2. Siete pesos, mi amigo, un regalo. *No, gracias, muy caro todavía. / ¡Seis! / Está bien.*

CONVERSATION STIMULUS

You want to buy a pair of shoes. Bargain with the salesman.

Note: In many Spanish-speaking countries bargaining with salesmen is a common practice.

¡Qué bonitos los zapatos! ¿Cuánto cuestan?
Diez pesos, un regalo.
¡Cinco!
No, no puedo. ¡Ocho!
Muy caros todavía. ¡Seis!
No no no y no. No puedo. ¡Siete pesos!
Muy bien, siete pesos.

III

EL HIJO	¿Qué buscas?
LA MADRE	El abrigo. Ah, aquí está. ¿Vas conmigo?
EL HIJO	¿Adónde? ¿al cine? ¡Claro!
LA MADRE	No, al centro, a las tiendas. Apúrate, vamos.
EL HIJO	¿Qué vas a comprar?
LA MADRE	Unos guantes y una falda para tu hermana.
EL HIJO	A propósito, mami, este . . . este . . .
LA MADRE	Ajá, ya sé, discos. Pero no. Cuestan muy caros.

QUESTIONS

1. ¿Qué busca la madre?
2. ¿Adónde va ella?
3. ¿Quiere el hijo ir con su mamá?
4. ¿Qué quiere comprar ella?
5. ¿Qué quiere comprar el hijo?
6. ¿Por qué no quiere comprar discos la madre?

Rejoinders

1. Mamá . . . ¿dónde están mis cosas? *Todo está en su lugar. / No sé. / En el baño.*
2. Hoy juega El Santos, campeón del mundo. *¿A qué hora? / ¿Dónde? / ¿Cuánto cuestan los boletos?*
3. ¡Ay caramba! ¡¡Pedro!! ¡¡Luisa!! *Aquí estamos. / ¿Qué pasa? / ¡Cómo gritas!*

Conversation Stimulus

You're looking for your things, but your mother has just cleaned your room and you can't find anything.

Start like this: ¡Mamá! ¡No encuentro nada!
¿Qué buscas? ¿Tu ___camisa___ ?
No, mi ___corbata. ¿Dónde está?___
Todo ___está en su lugar.___
¡Pero no encuentro mi corbata!

You want to go to the movies with a friend, but you haven't got enough money for a ticket, so you have to ask your father for some.

Start like this: Papá, este . . . este . . . Necesito tres pesos.
¡Cómo! ___¡Tres pesos!___
Quiero ir ___al cine con Arturo.___
¿Cuánto cuestan ___los boletos___ ?
Creo que ___cinco pesos___. Ya tengo ___dos___.
Muy bien. ¿Qué dan?
Una película americana.

LETTER ↔ SOUND CORRESPONDENCES

Lesson 1

READING: THE WRITTEN ACCENT

It is important to learn which syllable of a word is stressed. There are many pairs of words with different meanings which are pronounced alike except for the stress.

papa (*potato*)	papá (*Dad*)
llamo (*I call*)	llamó (*he called*)
tomas (*you take*)	Tomás (*Thomas*)
abra (*open*)	habrá (*there will be*)
estas (*these*)	estás (*you are*)

In words with a written accent, the syllable with the written accent is the one which is stressed.

FAMILIAR WORDS

mamá	Pérez	sábado
café	fútbol	película
inglés	miércoles	exámenes
después		

UNFAMILIAR WORDS

allá	álbum	público
allí	túnel	sótano
cortés	lápiz	lástima

SENTENCES

1. A propósito, ¿Tomás está aquí?
2. No, está en el café.
3. Ah, con razón. Hoy es sábado.

WRITING

Copy the above sentences and be prepared to write them from dictation.

Lesson 2

READING: WORDS WITH NO WRITTEN ACCENT

In words with no written accent that end with a vowel, an **n,** or an **s,** the stress falls on the next-to-the-last syllable. This is the most common stress pattern in Spanish.

FAMILIAR WORDS

todo	partido	inteligente
baño	barato	americano
sorda	boleto	españoles
tanta	arreglan	alemanes
llaman	problemas	señoritas
hablan	estamos	

UNFAMILIAR WORDS

mesa	viven	sentado	delante
cena	grises	cansado	conocen
saben	cartas	contenta	delgados

In words with no written accent that end in a consonant other than **n** or **s,** the stress falls on the last syllable.

FAMILIAR WORDS   UNFAMILIAR WORDS

pasar	comedor	pared	libertad
menor	español	Brasil	parasol
lugar	caminar	azul	Uruguay
usted	practicar	poner	universal
verdad	necesitar	calor	
Miguel			

SENTENCES

1. ¿Estudias ruso, francés, alemán, o español?
2. ¿Yo? Inglés.
3. José y yo vamos al café.
4. Después vamos al partido de fútbol.

WRITING

Copy the above sentences and be prepared to write them from dictation.

Spelling Notes:

1. Words ending in a vowel, in **n** or in **s,** in which the stress falls on the next-to-the-last syllable, require no written accent.

2. Words ending in a consonant other than **n** or **s,** in which the stress falls on the last syllable, require no written accent.

3. All other words require a written accent on the stressed syllable.

Lesson 3

SPELLING NOTES: WRITTEN ACCENT IN PLURAL NOUNS AND ADJECTIVES

1. A noun or an adjective which ends in **n** or **s,** and has a written accent on the last syllable in the singular, will not require a written accent in the plural.

calcetín	calcetines
canción	canciones
campeón	campeones

alemán	alemanes
inglés	ingleses
francés	franceses

2. A noun or an adjective of two or more syllables which ends in **n** or **s,** and has no written accent in the singular, will require a written accent in the plural.

examen   exámenes

SPELLING NOTES: OTHER USES OF THE WRITTEN ACCENT

1. In certain special cases the written accent does not indicate the position of stress within a word, but rather serves to distinguish two words of different meaning or function which are spelled the same except for the accent mark.

   These special written accents do correspond to stresses in spoken phrases: the word with the written accent is stressed, the word without the written accent is not.

Tú no buscas.	Tu amigo no busca.
(**Tú** stressed in sentence.)	(**Tu** unstressed in sentence.)

tú (*you*)	tu (*your*)
sí (*yes*)	si (*if*)
sé (*I know*)	se (*to him*)
dé (*give*)	de (*of, from*)
mí (*me*)	mi (*my*)
más (*more*)	mas (*but*)

2. Interrogative and exclamatory words are always written with an accent and stressed: **cómo, cuándo, cuánto, dónde, quién, qué, cuál.** Note that these same words are not written with an accent and not stressed when they are not used in an interrogative or exclamatory sense.

¡**Cómo** juega ese chico!	Juega **como** (*like*) un campeón.
¿**Cuándo** limpian la sala?	**Cuando** limpian la sala, no encuentro nada.

SENTENCES

1. ¿Cuánto cuestan los boletos? No sé.
2. ¡Cómo gritas, hijo! ¿Qué quieres?
3. ¿Tú estás en tu cuarto?

WRITING

Copy the above sentences and be prepared to write them from dictation.

BASIC DIALOG

Álbum de familia

Note: At this time, you may wish to assign the section on Home and the Family in *Glimpses of the Spanish World.*

HERNÁN   ¿Puedo ver este álbum?
CARLOS   Sí, claro, son fotos de mi familia.   6-1
HERNÁN   ¡Qué bonita es esta chica! ¿Quién es?
CARLOS   Una prima. Está bonita en la foto, pero ella no es muy linda, francamente.   6-2

HERNÁN   ¡Qué graciosa esta otra foto! ¿Dónde es la fiesta?
CARLOS   En mi casa. A ver si adivinas cuál soy yo.   6-3
HERNÁN   No tengo la menor idea. ¿Dónde estás?
CARLOS   Ése que está sentado en el suelo. Ése soy yo.   6-4

Family Album

HERNÁN   Can I see this album?
CARLOS   Yes, of course, they're pictures (photos) of my family.
HERNÁN   What a pretty girl this is! Who is she?
CARLOS   A cousin. She's cute in the picture, but she isn't very pretty, really (frankly).

HERNÁN   What a funny picture this other one is! Where's the party?
CARLOS   At my house. Let's see if you guess which one is me.
HERNÁN   I don't have the slightest (least) idea. Where are you?
CARLOS   The one (that) who's sitting (seated) on the floor. That's me.

◀ *A large family poses for a portrait during a reunion.*

Supplement

álbum 6-1	
¿Puedo ver este periódico? 6-2	Can I see this newspaper?
libro 6-3	book
primo 6-4	
Son fotos de mi padre. 6-4	They're pictures of my father.
abuelo 6-4	grandfather
novio 6-5	boy friend
familia 6-4	
¡Qué guapo[1] es ese chico!	What a handsome boy that is!
feo	homely (ugly)
delgado	thin
gordo } 6-6	fat
Es una foto. 6-7	

¿Dónde es la cena?	Where is the dinner?
el almuerzo	the lunch
la reunión 6-8	the meeting
La comida está en la mesa. 6-9	The food is on the table.
el suelo 6-10	
Ése que está sentado en la silla. 6-11	The one who's sitting on the chair.
Ése que está cansado. 6-12	That one who's tired.
enfermo 6-13	sick
contento 6-14	happy
trece, catorce, quince,	13, 14, 15,
dieciséis, diecisiete, dieciocho,	16, 17, 18,
diecinueve, veinte	19, 20

Listening and Speaking Exercises 107, 108, 109*, p. T61 ⊗

BASIC FORMS

Verbs

adivinar

Nouns

álbum	*m.*	foto	*f.*
padre	*m.*	reunión	*f.*

Note: Point out that the sound [f] is always represented by the letter *f*, never by the combination *ph*. See Letter ↔ Sound Correspondences, p. 107.

---

[1] **Guapo** means *handsome* when used for a boy, *pretty* when used for a girl. **Bonito** and **lindo** are not used to refer to a boy.

Vocabulary Exercises

1. QUESTIONS

1. ¿Con quién habla Hernán? *Con Carlos.*
2. ¿De qué hablan ellos? *De un álbum.*
3. ¿Qué quiere ver Hernán? *El álbum.*
4. ¿Quién es la chica que está en la foto? *Una prima de Carlos.*
5. ¿Es la hermana de Carlos? *No, no es su hermana.*
6. ¿Es su novia? *No, es su prima.*

2. DIALOG RECALL

álbum	*¿Puedo ver este álbum?*
familia	*Sí, claro, son fotos de mi familia.*
bonita	*¡Qué bonita es esta chica!*
francamente	*Está bonita en la foto, pero ella no es muy linda, francamente.*
libro	*¿Puedo ver este libro?*
padre	*Sí, claro, son fotos de mi padre.*
guapa	*¡Qué guapa es esta chica!*

---

3. QUESTIONS

1. ¿Es graciosa la otra foto? *Sí, es muy graciosa.*
2. ¿De qué es? *Es de una fiesta.*
3. ¿Dónde es la fiesta? *En la casa de Carlos.*
4. ¿Adivina Hernán cuál es Carlos? *No, no adivina.*
5. ¿Tiene usted un álbum?
6. ¿Es un álbum de familia?
7. ¿Cuántas fotos tiene usted? ¿De quiénes son?
8. ¿Tiene usted fotos de su novio? ¿de sus amigos? ¿de su familia?
9. Y un álbum de la escuela, ¿no tiene?
10. ¿Cuántos hermanos tiene usted?
11. ¿Tiene muchos primos?
12. ¿Cuántos primos tiene usted? ¿Cuántos abuelos tiene? ¿Cuántos tíos?
13. A ver si usted adivina cuántos hermanos tengo yo.

4. DIALOG RECALL

graciosa	*¡Qué graciosa esta otra foto!*
adivinas	*A ver si adivinas cuál soy yo.*
idea	*No tengo la menor idea.*
sentado	*Ése que está sentado en el suelo.*
reunión	*¿Dónde es la reunión?*
silla	*Ése que está sentado en la silla.*

5. NUMBER DRILL

1. Say the following numbers in Spanish:
   5, 15, 2, 12, 7, 17, 10, 20, 16, 19, 14

   Note: Use the chalkboard to cue these and other numbers.

cinco, quince, dos, doce, siete, diecisiete, diez, veinte, dieciséis, diecinueve, catorce

2. Say the number which is one digit higher:

3	cuatro	18	*diecinueve*	19	*veinte*	17	*dieciocho*
14	*quince*	15	*dieciséis*	12	*trece*	10	*once*

VARIATION: Say the number which is one digit lower.
VARIATION: Say the number which is two digits higher.

6. ENGLISH CUE DRILL

¡Qué bonita es la casa! ⊗   ¡Qué bonita es la casa!
It sure is a funny movie!   ¡Qué graciosa es la película!
What a nice album it is!   ¡Qué lindo es el álbum!
Is he a handsome boy!   ¡Qué guapo es el chico!
It sure is a big family!   ¡Qué grande es la familia!
What a homely girl she is!   ¡Qué fea es la chica!
It's a really pretty house!   ¡Qué bonita es la casa!

7. REJOINDERS

A ver si adivinas cuál soy yo.   *No sé. / No tengo la menor idea. / ¿Ése que está sentado allí? /*
Ése que está sentado en el suelo. / Ése que está sentado con todas
las chicas. / No sé, ¿cuál eres tú?

GRAMMAR

ser *and* estar *with Predicate Nouns and Adverbs*

TEACHER PRESENTATION: p. T164
GENERALIZATION

As a speaker of English, you are used to a single verb *be*. In Spanish you will have to learn to choose correctly between two verbs, **ser** and **estar,** both of which correspond to *be*.

In certain situations **estar** is always used; in others **ser** is always used.

1. Only **estar** is used to refer to the location of something or someone.

> **Todo está en su lugar.**
> **Mis cosas están en la cocina.**
> **¿Dónde estás?**
> **Aquí estoy.**

2. Only **ser** is used to link two noun phrases. (A noun phrase is a noun or a pronoun and any modifiers it may have.)

> **Yo soy Cristina.**
> **El señor alto es don Pedro.**
> **El lunes es el Día de la Madre.**

3. Only **ser** is used to link a noun phrase and adverbial expressions that indicate source or destination.

> **María es de los Estados Unidos.** (source)
> **Los regalos son para mi mamá.** (destination)

4. Only **ser** is used to refer to the time and place of events.

> **La reunión es a las ocho.**
> **¿Dónde es la fiesta?**
> **El examen es aquí.**

In these sentences **ser** means *take place, occur, be held.*

5. Some Spanish nouns can refer to either objects or events. With these nouns you must take special care to distinguish between location of an object and occurrence of an event. For example, **comida** may mean *food* (the actual objects eaten) or *meal* (the event of eating that food); **película** may mean *film* (the object that goes into a camera or projector) or *movie* (the event of showing a film). Nouns like **comida** and **película** may occur with either **ser** or **estar,** but the choice is not free: if the noun refers to an object, **estar** must be used (to express location); if the noun refers to an event, **ser** must be used (with the meaning *occur, take place*).

object	*event*
La comida está en la mesa.	**La comida es en mi casa.**
La película está en el suelo.	**La película es en el Cine Apolo.**

6. Summary:

estar	ser
Noun Phrase + **estar** + Location (other than an event)	Noun Phrase + **ser** + Noun Phrase
	Noun Phrase + **ser** + { Source / Destination }
	Noun Phrase (event) + **ser** + { Time / Place }

STRUCTURE DRILLS

Note: Before beginning these exercises, you may find it useful to say a few English sentences with a form of *be,* and have students tell whether a form of *ser* or *estar* would be used in the Spanish equivalent. For example: *John is here. (estar) John is a student. (ser) This is for you. (ser) We're in class. (estar)*

8. PERSON-NUMBER SUBSTITUTION

Está aquí, pero es de Colombia. ⊗   Está aquí, pero es de Colombia.
  (yo)   Estoy aquí, pero soy de Colombia.
  (ella y yo)   Estamos aquí, pero somos de Colombia.
  (tú)   Estás aquí, pero eres de Colombia.
  (ellos)   Están aquí, pero son de Colombia.
  (él)   Está aquí, pero es de Colombia.
  (ustedes)   Están aquí, pero son de Colombia.

9. PATTERNED RESPONSE

¿Don Pedro?, ¿el maestro? ⊗   Sí, don Pedro es el maestro.
¿El periódico?, ¿en el suelo?   Sí, el periódico está en el suelo.
¿Doña Marta?, ¿la abuela de Ana?   Sí, doña Marta es la abuela de Ana.
¿Ese libro?, ¿para la Sra. García?   Sí, ese libro es para la Sra. García.
¿Nosotros?, ¿en el aeropuerto?   Sí, nosotros estamos en el aeropuerto.
¿Pepe y Pedro?, ¿los campeones?   Sí, Pepe y Pedro son los campeones.
¿Ellas?, ¿aquí?   Sí, ellas están aquí.
¿Ellas?, ¿de aquí?   Sí, ellas son de aquí.
¿Esta silla?, ¿para el comedor?   Sí, esta silla es para el comedor.
¿Los gemelos?, ¿de California?   Sí, los gemelos son de California.

10. DIRECTED DIALOG

Pregúntele a *Pepe* si él está en la foto.   ¿Estás en la foto?
Pepe, diga que sí, y a ver si adivina cuál es usted.   Sí, a ver si adivinas cuál soy yo.
Diga que claro: ése que está sentado en el sofá.   Claro: ése que está sentado en el sofá.
Pepe, diga que no, que ése es *Camilo.*   No, ése es *Camilo.*

11. PAIRED SENTENCES

¿Dónde es la cena?   ¿Dónde es la cena?
Where's the dinner (food)?   ¿Dónde está la cena?
Where's the dinner (being held)?   ¿Dónde es la cena?

¿Es aquí el almuerzo?   *¿Es aquí el almuerzo?*
Is the lunch (food) here?   *¿Está aquí el almuerzo?*
Is the luncheon (being held) here?   *¿Es aquí el almuerzo?*

La película es en la sala.
The movie (reels of film) is in the living room.
The movie is (being shown) in the living room.

La película es en la sala.
La película está en la sala.

La película es en la sala.

¿Dónde son los exámenes?
Where are the exam papers?
Where are the exams (being given)?

¿Dónde son los exámenes?
¿Dónde están los exámenes?
¿Dónde son los exámenes?

La comida es aquí.
The food is here.
The dinner is (taking place) here.

La comida es aquí.
La comida está aquí.
La comida es aquí.

12. DOUBLE ITEM SUBSTITUTION

La fiesta es mañana. ⊗
El baile _____.
_____ aquí.
Mi padre _____.
_____ de California.
Mis abuelos _____.
_____ en mi casa.
La reunión _____.
_____ en la sala.
El libro _____.
_____ para Juan.

	VARIATION
La fiesta es mañana.	*la cena*
El baile es mañana.	
El baile es aquí.	*en la escuela*
Mi padre está aquí.	*la maestra*
Mi padre es de California.	*de Colombia*
Mis abuelos son de California.	*los señores*
Mis abuelos están en mi casa.	*aquí*
La reunión es en mi casa.	*el baile*
La reunión es en la sala.	*en la casa de Ana.*
El libro está en la sala.	*los regalos*
El libro es para Juan.	*para ellos*

→La cena es mañana.
El baile es en la escuela.
La maestra está aquí.
Mi padre es de Colombia.
Los señores son de Colombia.
Mis abuelos están aquí.
El baile es en mi casa.
La reunión es en la casa de Ana.
Los regalos están en la sala.
Los regalos son para ellos.

13. FREE RESPONSE

Buenos días, ¿cómo está usted?
Usted es el *Sr. García,* ¿no?
¿Cómo está su familia?
¿De dónde son ustedes?
¿Tiene usted un hermano?
¿Dónde está él ahora?
¿Dónde está su mamá?
¿De dónde es su mamá, de Nueva York?
Y su padre, ¿de dónde es él?
A ver si adivina de dónde soy yo.
¿Cuándo es el partido de fútbol? ¿Dónde es?
¿A qué hora es el partido?
A propósito, ¿cuánto cuestan los boletos?

14. DOUBLE ITEM SUBSTITUTION

El partido es esta tarde. ⊗

_____ en el estadio.

Los chicos _____.

_____ de los Estados Unidos.

Nosotros _____.

_____ en la sala.

La reunión _____.

_____ a las ocho.

La cena _____.

_____ en la mesa.

Las cosas _____.

_____ aquí.

El baile _____.

El partido es esta tarde.
El partido es en el estadio.
Los chicos están en el estadio.
Los chicos son de los Estados Unidos.
Nosotros somos de los Estados Unidos.
Nosotros estamos en la sala.
La reunión es en la sala.
La reunión es a las ocho.
La cena es a las ocho.
La cena está en la mesa.
Las cosas están en la mesa.
Las cosas están aquí.
El baile es aquí.

VARIATION: Substitute the following cues: aquí–los gemelos–de Nueva York–usted y yo–en la escuela–el baile–mañana–la comida–en el comedor–el libro–en la casa de Ana–la fiesta

15. FREE SUBSTITUTION

El maestro está aquí. _los chicos, la fiesta, el libro / ser or estar, depending on which is appropriate / en el comedor, en la escuela, en la mesa_

16. WRITING EXERCISE

Write the responses to Drill 11.

EXERCISE BOOK: EXERCISES 1, 2 AND 3.

ser _and_ estar _with Predicate Adjectives_

TEACHER PRESENTATION, p. T167

GENERALIZATION

1. On pages 92 and 93 you learned about situations in which only **ser** or **estar** can be used; the choice depends upon specific words or phrases in the rest of the sentence.

   There is also a construction in which either verb may occur: noun phrase + **ser** or **estar** + adjective. Both of the following sentences are correct:

   María es linda.
   María está linda.

They are, however, quite different in meaning. The choice of **ser** or **estar** with adjectives is determined by the relationship of the adjective to the rest of the sentence.

a. **Ser** expresses a <u>norm</u>. The sentence **María es linda** says that the adjective **linda,** *pretty,* normally applies to María—that being pretty is her normal condition.

b. **Estar** expresses an <u>attribute</u> of the subject <u>at a particular time</u>. The sentence **María está linda** says that the adjective **linda** happens to describe María at a particular time —whether or not she is normally pretty.

2. The difference in the relationships expressed by **estar** and **ser** is illustrated clearly in the dialog line <u>Está</u> (she happens to look) **bonita en la foto, pero ella no es** (normally) **muy linda, francamente.** Let us imagine a different situation: the girl not only looks pretty in the photograph, but also is, in fact, a very pretty girl. Then the speaker might have said: <u>Está</u> **bonita en la foto porque ella** <u>es</u> **muy linda.**

3. English, lacking the distinction between **ser** and **estar** with adjectives, frequently makes a roughly equivalent distinction by using expressions like these:

> *She <u>looks</u> pretty.* **(Está linda.)**
> *He's <u>gotten</u> sick.* **(Está enfermo.)**
> *We haven't <u>gone</u> deaf.* **(No estamos sordas.)**
> *He sure <u>has grown</u>!* **(¡Qué grande está!)**

Listening and Speaking Exercises 113, 114, 115*, 116*, p. T64 ⊗ | SECTION C

STRUCTURE DRILLS

17. PATTERNED RESPONSE

¡Qué bonita es esa chica! ⊗

Está bonita en la foto, pero ella no es muy bonita, francamente.

¡Qué gordo es ese señor!

Está gordo en la foto, pero él no es muy gordo, francamente.

¡Qué lindas son las primas de Juan!

Están lindas en la foto, pero ellas no son muy lindas, francamente.

¡Qué delgada es doña Delia!

Está delgada en la foto, pero ella no es muy delgada, francamente.

18. PAIRED SENTENCES

Esta mesa es bastante nueva. ⊗
This table looks quite new.
This table is quite new.

Esta mesa es bastante nueva.
Esta mesa está bastante nueva.
Esta mesa es bastante nueva.

¡Qué gordo es Alfonso!
Alfonso has certainly gotten fat!
Alfonso surely is fat!

¡Qué gordo es Alfonso!
¡Qué gordo está Alfonso!
¡Qué gordo es Alfonso!

(*continued*)

(continued)

¿Soy muy delgado?
Do I look very thin?
Am I very thin?

¿Soy muy delgado?
¿Estoy muy delgado?
¿Soy muy delgado?

¡Qué feos son mis zapatos!
My shoes look so ugly!
My shoes are so ugly!

¡Qué feos son mis zapatos!
¡Qué feos están mis zapatos!
¡Qué feos son mis zapatos!

¿Por qué gritas? No soy sordo.
Why are you shouting? I haven't gone deaf.
Why are you shouting? I'm not deaf.

¿Por qué gritas? No soy sordo.
¿Por qué gritas? No estoy sordo.
¿Por qué gritas? No soy sordo.

19. PATTERNED RESPONSE

¿Cómo es Pedrito? ⊗
¿Cómo está Pedrito?
¿Cómo son los gemelos?
¿Cómo están los gemelos?
¿Cómo es usted?
¿Cómo está usted?
¿Cómo es su novia?
¿Cómo está su novia?

Es alto y guapo.
Está enfermo hoy.
Son altos y guapos.
Están enfermos hoy.
Soy alto y guapo.
Estoy enfermo hoy.
Es alta y guapa.
Está enferma hoy.

20. FREE RESPONSE

¿De qué son las fotos de Carlos?
¿Quién es la chica que está en la foto?
¿Es ella muy linda?
¿Cómo está en la foto?
¿Cómo es la otra foto?
¿De qué es la foto?
¿Es la fiesta en casa de Carlos o de Hernán?
¿Dónde está Carlos en la foto?
¿Qué día es hoy?
¿Está bonito el día?
¿Cómo es esta escuela?
¿Cómo es su mamá?
¿Cómo es su casa?
¿Cómo están ustedes?
¿Y cómo son ustedes? ¿Son buenos?

Son fotos de su familia.
Es una prima de Carlos.
Está bonita en la foto, pero ella no es muy linda.
Está bonita.
Es graciosa.
Es de una fiesta.
Es en la casa de Carlos.
Está sentado en el suelo.

21. QUESTION-ANSWER FORMATION

Ask questions about don Pedro which will elicit answers containing the following information about him. Use the correct form of **ser** or **estar** in each of your questions.

Information	Question	Answer
un señor	¿Quién es don Pedro?	Don Pedro es un señor.
aquí	¿Dónde está don Pedro?	Está aquí.
un maestro	¿Quién es don Pedro?	Es un maestro.
sí, en esta foto	¿Está en esta foto?	Sí, está en esta foto.
ése que está sentado en el sofá	¿Cuál es don Pedro?	Ése que está sentado en el sofá.
no, no muy gordo	¿Es (está) muy gordo?	No, no es (está) muy gordo.
en la escuela ahora	¿Dónde está?	Está en la escuela ahora.
sí, mayor que el Sr. García	¿Es mayor que el Sr. García?	Sí, es mayor que el Sr. García.
sí, muy contento con el álbum	¿Está contento con el álbum?	Sí, está muy contento.
sí, bastante simpático	¿Es simpático?	Sí, es bastante simpático.
muy bien	¿Cómo está don Pedro?	Está muy bien.
no, no muy cansado	¿Está cansado?	No, no está muy cansado.

22. WRITING EXERCISE

Write the responses to Drills 18 and 19.

EXERCISE BOOK: EXERCISES 4, 5, 6, AND 7

The Suffix -ito

TEACHER PRESENTATION, p. T167

GENERALIZATION

Spanish has a number of suffixes, called diminutive suffixes, which can be added to noun stems and sometimes to adjective stems to indicate smallness, cuteness, or a feeling of affection on the part of the speaker. (The stem is the noun or adjective minus the last vowel, if there is one.) The most common diminutive suffix is **-ito** (**-ita** feminine), which can be added to the stem of many, although not all, nouns. The gender of a noun is never changed by the addition of **-ito, -ita.**

perro	**perrito** (*little dog, puppy*)
casa	**casita** (*little house*)
mesas	**mesitas** (*little tables*)
Juan	**Juanito** (*Johnny*)

The Suffix -ísimo

TEACHER PRESENTATION, p. T168

The suffix **-ísimo** has the meaning *extremely* and can be affixed to the stem of most adjectives. The **-ísimo** form of the adjective is usually called the superlative form.

alto	**altísimo**
grande	**grandísimo**
fácil	**facilísimo**

The **-ísimo** form of the adjective must, of course, be masculine or feminine, singular or plural, to agree with the noun it modifies.

María está **lindísima** esta noche.
Los exámenes son **dificilísimos.**

Note: Teach Letter ↔ Sound Correspondences (Spelling Changing with Suffixes, page 106) at this point.

STRUCTURE DRILLS

23. **NOUN → DIMINUTIVE FORM**

¿Cómo estás, Lupe? ⊗	¿Cómo estás, Lupita?
Son unos regalos.	*Son unos regalitos.*
¡Qué bonito es ese perro!	*¡Qué bonito es ese perrito!*
Busco unas mesas.	*Busco unas mesitas.*
¿Quién es ese chico?	*¿Quién es ese chiquito?*
Vamos con mi abuela.	*Vamos con mi abuelita.*
¿Cuándo llegan tus hermanos?	*¿Cuándo llegan tus hermanitos?*

24. **ADJECTIVE → SUPERLATIVE FORM**

El álbum es lindo. ⊗	El álbum es lindísimo.
Todos los chicos son altos.	*Todos los chicos son altísimos.*
Las gemelas son inteligentes.	*Las gemelas son inteligentísimas.*
Juana está gorda ahora.	*Juana está gordísima ahora.*
Estamos cansados.	*Estamos cansadísimos.*
El examen es fácil.	*El examen es facilísimo.*
Esta escuela es grande.	*La escuela es grandísima.*

25. **CUED DIALOG**

1. (ese chico)

1ST STUDENT	¿Es guapo ese chico?
2ND STUDENT	Sí, es guapísimo.

(tu novia)   *¿Es guapa tu novia? / Sí, es guapísima.*
(las primas)   *¿Son guapas tus primas? / Sí, son guapísimas.*
(los gemelos)   *¿Son guapos los gemelos? / Sí, son guapísimos.*
(ese chico)   *¿Es guapo ese chico? / Sí, es guapísimo.*

2. (la biblioteca)   1ST STUDENT   ¿La biblioteca es muy grande?
                              2ND STUDENT   Sí, es grandísima.

(el estadio)   *¿El estadio es muy grande? / Sí, es grandísimo.*
(las casas)   *¿Las casas son muy grandes? / Sí, son grandísimas.*
(los parques)   *¿Los parques son muy grandes? / Sí, son grandísimos.*
(la biblioteca)   *¿La biblioteca es muy grande? / Sí, es grandísima.*

26. WRITING EXERCISES

Write the responses to Drills 23 and 24.

EXERCISE BOOK: EXERCISES 8 AND 9.

ir *and* dar, *Present Tense*

PRESENTATION *TEACHER PRESENTATION, p. T168*

¿Adónde quiere **ir**?
¿Adónde **voy**?
¿Adónde **vas**?
¿Adónde **va**?
¿Adónde **vamos**?
¿Adónde **van**?

What is the theme vowel of the infinitive **ir?** What is the theme vowel in the present tense forms? Which present tense form has an irregular ending?

GENERALIZATION

ir, PRESENT TENSE		
	Singular	*Plural*
1	**voy**	**vamos**
2	**vas**	**van**
3	**va**	

1. The present tense forms of **ir** consist of the stem **v** and the theme vowel **a** + an ending. The ending of the first person singular is **oy** (like that of **estar: estoy**; and **ser: soy**). The other endings are those of regular **a**-class verbs.

   The first person plural form of **ir**—**vamos**—may mean *let's go* as well as *we go, we're going.*

dar, PRESENT TENSE		
	Singular	*Plural*
1	**doy**	**damos**
2	**das**	**dan**
3	**da**	

2. **Dar** is regular in the present tense except for the first person singular **doy**, which ends in **oy** like **soy, estoy,** and **voy.**

Listening and Speaking Exercises 117, 118, 119*, p. T66   ⊗ | SECTION D |

STRUCTURE DRILLS

27. PERSON-NUMBER SUBSTITUTION

1. ¿Adónde vas? ⊗   ¿Adónde vas?
   (ustedes)   ¿Adónde van?
   (yo)   ¿Adónde voy?
   (los chicos)   ¿Adónde van?
   (nosotros)   ¿Adónde vamos?
   (él)   ¿Adónde va?
   (tú)   ¿Adónde vas?

2. Vamos a la reunión ahora. ⊗
   (yo–tú y Juan–Pedro–ellos–Susana y yo–tú) *voy–van–va–van–vamos–vas*

28. PATTERNED RESPONSE

Doy una fiesta el sábado. ⊗   ¿Ah, sí? ¿usted da una fiesta?
Damos una fiesta el sábado.   *¿Ah, sí? ¿ustedes dan (or nosotros damos) una fiesta?*
Las gemelas García dan una fiesta el   *¿Ah, sí? ¿las gemelas García dan una fiesta?*
   sábado.
Tú das una fiesta el sábado.   *¿Ah, sí? ¿yo doy una fiesta?*
Ana y yo damos una fiesta el sábado.   *¿Ah, sí? ¿Ana y usted dan una fiesta?*
Doy una fiesta el sábado.   *¿Ah, sí? ¿usted da una fiesta?*

ADDITIONAL STRUCTURE DRILL, p. T205 ⊗

29. FREE RESPONSE

¿Adónde va usted este sábado?
¿Va al cine?
¿Qué dan?
¿Van ustedes a un baile el sábado?
¿Va su mamá al mercado hoy?
¿Qué día va ella al mercado?
¿Va su padre con ella?
¿A usted le gusta dar fiestas?
¿Da muchas?
¿Le gusta más dar o ir a fiestas?

30. WRITING EXERCISE

Write the responses to Drills 27.2 and 28.
EXERCISE BOOK: EXERCISES 10 AND 11.

Writing

1. SENTENCE CONSTRUCTION

Write a sentence using the following items in the order given. Use the appropriate form of
ser or **estar** in each sentence.

MODEL   prima / linda / foto

Possible sentences

Tu prima está muy linda en la foto.
La prima de Juan no está muy linda en
esta foto.

1. libro / para / maestra   *es*
2. chicos / en / comedor   *están*
3. hermanito / guapo / foto   *está*
4. dónde / álbum / familia   *está*
5. novio / sentado / sofá   *está*

6. yo / cansadísimo / ahora   *estoy*
7. Juan y yo / en / cocina   *estamos*
8. chico / hijo / doña Delia   *es*
9. cuándo / fiesta / escuela   *es*
10. tú / no / foto   *estás*

2. PARAGRAPH COMPLETION

Copy the following paragraph, filling in the blanks with the correct form of **ser** or **estar**.

Aquí tengo una foto de mi familia. El señor que __1__ sentado en el sofá __2__ mi
abuelo. Las dos chicas que __3__ sentadas con él __4__ mis primas, Marta y Carmen. Marta
no __5__ muy bonita en la foto, pero francamente, ella __6__ mucho más linda que su
hermana. Mi hermano y yo __7__ en la foto también. A ver si usted adivina dónde __8__ yo.
Sí, yo __9__ ése que __10__ sentado en la silla. Y mi hermano __11__ ése que __12__ con todas
las chicas.

1	2	3	4	5	6	7	8	9	10	11	12
está	es	están	son	está	es	estamos	estoy	soy	está	es	está

Listening and Speaking Exercise 120*, p. T67 ⊗

RECOMBINATION MATERIAL

Dialogs

I

MIGUELITA	A ver si adivina quién soy yo, don Francisco.
DON FRANCISCO	Mmm . . . no, no sé, no recuerdo. ¿Quién eres?
MIGUELITA	La hermana menor de Manolo.
DON FRANCISCO	Ah, sí, claro, ahora recuerdo. ¡Qué alta estás!

El hermano menor . . . ←
¡Qué alto estás!

VARIATION: Don Francisco is talking
to Miguel, Manolo's younger brother.

QUESTIONS

1. ¿Recuerda don Francisco quién es Miguelita?
2. ¿Quién es Miguelita?
3. ¿Es ella mayor o menor que Manolo?
4. ¿Cómo está Miguelita ahora?

II

CAROLINA	¡Qué bonita está la fiesta!
CRISTINA	¿Te gusta?
CAROLINA	Sí, mucho. ¿Cuál es tu primo?
CRISTINA	Ése que está sentado en el sofá.

. . . ¿Cuál es tu prima? ←
Ésa que está sentada . . .

VARIATION: Carolina's cousin is a girl. ─

QUESTIONS

1. ¿Dónde están las dos chicas?
2. ¿Está Carolina contenta con la fiesta?
3. ¿Cuál chico es el primo de Carolina?
4. ¿Dónde está sentado?

III

MANUEL	Hola, Blanca. ¿Cómo estás?
BLANCA	Muy bien.
MANUEL	¿Quieres caminar por el parque conmigo?
BLANCA	No puedo. Me aprietan mucho los zapatos.

REJOINDERS

¿Quieres caminar por el parque conmigo? *Claro, vamos. / Muy bien. / No puedo. / No, me aprietan mucho los zapatos. / Más tarde.*

IV

PATRICIO	Ése que está sentado en el sofá, ¿es tu padre?
MAURICIO	No, es mi abuelo.
PATRICIO	Y la señora que está sentada con él, ¿es tu abuela?
MAURICIO	No, es mi madre.

QUESTIONS

1. ¿Quiénes hablan?
2. ¿Quién está sentado en el sofá, el padre de Mauricio?
3. ¿Y quién es la señora que está sentada con él?

V

RODRIGO	A ver si adivinas quién es el chico que está en la . . . la chica . . . ←
	foto conmigo.
GONZALO	Mmm . . . tu hermano gemelo. . . . tu hermana gemela.
RODRIGO	No, es Carlos, mi primo. No, es Susana, mi prima.
GONZALO	¿Es verdad? Pero . . . son idénticos. . . . . son idénticas.

QUESTIONS

VARIATION: The conversation is between two girls, one of whom has a cousin named Susana.

1. ¿Qué tiene Rodrigo?
2. ¿Adivina Gonzalo quién está en la foto con Rodrigo?
3. ¿Quién piensa Gonzalo que está en la foto?
4. ¿Quién es Carlos?
5. ¿Cómo son Carlos y Rodrigo?

Narrative | *Note:* For teaching suggestions see p. T18.

Yo

Yo soy Francisco Castro, alumno de la Escuela Americana. Es una escuela muy bonita y moderna*. Me gusta mucho. Mis compañeros son todos muy buenos y simpáticos. Aquí tengo dos fotos: una es de la escuela; bonita ¿no? La otra es de todos los
5 chicos y chicas que están en mi clase*, y del maestro, don Pedro. Ése que está sentado con la chica rubia soy yo.

Note: Point out that many nouns and adjectives are written alike in Spanish and English: *álbum, animal, musical;* and that many others are almost alike, except that the Spanish word ends in a vowel: *moderno, clase.*

---

*Cognates are indicated by an asterisk (*).

QUESTIONS

Answer begins on line ⟶↓

1. ¿Quién es el chico que habla en la narración*? *1*
2. ¿Es él un alumno o el maestro? *1*
3. ¿Dónde estudia? *1*
4. ¿Cómo es la Escuela Americana? *2*
5. ¿Cómo son los compañeros de Francisco? *3*
6. ¿Cuántas fotos tiene Francisco? *3*
7. ¿De qué es una de las fotos? *4*
8. ¿De qué es la otra foto? *4*
9. ¿Está el maestro en la foto también? *5*
10. ¿Con quién está sentado Francisco en la foto? *6*

Rejoinders

1. ¡Qué guapo es ese chico! *Está guapo en la foto, pero él no es muy guapo, francamente. / Es muy simpático también. / Es mi primo. / Su primo es más guapo que él.*
2. A ver si adivinas cuál soy yo. *¡Tú no estás en la foto! / ¿Ése que está sentado en el sofá?*
3. ¿Dónde es la fiesta? *En mi casa. / En la escuela. / En la casa de mis abuelos. / En la casa de mi tía Luisa. / No tengo la menor idea.*

Conversation Stimulus

You are looking at a family album with a friend.

Start like this: ¡Qué graciosa es esa foto! ¿Dónde <u>es la fiesta</u>?
En la casa de <u>mis abuelos.</u>
¿Quién es <u>esa chica? Es muy bonita.</u>
¿Ella? <u>Es mi hermana mayor.</u>
¿Y quiénes son <u>ese señor y esa señora?</u>
Son mis tíos. Son muy simpáticos.

LETTER ↔ SOUND CORRESPONDENCES

Note: Teach this lesson with grammar section beginning on page 99 (The Suffix *-ito,* The Suffix *-ísimo*).

SPELLING NOTES: SPELLING CHANGES WITH SUFFIXES

c → qu

1. If the stem of a word ends in **c,** the **c** changes to **qu** before the suffixes **-ito** and **-ísimo** in order to retain the sound [k].

chico	chiquito
chica	chiquita
Marco	Marquito
simpático	simpatiquísimo

g → gu

2. If the stem of a word ends in **g,** the **g** changes to **gu** before the suffixes **-ito** and **-ísimo** in order to retain the sound [g] or [g̶].

amigo	amiguito
abrigo	abriguito

z → c

3. If the stem of a word ends in **z,** the **z** changes to **c** before the suffixes **-ito** and **-ísimo.** This change is just a convention; it is not needed to retain the sound [s].

Beatriz   Beatricita

WRITING

Spelling Note: [f] = **f**

The sound [f] is always represented by the letter **f.** The letter combination *ph* does not occur in Spanish.

SENTENCES

1. ¿Puedo ver la foto de la fiesta?
2. Claro, Felipe.
3. ¿Quién es esta chiquita?
4. Mi prima Beatricita. Es simpatiquísima.

WRITING

Copy the above sentences and be prepared to write them from dictation.

BASIC DIALOG

Con Conchita: durante el recreo

ENRIQUE	Tú sabes hablar inglés, ¿verdad? 7-1
CONCHITA	No mucho. Leo y escribo un poco solamente. ¿Por qué? 7-2
ENRIQUE	¿Qué dice esta carta? Es de una chica que vive en Canadá. 7-3
CONCHITA	Necesito un diccionario. Vamos a la biblioteca.

CONCHITA	Dice que se llama Sue, que es rubia, de ojos azules . . . ⎫
ENRIQUE	Mmm . . . debe ser muy bonita. ¿Qué más dice? ⎭ 7-4
CONCHITA	Quiere saber cómo eres tú . . . cuántos años tienes . . . ⎫
ENRIQUE	Yo no sé cómo soy yo. ¿Cómo soy yo, Conchita? ⎭ 7-5
CONCHITA	Yo creo que tú eres un gordito muy simpático. 7-6

Note: Nicknames which refer to physical characteristics, such as Gordo and Flaco, are common in Spanish-speaking countries. It is not considered in poor taste to call a friend *gordito*.

With Conchita: During Recess

ENRIQUE	You know how to speak English, don't you?
CONCHITA	Not very well (much). I only read and write a little. (I read and write a little only.) Why?
ENRIQUE	What does this letter say? It's from a girl who lives in Canada.
CONCHITA	I need a dictionary. Let's go to the library.

CONCHITA	She says her name is (she calls herself) Sue, that she's blond, with blue eyes . . .
ENRIQUE	Mmm . . . she must be very pretty. What else (more) does she say?
CONCHITA	She wants to know what you're like (how you are) . . . how old you are (how many years you have) . . .
ENRIQUE	I don't know what I'm like. What am I like, Conchita?
CONCHITA	I think you're a very nice little fat boy.

◀ *Youngsters gather in a school patio during recess.*

◀ Patios like this one, where children may play during recess, are typical.   **109**

Supplement

Vamos sin Conchita.	Let's go without Conchita.

Está delante de Conchita. 7-1   He's in front of Conchita.
    detrás de   7-2   back of

¿De qué color es tu vestido? Amarillo.   What color is your dress? Yellow.
                  Rojo.   Red.
                  Café.   Brown.
                  Blanco.   White.

Necesito un diccionario. 7-3
       la carta   7-4

¿Cómo te llamas?   What's your name?
Me llamo Conchita.   My name's Conchita.

Dice que es trigueña.   She says she's brunette.
       pelirroja   redheaded

Note: the meaning of *trigueño* varies from country to country; the most common meaning is *brunette.* In some countries, *moreno* is the equivalent of *brunette.* In others, *moreno* means dark-complexioned.

Dice que tiene pelo rubio.   She says she has blond hair.

Tiene ojos negros.   She has black eyes.
       castaños[1]   brown
       grises   grey
       verdes   green

Tú eres un gordito muy perezoso.   You're a very lazy little fat boy.
               listo   clever
               distraído   absent-minded

Vamos a la calle.   7-5   Let's go to the street.
           plaza   7-6   square (plaza)
           esquina   7-7   corner
           estación   7-8   station

Voy a la biblioteca contigo.   I'll go to the library with you.

¿Qué quieres comer? 7-9   What do you want to eat?
             hacer   do (make)
            escribir   7-10
            leer   7-11

Vamos durante el recreo   7–12

---

[1] **Castaño** is generally used only to indicate color of hair and eyes. Otherwise, one common Spanish equivalent of *brown* is **café**, although there are other equivalents used throughout Spanish America. Expressions like **unos zapatos de color café** may be shortened to **unos zapatos café,** where **café** remains singular in spite of the plural **zapatos.**

Note: Other equivalents for *brown* are *marrón, pardo,* and *caramelo.*

Listening and Speaking Exercises 121, 122, 123*, and 124*, p. T68 ⊗

BASIC FORMS

Verbs

*creer	*saber
*deber	*escribir
*leer	*vivir

Nouns

color *m.*   calle *f.*
                     estación *f.*

Adjectives

azul   gris
café   verde

Vocabulary Exercises

1. QUESTIONS

1. ¿Habla inglés Enrique? *No.*
2. ¿Habla inglés Conchita? *No mucho.*
3. ¿De quién es la carta de Enrique? *De una chica.*
4. ¿Dónde vive la chica? *En Canadá.*
5. ¿Qué necesita Conchita? *Un diccionario.*
6. ¿Adónde va Conchita a buscar el diccionario? *A la biblioteca.*
7. ¿Tiene usted un diccionario español-inglés?
8. ¿Estudia usted con diccionario o sin diccionario?

2. DIALOG RECALL

un poco *Leo y escribo un poco solamente.*
carta *¿Qué dice esta carta?*
Canadá *Es de una chica que vive en Canadá.*
diccionario *Necesito un diccionario.*

3. QUESTIONS

1. ¿Cómo se llama la chica que vive en Canadá? *Se llama Sue.*
2. ¿Es bonita ella? *Sí, debe ser muy bonita.*
3. ¿Cómo es ella? *Rubia, de ojos azules.*
4. ¿Qué quiere saber Sue en la carta? *Cómo es Enrique . . . cuántos años tiene . . .*
5. ¿Cómo es Enrique? *Es un gordito muy simpático.*
6. ¿Con quién habla usted durante el recreo?
7. ¿Es el recreo antes o después de esta clase?

4. ANTONYM DRILL

Hablo <u>poco</u> español.   *mucho*

¿Vamos <u>con</u> Conchita?   *sin*

¿Quién es ese chico que está <u>detrás</u> de
   Luis?   *delante*

Sue debe ser muy <u>bonita</u>.   *fea*

¡Qué <u>gordo</u> está Enrique!   *delgado*

Practicamos <u>antes</u> de la cena.   *después*

¿De qué color es? ¿<u>Blanco</u>?   *negro*

5. ENGLISH CUE DRILL

¿Cómo es Enrique? ⊗

What is Conchita like?

What is the station like?

What are the students like?

What is the school like?

What are the twins like?

What is Enrique like?

¿Cómo es Enrique?

¿Cómo es Conchita?

¿Cómo es la estación?

¿Cómo son los alumnos?

¿Cómo es la escuela?

¿Cómo son los gemelos?

¿Cómo es Enrique?

GRAMMAR

Position of Descriptive Adjectives

PRESENTATION *TEACHER PRESENTATION, p. T169*

¿A quién llamas? A la **chica americana.**
Excepto ese **chico rubio.**
Tiene **ojos azules.**
Eres un **gordito muy simpático.**

In each of these sentences, what is the position of the adjective in relation to the noun?

GENERALIZATION

1. Adjectives which specify some quality or characteristic of the noun they modify are called descriptive adjectives. The underscored adjectives in the following examples are descriptive adjectives:

   Está <u>bonita</u> en la foto, pero ella no es muy <u>linda</u>.
   Los boletos son <u>caros</u>.
   ¡Qué <u>feos</u> están mis zapatos!

2. As the above examples illustrate, descriptive adjectives may occur—with **ser, estar,** and a few other verbs—as the predicate adjective of a sentence.

SUBJECT   PREDICATE

Los boletos son caros.

PREDICATE   SUBJECT

¡Qué feos están mis zapatos!

3. Descriptive adjectives may also occur inside a noun phrase after the noun they modify. Noun + adjective is a normal word order in Spanish.

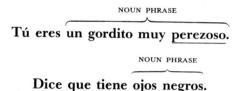

NOUN PHRASE

Tú eres un gordito muy perezoso.

NOUN PHRASE

Dice que tiene ojos negros.

Listening and Speaking Exercises 125, 126, 127, 128*, p. T70 ⊗

SECTION B

STRUCTURE DRILLS

6. ITEM SUBSTITUTION

1. Tengo unas amigas muy listas. ⊗	Tengo unas amigas muy listas. *VARIATION*
_____ una hermana _____.	Tengo una hermana muy lista. un hermano / listo
_____ unos compañeros _____.	Tengo unos compañeros muy listos. una amiga / lista
_____ un novio _____.	Tengo un novio muy listo. un primo / listo
_____ una prima _____.	Tengo una prima muy lista. unos primos / listos
_____ unos amigos _____.	Tengo unos amigos muy listos. unas amigas / listas
_____ un perro _____.	Tengo un perro muy listo. una novia / lista

2. ¿Buscas una corbata verde? ⊗ un pañuelo verde–unos guantes verdes–un vestido verde–unas medias
   (un pañuelo–unos guantes–un vestido–unas medias–una blusa) verdes–una blusa verde

3. ¿Vas con la chica francesa? ⊗ los señores franceses–el alumno francés–la familia francesa–las
   (los señores–el alumno–la familia–las señoras–el maestro) señoras francesas–el maestro
   francés

7. TRANSFORMATION DRILL

El diccionario es nuevo. Está aquí. ⊗	El diccionario nuevo está aquí.
La corbata es amarilla. Es de Juan.	La corbata amarilla es de Juan.
Los pañuelos son blancos. Están en mi cuarto.	Los pañuelos blancos están en mi cuarto.

(continued)

(*continued*)

La chica es pelirroja. Se llama Susana.
Los alumnos son americanos. Hablan bien español.
Las chicas son rubias. Son gemelas.
Los guantes son rojos. Son de María.

La chica pelirroja se llama Susana.
Los alumnos americanos hablan bien español.
Las chicas rubias son gemelas.
Los guantes rojos son de María.

8. FREE RESPONSE

¿Tiene *Juana* ojos verdes?
¿Y *Pedro*?
¿Y usted?
¿Tiene usted pelo rubio?
¿Y su mamá?
¿Y el maestro?
¿Es blanco el vestido de *Ana*?
¿Y los zapatos de *María*?
¿Y la camisa de *Juan*?
¿De qué color es la blusa de *Susana*?
¿Y los pantalones de *Camilo*?

Progressive Substitution Variation ←

El diccionario nuevo está aquí.
Las corbatas nuevas están aquí.
La corbata blanca está aquí.
Las corbatas blancas están aquí.
El zapato blanco está aquí.
Los zapatos negros están aquí.
El zapato negro está aquí.
Los guantes negros están aquí.
El guante azul está aquí.
Los guantes azules están aquí.

9. PROGRESSIVE SUBSTITUTION

El diccionario nuevo está aquí. ⊗

__ camisas _____ .	*El diccionario nuevo está aquí.*	VARIATION
_____ amarilla _____ .	*Las camisas nuevas están aquí.*	corbatas
_____ están __ .	*La camisa amarilla está aquí.*	blanca
__ guante _____ .	*Las camisas amarillas están aquí.*	están
_____ rojos _____ .	*El guante amarillo está aquí.*	zapato
_____ está __ .	*Los guantes rojos están aquí.*	negros
__ zapatos _____ .	*El guante rojo está aquí.*	está
_____ gris _____ .	*Los zapatos rojos están aquí.*	guantes
_____ están __ .	*El zapato gris está aquí.*	azul
	Los zapatos grises están aquí.	están

10. FREE SUBSTITUTION

El maestro nuevo está aquí. *la maestra, los alumnos, el chico / francés, alemán, rubio*

11. WRITING EXERCISE

Write the responses to Drills 6.2, 6.3 and 9.
EXERCISE BOOK: EXERCISES 1, 2, AND 3

12. DIRECTED DIALOG

Pregúntele a *Gloria* si recuerda la fiesta del otro día.

¿Recuerdas la fiesta del otro día?

Dígale que claro, y pregúntele por qué.

Claro, ¿por qué?

Pregúntele si recuerda al chico alto de ojos negros.

¿Recuerdas al chico alto de ojos negros?

→ a la chica alta

Dígale que claro, que es muy guapo.

Claro, es muy guapo. guapa

Dígale que usted va a una fiesta con él este domingo.

Yo voy a una fiesta con él este domingo.

con ella

13. DIRECTED DIALOG VARIATION

1. Do the directed dialog again, reading the directions to another student and using adjectives of your own choice.

2. Do the directed dialog again, reading the directions to another student and making it a conversation between two boys talking about a girl.

14. ENGLISH CUE DRILL

Es un chico rubio de ojos azules. ⊗

Es un chico rubio de ojos azules.

She's a redheaded girl with green eyes.

Es una chica pelirroja de ojos verdes.

She's a brunette lady with brown eyes.

Es una señora trigueña de ojos castaños.

He's a tall gentleman with grey eyes.

Es un señor alto de ojos grises.

She's a pretty young lady with black eyes.

Es una señorita bonita de ojos negros.

He's a blond boy with blue eyes.

Es un chico rubio de ojos azules.

15. FREE RESPONSE

¿Cómo se llama usted?

¿Cómo es usted? ¿alto? ¿gordo? ¿de ojos castaños?

¿Cuántos años tiene usted?

¿Cómo son sus compañeros?

¿Es usted perezoso o le gusta estudiar?

¿Cómo es su casa?

¿Tiene novia?

¿Cómo es ella?

¿Cuántos años tiene ella?

16. WRITING EXERCISE

Write the responses to Drill 14.

Prepositions

TEACHER PRESENTATION, p. T170

GENERALIZATION

1. Spanish, like English, has a number of simple prepositions, consisting of a single word. The following are the simple prepositions you have encountered so far:

a, *to*	**Vamos <u>a</u> las carreras.**
con, *with*	**Más tarde hablo <u>con</u> ella.**
de, *from, of*	**No llega <u>de</u> la escuela todavía.**
durante, *during*	**<u>Durante</u> el recreo.**
en, *in, on, at*	**Está <u>en</u> la mesa.**
para, *for*	**Es un regalo <u>para</u> tu mamá.**
por, *through, by, for*	**Pasa <u>por</u> el parque.**
sin, *without*	**Vamos <u>sin</u> Conchita.**

2. Spanish, like English, also has a number of compound prepositions. These consist of an adverb plus the simple preposition **de.**

delante (*in front, ahead*)		**delante de** (*in front of, ahead of*)
detrás (*in back, behind*)	**+ de →**	**detrás de** (*in back of, behind*)
después (*afterwards, later*)		**después de** (*after*)
antes (*before, beforehand*)		**antes de** (*before, prior to*)

Listening and Speaking Exercises 129, 130, 131, 132*, 133*, p. T73 ⊗

STRUCTURE DRILLS

SECTION C

17. PAIRED SENTENCES

Vamos después del recreo. ⊗	Vamos después del recreo.
We'll go later.	Vamos después.
We'll go after recess.	Vamos después del recreo.
Estudian antes del examen.	*Estudian antes del examen.*
They study beforehand.	*Estudian antes.*
They study before the exam.	*Estudian antes del examen.*
Es ése que está delante de Ana.	*Es ése que está delante de Ana.*
He's the one who's in front.	*Es ése que está delante.*
He's the one who's in front of Ana.	*Es ése que está delante de Ana.*
El carro está detrás de la casa.	*El carro está detrás de la casa.*
The car's in back.	*El carro está detrás.*
The car's in back of the house.	*El carro está detrás de la casa.*

18. FREE RESPONSE

¿Con quién estudia usted?

¿De dónde es usted?

¿Necesita usted comprar un regalo para su mamá?

¿Necesitan ustedes comprar un regalo para la maestra?

¿Estudia usted con diccionario o sin diccionario?

¿Juegan fútbol los chicos durante el recreo?

¿Y las chicas también?

¿Pasa usted por la biblioteca hoy?

EXERCISE BOOK: EXERCISE 4

Pronouns as Objects of Prepositions

PRESENTATION *TEACHER PRESENTATION, p. T171*

¿Quién está sentado delante de **ti?**
¿Delante de **mí?** Fernando Gómez.

Tengo un regalo para **ti.**
¿Para **mí?** Muchas gracias.

Which Spanish word corresponds to *me* after a preposition? Which word corresponds to *you* (familiar)?

GENERALIZATION

1. In English, pronouns used as the objects of verbs and pronouns used as the objects of prepositions are the same.

$$He\ hit \begin{cases} me. \\ you. \\ her. \\ them. \end{cases} \qquad The\ book\ is\ for \begin{cases} me. \\ you. \\ her. \\ them. \end{cases}$$

2. In Spanish, however, pronouns used as the objects of prepositions are the same as subject pronouns, except for the first person singular and the second person singular (familiar).

$$\textbf{El libro es para} \begin{cases} \textbf{usted.} \\ \textbf{él, ella.} \\ \textbf{nosotros.} \\ \textbf{ustedes.} \\ \textbf{ellos, ellas.} \end{cases}$$

3. For the first person singular and the second person singular (familiar), Spanish has two special forms.

$$\text{El libro es para } \begin{cases} \text{mí.} \\ \text{ti.} \end{cases}$$

Furthermore, **mí** and **ti** have special forms after the preposition **con.**

$$\text{con} + \text{mi} \rightarrow \text{conmigo} \qquad \text{con} + \text{ti} \rightarrow \text{contigo}$$

$$\text{Ellos van } \begin{cases} \text{conmigo.} \\ \text{contigo.} \end{cases}$$

STRUCTURE DRILLS

19. PATTERNED RESPONSE

1. ¿Es la carta para ti? ⊗   Sí, es para mí.
   ¿Van las chicas sin ella?   Sí, van sin ella.
   ¿Está Juan delante de usted?   Sí, está delante de mí.
   ¿Piensan los chicos en mí?   Sí, piensan en usted.
   ¿Estudia el chico rubio con ellos?   Sí, estudia con ellos.
   ¿Es el regalo para nosotros?   Sí, es para ustedes. (*or* para nosotros.)

Pupils learn to read and write in an open-air school in rural Costa Rica.

2. ¿Puedo ir con ustedes? ⊗   ¿Con nosotros? Sí, claro.
¿Van a la estación conmigo?   *¿Con usted? Sí, claro.*
¿Juan estudia con ella?   *¿Con ella? Sí, claro.*
¿Quieres ir a la plaza con nosotros?   *¿Con ustedes? Sí, claro.*
¿Puedo practicar contigo?   *¿Conmigo? Sí, claro.*
¿María vive con ellas?   *¿Con ellas? Sí, claro.*
¿Necesitan hablar con usted?   *¿Conmigo? Sí, claro.*

20. FREE RESPONSE

¿Le gusta más jugar, o hablar con sus amigos durante el recreo?
¿Con quién va usted al cine?
¿Va antes o después de la cena?
¿Quién está sentado detrás de usted? ¿y delante de usted?
¿Quién habla español con ustedes?
¿Quién practica español con usted?

21. WRITING EXERCISE

Write the responses to Drill 19.2.

EXERCISE BOOK: EXERCISES 5, 6, AND 7

Regular e-Class Verbs

PRESENTATION   *TEACHER PRESENTATION, p. T172*

¿Qué quieres **comer**?
¿Qué **como**?
¿Qué **comes**?
¿Qué **come**?
¿Qué **comemos**?
¿Qué **comen**?

What is the stem of the verb **comer**? What is the theme vowel? What are the endings added to the stem + theme vowel to agree with the subject? Are these endings the same as those added to the stem + theme vowel of regular **a**-class verbs?

GENERALIZATION

1. In Unit 2 you studied the present tense of regular verbs whose theme vowel is **a**. There is also a large class of verbs whose theme vowel is **e**. The regular verbs of this class which you have encountered so far are **comer, creer, deber,** and **leer**.

2. The present tense of regular **e**-class verbs is just like that of **a**-class verbs, except for the theme vowel.

comer, PRESENT TENSE

	Singular	Plural
1	com – o	com e mos
2	com e s	com e n
3	com e –	

STRUCTURE DRILLS

22. PERSON-NUMBER SUBSTITUTION

1. Como a las ocho. ⊗   Como a las ocho.
   (tú)   Comes a las ocho.
   (ellos)   Comen a las ocho.
   (usted)   Come a las ocho.
   (mi hermano y yo)   Comemos a las ocho.
   (ustedes)   Comen a las ocho.
   (él)   Come a las ocho.

2. Leo español un poco solamente. ⊗ *lee—leo—lee—lees—leen—leen—leemos*
   (usted–yo–ella–tú–ellos–Juana y usted–nosotros)

3. Francamente, debe estudiar más. *debo—debes—deben—debemos—debe—deben—debe*
   (yo–tú–ellos–Pedro y yo–él–ustedes–ella)

23. WRITING EXERCISE

Write the responses to Drills 22.2 and 22.3.

Regular i-Class Verbs

PRESENTATION *TEACHER PRESENTATION, p. T173*

Sé **escribir** un poco solamente.
Escribo un poco solamente.
Escribes un poco solamente.

Escribe un poco solamente.
Escribimos un poco solamente.
Escriben un poco solamente.

What is the stem of the verb **escribir?** What is the theme vowel? In which present tense forms is the theme vowel different? How is it different? What difference do you notice between the present tense forms of **i**-class verbs and those of **e**-class verbs?

GENERALIZATION

There is a third class of verbs, called **i**-class verbs, whose theme vowel is **i** when stressed and **e** when unstressed.

escribir, PRESENT TENSE

	Singular	Plural
1	escrib – o	escrib i mos
2	escrib e s	escrib e n
3	escrib e –	

The present tense forms of this class of verbs are like those of **e**-class verbs except for the first person plural. The regular **i**-class verbs which you have encountered so far are **escribir** and **vivir.**

STRUCTURE DRILLS

24. PERSON-NUMBER SUBSTITUTION

1. Escribo una carta en inglés. ⊗   Escribo una carta en inglés.
   (tú)   Escribes una carta en inglés.
   (ellos)   Escriben una carta en inglés.
   (usted)   Escribe una carta en inglés.
   (él y yo)   Escribimos una carta en inglés.
   (ustedes)   Escriben una carta en inglés.
   (él)   Escribe una carta en inglés.

2. Viven en la esquina.   *vivimos–viven–vivo–vives–vive–viven*
   (nosotros–María y ella–yo–tú–él–ustedes)

25. SINGULAR → PLURAL

Debo estudiar más. ⊗   Debemos estudiar más.
Escribo una carta ahora.   *Escribimos una carta ahora.*
Leo el periódico.   *Leemos el periódico.*
Vivo en la esquina.   *Vivimos en la esquina.*
No creo a Juan.   *No creemos a Juan.*
¿Como ahora?   *¿Comemos ahora?*

26. FREE RESPONSE

¿Qué necesita Conchita para leer la carta de Sue?   *Necesita un diccionario para leer la carta.*
¿Lee Enrique muy bien en inglés?   *No, Enrique no lee inglés.*
¿Lee y escribe inglés Conchita?   *Ella lee y escribe un poco solamente.*
¿Cuándo escribe usted cartas?
¿Necesita un diccionario para leer en español?
¿Y para escribir una carta en español?
¿Leen ustedes mucho o poco?
¿En qué calle vive usted?
¿Vive usted en la esquina?
¿Cree usted que es fácil o difícil leer en español?
¿Escriben los alumnos mucho durante el día?
¿A quién debe usted llamar después de la cena?
¿A qué hora come usted? ¿Come mucho?
¿Dónde viven ustedes, en Canadá?

27. PROGRESSIVE SUBSTITUTION

Juana escribe una carta. ⊗   *Juana escribe una carta.*
Mi amigo y yo _____.   *Mi amigo y yo escribimos una carta.*
_____ leemos _____.   *Mi amigo y yo leemos una carta.*
_____ periódico.   *Mi amigo y yo leemos un periódico.*
Mi padre _____.   *Mi padre lee un periódico.*
_____ encuentra _____.   *Mi padre encuentra un periódico.*
_____ boletos.   *Mi padre encuentra unos boletos.*
Los chicos _____.   *Los chicos encuentran unos boletos.*
_____ compran _____.   *Los chicos compran unos boletos.*
_____ cosas.   *Los chicos compran unas cosas.*

28. WRITING EXERCISE

Write the responses to Drills 24.2, 25, and 27.

EXERCISE BOOK: EXERCISES 8 AND 9

saber, ver, hacer, *Present Tense*

TEACHER PRESENTATION, p. T174

GENERALIZATION

saber, PRESENT TENSE

	Singular	Plural
1	sé	sabemos
2	sabes	saben
3	sabe	

Saber is a regular **e**-class verb except for the first person singular form <u>sé</u>.

ver, PRESENT TENSE

	Singular	Plural
1	veo	vemos
2	ves	ven
3	ve	

Ver is a regular **e**-class verb except for the first person singular form <u>veo</u>.

hacer, PRESENT TENSE

	Singular	Plural
1	hago	hacemos
2	haces	hacen
3	hace	

Hacer is a regular **e**-class verb except for the first person singular form <u>hago</u>.

STRUCTURE DRILLS

29. PERSON-NUMBER SUBSTITUTION

1. Sabe hablar inglés, pero no mucho. ⊗
   (yo)
   (tú)
   (Juanita)
   (Juan y María)
   (nosotros)

   Sabe hablar inglés, pero no mucho.
   Sé hablar inglés, pero no mucho.
   Sabes hablar inglés, pero no mucho.
   Sabe hablar inglés, pero no mucho.
   Saben hablar inglés, pero no mucho.
   Sabemos hablar inglés, pero no mucho.

2. No ven la calle. ⊗
   (tú–ustedes–Ana y yo–yo–usted)   *ves–ven–vemos–veo–ve*

3. ¿Qué haces? ⊗
   (nosotros–la maestra–los alumnos–yo–tú)   *hacemos–hace–hacen–hago–haces*

30. PLURAL → SINGULAR

Sabemos leer en español. ⊗   Sé leer en español.
¿Qué hacemos aquí?   *¿Qué hago aquí?*
No vemos nada.   *No veo nada.*
No sabemos cómo se llama.   *No sé cómo se llama.*
¿Por qué no hacemos el almuerzo?   *¿Por qué no hago el almuerzo?*
Vemos el álbum.   *Veo el álbum.*

31. DIRECTED DIALOG

Pregúntele a *Juan* qué dice esta carta.   ¿Qué dice esta carta?
Juan, diga que usted no sabe, que está   No sé, está en alemán.
   en alemán.
Pregúntele a *Pepe* si él sabe alemán.   *Pepe,* ¿tú sabes alemán?
Pepe, dígale que no mucho, que usted   No mucho. Yo estudio inglés.
   estudia inglés.
Pregunte quién sabe alemán aquí.   ¿Quién sabe alemán aquí?
Susana, diga que María y usted saben   María y yo sabemos alemán. Nosotras somos
   alemán, que ustedes son alemanas.   alemanas.

32. FREE RESPONSE

¿Qué ven ustedes en el libro de español? ¿muchas fotos?
¿Qué ve usted en las fotos?
¿Quién hace la cena en su casa?

¿Hace usted la cena?

¿Hace usted todas las comidas?

¿Sabe usted dónde está su mamá? ¿Dónde está ahora?

¿Sabe usted hablar español? ¿y francés?

¿Sabe su padre hablar español?

33. WRITING EXERCISE

Write the responses to Drills 29.2, 29.3, and 30.

EXERCISE BOOK: EXERCISE 10

Listening and Speaking Exercise 137*, p. T76 ⊗

Writing

1. MULTIPLE ITEM SUBSTITUTION

Write a new sentence substituting the items given for the corresponding words in the original sentence. Make any necessary changes.

MODEL   María compra una blusa nueva.
chicos / necesitar / carro
<u>Los chicos necesitan un carro nuevo.</u>

1. Los chicos juegan en el parque.
Sra. García / vivir / esquina
La Sra. García vive en la esquina.

2. Ana no estudia conmigo.
mis amigos / ir / sin
Mis amigos no van sin mí.

3. Tiene unos regalos para ti.
escribir / carta / con
Escribe una carta contigo.

4. Quiero practicar con las chicas españolas.
deber / estudiar / chico
Debo estudiar con el chico español.

5. ¿Quién es el chico rubio, un alumno nuevo?
señora / pelirrojo / maestra
¿Quién es la señora pelirroja, una maestra nueva?

2. DIALOG COMPLETION

Copy the following dialog, filling in each blank with any appropriate word.

Carlos, aquí tengo una carta para ti.

¿Para __1__? Debe ser de Bárbara.

¿Quién es Bárbara?

Una chica que __2__ en los Estados Unidos. ¿Quieres ver? Qué bien __3__ español, ¿verdad?

Creo que __4__ ser una chica muy __5__.

¿Cuántos años __6__?

Yo no __7__. ¿Trece? ¿Catorce? ¿Quién __8__? Pero yo __9__ que debe ser menor que nosotros.

Dice que es __10__, y que tiene ojos __11__.

Sí, ella es muy __12__.

1	2	3	4	5
mí	vive estudia	escribe sabe	debe	lista inteligente

6	7	8	9	10	11	12
tiene	sé	sabe	creo pienso sé	rubia triqueña pelirroja	verdes castaños negros azules	linda bonita guapa

EXERCISE BOOK: EXERCISE 11

RECOMBINATION MATERIAL

Dialogs

I

JORGE	¿Cuántos años tienes?
ESTEBAN	Once. Casi doce.
JORGE	Yo soy mayor que tú. Yo tengo trece.
ESTEBAN	Yo sé. Pero yo soy más alto. . . . Pero yo soy más alta. ←

QUESTIONS

VARIATION: The conversation takes ⎤
place between two girls.

1. ¿Con quién habla Jorge?
2. ¿Cuántos años tiene Esteban?
3. ¿Quién es mayor, Jorge o Esteban?
4. ¿Cuál chico es más alto?

II

TERESA	¿Quién es ese chico que está delante de nosotras? . . . esa chica . . . no- ← sotros
ROSITA	¿Cuál? ¿Ése de la camisa roja? . . . ¿Ésa de la blusa roja?
TERESA	No, el otro. No, la otra.
ROSITA	Se llama Juan Gómez. Es nuevo. . . . Juana Gómez. Es nueva.
TERESA	Es guapo, ¿verdad? Es guapa, ¿verdad?

QUESTIONS

VARIATION: Two boys are talking about ⎤
a girl named Juana Gómez.

1. ¿Cómo se llama la amiga de Rosita?
2. ¿De quién hablan las dos chicas?
3. ¿Dónde está Juan?
4. ¿Es nuevo Juan?
5. ¿Cómo es él?

III

SUSANA	A ver si adivinas cuántos años tengo.
ARTURO	Mmm, catorce.
SUSANA	No, más.
ARTURO	¿Quince?

SUSANA	Más todavía.
ARTURO	¿Diecisiete?
SUSANA	No, tengo dieciséis solamente.

CONVERSATION STIMULUS

Have a friend try to guess your age.

A ver si adivinas cuántos años tengo.
¿Doce?
No, más.
¿Catorce?
No, menos.
¡Trece!

Narrative

El gordito contesta la carta de Sue

Señorita Sue Richardson
2105 De Neve Circle
Toronto, Canadá

Estimada[2] amiga:

5   Muchas gracias por tu carta tan bonita. Tú debes ser una chica muy inteligente. Y muy bonita también. ¿Cuántos años tienes? ¿No tienes una foto?

Yo tengo casi quince años. Soy pelirrojo, y tengo ojos castaños. También soy un poco gordo, no muy gordo, un poco
10   solamente.

Tengo dos hermanos: una hermana mayor que se llama Vera (bastante fea y pretenciosa), y un hermano menor, Chucho[3], que tiene diez años.

Yo sé jugar fútbol americano, pero me gusta más el fútbol de
15   aquí. También juego tenis*. ¿Sabes tú jugar tenis?

Bien, no puedo escribir más porque tengo que estudiar. Hasta luego.

Tu amigo,

Quique

Quique[4]
Enrique Alberto (Quique) González

Note: Point out that there are many cognates which differ only in that the English word contains a double letter, while the Spanish word does not: *tenis.*

---

[2] *Dear,* literally *esteemed:* a normal salutation in letters.

[3] **Chucho** is short for the name **Jesús**.

[4] **Quique** is short for **Enrique**.

QUESTIONS

1. ¿Dónde vive Sue?   *3*
2. ¿Cómo empieza la carta Enrique? *4*
3. ¿Cómo debe ser Sue?   *5*
4. ¿Qué quiere Enrique?   *7*
5. ¿Cuántos años tiene él?   *8*
6. ¿Cómo es Enrique?   *8*
7. ¿Es delgado?   *9*
8. ¿Cuántos hermanos tiene?   *11*
9. ¿Cómo se llama la hermana de Enrique? *11*
10. ¿Cómo es Vera?   *12*
11. ¿Quién es Chucho?   *12*
12. ¿Cuántos años tiene?   *13*
13. ¿Sabe Enrique jugar fútbol?   *14*
14. ¿Sabe jugar fútbol americano?   *14*
15. ¿Qué más sabe jugar?   *15*
16. ¿Por qué no puede escribir más?   *16*

Rejoinders

1. Tú sabes hablar inglés, ¿verdad? *No mucho. / Un poco solamente. / No, yo estudio francés.*
2. Sue es rubia y tiene ojos azules. *Debe ser muy bonita. / ¿Qué más? / ¿Es alta o baja? / ¿Quién es Sue?*
3. Necesito un diccionario. *¿Por qué? / Vamos a la bibioteca, entonces. / Yo tengo uno. / ¿Un diccionario español-inglés?*

LETTER ↔ SOUND CORRESPONDENCES

READING: i = [y]

Before another vowel, the letter **i** without an accent mark represents the sound [y]. Thus, the letter combinations **ia, ie, io,** and **iu** represent one syllable each: [ya], [ye], [yo], [yu].

FAMILIAR WORDS familia, pronuncia, noticias, fiesta, pienso, estudio, biblioteca

UNFAMILIAR WORDS hacia, piano, septiembre, noviembre, julio, silencio, ciudad

READING: u = [w]

Before another vowel, the letter **u** without an accent mark represents the sound [w]. Thus, the letter combinations **ua, ue, ui,** and **uo** represent one syllable each: [wa], [we], [wi], [wo].

FAMILIAR WORDS cuarto, cuatro, guantes, escuela, puedo, juego, nuevo, Luisa

UNFAMILIAR WORDS gradual, cuaderno, duelo, muela, cuidado, continuo

READING: í = [i]; ú = [u]

The letters **í** (**i** with a written accent) or **ú** (**u** with a written accent) before another vowel represent a separate, stressed syllable.

FAMILIAR WORDS día, tía, todavía, García, María, tío

UNFAMILIAR WORDS comía, vivía, policía, librería, mío, río, sitúa,
continúa, gradúa

PAIRS

hacia	gracia	media	su novia	Mario	sitio	julio
hacía	García	medía	todavía	María	mi tío	un lío

continua
continúa

READING: cc = [ks]

The double consonant **cc,** which occurs only before **e** or **i,** represents the sounds [ks].

FAMILIAR WORDS diccionario

UNFAMILIAR WORDS acceso, acción, lección, dirección, sección,
ficción, accidente

SENTENCES

1. María todavía pronuncia muy mal.
2. ¿Qué día es la fiesta? El viernes.
3. ¿Vas al estadio con tu tío?
4. ¿Dónde está el diccionario? En tu cuarto.

WRITING

Copy the above sentences and be prepared to write them from dictation.

Spelling Notes:

1. Whenever **i** or **u** comes before any other vowel sound and is pronounced as a separate, stressed syllable, it is written with an accent mark.

2. Double consonants are extremely rare in Spanish. In fact, with the exception of **cc,** they almost never occur. (The **rr** and **ll** are separate letters, not double consonants.) Notice that the letter combination **cc** represents two sounds: the first **c** corresponds to the sound [k], the second to the sound [s]. The **cc** follows the generalizations, then, that **c** before a consonant represents the sound [k], and that **c** before **e** or **i** represents the sound [s].

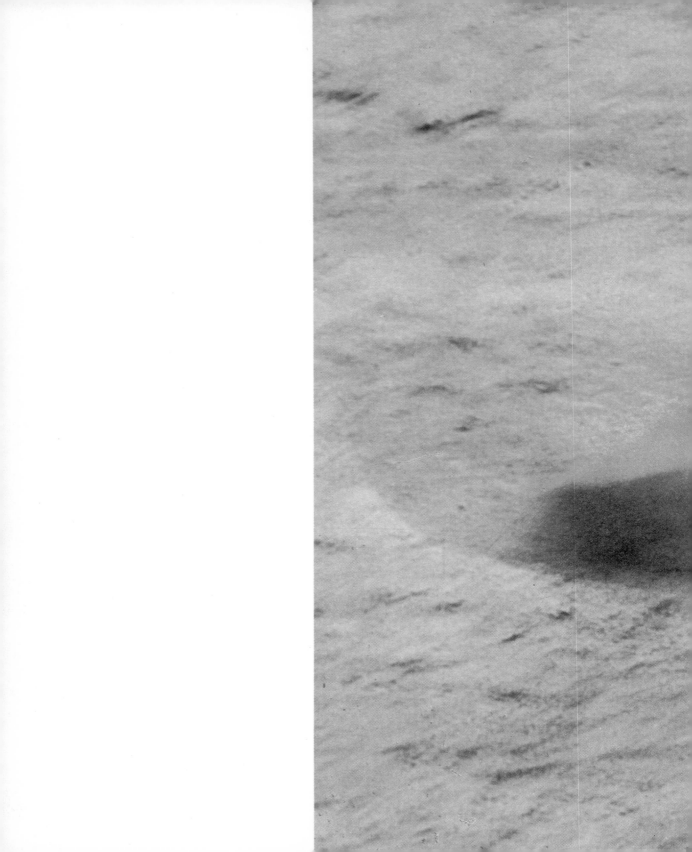

Glimpses of the Spanish World

OCÉANO

ATLÁNTICO

ESTADOS UNIDOS

ISLAS BAHAMAS
CUBA
HOND. BR.
HAITÍ
REPÚBLICA DOMINICANA
PUERTO RICO
JAMAICA
GUATEMALA
EL SALVADOR
HONDURAS
NICARAGUA
COSTA RICA
PANAMÁ
MÉXICO

VENEZUELA
GUAYANA
SURINAM
GUAYANA FRANCESA
BARBADOS
TRINIDAD Y TOBAGO

COLOMBIA

BRASIL

ECUADOR

PERÚ

BOLIVIA

PARAGUAY

CHILE

ARGENTINA

URUGUAY

Georgetown

TRÓPICO DE CÁNCER

CALIFORNIA

ARIZONA

NEW MEXICO

TEXAS

LOUISIANA

Mississippi

FLORIDA

GOLFO DE MÉXICO

Tijuana

Nogales

Ciudad Juárez

Chihuahua

Río Grande

Nuevo Laredo

Monterrey

SIERRA MADRE ORIENTAL

San Luis Potosí

Tampico

Mazatlán

Durango

Guadalajara

Manzanillo

San Miguel de Allende

SIERRA MADRE OCCIDENTAL

BAJA CALIFORNIA

GOLFO DE CALIFORNIA

San Juan Teotihuacán

Taxco

México, D.F.

Puebla

Veracruz

Oaxaca

Acapulco

SIERRA MADRE DEL SUR

GOLFO DE TEHUANTEPEC

GOLFO DE CAMPECHE

Mérida

PENÍNSULA DE YUCATÁN

Belice

Chichen Itza

La Habana

Santiago de Cuba

Kingston

Puerto Príncipe

ANTILLAS

MAR CARIBE

GOLFO DE DARIÉN

Tegucigalpa

Guatemala

San Salvador

Managua

San José

Panamá

GOLFO DE PANAMÁ

Santo Domingo

Ponce

San Juan

Barranquilla

Cartagena

Maracaibo

ARUBA

CURAZAO

BUENAIRE

Coro

Caracas

Cumaná

ISLA DE MARGARITA

Río Orinoco

SIERRA DE LAS GUAYANAS

ANTILLAS

Medellín

Bogotá

Río Magdalena

Quito

Guayaquil

Río Guayas

ECUADOR

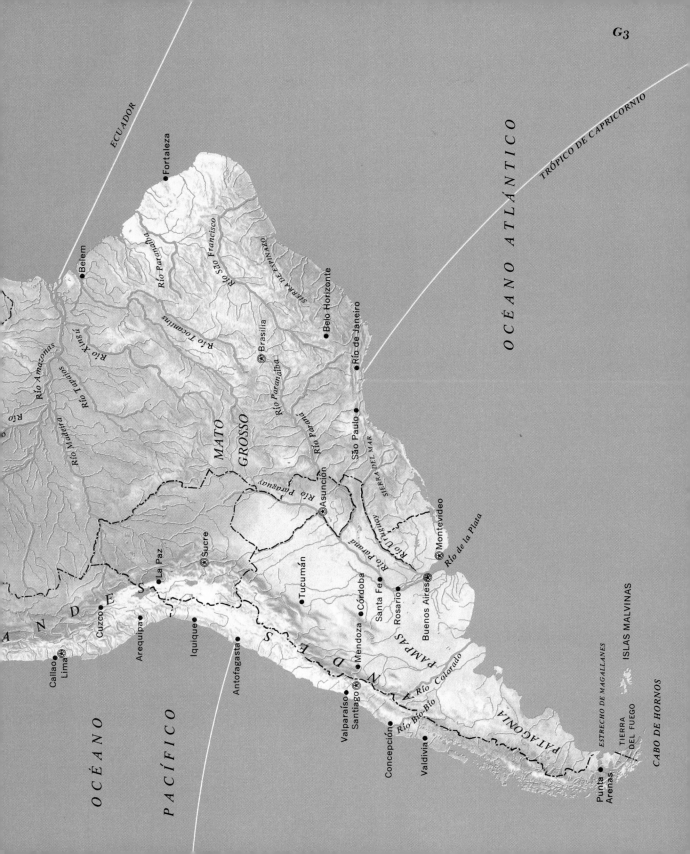

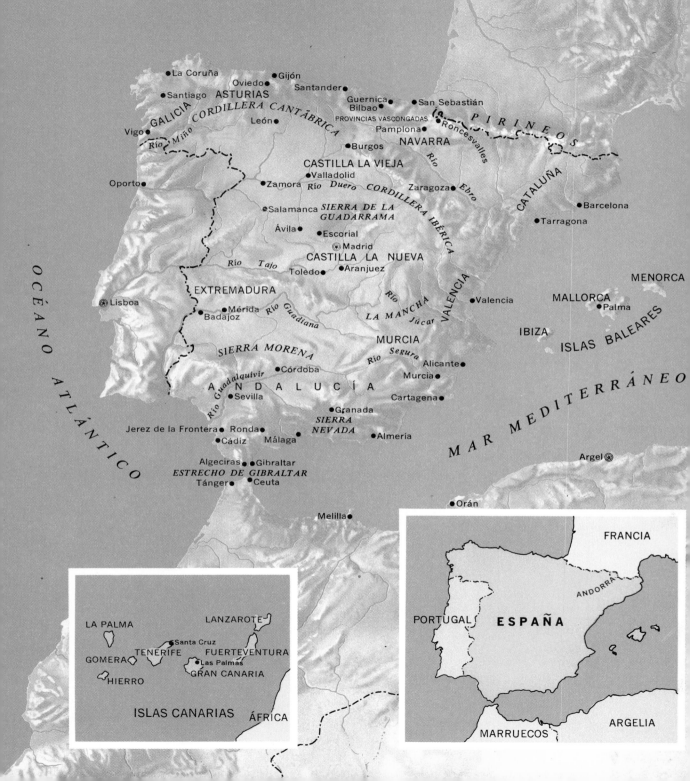

MAR CANTÁBRICO

La Coruña
Gijón
Oviedo
Santander
Santiago
ASTURIAS
Guernica
San Sebastián
GALICIA
CORDILLERA CANTÁBRICA
Bilbao
PROVINCIAS VASCONGADAS
PIRINEOS
León
Pamplona
Roncesvalles
Vigo
Río Miño
Burgos
NAVARRA
CASTILLA LA VIEJA
Río Ebro
CATALUÑA
Valladolid
Oporto
Zamora
Río Duero
Zaragoza
CORDILLERA IBÉRICA
Barcelona
Salamanca
SIERRA DE LA GUADARRAMA
Tarragona
Ávila
Escorial
Madrid
CASTILLA LA NUEVA
Río Tajo
Toledo
Aranjuez
EXTREMADURA
VALENCIA
Lisboa
Mérida
Río
MALLORCA
MENORCA
Badajoz
Río Guadiana
LA MANCHA
Júcar
Valencia
Palma
IBIZA
ISLAS BALEARES
MURCIA
SIERRA MORENA
Río Segura
Alicante
OCÉANO ATLÁNTICO
Río Guadalquivir
Córdoba
Murcia
ANDALUCÍA
Sevilla
Cartagena
Granada
MAR MEDITERRÁNEO
Jerez de la Frontera
Ronda
SIERRA NEVADA
Cádiz
Málaga
Almería
Argel
Algeciras
Gibraltar
ESTRECHO DE GIBRALTAR
Tánger
Ceuta
Orán
Melilla

LA PALMA
LANZAROTE
FRANCIA
Santa Cruz
TENERIFE
FUERTEVENTURA
ANDORRA
GOMERA
Las Palmas
PORTUGAL
ESPAÑA
HIERRO
GRAN CANARIA
ISLAS CANARIAS
ÁFRICA
MARRUECOS
ARGELIA

The Land and the People

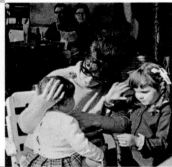

The Spanish-speaking peoples are varied in background. The magnificent pre-Columbian Indian civilizations were toppled by the Spanish conquistadors, but Indians still compose a large part of Latin America's population. The Spaniards settled throughout their new Empire, establishing important centers in Mexico and Peru. Large numbers of Africans were brought to work on plantations. Their descendants settled principally in the warm coastal areas and on the islands. People of Northern

Difficulty in exploiting tropical lands has been an obstacle to social and economic development. Most of Latin America lies within the tropics.

Buenos Aires, one of Latin America's most cosmopolitan cities, is an important center of cultural and economic activity.

The Andes are part of an immense chain which extends from Alaska to the tip of South America. The Andean plateaus and valleys include rich agricultural areas.

European origin have also settled throughout Latin America, particularly in the temperate areas. In Mexico and several Central and South American nations, people of mixed Indian and Spanish background make up a dominant part of the population.

Harvesting hay in one of Ecuador's fertile valleys.

Caracas, scene of immense urban construction and expansion projects.

Along the Peruvian coast the high Andes meet the sea.

The great Argentine plains, the Pampa, possess some of the world's richest soil. Argentina is a major producer of grain and meat.

The Home and the Family

A family enjoys a Sunday picnic in the Floating Gardens at Xochimilco, Mexico.

This upper-class living room combines modern and antique furnishings.

A housing project built by a textile workers' cooperative in Lima.

A group of cousins at a family gathering in Buenos Aires.

A rural family in Mexico.

*F*amily activities in Spanish-speaking countries often include grandparents, uncles, aunts, cousins, in-laws, godparents, and more distant relatives. Family gatherings are an important part of social life in these countries.

A family relaxes at a café during the Sherry Festival in Jerez, Spain.

Education

University of Mexico: Medical School and Laboratory for Cosmic Rays

*E*ducation in Spanish-speaking countries has traditionally emphasized the humanities and preparation for the professions of law, medicine and engineering. In recent years, however, more importance has been placed on the general education of all of the people, and there has been a growing interest in the physical and social sciences as well as in vocational training.

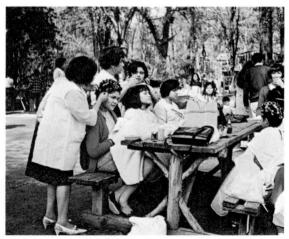

Girls learn to be beauticians in this open-air class in Mexico City.

A rural school in Guatemala. The need for more efficient farmers and a growing interest in mass education has prompted the establishment of rural schools in many Latin American countries.

The University of Salamanca, established in 1230, was for many centuries one of the principal seats of learning of the western world.

A Catholic school in Spain. Most private schools in Spain and in Latin America are run by the Church.

A modern classroom in Lima. Children in Spanish-speaking countries typically wear uniforms to school.

Age-old techniques compete with modern machinery in many phases of production.

Marketing produce in open-air stalls in Ecuador.

People at Work

A synthetic fiber plant in Colombia.

Agriculture remains by far the most important form of economic activity in Latin America and Spain. In some countries, mining and oil production are also important. Industry is growing rapidly. Mexico, Argentina, and Chile are self-sufficient in a large number of manufactured products, and other nations are making intensive efforts to develop both heavy and light industry.

Architects and city planners discuss a project.

Girls sorting olives in the southwestern part of Spain. The olive industry is one of Spain's main sources of agricultural wealth.

Indian laborers picking coffee on a plantation in Guatemala. Coffee is grown extensively in Colombia and in Central America.

Mexico is one of the world's leading suppliers of silver. Here, a Mexican artisan makes silver ornaments.

An Indian festival in the Andes.

Boys playing soccer in Uruguay. Soccer is widely played by amateurs as well as professionals.

An opera crowd during intermission. Latin America has produced internationally famous celebrities in the field of classical music, including the pianists Claudio Arrau of Chile and Jesús María Sanromá of Puerto Rico, and the composer Alberto Ginastera of Argentina.

Leisure
Time

Skiing is a popular sport in Chile. Here, some skiers relax in a ski lodge at Farellones.

Indian music and dances highlight this carnival at Copacabana, Bolivia.

Leisure activities reflect a variety of influences and ways of life in the Spanish-speaking world. Sophisticated European sports contrast with colorful festivals revealing a rich folk heritage. The arts are of increasing importance. Music, painting, and literature often combine European and native American elements.

A polo match in Buenos Aires. Polo has long been a favorite among Argentina's upper classes.

Religion

A golden altar dating from the mid-eighteenth century. The Colonial period produced some of Spanish America's most impressive religious art.

A modern church in San Salvador.

School girls with nuns in Spain. A very large percentage of the schools in Spain are run by the Church. Most schools in Latin America, however, are state-controlled.

The great majority of Spaniards and Latin Americans are Catholic. Religion is an important part of the daily life of a large number of Spanish-speaking people, and the Church plays a significant role in politics and education in Spain and many Latin American countries. Some Spanish-Americans are Protestants, and both Buenos Aires and Mexico City have sizable Jewish populations.

Indians attend mass in an Andean village near Cuzco, Peru.

Crowds stroll through the plaza after Mass in Burgos, Spain.

UNIT 8

BASIC DIALOG

A la hora de almuerzo

LA SEÑORA	¡Qué temprano viene el correo! ¿Qué hora es, don Chico? 8-1
EL CARTERO	Son las doce, según mi reloj. Aquí tiene. ⎤
LA SEÑORA	¿Sólo esto? ¿No hay cartas? 8-2
EL CARTERO	No, señora, eso es todo. Lo siento.
LA SEÑORA	Gracias. Con permiso[1], ya oigo a mi hijo. 8-3
LUISITO	¡Tengo mucha hambre! Mami, ¿conoces a Toni? 8-4
LA SEÑORA	Sí. ¡Hola, Toni! Y tú, ¿qué traes en esa bolsa? ⎤
LUISITO	Nada. Toni va a almorzar aquí. 8-5
LA SEÑORA	Bueno, ¿y qué tienes en la bolsa?
LUISITO	Una culebra. ¿Por qué pones esa cara, mami? 8-6

Note: The lunch hour varies from country to country. In some areas it is at noon, while in others it is at two o'clock. The midday meal is usually the heaviest of the day.

| *Note: Bolsa* may mean either *paper bag* or *handbag.*

At Lunch Time

THE LADY	The mail is certainly early! (How early comes the mail!) What time is it, don Chico?
THE MAILMAN	It's twelve o'clock, according to my watch (clock). Here you are (you have).
THE LADY	Only this? Aren't there any letters?
THE MAILMAN	No, ma'am, that's all. I'm sorry. (It I regret.)
THE LADY	Thanks. Excuse me (with permission), I hear my son now.
LUISITO	I'm very hungry! (I have much hunger!) Mom, do you know Toni?
THE LADY	Yes. Hi, Toni! And you, what do you have (bring) in that bag?
LUISITO	Nothing. Toni's going to have lunch here.
THE LADY	All right, and what do you have in the bag?
LUISITO	A snake. Why are you making (putting) that face, mom?

---

[1] **Con permiso** is used in some situations where in English we would say *excuse me*—principally in leave-taking or in passing someone.

◀ *A maid chats with the mailman. It is usual for families to have one or more servants.*

Supplement

¿Qué hora es? Es la una en punto.

        Es la una y diez.
        Es la una y cuarto.
        Es la una y veinticinco.
        Es la una y media.
        Son las dos menos cuarto.
        Son las dos menos cinco.
Según mi reloj. *(watch)* 8-1, *(clock)* 8-2
Es la hora del desayuno.

Ya sale mi hijo.
    el cartero 8-3

    mucha hambre 8-4
Tengo mucha sed. 8-5
    mucho frío 8-6
    mucho calor 8-7

¿Qué hay de comer? Carne. 8-8
        Huevos. 8-9
        Ensalada. 8-10
        Papas fritas. 8-11

        Pan y mantequilla. 8-12
        Helado. 8-13

¿Qué hay de tomar? Leche. 8-14
        Café. 8-15
        Agua fría. 8-16
¿Qué tienes en la bolsa? 8-18 Té caliente[2]. 8-17
Tengo una culebra. 8-19
Toni va a desayunar allí. 8-20
    cenar 8-21
    almorzar 8-22
¿Reconoces a Toni?
Entiendes
Prefieres

What time is it? It's exactly one o'clock.
(It's one on the dot.)
It's one ten.
It's a quarter past one.
It's one twenty-five.
It's half past one.
It's a quarter to two.
It's five to two.

It's breakfast time.

My son is leaving (going out) now.

I'm very thirsty. (I have much thirst.)
very cold (much cold)
very warm (much heat)

What's there to eat? Meat.
Eggs.
Salad.
French fries. (potatoes fried)
Bread and butter.
Ice cream.

What's there to drink (take)? Milk.
Coffee.
Cold water.
Hot tea.

Toni is going to have breakfast there.
have dinner

Do you recognize Toni?
understand
prefer

---

[2] **Caliente** is an adjective, while **calor** is a noun: **El café está muy caliente,** but **Tengo mucho calor.**

Listening and Speaking Exercises 138, 139*, 140*, p. T77 ⊗

BASIC FORMS

Verbs

almorzar (ue)	*oír	*sentir
cenar	*poner	*tener
*conocer	*preferir	tomar
desayunar	*reconocer	*traer
*entender	*salir	*venir

Nouns

café *m.*	agua *f.*[3]
calor *m.*	carne *f.*
pan *m.*	hambre *f.*[3]
reloj *m.*	leche *f.*
té *m.*	sed *f.*

Vocabulary Exercises

1. QUESTIONS

1. ¿Viene el correo tarde o temprano? *Temprano.*
2. ¿Cómo se llama el cartero? *Don Chico.*
3. ¿Qué hora es según el reloj del cartero? *Las 12.*
4. ¿A qué hora empieza esta clase?
5. ¿Qué hora es según su reloj?
6. ¿A qué hora es el recreo?
7. ¿Tiene el cartero cartas para la señora? *No.*
8. ¿Quién viene después? *El hijo de la señora.*

2. DIALOG RECALL

correo	*¡Qué temprano viene el correo!*
una en punto	*Es la una en punto, según mi reloj.*
reloj	*Son las doce, según mi reloj.*
cartas	*¿No hay cartas?*
todo	*No, señora, eso es todo.*
siento	*Lo siento.*
hijo	*Ya oigo a mi hijo.*

3. QUESTIONS

1. ¿Cómo se llama el hijo de la señora? *Se llama Luisito.*
2. ¿Quién dice que tiene hambre? *Luisito dice que tiene hambre.*
3. ¿Tiene usted hambre ahora?
4. ¿Tiene sed?

(continued)

---

[3] Even though **agua** and **hambre** are feminine, the form of the singular definite article which is used with them is **el**: **el agua,** but **las aguas frías; el hambre,** but **mucha hambre.** The same is true of all feminine nouns whose first sound is stressed [a].

(continued)

5. ¿Cómo se llama el amigo de Luisito?   *Se llama Toni.*
6. ¿Va a cenar Toni con Luisito?   *No, va a almorzar con él.*
7. A propósito, ¿a usted qué le gusta comer para el desayuno? ¿para el almuerzo? ¿para la cena?
8. ¿Qué le gusta tomar? ¿leche? ¿té? ¿café?
9. ¿A qué hora almuerza usted?
10. ¿A qué hora desayuna?
11. ¿Qué tiene Luisito en la bolsa?   *Una culebra.*
12. ¿Está la señora contenta con la culebra?   *No, no muy contenta.*

4. FREE COMPLETION

1. Tengo mucha _____.   *hambre, sed*
2. ¿Almorzamos en _____?   *un restaurante, el comedor, el centro, casa*
3. No me gusta tomar _____.   *leche, agua, té, café*
4. Todavía no es la hora de _____.   *almuerzo*
5. ¿En la bolsa? Sólo tengo una _____.   *culebra, cosa, foto, corbata*

5. REJOINDERS

Aquí viene el correo. *¡Qué temprano viene! / ¿Dónde está el cartero? / ¡Tan tarde! / ¿Es verdad?*
Tengo mucha hambre. *¿Qué quiere comer? / Todavía no es la hora de almuerzo. / Yo también.*
¡Hola, Toni! *Buenos días, señor. / Buenas tardes, señora. / ¡Hola, Juan! ¿Cómo estás?*

A market in Mexico City. Farmers from outlying areas bring their produce to the city to sell.

GRAMMAR

Stem Alternation: e-ie
e-*Class and* i-*Class Verbs*

PRESENTATION *TEACHER PRESENTATION, p. T174*

Quie**ro** unos discos.
Que**remos** unos discos.

¿**Prefi**e**res** a Toni?
¿**Pref**e**rimos** a Toni?

Is the stem stressed or unstressed in each one of the verb forms? What is the vowel sound in the stem when stressed? How is the sound written? What is the vowel sound in the stem when unstressed? How is the sound written? Do **e**-class and **i**-class verbs with **e-ie** stem alternation follow the same pattern as **a**-class verbs like **pensar**?

GENERALIZATION

1. Some **e**-class and **i**-class verbs have the same alternation in their stems between unstressed **e** and stressed **ie** [ye] as **a**-class verbs like **pensar.**

Stressed Stem	*Unstressed Stem*
qui**e**ro	qu**e**rer
qui**e**res	qu**e**remos
qui**e**re	
qui**e**ren	
prefi**e**ro	pref**e**rir
prefi**e**res	pref**e**rimos
prefi**e**re	
prefi**e**ren	

2. Other verbs like **querer** and **preferir** are **entender** and **sentir.**

Listening and Speaking Exercises 141, 142, 143*, p. T78 ⊗

STRUCTURE DRILLS

6. PATTERNED RESPONSE

¿Entiende eso? ⊗	Claro, debe entender eso.
¿Prefiere eso?	Claro, debe preferir eso.
¿Siente eso?	Claro, debe sentir eso.
¿Quiere eso?	Claro, debe querer eso.
¿Entiende eso?	Claro, debe entender eso.

7. PERSON-NUMBER SUBSTITUTION

1. No quieren almorzar aquí. ⊗   No quieren almorzar aquí.
   - (yo)   No quiero almorzar aquí.
   - (usted)   No quiere almorzar aquí.
   - (nosotros)   No queremos almorzar aquí.
   - (tú)   No quieres almorzar aquí.
   - (ella)   No quiere almorzar aquí.
   - (Susana y yo)   No queremos almorzar aquí.

2. Sólo entiende alemán. ⊗   *entiendo–entiendes–entiende–*
   - (yo–tú–él–ustedes–nosotros–Juan y María)   *entienden–entendemos–entienden*

3. Prefiero llegar temprano. ⊗   *preferimos–prefieren–prefiere–*
   - (nosotros–ellas–usted–él y yo–tú–Juan)   *preferimos–prefieres–prefiere*

8. PAIRED SENTENCES

Quiere cenar ahora. ⊗   Quiere cenar ahora.
- (nosotros)   Queremos cenar ahora.
- (él)   Quiere cenar ahora.

¿Entiendes el problema?   *¿Entiendes el problema?*
- (nosotros)   *¿Entendemos el problema?*
- (tú)   *¿Entiendes el problema?*

Lo siento mucho.   *Lo siento mucho.*
- (nosotros)   *Lo sentimos mucho.*
- (yo)   *Lo siento mucho.*

Prefieren almorzar en el restaurante.   *Prefieren almorzar en el restaurante.*
- (nosotros)   *Preferimos almorzar en el restaurante.*
- (ellos)   *Prefieren almorzar en el restaurante.*

9. SINGULAR → PLURAL

No quiero comer en ese restaurante. ⊗   No queremos comer en ese restaurante.
Prefiero almorzar aquí.   *Preferimos almorzar aquí.*
No entiendo a ese chico.   *No entendemos a ese chico.*
Lo siento mucho.   *Lo sentimos mucho.*
No quiero ir contigo.   *No queremos ir contigo.*

VARIATION: Use right-hand column as stimulus and have student give singular form.

10. FREE RESPONSE

¿Entiende usted francés?
¿Usted prefiere hablar inglés o español?
Y ustedes, ¿qué prefieren hablar?
¿Entiende usted español bien o un poco solamente?
¿Quieren ustedes almorzar ahora?
¿Qué prefiere usted comer para el desayuno, huevos fritos o carne?
¿Qué prefiere usted comer para la cena?
Mañana hay un examen. ¿Ustedes lo sienten o están contentos?
Cuando usted tiene calor, ¿qué prefiere tomar, té frío o caliente?

11. WRITING EXERCISE

Write the responses to Drills 7.2, 7.3, and 9.

EXERCISE BOOK: EXERCISES 1 AND 2

TEACHER PRESENTATION, p. T175   **allí *and* haber**

GENERALIZATION

1. In English, *there* is used two ways: to indicate location, meaning *that place;* and—followed by a form of *be*—to indicate the presence or occurrence of something.

    John is there. (location)
    There has to be more food. (More food must be present.)

2. Spanish has separate equivalents for these two uses of *there.*

   a. If *there* indicates location, it is expressed by **allí**.

    Juan está <u>allí</u>.
    John is <u>there</u>.

   b. If *there* + *be* indicates presence, it is expressed by the irregular verb **haber.**

    Tiene que <u>haber</u> más comida.
    There has to <u>be</u> more food.

One present tense form of **haber, hay,** corresponds to both *there is* and *there are*.

Hay un reloj en la mesa.
There is a clock on the table.

¿No hay cartas?
Aren't there any letters?

Both **allí** and a form of **haber** may occur in the same sentence:

Hay culebras allí.

STRUCTURE DRILLS

12. PAIRED SENTENCES

Allí está el reloj. ⊗
(Over) there there is a clock.
There is the clock.

Allí está el reloj.
Allí hay un reloj.
Allí está el reloj.

El cartero está allí.
There is a mailman there.
The mailman is there.

El cartero está allí.
Hay un cartero allí.
El cartero está allí.

Allí están las bolsas.
There are some bags there.
There are the bags.

Allí están las bolsas.
Hay unas bolsas allí.
Allí están las bolsas.

¿Está el restaurante allí?
Is there a restaurant there?
Is the restaurant there?

¿Está el restaurante allí?
¿Hay un restaurante allí?
¿Está el restaurante allí?

13. DIRECTED DIALOG

Pregúntele a *tía Luisa* que hay de comer.
Tía Luisa, diga que hay huevos con papas fritas.
Diga que usted no quiere comer eso.
Tía Luisa, diga que usted lo siente mucho.
Diga que usted prefiere carne con ensalada.
Tía Luisa, dígale que hay un restaurante muy bueno en la esquina.

¿Qué hay de comer?
Hay huevos con papas fritas.

Yo no quiero comer eso.
Lo siento mucho.
Prefiero carne con ensalada.

Hay un restaurante muy bueno en la esquina.

14. WRITING EXERCISE

Write the responses to Drill 12.

EXERCISE BOOK: EXERCISE 3

Demonstrative Adjectives

PRESENTATION *TEACHER PRESENTATION, p. T176*

¿Puedo ver **este** periódico?
¿Puedo ver **estos** periódicos?

Esta blusa es muy linda.
Estas blusas son muy lindas.

What word meaning *this* is used with masculine singular nouns? with masculine plural nouns?
What word meaning *this* is used with feminine singular nouns? with feminine plural nouns?

Excepto **ese chico.**
Excepto **esos chicos.**

¿Qué traes en **esa bolsa**?
¿Qué traes en **esas bolsas**?

What word meaning *that* is used with masculine singular nouns? with masculine plural nouns?
What word meaning *that* is used with feminine singular nouns? with feminine plural nouns?

GENERALIZATION

1. The English and Spanish demonstrative adjectives are shown in the following chart:

		Singular	*Plural*
this/these	MASCULINE	este (chico)	estos (chicos)
	FEMININE	esta (chica)	estas (chicas)
that/those	MASCULINE	ese (chico)	esos (chicos)
	FEMININE	esa (chica)	esas (chicas)

2. In Spanish, the demonstrative adjectives agree in gender and number with the noun they modify.

| *Note: Aquel* will be introduced in Level II.

STRUCTURE DRILLS

15. ITEM SUBSTITUTION

1. No quiero comer esta carne. ⊗   No quiero comer esta carne.
   _____ helado.   No quiero comer este helado.
   _____ papas.   No quiero comer estas papas.
   _____ huevos.   No quiero comer estos huevos.
   _____ ensalada.   No quiero comer esta ensalada.
   _____ pan.   No quiero comer este pan.

2. ¿Adónde vas con ese libro? ⊗   *esas cartas—esa comida—esos periódicos—*
   (cartas–comida–periódicos–diccionario–bolsa) *ese diccionario—esa bolsa*

16. FREE COMPLETION

No queremos tomar este _____.   *té, café*
¡Qué bonitos son estos _____!   *regalos, guantes, vestidos, pantalones*
No me gusta esta _____.   *comida, ensalada, carne, leche*
¿Son inteligentes esos _____?   *chicos, alumnos, gemelos*
¿Quieres comer estas _____?   *papas*

17. PATTERNED RESPONSE

¿Es nuevo ese reloj? ⊗   ¿Este reloj? No, no es nuevo.
¿Es francesa esa corbata?   *¿Esta corbata? No, no es francesa.*
¿Son caros esos libros?   *¿Estos libros? No, no son caros.*
¿Es bueno ese diccionario?   *¿Este diccionario? No, no es bueno.*
¿Son italianas esas camisas?   *¿Estas camisas? No, no son italianas.*
¿Está caliente ese café?   *¿Este café? No, no está caliente.*
¿Está fría esa agua?   *¿Esta agua? No, no está fría.*
VARIATION: ¿Es nuevo este reloj?   *¿Ese reloj? No, no es nuevo.*

18. PROGRESSIVE SUBSTITUTION

Esa maestra es muy distraída. ⊗   *Esa maestra es muy distraída.*
Ese _____.   *Ese maestro es muy distraído.*
___ alumnos _____.   *Esos alumnos son muy distraídos.*
_____ listas.   *Esas alumnas son muy listas.*
Esta _____.   *Esta alumna es muy lista.*
___ chicos _____.   *Estos chicos son muy listos.*
_____ perezoso.   *Este chico es muy perezoso.*
Estas _____.   *Estas chicas son muy perezosas.*
___ señor _____.   *Este señor es muy perezoso.*
_____ antipáticos.   *Estos señores son muy antipáticos.*

19. FREE SUBSTITUTION

¿<u>Almuerza</u> usted con <u>ese chico</u>? *estudia, cena, habla / ese señor, esa maestra, esos chicos*

20. WRITING EXERCISE

Write the responses to Drills 15.2, 17, and 18.

EXERCISE BOOK: EXERCISES 4 AND 5

The Neuter Demonstratives esto *and* eso

TEACHER PRESENTATION, p. T177
GENERALIZATION

Masculine	*Feminine*	*Neuter*
este, estos	**esta, estas**	**esto**
ese, esos	**esa, esas**	**eso**

1. Masculine and feminine demonstrative adjectives modify nouns, and agree in gender and number with the nouns they modify. **Esto** and **eso** never modify a noun, and thus never show number or gender agreement. The word neuter is used simply to indicate that these demonstratives do not belong to any gender class.

   a. If a noun is present, a masculine or feminine demonstrative is used.

      No quiero comer <u>este</u> huevo.
      <u>Esa</u> cosa es buena.

   b. If no noun is present, a neuter demonstrative is used.

      No quiero comer <u>esto</u>.
      <u>Eso</u> es bueno.

2. Three situations commonly require the use of neuter demonstratives:

   a. When the speaker does not know what something is.

      ¿Qué es <u>esto</u>?

b. To identify a previously unidentified object.

Eso es un huevo.

c. To refer to situations, ideas, and actions which are not associated with any particular noun from which the demonstrative may receive gender.

Hay un examen mañana. No, eso no es verdad.

Note: Aquello will be introduced in Level II.

STRUCTURE DRILLS

21. ENGLISH CUE DRILLS

1. ¿Qué es eso? ¿Helado? ☻   *¿Qué es eso? ¿Helado?*
   What's that? Water?   *¿Qué es eso? ¿Agua?*
   What's that? Tea?   *¿Qué es eso? ¿Té?*
   What's that? Milk?   *¿Qué es eso? ¿Leche?*
   What's that? Bread and butter?   *¿Qué es eso? ¿Pan y mantequilla?*
   What's that? Ice cream?   *¿Qué es eso? ¿Helado?*

2. ¿Esto? Es café. ☻   *¿Esto? Es café.*
   This? It's meat.   *¿Esto? Es carne.*
   This? It's food.   *¿Esto? Es comida.*
   This? It's salad.   *¿Esto? Es ensalada.*
   This? It's tea.   *¿Esto? Es té.*
   This? It's coffee.   *¿Esto? Es café.*

22. PAIRED SENTENCES

Esto es difícil. ☻   Esto es difícil.
This exam is difficult.   Este examen es difícil.
This is difficult.   Esto es difícil.

¿Qué es eso?   *¿Qué es eso?*
What's that thing?   *¿Qué es esa cosa?*
What's that?   *¿Qué es eso?*

Sólo tengo esto.   *Sólo tengo esto.*
I only have these letters.   *Sólo tengo estas cartas.*
I only have this.   *Sólo tengo esto.*

23. FREE RESPONSE

¿Es esto un sombrero?
¿Qué es esto?
Y eso, ¿qué es? ¿un libro?
¿Es bueno ese libro?
¿Es nueva esa camisa? ¿y esos pantalones?
¿Quién es ese chico?
Y esas chicas, ¿quiénes son?
¿De qué color es esta blusa? ¿y esta falda?
   ¿y esos guantes? ¿y esas medias? ¿y esto?
¿Qué estudiamos en esta clase?
¿Estudiamos francés en esta clase?
¿De quién son estos libros?
¿Está en español o en inglés este periódico?
¿Cómo se llama esa chica?

24. WRITING EXERCISE

Write the responses to Drills 21.1, 21.2, and 22.
EXERCISE BOOK: EXERCISE 6

Verbs with Stem Irregularities: conocer, poner, salir

PRESENTATION *TEACHER PRESENTATION, p. T177*

Cono<u>zc</u>o a Toni.
Conoces a Toni.
Conoce a Toni.
Conocemos a Toni.
Conocen a Toni.

Which form of **conocer** is irregular? What sound is added to the stem of the first person singular? How is the spelling affected by this change?

Ya **sal<u>g</u>o.**
Ya **sales.**
Ya **sale** mi hijo.
Ya **salimos.**
Ya **salen** mis hijos.

Which form of **salir** is irregular? What sound is added to the stem of the first person singular?

GENERALIZATION

conocer, PRESENT TENSE		
	Singular	*Plural*
1	conoz **c** – o	conoc e mos
2	conoc e s	conoc e n
3	conoc e –	

1. Certain verbs add the sound [k] (spelled **c**) to the stem of the first person singular. The other forms are regular.

   The letter **z** in **conozco** is simply a spelling convention; the sound remains [s]. **Reconocer** follows the same pattern as **conocer.**

poner, PRESENT TENSE		
	Singular	*Plural*
1	pon **g** – o	pon e mos
2	pon e s	pon e n
3	pon e –	

salir, PRESENT TENSE		
	Singular	*Plural*
1	sal **g** – o	sal i mos
2	sal e s	sal e n
3	sal e –	

2. Certain verbs add the sound [g] to the stem of the first person singular. The other forms are regular.

Listening and Speaking Exercises 146, 147, 148*, p. T81 ⊗   SECTION D

STRUCTURE DRILLS

25. PERSON-NUMBER SUBSTITUTION

1. No conoce al Sr. López. ⊗   No conoce al Sr. López.
   (mi hermano y yo)   No conocemos al Sr. López.
   (usted)   No conoce al Sr. López.
   (yo)   No conozco al Sr. López.
   (Susana y él)   No conocen al Sr. López.
   (tú)   No conoces al Sr. López.

2. Pone las cartas aquí. ⊗
    (el cartero–yo–tú–los chicos–nosotros) *pone–pongo–pones–ponen–ponemos*

3. Salen temprano hoy.
    (Toni y yo–usted–yo–los alumnos–tú) *salimos–sale–salgo–salen–sales*

26. WRITING EXERCISE

Write the responses to Drills 25.2 and 25.3.

EXERCISE BOOK: EXERCISE 7

Verbs with Stem Irregularities: traer, oír

TEACHER PRESENTATION, p. T178
GENERALIZATION

1. **Traer** adds **ig** to the stem of the first person singular. The other forms are regular.

traer, PRESENT TENSE		
	Singular	*Plural*
1	tra <u>ig</u> – o	tra e mos
2	tra e s	tra e n
3	tra e –	

Traigo has two syllables: [tray-go].

2. **Oír** adds **ig** to the stem of the first person singular, and **y** to the stem of all the other forms, except the first person plural.

oír, PRESENT TENSE		
	Singular	*Plural*
1	o <u>ig</u> – o	o í mos
2	o <u>y</u> e s	o <u>y</u> e n
3	o <u>y</u> e –	

Oigo has two syllables: [oy-go].

STRUCTURE DRILLS

27. PERSON-NUMBER SUBSTITUTION

1. ¿Qué traen a la fiesta? ⊗   ¿Qué traen a la fiesta?
   (tú)   ¿Qué traes a la fiesta?
   (yo)   ¿Qué traigo a la fiesta?
   (él)   ¿Qué trae a la fiesta?
   (nosotros)   ¿Qué traemos a la fiesta?
   (Pedro y tú)   ¿Qué traen a la fiesta?

2. No oye el reloj. ⊗
   (yo–ustedes–el maestro–Susana y yo–tú) *oigo–oyen–oye–oímos–oyes*

28. PLURAL → SINGULAR

No conocemos Canadá. ⊗   No conozco Canadá.
¿Ponemos el correo aquí?   *¿Pongo el correo aquí?*
Salimos a las ocho y cuarto.   *Salgo a las ocho y cuarto.*
No oímos nada.   *No oigo nada.*
No reconocemos este lugar.   *No reconozco este lugar.*
Traemos algo para Luisito.   *Traigo algo para Luisito.*

VARIATION: Use right-hand column as stimulus and have student give plural form.

29. SINGULAR → PLURAL

¿Dónde pongo el libro? ⊗   ¿Dónde ponemos el libro?
No reconozco esa cara.   *No reconocemos esa cara.*
Oigo al cartero.   *No oímos al cartero.*
Salgo ahora.   *Salimos ahora.*
Traigo un regalo en esta bolsa.   *Traemos un regalo en esta bolsa.*
No conozco a don Chico.   *No conocemos a don Chico.*

VARIATION: Use right-hand column as stimulus and have student give singular form.

30. FREE RESPONSE

¿A qué hora sale usted para la escuela? ¿a las ocho y media?
¿Conoce usted a este chico? ¿Cómo se llama?
¿Qué trae usted a la escuela?
¿Qué traen ustedes a esta clase?
¿Qué pone el maestro en la mesa?
¿Reconocen ustedes este periódico? ¿Es un periódico en español o en inglés?
¿A qué hora salen ustedes de la escuela?
¿Sabe a qué hora salgo yo?
¿Conoce usted a la maestra de francés?

31. WRITING EXERCISE

Write the responses to Drills 27.2, 28 and 29.

Verbs with Stem Irregularities: tener, venir

TEACHER PRESENTATION, p. T178

GENERALIZATION

Tener and **venir** have two irregularities: they add **g** to the stem of the first person singular, and the stem vowel alternates between unstressed **e** and stressed **ie,** except in the irregular first person singular.

tener, PRESENT TENSE		
	Singular	*Plural*
1	ten g – o	ten e mos
2	tien e s	tien e n
3	tien e –	

venir, PRESENT TENSE		
	Singular	*Plural*
1	ven g – o	ven i mos
2	vien e s	vien e n
3	vien e –	

STRUCTURE DRILLS

32. PERSON-NUMBER SUBSTITUTION

1. Tienen mucho dinero. ⊗
   (yo)
   (tú)
   (Juan y yo)
   (el maestro)
   (María y ella)

   Tienen mucho dinero.
   Tengo mucho dinero.
   Tienes mucho dinero.
   Tenemos mucho dinero.
   Tiene mucho dinero.
   Tienen mucho dinero.

2. Viene a las doce en punto. ⊗
   (ellos–Susana y yo–ella–ustedes–yo)

   vienen–venimos–viene–vienen–vengo

33. PATTERNED RESPONSE

¿Quiere Juan comer ahora?
¿Quieres tú comer ahora?

Sí, tiene mucha hambre.
Sí, tengo mucha hambre.   (*continued*)

(continued)

¿Quieren los chicos comer ahora?   *Sí, tienen mucha hambre.*
¿Quieren ustedes comer ahora?   *Sí, tenemos mucha hambre.*
¿Quiere don Chico comer ahora?   *Sí, tiene mucha hambre.*

VARIATION

¿Quiere Juan tomar algo?   *Sí, tiene mucha sed.*

34. ENGLISH CUE DRILLS

1. Tenemos mucho calor.   *Tenemos mucho calor.*
   He's very thirsty.   *Tiene mucha sed.*
   I'm very cold.   *Tengo mucho frío.*
   They're very hungry.   *Tienen mucha hambre.*
   We're very warm.   *Tenemos mucho calor.*

2. Tengo que desayunar ahora.   *Tengo que desayunar ahora.*
   We have to have dinner now.   *Tenemos que cenar ahora.*
   They have to leave now.   *Tienen que salir ahora.*
   He has to have lunch now.   *Tiene que almorzar ahora.*
   You have to study now. (*tú*)   *Tienes que estudiar ahora.*
   I have to have breakfast now.   *Tengo que desayunar ahora.*

35. FREE RESPONSE

¿A qué hora vienen ustedes a la escuela?
¿Qué toma usted cuando tiene sed?
¿Tiene sed ahora?
¿Qué come usted cuando tiene hambre?
¿Cuáles días vienen los alumnos a la escuela?
¿Cuáles días no vienen?
¿Tiene usted frío ahora? ¿Tiene calor?

36. CHAIN DRILL

Pregúntele a *Juan* cuántos años tiene.   ¿Cuántos años tienes?
Juan, dígale cuántos años tiene y pregún-   Tengo _____ años. Y tú, María, ¿cuántos
  tele a *María* cuántos años tiene ella.   años tienes?
María, dígale cuántos años tiene y pre-   Tengo _____ años. Y tú, Camilo, ¿cuántos
  gúntele a *Camilo* cuántos años tiene él.   años tienes?

37. WRITING EXERCISE

Write the responses to Drills 32.2, 33, 34.1, and 34.2.

EXERCISE BOOK: EXERCISES 8, 9, 10, 11, AND 12.

Listening and Speaking Exercise 149*, p. T82 ⊗

Writing

1. MULTIPLE ITEM SUBSTITUTION

MODEL   Yo no entiendo a ese chico.
Mamá / leer / periódico
Mamá no lee ese periódico.

1. Toni vive en esa esquina.
   mis amigos y yo / almorzar / restaurante   *Mis amigos y yo almorzamos en ese restaurante.*

2. Esos señores no hablan inglés.
   chica / entender / español   *Esa chica no entiende español.*

3. ¿Qué quiere usted, este periódico o esos libros?
   preferir / falda / vestido   *¿Qué prefiere usted, esta falda o ese vestido?*

4. ¿Quién es ese señor pelirrojo, el cartero?
   señora / trigueño / maestra   *¿Quién es esa señora trigueña, la maestra?*

5. Juanito, ¿qué tienes en ese álbum?
   Sr. Castro / traer / bolsa   *Sr. Castro, ¿qué trae en esa bolsa?*

6. ¡Qué temprano llegan las maestras!
   tarde / venir / cartero   *¡Qué tarde viene el cartero!*

7. La señora no ve el periódico.
   yo / oír / maestro   *Yo no oigo al maestro.*

2. DIALOG COMPLETION

Copy the following dialog, filling in each of the blank spaces with the appropriate form of one of the verbs listed below. You may use the same verb more than once.

poner	tener	querer	traer
entender	conocer	venir	oír

—¡Qué temprano __1__ usted, don Chico!
—Yo siempre __2__ a las once, señora.
—¿__3__ algo para nosotros? Con permiso, don Chico, __4__ a mi hijo.
—¿Qué hay de comer, mami? Toni y yo __5__ mucha hambre. Tú __6__ a Toni, ¿verdad, mami?
—Claro, yo __7__ a todos tus amigos. ¿Qué __8__ comer ustedes?
—¡Helado con papas fritas! ¿Por qué __9__ esa cara?
—¡Ay, caramba, yo no __10__ a estos chicos!

1	2	3	4	5	6	7	8	9	10
viene	vengo	trae tiene	oigo	tenemos	conoces	conozco	quieren	pones	entiendo

RECOMBINATION MATERIAL

Dialogs

I

EL SEÑOR	Señorita, ¿sabe usted dónde está el Cine California?
LA SEÑORITA	No, lo siento. No tengo la menor idea.
EL SEÑOR	El cine donde dan películas americanas.
LA SEÑORITA	Ah sí, creo que está en la esquina del Parque Colón.
EL SEÑOR	Gracias, señorita.

QUESTIONS

1. ¿Qué quiere saber el señor?
2. ¿Sabe la señorita dónde está el Cine California?
3. ¿Qué dice ella?
4. ¿Cuáles películas dan en el Cine California?
5. ¿Dónde cree la señorita que está el cine?

II

TONI	¡Caramba! Ya son las once y media.
LUIS	¡Qué tarde! El partido empieza a la una.
TONI	¡Y todavía tenemos que almorzar!
LUIS	Yo no tengo hambre. ¿Y tú?
TONI	Tampoco.
LUIS	Mejor. Después comemos algo en el estadio.

QUESTIONS

1. ¿Qué hora es?
2. ¿Adónde van los dos chicos?
3. ¿A qué hora empieza el partido?
4. ¿Almuerzan Toni y Luis? ¿Por qué no?
5. Entonces, ¿cuándo comen? ¿Dónde?

III

EL HIJO	¿Qué tienes en esa bolsa, mami?
LA MADRE	Nada.
EL HIJO	¿Algo para la casa?
LA MADRE	No, nada.
EL HIJO	¿Un regalo para mí?
LA MADRE	Mmm, tal vez. . .
EL HIJO	¿Unos discos?
LA MADRE	No, una camisa nueva. Aquí tienes.

REJOINDERS

A ver si adivinas qué tengo en esta bolsa.

*¿Algo para la casa? / ¿Algo para mí? / ¿Un regalo? /
No sé. / No tengo la menor idea. / ¿Algo para comer?
¿Algo para tomar? / ¿Unos discos? / Mmm . . . a ver, ¿de
qué color es?*

Narrative

Lunes: día feo

¿Qué oigo? ¿Es el radio*? Ah no, es el reloj de la catedral* . . .
(¡TLONG!) . . . creo que es temprano todavía; a ver . . .
(¡TLONG!) . . . (¡TLONG!) cinco . . . las cinco, qué bueno, es
temprano todav . . . (¡TLONG!) (¡TLONG!) . . . ¡ay, caramba!
5 siete, ¡son las siete! ¡Imposible*! ¡Qué tarde! ¡Lunes! ¡Las siete de
la mañana! ¡Escuela! ¡Examen de geografía*! ¡Qué horrible*! ¡Y
no sé nada, ab-s-olu-ta-men-te* nada! ¡Examen con don Pedro, el
maestro más estricto* del mundo! No, imposible, no puedo ir a la
escuela hoy, estoy enfermo, tengo temperatura*. Yo sé que no sé
10 nada . . . a ver: ¿la capital* de Brasil*? Este . . . este . . . ¡Río de
Janeiro! . . . No no no, no es Río de Janeiro, ahora tienen otra
nueva, ¿cómo se llama? . . . no recuerdo. ¿Los productos* princi-
pales* de Colombia? No tengo la menor idea. No, no puedo ir a la
escuela, tengo una temperatura muy alta . . . Ay, caramba, aquí
15 viene mamá.

—Buenos días, hijo . . . ¡Qué! Luis, ¿sabes qué hora es? Vas a
llegar tarde a la escuela. ¡Vamos, apúrate!

—Mami . . . este . . .

—Ajá, ya sé, tienes temperatura. Todos los lunes estás en-
20 fermo. ¡No, señor! ¡Perezoso! ¡Apúrate! ¡Vamos!

—Pero mami . . .

—¡In-me-dia-ta-men-te*!

Note: Point out that many
Spanish words which end in *ía*
have the same meaning as
English words which end in *y:*
geografía.

Note: Point out that many
Spanish words which end in
mente have the same meaning
as English words which end in
ly: inmediatamente.

—Pero mami . . .

—¡NO! Tienes que ir a la escuela, ¿entiendes?

25 —Sí, mami.

(más tarde, en el comedor) *Note:* Kitchens in Spanish-speaking countries do not commonly have breakfast nooks. All meals are taken in the dining room.

—¡Hmm, qué guapo estás con esos pantalones nuevos!

—. . . Mm . . .

—¿Quieres más café? *Note:* In some Spanish-speaking countries it is not unusual for young children to drink coffee.

30 —Mm-mm.

—¿Mm-mm sí o mm-mm no?

—No.

—Hoy vienes a almorzar temprano, ¿no? ¿ah, Luisito? ¡Luisito! ¿En qué piensas?

35 —¿Mm? Mami, ¿tú sabes cómo se llaman todos los estados de los Estados Unidos?

—Claro, muy fácil: Nueva York, California . . . Tejas . . . este . . . Miami . . .

A cathedral dating from the Colonial period is a familiar sight in many Spanish American cities.

—Miami no es un estado.

40 —¡Arizona! . . . California . . . este . . . Nueva York . . . Arizona . . . este . . . Arizona . . .

—Hasta luego, mami.

QUESTIONS

1. ¿Qué día es, en la narración? *Title*
2. ¿Qué oye Luis, el radio? *1*
3. ¿Qué cree Luis cuando oye el reloj de la catedral? *1*
4. ¿Qué hora es? *5*
5. ¿Qué pasa hoy en la escuela? *6*
6. ¿Cómo se llama el maestro de geografía? *7*
7. ¿Cómo es don Pedro? *8*
8. ¿Por qué dice Luis que está enfermo? *9*
9. ¿Sabe él cuál es la capital de Brasil? *12*
10. ¿Tiene idea de cuáles son los productos principales de Colombia? *13*
11. ¿Por qué no puede ir a la escuela, según él? *14*

12. ¿Quién viene al dormitorio? *15*
13. ¿Qué pasa todos los lunes, según la mamá? *20*
14. ¿Dice la mamá que él tiene que ir a la escuela? *20*
15. ¿Dónde desayunan, en la cocina o en el comedor? *26*
16. ¿Por qué está Luis tan guapo hoy, según la mamá? *27*
17. ¿Quiere él más café? *32*
18. ¿Entiende la mamá cuando él contesta? *31*
19. ¿Qué quiere saber el hijo? *35*
20. ¿Sabe la mamá cómo se llaman todos los estados? *40*
21. ¿Cómo es el lunes, un día bonito? *Title*

Conversation Stimulus

You and your friend have a geography test and neither one of you is prepared. What do you say to each other?

Start like this: ¡Caramba! Mañana *tenemos un examen de geografía.*

Yo no *sé nada. Yo sé que no sé nada.*

¿Tú sabes cuál es la capital de *Brasil?*

No tengo la menor idea. ¿Cuáles son los productos principales de *los Estados Unidos?*

A ver . . . a ver . . . No sé. ¿Cuáles son? ¿Tú sabes?

No, yo no sé tampoco.

BASIC DIALOG

Note: At this time, you may wish to assign the section on the Land and the People in Glimpses of the Spanish World.

SECTION A

Unas vacaciones[1] en Perú

SR. RAMOS	A ver si sabes cuál es la capital de Perú.
HIJA	¡Lima! Aquí está en el mapa.

9-1

SR. RAMOS	Creo que vamos a hacer un viaje allá[2]. ¿Qué te parece la idea?

9-2

HIJA	Me encanta. ¿De veras? ¿Cuándo?

9-3

SR. RAMOS	A fines de agosto, y volvemos en septiembre.
HIJA	¿Cómo es Lima, papi? ¿Es verdad que allá nunca llueve?
SR. RAMOS	Sí, el clima es muy bueno; no hace ni frío ni calor.

9-4

HIJA	¡Mañana le cuento a todo el mundo!

A vacation in Peru

MR. RAMOS	Let's see if you know (which is) the capital of Peru.
DAUGHTER	Lima! Here it is on the map.
MR. RAMOS	I think we're going to take (make) a trip there. What do you think of the idea? (How to you seems the idea?)
DAUGHTER	I love it. (To me it delights.) Really? When?
MR. RAMOS	Towards the end of August, and we'll come back in September.
DAUGHTER	What's Lima like, dad? Is it true it never rains there?
MR. RAMOS	Yes, the climate is very nice; it's neither cold nor hot. (It makes neither cold nor heat.)
DAUGHTER	Tomorrow I'll tell everybody (all the world)!

---

[1] **Vacación** is normally used in the plural.

[2] **Allá** is used to refer to a more distant point than **allí,** and is more vague in reference.

◀ *Crowds flock to this beach area near Lima, once reserved for the very wealthy.*

Supplement

¿Vas a pasar las vacaciones en España?	Are you going to spend your vacation in Spain?

A principios de enero. | *Note:* Point out that the months are not capitalized. | At the beginning of January.

febrero	February
marzo	March
abril	April
mayo	May
junio	June

A mediados de julio.	Around the middle of July.
agosto	August
septiembre	September
octubre	October
noviembre	November
diciembre	December

Volvemos el primero[3] de septiembre.	We'll return on September first.
dos	second
tres	third

¿En qué mes estamos?	What month is this?
¿Qué fecha es hoy?	What's the date today?

Aquí está en el mapa. 9-1

Mañana le pregunto a todo el mundo.	Tomorrow I'll ask everyone.
llueve mucho. 9-2	
Allá hace buen tiempo. 9-3	The weather is nice there.
mal 9-4	bad
calor 9-5	
Voy a viajar en tren. 9-7 frío 9-6	I'm going to travel by train.
barco 9-8	boat
bicicleta 9-9	bicycle
autobús 9-10	bus
avión 9-11	plane

Tu mamá trabaja mucho. 9-12	Your mother works a lot.
duerme 9-13	sleeps
Vamos a hacer un viaje. 9-14	

21	22	23	24	25	26
veintiuno,	veintidós,	veintitrés,	veinticuatro,	veinticinco,	veintiséis,

---

[3] Except for **primero,** the cardinal numbers are used for the date in Spanish.

27	28	29	30	31	32

veintisiete, veintiocho, veintinueve, treinta, treinta y uno, treinta y dos,

40	50	60	70	80	90	100	101

cuarenta, cincuenta, sesenta, setenta, ochenta, noventa, cien, ciento uno

Listening and Speaking Exercises 150, 151, 152*, 153*, p. T83 ⊗

BASIC FORMS

Verbs

contar (ue)	preguntar
*dormir	trabajar
*llover	viajar
parecer (zc)	*volver

Nouns

autobús *m.*	fin *m.*	viaje *m.*
avión *m.*	mapa *m.*	capital *f.*
calor *m.*	mes *m.*	vacaciones *f.pl.*
clima *m.*	tren *m.*	

Vocabulary Exercises

1. QUESTIONS

1. ¿Sabe la hija del Sr. Ramos cuál es la capital de Perú? *Sí, sabe.*
2. ¿Cuál es la capital de Perú? *Lima.*
3. Según el Sr. Ramos, ¿dónde van a pasar ellos las vacaciones? *En Lima.*
4. ¿Está la hija contenta con la idea? *Sí, está muy contenta.*
5. ¿Cuándo va la familia Ramos a Perú? *A fines de agosto.*
6. ¿Dónde quiere usted pasar sus vacaciones? ¿en España? ¿en Canadá?
7. ¿Cuándo empiezan las vacaciones aquí? ¿a principios de mayo?
8. ¿En qué mes estamos?
9. ¿Qué día es hoy? ¿lunes?
10. ¿Qué día es mañana?
11. ¿Qué fecha es hoy? ¿primero de mayo?
12. ¿En qué mes empiezan las clases?
13. ¿Cuántos meses hay en el año? ¿Cuáles son? *Doce. Enero, febrero, marzo, abril, mayo, junio, julio, agosto, septiembre, octubre, noviembre, diciembre.*

2. QUESTIONS

1. ¿Llueve mucho en Lima, según el Sr. Ramos? *No, nunca llueve allí, según él.*
2. ¿Hace mucho calor allá? *No, no hace ni frío ni calor.*
3. ¿Hace mucho calor aquí?
4. ¿Hace mucho frío hoy o hace buen tiempo?
5. ¿Cómo está el día hoy? ¿Hace mal tiempo?
6. ¿En qué meses hace frío aquí?
7. ¿A usted le gusta el frío?
8. ¿En qué meses hace calor?
9. ¿Hace buen tiempo ahora?
10. ¿Cuándo hace mal tiempo aquí?
11. Cuando usted viaja, ¿prefiere ir en tren o en avión?
12. Y usted, ¿prefiere viajar en carro o en tren?
13. ¿Trabaja usted? ¿Dónde?

3. FREE COMPLETION

1. ¿Es verdad que allá nunca _____? *hace frío, llueve*
2. Lima es _____. *la capital de Perú, muy bonita*
3. Prefiero viajar en _____. *tren, avión*
4. Hoy es el veinte de _____. *enero, febrero*
5. Allá nunca hace _____. *frío, calor*

EXERCISE BOOK: EXERCISE 1

4. NUMBER DRILL

Note: Use chalkboard to cue these and other numbers.

Say the following numbers:
22, 30, 44, 57, 63, 78, 95, 100

veintidós, treinta, cuarenta y cuatro, cincuenta y siete, sesenta y tres, setenta y ocho, noventa y cinco, cien

VARIATION: Say the number which is one digit higher.
VARIATION: Say the number which is one digit lower.

A family spends the afternoon boating in one of Lima's lovely parks.

GRAMMAR

Stem Alternation: o-ue
e-*Class and* i-*Class Verbs*

PRESENTATION *TEACHER PRESENTATION, p. T179*

> **Vuelvo** en septiembre.
> **Volvemos** en septiembre.
>
> **Duerme** mucho.
> **Dormimos** mucho.

Is the stem stressed or unstressed in each verb form? What is the vowel sound in the stem when stressed? How is the sound written? What is the vowel sound in the stem when unstressed? How is the sound written?

GENERALIZATION

1. You have already learned that **o** alternates with **ue** [we] in the stems of certain **a**-class verbs. Several **e**-class and **i**-class verbs also have this **o-ue** stem alternation, **o** occurring when the stem is unstressed, **ue** occurring when the stem is stressed.

Stressed Stem	*Unstressed Stem*
vuelvo	volver
vuelves	volvemos
vuelve	
vuelven	
duermo	dormir
duermes	dormimos
duerme	
duermen	

2. The infinitives of **e**-class and **i**-class verbs you have learned so far which have this alternation are **llover, poder, volver,** and **dormir.**

Listening and Speaking Exercises 154, 155, 156*, p. T84 ⊗ | SECTION B |

STRUCTURE DRILLS

5. PATTERNED RESPONSE

No vuelvo ahora. ⊗   ¿Cuándo vas a volver?
No duermo ahora.   ¿Cuándo vas a dormir?
No puedo ahora.   ¿Cuándo vas a poder?
No vuelvo ahora.   ¿Cuándo vas a volver?

6. PERSON-NUMBER SUBSTITUTION

1. ¿Vuelve en mayo? ⊗   ¿Vuelve en mayo?
   (yo)   ¿Vuelvo en mayo?
   (nosotros)   ¿Volvemos en mayo?
   (tú)   ¿Vuelves en mayo?
   (ellos)   ¿Vuelven en mayo?
   (Ana y yo)   ¿Volvemos en mayo?
   (usted)   ¿Vuelve en mayo?

2. No duermo mucho. ⊗ *dormimos–duermo–duermen–dormimos–*
   (nosotros–yo–ustedes–mis hermanos y yo–tú–él) *duermes–duerme*

7. PAIRED SENTENCES

¿Puedes ir al baile? ⊗   ¿Puedes ir al baile?
   (nosotros)   ¿Podemos ir al baile?
   (tú)   ¿Puedes ir al baile?

Vuelven el primero de junio.   *Vuelven el primero de junio.*
   (nosotros)   *Volvemos el primero de junio.*
   (ellos)   *Vuelven el primero de junio.*

Nunca duermo durante el día.   *Nunca duermo durante el día.*
   (nosotros)   *Nunca dormimos durante el día.*
   (yo)   *Nunca duermo durante el día.*

8. FREE RESPONSE

¿Llueve mucho en Lima, según el Sr. Ramos? *No, no llueve mucho.*
¿Cuándo llueve allá?   *Nunca llueve allá.*

¿Cuándo va la familia Ramos a Perú? ¿Cuándo vuelve? *A fines de agosto. Vuelve en septiembre.*
¿En qué meses llueve mucho aquí?
¿Llueve ahora?
¿A qué hora vuelven ustedes a casa?
Cuando usted sale con sus amigos los sábados, ¿vuelve a su casa tarde o temprano?
¿Duerme usted mucho?
¿Duerme mucho cuando está enfermo?
Ustedes nunca duermen en esta clase, ¿verdad?

9. WRITING EXERCISE

Write the responses to Drills 6.2 and 7.

EXERCISE BOOK: EXERCISES 2 AND 3

ir + a + *Infinitive*

PRESENTATION *TEACHER PRESENTATION, p. T180*

> **Voy a viajar** en tren.
> **¿Vas a pasar** las vacaciones en España?
> **Vamos a hacer** un viaje allá.

What three parts make up the verb in each of these sentences?

GENERALIZATION

In English we often use a form of the verb *be* + *going to* + an <u>infinitive</u> when referring to an event that will take place in the future.

> *I <u>am going to</u> <u>travel</u> by train.*

The equivalent construction in Spanish consists of a form of the verb **ir** + **a** + <u>infinitive</u>.

> <u>**Voy**</u> <u>**a**</u> <u>**viajar**</u> en tren.

STRUCTURE DRILLS

10. PRESENT → **ir** + **a** + INFINITIVE

Damos una fiesta esta noche. ⊗
Compro las cosas ahora.

Vamos a dar una fiesta esta noche.
Voy a comprar las cosas ahora.   (*continued*)

(*continued*)

Todo el mundo viene.	*Todo el mundo va a venir.*
Empieza a las ocho y media.	*Va a empezar a las ocho y media.*
Los chicos traen discos.	*Los chicos van a traer discos.*
¿Cómo? ¿Llueve esta noche? ¡Imposible!	*¿Cómo? ¿Va a llover esta noche. ¡Imposible!*
Damos una fiesta esta noche.	*Vamos a dar una fiesta esta noche.*

11. FREE RESPONSE

¿Qué va a hacer la familia Ramos durante las vacaciones?	*Va a hacer un viaje.*
¿Adónde van a ir el Sr. Ramos y su familia?	*Van a ir a Lima.*
¿Cuándo van a empezar el viaje?	*Van a empezar el viaje en agosto.*
¿Cuándo van a volver?	*Van a volver en septiembre.*

¿Va a hacer un viaje usted durante las vacaciones?

¿Cómo va usted a viajar? ¿en carro?

¿Qué van a hacer ustedes después de la cena? ¿escuchar el radio? ¿estudiar?

¿Qué van a hacer ustedes mañana?

12. WRITING EXERCISE

Write the responses to Drill 10.

EXERCISE BOOK: EXERCISE 4

Indirect Object Pronouns

PRESENTATION *TEACHER PRESENTATION, p. T180*

Mañana **me** cuentan las noticias.
Mañana **te** cuentan las noticias.
Mañana **le** cuentan las noticias.
Mañana **nos** cuentan las noticias.
Mañana **les** cuentan las noticias.

Which word is the indirect object pronoun in each of these sentences? What is the position of the indirect object pronoun in relation to the verb?

GENERALIZATION

1. The Spanish indirect object pronouns are given in the following chart:

	Singular	Plural
1	me	nos
2	te	
		les
3	le	

2. In English sentences, the indirect object pronoun often occurs before the direct object.

> *I'm writing <u>him</u> a letter.*
> *He buys <u>me</u> a present.*

It may also occur after the direct object, following the prepositions *to* and *for*.

> *I'm writing a letter <u>to him</u>.*
> *He buys a present <u>for me</u>.*

In Spanish, however, the indirect object pronoun occurs immediately before a verb with a person-number ending.

<u>**Le**</u> **escribo una carta.** $\begin{cases}$ *I'm writing him a letter.*
 I'm writing a letter to him. $\end{cases}$

<u>**Me**</u> **compra un regalo.** $\begin{cases}$ *He buys me a present.*
 He buys a present for me. $\end{cases}$

Note: Affirmative command constructions, in which object pronouns may follow a verb with a person-number ending, will be discussed in Level II.

3. In Spanish, if there is an indirect object noun, there is normally an indirect object pronoun which repeats it. The indirect object noun is always preceded by **a.**

Le   escribo una carta   **a María.**
(*To her = Mary*)   *I'm writing a letter*   *to Mary.*

Les   traigo   unos regalos **a mis hermanas.**
(*For them = my sisters*)   *I'm bringing some presents*   *for my sisters.*

Le   compro   una casita **al perro.**
(*For him = the dog*)   *I'm buying a little house for the dog.*

Thus, in Spanish sentences of this type, the indirect object is actually stated twice, once by the indirect object noun, and again by the indirect object pronoun before the verb.

Note: Spanish does permit sentences like *Escribo una carta a María.* However, constructions of this type are not normally used in everyday language, although they do occur in more formal speech and writing.

4. Indirect object pronouns in Spanish are always unstressed. In order to emphasize an indirect object pronoun or to clarify the gender of **le(s)** or **nos, <u>a</u>** + a prepositional pronoun is used.

Le escribo.	*I'm writing to him.*
Le escribo a él.	*I'm writing to <u>him</u> (not <u>her</u> or <u>you</u>).*
Me escribe mucho.	*He writes to me a lot.*
A mí me escribe mucho.	*He writes to <u>me</u> (not <u>us</u> or <u>her</u>) a lot.*

Listening and Speaking Exercises 157 and 158*, p. T86 ⊗   SECTION C

STRUCTURE DRILLS

13. PERSON-NUMBER SUBSTITUTION

VARIATION
¿Por qué no me pregunt.

1. ¿Por qué no me contesta? ⊗   ¿Por qué no me contesta?
   (a él)   ¿Por qué no le contesta?
   (a ellos)   ¿Por qué no les contesta?
   (a nosotros)   ¿Por qué no nos contesta?
   (a mí)   ¿Por qué no me contesta?
   (a ti)   ¿Por qué no te contesta?

2. Le dan un regalo. ⊗
   (a ti–a ellos–a nosotros–a ella–a mí)   *te–les–nos–le–me*
   VARIATION: Le traen unas cosas.
3. ¿Qué les compra? ⊗
   (a él–a usted–a ti–a nosotros–a mí–a ustedes)   *le–le–te–nos–me–les*
   VARIATION: ¿Qué les da?

14. ENGLISH CUE DRILLS

1. Nos traen un regalo.   Nos traen un regalo.
   They bring us a gift.   Nos traen un regalo.
   They bring a gift for us.   Nos traen un regalo.
   They bring a gift to us.   Nos traen un regalo.

2. Le escribo una carta.   *Le escribo una carta.*
   I'm writing him a letter.   *Le escribo una carta.*
   I'm writing a letter for him.   *Le escribo una carta.*
   I'm writing a letter to him.   *Le escribo una carta.*

15. PAIRED SENTENCES

Le hablo a él. ⊗   Le hablo a él.
I'm speaking to him.   Le hablo.
I'm speaking to <u>him</u>.   Le hablo a él.

Nunca me gritan a mí.   *Nunca me gritan a mí.*
They never yell at me.   *Nunca me gritan.*
They never yell at me.   *Nunca me gritan a mí.*

¿Por qué nos pregunta a nosotros?   *¿Por qué nos pregunta a nosotros?*
Why is he asking us?   *¿Por qué nos pregunta?*
Why is he asking us?   *¿Por qué nos pregunta a nosotros?*

16. CUED RESPONSE

1. ¿A quién le escribes? 🌀
   (a mi mamá)   Le escribo a mi mamá.
   (a Juana)   Le escribo a Juana.
   (a Juana y a María)   Les escribo a Juana y a María.
   (a ti)   Te escribo a ti.

2. ¿A quién le habla el maestro? 🌀
   (a Pepe y a Pedro–a mí–a Pepe y a mí–a ustedes)   *Les habla a Pepe y a Pedro. Me habla a mí.*
                                                     Nos habla a Pepe y a mí. Les habla a ustedes.

17. DIRECTED DRILL

Dígale a *Lupe* que usted le trae un   Te traigo un regalo.
regalo. 🌀
Dígales a *Lupe* y a *Rosa* que usted les   Les traigo un regalo.
trae un regalo.
Diga que usted me habla a mí.   Le hablo a usted.
Diga que usted nos habla a *Marta* y a mí.   Les hablo a *Marta* y a usted.
Diga que *Pepe* le lee una carta a usted.   *Pepe* me lee una carta.
Díga que *Pepe* les lee una carta a *Luisa*   *Pepe* nos lee una carta a *Luisa* y a mí.
y a usted.

18. PATTERNED RESPONSE

1. ¿Me compra unos discos? 🌀   Bueno, le compro dos.
   ¿Les compra unos discos a mis amigos?   Bueno, les compro dos.
   ¿Nos compra unos discos?   Bueno, les compro dos.
   ¿Le compra unos discos a Pedro?   *VARIATION*   Bueno, le compro dos.
   ¿Me compra unos libros?   *Bueno, le compro dos.*
2. Le traigo algo a usted. 🌀   ¿De veras? ¿Qué me trae?
   Le traigo algo a Juan.   *¿De veras? ¿Qué le trae?*
   Les traigo algo a ustedes.   *¿De veras? ¿Qué nos trae?*
   Les traigo algo a las gemelas.   *¿De veras? ¿Qué les trae?*
   VARIATION
   Le traigo un regalo a usted.   *¿De veras? ¿Qué me trae?*

19. FREE RESPONSE

Cuando usted sale con sus amigos, ¿su padre le da dinero?

¿Qué le compra usted a su mamá para el Día de la Madre?

¿Su mamá le compra muchas cosas a usted?

¿Cuándo les escribe a sus amigos?

¿Ellos le escriben muchas cartas a usted?

¿Quién les habla en español a ustedes?

20. WRITING EXERCISE

Write the responses to Drills 13.2, 13.3, and 18.2.

EXERCISE BOOK: EXERCISES 5, 6, 7, 8, AND 9

More Indirect Object Constructions

TEACHER PRESENTATION, p. T183

GENERALIZATION

1. In Spanish, the indirect object is often used to indicate persons for whom a service (or disservice) is performed. The direct object in such sentences is normally preceded by the definite article in cases where English would require a possessive construction.

2. Paragraph 1 shows that indirect objects in Spanish are used to indicate persons or things involved in the action of the verb. The kinds of involvement expressed by indirect objects are more varied in Spanish than in English. In fact, with some verbs, such as **comprar,** an indirect object construction may have more than one English equivalent.

Le compro la bicicleta a Juan.

I'm buying the bicycle {*for John.* / *from John.*}

The construction **le . . . a Juan** indicates that **Juan** is involved in the purchase, but exactly in what way is understood only from the context of the conversation, not from the sentence itself.

Listening and Speaking Exercises 159, 160, 161*, p. T87 ⊗ **SECTION D**

STRUCTURE DRILLS

21. PATTERNED RESPONSE

¿Arregla mamá la casa? ⊗   No, yo le arreglo la casa a mamá.
¿Cierra la maestra las ventanas?   No, yo le cierro las ventanas a la maestra.
¿Compran los señores los boletos?   No, yo les compro los boletos a los señores.
¿Contesta papá el teléfono?   No, yo le contesto el teléfono a papá.
¿Hago yo el mapa?   No, yo le hago el mapa a usted.
¿Limpiamos nosotros el cuarto?   No, yo les limpio el cuarto a ustedes.

VARIATION 1 No, nosotros le arreglamos la casa a mamá.
VARIATION 2 No, Juan le arregla la casa a mamá.

22. CUED RESPONSE

Le busco un regalo a mi hermano.
¿Qué busco?   Busca un regalo.
¿A quién?   Le busca un regalo a su hermano.

Les limpio el carro a mis tíos.
¿Qué limpio?   *Limpia el carro.*
¿A quién?   *Les limpia el carro a sus tíos.*

Le arreglo la sala a mi mamá.
¿Qué arreglo?   *Arregla la sala.*
¿A quién?   *Le arregla la sala a su mamá.*

23. ENGLISH CUE DRILLS

1. Mi mamá me arregla el cuarto. ⊗   Mi mamá me arregla el cuarto.
   She cleans my shoes.   Me limpia los zapatos.
   She makes my dinner.   Me hace la cena.
   She buys my shirts.   Me compra las camisas.
   She takes my temperature when I'm sick. Me toma la temperatura cuando estoy en-
                                          fermo.
   She puts my room in order.   Me arregla el cuarto.

2. Le compro una bicicleta a Juan.   *Le compro una bicicleta a Juan.*
   I'm buying Juan a bicycle.   *Le compro una bicicleta a Juan.*
   I'm buying a bicycle for Juan.   *Le compro una bicicleta a Juan.*
   I'm buying a bicycle from Juan.   *Le compro una bicicleta a Juan.*

24. WRITING EXERCISE

Write the responses to Drills 22, 23.1, and 23.2.
EXERCISE BOOK: EXERCISE 10

Indirect Objects: Further Details

TEACHER PRESENTATION, p. T184
GENERALIZATION

1. The following verbs take only indirect objects when used with the meanings given:

encantar
{
Le encanta la idea.
She loves the idea.
(The idea delights her.)
}

parecer
{
¿Qué te parece la idea?
What do you think of the idea?
(How does the idea seem to you?)
}

gustar
{
Le gusta viajar en barco.
She likes to travel by boat.
(To travel by boat pleases her.)
}

pasar
{
¿Qué les pasa?
What's the matter with them?
}

2. Reread the examples just given for **encantar, gustar,** and **parecer.** Two English equivalents are given: one is natural English and one is a literal translation. Note that when natural English is used, the roles of subject and object are the reverse of what they are in the Spanish examples. That is, the indirect objects in the Spanish sentences correspond to the subjects in the English sentences; conversely, the objects (of one kind or another) in the English sentences correspond to the subjects in the Spanish sentences. You must pay careful attention to subject-verb agreement in Spanish sentences of this type.

Singular Subject	*Plural Subject*
Le encanta la idea	**Le encantan las ideas.**
¿Qué te parece la idea?	**¿Qué te parecen las ideas?**
No me gusta ese chico.	**No me gustan esos chicos.**

STRUCTURE DRILLS

25. ITEM SUBSTITUTION

1. No me gustan esas chicas. ⊗
   _____ ese carro.
   _____ esos mapas.
   _____ esos colores.
   _____ esa bicicleta.

No me gustan esas chicas. *VARIATION*
No me gusta ese carro. ese libro
No me gustan esos mapas. esas fotos
No me gustan esos colores. esas cosas
No me gusta esa bicicleta. esa casa

2. ¿Qué te parece la idea? ⊗   *parece–parecen–parece–parecen–parece*
   (ese maestro–los alumnos–el partido–las gemelas–la nueva escuela)
   VARIATION: (esa maestra–los compañeros–el desfile–los gemelos–el libro)

26. PATTERNED RESPONSE

1. ¿A Juana le gusta el barco? ⊗   Claro, le encanta.
   ¿y a ti?   *Claro, me encanta.*
   ¿y a ustedes?   *Claro, nos encanta.*
   ¿y a Elena y a Marta?   *Claro, les encanta.*
   ¿y a usted?   *Claro, me encanta.*
   ¿y a mí? *VARIATION*   *Claro, le encanta.*
   ¿A Juana le gusta el regalo?   *Claro, le encanta.*
2. ¿Qué les parece la idea a los alumnos? ⊗   Les gusta mucho.
   ¿y a ti?   *Me gusta mucho.*
   ¿y a Susana?   *Le gusta mucho.*
   ¿y a usted?   *Me gusta mucho.*
   ¿y a ustedes?   *Nos gusta mucho.*
   ¿y a Miguel y a Luis?   *Les gusta mucho.*
   VARIATION
   ¿Qué les parece el álbum a los chicos?   *Les gusta mucho.*

27. PROGRESSIVE SUBSTITUTION

A los señores les encanta la idea. ⊗   *A los señores les encanta la idea.*
A nosotros _____.   *A nosotros nos encanta la idea.*
_____ gusta _____.   *A nosotros nos gusta la idea.*
_____ los zapatos.   *A nosotros nos gustan los zapatos.*
A mí _____.   *A mí me gustan los zapatos.*
_____ aprietan _____.   *A mí me aprietan los zapatos.*
_____ la corbata.   *A mí me aprieta la corbata.*
Al chico _____.   *Al chico le aprieta la corbata.*

28. FREE RESPONSE

¿Le gusta más viajar en tren o en avión?
¿Qué le gusta hacer durante las vacaciones? ¿trabajar? ¿viajar?
A las chicas les encantan las culebras, ¿verdad?
¿Le aprietan los zapatos a usted ahora?
A los alumnos, ¿qué les parecen los exámenes? ¿Les gustan?
¿Cuál clase le gusta más a usted?
A ustedes les encanta la clase de español, ¿verdad?
Y la clase de geografía, ¿qué les parece? ¿y la clase de inglés?
A ver si adivinan cuál clase me gusta más a mí.

29. BASIC DIALOG VARIATION

Change the second part of the Basic Dialog to narrative form. *Start like this:* La hija del Sr. Ramos le pregunta a su papá cómo es Lima, y si . . . *es verdad que allá nunca llueve. Él le contesta sí, que el clima es muy bueno, que no hace ni frío ni calor. Ella le dice que mañana le va a contar (or cuenta) a todo el mundo.*

30. WRITING EXERCISE

Write the responses to Drills 25.2, 26.1, and 27.

EXERCISE BOOK: EXERCISES 11 AND 12

Listening and Speaking Exercise 162*, p. T88 ⊗

Writing

1. MULTIPLE ITEM SUBSTITUTION

    MODEL   Le doy un regalo a Juana.
               escribir / carta / mis tíos
               <u>Les escribo una carta a mis tíos.</u>

1. Mañana le cuento a todo el mundo.
   más tarde / preguntar / ellos   *Más tarde les pregunto a ellos.*

2. A los chicos les gusta el carro.
   a mí / encantar / discos   *A mí me encantan los discos.*

3. Ana no quiere viajar.
   tú y yo / poder / trabajar   *Tú y yo no podemos trabajar.*

4. Yo siempre leo en el avión.
   nosotros / dormir / tren   *Nosotros siempre dormimos en el tren.*

5. A ti te traen un regalo.
   a nosotros / dar / mapas   *A nosotros nos dan unos mapas.*

6. Le escribo una carta a mi tío.
   leer / libro / ellas   *Les leo un libro a ellas.*

7. Juana llega en diciembre.
   las chicas / volver / junio   *Las chicas vuelven en junio.*

8. A ese señor le aprietan los zapatos.
   señoritas / encantar / baile   *A esas señoritas les encanta el baile.*

9. Me compran los discos a mí.
   limpiar / carro / mi padre   *Le limpian el carro a mi padre.*

10. Le hago el desayuno a mi mamá.
    arreglar / cuarto / ustedes   *Les arreglo el cuarto a ustedes.*

2. PARAGRAPH REWRITE

Rewrite the following paragraph, changing the verbs to the form **ir** + **a** + infinitive.

¿Dónde pasan ustedes las vacaciones? ¿En Lima? ¿En Buenos Aires? Ricardo sale para España mañana y Susana va a Nueva York el 20 de enero y no vuelve hasta mediados de febrero. Pero yo tengo que pasar las vacaciones aquí. No puedo hacer un viaje este año porque no tengo bastante dinero. Pero le cuento una cosa: yo trabajo, y tal vez uno de estos días mi hermano y yo hacemos un viaje muy bonito. Y tú, Pedro, ¿qué haces durante las vacaciones?

*van a pasar   va a salir   va a ir   va a volver   voy a tener   voy a poder   voy a tener   voy a contar
voy a trabajar   vamos a hacer   vas a hacer*

RECOMBINATION MATERIAL

Dialogs

I

CONSUELO	¿Quieres ir al cine?
ALICIA	No, quiero dormir. Estoy muy cansada. . . . cansado.
CONSUELO	Van a dar una película muy buena.
ALICIA	¿Cuál?
CONSUELO	Una película inglesa. No recuerdo cómo se llama.
ALICIA	No gracias. Prefiero dormir.
CONSUELO	¡Qué perezosa! ¡Qué perezoso!

VARIATION: The conversation takes place between two brothers.

QUESTIONS

1. ¿Qué quiere hacer Consuelo?
2. Y Alicia, ¿qué quiere hacer ella?
3. ¿Por qué quiere dormir Alicia?
4. Según Consuelo, ¿cómo es la película que van a dar?
5. ¿Cuál película van a dar?
6. ¿Recuerda Consuelo cómo se llama?
7. ¿Qué prefiere hacer Alicia, ir al cine o dormir?
8. ¿Qué le dice Consuelo?

REJOINDERS

¿Quieres ir al cine?   *No, quiero dormir. / No, quiero estudiar. / No, prefiero ir al parque. / ¿Qué dan? / Claro, vamos. / ¿Cuándo? / Muy bien. / Sí, ¿cuándo empieza la película? / No sé, estoy muy cansado.*

II

EL HIJO	Papi, este . . . ¿Puedo comprar un carro?
EL PADRE	¡¡UN CARRO!! ¡Tú quieres comprar un carro!
EL HIJO	Sí, este . . . un carro viejo . . . pequeño . . . barato . . .
EL PADRE	¿Para qué necesitas un carro? Ya tienes una bicicleta muy bonita.
EL HIJO	Pero . . . papi . . .

QUESTIONS

1. ¿Qué quiere comprar el hijo?
2. ¿Qué le contesta el padre? ¿Le parece buena la idea a él?
3. ¿Quiere el chico un carro nuevo y caro?
4. ¿Por qué no necesita un carro, según el padre?
5. ¿Qué le dice el hijo al padre?

III   *VARIATION:* The two speakers address each other as *usted.*

CARLOS	¿Sabes dónde vamos a pasar las vacaciones? ¿Sabe . . .
CLARA	¿Dónde?
CARLOS	A ver si adivinas. A ver si adivina.

Relics of great Indian civilizations—such as these clay figures from Veracruz—abound in Mexico.

CLARA   Pero no tengo la menor idea . . . a ver . . . ¿en España? ¿en Nueva York?

CARLOS   No, en Perú.

CLARA   ¿De veras? ¡Qué bien!

CARLOS   Sí, vamos a fines de junio y no volvemos hasta septiembre.

REJOINDERS

A ver si adivinas dónde vamos a pasar las vacaciones.   *A ver . . . ¿en España? / No sé. / No tengo la menor idea. / ¿En los Estados Unidos?*

Narrative

Jeem, Beel y Beector

Note: The names in the title are American names written, in English, to sound the way a Spanish-speaking person might pronounce them.

I

Durante los meses de junio, julio, y agosto, los alumnos de las escuelas norteamericanas pasan sus vacaciones de diferentes* maneras*. Unos viajan y van de Tejas a Vermont, de Nueva York a California, o simplemente* de una Carolina a la otra. Muchos
5 otros juegan, trabajan, o estudian durante sus vacaciones. Unos prefieren no hacer absolutamente nada, y si en sus casas les permiten* hacer eso, eso es exactamente* lo que hacen: no hacen nada. Pero ésta es la excepción*. Estos chicos perezosos son casos* extremos* y no son muchos.

Note: Point out that many Spanish verbs are the same as English verbs, except that they have Spanish person-number endings: *permitir, consultar.*

10 En el otro extremo encontramos a unos pocos a quienes les gusta hacer mucho, muchísimo. Son activos*, ambiciosos*, con mucha energía*, y les encanta todo lo que es aventura*, especialmente* las aventuras de viajes a lugares muy distantes*. Éste es el caso de Jeem, Beel y Beector.

Note: Point out that many Spanish nouns ending in *-ción* have the same meaning as corresponding English nouns ending in *-tion: excepción.* Many Spanish adjectives ending in *-oso* have the same meaning as corresponding English adjectives ending in *-ous.*

15 Estos tres chicos, de quince, dieciséis, y diecisiete años respectivamente*, van a hacer un viaje en jeep* y en barco a México*[4] y Centroamérica* este año. Y después de consultar* muchos mapas y muchos libros, éste es el plan* de viaje que ellos tienen:

Salen de Washington el día 25 de junio y calculan* llegar a
20 Laredo, Tejas, cinco días más tarde. El jueves salen de Laredo,

---

[4] **México** is frequently written **Méjico.** Both spellings are correct.

pasan el Río Grande y entran* a México por Nuevo Laredo, donde pasan la noche, para luego continuar* su viaje hasta llegar al Distrito Federal, la capital, que también se llama México, D.F.

Note: Also called the Río Bravo. Both names are correct.

25 En México van a pasar unos diez días, más o menos, porque quieren visitar* muchos lugares. Quieren ver, por ejemplo*, las famosas* pirámides* de San Juan Teotihuacán, los museos* que tienen las reliquias* de las grandes civilizaciones* indias* de México, los puertos* de Acapulco en el Pacífico* y Veracruz en el Atlántico*. Y muchas cosas más.

Note: Immense pyramids near Mexico City, built by an empire which preceded the Aztec.

Note: Point out that a number of Spanish words with *ue* correspond to English nouns with a single vowel: *puerto.*

QUESTIONS

1. ¿Cómo se llaman los tres chicos en la narración?   *Title*
2. ¿Durante cuáles meses están de vacaciones los alumnos norteamericanos?   *1*
3. ¿Cómo pasan sus vacaciones ellos?   *2*
4. ¿Qué hacen los chicos activos?   *3*
5. ¿Qué hacen los chicos perezosos?   *6*
6. ¿Qué les gusta hacer a esos chicos que son especialmente activos y ambiciosos?   *10*
7. ¿Cuáles aventuras les gustan más?   *13*
8. ¿Cuántos años tienen Jeem, Beel, y Beector respectivamente?   *15*
9. ¿Qué van a hacer durante los meses de junio, julio, y agosto estos tres chicos? *16*

10. ¿Cómo van a viajar, en avión?   *16*
11. ¿Dónde y cuándo van a empezar su viaje? *19*
12. ¿Adónde van primero?   *20*
13. ¿Cuándo salen de Laredo?   *20*
14. ¿Por dónde entran a México?   *21*
15. ¿Hasta dónde van a continuar su viaje después de salir de Nuevo Laredo?   *22*
16. ¿Por qué van a pasar tantos días en la capital?   *25*
17. ¿Qué quieren visitar en México?   *26*
18. ¿Cómo se llaman las grandes pirámides? *26*
19. ¿Qué hay en los museos de México?   *27*

II ←————————————————————

NOTE: PART II OF NARRATIVE IS NOT INCLUDED IN RECORDED PROGRAM.

30 A mediados de julio Jeem, Beel, y Beector salen de México y continúan su viaje. Pasan por las seis pequeñas pero interesantes y pintorescas* repúblicas* de Centroamérica hasta llegar a Panamá, la capital de la república de Panamá.

En Panamá, según el plan de viaje, los chicos van a poner el 35 jeep en un barco de carga*. Panamá (la capital) está en la costa* del Pacífico y el barco tiene que pasar por el Canal* de Panamá para llegar a la costa del Atlántico. Los chicos también van a pasar el canal en barco, pero sentados en el jeep; de esta manera van a continuar el viaje por barco hasta Nueva Orleáns. No es 40 la manera ideal* de viajar, pero es barata.

Finalmente,* continúan en jeep hasta Washington, con la intención* de llegar allá a mediados de agosto.

Jeem, Beel, y Beector están muy contentos con respecto* a su proyecto*. Ya tienen los pasaportes* y las visas*, y tienen también
45 el permiso de sus padres, que es la cosa principal*. Necesitan dinero para comprar un jeep usado*, para la gasolina*, para la comida, y para los hoteles*.

Beel y Beector trabajan los sábados en un supermercado* y Jeem tiene una ruta* de periódicos. Ya tienen cien dólares*
50 economizados*, pero necesitan mucho más porque sólo el jeep, que van a comprar en un lugar de carros usados que se llama "Juan el Honesto", cuesta ciento noventa y nueve. Es un jeep del año '47 pero, según el Sr. Honesto, está en perfecta* condición*. Ellos creen que antes del quince de junio van a poder comprar el
55 jeep, y van a estar totalmente* preparados* para empezar el viaje.

Note: Point out that many Spanish words written with *y* have the same meaning as English words written with *j: proyecto.*

QUESTIONS

1. ¿Cuándo salen los tres chicos de México? 30
2. ¿Por cuáles repúblicas van a pasar? 31
3. ¿Qué van a hacer los chicos en Panamá? 34
4. ¿Dónde está Panamá (la capital)? 35
5. ¿Por dónde tiene que pasar el barco para llegar a la costa del Atlántico? 36
6. ¿Cómo van a pasar el canal los chicos? 38
7. ¿Adónde van a ir luego? ¿Cómo? 39
8. ¿Cuándo calculan llegar a Washington? 42
9. ¿Ya tienen sus pasaportes y sus visas? 44
10. ¿Tienen el permiso de sus padres para hacer el viaje? 45
45
11. ¿Para qué necesitan dinero? 45
12. ¿Dónde trabajan Beel y Beector? ¿y Jeem? 48
13. ¿Cuánto dinero tienen economizado ya? 49
14. ¿Ya tienen bastante para comprar el jeep? 52
15. ¿Van a comprar un carro nuevo? 53
16. ¿En qué condición está el jeep, según el Sr. Honesto? 53

Conversation Stimulus

¿Puede usted contar el proyecto de Jeem, Beel, y Beector?
¿Puede indicar* en un mapa la ruta de los tres chicos?

BASIC DIALOG

Mal servicio telefónico

CLIENTE   Tres veces he llamado y sigue ocupada la línea. ¡Ah, por fin! ¿Aló?   10-1
SECRETARIA   Salón de Belleza Venus, a sus órdenes.
CLIENTE   ¿No es el veinte-trece-cero cero? ¿Librería Campos?   10-2
SECRETARIA   No, está equivocado. Habla con el veinte-doce-cero cero.

CLIENTE   ¡Quinta vez! ¿Aló? ¿Está el Sr. Campos, por favor?   10-3
EMPLEADO   Acaba de salir. ¿Desea dejar algún recado?
CLIENTE   ¿Usted sabe si ya han recibido la segunda edición de . . .
EMPLEADO   Yo no sé nada. Ya todos han salido a almorzar.
CLIENTE   ¡Qué mala suerte! ¿Usted sabe el número de la ca . . . ¿aló? . . . Mmm . . .   10-4
colgó.

Bad Telephone Service

CUSTOMER   I've called three times and the line's still (continues) busy. Ah, at last! Hello?
SECRETARY   Venus Beauty Salon, at your service (orders).
CUSTOMER   Isn't this 20-13-00? Campos Bookstore?
SECRETARY   No, you have the wrong number (you're mistaken). This is 20-12-00.

CUSTOMER   Fifth time! Hello? Is Mr. Campos there, please?
CLERK   He has just left. Do you wish to leave a (some) message?
CUSTOMER   Do you know if they've received the second edition of . . .
CLERK   I don't know anything. They've all gone out to lunch already.
CUSTOMER   What (bad) luck! Do you know their home numb . . . hello? . . . Mmm . . .
He hung up.

◀ *Students leaf through books at an open-air bookstore in Spain.*

Supplement

Tres veces he marcado el número.		I've dialed the number three times.
Librería	10-1	
¿La Zapatería Campos?	10-2	Campos Shoe Store?
Peluquería	10-3, 10-4	Barber Shop, Beauty Shop
Oficina	10-5	Office
¿El Salón de Belleza?	10-4	
Está preocupado.	10-6	He's worried.
enojado	10-7	angry
mojado	10-8	wet
asustado	10-9	frightened
aburrido	10-10	bored
Está resfriado.	10-11	He has a cold.

Ésta es la primera vez.		This is the first time.
segunda		second
tercera		third
cuarta		fourth
quinta		fifth
sexta		sixth
séptima		seventh
octava		eighth
novena		ninth
décima		tenth

Note: Point out that in words in which the final consonant is z, the z changes to c before the plural ending -es. See Letter-Sound Correspondences, page 197.

Habla con el zapatero.	10-12	You're speaking with the shoemaker.
peluquero	10-13	barber, hairdresser
camarero	10-14	waiter
médico	10-15	doctor
dentista	10-16	dentist
jefe	10-17	boss
la criada	10-18	maid
la peluquería	10-19	
Todos han salido a bailar.	10-20	They've all gone out to dance.
cantar	10-21	sing
nadar	10-22	swim
¿Sabe usted la dirección de la casa?		Do you know the home address?

Note: At this time, you may wish to assign the section on People at Work in *Glimpses of the Spanish World.*

Listening and Speaking Exercises 163, 164, 165*, 166*, p. T89 ⊗

BASIC FORMS

Verbs

aburrir	dejar	nadar
acabar	enojar	ocupar
asustar	equivocar	preocupar
bailar	marcar	recibir
cantar	mojar	resfriar
colgar (ue)		

Nouns

cliente[1] *m.*	salón *m.*	orden *f.*
dentista *m.*	dirección *f.*	suerte *f.*
jefe[2] *m.*	edición *f.*	vez *f.*

Vocabulary Exercises

1. QUESTIONS

1. ¿Cuántas veces marca el número el cliente antes de hablar con la secretaria? *Tres veces.*
2. ¿Por qué no contestan? *La línea esta ocupada.*
3. ¿Contestan por fin? *Sí, contestan.*
4. ¿Qué dice la secretaria cuando contesta el teléfono? *Salón de Belleza Venus, a sus órdenes.*
5. ¿Con cuál número quiere hablar el cliente? *Con el veinte-trece-cero cero.*
6. ¿Es ése el número del salón de belleza? *No.*
7. ¿Cuál es el número de teléfono del Salón Venus? *Veinte-doce-cero cero.*
8. ¿Cómo es el servicio telefónico, bueno o malo? *Es malo.*
9. ¿Cuál es el número de teléfono de su casa?
10. ¿Sabe usted el número de teléfono de la oficina de su padre?
11. ¿Le gusta a usted ir a la peluquería?
12. ¿Cuántas veces va al mes?

---

[1] **Cliente** has a special feminine form: **clienta.**

[2] **Jefe** has a special feminine form: **jefa.**

2. QUESTIONS

1. ¿A quién llama el cliente? Al Sr. Campos.
2. ¿Quién contesta la quinta vez que llama? Un empleado de la Librería Campos.
3. ¿Está el Sr. Campos? No, no está.
4. ¿Dónde trabaja el Sr. Campos, en una oficina? No, en una librería.
5. ¿Dónde trabaja su padre, en una oficina o en otro lugar?
6. ¿Cuál es la dirección de su casa?
7. ¿Deja un recado el cliente? No, no deja un recado.
8. ¿Qué desea saber el cliente? Si han recibido la segunda edición de un libro.
9. ¿Sabe el empleado si tienen el libro que el cliente quiere? No, él no sabe nada.
10. ¿Qué le quiere preguntar el cliente? El número de la casa del Sr. Campos.
11. ¿Le contesta el empleado? No, no le contesta.
12. ¿Qué hace el empleado? Cuelga el teléfono.
13. ¿Cómo se llama un señor que arregla zapatos? ¿y el lugar donde uno compra zapatos? Un zapatero. Una zapatería.
14. ¿Cómo se llama un señor que arregla pelo? Un peluquero.
15. Y un peluquero, ¿dónde trabaja? En una peluquería. (En un salón de belleza.)
16. ¿Dónde trabaja un camarero? En un restaurante.
17. ¿A usted le gusta bailar? ¿Baila bien?
18. ¿Sabe usted cantar? ¿Cuáles canciones sabe?

In areas where many people do not have private phones, one can place a call from a small shop.

3. SYNONYMS

Repeat each of the following sentences, replacing the underlined words with a word or expression that has the same meaning.

La señora está en el salón de belleza.   *La señora esta en la peluquería.*
La línea todavía está ocupada.   *La línea sigue ocupada.*
Finalmente contestan.   *Por fin contestan.*
¿Quiere dejar un recado?   *¿Desea dejar un recado?*
Es un señor que arregla zapatos.   *Es un zapatero.*

4. PATTERNED RESPONSE

¡Tres veces han llamado! ⊗   Sí, y ésta es la cuarta vez.
¡Dos veces han llamado!   *Sí, y ésta es la tercera vez.*
¡Cinco veces han llamado!   *Sí, y ésta es la sexta vez.*
¡Cuatro veces han llamado!   *Sí, y ésta es la quinta vez.*
¡Seis veces han llamado!   *Sí, y ésta es la séptima vez.*
¡Nueve veces han llamado!   *Sí, y ésta es la décima vez.*

5. BASIC DIALOG VARIATION

Change the second part of the Basic Dialog to narrative form. *Start like this:*
El cliente le pregunta al empleado si está el Sr. Campos. *El empleado le contesta que acaba de salir, y le pregunta si desea dejar algún recado. El cliente le empieza a preguntar al empleado si han recibido la segunda edición de un libro, pero el empleado le dice que él no sabe nada y que ya todos han salido a almorzar. El cliente dice ¡qué mala suerte!, y le quiere preguntar el número de la casa del Sr. Campos, pero el empleado cuelga el teléfono.*

GRAMMAR

The Present Perfect

PRESENTATION *TEACHER PRESENTATION, p. T185*

Tres veces **he llamado.**
Ya **he comido.**
Han recibido la segunda edición.
Todos **han salido** a almorzar.

Which two parts make up the verb in each of these sentences? Which ending is added to the stem + theme vowel of the second verb form? What is the theme vowel for the **-do** form of **e-** and **i**-class verbs?

GENERALIZATION

1. The present perfect is a compound tense in both Spanish and English. It consists of two parts: an auxiliary verb (**haber** in Spanish, *have* in English), and a form of the main verb called a past participle (**llamado** / *called*).

He llamado tres veces.
I have called three times.

2. For all but a few irregular verbs, the past participle is formed by adding **-do** to the stem + theme vowel. The theme vowel is **i** for both **e-** and **i-**class verbs.

	Stem	Theme vowel	Ending
a-class	**llam**	**a**	**do**
e-class	**com**	**i**	**do**
i-class	**recib**	**i**	**do**

3. Only the auxiliary **haber** changes form to show agreement with the subject.

he
has
ha   } **llamado, comido, recibido**
hemos
han

4. The present perfect in English and Spanish correspond closely in both form and meaning. There is one exception: the auxiliary **haber** and the main verb are not usually separated in Spanish, although they frequently are in English.

Ya he llamado tres veces.
I've already called three times.

¿Ya han salido ustedes a almorzar?
Have you already gone out to lunch?

5. The auxiliary verb **haber** must not be confused with the verb **tener**.

He comido.   **Tengo dinero.**
I have eaten.   *I have money.*

| *Note:* Teach Letter-Sound Correspondences (page 196) at this point.

STRUCTURE DRILLS

6. PERSON-NUMBER SUBSTITUTION

1. No han almorzado todavía. ⊗
   - (usted)
   - (mi compañero y yo)
   - (la secretaria)
   - (yo)
   - (tú)
   - (los camareros)

   No han almorzado todavía.
   No ha almorzado todavía.
   No hemos almorzado todavía.
   No ha almorzado todavía.
   No he almorzado todavía.
   No has almorzado todavía.
   No han almorzado todavía.

2. Ya ha recibido la carta. ⊗
   (yo–los señores–tú–mi padre y yo–ustedes)

   he recibido–han recibido–has recibido–
   hemos recibido–han recibido

7. ITEM SUBSTITUTION

1. Todo el mundo ha bailado. ⊗
   - (venir)
   - (ir)
   - (trabajar)
   - (comer)

   Todo el mundo ha bailado.   *VARIATION*
   Todo el mundo ha venido.   *hablar / hablado*
   Todo el mundo ha ido.   *llamar / llamado*
   Todo el mundo ha trabajado.   *salir / salido*
   Todo el mundo ha comido.   *oír / oído*

2. No han llegado todavía. ⊗
   (salir–empezar–leer–almorzar–cantar–entrar)

   salido–empezado–leído–almorzado–
   cantado–entrado

   VARIATION: Use infinitives in Drill 7.1

8. PRESENT → PRESENT PERFECT

El cliente deja un recado. ⊗
¿Nunca comes en ese restaurante?
Todo el mundo sale.
¿Cuelga el teléfono la secretaria?
Pasan horas en el salón de belleza.
El camarero trae el café.
Recibo muchas ediciones.
La línea está ocupada.

El cliente ha dejado un recado.
¿Nunca has comido en ese restaurante?
Todo el mundo ha salido.
¿Ha colgado el teléfono la secretaria?
Han pasado horas en el salón de belleza.
El camarero ha traído el café.
He recibido muchas ediciones.
La línea ha estado ocupada.

VARIATION: Use the right-hand column as stimulus and have student give present tense forms.

9. WRITING EXERCISE

Write the responses to Drills 6.2, 7.2, and 8.

EXERCISE BOOK: EXERCISES 1, 2, AND 3

10. PATTERNED RESPONSE

Ustedes van a estudiar ahora, ¿verdad? ⊗	No, señor, ya hemos estudiado.
Usted va a marcar el número ahora, ¿verdad?	*No, señor, ya he marcado el número.*
Los alumnos van a cantar ahora, ¿verdad?	*No, señor, ya han cantado.*
El jefe va a ir al banco ahora, ¿verdad?	*No, señor, ya ha ido al banco.*
La criada va a limpiar el cuarto ahora, ¿verdad?	*No, señor, ya ha limpiado el cuarto.*

11. FREE RESPONSE

¿Ha estado usted en México? ¿en Puerto Rico?
¿Ha viajado mucho?
¿Adónde ha ido?
¿Ha visitado muchos lugares interesantes?
¿Cuántas veces ha ido usted a nadar este año?
¿Cuántas veces ha tenido que venir su mamá a la escuela?
¿Ya han almorzado ustedes? ¿A qué hora almuerzan?

acabar de + *Infinitive*

TEACHER PRESENTATION, p. T186
GENERALIZATION

The English construction (*he*) *has just* + past participle is not expressed by the present perfect in Spanish, but by the special construction **acabar de** + infinitive. (*He*) *just* + past tense is expressed by the same special construction.

Listening and Speaking Exercises 171, 172, 173*, p. T93 ⊗   SECTION C

STRUCTURE DRILL

12. ENGLISH CUE DRILL

Acaba de llamar. ⊗	*Acaba de llamar.*
I've just come.	*Acabo de venir.*
He just hung up.	*Acaba de colgar.*
She just dialed.	*Acaba de marcar.*
We've just had breakfast.	*Acabamos de desayunar.*
They've just begun.	*Acaban de empezar.*
They just began.	*Acaban de empezar.*
He just called.	*Acaba de llamar.*

13. WRITING EXERCISE

Write the responses to Drill 12.

EXERCISE BOOK: EXERCISE 4

Past Participles as Adjectives

PRESENTATION *TEACHER PRESENTATION, p. T186*

El cliente está **equivocado.**
Los alumnos están **aburridos.**
Las chicas están **asustadas.**
La línea sigue **ocupada.**

Does the past participle show number and gender agreement with the noun it modifies in these sentences? Does it then function as a verb or as an adjective?

GENERALIZATION

1. In both Spanish and English, past participles are used not only in the present perfect tense but also as adjectives.

El banco está <u>cerrado.</u>   *The bank is <u>closed.</u>*
El chico está <u>equivocado.</u>   *The boy is <u>mistaken.</u>*
Un alumno <u>aburrido</u> no pone   *A <u>bored</u> student doesn't*
   atención.   *pay attention.*

2. Past participles do not change form to agree with the subject when they are part of the verb.

El chico ha comido.
Las chicas han comido.

Past participles used as adjectives do, however, agree in number and gender with the noun they modify, just like other adjectives.

El <u>banco</u> está cerrad<u>o.</u>
Los <u>bancos</u> están cerrad<u>os.</u>

La <u>puerta</u> está cerrad<u>a.</u>
Las <u>puertas</u> están cerrad<u>as.</u>

STRUCTURE DRILLS

14. ITEM SUBSTITUTION

1. Los alumnos están equivocados. ⊗   Los alumnos están equivocados.   *VARIATION*

   La secretaria _____.   La secretaria está equivocada.   La criada

   El empleado _____.   El empleado está equivocado.   El jefe

   Los médicos _____.   Los médicos están equivocados.   Los clientes

   Las chicas _____.   Las chicas están equivocadas.   Las señoras

2. El jefe sigue resfriado. ⊗   siguen resfriados–sigue resfriada–siguen resfriadas–sigue resfriado

   (los señores–la secretaria–las dos empleadas–el alumno)

   VARIATION: (los chicos–la maestra–las dos criadas–el empleado)

15. TRANSFORMATION DRILL

Han arreglado la sala. ⊗   La sala está arreglada.

Han cerrado los bancos.   *Los bancos están cerrados.*

Han mojado las ventanas.   *Las ventanas están mojadas.*

Han asustado al empleado.   *El empleado está asustado.*

Han cerrado la zapatería.   *La zapatería está cerrada.*

16. PROGRESSIVE SUBSTITUTION

La línea sigue ocupada. ⊗   *La línea sigue ocupada.*

___ señor _____.   *El señor sigue ocupado.*

_____ parece _____.   *El señor parece ocupado.*

_____ preocupados.   *Los señores parecen preocupados.*

___ maestra _____.   *La maestra parece preocupada.*

_____ sale _____.   *La maestra sale preocupada.*

_____ asustadas.   *Las maestras salen asustadas.*

___ chico _____.   *El chico sale asustado.*

ADDITIONAL STRUCTURE DRILL, p. T205 ⊗

17. WRITING EXERCISE

Write the responses to Drills 14.2, 15, and 16.

EXERCISE BOOK: EXERCISES 5, 6, AND 7

18. FREE RESPONSE

¿Dónde está *Pedro*? ¿Está resfriado hoy?

¿Y *Susana*? ¿Sigue resfriada ella?

¿Están ustedes cansados ahora?

¿Por qué? ¿Han estudiado mucho?

Pero ustedes nunca están aburridos en esta clase, ¿verdad?

¿Estudia bien un alumno cansado?
¿Parezco yo preocupado? ¿parezco cansado?
¿Están ustedes sentados ahora?

Adjective Position

TEACHER PRESENTATION, p. T186

GENERALIZATION

1. In Unit 7 you learned that the usual position of descriptive adjectives within a noun phrase is after the noun.

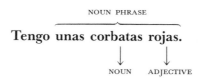

NOUN PHRASE

Tengo unas corbatas rojas.

↓ ↓
NOUN   ADJECTIVE

2. There is another class of adjectives called limiting adjectives. The usual position of limiting adjectives is before the noun they modify. The underlined adjectives in the following examples are limiting adjectives.

> **Tengo tres corbatas rojas.**
> **Hay muchas corbatas en esa tienda.**
> **¡Tiene tanto dinero!**

Limiting adjectives include:

a. cardinal and ordinal numbers: **uno, dos, . . . ; primero, segundo, . . .**

b. quantifiers (adjectives which indicate quantity): **mucho, poco, tanto, bastante, alguno, ninguno, . . .**

c. the possessive adjectives **mi, tu, su, . . .**

3. Some adjectives occur freely either before or after the noun they modify.

> **Es una maestra buena.**
> **Es una buena maestra.**
>
> **Es una película mala.**
> **Es una mala película.**
>
> **Es un baile nuevo.**
> **Es un nuevo baile.**

Note: Cases in which the meaning of an adjective varies according to whether it is placed before or after the noun will be discussed in Level III.

4. Some adjectives drop the final **o** before a masculine singular noun.

algún chico	*but*	**algunos chicos, alguna chica, algunas chicas**
buen chico	*but*	**buenos chicos, buena chica, buenas chicas**
mal chico	*but*	**malos chicos, mala chica, malas chicas**
primer chico	*but*	**primeros chicos, primera chica, primeras chicas**
tercer chico	*but*	**tercera chica**
ningún chico	*but*	**ninguna chica**

5. **Grande** has a shortened form which is used before any singular noun.

gran señor	*but*	**grandes señores**
gran señora	*but*	**grandes señoras**

Gran(de) means *great* when used before a noun, *large* or *big* when used after a noun.

un gran señor	*a great gentleman*
un señor grande	*a large (tall) gentleman*

STRUCTURE DRILLS

19. DOUBLE ITEM SUBSTITUTION

Tengo poco dinero.		Tengo poco dinero.	*VARIATION*
_____ amigos.	*Note:* Point out that *poco* means *few* when used with a plural noun.	Tengo pocos amigos.	tíos
_____ muchas ___.		Tengo muchas amigas.	algunas
_____ primos.		Tengo muchos primos.	amigos
_____ un _____.		Tengo un primo.	un
_____ hermana.		Tengo una hermana.	compañera
_____ tres _____.		Tengo tres hermanas.	tantos

Listening and Speaking Exercises 174, 175, 176*, p. T94 ⊗   SECTION D

20. EXPANSION DRILL

Hay médicos aquí. ⊗   Hay médicos aquí.
   (algunos)   Hay algunos médicos aquí.
   (franceses)   Hay algunos médicos franceses aquí.

Hay dentistas también.   *Hay dentistas también.*
   (italianos)   *Hay dentistas italianos también.*
   (tres)   *Hay tres dentistas italianos también.*

Es la chica que ha venido.   *Es la chica que ha venido.*
   (primera)   *Es la primera chica que ha venido.*
   (bonita)   *Es la primera chica bonita que ha venido.*

He comprado camisas.
   (dos)
   (rojas)

He comprado camisas.
He comprado dos camisas.
He comprado dos camisas rojas.

Hay restaurantes en Lima.
   (caros)
   (muchos)

Hay restaurantes en Lima.
Hay restaurantes caros en Lima.
Hay muchos restaurantes caros en Lima.

Es el cliente que ha llamado.
   (cuarto)
   (americano)

Es el cliente que ha llamado.
Es el cuarto cliente que ha llamado.
Es el cuarto cliente americano que ha llamado.

21. FREE RESPONSE

¿Conoce usted a algunos alumnos españoles? ¿a cuántos?
¿Tiene usted muchos compañeros simpáticos?
¿Hay muchas o pocas chicas bonitas en esta clase?
¿Cuántas? ¿Bastantes?
Y chicos guapos, ¿hay muchos?
Si hacemos una fiesta ahora, ¿le parece una mala idea, una buena idea, o una gran idea?

22. PAIRED SUBSTITUTIONS

Es una buena maestra. ⊗
_____ dentista.

Es una buena maestra.
Es un buen dentista.

¿Tienes algunas ideas?
¿_____ problema?

¿Tienes algunas ideas?
¿Tiene algún problema?

Es la primera vez que viene.
_____ día _____.

Es la primera vez que viene.
Es el primer día que viene.

¡Qué mal servicio!
¡_____ suerte!

¡Qué mal servicio!
¡Qué mala suerte!

Es la tercera cosa que he comprado hoy.
_____ libro _____.

Es la tercera cosa que he comprado hoy.
Es el tercer libro que he comprado hoy.

Estudia con un gran médico.
_____ maestros.

Estudia con un gran médico.
Estudia con unos grandes maestros.

No ha dejado ningún recado.
_____ cosa.

No ha dejado ningún recado.
No ha dejado ninguna cosa.

23. FREE SUBSTITUTION

Hay <u>muchas</u> <u>cosas</u> <u>bonitas</u> aquí.   *pocos, bastantes, algunos / vestidos, regalos, faldas / lindos, caros, baratos*

24. WRITING EXERCISE

Write the responses to Drills 20 and 22.
EXERCISE BOOK: EXERCISE 8

conocer *and* saber

TEACHER PRESENTATION, p. T187

GENERALIZATION

1. Two verbs must be distinguished in Spanish which correspond to two meanings of *know:* **conocer** and **saber.**

2. **Conocer** means *know* in the sense of *be acquainted with personally, know about from first hand experience.* Such knowledge cannot be communicated from one person to another. Thus, the objects of **conocer** are typically nouns referring to people one has met and places one has been to.

> **Mami, ¿conoces a Toni?**
> **Enrique conoce Perú porque ha estado allí.**

3. **Saber** means know in the sense of *possess factual information* or *know how to.* Such knowledge can be communicated from one person to another. **Saber,** unlike **conocer,** can be followed by an infinitive.

> **Mamá sabe dónde vive Toni.**
> **¿Sabes cuál es la capital de Perú?**
> **Patricio no sabe bailar.**

STRUCTURE DRILLS

Note: Before beginning these exercises, you may find it useful to say a few English sentences with a form of know, and have students tell whether a form of conocer or saber would be used in the Spanish equivalent. For example, I know John. (conocer) I know his name. (saber) I know how to swim. (saber)

25. PAIRED SENTENCES

No conocen España. ⊗
They don't know Spanish.
They don't know Spain.

No conocen España.
No saben español.
No conocen España.

Sé cuál es la capital de Colombia.
I know Colombia.
I know what the capital of Colombia is.

Sé cuál es la capital de Colombia.
Conozco Colombia.
Sé cuál es la capital de Colombia.

No sabe llegar al centro.
She doesn't know the downtown area.
She doesn't know how to get downtown.

No sabe llegar al centro.
No conoce el centro.
No sabe llegar al centro.

¿Sabes escribir "Susana"?	*¿Sabes escribir "Susana"?*
Do you know Susana?	*¿Conoces a Susana?*
Do you know how to write "Susana"?	*¿Sabes escribir "Susana"?*

26. PATTERNED RESPONSE

¿Ella? ¿al Sr. Fernández? ⊗	Sí, ella conoce al Sr. Fernández.
¿Juan? ¿leer francés?	*Sí, Juan sabe leer francés.*
¿Usted? ¿Buenos Aires?	*Sí, yo conozco Buenos Aires.*
¿Las chicas? ¿a todo el mundo?	*Sí, las chicas conocen a todo el mundo.*
¿El perro? ¿cerrar la puerta?	*Sí, èl perro sabe cerrar la puerta.*

27. WRITING EXERCISE

Write the responses to Drill 26.

EXERCISE BOOK: EXERCISES 9 AND 10

Listening and Speaking Exercise 177, p. T95 ⊗

Writing

1. MULTIPLE ITEM SUBSTITUTION

MODEL   Ha leído la carta.
          (yo) / empezar / examen
          <u>He empezado el examen.</u>

1. He visitado muchos lugares interesantes.
   (nosotros) / recibir / cartas   *Hemos recibido muchas cartas interesantes.*

2. ¿Has conocido a algunos señores importantes?
   (ellos) / dejar / recado   *¿Han dejado algún recado importante?*

3. Hemos comprado unos guantes lindísimos.
   (ella) / cantar / canciones   *Ha cantado unas canciones lindísimas.*

4. Ese señor es el primer cliente americano que ha venido.
   señoras / maestras / llamar   *Esas señoras son las primeras maestras americanas que han llamado.*

5. Ha estudiado con un gran maestro italiano.
   (yo) / trabajar / médicos   *He trabajado con unos grandes médicos italianos.*

6. Es la quinta vez que Juan ha llamado.
   libro / chicos / leer   *Es el quinto libro que los chicos han leído.*

7. ¿Usted conoce España?
   la criada / español   *¿La criada sabe español?*   (*continued*)

(*continued*)

8. El empleado no ha arreglado la tienda.
   camareros / limpiar / mesas   *Los camareros no han limpiado las mesas.*

9. La secretaria está enojada con el jefe.
   jefe / secretaria   *El jefe está enojado con la secretaria.*

10. La chica francesa está encantada con la idea.
    peluqueros / regalo   *Los peluqueros franceses están encantados con el regalo.*

2. PARAGRAPH COMPLETION

Copy the following paragraphs, filling in each of the blank spaces with the correct form of one of the verbs listed below.

economizar	leer	recibir	usar
empezar	tener	dar	consultar
preparar	ir	comprar	preocupar

Ya estamos totalmente __1__ para empezar el viaje. Hemos __2__ un jeep, y papá nos ha __3__ cien dólares para gasolina. Mi mamá está muy __4__ porque piensa que no vamos a tener bastante dinero, pero hemos __5__ durante todo el año y yo creo que sí, que vamos a tener bastante.

Hemos __6__ a la biblioteca dos o tres veces y hemos __7__ muchos mapas y libros. Yo ya he __8__ tres libros de viajes.

Las vacaciones no han __9__ todavía y he __10__ que estudiar mucho para los exámenes en estos días, pero acabo de __11__ mi pasaporte en el correo ¡y casi no puedo pensar en otra cosa que el viaje!

1	2	3	4	5	6	7	8	9
preparados	comprado	dado	preocupada	economizado	ido	consultado	leído	empezado

10	11
tenido	recibir

RECOMBINATION MATERIAL

Dialogs

I

PEDRO	Este . . . ¿Cómo te llamas?
ANITA	Anita.
PEDRO	Este . . . este . . . . ¿Quieres bailar conmigo, Anita?
ANITA	No gracias, me aprietan mucho los zapatos.
PEDRO	Bueno, ¿quieres tomar algo, entonces?

ANITA	No, no tengo sed.
PEDRO	Pero, este . . . ¿Me das tu dirección?
ANITA	¡Caramba! ¡Qué chico!

REJOINDERS

¿Quieres bailar conmigo? *Sí, gracias. / Claro. / No, gracias. / No, me aprietan los zapatos. / No, yo no sé bailar bien. / No, estoy muy cansada.*

II

EL SEÑOR	Señorita, ¿me puede dar el quince-dieciséis-treinta y cuatro, por favor?
LA SEÑORITA	¿Quince-diecisiete-treinta y cuatro?
EL SEÑOR	No, señorita, dieciséis.
LA SEÑORITA	¿Dieciséis-diecisiete-treinta y cuatro?
EL SEÑOR	. . . QUINCE-DIECISÉIS-TREINTA Y CUATRO.
LA SEÑORITA	Sí señor . . . . lo siento señor, la línea está ocupada. . .

CONVERSATION STIMULUS

You are trying to make a telephone call but the operator can't get the number right.

III

EL CLIENTE	Señorita, me trae dos huevos fritos, por favor.
LA CAMARERA	Lo siento, señor, no hay huevos.
EL CLIENTE	Bueno, carne con ensalada, entonces.
LA CAMARERA	Imposible. No hay más ensalada.
EL CLIENTE	¡El servicio en este restaurante es horrible!
LA CAMARERA	Lo siento mucho, señor. ¿Quiere carne con papas fritas, mejor?
EL CLIENTE	Bueno, y un poco de agua, por favor.
LA CAMARERA	Sí señor.
EL CLIENTE	¡¡Señorita!! Me ha mojado la camisa, la corbata, y los pantalones también. ¡Voy a hablar con su jefe inmediatamente! ¡¡¡IN-ME-DIA-TA-MEN-TE!!!

QUESTIONS

1. ¿Qué quiere comer el cliente?
2. ¿Qué le dice la camarera?

3. ¿Qué quiere el cliente entonces?
4. ¿Le trae carne con ensalada la camarera?

(*continued*)

(*continued*)

5. ¿Por qué no?
6. ¿Qué dice el cliente del servicio?
7. ¿Qué le quiere traer la camarera?
8. ¿Quiere él carne con papas fritas?
9. ¿Qué más quiere?

10. ¿Le trae agua la camarera?
11. ¿Está contento el cliente?
12. ¿Por qué no? ¿Qué le hace la camarera?
13. ¿Con quién quiere hablar el cliente?
14. ¿Cuándo? ¿Más tarde?

Note: Point out that many Spanish adjectives ending in *-ico* correspond to English adjectives ending in *-ic*: *artístico*. Many which end in *-cional* correspond to English adjectives ending in *-tional*. Many nouns ending in *-dad* correspond to English nouns ending in *-ty*: *personalidad, electricidad*.

Narrative

El teléfono

Ese aparato* feo y de color negro, de figura* poco artística*, frío de personalidad*, ese instrumento* que un señor con uniforme* de la Compañía* Nacional* de Electricidad* colgó en una pared° de la cocina de mi casa, ése es nuestro° indispensable* y
5 sincero* amigo, el teléfono.

Si de todos los aparatos eléctricos* que la técnica* moderna ha creado*, alguien me dice que solamente uno puedo tener en mi casa, y me ordena* eliminar* todos los otros, yo inmediatamente selecciono* el teléfono y elimino el refrigerador*, el
10 radio, y todos los otros que tenemos en la casa, inclusive* la televisión* en colores que es tan bonita.

Yo no puedo vivir sin el teléfono. Y si puedo, no quiero. Yo he estado acostumbrado* toda mi vida° a tener ese intermediario*, ese contacto* inmediato* con mis compañeros de escuela,
15 con mi novia, con el médico, con el mercado, con el cine, con la persona* que nos informa* si va a llover o va a hacer frío o calor, con la señorita que nos dice qué hora es. Y ese intermediario es mi amigo, nuestro teléfono.

¿Pero quién soy yo? Yo soy yo, pero puede ser mi madre quien
20 escribe esto, o mi padre, o uno de mis hermanos o la criada* Concepción, o la tía que vive con nosotros; porque todos tenemos ese gran afecto* por el teléfono, un afecto más grande que el que le tenemos al perro y a los otros animales* domésticos* de mi casa.

Especialmente* mi tía y mi "simpática" hermanita de catorce
25 años; ellas son las mejores amigas del teléfono, ellas monopolizan* sus servicios por dos y tres horas todos los días°. Pero todos

¿Qué hay en la pared?
¿Una foto?
¿De qué color es la pared?
¿Cuántas paredes hay?
pared *f: wall*
nuestro: *our*
¿Cuántos alumnos hay en nuestra clase?

vida: *life*
¿Es fácil o difícil la vida de un alumno? ¿Por qué?

Note: In Spanish-speaking countries, many families have full-time live-in servants.
¿Estudian ustedes todos los días?
¿Qué hacen ustedes todos los días?
todos los días: *every day*

Note: In Spanish-speaking countries it is not unusual for a widowed grandmother or an unmarried aunt to live with the family.

nosotros también debemos confesar* que somos adictos*, unos
más y otros menos, que todos sufrimos* de "telefonitis*" crónica*
y que a todos nos parece que este hábito* es un buen hábito.

30   Mi padre también sufre de "telefonitis", pero él casi no tiene
oportunidad* de usar el teléfono. No es que no quiere, es que no
puede. Cada° vez que quiere usar* el teléfono, está ocupado por
alguien; o es mamá que habla con mi abuela, o mi hermana que
escucha un disco nuevo que una de sus amigas acaba de comprar,

35 o mi tía que llama a otra tía, o la criada que conversa* con su
novio, el zapatero. Entonces, y esto ocurre* frecuentemente*, mi
papá* pierde° la paciencia* y furioso* comienza* a gritar:
    —¡¡POR QUÉ SÓLO YO, EL JEFE DE LA CASA, NO
PUEDO USAR EL TELÉFONO NUNCA!! ¡¡QUIERO SABER

40 QUIÉN ES EL JEFE EN ESTA CASA!! (Silencio*, nadie°
contesta.)
    —¡Si quiero llamar de mi casa a la oficina, el teléfono está
ocupado! ¡Si quiero llamar de la oficina a mi casa, la línea está
ocupada! (Nadie dice nada.)

45   —¡Caramba! —grita papá repetidas* veces en protesta*, pero
el silencio continúa. Finalmente, después de tanta protesta,
reaccionan* mamá y mi tía.
    —Shh, Mauricio, por favor. ¡Cómo gritas, no estamos sordas!
    Ése es el teléfono de la casa, nuestro bueno y estimado amigo,

50 siempre° ocupado.

cada: *each*
¿Tiene cada alumno un libro de español?

perder (ie): *lose*
¿Su padre pierde la paciencia con usted?

nadie: *no one*
Nadie habla ruso aquí, ¿verdad?
¿Habla alemán alguién?

siempre: *always*
¿Está siempre ocupado el teléfono de su casa? ¿Por qué?

QUESTIONS

1. ¿Cómo es el teléfono del narrador*?   *1*
2. ¿Quién colgó el teléfono en su casa?   *2*
3. ¿Dónde colgó el teléfono?   *4*
4. ¿Cuáles aparatos eléctricos modernos menciona* el autor?   *9*
5. ¿Dice el autor que puede vivir sin el teléfono?   *12*
6. ¿Quiere vivir sin él?   *12*
7. ¿A quiénes está acostumbrado a llamar?   *14*
8. ¿Quiénes más usan el teléfono en la casa del narrador?   *19*
9. ¿Quién es Concepción?   *20*
10. ¿Qué prefiere el narrador, el teléfono o sus animales domésticos?   *23*

11. ¿Cuáles son las personas que más monopolizan el teléfono?   *24*
12. ¿El narrador realmente* cree que su hermana es simpática?   *24*
13. ¿De qué sufre toda la familia?   *28*
14. ¿A la familia le parece su "telefonitis" un buen o un mal hábito?   *29*
15. ¿Sufre el padre de "telefonitis" también?   *30*
16. ¿Por qué no tiene oportunidad de usar el teléfono?   *32*
17. ¿Por quiénes está ocupado casi siempre el aparato?   *33*
18. ¿Con quién habla la mamá?   *33*

(*continued*)

(continued)

19. ¿Qué hace la hermana por teléfono? 34
20. ¿A quién llama la tía? 35
21. ¿Con quién conversa la criada? 35
22. ¿Qué ocurre cuando el padre quiere usar el teléfono y no puede? 37

23. ¿Qué grita él? 38
24. ¿Qué dice la familia cuando él empieza a gritar? 46
25. ¿Quiénes reaccionan por fin? 47
26. ¿Qué dicen ellas? 48

Conversation Stimulus

Usted habla de algo muy interesante con un amigo, pero su papá quiere usar el teléfono.

Start like this: José, te tengo que contar algo
muy importante: *Mañana hay un examen de geografía y . . .*
¿TODAVÍA ESTÁS *hablando* ?
Sí papi, *le tengo que contar algo a José.*
Necesito *usar el teléfono inmediatamente.*
Pero, papi, esto es importante.
¡Por qué sólo yo, el jefe de la casa, no puedo usar el teléfono nunca!
No puedo hablar más, José. Mi papá quiere usar el teléfono.

LETTER ↔ SOUND CORRESPONDENCES

Note: Teach this lesson with Grammar section beginning on page 181 (The Present Perfect).

READING: i, y, u AFTER ANOTHER VOWEL

When the letters **i, y,** or **u** follow another vowel, the two vowel sounds together are pronounced as one syllable.

FAMILIAR WORDS   baile, traigo, seis, veinte, treinta, oigo,
hoy, soy, estoy, muy, Luis, Luisa,
restaurante, reunión

UNFAMILIAR WORDS   caigo, Zoila, peine, auto, causa, Mauro, Europa

READING: í = [í]; ú = [ú]

The letters **í** (i with a written accent) and **ú** (u with a written accent) after another vowel are a separate, stressed syllable.

FAMILIAR WORDS   distraído, traído, leído, oído, Raúl |*Note:* Point out the past participles.

UNFAMILIAR WORDS   caído, país, aún, baúl

PAIRS   traigo   caigo   oigo   ley   rey   aunque
                        traído   caído   oído   leído   reído   aún

WRITING

Spelling Note: Whenever **i** or **u** follows any other vowel and is pronounced as a separate stressed syllable, it must be written with an accent mark.

WRITING: SPELLING CHANGES IN THE PLURAL

z → c

In words in which the final consonant is **z**, the **z** changes to **c** before the plural ending **es**. This change is just a convention. It is not needed to retain the sound [s].

vez   veces

SENTENCES

1. Luis, ¿cuántas veces has leído este libro? ¡Seis!
2. ¿Qué te han traído? Veinte pesos.
3. Yo no oigo nada. ¿Tú has oído algo?

WRITING

Copy the above sentences and be prepared to write them from dictation.

BASIC DIALOG

Un dictado

MAESTRA	¿Están listos? ¿Dónde está Eugenio? `11-1`
GARCÍA[1]	Acaba de salir. Anda tomando agua.
MAESTRA	¡Qué barbaridad! Ni siquiera pide permiso. Bien, ¿listos? `11-2`
SALGADO	¡Pst, García! ¿Me prestas tu pluma? Esta cosa no sirve. `11-3`
GARCÍA	¿Mi pluma? ¿Estás loco? ¿Y con qué escribo yo?
MAESTRA	¡Sh, silencio! ". . . No es el indio ni el español . . . coma . . ." `11-4`
SALGADO	No tan rápido, por favor. ¿Puede repetir la frase? `11-5`
MAESTRA	Usted no está poniendo atención, ¡eso es lo que pasa!
SALGADO	Es que García está molestando. `11-6`
GARCÍA	¡YO! ¡Qué mentira! ¡Yo no estoy haciendo nada!

A Dictation

TEACHER	Are you ready? Where's Eugenio?
GARCÍA	He just left. He's out drinking water.
TEACHER	That's awful! He doesn't even ask permission. All right, ready?
SALGADO	Pst, García! Will you lend me your pen? This thing's no good (doesn't serve).
GARCÍA	My pen? Are you crazy? And what'll I write with?
TEACHER	Shh, quiet! ". . . It's neither the Indian nor the Spaniard . . . comma . . ."
SALGADO	Not so fast, please. Can you repeat the sentence?
TEACHER	You're not paying (putting) attention, that's what's the matter!
SALGADO	It's that García's fooling around (bothering).
GARCÍA	ME! What a lie! I'm not doing anything!

---

[1] Boys and men are often addressed by their last name in Spanish-speaking countries.

◀ *Most Catholic schools—and many public schools, too—are not co-educational.*

◀ *Note:* Except in some rural areas, schools in Spain are not co-ed. In Spanish America, the percentage of co-ed schools varies from country to country.

199

Supplement

Es un trabajo muy difícil.		It's a very difficult job (work).
una tarea		assignment
una lección		lesson
tu pluma	11-1	
¿Me prestas tu cuaderno?	11-2	Will you lend me your notebook?
tus apuntes		your notes
Este papel no sirve.	11-3	This paper's no good.
lápiz	11-4	pencil
pupitre²	11-5	desk
escritorio	11-6	desk

No es el español . . . punto.	It's not the Spaniard . . . period.
dos puntos	colon
punto y coma	semicolon
signo de interrogación	question mark
signo de exclamación	exclamation mark
No tan despacio.	Not so slowly.
pronto	soon
¿Puede repetir la palabra?	Can you repeat the word?
el párrafo	the paragraph

Listening and Speaking Exercises 178, 179, 180*, 181*, p. T96 ⊗

BASIC FORMS

Verbs

andar   prestar
molestar   *repetir
*pedir   *servir

Nouns

apunte *m.*	atención *f.*	frase *f.*
lápiz *m.*	barbaridad *f.*	interrogación *f.*
papel *m.*	exclamación *f.*	lección *f.*
pupitre *m.*		

---

²**Pupitre** refers to a small desk used by students in a classroom. Otherwise, the equivalent of *desk* is **escritorio**.

Vocabulary Exercises

1. QUESTIONS

1. ¿Qué les pregunta la maestra a los alumnos?
2. ¿Están los alumnos listos para el dictado?
3. ¿Está Eugenio en su lugar?
4. ¿Dónde anda?
5. ¿Por qué está enojada la maestra?
6. ¿Qué le pide Salgado a García?
7. ¿García le quiere prestar su pluma?
8. ¿Por qué no? ¿No tiene otra?
9. ¿Hay muchos dictados en esta clase?
10. ¿Hay un dictado todos los días?
11. ¿Tienen ustedes mucha tarea?
12. ¿Dónde está su pupitre? Y mi escritorio, ¿dónde está?
13. ¿Tiene usted un lápiz? ¿y una pluma? ¿y un cuaderno?

Les pregunta si están listos.

No. Eugenio no está en clase, y Salgado no tiene pluma.

No, no está en su lugar.

Anda tomando agua.

Ni siquiera pide permiso.

Le pide una pluma.

No, no le quiere prestar su pluma.

No, no tiene otra.

2. DIALOG RECALL

listos

anda

ni siquiera

prestas

loco

cuaderno

lápiz

escritorio

¿Están listos?

Anda tomando agua.

Ni siquiera pide permiso.

¿Me prestas tu pluma?

¿Estás loco?

¿Me prestas tu cuaderno?

Este lápiz no sirve.

Este escritorio no sirve.

---

3. QUESTIONS

1. ¿Cómo empieza el dictado?
2. ¿Cómo habla la maestra, según Salgado, rápido o despacio?
3. ¿Qué le pregunta Salgado a la maestra?
4. ¿Qué le contesta ella?
5. ¿Por qué no entiende Salgado, según la maestra?
6. ¿Y según Salgado?
7. ¿Qué dice García?
8. Usted siempre pone atención en clase, ¿verdad?
9. ¿Pierde la paciencia el maestro cuando ustedes no ponen atención?

No es el indio ni el español . . .

Habla rápido.

Si puede repetir la frase.

Que él no está poniendo atención.

No está poniendo atención.

García esta molestando.

¡Qué mentira!

4. WORD REPLACEMENT

Repeat each of the following sentences, replacing the underlined words with any other appropriate word.

1. Es un dictado muy fácil.
2. Nunca tomamos café.
3. Necesito una pluma para el dictado.
4. La maestra repite la palabra.
5. ¡No tan pronto!

Es una lección muy fácil.   *(una tarea, un trabajo)*
Nunca tomamos té (agua, leche).
Necesito un lápiz (un papel) para el dictado.
La maestra repite el párrafo (la frase, el número).
¡No tan rápido! (despacio).

5. PUNCTUATION DRILL

Read the following sentences aloud, including the punctuation marks.

¿Estás loco?
¡Shh, silencio!
No tan rápido, por favor.
Anda tomando agua; siempre toma agua.
Éste es el problema: nadie está poniendo atención.
¡Qué mentira! ¿Qué estoy haciendo yo?

signo de interrogación / signo de interrogación
signo de exclamación / coma / signo de exclamación
coma / punto
punto y coma / punto
dos puntos / punto
signo de exclamación / signo de exclamación / signo de interrogación / signo de interrogación

GRAMMAR

Stem Alternation: e-i
i-*Class Verbs*

PRESENTATION   *TEACHER PRESENTATION, p. T187*

Ni siquiera **pi**do permiso.
Ni siquiera **pi**de permiso.
Ni siquiera **pe**dimos permiso.

Which vowel occurs in the stem of the verb forms in the first two sentences? in the third? Which vowel occurs in the stem when there is a stressed **i** in the next syllable? Which vowel occurs otherwise?

GENERALIZATION

1. Some **i**-class verbs have a type of stem alternation not found in **a**-class and **e**-class verbs: the last stem vowel is **e** if a stressed **i** occurs in the next syllable; otherwise the last stem vowel is **i**.

No stressed **i** in next syllable	Stressed **i** in next syllable
p<u>i</u>do	p<u>e</u>dir
p<u>i</u>des	p<u>e</u>dimos
p<u>i</u>de	
p<u>i</u>den	

2. Other verbs which show **e-i** alternation are **seguir**,[3] **repetir,** and **servir.**

Listening and Speaking Exercises 182, 183, 184*, p. T98 ⊗   SECTION B

STRUCTURE DRILLS

6. PERSON-NUMBER SUBSTITUTION

1. No pide permiso. ⊗   No pide permiso.
   (yo)   No pido permiso.
   (tú)   No pides permiso.
   (Ana y yo)   No pedimos permiso.
   (ustedes)   No piden permiso.
   (ella)   No pide permiso.

2. Repito el número. ⊗   *repite–repetimos–repiten–*
   (usted–nosotros–Susana y él–yo–tú)   *repito–repites*

7. PAIRED SENTENCES

   Sirvo el té ahora. ⊗   Sirvo el té ahora.
   (nosotros)   Servimos el té ahora.
   (yo)   Sirvo el té ahora.   (*continued*)

---

[3] The first person singular of **seguir** is **sigo.** The **u** which occurs in the other present tense forms is not required in order to retain the sound [g̸] in the first person singular. See page 65.

(*continued*)

Sigue ocupado.
   (nosotros)
   (él)

Sigue ocupado.
Seguimos ocupados.
Sigue ocupado.

Repiten el párrafo.
   (nosotros)
   (ellos)

Repiten el párrafo.
Repetimos el párrafo.
Repiten el párrafo.

Le pido un lápiz.
   (nosotros)
   (yo)

Le pido un lápiz.
Le pedimos un lápiz.
Le pido un lápiz.

¿Cuándo sirven la cena?
   (nosotros)
   (ellos)

¿Cuándo sirven la cena?
¿Cuándo servimos la cena?
¿Cuándo sirven la cena?

Sigo enojado.
   (nosotros)
   (yo)

Sigo enojado.
Seguimos enojados.
Sigo enojado.

8. WRITING EXERCISE

Write the responses to Drills 6.2 and 7.

EXERCISE BOOK: EXERCISE 1

The Irregular Verb decir

TEACHER PRESENTATION, p. T188

GENERALIZATION

Decir is like other **i**-class verbs with **e-i** stem alternation, except that the first person singular is **digo.**

No stressed **i** in next syllable	Stressed **i** in next syllable
digo	de̲cir
di̲ces	de̲cimos
di̲ce	
di̲cen	

STRUCTURE DRILLS

9. PERSON-NUMBER SUBSTITUTION

Siempre dice la verdad. ⊗   Siempre dice la verdad.
   (nosotros)   Siempre decimos la verdad.
   (yo)   Siempre digo la verdad.
   (ustedes)   Siempre dicen la verdad.
   (Juan)   Siempre dice la verdad.
   (mis amigos y yo)   Siempre decimos la verdad.
   (tú)   Siempre dices la verdad.

10. SINGULAR → PLURAL

Nunca pido permiso. ⊗   Nunca pedimos permiso.
Repito el párrafo.   *Repetimos el párrafo.*
Digo la verdad.   *Decimos la verdad.*
Sigo ocupado.   *Seguimos ocupados.*
¿Sirvo la cena ahora?   *¿Servimos la cena ahora?*

11. PLURAL → SINGULAR

No pedimos nada. ⊗   No pido nada.
Repetimos la lección.   *Repito la lección.*
No decimos eso.   *No digo eso.*
Seguimos resfriados.   *Sigo resfriado.*
¿Servimos té o café?   *¿Sirvo té o café?*

12. FREE RESPONSE

¿Piden permiso ustedes cuando salen de la clase?
¿Pide usted permiso cuando sale de la casa? ¿a quién? ¿a su padre?
¿A qué hora sirven la cena en su casa?
¿Quién sirve la cena, usted o su mamá, o ustedes dos?
¿Dice usted siempre la verdad? ¿casi siempre?
¿Sirve la pluma de Salgado?
¿Sirve esta pluma? ¿y estos lápices?
¿Para qué sirve un lápiz?

13. WRITING EXERCISE

Write the responses to Drills 10 and 11.
EXERCISE BOOK: EXERCISES 2 AND 3

The Present Progressive

PRESENTATION *TEACHER PRESENTATION, p. T188*

Anda tomando agua.
García **está molestando.**

Which two parts make up the verb in each of these sentences? What is the theme vowel of the verbs which constitute the second part? What ending is added to the stem + theme vowel?

Usted no **está poniendo** atención.
Yo no **estoy haciendo** nada.
¿**Está escribiendo** una carta?

Which two parts make up the verb in each of these sentences? To which verb classes do the verbs which constitute the second part belong? What is the theme vowel of **e**-class and **i**-class verbs when the **-ndo** ending is attached?

GENERALIZATION

1. Like the present perfect, the present progressive is a compound tense in both English and Spanish. It consists of an auxiliary verb (**estar** in Spanish, *be* in English) followed by a form of the main verb called the present participle (**poniendo** / *paying*).

   Usted no está <u>poniendo</u> atención.
   You <u>aren't</u> <u>paying</u> attention.

2. In Spanish the present participle is formed by attaching the ending **-ndo** to the stem + theme vowel. In the present participle of **e**-class and **i**-class verbs, the theme vowel is **-ie** [ye].

	Stem	Theme Vowel	Ending
a-class	**llam**	**a**	**ndo**
e-class	**com**	**ie**	**ndo**
i-class	**recib**	**ie**	**ndo**

In **e**-class and **i**-class verbs whose stem ends in a vowel, and in the verb **ir,** the **ie** of the present participle is spelled **ye.**

leer	→	le<u>y</u>endo
creer	→	cre<u>y</u>endo
ir	→	<u>y</u>endo

In the small group of **i**-class verbs with **e-i** stem alternation, the vowel which occurs in the stem of the present participle is **i,** since there is no stressed **i** in the next syllable.

decir	→	diciendo
pedir	→	pidiendo
repetir	→	repitiendo
seguir	→	siguiendo
servir	→	sirviendo

3. In the present progressive only **estar**—never the present participle—changes form to show agreement with the subject.

El chico est<u>á</u> molestando.
Los chicos est<u>án</u> molestando.
Nosotros est<u>amos</u> molestando.

4. In Spanish, the present progressive is used only to refer to events going on at the moment of speaking. In English, the present progressive may be used to indicate future events; in such cases Spanish normally requires the simple present.

Juan sale mañana.
John is leaving tomorrow.

In English, the simple present may be used to refer to events which occur repeatedly, but which may not be going on at the moment of speaking: *John eats a lot* (usually, although he may be sleeping right now); but only the present progressive—never the simple present —is used for on-going events: *John is eating right now.* Spanish speakers, however, use the simple present both for events which occur repeatedly and for on-going events.

Juan come ahora.
Juan está comiendo ahora.

What is the difference between these two sentences? The first one simply names the activity. The second not only names the activity, but also emphasizes the fact that it is in progress at the moment of speaking.

5. Several verbs besides **estar** may occur as auxiliaries before a present participle. So far you have learned **seguir** and **andar.**

(*continued*)

(continued)

a. Literally, **seguir** means *continue, follow*. When used as an auxiliary in the present progressive, the usual English equivalents are *keep on ...ing, still be ...ing.*

García sigue molestando.
García keeps on fooling around.

Los alumnos siguen poniendo atención.
The students are still paying attention.

b. The literal meaning of **andar** is *walk, go*. When used as an auxiliary in the present progressive, the usual English equivalents are *be out ...ing* or *go around ...ing.*

Anda tomando agua.
He's out drinking water.

¿Por qué andas diciendo eso?
Why do you go around saying that?

Listening and Speaking Exercises 185, 186, 187*, p. T100 ⊗   SECTION C

STRUCTURE DRILLS

14. INFINITIVE → PRESENT PARTICIPLE

1. García está molestando. ⊗   García está molestando.   *VARIATION*
   - (nadar)   García está nadando.   (escribir)   *escribiendo*
   - (salir)   García está saliendo.   (jugar)   *jugando*
   - (comer)   García está comiendo.   (desayunar)   *desayunando*
   - (leer)   García está leyendo.   (almorzar)   *almorzando*
   - (pensar)   García está pensando.
   - (perder)   García está perdiendo.
   - (gritar)   García está gritando.

2. ¿Siguen trabajando en México? ⊗
   - (vivir, estudiar, viajar)   *viviendo–estudiando–viajando*

3. ¿Qué andan diciendo? ⊗
   - (repetir, seguir, pedir)   *repitiendo–siguiendo–pidiendo*

15. PRESENT → PRESENT PROGRESSIVE

La maestra hace un dictado. ⊗   La maestra está haciendo un dictado.
Los alumnos no ponen atención.   *Los alumnos no están poniendo atención.*
Un chico sale.   *Un chico está saliendo.*
Otro chico habla con su amigo.   *Otro chico está hablando con su amigo.*

Nadie escucha a la maestra.   *Nadie está escuchando a la maestra.*
La maestra les grita.   *La maestra les está gritando.*
Todos los alumnos escriben el dictado.   *Todos los alumnos están escribiendo el dictado.*

16. WRITING EXERCISE

Write the responses to Drills 14.2, 14.3, and 15.
EXERCISE BOOK: EXERCISES 4, 5 AND 6

More about Negation

PRESENTATION *TEACHER PRESENTATION, p. T190*

Nada le gusta.
Nadie pone atención.
Ninguno de los dos es mayor.
Allá **nunca** llueve.
Eugenio **tampoco** pide permiso.
Ni el indio **ni** el español están aquí.

Which is the negative word in each of these sentences? What is its position in relation to the verb?

No le gusta **nada.**
No pone atención **nadie.**
No es mayor **ninguno** de los dos.
Allá **no** llueve **nunca.**
Eugenio **no** pide permiso **tampoco.**
No están aquí **ni** el indio **ni** el español.

Which is the negative word in each of these sentences, aside from **no**? What is its position in relation to the verb? Which word precedes the verb when these negative words follow it?

GENERALIZATION

1. In Unit 2 you learned that in the simplest cases Spanish sentences are made negative by the insertion of **no** before the verb form which has a person-number ending.

   Juan <u>no</u> estudia mucho.

2. There are other negative words in Spanish in addition to **no.** Each Spanish word in the left-hand box of the following chart has a negative counterpart, shown on the right.

algo	*something*	**nada**	*nothing*
alguien	*someone, somebody*	**nadie**	*no one, nobody*
alguno	*some* (particular one)	**ninguno**	*none, no*
algunas veces	*sometimes*	**nunca**	*never*
también	*also, too*	**tampoco**	*either, neither*
o	*or*	**ni**	*nor*

a. Like **uno, ninguno** and **alguno** have no final <u>o</u> before a masculine singular noun: **ningún chico,** but **ninguna chica, ninguno de los chicos** (*none of the boys*), and **ninguna de las chicas** (*none of the girls*). **Ninguno** does not normally occur in the plural.

b. There is no one-word Spanish equivalent for *sometimes;* literally, **algunas veces** means *some times.*

c. Both **o** and **ni** may be used in pairs, meaning *either . . . or* and *neither . . . nor:* **o** el español <u>o</u> el indio, <u>*either*</u> *the Spaniard* <u>*or*</u> *the Indian;* **ni** el español **ni** el indio, <u>*neither*</u> *the Spaniard* <u>*nor*</u> *the Indian.*

d. The equivalent for *not even* is **ni siquiera.**

> **Ni siquiera estudia.**
> *He doesn't even study.*

3. Sentences using any of these negative words may occur in two forms, both with the same meaning.

Negative + Verb	*No + Verb + Negative*	
Nada le gusta.	**No le gusta nada.**	*Nothing pleases him.*
Nadie va a ir.	**No va a ir nadie.**	*Nobody is going to go.*
Ninguno de los chicos estudia.	**No estudia ninguno de los chicos.**	*None of the boys study.*
Yo nunca voy.	**Yo no voy nunca.**	*I never go.*
Tampoco estudia	**No estudia tampoco.**	*He doesn't study either.*
Ni Juan ni Pedro van.	**No van ni Juan ni Pedro.**	*Neither John nor Peter is going.*

4. If a negative word appears after the verb, **no** or another negative word must appear before the verb. In Spanish, negation is marked at every opportunity.

Yo <u>no</u> le doy <u>nada</u> a <u>nadie</u> <u>nunca</u>.

I never give anybody anything.

STRUCTURE DRILLS

17. AFFIRMATIVE → NEGATIVE

¿Entiende alguien la lección? ⊗	¿No entiende nadie la lección?
Estudio con ellos algunas veces.	*No estudio con ellos nunca.*
¿Hay algo en el escritorio?	*¿No hay nada en el escritorio?*
Quiero ir o con Pedro o con Juan.	*No quiero ir ni con Pedro ni con Juan.*
La maestra habla con algunos de los alumnos.	*La maestra no habla con ninguno de los alumnos.*
¿Tú estudias español también?	*¿Tú no estudias español tampoco?*

18. no + NEGATIVE WORD → NEGATIVE WORD

No está listo nadie. ⊗	Nadie está listo.
No es español ninguno de los dos.	*Ninguno de los dos es español.*
No me prestas nunca tus apuntes.	*Nunca me prestas tus apuntes.*
No le gusta nada a García.	*Nada le gusta a García.*
No hace la tarea nadie.	*Nadie hace la tarea.*
No quiero estudiar tampoco.	*Tampoco quiero estudiar.*
No sirven ni el lápiz ni la pluma.	*Ni el lápiz ni la pluma sirven.*

VARIATION

Cue answers in right-hand column and have student give *no* + negative word construction.

19. NEGATIVE WORD → no + NEGATIVE WORD

Nunca tomo café. ⊗	No tomo café nunca.
Tampoco quiero agua.	*No quiero agua tampoco.*
Nada le gusta.	*No le gusta nada.*
Nadie está poniendo atención.	*No está poniendo atención nadie.*
Ninguno entiende.	*No entiende ninguno.*
Ni el español ni el francés hablan inglés.	*No hablan inglés ni el español ni el francés.*

VARIATION

Cue answers in right-hand column and have student give negative word construction.

20. NEGATIVE RESPONSE DRILL

Give a negative answer to each of the following questions.

A usted le encantan los exámenes, ¿verdad?

¿Los exámenes de geografía y los dictados de español?

También le gustan mucho las tareas difíciles, ¿verdad?

Answer should contain the following negative words:

no

(no) / ni . . . ni . . .

(no) / tampoco   *(continued)*

Note: Words in parentheses may be omitted in answer.

(*continued*)

Y algunas veces estudia con los otros alumnos, ¿no?	*(no) / nunca*
¿Practica usted con alguien para los dictados?	*no / nadie*
¿La maestra algunas veces habla muy despacio durante los dictados?	*(no) / nunca*
Y usted entiende todo, ¿verdad?	*no / (nada)*
¿Hace usted las lecciones con algunos de sus amigos?	*no / ninguno*
¿Trae usted algo a la clase de español?	*no / nada*

21. ENGLISH CUE DRILL

¡Qué perezoso! Ni siquiera ha estudiado. ⊗	*¡Qué perezoso! Ni siquiera ha estudiado.*
He hasn't even begun the assignment.	*Ni siquiera ha empezado la tarea.*
He hasn't even thought about the lesson.	*Ni siquiera ha pensado en la lección.*
He hasn't even looked for his notes.	*Ni siquiera ha buscado sus apuntes.*
Is he lazy! He hasn't even studied.	*¡Qué perezoso! Ni siquiera ha estudiado.*

22. CHAIN DRILL

¿Está usted listo para el dictado?	Sí, ¿y tú, *Roberto*?
	Yo también, ¿y tú, *Elena*?
	Yo, no ¿y tú, *Camilo*?
	Yo tampoco.
¿Va usted a las carreras hoy?	Sí, ¿y tú, *Lupita*?
	etc. . . . *Yo también, ¿y tú, Roberto?*
¿Sabe usted nadar?	*Yo, no, ¿y tú, Juana?*
	Yo tampoco.

23. WRITING EXERCISE

Write the responses to Drills 17, 18, and 19.
EXERCISE BOOK: EXERCISES 7, 8, 9, AND 10

Possessive Adjectives

PRESENTATION *TEACHER PRESENTATION, p. T191*

<u>Mi</u> pluma y <u>mi</u> cuaderno.
<u>Mis</u> plumas y <u>mis</u> cuadernos.

Does **mi** show gender agreement? Does it show number agreement?

¿Me prestas <u>tu</u> pluma y <u>tu</u> libro?
¿Me prestas <u>tus</u> plumas y <u>tus</u> libros?

Does **tu** show gender agreement? Does it show number agreement?

Es <u>su</u> tía y <u>su</u> tío.
Son <u>sus</u> tías y <u>sus</u> tíos.

Does **su** show gender agreement? Does it show number agreement?

Es <u>nuestro</u> abuelo y <u>nuestra</u> tía.
Son <u>nuestros</u> abuelos y <u>nuestras</u> tías.

Does **nuestro** show gender agreement? Does it show number agreement?

GENERALIZATION

1	mi, mis	**nuestro, nuestros** **nuestra, nuestras**
2	tu, tus	
3	su, sus	

1. All possessive adjectives show number agreement. Only **nuestro / nuestra** show gender agreement. The possessive adjectives agree with what is possessed, not with the possessor. This is just another instance of grammatical agreement: *our book* must be **nuestro libro** even if the possessors are female, and *our house* must be **nuestra casa** even if the possessors are male.

2. When it is not clear from context which of the possible meanings of **su(s)** is the one intended, **su(s)** can be replaced by the appropriate form of the definite article before the noun, and **de** + **ustedes, él, ella, ellos,** or **ellas** after the noun.

Éste es su cuaderno. → Éste es el cuaderno de él.
Éstos son sus apuntes. → Éstos son los apuntes de ella.
¿Cuál es su casa? → ¿Cuál es la casa de ellos?

Students from the University of Puerto Rico at a freshman party.

3. The possessive adjectives **mi** and **tu** do not have a written accent (as distinct from the pronouns **mí** and **tú**).

4. Unlike English, Spanish often uses the definite article rather than a possessive adjective when it is obvious who the possessor is. Typical instances are with parts of the body and articles of clothing.

> **Me aprietan mucho los zapatos.**
> *My shoes are too tight.*
>
> **Tengo algo en el ojo.**
> *I have something in my eye.*
>
> **Ella tiene el pelo rubio.**
> *She has blond hair. (Her hair is blond.)*

Listening and Speaking Exercises 188, 189, 190*, p. T101 ⊗

SECTION D

STRUCTURE DRILLS

24.ITEM SUBSTITUTION

			VARIATION	
1. No encuentro mi pluma. ⊗		No encuentro mi pluma.	(tarea)	*mi*
_____ lápiz.		No encuentro mi lápiz.	(trabajo)	*mi*
_____ cosas.		No encuentro mis cosas.	(lecciones)	*mis*
_____ apuntes.		No encuentro mis apuntes.	(papeles)	*mis*

2. ¿Estás buscando tu cuaderno? ⊗
    (tarea–boletos–cartas)   *tu tarea–tus boletos–tus cartas*
    VARIATION: sombrero–corbata–guantes–cosas
3. Viene con sus hijas. ⊗
    (hijo–amigos–amiga)   *su hijo–sus amigos–su amiga*
    VARIATION: amigas–padre–tíos–prima
4. ¿Conoces a nuestro padre? ⊗
    (primas–abuelos–tía)   *nuestras primas–nuestros abuelos–nuestra tía*
    VARIATION: compañero–amigas–primos–maestra

25. de CONSTRUCTION → POSSESSIVE ADJECTIVE

Es la bicicleta de García. ⊗   Es su bicicleta.
Son los libros de ella.   *Son sus libros.*
Son las cosas de ustedes.   *Son sus cosas.*
Es la casa de los gemelos González.   *Es su casa.*
Son las lecciones de Camilo y Miguel. *Son sus lecciones*

26. PERSON-NUMBER SUBSTITUTION

1. Tú y tu familia siempre llegan tarde. ⊗   Tú y tu familia siempre llegan tarde.
   Juan _____.   Juan y su familia siempre llegan tarde.
   Las gemelas _____.   Las gemelas y su familia siempre llegan tarde.
   Usted _____.   Usted y su familia siempre llegan tarde.
   Ustedes _____.   Ustedes y su familia siempre llegan tarde.

2. Tú no arreglas tu cuarto. ⊗
   (mis hermanos y yo–Eva–ustedes–yo–nosotros)   *arreglamos nuestro cuarto—arregla su cuarto*
                                     —arreglan su cuarto—arreglo mi cuarto—
                                     arreglamos nuestro cuarto

27. PATTERNED RESPONSE

¿Me prestas tu pluma?   ¿Mi pluma? Sí, claro.
¿Puedo ver el álbum de ustedes?   ¿Nuestro álbum? Sí, claro.
¿Conoce usted a los abuelos de Juan?   *¿A sus abuelos? Sí, claro.*
¿Sabe usted nuestra dirección?   *¿Su dirección? Sí, claro.*
¿Ha recibido usted mi carta?   *¿Su carta? Sí, claro.*
¿Me da usted su número de teléfono?   *¿Mi número de teléfono? Sí, claro.*

28. FREE RESPONSE

¿Cómo es su madre? ¿alta? ¿bonita?
¿De qué color tiene los ojos ella?
¿Y el pelo?
Y su padre ¿cómo es él? ¿guapo? ¿inteligente?   *(continued)*

(*continued*)

¿Cómo es la casa de ustedes? ¿grande? ¿pequeña?
¿De qué color es?
¿Cuántos cuartos hay en la casa de ustedes?
¿De qué color es su cocina? ¿y su baño?
¿Cómo es usted? ¿alto? ¿bajo?
¿De qué color tiene los ojos?
¿De qué color tengo los ojos yo? ¿y el pelo?
¿Dónde está mi escritorio? ¿y su pupitre?

29. WRITING EXERCISE

Write the responses to Drills 25, 26.2, and 27.

EXERCISE BOOK: EXERCISES 11 AND 12

Listening Exercise 191*, p. T103 ⊗

Writing

1. MULTIPLE ITEM SUBSTITUTION

MODELS   Ana va a decir algo.
los chicos / estar / nada
Los chicos no están diciendo nada.

Papá habla con alguien.
yo / estudiar / nadie
Yo no estudio con nadie.

1. Mi hermano va a hacer algo ahora.
amigos / estar / nada

    Mis amigos no están haciendo nada ahora.

2. Juan me presta algunas veces sus apuntes.
esos chicos / nunca / tarea

    Esos chicos no me prestan nunca su tarea.

3. Nuestra maestra va a consultar con alguien.
jefe / estar / nadie

    Nuestro jefe no está consultando con nadie.

4. La secretaria lee el párrafo.
alumnos / repetir / frase

    Los alumnos repiten la frase.

5. ¿Le pides algo a los señores?
decir / nada / a nosotros

    ¿No nos dices nada a nosotros?

6. Este lápiz sirve también.
estos / tampoco

    Estos lápices no sirven tampoco.

7. El médico parece o francés o alemán.
empleada / ni / ni

    La empleada no parece ni francesa ni alemana.

8. Mi prima va a comprar algo.
   Blanca y yo / estar / nada   *Blanca y yo no estamos comprando nada.*

9. Yo sigo estudiando los apuntes.
   él / andar / mapa   *Él anda estudiando el mapa.*

10. La maestra repite la frase muy despacio.
    yo / decir / palabras / rápido   *Yo digo las palabras muy rápido.*

2. DIALOG REWRITE

Rewrite the following dialog, changing the verbs to the present progressive.

MAMÁ	Yo te hablo y tú no me pones atención.	*estoy hablando / estás poniendo*
PAPÁ	Es que leo el periódico.	*estoy leyendo*
MAMÁ	Pero yo te digo algo importante.	*estoy diciendo*
PAPÁ	Pero yo leo algo importante. Bien, bien . . . a próposito, ¿qué hace Carlitos ahora?	*estoy leyendo* / *está haciendo*
MAMÁ	Escucha el radio.	*está escuchando*
PAPÁ	¿Y Luisito?	
MAMÁ	Juega con sus amigos.	*está jugando*
PAPÁ	¿Cómo? ¿Y no estudian?	*están estudiando*
MAMÁ	¡Ay, caramba! ¡Yo te hablo y tú no me pones atención!	*estoy hablando / estás poniendo*

A class in Guatemala. Subjects related to farming are part of the curriculum in many rural schools.

RECOMBINATION MATERIAL

Dialogs

I

PADRE ¿Estás lista? Ya salgo para la oficina.

HIJA Sí, casi. A ver, ¿dónde está mi cuaderno?

PADRE Apúrate si quieres ir en carro.

HIJA Sí, papi. ¡Qué barbaridad! Ahora no encuentro mi abrigo.

PADRE ¡Caramba! ¡No vamos a salir nunca!

QUESTIONS

1. ¿Adónde va el padre?
2. ¿Está listo para salir, o todavía no?
3. ¿Cómo va, en autobús?
4. ¿Está lista para salir la hija?
5. ¿Qué busca ella?
6. ¿Qué dice el padre?

II

CHUCHO ¡Ay! ¡Tanto trabajo que tenemos!

QUIQUE Es verdad. Yo creo que esos maestros nunca han sido alumnos.

CHUCHO Tengo un dictado en inglés mañana y también un examen de geografía.

QUIQUE ¡Qué barbaridad! Yo tengo un examen de español.

CHUCHO Y yo no sé absolutamente nada. Es imposible saber tantas cosas.

QUESTIONS

1. ¿Están contentos los dos chicos?
2. ¿Por qué no?
3. ¿Qué dicen de los maestros?
4. ¿Es verdad lo que dicen?
5. ¿En cuál clase tiene un dictado Chucho?
6. ¿En cuál clase tiene un examen?

7. ¿Qué va a pasar mañana en la clase de español de Quique?
8. ¿Está Chucho listo para los exámenes?
9. ¿Qué dice él?

III

MARINA	¿Qué vas a pedir? ¿Un helado?	. . . va . . .
ELENA	No, yo estoy muy gorda. Sólo voy a tomar un café.	
MARINA	¿Estás loca? ¿No tienes hambre?	Está / tiene . . .
ELENA	No, chica. No quiero nada. Estoy gordísima.	
MARINA	No me parece. Estás muy delgada.	Está . . .
ELENA	Bueno. Voy a pedir un heladito también.	

QUESTIONS

VARIATION: The conversation takes place between two ladies who address each other as *usted*. Omit the word *chica*.

1. ¿Dónde están las dos chicas?
2. ¿Por qué no quiere Elena pedir un helado?
3. ¿Qué quiere tomar ella?
4. ¿Qué le dice Marina?
5. ¿Qué contesta Elena?
6. ¿Está Elena gorda, según Marina?
7. ¿Qué va a pedir Elena por fin?

IV

LUIS	Juan, ¿me prestas un lápiz?
JUAN	No tengo.
LUIS	Tu pluma, entonces, por favor.
JUAN	Bueno, ¿no tienes pluma tú?
LUIS	Yo no encuentro nada en este cuarto . . . y un papel, por favor, Juanito . . .
JUAN	¡Pero acabas de comprar papel!
LUIS	Estoy buscando, pero no encuentro.
JUAN	¿¿¿Has buscado en tu escritorio???
LUIS	Ah . . .

REJOINDERS

¿Me prestas tu lápiz?

No tengo.

Sí, claro.

¿Quieres esta pluma, mejor?

¿No tienes lápiz tú?

Narrative

América y los americanos

"¡Todos los habitantes* de este Hemisferio* somos americanos, no sólo la población* de los Estados Unidos! ¡Porque América es Canadá, es Argentina, es todo el Hemisferio Occidental*!"

Ésta es la eterna* protesta de unos pocos extremistas*, quienes
5   no están contentos porque los americanos han monopolizado esta palabra y han limitado* su aplicación* a la nacionalidad* de los Estados Unidos. Es una protesta sin mucha importancia*. Técnicamente* es verdad que todos nosotros somos americanos, pero la realidad de las cosas es que cuando hablamos
10 de "nacionalidad americana" o de "productos americanos", sabemos muy bien que esa nacionalidad y esos productos no corresponden* a ningún otro país° del Hemisferio sino a los Estados Unidos. Es simplemente una conveniencia*, un término* que ha sido adaptado* por los Estados Unidos y aceptado* en todo el
15 mundo, inclusive en el resto de América.

Es fácil, si queremos, encontrar la explicación* de cómo esto ha ocurrido. Las palabras que denominan* la nacionalidad de un país son siempre derivaciones* del nombre° principal. Así, guatemalteco* está derivado* de Guatemala, mexicano* de México,
20 cubano* de Cuba, colombiano* de Colombia, puertorriqueño* de Puerto Rico, japonés* de Japón*, ruso de Rusia*, chino* de China, y cien más. Todas son derivaciones fáciles. Pero, de Estados Unidos, ¿qué palabra vamos a derivar? ¡Estadounidense, nada menos! Sí, es-ta-dou-ni-den-se, seis sílabas*, y de difícil y horrible
25 pronunciación.* Y si esto ocurre en español, ¿qué derivación pueden producir* los americanos con su "United States"? (¿United Statian?) Una catástrofe* completa.*

Pero ellos, siempre tan prácticos*, han encontrado dos soluciones* al problema: primera, usar solamente las iniciales* U.S.
30 Pero como ellos deben saber que el uso* de iniciales para hablar de nacionalidades no es muy satisfactorio* en otras lenguas°, nuestros primos del norte han encontrado otra solución: ¡otro nombre para Estados Unidos! Con fácil derivación para la nacionalidad, naturalmente*: "America → American", excelente*.
35 Y nosotros, por nuestra parte, que somos de una de esas lenguas

país *m: country*
¿De qué país es usted?
¿En cuáles países hablan español?
¿De qué país es un japonés? un ruso? un mexicano?
nombre *m: name*
¿Es español su nombre?
¿Es italiano?

lengua: *language* (*tongue*)
¿Qué lengua habla usted en su casa?

donde no podemos hablar con iniciales, y sin poder decir fácilmente "estadounidense", hemos aceptado con absoluta satisfacción* la adaptación* de la palabra "americano" a la nacionalidad
de los Estados Unidos.

40   Esta teoría* puede no ser cierta°, pero si˜no hay otra, a mí
me parece aceptable*.

cierto-a: *correct*
Ustedes hablan español
muy bien, ¿no es cierto?
¿A usted le parece cierta
la teoría del autor?

QUESTIONS

1. ¿Qué dicen los extremistas con respecto a *1* la palabra "americano?"
2. ¿Limitan la aplicación de esta palabra a *6* los habitantes de los Estados Unidos?
3. Según el autor de este artículo*, ¿tiene *7* mucha importancia la protesta de los extremistas?
4. ¿Son americanos todos los habitantes de *8* este Hemisferio, técnicamente?
5. En realidad, ¿a los habitantes de cuál país *11* corresponde la palabra "americano"?
6. Los nombres de las nacionalidades, ¿de *17* cuál palabra son derivados?
7. ¿Cuál es la nacionalidad de un habitante *18* de Guatemala?

Note: Point out that many Spanish nouns which end in *-ulo* correspond to English nouns which end in *-le: artículo.*

8. ¿Y de un habitante de Colombia? ¿y uno *20* de Cuba? ¿uno de Puerto Rico? ¿y uno de Japón?
9. ¿Qué nacionalidad podemos derivar de *23* la palabra Estados Unidos?
10. ¿Es fácil pronunciar esta palabra? *24*
11. ¿Han encontrado una solución al pro- *28* blema los americanos?
12. ¿Cuál es la primera solución? *29*
13. ¿Es satisfactoria en otras lenguas esta *31* solución?
14. ¿Cuál es la otra solución? *32*
15. ¿Aceptan esta solución las personas que *37* hablan español?

Rejoinders

1. ¿Dónde está García? *No sé. / Anda tomando agua. / En casa. / Allí está.*
2. Esta pluma no sirve. *¿Quieres usar mi lápiz? / ¿No tienes otra? / ¿Por qué no?*
3. ¡Todos los habitantes de este Hemisferio somos americanos!

Es verdad. / ¿Por qué dice usted eso? / Pero todos sabemos que cuando hablamos de "productos americanos", esos productos son de los Estados Unidos. / Esa protesta es sin mucha importancia.

BASIC DIALOG

La técnica de la mujer

INÉS	¡Viera usted qué liquidación de ropa tienen allí! ¿Vamos? `12-1`
PEPITA	Mi marido me mata si le hablo de ir de compras.
INÉS	Tan exagerada. Estoy segura que la deja. `12-2`
PEPITA	Quién sabe. En todo caso, yo la llamo.
MARIDO	¡No! Una y mil veces ¡NO! `12-3`
PEPITA	Pero Lorenzo, una amiga mía dice que . . .
MARIDO	Esas amigas tuyas no saben lo que cuesta el dinero. ¡NO! `12-4`
PEPITA	Está bien. Ya sé que tú no me quieres . . .
MARIDO	¡Pepita, mi amor! ¿Vas a llorar? ¡Claro que puedes ir! `12-5`
PEPITA	¿De veras? Qué bueno eres. Te prometo no gastar mucho. `12-6`

Woman's Technique

INÉS	You should see what a clothing sale they're having there! Shall we go?
PEPITA	My husband will kill me if I talk to him about going shopping.
INÉS	Don't exaggerate. (So exaggerated.) I'm sure he'll let you.
PEPITA	I don't know. (Who knows.) In any case, I'll call you.
HUSBAND	No! (One and) a thousand times NO!
PEPITA	But Lorenzo, a friend of mine says that . . .
HUSBAND	Those friends of yours don't know the value of a dollar (what money costs). NO!
PEPITA	All right. I (already) know you don't love me . . .
HUSBAND	Pepita, darling (my love)! Are you going to cry? Of course you can go!
PEPITA	Really? You're so sweet. (How good you are.) I promise you not to spend much.

◀ *Women window-shop in an elegant section of Mexico City.*

Supplement

ropa			
Tienen una liquidación de trajes.	12-1 12-2	They're having a sale on suits.	
trajes de baño	12-3	bathing suits	
sacos sport	12-4	sport coats (jackets)	
swéaters[1]	12-5	sweaters	

¡Qué gangas tienen en ese almacén! 12-6   What bargains they have in that department store!

Abren a las nueve de la mañana.   They open at nine o'clock in the morning.

¡Mi esposa[2] me mata!   My wife will kill me!
¡Mis padres me matan!   My parents will kill me!

De todos modos, yo la llamo.   Anyway, I'll call you.
Además   Besides
Por consiguiente   Therefore

Un pariente mío dice que . . .   A relative of mine says that . . .
    sobrino   nephew
    nieto   grandson
    cuñado   brother-in-law

Esos amigos tuyos no ganan nada.   Those friends of yours don't earn anything.
    venden   sell

Nosotros nunca ganamos.   We never win.

Es una amiga suya.   She's a friend of yours.
    nuestra   ours

Listening and Speaking Exercises 192, 193*, 194, 195, 196*, 197*, p. T103 ⊗

---

[1] **Swéater,** being a foreign word, has an irregular plural. It is formed by adding **s** where one would normally expect **es.**

[2] **Esposa** has a masculine form: **esposo. Marido,** however, has no feminine form.

BASIC FORMS

Verbs

abrir	matar
ganar	prometer
gastar	vender
llorar	

Nouns

almacén *m.*	traje *m.*
amor *m.*	traje de baño *m.*
pariente *m.f.*	liquidación *f.*
swéater *m.*	mujer *f.*

Vocabulary Exercises

1. QUESTIONS

1. ¿De qué hablan las dos señoras? *Hablan de una liquidación.*
2. ¿Quiere Inés ir de compras? *Sí, quiere ir.*
3. ¿Quiere Pepita ir con ella? *Sí, quiere ir con ella.*
4. ¿A usted le gusta ir de compras?
5. ¿Prefiere ir con su mamá o con un amigo?
6. ¿Le gustan las gangas?
7. ¿Le gustan las liquidaciones? ¿Por qué?
8. ¿Tiene usted mucha ropa?
9. ¿Qué necesita usted comprar, un traje de baño?
10. ¿Necesita usted comprar un saco sport? ¿un swéater?
11. ¿Prefiere usted comprar en un almacén grande o en una tienda pequeña?
12. ¿Cuál almacén prefiere usted?
13. ¿A qué hora abren los almacenes?
14. Según Pepita, ¿va a estar enojado su marido si ella va de compras? *Sí, muy enojado.*
15. ¿Cómo es Pepita, según Inés? *Es exagerada.*
16. ¿Cree Inés que el marido de Pepita la deja ir? *Sí, está segura que la deja.*
17. ¿Qué va a hacer Pepita, en todo caso? *Va a llamar a Inés.*

2. FREE COMPLETION

1. ¡Viera usted qué liquidación de _____!   *ropa, trajes, trajes de baño, sacos, swéaters*
2. Me encanta ir a _____.   *la tienda, ese almacén, las liquidaciones que tienen allí.*
3. Usted es tan _____.   *exagerado, simpático, inteligente*
4. ¿A qué hora abren los _____?   *almacenes, mercados, parques*

---

3. QUESTIONS

1. ¿Cómo se llama el marido de Pepita?   *Se llama Lorenzo.*
2. ¿Está enojado él?   *Sí, está muy enojado.*
3. ¿Qué dice Lorenzo de las amigas de Pepita?   *Dice que no saben lo que cuesta el dinero.*
4. ¿Creen sus padres que usted no sabe lo que cuesta el dinero?
5. Cuando usted quiere ir de compras, ¿le pide dinero a su padre?
6. ¿Gasta usted mucho dinero?
7. ¿Trabaja usted? ¿Gana mucho? ¿Trabaja en un almacén?
8. ¿Qué dice Pepita cuando Lorenzo empieza a hablar de sus amigas?   *"Ya sé que tú no me quieres."*
9. ¿Qué cree Lorenzo que Pepita va a hacer?   *Cree que va a llorar.*
10. ¿Usted llora mucho cuando sus padres le gritan?
11. ¿Qué le dice Lorenzo a su esposa? ¿Sigue enojado él?   *Dice que puede ir. No sigue enojado.*
12. ¿Está Pepita contenta ahora? ¿Qué le dice a su marido?   *Sí. Le dice que es muy bueno.*
13. ¿Qué le promete Pepita a Lorenzo?   *Le promete no gastar mucho.*
14. ¿Son todos los maridos como Lorenzo?
15. Y las mujeres, ¿son todas como Pepita?

4. SYNONYMS

¡Esa señora es tan exagerada!   *¡Esa mujer es tan exagerada!*
¡Mi esposo me mata!   *¡Mi marido me mata!*
Voy con mi padre y mi madre.   *Voy con mis padres.*
Juan es el marido de mi hermana.   *Juan es mi cuñado.*
Luisa es la hija de mi hermana.   *Luisa es mi sobrina.*

5. ANTONYMS

Compran muchas cosas.   *Venden muchas cosas.*
Siempre perdemos.   *Siempre ganamos.*
La ropa es muy cara en ese almacén.   *La ropa es muy barata en ese almacén.*
¿Por qué no cierras las ventanas?   *¿Por qué no abres las ventanas?*
¡Es verdad!   *¡Es mentira!*

GRAMMAR

Direct Object Pronouns

PRESENTATION *TEACHER PRESENTATION, p. T193*

Digo **el número.**
Lo digo.

Llamo a **la chica americana.**
La llamo.

Which direct object pronoun can replace a masculine singular noun phrase? a feminine singular noun phrase?

No encuentro a **los señores.**
No **los** encuentro.

No encuentro **las cosas.**
No **las** encuentro.

Which direct object pronoun can replace a masculine plural noun phrase? a feminine plural noun phrase?

Tú no **me** quieres.
Claro que **te** quiero.
Él no **nos** quiere.

Are the direct object pronouns **me, te,** and **nos** the same as the corresponding indirect object pronouns?

GENERALIZATION

	Singular	*Plural*
1	**me**	**nos**
2	**te**	**los, las**
3	**lo, la**	

1. The direct object pronouns **me, te,** and **nos** have the same form as the corresponding indirect object pronouns; the third person forms are the same as the corresponding forms of the definite article, except for **lo.**

2. Direct object pronouns, unlike indirect object pronouns, show gender agreement in the third person. As usual, the masculine plural form is used for groups of mixed gender.

> **Los llamo mañana.**
> *I'll call you (men and women) tomorrow.*

3. Direct object pronouns make no distinction between persons and things. **Lo** can replace both **al chico** and **el libro** in the following sentences:

> **Veo al chico.**
> **Veo el libro.** } **Lo veo.**

4. Direct object pronouns, like indirect object pronouns, precede a verb with a person-number ending.

> **Yo no los llamo.**
> **Yo no los he llamado.**

5. Like indirect object pronouns, direct object pronouns in Spanish are always unstressed. The same device is used to emphasize them as for indirect object pronouns: in addition to the unstressed pronoun before the verb, <u>a</u> + a prepositional pronoun are placed after the verb.

> **Lo llamo <u>a él</u>.**
> *I call <u>him</u>.*

> **Me quiere ver <u>a mí</u>.**
> *He wants to see <u>me</u>.*

Listening and Speaking Exercises 198, 199*, 200, 201*, p. T106   ⊗   **SECTION B**

STRUCTURE DRILLS

6. NOUN → PRONOUN

VARIATION: Substitute the following noun phrases for the ones in Drill 6.1 and 6.2.

1. No veo el mapa. ⊗
   No veo al empleado.
   No veo la televisión.
   No veo a la mujer.
   No veo los lápices.
   No veo a los camareros.
   No veo las cosas.
   No veo a las criadas.

No lo veo.	el libro
No lo veo.	al camarero
No la veo.	la carta
No la veo.	a la criada
No los veo.	los apuntes
No los veo.	a los chicos
No las veo.	las fotos
No las veo.	a las señoras

2. Vendemos los discos. ⊗
   ¿Llamas a las chicas americanas?
   ¡Siempre molestas a la maestra!

Los vendemos.	los libros
¿Las llamas?	a las gemelas
¡Siempre la molestas!	a la señora

¿Han leído el periódico?	*¿Lo han leído?*	el párrafo
¿Ya cierran la librería?	*¿Ya la cierran?*	la zapatería
¿Has encontrado los apuntes?	*¿Los has encontrado?*	los lápices
¿Conocen ustedes al Sr. Quezada?	*¿Lo conocen?*	al médico
No sé el nombre.	*No lo sé.*	el número

7. DIRECTED ADDRESS

Address the following statements to the persons indicated by the cue.

1. Lo voy a visitar mañana. ⊗   Lo voy a visitar mañana.
   - (a su compañero)   Te voy a visitar mañana.
   - (a dos de sus amigos)   Los voy a visitar mañana.
   - (al dentista)   Lo voy a visitar mañana.
   - (a mí)   Lo (*or* la) voy a visitar mañana.
   - (a Juan y a María)   Los voy a visitar mañana.

2. ¡Tres veces lo he llamado! ⊗
   - (al médico)   *¡Tres veces lo he llamado!*
   - (a su prima)   *¡Tres veces lo he llamado!*
   - (a mí)   *¡Tres veces te he llamado!*
   - (a la Sra. Delgado y a mí)   *¡Tres veces lo (or la) he llamado!*
   - (a la maestra de geografía)   *¡Tres veces los (or las) he llamado!*
        ¡Tres veces la he llamado!

Listening and Speaking Exercises 202, 203, 204, 205*, p. T108 ⊗   SECTION C

8. PATTERNED RESPONSE

¿Te dejan tomar café? ⊗	Sí, claro que me dejan.
¿Los dejan a ustedes ir al cine?	*Sí, claro que nos dejan.*
¿Me dejan gritar?	*Sí, claro que lo (or la) dejan.*
¿Dejan a Pepita ir de compras?	*Sí, claro que la dejan.*
¿Lo dejan gastar mucho dinero a usted?	*Sí, claro que me dejan.*
¿Nos dejan ir a la liquidación?	*Sí, claro que los (or nos) dejan.*
¿Te dejan trabajar?	*Sí, claro que me dejan.*

9. PAIRED SENTENCES

Lo llamo. ⊗	Lo llamo.
I'll call <u>you</u>.	Lo llamo a usted.
I'll call you.	Lo llamo.
No la encuentran.	*No la encuentran.*
They can't find <u>her</u>.	*No la encuentra a ella.*
They can't find her.	*No la encuentran.*

(*continued*)

(*continued*)

Nos busca.	*Nos busca.*
He's looking for <u>us</u>.	*Nos busca a nosotros.*
He's looking for us.	*Nos busca.*
No los conozco.	*No los conozco.*
I don't know <u>them</u>.	*No los conozco a ellos.*
I don't know them.	*No los conozco.*

10. WRITING EXERCISE

Write the responses to Drills 6.2, 7.2, and 8.

EXERCISE BOOK: EXERCISES 1, 2, 3 AND 4

Direct vs. Indirect Objects

TEACHER PRESENTATION, p. T195

GENERALIZATION

1. Whether a Spanish verb takes a direct or an indirect object is not always predictable from the corresponding English verb.

<u>Lo</u> dejo ir.
I let <u>him</u> go.

<u>Le</u> permito ir.
I permit <u>him</u> to go.

You must learn the kinds of objects a Spanish verb may take as you learn the verb.

2. Most Spanish verbs may take both direct and indirect objects. Verbs that have to do with some form of communication are typical: the person communicated with is an indirect object; the message communicated is a direct object.

I answer	*the letter.*	**Contesto la carta.**	<u>La</u> **contesto.**
	the teacher.	**Le contesto al maestro.**	<u>Le</u> **contesto.**
I'm writing	*the letter.*	**Escribo la carta.**	<u>La</u> **escribo.**
	my uncle.	**Le escribo a mi tío.**	<u>Le</u> **escribo.**

Llamar, though it seems like a verb of communication, takes a direct object for the person called.

I'm calling	*the number.*	**Llamo el número.**	<u>Lo</u> **llamo.**
	John.	**Llamo a Juan.**	<u>Lo</u> **llamo.**

Note: Remind students that in sentences in which the indirect object is stated, an indirect object pronoun precedes the verb: *Le escribo a María.* In sentences in which the direct object is stated, there is no direct object pronoun before the verb: *Llamo a María.*

STRUCTURE DRILLS

11. INDIRECT VS. DIRECT OBJECT

	1ST STUDENT	2ND STUDENT
1. Busco al médico.	Busco al médico.	Lo busco.
(escribo)	Le escribo al médico.	Le escribo.
(llamo)	Llamo al médico.	Lo llamo.
(hablo)	Le hablo al médico.	Le hablo. ✓
2. ¿Conoces a María?	¿Conoces a María?	¿La conoces?
(traes)	¿Traes a María?	¿La traes?
(gritas)	¿Le gritas a María?	¿Le gritas?
(contestas)	¿Le contestas a María?	¿Le contestas?
3. No ve a los chiquitos.	No ve a los chiquitos.	No los ve.
(grita)	No les grita a los chiquitos.	No les grita.
(lee)	No les lee a los chiquitos.	No les lee.
(reconoce)	No reconoce a los chiquitos.	No los reconoce.

12. CUED DIALOG

1.   (la tarea)   1ST STUDENT   ¿Escribes la tarea? ✓
                              2ND STUDENT   No, la escribo después.

      (al Sr. López)   1ST STUDENT   ¿Le escribes al Sr. López? ✓
                              2ND STUDENT   No, le escribo después.

      (las cartas)   ¿Escribes las cartas? / No, las escribo después.
      (a las gemelas)   ¿Les escribes a las gemelas? / No, les escribo después.

2.   (al maestro)   1ST STUDENT   ¿Le contestas al maestro?
                              2ND STUDENT   Sí, le contesto.

      (el teléfono)   ¿Contestas el teléfono? / Sí, lo contesto.
      (a los señores)   ¿Les contestas a los señores? / Sí, les contesto.
      (las cartas)   ¿Contestas las cartas? / Sí, las contesto.

13. FREE RESPONSE

¿Conoce usted a este chico? ¿y a esta chica?
¿Sabe el nombre de esta chica?
¿Sabe su dirección?
¿Yo los dejo a ustedes hablar en clase?
¿Los dejo hablar inglés?
¿Cuál lengua hablan ustedes en clase?
¿Cuándo va a traer usted a su mamá aquí?

(*continued*)

(*continued*)

¿Trae usted a sus amigos a la clase de español?

¿Sus amigos lo llaman a usted todas las noches?

¿Lo visitan frecuentemente?

¿Ve usted a sus amigos todos los días? ¿Dónde?

14. WRITING EXERCISE

Write the responses to Drills 11.2, 11.3, and 12.2.

EXERCISE BOOK: EXERCISES 5, 6, AND 7

The Infinitive as the Object of a Preposition

PRESENTATION   *TEACHER PRESENTATION, p. T195*

Me mata si le hablo **de ir** de compras.

Nunca viene **sin llamar.**

¿Siempre pides permiso **antes de salir**?

Which form of the verb follows the preposition?

Stores featuring a great variety of wares attact crowds during Sunday market in Madrid.

GENERALIZATION

1. Like the gerund of English verbs (the form that ends in *-ing*), the infinitive of Spanish verbs often functions as a noun.

Ver para creer.
Seeing is believing.

2. One common use of the infinitive functioning as a noun is as the object of a preposition.

Me mata si le hablo <u>de</u> <u>ir</u> de compras.
He'll kill me if I talk to him about going shopping.

STRUCTURE DRILLS

15. DOUBLE ITEM SUBSTITUTION

Nunca salgo antes de estudiar. ⊗	*Nunca salgo antes de estudiar.*
_____ cenar.	*Nunca salgo antes de cenar.*
_____ después de ___.	*Nunca salgo después de cenar.*
_____ comer.	*Nunca salgo después de comer.*
_____ sin _____.	*Nunca salgo sin comer.*
_____ almorzar.	*Nunca salgo sin almorzar.*
_____ para _____.	*Nunca salgo para almorzar.*

16. ENGLISH CUE DRILLS

1. ¿Qué haces después de cenar? ⊗
   What do you do after studying?
   What do you do after you practice?
   What do you do after going shopping?
   What do you do after you win a game?
   What do you do after losing a game?
   What do you do after you have dinner?

   ¿Qué haces después de cenar?
   ¿Qué haces después de estudiar?
   ¿Qué haces después de practicar?
   ¿Qué haces después de ir de compras?
   ¿Qué haces después de ganar un partido?
   ¿Qué haces después de perder un partido?
   ¿Qué haces después de cenar?

2. ¡Qué clase! ¡Todos estamos cansados de trabajar! ⊗
   Ana's tired of reading.
   Pedro's tired of writing.
   The twins are tired of speaking Spanish.
   I'm tired of repeating sentences.
   You're tired of studying. (*ustedes*)
   What a class! We're all tired of working!

   ¡Qué clase! ¡Todos estamos cansados de trabajar!
   Ana está cansada de leer.
   Pedro está cansado de escribir.
   Los gemelos están cansados de hablar español.
   Yo estoy cansado de repetir frases.
   Ustedes están cansados de estudiar.
   ¡Qué clase! ¡Todos estamos cansados de trabajar!

17. FREE RESPONSE

¿Está usted cansado de estudiar ahora?
¿Qué va a hacer después de salir de la escuela esta tarde?
¿Va a ir al almacén antes de volver a casa?
¿Para qué? ¿Para comprar algo?
¿Le gusta ir al almacén sin poder gastar mucho?
Y usted, ¿adónde va a ir antes de volver a casa?
¿Hace sus lecciones antes o después de cenar?
¿Qué hace usted después de estudiar? ¿Llama a sus amigos?

18. WRITING EXERCISE

Write the responses to Drills 15 and 16.2.
EXERCISE BOOK: EXERCISE 8

Possessive Adjectives: Long Forms

PRESENTATION *TEACHER PRESENTATION, p. T195*

Una amiga **mía** dice eso.
Esas amigas **tuyas** no saben nada.
¿Es un amigo **suyo**?
Son unos amigos **nuestros.**

Which is the word that expresses possession in each of these sentences? What is its position in relation to the noun? Does it agree in number and gender with the noun it modifies?

GENERALIZATION

1	mío,	míos	nuestro,	nuestros
	mía,	mías	nuestra,	nuestras
2	tuyo,	tuyos		
	tuya,	tuyas		
3		suyo,	suyos	
		suya,	suyas	

1. The long form possessive adjectives agree in number and gender with the noun they modify.

> **Esa <u>amiga mía</u> es simpática.**
> **Esos <u>amigos tuyos</u> son antipáticos.**

2. Long form possessive adjectives are used in these situations:

   a. After **ser** and **parecer.**

   > **¿<u>Son tuyos</u> estos guantes?**
   > *Are these gloves yours?*

   > **Sí, <u>parecen míos</u>.**
   > *Yes, they look like mine.*

   b. After a noun, to express *of mine, of yours, of ours,* etc.

   > **Una <u>amiga mía</u> dice que . . .**
   > *A friend of mine says that . . .*

   > **Esas <u>amigas tuyas</u> . . .**
   > *Those friends of yours . . .*

   > **Son unos <u>primos nuestros</u>.**
   > *They're some cousins of ours.*

   c. After a noun, to emphasize that one possessor rather than another is referred to.

   > **mi casa**   *my house*
   > **la casa mía** *<u>my</u> house*
   >
   > **tus ideas**   *your ideas*
   > **las ideas tuyas** *<u>your</u> ideas*

3. **Suyo,** like **su,** can refer to any third person possessor. When it is not clear from the context which one is intended, **suyo** may be replaced by **de** + the appropriate prepositional object pronoun.

   > **Estos periódicos no son** { **suyos.**
   >   { **de él.**

   > **¿Son** { **suyas** } **estas cosas?**
   >   { **de ustedes** }

   > **El libro es** { **suyo.**
   >   { **de ella.**

   > **La casa es** { **suya.**
   >   { **de ellos.**

Listening and Speaking Exercises 206, 207, 208, 209*, p. T110 ⊗ SECTION D

STRUCTURE DRILLS

19. ITEM SUBSTITUTION

1. Ese lápiz no es mío. ⊗   *VARIATION*   Ese lápiz no es mío.
   Esa pluma _____.   esa casa   Esa pluma no es mía.
   Esos apuntes _____.   esos guantes   Esos apuntes no son míos.
   Esas cosas _____.   esas fotos   Esas cosas no son mías.

2. ¿Es tuyo el saco? ⊗   *¿Es tuya la bicicleta?— ¿Son tuyos los pesos? ¿Son tuyas*
   (la bicicleta–los pesos–las fotos) *las fotos?*
   VARIATION: Use nouns in Drill 19.1

3. Esos amigos suyos nunca estudian. ⊗   *Ese sobrino suyo nunca estudia.–Esa hija suya nunca estudia.–*
   (ese sobrino–esa hija–esas compañeras) *Esas compañeras suyas nunca estudian.*
   VARIATION: (ese hijo-esa amiga-esas primas)

4. Es un tío nuestro. ⊗   *Son unos parientes nuestros.–Es una sobrina nuestra.–*
   (unos parientes–una sobrina–unas primas) *Son unas primas nuestras.*
   VARIATION: (unos amigos-una compañera-unas tías)

20. PERSON-NUMBER SUBSTITUTION

1. Este carro es mío. ⊗   Este carro es mío.
   (de usted)   Este carro es suyo.
   (de Luis)   Este carro es suyo.
   (de mis amigos)   Este carro es suyo.

2. ¿Es tuya esta casa? ⊗   *¿Es suya esta casa?*
   (de ustedes–del nuevo médico–de las gemelas)   *¿Es suya esta casa?*
                                                  ¿Es suya esta casa?

3. Estos libros no son nuestros.   *Estos libros no son suyos.*
   (de los alumnos–de usted–de mi sobrina)   *Estos libros no son suyos.*
                                                  Estos libros no son suyos.

21. PATTERNED RESPONSE

¿Es una prima de Juan?   Sí, es una prima suya.
¿Son unas amigas de las gemelas?   *Sí, son unas amigas suyas.*
¿Es su sobrino?   *Sí, es un sobrino suyo (or mío).*
¿Es un nieto de la señora?   *Sí, es un nieto suyo.*
¿Son unos compañeros de ustedes?   *Sí, son unos compañeros nuestros.*
¿Son mis alumnos?   *Sí, son (or somos) unos alumnos suyos.*
¿Es nuestro pariente?   *Sí, es un pariente suyo (or nuestro).*

22. FREE RESPONSE

¿Es de usted este cuaderno?
Y este lápiz, ¿también es suyo?

¿Y esta cosa? ¿y estas dos plumas?
¿Es mío este periódico? ¿y estos libros?
¿Son de *Juan* estos papeles?
Y estos apuntes, ¿de quién son?
¿Es de ustedes este mapa? ¿y esas fotos, también son suyas?
¿Es de *Luisa* este swéater? ¿y estos guantes también?
Juan, ¿es de su padre este saco? ¿y esta corbata?
Susana, ¿es *Cristina* una amiga suya?
¿Esos dos chicos son amigos suyos? ¿y esas dos chicas?
¿Son ustedes alumnos míos? ¿Son alumnos de la *Sra. Delgado?*

23. WRITING EXERCISE

Write the responses to Drills 19.2, 19.3, 19.4, and 21.

EXERCISE BOOK: EXERCISES 9 AND 10

Generic Use of the Definite Article

TEACHER PRESENTATION, p. T196
GENERALIZATION

Generic means "referring to a class of things as a whole, rather than to any particular member of the class." The underlined nouns in the following examples are used in a generic sense:

<u>Cars</u> are expensive.
<u>Women</u> talk a lot.
<u>Geography</u> is easy.

In the Spanish equivalents of sentences like the above, the subject noun used in a generic sense is preceded by the definite article.

<u>Los carros</u> son caros.
<u>Las mujeres</u> hablan mucho.
<u>La geografía</u> es fácil.

STRUCTURE DRILLS

24. ENGLISH CUE DRILLS

1. La geografía es difícil. ⊗   La geografía es difícil.
   Spanish is easy.   El español es fácil.
   English is boring.   El inglés es aburrido.
   Geography is difficult.   La geografía es difícil.   *(continued)*

(*continued*)

2. Los maestros trabajan mucho. ⊗   *Los maestros trabajan mucho.*
   Students study a lot.   *Los alumnos estudian mucho.*
   Women spend a lot.   *Las mujeres gastan mucho.*
   Girls talk a lot.   *Las chicas hablan mucho.*
   Boys fool around a lot.   *Los chicos molestan mucho.*
   Teachers work a lot.   *Los maestros trabajan mucho.*

25. PATTERNED RESPONSE

Aquí venden carros. ⊗   Los carros son muy caros.
Aquí venden gasolina.   *La gasolina es muy cara.*
Aquí venden bicicletas.   *Las bicicletas son muy caras.*
Aquí venden ropa.   *La ropa es muy cara.*
Aquí venden trajes de baño.   *Los trajes de baño son muy caros.*
Aquí venden café.   *El café es muy caro.*

26. WRITING EXERCISE

Write the responses to Drills 24.2 and 25.
EXERCISE BOOK: EXERCISE 11

Listening and Speaking Exercise 210*, p. T111 ⊗

Friends spend long hours discussing politics and local news in a café.

Writing

1. MULTIPLE ITEM SUBSTITUTION

MODEL   ¿A la chica americana? La llamo ahora.
maestro / (nosotros) / buscar
¿Al maestro americano? Lo buscamos ahora.

1. ¿Ese libro? No lo he leído.
canción / (nosotros) / escuchar

¿Esa canción? No la hemos escuchado.

2. ¿A su sobrino? No lo conocemos.
cuñada / (yo) / ver

¿A su cuñada? No la veo.

3. ¿La casa? No la venden.
guantes / (ella) / encontrar

¿Los guantes? No los encuentra.

4. ¿La librería? La arregla el empleado.
cuartos / limpiar / criada

¿Los cuartos? Los limpia la criada.

5. Esas amigas tuyas no estudian nunca.
parientes / trabajar

Esos parientes tuyos no trabajan nunca.

6. De todos modos, yo te llamo a ti.
en todo caso / tú / a mí

En todo caso, tú me llamas a mí.

7. Esas amigas suyas no me gustan a mí.
compañeros / a ellas

Esos compañeros suyos no les gustan a ellas.

8. Estamos cansados de estudiar.
(ella) / llorar

Está cansada de llorar.

9. ¿Vas a la tienda después de hacer tu trabajo?
(ellos) / museo / escribir / lecciones

¿Van al museo después de escribir sus lecciones?

10. Los chicos nunca vienen sin llamar.
mi hermana y yo / salir / pedir permiso

Mi hermana y yo nunca salimos sin pedir permiso.

2. DIALOG COMPLETION

Copy the following dialog, filling in each blank with the correct object pronoun.

INÉS   Aló, ¿está Pepita?
LORENZO   Sí, __1__ voy a llamar.
INÉS   ¿Aló? Pepita, ¿quiere usted ir a esa liquidación conmigo?
PEPITA   No sé. Mi marido __2__ mata si __3__ digo que voy a otra
liquidación.

(*continued*)

(*continued*)

INÉS   ¿Por qué?

PEPITA   Siempre __4__ prometo no gastar mucho, pero . . .

INÉS   Sí, yo sé. Primero __5__ grita un poco, pero después __6__ dice que __7__ quiere y __8__ deja ir.

PEPITA   No, usted no __9__ conoce. De todos modos, __10__ llamo más tarde.

1	2	3	4	5	6	7	8	9	10
la	me	le	le	le	le	la	la	lo	la

RECOMBINATION MATERIAL

Dialogs

I

PEPITA   ¡Qué ganga! Sólo cuatro veinticinco por este swéater.

INÉS   ¡Un regalo! ¿Lo compra? Es muy bonito.   . . . ¿Lo compras? ←

PEPITA   No sé. Mi marido me mata. . .

INÉS   Pero Pepita, va perfecto con la falda que acaba de comprar. . . . que acabas de

PEPITA   Sí, es de exactamente ese color.

INÉS   ¡Y sólo cuesta cuatro vienticinco!

PEPITA   Bueno, lo compro, ¡pero ahora tengo que comprar unos zapatos para el swéater y la falda!

QUESTIONS

VARIATION: Pepita and Inés address each other as *tú*.

1. ¿Cuánto cuesta el swéater que Pepita quiere comprar?
2. ¿Está barato, según Inés?
3. ¿Lo encuentra bonito ella?
4. Según Pepita, ¿qué le hace su marido si ella compra el swéater?
5. ¿Es exagerada ella?
6. ¿Por qué lo debe comprar, según Inés?
7. ¿Qué dice Pepita?
8. ¿Qué hace Pepita, por fin?
9. ¿Qué más va a tener que comprar ella?

REJOINDER

¡Sólo quince noventa y cinco por este saco!

¡Qué ganga! / ¿Lo va a comprar? / ¡Qué barato está! / ¡Un regalo! / ¡Qué bonito! / No me gusta. / Éste otro es más barato todavía.

II

PEDRO	¡Qué graciosa esta foto! ¿Dónde es la fiesta?
ÁNGEL	En la casa de unos parientes míos.
PEDRO	Ésta es tu prima, ¿no es cierto?
ÁNGEL	No, mi cuñada, esposa de Antonio, mi hermano mayor.
PEDRO	Y estos chiquitos, ¿son hijos de ella?
ÁNGEL	Sí, mis sobrinitos, Toño y Chucho. Son gemelos.

Note: Toño is short for Antonio. It is common in Spanish-speaking countries for the first-born son to have the same name as his father.

QUESTIONS

1. ¿De qué es la foto?
2. ¿Dónde es la fiesta?
3. ¿Quién es la señora que Pedro ve en la foto?
4. ¿Cómo se llama el marido de esa señora?
5. ¿Es Antonio el primo de Ángel?
6. ¿Cómo se llaman los hijos de Antonio y su esposa?

III

ARTURO	¡Vieras los carros usados que venden allí!	¡Viera . . .
MIGUEL	¿De veras? ¿Tu padre te va a comprar un carro?	¿Su padre le va . . .
ARTURO	No, lo voy a comprar yo. He estado economizando.	
MIGUEL	¿Sí? Tú debes ganar mucho.	Usted debe . . .
ARTURO	No tanto. Tengo una ruta de periódicos.	
MIGUEL	¡Qué suerte!	

VARIATION: Arturo is talking to his teacher who addressed him as *usted.*

QUESTIONS

1. ¿De qué hablan los dos chicos?
2. ¿Quiere Arturo comprar un carro nuevo o uno usado?
3. ¿El padre de Arturo le va a comprar el carro?
4. ¿Qué ha estado haciendo Arturo?
5. ¿Por qué puede economizar tanto dinero Arturo, según Miguel?
6. ¿Gana Arturo mucho dinero en realidad?
7. ¿En qué trabaja él?
8. ¿Tiene un trabajo difícil?
9. ¿Cree Miguel que Arturo tiene suerte?

REJOINDER

Voy a comprar un carro nuevo. *¿De veras? / ¿Cuándo? / ¡Tú debes ganar mucho! / ¡Qué suerte! / ¿Dónde? / ¿Has estado economizando? / ¿Con el dinero que ha ganado vendiendo periódicos?*

Narrative

El Nuevo Mundo

Si miramos° un mapa del Hemisferio Occidental, podemos observar* que el Nuevo Mundo tiene la forma* de dos triángulos* unidos por una delgada faja° de tierra°. El triángulo superior* contiene* tres grandes países: Canadá, Estados Unidos, y
5 México, y llamamos esta parte del continente "Norteamérica"*. Por esta razón también les decimos "norteamericanos"* a los americanos. Sin embargo°, nadie les aplica* este término a los habitantes de Canadá y México, que por su posición* geográfica* también son norteamericanos. La nacionalidad de cada una de
10 estas dos repúblicas es una palabra tan claramente derivada del nombre del país—canadiense* y mexicano—que para no hacer confusión* preferimos reservar* "norteamericanos" para los habitantes de los Estados Unidos.

La delgada faja de tierra que une* los dos triángulos consiste
15 en seis pequeñas repúblicas llamadas, de norte* a sur*: Guatemala, Honduras, El Salvador, Nicaragua, Costa Rica y Panamá. Lógicamente*, llamamos esta región* Centroamérica, y a sus habitantes, centroamericanos*.

Al sur, está el segundo triángulo: Suramérica*. En esa enorme*
20 extensión* de territorio* encontramos diez naciones* latinas[3]*, unas de gran tamaño°, otras de tamaño mediano* y otras más pequeñas. Son Venezuela, Colombia, Ecuador, Perú, Chile, Bolivia, Paraguay, Argentina, Uruguay, y Brasil.

Éstas son todas las naciones del continente, pero no son todas
25 las repúblicas del Hemisferio. Debemos incluir* también Cuba, la República Dominicana, Haití, Jamaica, y el territorio de Puerto Rico, estado libre° asociado* a los Estados Unidos, situadas* todas en el mar° Caribe[4].

Finalmente debemos mencionar dos clasificaciones* más de
30 nuestra América, que no son clasificaciones geográficas sino lingüísticas*: Hispanoamérica* y Latinoamérica*. Hispano-

---

mirar: *look at*
¿Qué está mirando?
faja: *strip*
tierra: *land*
¿Cómo se llama la faja de tierra que es la parte mexicana de California?
sin embargo: *nevertheless*
¿A usted le gusta estudiar? (When a student answers "No" ask:) ¿Tiene que estudiar mucho, sin embargo?

tamaño: *size*
¿Es Brasil un país de gran tamaño?
Y Chile, ¿es de gran tamaño o de tamaño mediano?

libre: *free*
mar *m: sea*
¿Cuándo va a estar usted libre esta tarde?
¿Está libre esta noche, o va a salir?
¿En qué mar están situadas Cuba y Puerto Rico?
¿Es bonito el mar Caribe?

---

[3] Plus the territory of the Guianas (French, British, and Dutch). The independent country of Guyana was formerly British Guiana. Dutch Guiana is officially Surinam, an autonomous overseas territory of the Kingdom of the Netherlands.

[4] Two more islands that have recently become independent nations are Trinidad-Tobago and Barbados.

américa incluye solamente los países de lengua española. Latinoamérica comprende* todos los países donde la lengua oficial* es
una de las tres lenguas romances* habladas en el Nuevo Mundo:
35 español, portugués*, y francés.

Norteamericanos, hispanoamericanos*, centroamericanos,
americanos, suramericanos*, latinoamericanos*: éstos son los
habitantes del Hemisferio Occidental, el Nuevo Mundo, América.

QUESTIONS

1. ¿Qué forma tiene el Nuevo Mundo?   2
2. ¿Cuáles países contiene el triángulo superior?   3
3. ¿Cómo se llama este gran triángulo?   5
4. ¿Cuál otro nombre usamos para hablar de los "americanos"?   6
5. ¿Son norteamericanos los mexicanos y los canadienses por su posición geográfica?   8
6. ¿Les decimos normalmente "norteamericanos" a los habitantes de México y de Canadá?   7
7. ¿Por qué no?   10
8. ¿Cómo se llama la delgada faja de tierra que une Norteamérica y Suramérica?   17
9. ¿De cuáles países consiste Centroamérica?   15
10. ¿Cómo se llaman los habitantes de Centroamérica?   18

11. ¿Cuántas naciones latinas hay en Suramérica?   20
12. ¿Recuerda usted cuáles son?   22
13. ¿Son todas de gran tamaño?   21
14. ¿Cuáles son las repúblicas que no hemos mencionado todavía?   25
15. ¿Es Puerto Rico una nación completamente independiente? ¿Qué es?   27
16. ¿Cuáles dos clasificaciones linguísticas menciona el autor?   31
17. ¿Cuáles países incluye la clasificación "Hispanoamérica"?   32
18. ¿Cuáles países están comprendidos en la clasificación "Latinoamérica"?   35
19. ¿Cuáles son las tres lenguas romances habladas en Latinoamérica?   31

Conversation Stimulus

Usted va a hacer un viaje por Latinoamérica. ¿Cuáles países prefiere visitar? ¿Cuál ruta va a seguir? ¿A cuál país va primero? ¿A cuáles países va después? ¿Con quiénes va a viajar? ¿Cómo va a viajar? ¿Cuándo empieza su viaje? ¿Cuándo vuelve? ¿Cuáles son las cosas principales que usted quiere ver en cada país?

Suggested responses:
Voy a hacer un viaje por Latinoamérica. Quiero visitar México, Venezuela, Perú y Argentina. Voy primero a México, y después de pasar unas semanas allí, voy a Caracas. Paso una semana en la capital de Venezuela, y después voy a Perú, donde quiero ver las reliquias de la civilización inca. Entonces quiero continuar mi viaje hasta Buenos Aires, y de allí vuelvo en avión a Nueva York. Voy a viajar con mi hermano mayor. Empezamos el viaje el primero de julio y volvemos a principios de septiembre. En cada país quiero ver los museos, las reliquias de las civilizaciones indias si hay, las catedrales importantes, las calles y tiendas típicas, y más importante, quiero conocer a muchos hispanoamericanos.

◄ *Note:* On her fifteenth birthday, a girl officially becomes a "young lady." Parties range from elaborate
affairs to small get-togethers in the home. Here, the
birthday girl dances with her *novio.*

BASIC DIALOG

Las quince primaveras[1]

BÁRBARA	¿Ya te vas? ¿Por qué no te quedas un rato más?	
CECILIA	No, si no me acuesto temprano, no me levanto mañana.	13-1
BÁRBARA	¿Tú estás invitada a la fiesta de Ana? Yo, no, fíjate.	13-2
CECILIA	Yo tampoco. Tal vez no ha hecho la lista todavía.	13-3

BÁRBARA	Tu cumpleaños es muy pronto también, ¿no?	13-4
CECILIA	Sí, pero yo no voy a hacer una fiesta muy grande.	
BÁRBARA	¿A quiénes piensas invitar?	
CECILIA	A unos veinte muchachos y a unas diez amigas.	13-5
BÁRBARA	Me parece muy bien. El doble de hombres.	
CECILIA	Sí, ¡porque siempre se presenta la mitad!	13-6

Sweet Sixteen (The Fifteen Springs)

BÁRBARA	Are you going already? Why don't you stay a while longer?
CECILIA	No, if I don't go to bed early, I won't get up tomorrow.
BÁRBARA	Are you invited to Ana's party? I'm not, just imagine.
CECILIA	Neither am I. Maybe she hasn't made the list yet.

BÁRBARA	Your birthday's very soon too, isn't it?
CECILIA	Yes, but I'm not going to have a very big party.
BÁRBARA	Who do you intend to invite?
CECILIA	About (some) twenty boys and about ten girl friends.
BÁRBARA	That seems fine to me. Twice as many (the double) men.
CECILIA	Yes, because half always show up (present themselves)!

---

[1] It is the custom in some Spanish-speaking countries for girls to celebrate their fifteenth birthday **(las quince primaveras)** in much the same way girls celebrate their "sweet sixteen" in many parts of the United States.

◄ *A Mexican girl celebrates her fifteenth birthday at a party as elegant as a debutante ball.*

Supplement

¿Te aburres mucho?		Do you get very bored?
¿Te asustas mucho?		Do you get very frightened?
¿Te cansas mucho?		Do you get very tired?
¿Te enojas mucho?		Do you get very angry?
¿Te preocupas mucho?		Do you get very worried?

¿Por qué no te sientas ahora?	13-1		Why don't you sit down now?
te vistes	13-2		get dressed
te bañas	13-3		bathe
me acuesto	13-4		
Si no me duermo ahora,	13-5		If I don't go to sleep now,
me levanto	13-6		
no me despierto mañana.	13-7		I won't wake up tomorrow.

¿Me puedo lavar las manos?	13-8	May I wash my hands?
manos	13-9	

Note: The use of the reflexive pronoun with *despertar* is optional for many Spanish speakers.

No ha escrito la lista.	She hasn't written the list.
dicho	said
visto	seen
abierto	opened

¿Dónde ha puesto la lista?	Where has she put the list?
¿Han vuelto solos?	Have they come back by themselves (alone)?

Ella cumple quince en el verano.	13-10	She'll be (fulfill) fifteen in the summer.
el otoño	13-11	the autumn
el invierno	13-12	the winter
la primavera	13-13	

¿En qué estación estamos?	What season is this?
¿Cuándo es tu aniversario?	When is your anniversary?
santo[2]	saint's day
cumpleaños } 13-14	

¿Me quito el abrigo?	13-15	Shall I take off my coat?
Me pongo	13-16	put on

Listening and Speaking Exercises 211, 212, 213*, 214*, p. T112 ⊗

---

[2] In many Spanish-speaking countries it is the custom for a person to celebrate the day of the saint for which he was named, instead of, or as well as, his own birthday. In certain areas women celebrate only their saint's day while men celebrate only their birthday.

BASIC FORMS

Verbs

*aburrirse	*dormirse (ue)	*ponerse
*acostarse (ue)	*enojarse	*preocuparse
*asustarse	*fijarse	*presentarse
*bañarse	invitar	*quedarse
*cansarse	*irse	*quitarse
cumplir	*lavarse	*sentarse (ie)
*despertarse (ie)	*levantarse	*vestirse (i)

Nouns

cumpleaños	*m.*	mano	*f.*
doble	*m.*	mitad	*f.*
hombre	*m.*		

Vocabulary Exercises

1. QUESTIONS

1. ¿Está Bárbara invitada a la fiesta de Ana?   *No, no está invitada.*
2. Y Cecilia, ¿está invitada ella?   *No, tampoco.*
3. ¿Por qué no están invitadas, según Cecilia?   *Tal vez Ana no ha hecho la lista todavía.*
4. ¿A usted le gusta dar fiestas?
5. ¿Cuándo va a dar una?
6. ¿A quiénes va a invitar?
7. ¿Va a invitar al maestro de español?
8. ¿A usted le gusta invitar a sus amigos a la casa?
9. ¿Le gusta bailar? ¿Cuáles bailes le gustan más?
10. ¿Le gusta hablar por teléfono?

2. FREE COMPLETION

1. Siempre me acuesto muy _____.   *tarde, temprano*
2. ¿Por qué no te sientas en el _____?   *sofá, suelo, comedor*
3. Los domingos me levanto a las _____.   *diez, once*
4. No he escrito la _____.   *lista, carta, tarea, lección*
5. Me voy a lavar _____.   *las manos, la cara, el pelo*

3. QUESTIONS

1. ¿Va a ser pronto el cumpleaños de Cecilia? *Sí, muy pronto.*
2. ¿Va a hacer una fiesta de cumpleaños ella? *Sí, pero no una fiesta grande.*
3. ¿A cuántos muchachos piensa invitar? ¿A cuántas muchachas? *A unos veinte; a unas diez.*
4. ¿Qué le parece la idea a Bárbara? ¿Por qué le parece bien? *Le parece bien; siempre se presenta la mitad de los hombres.*
5. ¿Cuándo es su cumpleaños?
6. ¿Cuántos años va a cumplir?
7. ¿Piensa dar una fiesta?
8. ¿Va a invitar a más muchachos o a más muchachas? ¿Por qué?
9. ¿Sabe usted cuándo es su santo?
10. ¿Sabe cuándo es el aniversario de sus padres? ¿Cuándo es?
11. ¿En qué estación estamos?
12. ¿Cuál estación prefiere usted? ¿Por qué?
13. ¿Cuántas estaciones hay en un año? ¿Cuáles son? *Cuatro: primavera, verano, otoño, invierno*
14. ¿En cuál estación hace calor? ¿En cuál estación hace frío? *Hace calor en el verano. Hace frío en el invierno.*

4. ANTONYMS

Me acuesto temprano.	*Me levanto temprano.*
Voy a hacer una fiesta grande.	*Voy a hacer una fiesta pequeña.*
Me quito los guantes.	*Me pongo los guantes.*
Me acuesto tarde.	*Me acuesto temprano.*
El almacén está cerrado.	*El almacén está abierto.*

GRAMMAR

Irregular Past Participles

TEACHER PRESENTATION, p. T196
GENERALIZATION

Some verbs have an irregular past participle. The most common irregular past participles are these:

abierto	(abrir)	puesto	(poner)
dicho	(decir)	visto	(ver)
escrito	(escribir)	vuelto	(volver)
hecho	(hacer)		

STRUCTURE DRILLS

5. PERSON-NUMBER SUBSTITUTION

1. No he abierto la puerta. ⊗
    (nosotros)
    (ellos)
    (tú)
    (él)

No he abierto la puerta.
No hemos abierto la puerta.
No han abierto la puerta.
No has abierto la puerta.
No ha abierto la puerta.

2. ¿Has visto al jefe? ⊗
    (ella–ustedes–usted y yo–tú)

ha visto–han visto–
hemos visto–has visto

6. ITEM SUBSTITUTION

1. No he visto la lista. ⊗
    (escribir)
    (hacer)
    (decir)
    (ver)

No he visto la lista.
No he escrito la lista.
No he hecho la lista.
No he dicho la lista.
No he visto la lista.

2. ¿Qué has puesto en la cocina? ⊗
    (ver–hacer–decir–poner)

has visto–has hecho–
has dicho–has puesto

7. PRESENT → PRESENT PERFECT

¿Ya vuelven los muchachos? ⊗
¿Qué haces?
¿Abres las cartas?
No vuelve todavía.
Yo no digo nada.
¿La lista? No la hago todavía.
¿El correo? Lo pongo en su escritorio.
¿Él? Nunca nos escribe.

¿Ya han vuelto los muchachos?
¿Qué has hecho?
¿Has abierto las cartas?
No ha vuelto todavía.
Yo no he dicho nada.
¿La lista? No la he hecho todavía.
¿El correo? Lo he puesto en su escritorio.
¿Él? Nunca nos ha escrito.

VARIATION: Use right-hand column as stimulus and have student give present tense forms.

8. DOUBLE ITEM SUBSTITUTION

VARIATION

1. He escrito la lista. ⊗   visto
    Voy a _____.
    _____ escribiendo _____.   viendo
    _____ hacer _____.   decir
    He _____.
    Estoy _____.

He escrito la lista.   *He visto la lista.*
Voy a escribir la lista.   *Voy a ver la lista.*
Estoy escribiendo la lista. *Estoy viendo la lista.*
Voy a hacer la lista.   *Voy a decir la lista.*
He hecho la lista.   *He dicho la lista.*
Estoy haciendo la lista.   *Estoy di-*   (*continued*)
ciendo la lista.

(*continued*)

	VARIATION	

2. No hemos dicho nada.    hecho

    ___ vamos a _____.

    ___ estamos _____.

    _____ visto _____.   abierto

    ___ vamos a _____.

No hemos dicho nada.   → *No hemos hecho nada.*

No vamos a decir nada.   *No vamos a hacer nada.*

No estamos diciendo nada.   *No estamos haciendo nada.*

No hemos visto nada.   *No hemos abierto nada.*

No vamos a ver nada.   *No vamos a abrir nada.*

9. FREE RESPONSE

¿Ya ha hecho usted toda su tarea para mañana?

¿Ha escrito la lección de español?

¿Ya la ha puesto en mi escritorio?

¿Este libro está escrito en inglés o en español?

¿Qué han tenido que leer ustedes para hoy?

¿Ya ha vuelto su padre del trabajo? ¿A qué hora vuelve él?

¿Está abierta la puerta? ¿Están abiertas todas las ventanas?

¿Alguno de ustedes ha visto al maestro de geografía hoy?

10. WRITING EXERCISE

Write the responses to Drills 6.2, 7, 8.2.

EXERCISE BOOK: EXERCISES 1 AND 2

Girls attend a bullfight in Mexico. Bullfighting is popular in only six Spanish American countries.

Reflexive Pronouns

PRESENTATION *TEACHER PRESENTATION, p. T197*

Sólo yo <u>me</u> **presento.**
Sólo tú <u>te</u> **presentas.**
Sólo él <u>se</u> **presenta.**
Sólo nosotros <u>nos</u> **presentamos.**
Sólo ellos <u>se</u> **presentan.**

Which word means *myself? yourself* (familiar)? *himself? ourselves? themselves?* What is the position of these words in relation to the verb?

GENERALIZATION

1. Reflexive pronouns are object pronouns which are the same in reference as the subject. In English they end in *self* or *selves*.

John cut himself.

We saw ourselves in the mirror.

2. These are the reflexive pronouns in Spanish:

	Singular	Plural
1	me	nos
2	te	
3		se

Me, te, and **nos** have the same form as the corresponding direct and indirect object pronouns. The third person pronoun **se** is invariable; it does not change to show either number or gender agreement.

3. The reflexive pronouns occupy the same position in sentences as the direct and indirect object pronouns.

> **No <u>se</u> reconoce en la foto.**
> *She doesn't recognize herself in the picture.*

> **Nunca <u>se</u> han visto en televisión.**
> *They've never seen themselves on television.*

Listening and Speaking Exercises 219 and 220*, p. T117 ⊗   SECTION C

STRUCTURE DRILLS

11. PERSON-NUMBER SUBSTITUTION

1. No se presenta. ⊗   No se presenta.
   (yo)   No me presento.
   (los muchachos)   No se presentan.
   (nosotros)   No nos presentamos.
   (Ana)   No se presenta.
   (usted)   No se presenta.
   (tú)   No te presentas.
   (ella)   No se presenta.
   (ellas)   No se presentan.

2. Me veo en la foto. ⊗   *se ve–se ven–me veo–te ves–nos vemos*
   (usted–Cecilia y Carlos–yo–tú–Hernán y yo)

12. PAIRED SENTENCES

¿Nunca se ha visto en televisión? ⊗   ¿Nunca se ha visto en televisión?
Hasn't he ever seen him on television?   ¿Nunca lo ha visto en televisión?
Hasn't he ever seen himself on television? ¿Nunca se ha visto en televisión?

No se reconocen en esa foto.   *No se reconocen en esa foto.*
They don't recognize them in that pic-   *No los reconocen en esa foto.*
ture.
They don't recognize themselves in that   *No se reconocen en esa foto.*
picture.

13. WRITING EXERCISE

Write the responses to Drills 11.2 and 12.

EXERCISE BOOK: EXERCISES 3 AND 4

Reflexive Pronouns with Service-Disservice Verbs

TEACHER PRESENTATION, p. T198
GENERALIZATION

You learned in Unit 9 that the person or thing for whom a service or a disservice is performed is usually expressed as an indirect object in Spanish. When someone performs a service (or disservice) for himself, the appropriate reflexive pronoun is used. Note the use of the definite article—not a possessive—with the direct object.

Juan se lava las manos.
John is washing his hands.

Yo me quito los guantes.
I'm taking off my gloves.

STRUCTURE DRILLS

14. PERSON-NUMBER SUBSTITUTION

1. Me lavo las manos. ⊗
   (tú)
   (nosotros)
   (él)
   (los chicos)
   (yo)

   Me lavo las manos.
   Te lavas las manos.
   Nos lavamos las manos.
   Se lava las manos.
   Se lavan las manos.
   Me lavo las manos.

2. ¿Cómo? ¿Te compras un carro nuevo? ⊗
   (usted–la maestra–ustedes–yo–tú)

   se compra–se compra–se compran–me compro–te compras

15. PAIRED SENTENCES

Me quito los zapatos. ⊗
I take off their shoes.
I take off my shoes.

Me quito los zapatos.
Les quito los zapatos.
Me quito los zapatos.

Me pongo los guantes.
I put his gloves on (him).
I put my gloves on.

Me pongo los guantes.
Le pongo los guantes.
Me pongo los guantes.

Se compra un carro.
He buys them a car.
He buys himself a car.

Se compra un carro.
Les compra un carro.
Se compra un carro.

(continued)

(continued)

¿Te haces un vestido?	*¿Te haces un vestido?*
Are you making her a dress?	*¿Le haces un vestido?*
Are you making yourself a dress?	*¿Te haces un vestido?*

16. PATTERNED RESPONSE

¿Su mamá les pone la ropa a los chiqui-
   tos? ⊗

No, ellos se ponen la ropa solos.

¿El peluquero le lava el pelo a usted?

No, yo me lavo el pelo solo.

¿Usted le limpia los zapatos a su hermanito?

No, él se limpia los zapatos solo.

¿La criada le hace la comida a su mamá?

No, ella se hace la comida sola.

¿Usted les quita los guantes a los geme-
   litos?

No, ellos se quitan los guantes solos.

17. FREE RESPONSE

¿Qué se pone usted para ir a una fiesta? ¿y para venir a la escuela?

¿Qué se pone cuando hace frío?

¿Se quitan ustedes el abrigo cuando llegan a la escuela? ¿y los guantes? ¿y los zapatos?

¿Su mamá le hace la ropa a usted?

¿Cuándo se lava el pelo usted?

¿Quién le lava el pelo? ¿su mamá? ¿la peluquera?

¿Usted se limpia los zapatos todos los días?

¿Su papá se compra un carro nuevo cada año?

¿Le va a comprar uno a usted este año?

18. WRITING EXERCISE

Write the responses to Drills 14.2, 15, and 16.

More about Reflexive Pronouns

TEACHER PRESENTATION, p. T198
GENERALIZATION

1. Some Spanish verbs, like **lavar**, **sentar**, and **preocupar**, always have a direct object. If the direct object is not the same in reference as the subject, the pattern of the Spanish sentence is like that of the English equivalent.

Juan está lavando las paredes.
John is washing the walls.

Rosa sienta a su tía.
Rose is seating her aunt.

Yo preocupo a mi mamá.
I worry my mother.

If, however, the direct object is the same in reference as the subject, a reflexive direct object pronoun is used in the Spanish sentence, while the English equivalent may show no object at all (*I worry*), use *get* + an adjective (*I get worried*), or use some word like *up* or *down* (*She sits down*).

Juan se está lavando.
John is washing (up).

Rosa se sienta.
Rose sits (down).

Yo me preocupo.
I worry (get worried).

2. Other verbs like **lavar, sentar,** and **preocupar** which you have learned are these:

	Used with a Direct Object	*Used with a Reflexive Direct Object*
aburrir	*bore (someone)*	*get bored*
acostar	*put (someone) to bed*	*go to bed*
asustar	*scare, frighten (someone)*	*get scared, frightened*
bañar	*bathe (someone)*	*bathe, take a bath*
cansar	*tire (someone)*	*tire, get tired*
despertar	*wake (someone) up*	*wake up*
enojar	*make (someone) angry*	*get angry*
levantar	*lift, raise (something)*	*rise*
	get (someone) up, out of bed	*get up, out of bed*
llamar	*call (someone)*	*be named*
mojar	*wet (someone, something)*	*get wet*
presentar	*present (someone, something)*	*show up*
vestir	*dress (someone)*	*dress, get dressed*

3. The following verbs are always reflexive with the meanings given:

Note: Quedar is used without a reflexive pronoun with the meaning be left (Sólo dos pesos me quedan. Es el único que queda.) and agree (Quedé en llamarlo.)

quedarse	*stay*
resfriarse	*catch a cold*
equivocarse	*be mistaken, make a mistake*

4. **Dormir** means *sleep;* **dormirse** means *fall asleep.*

> **Todos duermen.**
> *They're all sleeping.*

> **Juan se duerme inmediatamente.**
> *Juan falls asleep immediately.*

5. *Go* has two Spanish equivalents: **ir** and **irse**. **Ir** is used when the destination is expressed or at least clearly understood.

> **¿Vas a la fiesta? No, no voy.**

Irse is used when the destination is not mentioned, or when it is mentioned but the emphasis is on the departure rather than the destination. In addition to *go*, common English equivalents for **irse** are *leave* and *go away.*

> **¿Ya te vas?**
> *Are you going (leaving) already?*

> **Me voy a México mañana.**
> *I'm leaving for Mexico tomorrow.*

STRUCTURE DRILLS

19. PERSON-NUMBER SUBSTITUTION

1. ¿Te sientas aquí? ⊗   ¿Te sientas aquí?
   (nosotros)   ¿Nos sentamos aquí?
   (yo)   ¿Me siento aquí?
   (ustedes)   ¿Se sientan aquí?
   (su cuñado)   ¿Se sienta aquí?
   (tú)   ¿Te sientas aquí?

2. Nunca se aburren en esta clase. ⊗ *nos aburrimos–me aburro–nos aburrimos–se aburren–se aburre–*
   (nosotros–yo–mis compañeros y yo–los alumnos–el maestro–tú) *te aburres*

3. Me quedo un rato más: *nos quedamos–se quedan–se queda–te quedas–se quedan–nos quedamos*
   (nosotros–ustedes–Bárbara–tú–los muchachos–mi mamá y yo)

20. PATTERNED RESPONSE

¿Ya te vas?   No, me voy a las cinco.
¿Ya se van los muchachos?   No, se van a las cinco.
¿Ya se van ustedes?   No, nos vamos a las cinco.

¿Ya se va la señora?   No, se va a las cinco.
¿Ya te vas?   No, me voy a las cinco.

Listening and Speaking Exercises 221 and 222*, p. T118 ⊗

SECTION D

21. PAIRED SENTENCES

Estoy muy cansado. ⊗   Estoy muy cansado.
I get very tired.   Me canso mucho.
I am very tired.   Estoy muy cansado.

¿Ya estás vestido?   *¿Ya estás vestido?*
Are you getting dressed already?   *¿Ya te vistes?*
Are you dressed already?   *¿Ya estás vestido?*

¿Por qué están enojados?   *¿Por qué están enojados?*
Why are they getting angry?   *¿Por qué se enojan?*
Why are they angry?   *¿Por qué están enojados?*

22. ADJECTIVE → REFLEXIVE CONSTRUCTION

Los muchachos están aburridos. ⊗   Los muchachos se aburren.
La maestra está enojada.   *La maestra se enoja.*
Yo estoy preocupado.   *Yo me preocupo.*
Mis amigos y yo estamos cansados.   *Mis amigos y yo nos cansamos.*
El jefe está equivocado.   *El jefe se equivoca.*
Las chicas están asustadas.   *Las chicas se asustan.*
Los chicos están resfriados.   *Los chicos se resfrían.*

VARIATION: Use the right-hand column as stimulus.

23. WRITING EXERCISE

Write the responses to Drills 19.2 and 22.
EXERCISE BOOK: EXERCISES 5, 6, AND 7

24. PROGRESSIVE SUBSTITUTION

		VARIATION
Los alumnos se aburren mucho. ⊗	*Los alumnos se aburren mucho.*	se preocupan
Yo _____.	*Yo me aburro mucho.*	
_____ nos _____.	*Nosotros nos aburrimos mucho.*	
_____ cansas ____.	*Tú te cansas mucho.*	enojas
Él _____.	*Él se cansa mucho.*	
_____ te _____.	*Tú te cansas mucho.*	
_____ preocupamos _.	*Nosotros nos preocupamos mucho.*	resfriamos

25. FREE SUBSTITUTION

La maestra nunca se enoja.   los alumnos, ese chico, tú y yo / aburrirse, preocuparse, cansarse

26. DIRECTED DIALOG

Pregúntele a *Juana* a qué hora se levanta.
Juana, contéstele.

Juana, ¿a qué hora te levantas?

Pregúntele a *Pepe* a qué hora se acuesta.
Pepe, contéstele.

Pepe, ¿a qué hora te acuestas?

Pregúnteles a *Elena* y a *Susana* hasta qué hora se quedan aquí.
Elena, contéstele.

¿Hasta qué hora se quedan aquí?

Pregúnteme a mí si yo me enojo mucho.

¿Se enoja usted mucho?

27. BASIC DIALOG VARIATION

Say the first part of the Basic Dialog again, this time making it a conversation between two ladies who address each other as **usted.** Omit the expression **fíjate.** *Bárbara le pregunta a Cecilia si ya se va y por qué no se queda un rato más. Cecilia le dice que no, que si no se acuesta temprano, no se levanta mañana. Bárbara le pregunta si está invitada a la fiesta de Ana, y le dice que ella no está invitada. Cecilia le dice*

28. TÚ → USTED

que ella tampoco, y que tal vez es que Ana no ha hecho la lista todavía.

Te llamas Juan. ⊗	Se llama Juan.
Te reconozco.	Lo (*or* la) reconozco.
Te hablo mañana.	Le hablo mañana.
Siempre te enojas.	*Siempre se enoja.*
¿Ya te vas?	*¿Ya se va?*
Te traigo un regalo.	*Le traigo un regalo.*
No te veo.	*No lo veo.*

VARIATION: Use right-hand column as stimulus.

29. PAIRED SENTENCES

No se asusta. ⊗	No se asusta.
He doesn't frighten me.	No me asusta.
He doesn't get frightened.	No se asusta.
Me despierto.	*Me despierto.*
I wake him up.	*Lo despierto.*
I wake up.	*Me despierto.*
Tú te preocupas mucho.	*Tú te preocupas mucho.*
You worry me a lot.	*Tú me preocupas mucho.*
You worry a lot.	*Tú te preocupas mucho.*
Nunca se aburren.	*Nunca se aburren.*
They never bore us.	*Nunca nos aburren.*
They never get bored.	*Nunca se aburren.*

30. FREE RESPONSE

¿A qué hora se despierta usted?

¿Quién lo despierta?

¿A qué hora se levanta?

¿Se lava la cara cuando se levanta?

¿Se baña o solamente se lava la cara?

¿A qué hora se acuesta usted?

¿Se duerme inmediatamente?

¿Cuántas horas duerme usted?

¿Va usted a muchas fiestas?

¿Se preocupa su mamá cuando usted llega tarde de una fiesta?

¿Y usted se enoja cuando ella se preocupa?

¿Tienen ustedes muchos exámenes?

¿Se asustan cuando tienen un examen?

¿Hasta qué hora se quedan los alumnos en la escuela?

¿A qué hora se va usted?

¿Hasta qué hora se quedan los maestros?

¿Cómo se llama usted?

¿Tiene usted hermanos? ¿Cómo se llaman ellos?

¿Sabe cómo me llamo yo?

31. WRITING EXERCISE

Write the responses to Drills 24, 28 and 29.

EXERCISE BOOK: EXERCISES 8, 9, AND 10

Listening and Speaking Exercise 223*, p. T119 ⊗

Writing

11. SENTENCE CONSTRUCTION

MODELS: Yo / levantarse / temprano   Juana / haber / escribir / carta
Yo me levanto temprano.   Juana ha escrito la carta.

1. alumnos / siempre / presentarse / tarde   *Los alumnos siempre se presentan tarde.*
2. primos y yo / sentarse / suelo   *Mis primos y yo nos sentamos en el suelo.*
3. hermanito / vestirse / solo   *Mi hermanito se viste solo.*
4. todo el mundo / irse / ahora   *Todo el mundo se va ahora.*
5. mamá / quitar / guantes / hermanita   *Mi mamá le quita los guantes a mi hermanita.*
6. criada / haber / abrir / puerta   *La criada ha abierto la puerta.*
7. Ana y yo / haber / hacer / lista   *Ana y yo hemos hecho la lista.*
8. chicos / no / haber / volver / todavía   *Los chicos no han vuelto todavía.*

2. PARAGRAPH COMPLETION

Copy the following paragraphs, filling in the blank spaces with the appropriate reflexive pronoun.

¡Qué aburrida es mi vida! Todos los días cuando __1__ despierto, mi mamá me grita: ¡Apúrate, Juan! ¿No __2__ has vestido todavía? ¿Ni siquiera __3__ has levantado? Yo __4__ levanto, __5__ baño, __6__ visto y voy al comedor.

Mi hermana Teresa __7__ sienta conmigo y empieza a hablar y hablar. Mi mamá y mi papá __8__ enojan porque creen que vamos a llegar tarde a la escuela. Por fin __9__ levantamos. Yo __10__ pongo el saco y Teresa __11__ pone el swéater y __12__ vamos a la escuela. ¡Cómo yo __13__ aburro!

1	2	3	4	5	6	7	8	9	10	11	12	13
me	te	te	me	me	me	se	se	nos	me	se	nos	me

RECOMBINATION MATERIAL

Dialogs

I

→ *VARIATION*

BÁRBARA	Elena, ¿me prestas tu swéater nuevo?	Juan / corbata nueva
ELENA	¿Estás loca? ¿Para qué lo necesitas?	loco / la
BÁRBARA	Ay, tú siempre te enojas cuando yo te pido algo.	
ELENA	Es que tú siempre quieres usar mi ropa.	
BÁRBARA	¡Qué hermana más antipática! Lo necesito para la fiesta de Ana.	hermano / la
ELENA	Bueno, pero si algo le pasa a ese swéater, yo te MATO.	esa corbata

QUESTIONS

1. ¿Qué le pide Bárbara a Elena?
2. ¿Qué le pregunta Elena?
3. ¿Cuándo se enoja siempre Elena, según Bárbara?
4. ¿Qué quiere siempre Bárbara, según Elena?
5. ¿Para qué necesita el swéater Bárbara?
6. ¿Le presta el swéater por fin Elena?
7. ¿Qué dice Elena que va a hacer si algo le pasa al swéater?
8. ¿Es exagerada ella?

DIALOG VARIATION

Read the dialog once again. This time it will be an argument between two brothers, one of whom wants to borrow a tie from the other.

II

MAESTRO	¡Viera usted la clase de español que tengo! Esos chicos son imposibles.
MAESTRA	No lo creo, Sr. Almanza. Usted es tan exagerado.
MAESTRO	¡Ja! Uno se levanta; el otro sale sin pedir permiso; el otro se aburre y se duerme . . .
MAESTRA	Es que usted los hace trabajar mucho.
MAESTRO	No es eso, es que son imposibles.

QUESTIONS

1. ¿Quién es el Sr. Almanza?
2. ¿Qué dice de su clase de español?
3. ¿Cree la maestra lo que dice él? ¿Por qué no?
4. ¿Qué hacen los alumnos del Sr. Almanza?
5. ¿Por qué hacen eso, según la maestra?
6. ¿Y según el Sr. Almanza?

III

HERMANO	¿Sigues hablando? ¿No te puedes apurar un poco?
HERMANA	Sí, sí, —y fíjate, Marta, que hay una liquidación de . . .
HERMANO	¡Caramba! Esta hermana mía pasa horas hablando por teléfono. ¡¡¡APÚRATE!!!
HERMANA	¡Shhh! ¡Cómo gritas! —y otra cosa que te tengo que contar, Martita. . . .
HERMANO	¿ME VAS A DEJAR USAR EL TELÉFONO?
HERMANA	—Bueno, Martita, no puedo hablar más. Parece que mi hermanito quiere usar el teléfono. Hasta luego, chica.

QUESTIONS

1. ¿Qué está haciendo la hermana?
2. ¿Qué quiere el hermano?
3. ¿Por qué necesita usar el teléfono él?
4. ¿De qué están hablando la hermana y su amiga?
5. ¿Cómo pasa horas la hermana?
6. ¿Se apura en colgar ella?
7. ¿Qué cosa grita el hermano, por fin?
8. ¿Cuelga la hermana, por fin?

Narrative

Problemas entre° hermanos

A mí me encanta ver la televisión, pero desgraciadamente°, a mi hermanito también le gusta mucho. Él siempre quiere ver esos programas* para niños°, esos programas aburridos de cowboys*. Me cansa tener que pelear° con él cada vez que quiero
5   ver algo interesante. A mí me gustan los programas para adultos*. . . las noticias, por ejemplo, o un buen programa musical*. También me gustan esas películas que dan en las noches, muy tarde. Pero no me gustan esos programas ridículos* de indios y cowboys.

10 Pero mi hermano es un niño todavía, tiene solamente nueve años. Él no entiende ni las noticias ni la música* ni ninguna de las cosas que a mí me interesan*. Y ahora que tenemos una nueva televisión en colores, la situación* está peor°.

El otro día, por ejemplo, llego yo de la escuela, y después
15 de comer algo y estudiar un poco, voy a la sala para ver uno de mis programas favoritos*. Diez minutos* después llega mi hermanito. Se queda viendo el programa un rato, y luego se levanta y se acerca° a la televisión. ¡Ni siquiera pide permiso! Cambia° el canal* sin decir una palabra, ni una sola palabra. ¡Nunca he
20 visto a un chico como ese hermano mío! A veces creo que hace estas cosas para molestar, nada más. ¡Qué muchacho más antipático!

Bueno, él se sienta otra vez, y allí estoy yo, teniendo que ver uno de esos programas ridículos. Primero aparece* el héroe*,
25 guapo, simpático, inteligente . . . un cowboy típico* con un gran sombrero y dos pistolas*. Luego sale el indio y empiezan a pelear. ¡Qué absurdo*! Claro que yo me aburro viendo esas cosas, y entonces, después de dos o tres minutos, me levanto, voy a la televisión, y cambio el canal. No le digo nada a mi hermano.
30 ¿Para qué? Él no entiende nada. Además, él también cambia el canal cuando quiere y no le pide permiso a nadie. Ésta no es la primera vez, no señor. Esto ocurre casi todos los días en mi casa. Él siempre hace lo que quiere. Bueno, vieran ustedes cómo llora y grita ese chiquito porque yo cambio el canal. ¡Qué barbaridad!
35 En ese momento* llega mi papá, enojadísimo. Mi hermano y yo estamos muy asustados porque cuando nuestro padre se enoja, se enoja de verdad. Pero mi papá no nos dice nada. Ni siquiera nos mira. Va a la televisión y cambia el canal una vez más. Y se

¿Hay muchos problemas entre hermanos en su casa? Entre usted y yo ¿es esta su clase favorita?
entre: *between, among*

desgraciadamente: *unfortunately*
niño: *child*
pelear: *fight*
¿Hay niños pequeños en su familia? ¿Lloran mucho? ¿Molestan?
¿Hay niños pequeños en esta escuela?
¿Pelea usted con su hermano? ¿Quién gana?
¿Pelea usted con los otros alumnos?
peor: *worse*
¿Cuál es peor, un examen de inglés o un dictado en español?

acercarse: *approach, go towards*
cambiar: *change*
¿Cuál es peor, un examen de geografía o un examen de inglés?

¿Para qué se acerca a la televisión el hermanito de la narradora?
¿Quién se acerca a la televisión después? ¿Para qué?
¿Usted cambia el canal cuando su hermanito está viendo la televisión?
¿Él también cambia el canal?
¿Qué hace usted cuando él cambia el canal?

sienta a ver las noticias. Mi hermano y yo salimos sin abrir la
40 boca°. Él se va a su dormitorio y cierra la puerta. Yo me voy a
mi escritorio y me siento a hacer mis lecciones. Y en la sala, con
excepción de la voz° del comentador* de las noticias, silencio
total* y absoluto.

¿Por qué salen la narradora
y su hermano sin abrir la
boca?
boca: *mouth*
¿A usted le gusta cantar?
¿Tiene bonita voz?
voz (*f*): *voice*
¿Tienen bonita voz los
comentadores de la tele-
visión?

QUESTIONS

Yo soy Juanita Martínez, la autora de la narración que ustedes acaban de leer.

1. ¿Qué me encanta a mí? ¿y a mi hermano? *1*
2. ¿Qué programas le gustan a él? *3*
3. ¿Qué tengo que hacer cada vez que quiero ver algo interesante? *4*
4. ¿Qué programas me gustan a mí? *5*
5. ¿Por qué está peor la situación ahora? *12*
6. El otro día, cuando llego de la escuela, ¿que hago primero? ¿y luego? *15*
7. ¿Quién llega diez minutos después? *16*
8. ¿Qué hace él por un rato? *17*
9. ¿Qué hace después? *17*
10. ¿Qué me dice cuando cambia el canal? *19*
11. ¿Por qué hace estas cosas, probablemente? *20*
12. ¿Cómo es el programa que él quiere ver? *24*
13. ¿Quién aparece primero? *.24*
14. ¿Cómo es el héroe? *25*
15. ¿Quién aparece luego? *26*
16. ¿Qué empiezan a hacer? *26*
17. ¿Qué hago yo después de dos o tres minutos? *28*
18. ¿Le digo algo a mi hermano? ¿Por qué no? *31*
19. ¿Qué hace mi hermanito cuando yo cambio el canal? *33*
20. ¿Quién llega en ese momento? *35*
21. ¿Qué hace mi papá? *38*
22. ¿Qué hacemos mi hermano y yo? *39*
23. ¿Adónde va él? ¿Y yo qué hago? *40*
24. ¿Qué hay en la sala? *43*

Conversation Stimulus

Usted quiere ver las noticias en la televisión, pero su hermano quiere ver un partido de tenis.

Start like this:

Las noticias empiezan en cinco minutos.
¿Cómo? Tú quieres ver las noticias ahora?
Sí, _siempre veo las noticias a las seis y media._
¡Qué aburrido! _Yo quiero ver el partido de tenis._
Ay, esos partidos son tan aburridos. ¿Por qué no vemos la noticias, mejor?

¿Puede usted describir un programa de televisión típico?

Use the following questions as a guide:

1. ¿Quién es el héroe?
2. ¿Cómo es él?
3. ¿Quién es la novia del héroe?
4. ¿Cómo es ella?
5. ¿Pelean el héroe y su novia?
6. ¿Pelea el héroe con otra persona?
7. ¿Con quién?
8. ¿Termina* el programa con todos contentos?

El programa que voy a describir se llama _____. El héroe es _____, un cowboy alto y guapo. Su novia se llama _____. Ella es bonita y rubia, pero no muy inteligente. El héroe nunca pelea con su novia. Pelea con un hombre malo que se llama _____. Al fin del programa, el héroe mata al hombre malo y todos están muy contentos.

BASIC DIALOG

Regreso de los Estados Unidos

CLAUDIA	Ay, no nos oye. ¡Señor! ¡Por favor, mi maleta!
GLORIA	Y la mía también. ¡Por favor, que tenemos prisa!

14-1 *Note:* Point out *Aduana* sign in poster.

EMPLEADO	No tengo mil manos. Paciencia, ya se la doy. ¿Cuál es la suya? 14-2
CLAUDIA	La negra. Ésa no, la otra. La que acaba de tocar. Ésa. Gracias. 14-3

GLORIA	¡Allá arriba está toda la familia! 14-4
CLAUDIA	El de anteojos negros . . . ¿es Alberto ése?
GLORIA	Sí. ¡Qué alto está nuestro hermanito! 14-5
CLAUDIA	¡Altísimo! ¡Qué emoción[1] estar de vuelta en Colombia!
GLORIA	¡Y no tener que hablar más inglés!

14-6

Back (Return) from the United States

CLAUDIA	Darn, he doesn't hear us. Mister! Please, my suitcase!
GLORIA	And mine too. Please, we're in a hurry.
EMPLOYEE	I only have two hands. (I don't have a thousand hands.) Patience, I'll give it to you in a second (now). Which is yours?
CLAUDIA	The black one. Not that one, the other one. The one you just touched. That one. Thanks.

GLORIA	The whole family's up there!
CLAUDIA	The one with sunglasses . . . is that Alberto?
GLORIA	Yes. Our little brother certainly has got tall!
CLAUDIA	Very tall! It's so exciting (what emotion) to be back in Colombia!
GLORIA	And not have to speak English any more!

---

[1] ¡Qué emoción! is an expression more commonly used by women than by men.

◀ *An aerial view of Bogotá, Colombia. The city is built on a sloping plain at the foot of two mountains.*

Note: It is not unusual for wealthy Spanish-American families to send their children to secondary school in Europe or the United States.

Supplement

¿Cuándo regresan?		When are they returning?
maleta	14-1	
¡Por favor, mi baúl!	14-2	Please, my trunk!
equipaje	14-3	baggage

Están en la ciudad.	14-4	They're in the city.
el edificio	14-5	the building
el departamento	14-6	the apartment
el jardín	14-7	the garden

Me das mis llaves, por favor.	14-8	Will you give me my keys, please.
mi cartera	14-9	my purse
mi paraguas	14-10	my umbrella
mi impermeable	14-11	my raincoat
mi cepillo	14-12	my brush
mi peine	14-13	my comb
mis anteojos	14-14	
Gracias. De nada.		Thank you. You're welcome.

Allá abajo está toda la familia.	The whole family is down there.
A la derecha	on the right
A la izquierda	on the left

¡Qué joven está!	14-15	How young he looks!
viejo		old

¡Qué brutal!	That's terrific (brutal)!
estupendo	wonderful
espantoso	awful

¡Y no tener que aprender más inglés!	And not have to learn English any more!
enseñar	teach

Vamos a hacer las maletas ahora.	14-16	We're going to pack now.

Listening and Speaking Exercises 224, 225, 226, 227*, 228*, p. T120 ⊗

BASIC FORMS

Verbs

aprender   regresar
enseñar   tocar

Nouns

anteojos *m.pl.*   peine *m.*
baúl *m.*   ciudad *f.*
impermeable *m.*   emoción *f.*
jardín *m.*   llave *f.*
paraguas *m.*

Adjectives

brutal   joven

Vocabulary Exercises

1. QUESTIONS

1. ¿De dónde acaban de regresar Claudia y Gloria?   *De los Estados Unidos.*
2. ¿Qué le están pidiendo al empleado?   *Su maleta.*
3. ¿Qué tiene Gloria, paciencia o prisa?   *Tiene prisa.*
4. ¿Qué les dice el empleado?   *Les dice que no tiene mil manos.*
5. ¿De qué color es la maleta de Claudia?   *Es negra.*
6. ¿Tienen mucho equipaje las chicas?   *No, cada una tiene solamente una maleta.*
7. ¿Tengo yo paciencia con ustedes?
8. ¿A usted le gusta viajar?
9. ¿Tiene usted un baúl?
10. ¿Tiene unas maletas?
11. ¿Qué pone en su maleta cuando hace un viaje?
12. ¿Hay edificios grandes en esta ciudad?
13. ¿Vive usted en una casa o en un departamento?
14. ¿Tiene su casa un jardín?
15. ¿Tiene usted una llave de la casa?
16. *María,* ¿qué tiene usted en la cartera?

2. SENTENCE COMPLETION

1. ¡Cómo llueve! Necesito mi _____. *paraguas, impermeable*
2. Por favor, ¿me da mi _____? *cartera, maleta, equipaje, llave, paraguas*
3. Vivo en _____. *ese edificio, un departamento, la ciudad*
4. Los niños están jugando en el _____. *jardín, parque*
5. No encuentro nada en esta _____. *cartera, maleta*

3. QUESTIONS

1. ¿Quiénes están en el aeropuerto cuando llegan Claudia y Gloria? *Toda la familia está allí.*
2. ¿En qué parte del edificio están, arriba o abajo? *Están arriba.*
3. ¿Quién es el muchacho de anteojos negros? *Es Alberto, su hermano.*
4. ¿Está muy alto él? *Sí, altísimo.*
5. ¿Usa usted anteojos para leer?
6. ¿Están contentas de estar de vuelta las dos chicas? *Sí, están contentas.*
7. ¿Por qué están tan contentas? *Porque no van a tener que hablar más inglés.*
8. ¿Piensa usted hacer un viaje este verano?
9. ¿Va a tener que hablar español durante el viaje?
10. ¿Qué tiene que hacer cuando hace un viaje? ¿comprar los boletos, y qué más?
11. ¿Quién les enseña español a ustedes?
12. ¿Enseñan francés en esta escuela? ¿Cuáles otras lenguas enseñan?
13. ¿Quién está a su derecha? ¿a su izquierda?
14. ¿Quién está delante de usted? ¿y detrás de usted?

4. SYNONYMS

Están de regreso. *vuelta*
¡Qué horrible! *espantoso*
¿Cuándo van a volver? *regresar*
Es un hombre muy simpático. *señor*

5. ANTONYMS

Alberto es tan alto. *bajo*
¡Allí están, a la derecha! *izquierda*
¡Qué espantoso! *estupendo*
La Sra. López aprende inglés ahora. *enseña*
¿Quién es esa mujer? *ese hombre*
Todo el mundo está arriba. *abajo*

6. REJOINDERS

Hay un examen de español mañana. *¡Es imposible aprender tantas cosas! / ¿De veras?*
¡Por fin estamos de vuelta en los Estados Unidos! *¡Qué emoción! / ¡Y no tenemos que hablar más español!*
¡Gracias! *De nada.*

GRAMMAR

Object Pronouns in Sequence

TEACHER PRESENTATION, p. T199
PRESENTATION

¿**Me** da **la maleta,** por favor?
¿**Me la** da, por favor?

Te presto **los apuntes.**
Te los presto.

Nos dice **el nombre.**
Nos lo dice.

Se pone **los guantes.**
Se los pone.

What is the position of the direct object pronoun in relation to the indirect object pronoun in the second sentence in each pair?

Ya **le** doy **la maleta.**
Ya **se la** doy.

¿**Les** prestas **el carro?**
¿**Se lo** prestas?

Which single pronoun replaces **le** and **les** immediately preceding a direct object pronoun beginning with the letter <u>l</u>?

GENERALIZATION

In the kinds of sentences you have learned so far, two object pronouns in the same sentence must occur in the following order:

$$\boxed{\begin{matrix} \textbf{me} \\ \textbf{te} \\ \textbf{nos} \\ \textbf{se} \end{matrix}} \quad + \quad \boxed{\begin{matrix} \textbf{lo(s)} \\ \textbf{la(s)} \end{matrix}}$$

This chart summarizes the following facts: *(continued)*

(*continued*)

a. The third person direct object pronouns **lo, los, la, las** never precede another object pronoun.

Me da el libro.	→	Me lo da.
¿Te vende la casa?	→	¿Te la vende?
Nos trae los libros.	→	Nos los trae.
Nos presta las maletas.	→	Nos las presta.

b. Spanish does not permit two object pronouns beginning with **l** to occur together: **se** replaces **le** and **les** before **lo, los, la, las.**

Le da el libro.	→	Se lo da.
Les vendo la casa.	→	Se la vendo.
Le trae los libros.	→	Se los trae.
Les presto las maletas.	→	Se las presto.

Listening and Speaking Exercises 229 and 230*, p. T121 ⊗   SECTION B

STRUCTURE DRILLS

7. NOUN → PRONOUN

VARIATION: Substitute the following nouns for the ones in Drills 7.1 and 7.2

1. Se pone el impermeable. ⊗ — Se lo pone. — el abrigo
   ¿No te quitas los guantes? — ¿No te los quitas? — los zapatos
   Se lavan las manos. — Se las lavan.
   Me limpio los zapatos. — Me los limpio. — los guantes
   Se compra la cartera. — Se la compra. — la falda

2. Le presto el paraguas. ⊗ — Se lo presto. — el impermeable
   Les doy las llaves. — *Se las doy.* — las cosas
   ¿Nos traen el equipaje? — *¿Nos lo traen?* — el regalo
   No me han dicho la dirección. — *No me la han dicho.* — la palabra
   Les damos los papeles mañana. — *Se los damos mañana.* — los boletos
   ¿Te han pedido los pasaportes? — *¿Te los han pedido?* — los discos
   ¿No les cuentas las noticias? — *¿No se las cuentas?* — las aventuras

8. PERSON-NUMBER SUBSTITUTION

1. ¿Me la da, por favor? ⊗ — ¿Me la da, por favor? — *VARIATION*
   (a él) — ¿Se la da, por favor? — a ella
   (a mi hermana) — ¿Se la da, por favor? — a ese muchacho
   (a nosotros) — ¿Nos la da, por favor? — a ella y a mí
   (a los niños) — ¿Se la da, por favor? — a los empleados
   (a mí) — ¿Me la da, por favor?

2. Ya te las doy. ⊗ *Ya se las doy.–Ya se las doy.–Ya se las doy.–Ya te las doy.–Ya se las doy.*
   (a usted–a ellos–a ustedes–a ti–a usted y a ella)

3. ¿Cuándo me lo trae? ⊗ *¿Cuándo nos lo trae?–¿Cuándo se lo trae?–¿Cuándo se lo trae?*
   (a Juana y a mí–a Marta y a Luisa–a Juan y a usted)

VARIATION: (a usted y a mí–a Juana y a las gemelas–a él y a ti)

9. WRITING EXERCISE

Write the responses to Drills 7.2, 8.2 and 8.3.

10. CUED RESPONSE

		VARIATION
¿A quiénes les trae el papel? ⊗	Se lo traigo a esos señores.	
(a esos señores)		a esos chicos
¿A quién le presta las llaves?	*Se las presto a Juan.*	
(a Juan)		a Juana
¿A quiénes les enseña la canción?	*Se la enseño a los niños.*	
(a los niños)		a los muchachos
¿A quién le pide los apuntes?	*Se los pido a ustedes.*	
(a ustedes)		a ellos
¿A quién le trae este regalo?	*Se lo traigo a Luisa.*	
(a Luisa)		a Luis
¿A quién le cuenta sus problemas?	*Se los cuento a mi mejor amigo.*	
(a mi mejor amigo)		a mi mamá
¿A quién le da el dinero?	*Se lo doy a él.*	
(a él)		a ella
¿A quién le escribe la carta?	*Se la escribo a ella.*	
(a ella)		a usted

11. DIRECTED DIALOG

Pregúntele a *Marta* quién le compra la ropa.	*Marta,* ¿quién te compra la ropa?
Marta, contéstele.	Mi mamá me la compra.
Pregúntele a *Diana* si ella se compra la ropa sola.	*¿Tú te compras la ropa sola?*
Diana, contéstele.	
Pregúntele a *Pedro* quién le presta los apuntes cuando no viene a clase.	*¿Quién te presta los apuntes cuando no vienes a clase?*
Pedro, contéstele.	

(*continued*)

(continued)

    Pregúntele a *Roberto* quién le hace el desayuno.
    Roberto, contéstele.

        ¿Quién te hace el desayuno?

    Pregúntele a *Lupe* si ella se lava el pelo sola.
    Lupe, contéstele.

        ¿Tú te lavas el pelo sola?

    Pregúntele a *Juan* si él le lava el carro a su papá.
    Juan, contéstele.

        ¿Tú le lavas el carro a tu papá?

12. PATTERNED RESPONSE

¿Le dan el dinero a Pepe?   No, no se lo dan a él.
¿Le venden los boletos a usted?   *No, no me los venden a mí.*
¿Nos enseñan los bailes a nosotros?   *No, no se los enseñan a ustedes.*
¿Les leen la carta a sus compañeros?   *No, no se la leen a ellos.*
¿Me traen el diccionario a mí?   *No, no se lo traen a usted.*
¿Les piden la visa a ustedes?   *No, no nos la piden a nosotros.*
¿Le compran el carro a su hijo?   *No, no se lo compra a él.*
¿Le hacen la fiesta a María?   *No, no se la hacen a ella.*
        (or, *no nos los enseñan a nosotros*)

13. WRITING EXERCISE

Write the responses to Drills 10 and 12.

EXERCISE BOOK: EXERCISES 1, 2, 3, 4, AND 5

14. FREE RESPONSE

¿A quién le pide los apuntes cuando usted no puede venir a clase?
¿Él se los presta?
¿Usted le presta los apuntes a él cuando no viene a clase?
¿Ustedes le dan la tarea a la maestra todos los días?
¿Ya se la han dado hoy?
¿Quién le lava la ropa a usted?
¿Usted se limpia los zapatos o alguien se los limpia?
¿Su mamá le arregla el cuarto?
¿Ella le hace las maletas cuando usted hace un viaje?
¿Le presta su padre las llaves del carro?
Usted no se las pierde, ¿verdad?

Position of Object Pronouns

PRESENTATION *TEACHER PRESENTATION, p. T199*

García **nos** está **molestando.**
García está **molestándonos.**

¿**Me** estás **poniendo** atención?
¿Estás **poniéndome** atención?

Where does the object pronoun occur in the first sentence in each pair? and in the second?

¿**Me** puedo lavar las manos?
¿Puedo **lavarme** las manos?

Mi papá **me lo** va a **comprar.**
Mi papá va a **comprármelo.**

Where do(es) the object pronoun(s) occur in the first sentence in each pair? and in the second?

GENERALIZATION

1. Object pronouns may precede a verb form with a person-number ending. In the kinds of sentences you have learned so far, they never immediately follow.

   No <u>nos</u> oye.
   <u>Se</u> <u>lo</u> ha dado.
   ¿<u>Me</u> puedo lavar las manos?
   <u>Te</u> estoy hablando.

2. Object pronouns may also be attached to the end of an infinitive or a present participle. If two or more pronouns follow the verb, they occur as an inseparable unit.

   ¿**Puedo lavar<u>me</u> las manos?**
   Voy a dár<u>selo</u>.
   Estoy hablándo<u>te</u>.

   The object pronoun never directly precedes an infinitive or present participle.
   The infinitive requires a written accent on the stressed syllable when more than one object pronoun is attached to the end. The present participle requires a written accent on the stressed syllable when one or more object pronouns are attached to the end. (See page 86.)

3. In phrases which consist of a verb form with a person-number ending and an infinitive or a present participle, object pronouns either precede or follow the whole phrase. They never occur between the two verbs.

¿<u>Me</u> puedo lavar las manos?
¿Puedo lavar<u>me</u> las manos?

<u>Te</u> estoy hablando.
Estoy hablándo<u>te</u>.

Listening and Speaking Exercises 231 and 232*, p. T123 ⊗

SECTION C

STRUCTURE DRILLS

15. TRANSFORMATION DRILL

Me voy a sentar aquí. ⊗	Voy a sentarme aquí.
Te estoy hablando.	Estoy hablándote.
No la debemos invitar.	No debemos invitarla.
El niño no se quiere acostar.	El niño no quiere acostarse.
¿Le estás escribiendo una carta?	¿Estás escribiéndole una carta?
Nos acaban de llamar.	Acaban de llamarnos.
Se lo tengo que comprar.	Tengo que comprárselo.
Te lo acabo de decir.	Acabo de decírtelo.
¿No me lo puede traer?	¿No puede traérmelo?
Se lo estoy trayendo.	Estoy trayéndoselo.

VARIATION: Use right-hand column as stimulus.

A laborer from the hot coastlands of Colombia.

16. PATTERNED RESPONSE

1. ¿Cuándo vas a hacer las maletas? ⊗   Estoy haciéndolas ahora.
   ¿Cuándo vas a arreglar el cuarto?   *Estoy arreglándolo ahora.*
   ¿Cuándo vas a leer el periódico?   *Estoy leyéndolo ahora.*
   ¿Cuándo vas a abrir los regalos?   *Estoy abriéndolos ahora.*
   ¿Cuándo vas a llamar a la chica?   *Estoy llamándola ahora.*

2. ¿Ya te has lavado las manos? ⊗   ¡Paciencia! Voy a lavármelas ahora.
   ¿Ya me has comprado las cosas?   *¡Paciencia! Voy a comprárselas ahora.*
   ¿Ya le has escrito la carta?   *¡Paciencia! Voy a escribírsela ahora.*
   ¿Ya te has puesto el abrigo?   *¡Paciencia! Voy a ponérmelo ahora.*
   ¿Ya nos has hecho el almuerzo?   *¡Paciencia! Voy a hacérselo ahora.*

17. WRITING EXERCISE

Write the responses to Drills 16.1 and 16.2.

EXERCISE BOOK: EXERCISES 6, 7, AND 8

Nominalization

TEACHER PRESENTATION, p. T200
PRESENTATION

> **La maleta negra.**
> **La negra.**
>
> **Esa maleta** no.
> **Ésa** no
>
> **La otra maleta.**
> **La otra.**
>
> **La maleta** que acaba de tocar.
> **La** que acaba de tocar.

What is the English equivalent of each of these phrases? Which word occurs in the English equivalent of the second phrase in each pair? In the examples in Spanish, how does the second phrase in each pair differ from the first?

GENERALIZATION

1. In English we normally say *"Not that suitcase, the other one,"* instead of *"Not that suitcase, the other suitcase." One* is substituted for *suitcase* in the second noun phrase. In similar Spanish

sentences, the repeated noun is simply omitted. Nothing is substituted in its place: **Esa maleta no, la otra maleta.** → **Esa maleta no, la otra.** The deletion of **maleta** from the noun phrase **la otra maleta** leaves the adjective **otra** functioning as the head of the noun phrase. This process is called <u>nominalization</u>.

2. The following lines from the Basic Dialog are examples of nominalization.

¡Por favor, mi maleta!	*Please, my suitcase!*
Y la mía también.	*And mine too.*

(**maleta** is dropped, leaving **mía** as a nominalized possessive)

¿Cuál es la suya?
    ↑   ↑
  maleta maleta
                           Which is yours?

La negra.
  ↑
maleta
                           The black one.

La que acaba de tocar. Ésa.
 ↑   ↑
maleta   **maleta**
                           The one you just touched. That one.

3. Nominalized demonstrative adjectives have a written accent on the stressed syllable. (See page 87.)

ese baúl	→	**ése**
esa maleta	→	**ésa**
esos cepillos	→	**ésos**
esta cartera	→	**ésta**
estos guantes	→	**éstos**

STRUCTURE DRILLS

18. DELETION DRILL

¿Es cara esa cartera? ⊗
¿Cuál cartera?
La cartera blanca.

¿De quién son esas llaves?
¿Cuáles llaves?
Las llaves que están en la mesa.

VARIATION: Substitute the following nouns for the ones in Drill 18.

¿Es cara ésa?
¿Cuál?
La blanca.
                 falda

¿De quién son ésas?
¿Cuáles?
Las que están en la mesa.
               cosas

Ese impermeable es muy bonito.   *Ése es muy bonito.*   **carro**
¿El impermeable amarillo?   *¿El amarillo?*
No, el impermeable rojo.   *No, el rojo.*

Los amigos tuyos son muy perezosos.   *Los tuyos son muy perezosos.*   **compañeros**
¿Los amigos míos?   *¿Los míos?*
Sí, los amigos que siempre invitas a la
casa.   *Sí, los que siempre invitas a la casa.*

19. PATTERNED RESPONSE

1. ¿Dónde está la cartera café?   ¿La café? No tengo la menor idea.
   ¿Dónde está el cepillo blanco?   *¿El blanco? No tengo la menor idea.*
   ¿Dónde está el peine negro?   *¿El negro? No tengo la menor idea.*
   ¿Dónde están las maletas nuevas?   *¿Las nuevas? No tengo la menor idea.*

2. ¿Es nuevo ese impermeable?   ¿Éste? No, no es nuevo.
   ¿Son nuevas esas llaves?   *¿Éstas? No, no son nuevas.*
   ¿Son nuevos esos anteojos?   *¿Éstos? No, no son nuevos.*
   ¿Es nuevo ese cepillo?   *¿Éste? No, no es nuevo.*

3. ¿Quién es el señor que está allí?   ¿El que está allí? No sé.
   ¿Quiénes son los muchachos que están allí?   *¿Los que están allí? No sé.*
   ¿Quién es la señora que está allí?   *¿La que está allí? No sé.*
   ¿Quiénes son las chicas que están allí?   *¿Las que están allí? No sé.*

4. Tus boletos están aquí, ¿verdad?   ¿Los míos? Sí.
   La cartera de Eva está aquí, ¿verdad?   ¿La suya? Sí.
   Las llaves de ustedes están aquí, ¿verdad?   *¿Las nuestras? Sí.*
   Mi peine está aquí, ¿verdad?   *¿El suyo? Sí.*
   Nuestras cosas están aquí, ¿verdad?   *¿Las suyas? Sí. (or ¿Las nuestras? Sí.)*

20. FREE RESPONSE

¿Cuál libro es el suyo? ¿Éste o ése?
¿Cuál cartera es la suya, *Ana*?
¿Y cuál es la suya, *Rosita*?
¿Son estos anteojos los míos o los de *Pepe*?
¿Y este swéater?
¿Y estas llaves?
¿Cuál cuaderno es el suyo, *Juan*? ¿el azul?
¿Cuál pluma es la suya? ¿la roja?
¿Cuál lápiz es el mío?   *(continued)*

(*continued*)

¿Son de *Juana* los guantes negros?
Y los blancos, ¿de quién son?
¿Cuál cartera es la mía, ésa o la que acabo de tocar?
¿Cuál libro está en mejor condición, éste o el que está en la mesa?
¿Cuál chico se llama *Pedro,* éste o el que está sentado allí?

21. WRITING EXERCISE

Write the responses to Drills 19.1, 19.2, 19.3, 19.4.
EXERCISE BOOK: EXERCISE 9

Comparatives: más/menos . . . que

PRESENTATION *TEACHER PRESENTATION, p. T201*

Esta escuela es **más** bonita **que** la otra.
Juan es **menos** alto **que** Pedro.

Which words mean *more . . . than* in these sentences? Which words mean *less . . . than?*

GENERALIZATION

1. The following sentences are called comparative sentences.

   Jack is smarter than Jill.
   Jill is more beautiful than Susan.
   Susan is less intelligent than George.

Spanish has no suffix like the comparative *-er* of English. With the exceptions given on the next page, comparatives of this type are expressed in Spanish with the following words:

$$\left.\begin{array}{l}\textbf{más} \\ \textbf{menos}\end{array}\right\} \;+\; \textbf{que}$$

Yo soy <u>más</u> perezoso <u>que</u> usted.
I'm laz<u>ier</u> than <u>you</u>.

Pedro es menos ambicioso que Juan.
Pedro is <u>less</u> ambitious <u>than</u> Juan.

2. If a pronoun follows **que,** it is the subject pronoun, not the prepositional pronoun.

Yo soy más perezoso que tú.

3. English has some irregular comparative adjectives, like *good → better,* and so does Spanish.

más bueno	→	mejor
más malo	→	peor
más joven	→	menor
más viejo	→	mayor

The regularly formed **más bueno, más malo,** and **más joven** are used interchangeably with the irregular **mejor, peor,** and **menor. Más viejo,** however, is not completely interchangeable with **mayor. Más viejo** classifies the person or object described as old: **Mi abuelo es más viejo que mi abuela. Mayor** simply describes an age relationship; it does not imply that the persons or objects described are old: **Ana es mayor que María.**

4. Except in a few special cases, **de** instead of **que** is used before numbers.

Tengo más de cien pesos.

Note: Constructions like *No tengo más que dos pesos* will be discussed in Level III.

5. To express the ideas *-est, most, least,* Spanish uses the definite article with **más, menos,** or an irregular comparative adjective.

María es la chica más linda del mundo.	*María is the prettiest girl in the world.*
Juan es el chico más inteligente de la clase.	*Juan is the most intelligent boy in the class.*
Josefina es la mejor alumna de la escuela.	*Josefina is the best student in the school.*
Paco es el menos perezoso.	*Paco is the least lazy.*

Note the use of **de** for *in* in this construction: **del mundo, de la clase, de la escuela.**

Listening and Speaking Exercises 233, 234, 235*, p. T124 ⊗ **SECTION D**

STRUCTURE DRILLS

22. PATTERNED RESPONSE

1. Pedro es listo, ¿y Pepe? ⊗	Pepe es más listo todavía.
Sue es linda, ¿y las gemelas?	*Las gemelas son más listas todavía.*
Esto es bueno, ¿y eso?	*Eso es mejor todavía.*
El abuelo es viejo, ¿y la abuela?	*La abuela es mayor todavía.* (or *La abuela es más vieja todavía.*)
Doña Delia es joven, ¿y doña Marta?	*Doña Marta es más joven todavía.*
Esto es malo, ¿y eso?	*Eso es peor todavía.* (*continued*)

(*continued*)

2. Elena es alta, ¿y Lupita? ⊗   Lupita es menos alta.

   Él es pretencioso, ¿y ella?   *Ella es menos pretenciosa.*

   El muchacho es simpático, ¿y su her-   *Su hermana es menos simpática.*
   mana?

   Los dictados son fáciles, ¿y los exámenes?   *Los exámenes son menos fáciles.*

23. CUED DIALOG

    (vestido)   1ST STUDENT Quiero un vestido más ba-
   rato, por favor.

   2ND STUDENT Éste es el más barato que
   tenemos.

    (camisas) *Quiero unas camisas más baratas . . . / Éstas son las más baratas . . .*

    (zapatos) *Quiero unos zapatos más baratos . . . / Éstos son los más baratos . . .*

    (traje) *Quiero un traje más barato . . . / Éste es el más barato . . .*

    (medias) *Quiero unas medias más baratas . . . / Éstas son las más baratas . . .*

    (paraguas) *Quiero un paraguas más barato . . . / Éste es el más barato . . .*

    (cartera) *Quiero una cartera más barata . . . / Ésta es la más barata . . .*

    (guantes) *Quiero unos guantes más baratos . . . / Éstos son los más baratos . . .*

24. PATTERNED RESPONSE

Yo soy muy perezoso. | *Note:* **Girls use the feminine form of the adjective.**   1ST STUDENT Yo soy más perezoso que
   usted.

   2ND STUDENT Pero yo soy el más perezoso de
   todos.

Blanca es ambiciosa.   *Yo soy más ambicioso que Blanca. / Pero yo soy el más ambicioso de todos.*

Ellos son muy distraídos.   *Yo soy más distraído que ellos. / Pero yo soy el más distraído de todos.*

María es muy joven.   *Yo soy menor que María. / Pero yo soy el menor de todos.*

Yo soy muy alto.   *Yo soy más alto que tú. / Pero yo soy el más alto de todos.*

Él es muy delgado.   *Yo soy más delgado que él. / Pero yo soy el más delgado de todos.*

25. ENGLISH CUE DRILLS

1. Jorge es más alto que Enrique. ⊗   *Jorge es más alto que Enrique.*

   Enrique is fatter than Pedro.   *Enrique es más gordo que Pedro.*

   Pedro is older than Juan.   *Pedro es mayor que Juan.*

   Juan is shorter than Jorge.   *Juan es más bajo que Jorge.*

   Jorge is taller than Enrique.   *Jorge es más alto que Enrique.*

2. ¡Qué chico! Es el alumno más inteligente de la clase. ⊗

He's the most ambitious son in the family.
He's the handsomest boy in the class.
He's the nicest classmate in the school.
He's the least pretentious boy in the world.
What a boy! He's the most intelligent student in the class.

¡Qué chico! Es el alumno más inteligente de la clase.

Es el hijo más ambicioso de la familia.
Es el chico más guapo de la clase.
Es el compañero más simpático de la escuela.
Es el chico menos pretencioso del mundo.

¡Qué chico! Es el alumno más inteligente de la clase.

26. PAIRED SENTENCES

Invita a más muchachos que muchachas. ⊗
She invites more than ten boys.
She invites more boys than girls.

Invita a más muchachos que muchachas.
Invita a más de diez muchachos.
Invita a más muchachos que muchachas.

Ellos han dado más fiestas que nosotros.
They've given more than five parties.
They've given more parties than we (have).

Ellos han dado más fiestas que nosotros.
Ellos han dado más de cinco fiestas.
Ellos han dado más fiestas que nosotros.

Ella tiene más dinero que yo.
She has more than a hundred pesos.
She has more money than I (do).

Ella tiene más dinero que yo.
Ella tiene más de cien pesos.
Ella tiene más dinero que yo.

27. FREE RESPONSE

¿Tiene usted un hermano? ¿Es mayor o menor que usted?
¿Es usted el mayor de la familia? ¿Es el menor?
¿Quién es el más perezoso de la familia? ¿Quién es el menos perezoso?
¿Quién es su mejor amigo? ¿Es él más o menos alto que usted?
¿Cuántos años tiene? ¿Es mayor o menor que usted?
¿Tiene usted más de diez años?
¿Son ustedes los mejores alumnos de la escuela?
¿Quiénes son los peores?
¿Quién es el mejor maestro de la escuela?
¿Quién es el maestro más estricto?
¿Quién es el más simpático?

28. WRITING EXERCISE

Write the responses to Drills 22.1, 22.2, 25.2, and 26.

EXERCISE BOOK: EXERCISES 10, 11, AND 12

Listening and Speaking Exercise 236*, p. T126 ⊗

Writing

1. MULTIPLE ITEM SUBSTITUTION

MODEL   El equipaje que usted acaba de tocar es el mío.
maleta / tú / abrir
La maleta que tú acabas de abrir es la mía.

1. ¿Cuál cartera te gusta más a ti? ¿La roja o la amarilla?
paraguas / a usted   *¿Cuál paraguas le gusta más a usted? ¿El rojo o el amarillo?*

2. Este edificio es más alto que el otro.
ciudad / menos / grande   *Esta ciudad es menos grande que la otra.*

3. ¿Cuál impermeable vas a comprar? ¿Éste o el que está en la silla?
anteojos / usar / escritorio   *¿Cuáles anteojos vas a usar? ¿Éstos o los que están en el escritorio?*

4. Este aeropuerto es más moderno que el de Quito.
tiendas / menos / Madrid   *Estas tiendas son menos modernas que las de Madrid.*

5. ¿Cuáles llaves necesita usted? ¿Éstas o las que acabo de tocar?
cepillo / querer / lavar   *¿Cuál cepillo quiere usted? ¿Éste o el que acabo de lavar?*

6. Este peine no es el mío. Es el de Juan.
llaves / suyo / María   *Estas llaves no son suyas. Son las de María.*

7. ¿Cuál maleta es la tuya? ¿Ésta o la que acaban de abrir?
baúl / cerrar   *¿Cuál baúl es el tuyo? ¿Éste o el que acaban de cerrar?*

8. Este departamento es más bonito que el de la Sra. Pérez.
casa / menos / Sr. García   *Esta casa es menos bonita que la del Sr. García.*

2. SENTENCE CONSTRUCTION

Construct a sentence using the following words, as shown in the model. Then write a second sentence, replacing the underlined noun with a pronoun.

MODEL   (yo) / dar / maleta / a Carmen
Le doy la maleta a Carmen.
Se la doy a Carmen.

1. (ella) / enseñar / bailes / a las muchachas   *Les enseña los bailes a las muchachas. / Se los enseña a las muchachas.*
2. (tú) / ponerse / impermeable   *Te pones el impermeable. / Te lo pones.*
3. Juan / abrir / puerta / al maestro   *Juan le abre la puerta al maestro. / Juan se la abre al maestro.*
4. los niños / nunca / decir / verdad / a ti   *Los niños nunca te dicen la verdad a ti. / Los niños nunca te la dicen a ti.*
5. (ellos) / prestar / carro / a mí   *Me prestan el carro a mí. / Me lo prestan a mí.*

RECOMBINATION MATERIAL

Dialogs

I

CLAUDIA	No encuentro nada en esta cartera.
GLORIA	¿Qué buscas, tus llaves?
CLAUDIA	Sí, para abrir la maleta. ¡Por fin! Aquí están.
GLORIA	Yo te la abro . . . ¿Qué pasa? No puedo abrirla.
CLAUDIA	A la izquierda . . . más . . . más . . . a la derecha ahora . . .
GLORIA	No, no puedo. Tal vez ésta no es la llave.
CLAUDIA	Sí, ésa es . . . ¡ay, caramba! ¡Todas mis cosas están en el suelo! Sí, chica, ésa es la llave.

QUESTIONS

1. ¿Cuál es el problema de Claudia?
2. ¿Es éste un problema típico de las mujeres?

(*continued*)

A department store in Mexico. Department store chains, with branches in different cities, are not common.

(continued)

  3. ¿Qué busca ella?

  4. ¿Para qué necesita sus llaves?

  5. ¿Las encuentra por fin?

  6. ¿Qué le dice Gloria?

  7. ¿Es fácil abrir la maleta?

  8. ¿Por qué no puede abrirla, según Gloria?

  9. ¿Es ésa la llave?

10. ¿Dónde encuentra su ropa Claudia cuando Gloria abre la maleta?

II

VARIATION

SEÑORA	Señorita, ¿dónde están los impermeables?	Señor / abrigos
EMPLEADA	¿Para hombres o mujeres?	
SEÑORA	Para mujeres.	hombres
EMPLEADA	¿Qué tamaño busca?	
SEÑORA	Cuarenta y dos[2].	cuarenta y ocho
EMPLEADA	A ver, no estoy segura. Tengo que preguntarle a mi jefe.	seguro
SEÑORA	Muy bien, señorita.	señor

DIALOG VARIATION

Usted está en un almacén y quiere comprar un abrigo.

| *Note:* **Call on two boys to do the variation.**

III

CHELA	¿Por qué no vienes a mi casa esta tarde?
MARÍA	No sé si puedo. Tengo que ir a la biblioteca.
CHELA	La chica americana va a enseñarnos unos bailes nuevos.
MARÍA	¿Bailes americanos? ¡Brutal!
CHELA	Claro. Va a enseñarnos los bailes "a gogo".
MARÍA	¡Estupendo! Y yo tengo unos discos nuevos . . .
CHELA	¿Pero no vas a ir a la biblioteca?
MARÍA	¿La biblioteca? ¿Estás loca?

---

[2] European measurements are used in most Latin American countries. Size 42 corresponds approximately to size 10 in the United States.

QUESTIONS

1. ¿Adónde invita Chela a María?
2. ¿Dice María que puede ir?
3. ¿Adónde tiene que ir ella esta tarde?
4. ¿A quién más ha invitado Chela a su casa?
5. ¿Qué va a enseñarles la chica americana?
6. ¿Quiere María aprender unos bailes americanos?
7. ¿Cuáles bailes va a enseñarles la americana?
8. ¿Qué tiene María?
9. ¿Qué le pregunta Chela a María?
10. ¿Ha cambiado María sus planes para la tarde?

Narrative

Folklore de pueblo° chico°

Los viejos de este pueblo cuentan muchas historias* misteriosas* y fantásticas*—historias que encantan y asustan a los jóvenes, quienes creen todo lo que sus abuelos les dicen. Yo no sé si esas leyendas* lindísimas que forman una parte tan impor-
5 tante* de nuestra tradición* folklórica* están basadas* en la verdad o si son productos de la imaginación de la gente° de aquí, pero sí sé que tienen una profunda* influencia* en la vida de cada uno de nosotros.

Mi abuelo es uno de los hombres más viejos del pueblo, y
10 conoce todas las leyendas de la región. Cuenta la historia de un marinero°—figura importante de nuestro folklore—que, ya viejo, abandona* su barco y viene a vivir a nuestro pueblo a la casa de su hija Consuelo y del marido de ella. Vive y trabaja en el pueblo, pero piensa constantemente* en el mar, su gran amor.
15 Por horas y horas contempla* el horizonte* y los barcos que pasan. Y cuando uno de éstos llega al puerto, busca a los marineros para conversar con ellos y escuchar las noticias que le traen de distantes lugares. "Algún día voy a volver al mar"—les dice a sus amigos.
20 Pero él está muy viejo ya, y un día, enfermo y cansado de la vida, muere°.

*   *   *

pueblo: *village*
chico: *pequeño*
¿Vive usted en un pueblo chico?
¿Hay muchos pueblos chicos en los Estados Unidos?

gente *f:* personas
¿Hay muchos pueblos chicos en Hispanoamérica?
¿Conoce usted a mucha gente?
marinero: *sailor*
¿Es marinero su papá?

morir (ue): *die*
p.p.: **muerto**
¿Está muerto de hambre usted? ¿Cuándo va a comer?

Pasan los años. Más barcos llegan al puerto; unos marineros se quedan en el pueblo; otros vuelven al mar. La vida continúa como siempre. Ya casi nadie recuerda al viejo marinero.

25 Una noche, en la casa de su hija, todos duermen. De repente° Consuelo se despierta.

—¡Hay alguien en el patio*!—dice nerviosa*, despertando a su marido—Oigo voces . . .

Pero él, completamente dormido, no le contesta.

30 —¡Juan!—le grita a su marido—estoy segura de que oigo voces, y creo que vienen del patio.

Juan se despierta por fin. —¿Voces?—le pregunta medio dormido—¿Quién es?

Consuelo está muy asustada y empieza a llorar. —No sé—le
35 dice—creo que es la voz de mi padre.

—Consuelo, mi amor, estás muy nerviosa y cansada. Tienes que dormir. Y Juan, cerrando los ojos otra vez, se duerme inmediatamente.

Pero ella no puede dormir. Se levanta y se pone la bata°.
40 Va a la cocina y busca una vela°. Encuentra una y se acerca a la puerta de la casita. Escucha . . . escucha . . . pero ni ve ni oye nada en el patio. De repente nota* algo en el suelo que le llama la atención. Está asustadísima, pero por fin se acerca.

de repente: *all of a sudden*

En la leyenda, ¿Juan se despierta de repente? ¿Por qué Consuelo se despierta de repente? ¿Qué oye ella?

¿Tiene usted una bata? ¿De qué color es?
¿Necesita una bata nueva?
bata: *robe*
vela: *candle*
¿Le gusta a usted cenar con velas?

Dock workers load a ship in Cartagena, one of Colombia's two major ports on the Caribbean.

—¿Qué es esto?—se pregunta—¿qué puede ser esto?

45 —Y de repente lo ve claramente. Es un charco° de agua— un charco de agua del mar.

Consuelo se tranquiliza*; ya no está asustada. —Mi padre ha vuelto a visitar a su hija—se dice. —Ha vuelto del mar.

Consuelo vuelve al dormitorio, y pocos minutos después, 50 duerme tranquilamente*.

charco: *puddle*

Cuándo llueve aquí, ¿hay charcos de aqua en la calle?
¿Hay charcos de agua en el patio de la escuela?

QUESTIONS

1. ¿Qué cuentan los hombres viejos del pueblo? 1
2. ¿Cree usted que estas historias están basadas en la verdad o que son solamente productos de la imaginación?
3. ¿Es el marinero una figura importante en el folklore del pueblo? 11
4. ¿Por qué abandona su barco el marinero? 12
5. ¿Adónde va a vivir? 12
6. ¿En qué piensa constantemente? 14
7. ¿Qué contempla por horas y horas? 15
8. ¿Qué pasa cuando un barco llega al puerto? 16
9. ¿Para qué busca a los marineros que llegan en el barco? 17
10. ¿Qué les dice a sus amigos? 18
11. ¿Qué pasa un día? 21
12. ¿Qué hacen todos en la casa de Consuelo? 25
13. ¿Quién se despierta de repente? 26
14. ¿Qué le dice a su marido? 27

15. ¿Le contesta él? ¿Por qué no? 29
16. ¿Qué hace Consuelo entonces? 30
17. ¿Se despierta Juan esta vez? 32
18. ¿Qué empieza a hacer Consuelo? 34
19. ¿De quién cree ella que es la voz? 35
20. ¿Qué le dice su marido? 36
21. ¿Qué hace él entonces? 37
22. ¿Puede dormir Consuelo? 39
23. ¿Qué hace ella? 39
24. ¿Qué se pone? 39
25. ¿Adónde va primero? 40
26. ¿Qué busca allí? 40
27. ¿Adónde va entonces? 41
28. ¿Oye algo en el patio? 41
29. ¿Qué nota de repente? 43
30. ¿Qué hace por fin? 43
31. ¿Qué es lo que está en el suelo? 45
32. ¿De dónde viene el agua? 46
33. ¿Se tranquiliza entonces Consuelo? 47
34. ¿Por qué? ¿Quién ha venido a visitarla? 47

Conversation Stimulus

¿Tú sabes la leyenda del marinero que vuelve del mar?
Claro, mi abuelo <u>*me la ha contado muchas veces.*</u>
¿Me la <u>*cuentas, por favor*</u>?
Ahora no, porque tengo que <u>*salir.*</u>
¿Cuándo, entonces?
No sé. Algún día.

Note: Most Spanish-American school systems are modeled after the Spanish system: six years of primary school followed by six years of secondary education in schools called *liceos, colegios* or *gimnasios.* Before entering a university, a student must pass the *bachillerato* exam.

UNIT 15

BASIC DIALOG

Los últimos días

MAESTRA	Si le presto el libro, ¿cuándo me lo devuelve?
JOSÉ LUIS	La semana próxima, sin falta.

15-1

MAESTRA	La semana próxima vamos a estar en vacaciones.

15-2

JOSÉ LUIS	El viernes, entonces. A propósito, ¿nos va a dar las notas hoy?
MAESTRA	Sí, esta tarde se las doy.

15-3

JOSÉ LUIS	¿No me puede dar la mía ahora? No sabe cómo estoy sufriendo.
MAESTRA	No. Lo siento mucho.

15-4

JOSÉ LUIS	¿Pero no puede decirme al menos si voy a pasar?
MAESTRA	Mmm, bien. Va a pasar, pero raspando, con un cinco[1].

15-5

JOSÉ LUIS	¡Gracias, señorita! ¡Gracias!

15-6

The Last Days

TEACHER	If I lend you the book, when will you return it to me?
JOSÉ LUIS	Next week, without fail (fault).
TEACHER	Next week we're going to be on vacation.
JOSÉ LUIS	Friday, then. By the way, are you going to give us our grades today?
TEACHER	Yes, this afternoon I'll give them to you.
JOSÉ LUIS	Can't you give me mine now? You don't know how I'm suffering.
TEACHER	No. I'm very sorry.
JOSÉ LUIS	But can't you tell me at least if I'm going to pass?
TEACHER	Mmm, all right. You're going to pass, but barely (scraping), with a five.
JOSÉ LUIS	Thank you, señorita! Thank you!

---

[1] Grades in Spanish-speaking countries are normally based on a number system. In some countries they are based on a scale of 10, 5 being the lowest passing grade. In others they are based on a scale of 7, 4 being the lowest passing grade.

◀ *Students receive a diploma called the* bachillerato *after six years of high school and a difficult exam.*

Supplement

Le presto la revista. 15-1	I'll lend you the magazine.
novela 15-2	novel
máquina de escribir 15-3	typewriter
Se lo traigo dentro de una semana.	I'll bring it to you in a week.
pasado mañana	the day after tomorrow
mañana por la mañana	tomorrow morning
de hoy en ocho² (días)	a week from today
de hoy en quince² (días)	two weeks from today
Vamos a la piscina. 15-4	We're going to the swimming pool.
a la playa 15-5	to the beach
al campo 15-6	to the country
a la hacienda 15-7	to the farm, ranch
Le mando una tarjeta. 15-8	I'll send you a card.
nota	note

No sabe cómo me duele la cabeza. 15-9	You don't know how my head is hurting.
la garganta 15-10	my throat
el estómago 15-11	my stomach
Me duelen los brazos. 15-12	My arms are hurting.
las piernas 15-13	My legs
los pies 15-14	My feet
Los otros no están tan tristes como yo. 15-15	The others aren't as sad as I am.
alegres 15-16	gay
Ellos no tienen tantos problemas como yo.	They don't have as many problems as I do.
Los otros no sufren tanto como yo.	The others don't suffer as much as I do.
Siempre saco un diez en matemáticas.	I always get a ten in mathematics.
historia	history
álgebra	algebra
dibujo	drawing

Listening and Speaking Exercises 237, 238, 239, 240*, p. T127 ⊗

---

²In the expressions **de hoy en ocho** and **de hoy en quince,** *today* is considered the first countable day. Thus, a week from today is eight days from today.

> ### BASIC FORMS
>
> *Verbs*
>
> devolver (ue)   raspar
> doler (ue)   sacar
> mandar   sufrir
>
> *Nouns*
>
> pie   *m.*
> álgebra[3]   *f.*
>
> *Adjectives*
>
> alegre
> triste

Vocabulary Exercises

1. QUESTIONS

1. ¿Qué le va a prestar la maestra a José Luis?   *Un libro.*
2. ¿Cuándo quiere devolvérselo él?   *La semana próxima.*
3. ¿Por qué no puede devolvérselo la semana próxima?   *Van a estar en vacaciones.*
4. Entonces, ¿cuándo va a devolverle el libro a la maestra?   *El viernes.*
5. ¿Cuándo empiezan las vacaciones en esta escuela? ¿pasado mañana?
6. ¿Cuándo es su último examen?
7. ¿Cuándo es el próximo examen en esta clase?
8. ¿Qué va a hacer usted durante las vacaciones?
9. ¿Va a ir a la playa todos los días?
10. ¿Prefiere ir a la playa o a una piscina?
11. ¿Prefiere nadar en el mar o en una piscina?
12. ¿Va a ir al campo durante las vacaciones?
13. Me va a mandar una tarjeta, sin falta, ¿verdad?
14. ¿Ha estado usted en una hacienda?
15. ¿Qué le pregunta José Luis a la maestra con respecto a las notas?   *Si se las va a dar hoy.*
16. ¿Cuándo les va a dar ella las notas a sus alumnos?   *Esta tarde.*
17. ¿Está usted contento con sus notas? ¿Por qué (no)?

---

[3] The masculine definite article is used with **álgebra: El álgebra es difícil.** (See page 133.)

2. FREE COMPLETION

1. Estoy leyendo una _____.   *novela, revista, carta*
2. Durante las vacaciones voy a ir a _____.   *una hacienda, la playa, la piscina, Lima*
3. ¿Vas a mandarme una _____?   *tarjeta, carta*
4. Escribo con una _____.   *máquina de escribir, pluma*

---

3. QUESTIONS

1. ¿Qué le pide José Luis a la maestra? *Su nota.*   *Porque está sufriendo.*
2. ¿Por qué necesita saber su nota inmediatamente, según él? ↑¿Se la da la maestra? *No.*
3. Si no puede saber su nota, ¿qué quiere saber José Luis, al menos? *Si va a pasar.*
4. ¿Qué le dice la maestra? *Que va a pasar, pero raspando.*
5. ¿A usted le duele la cabeza antes de un examen? ¿Le duele el estómago?
6. ¿Va a pasar raspando usted en esta clase?
7. ¿Qué nota va a sacar en la clase de historia? ¿y en la clase de álgebra? ¿y en la de dibujo?
8. ¿Estudia usted dibujo? ¿Estudia música? ¿Cuál clase le gusta más?
9. ¿Usted va a seguir estudiando español el año próximo? ¿Qué más va a estudiar?
10. ¿Están ustedes tristes porque las clases van a terminar pronto?
11. ¿Está usted resfriado hoy? ¿Le duele la garganta? ¿y la cabeza? ¿y el estómago?
12. *Juan,* ¿le duelen las piernas después de pasar todo el día jugando fútbol? ¿y los pies?
13. ¿Le duelen los pies después de hacer uno de esos bailes modernos? ¿y las piernas?
14. ¿Le duelen los brazos después de pasar todo el día nadando?

Private beach clubs are popular among Argentina's wealthy.

4. BASIC DIALOG VARIATION

Change the Basic Dialog to narrative form.

La maestra le pregunta a José Luis que si ella le presta el libro, cuándo se lo devuelve él. Él contesta que la semana próxima, sin falta. Ella le dice que la semana próxima van a estar en vacaciones. Él le dice que el viernes, entonces, y le pregunta si les va a dar las notas hoy. Ella le dice que sí, que esta tarde se las da. Él le pregunta que si no le puede dar la suya ahora, y le dice que ella no sabe cómo está sufriendo. Ella le dice que no, que lo siente mucho. José Luis le pregunta si puede decirle al menos si va a pasar. La maestra le dice que va a pasar, pero raspando, con un cinco. Y él grita ¡gracias, señorita, gracias!

GRAMMAR

Infinitives as Verb Complements

TEACHER PRESENTATION, p. T202

PRESENTATION

¿No me **puede dar** la mía ahora?
Prometo no **gastar** mucho.
¿**Desea dejar** algún recado?
¿**Quieres escuchar** unos discos?
Debe ser muy bonita.

Does the first verb in each sentence have a person-number ending? Does the second? What is the form of the second verb?

GENERALIZATION

In Spanish, as in English, many verbs may be followed by an infinitive (or an infinitive phrase), just as they may be followed by a noun phrase.

The structure of examples like the following is practically identical in English and Spanish. The English infinitive marker *to* is matched by the Spanish infinitive ending **r** in these examples.

Verb + Noun Phrase	*Verb + Infinitive (Phrase)*
Quiero el dibujo.	**Quiero leer.**
I want the drawing.	*I want to read.*

The infinitive marker *to* is not used in English after *can, must,* and a few other verbs.

Puedo salir.
I can leave.

Debo salir.
I must leave.

STRUCTURE DRILLS

5. DOUBLE ITEM SUBSTITUTION

VARIATION

Prefiero trabajar ahora. ⊗	*Prefiero trabajar ahora.*	
Quieren _____.	*Quieren trabajar ahora.*	desea
_____ sentarse _____.	*Quieren sentarse ahora.*	dormir
Necesita _____.	*Necesita sentarse ahora.*	debe
_____ llamarlo _____.	*Necesita llamarlo ahora.*	contármelo
Debemos _____.	*Debemos llamarlo ahora.*	quiere
_____ economizar __.	*Debemos economizar ahora.*	acostarse
Prometo _____.	*Prometo economizar ahora.*	prefiere
_____ estudiar _____.	*Prometo estudiar ahora.*	levantarse

6. SENTENCE COMBINATION

¿Desea un café? ¿Toma un café? ⊗	¿Desea tomar un café?
Queremos una tarjeta. Mandamos una tarjeta.	*Queremos mandar una tarjeta.*
Prefiero la hacienda. Visito la hacienda.	*Prefiero visitar la hacienda.*
No sabe el número. No marca el número.	*No sabe marcar el número.*
Necesito buenas notas. Saco buenas notas.	*Necesito sacar buenas notas.*

7. FREE RESPONSE

¿Sabe usted nadar?
¿Sabe jugar tenis?
¿Le duelen los brazos después de un partido de tenis? ¿y las piernas?
¿Piensa usted jugar tenis este sábado?
¿Piensa hacer una fiesta? ¿Son alegres las fiestas de la escuela?
¿Qué piensa hacer este sábado?
¿Qué prefiere hacer, escuchar discos o estudiar?

Double Item Substitution Variation ←

¿Qué deben ustedes hacer esta tarde?
¿Piensan estudiar esta tarde?
¿Necesitan estudiar mucho?
¿Me prometen estudiar más el año próximo, sin falta?
¿Piensa trabajar durante las vacaciones?
¿Prefiere usted trabajar o viajar?
¿Qué piensan hacer sus amigos?

Desea trabajar ahora.
Desea dormir ahora.
Debe dormir ahora.
Debe contármelo ahora.
Quiere contármelo ahora.
Quiere acostarse ahora.
Prefiere acostarse ahora.
Prefiere levantarse ahora.

8. WRITING EXERCISE

Write the responses to Drill 6.

EXERCISE BOOK: EXERCISE 1

More about Infinitives as Verb Complements

PRESENTATION *TEACHER PRESENTATION, p. T202*

Vamos <u>a</u> estar en vacaciones.
¿Aprenden <u>a</u> hablar español?
Acaba <u>de</u> salir.
¿Tienes <u>que</u> comprar algo?

Which word precedes the infinitive in the first two sentences? in the third? in the fourth?

GENERALIZATION

Some Spanish verbs, unlike those on page 293, require **a, de,** or **que** before an infinitive.

Verb		Examples
aprender		Aprenden a hablar español.
comenzar		Comienza a gritar.
empezar		¿Cuándo empezamos a estudiar?
enseñar		Inés nos enseña a cantar.
entrar	a	¿Entramos a ver la película?
invitar		¿Me invitas a bailar?
ir		Vamos a dar una fiesta.
llamar		Los llamo a almorzar.
salir		Salen a cenar todos los sábados.
venir		Vengo a ver a Pedro.
acabar	de	Acaba de salir.
terminar		¿Cuándo terminas de escribir la tarea?
tener	que	Tengo que estudiar.

Listening and Speaking Exercises 246, 247*, 248, 249*, p. T131 ⊗
⊗ SECTION C

STRUCTURE DRILLS

9. DOUBLE ITEM SUBSTITUTION

		VARIATION
Quiero estudiar. ⊗	*Quiere estudiar.*	
Empiezan _____.	*Empiezan a estudiar.*	terminan / de
_____ comer.	*Empiezan a comer.*	cenar
Prefieren _____.	*Prefieren comer.*	tienen / que
_____ volver.	*Prefieren volver.*	llamar
Puedes _____.	*Puedes volver.*	debes
_____ economizar.	*Puedes economizar.*	jugar
Aprenden _____.	*Aprenden a economizar.*	empiezan / a
_____ nadar.	*Aprenden a nadar.*	gritar
Vamos _____.	*Vamos a nadar.*	acaban / de
_____ contestar.	*Vamos a contestar.*	llegar
Acaba _____.	*Acaba de contestar.*	va / a
_____ levantarse.	*Acaba de levantarse.*	irse
Tienen _____.	*Tienen que levantarse.*	tienen / que

10. EXPANSION DRILL

Empiezan la novela. ⊗
    (leer)   Empiezan a leer la novela.
Por fin termina sus lecciones.
    (hacer)   *Por fin termina de hacer sus lecciones.*
¿Aprendes español?
    (hablar)   *¿Aprendes a hablar español?*
No sé el nombre.
    (escribir)   *No sé escribir el nombre.*
Me enseñan el cha-cha-cha.
    (bailar)   *Me enseñan a bailar el cha-cha-cha.*
Llamo a los niños.
    (comer)   *Llamo a comer a los niños.*
Tengo una máquina de escribir.
    (comprar)   *Tengo que comprar una máquina de escribir.*
¿Cuándo comienza su tarea?
    (hacer)   *¿Cuándo comienza a hacer su tarea?*

11. FREE RESPONSE

¿Va usted a pasar este año?
¿Va a pasar raspando, o va a sacar buenas notas?

Si pasa raspando, ¿me promete estudiar más el año próximo?
¿A qué hora empieza a hacer su tarea?
¿Ya sabe usted jugar tenis?
¿Piensa aprender a nadar este verano?
¿Quién va a enseñarle a nadar?

12. DOUBLE ITEM SUBSTITUTION

VARIATION

Prometo estudiar. ☺	prometemos	Prometo estudiar.	*Prometemos estudiar.*
Estoy _____.	estamos	Estoy estudiando.	*Estamos estudiando.*
_____ trabajado.	comido	He trabajado.	*Hemos comido.*
Tengo _____.	tenemos	Tengo que trabajar.	*Tenemos que comer.*
_____ comiendo.	preguntando	Estoy comiendo.	*Estamos preguntando.*
He _____.	hemos	He comido.	*Hemos preguntado.*
_____ vistiéndome.	sentándonos	Estoy vistiéndome.	*Estamos sentándonos.*
Acabo _____.	acabamos	Acabo de vestirme.	*Acabamos de sentarnos.*

13. WRITING EXERCISE

Write the responses to Drills 9 and 10.

EXERCISE BOOK: EXERCISES 2, 3, AND 4

Adverbs with -mente

PRESENTATION *TEACHER PRESENTATION, p. T203*

Ella no es muy bonita, **francamente.**
¡Es **absolutamente** imposible!
Voy a hablar con su jefe **inmediatamente.**

Which words are the adverbs in these sentences? What suffix do they end in? What part of speech is the word to which the suffix is attached? Is it attached to the masculine or the feminine form?

GENERALIZATION

In English, many adverbs are formed by adding -*ly* to an adjective.

$$\begin{array}{ccc} immediate & \rightarrow & immediate\underline{ly} \\ perfect & \rightarrow & perfect\underline{ly} \end{array}$$

In Spanish many adverbs are formed by adding **-mente** to the feminine singular form of an adjective.

inmediata	➜	**inmediata<u>mente</u>**
perfecta	➜	**perfecta<u>mente</u>**

STRUCTURE DRILLS

14. ADJECTIVE ➜ ADVERB

inmediato	inmediatamente
perfecto	*perfectamente*
absoluto	*absolutamente*
fácil	*fácilmente*
posible	*posiblemente*
principal	*principalmente*
seguro	*seguramente*
exagerado	*exageradamente*
triste	*tristemente*
loco	*locamente*
alegre	*alegremente*
franco	*francamente*
distraído	*distraídamente*
desgraciado	*desgraciadamente*

15. TRANSFORMATION DRILL

Aprendemos esa lección de una **manera fácil**. ⊗	Aprendemos esa lección fácilmente.
Los niños cantan de una manera alegre.	Los niños cantan alegremente.
Me duele la cabeza de una manera horrible.	Me duele la cabeza horriblemente.
Ella siempre habla de una manera exagerada.	Ella siempre habla exageradamente.
La criada grita de una manera loca.	La criada grita locamente.
La maestra nos mira de una manera triste.	La maestra nos mira tristemente.

16. FREE SUBSTITUTION

Es <u>absolutamente</u> <u>imposible</u>. *realmente, francamente, perfectamente / posible, fácil, malo, absurdo*

EXERCISE BOOK: EXERCISES 5 AND 6

Comparatives: tan/tanto . . . como

PRESENTATION *TEACHER PRESENTATION, p. T203*

> Ellos no están <u>tan</u> tristes <u>como</u> yo.
> Cristina no aprende <u>tan</u> fácilmente <u>como</u> tú.

Which words mean *as . . . as* in these sentences? Which part of speech is the word that follows **tan** in the first sentence? Which part of speech is the word that follows **tan** in the second sentence?

> Ellos no tienen <u>tantos</u> problemas <u>como</u> yo.
> Yo no tengo <u>tanta</u> prisa <u>como</u> ella.
> Los otros no sufren <u>tanto</u> <u>como</u> yo.

Which words mean *as much (as many) . . . as*? In which of these sentences does a form of **tanto** function as an adjective? Does **tanto** show number and gender agreement when it functions as an adjective? Does **tanto** function as an adjective or an adverb in the last sentence?

GENERALIZATION

Spanish	English
tan + { adjective / adverb } **como**	*as* + { adjective / adverb } *as*
tanto, -a + { singular / noun } **como**	*as much* + { singular / noun } *as*
tantos, -as + { plural / noun } **como**	*as many* + { plural / noun } *as*
tanto como	*as much as*

1. As an adjective, **tanto** agrees in number and gender with the noun it modifies: **tanto dinero, tanta prisa, tantos muchachos, tantas muchachas.**

2. If a pronoun follows **como,** it is the subject pronoun, not the prepositional pronoun.

> **Ellos no tienen tantos problemas como <u>yo</u>.**
> **María no es tan alta como <u>tú</u>.**

Listening and Speaking Exercises 250, 251*, 252*, p. T134 ⊗   SECTION D

STRUCTURE DRILLS

17. PAIRED SUBSTITUTIONS

1. Este edificio no es tan grande como el otro. ⊗
   ____ piscina _____.   *Esta piscina no es tan grande como la otra.*
   Esta playa es tan linda como la de Miami.
   ____ aeropuerto _____.   *Este aeropuerto es tan lindo como el de Miami.*
   Esta máquina de escribir es tan cara como la tuya.
   ____ carro _____.   *Este carro es tan caro como el tuyo.*

2. José Luis tiene tantos problemas como yo. ⊗
   _____ dinero _____.   *José Luis tiene tanto dinero como yo.*
   Yo no leo tantas revistas como tú.
   _____ libros _____.   *Yo no leo tantos libros como tú.*
   Ellos no tienen tanto trabajo como nosotros.
   _____ tarea _____.   *Ellos no tienen tanta tarea como nosotros.*

18. PATTERNED RESPONSE

1. Juan es guapo. Su hermano, también. ⊗   Su hermano es tan guapo como **Juan.**
   Ana es simpática. Isabel, también.   *Isabel es tan simpática como Ana.*
   Mamá está preocupada. Papá, también.   *Papá está tan preocupado como mamá.*
   Los niños están cansados. Yo también.   *Yo estoy tan cansado como los niños.*
   Los alumnos están aburridos. La maestra,   *La maestra está tan aburrida como los alumnos.*
   también.

2. Ella ha leído diez novelas. Él ha leído   Él no ha leído tantas novelas como ella.
   menos. ⊗
   Arturo ha mandado dos tarjetas. Juan ha   *Juan no ha mandado tantas tarjetas como Arturo.*
   mandado menos.
   José tiene muchos problemas. Los otros   *Los otros alumnos no tienen tantos problemas como José.*
   alumnos tienen menos.
   Enrique gana mucho dinero. Miguel   *Miguel no gana tanto dinero como Enrique.*
   gana menos.
   Este carro usa mucha gasolina. El jeep   *El jeep no usa tanta gasolina como este carro.*
   usa menos.

3. Pedro estudia más que Juan. ⊗   Juan no estudia tanto como Pedro.
   José Luis sufre más que sus compañeros.   *Sus compañeros no sufren tanto como José Luis.*
   El maestro se aburre más que los chicos.   *Los chicos no se aburren tanto como el maestro.*
   Mi papá se enoja más que mi mamá.   *Mi mamá no se enoja tanto como mi papá.*
   La garganta me duele más que la cabeza.   *La cabeza no me duele tanto como la garganta.*

19. CUED DIALOG

(carro)   1ST STUDENT   ¡Qué lindo es este carro!
                     2ND STUDENT   Sí, pero no es tan lindo como el otro.

(dibujos)   *¡Qué lindos son estos dibujos! / Sí, pero no son tan lindos como los otros.*
(hotel)   *¡Qué lindo es este hotel! / Sí, pero no es tan lindo como el otro.*
(tarjetas) *¡Qué lindas son estas tarjetas! / Sí, pero no son tan lindas como las otras.*
(piscina)   *¡Qué linda es esta piscina! / Sí, pero no es tan linda como la otra.*
(aviones)   *¡Qué lindos son estos aviones! / Sí, pero no son tan lindos como los otros.*
(tren)   *¡Qué lindo es este tren! / Sí, pero no es tan lindo como el otro.*
(casa)   *¡Qué linda es esta casa! / Sí, pero no es tan linda como la otra.*

20. FREE RESPONSE

Juan, ¿es usted tan alto como su papá?
¿Es usted tan inteligente como él?
¿Es él tan simpático como usted?
Ana, ¿es usted tan bonita como su mamá?
¿Es tan alta como ella?
¿Ella habla español tan bien como usted?
¿Estudia usted tanto como los otros alumnos?
¿Habla español tan bien como ellos?
¿Saca notas tan buenas como ellos?
¿Habla español tan rápido como el maestro?
¿A usted le gusta la clase de historia tanto como la de español?
¿Le gusta la clase de inglés tanto como la de matemáticas?
¿A usted le parece tan fácil hablar español como inglés?
¿Tienen ustedes tantos exámenes en la clase de historia como en ésta?
¿Tienen tanta tarea?
¿Está usted tan contento el primer día de clases como el último?

21. WRITING EXERCISE

Write the responses to Drills 18.1, 18.2, and 18.3.

EXERCISE BOOK: EXERCISES 7, 8, AND 9

Listening and Speaking Exercise 253*, p. T137 ⊗

Writing

1. MULTIPLE ITEM SUBSTITUTION

1. ¿A qué hora empiezan a estudiar los muchachos?
   terminar / trabajar / médico   *¿A qué hora termina de trabajar el médico?*

2. Aprendemos a hablar español ahora.
   preferir / estudiar / álgebra   *Preferimos estudiar álgebra ahora.*

3. ¿Desean dejar algún recado?
   tener / escribir / tarjetas   *¿Tienen que escribir algunas tarjetas?*

4. Pienso sacar un siete en historia.
   querer / diez / matemáticas   *Quiero sacar un diez en matemáticas.*

5. Tú y yo no hemos hecho tanto trabajo como ella.
   los otros alumnos / leer / novelas / yo   *Los otros alumnos no han leído tantas novelas como yo.*

6. Tú no has mandado tantas tarjetas como yo.
   los muchachos / recibir / recados / ella   *Los muchachos no han recibido tantos recados como ella.*

7. Este carro no es tan barato como el de Juan.
   máquina de escribir / mi hermana   *Esta máquina de escribir no es tan barata como la de mi hermana.*

8. Esta maleta no es tan bonita como la de la otra muchacha.
   baúl / grande / muchacho   *Este baúl no es tan grande como el del otro muchacho.*

9. Al niño le encanta la película.
   a mí / doler / pies   *A mí me duelen los pies.*

10. ¿A ti te aprietan los zapatos?
    a usted / doler / cabeza   *¿A usted le duele la cabeza?*

2. SENTENCE COMBINATION

MODELS   Esta tarjeta es bonita. La otra, también.
         <u>Esta tarjeta es tan bonita como la otra.</u>

         Yo mando muchas cartas. Ella, también.
         <u>Yo mando tantas cartas como ella.</u>

1. El álgebra es difícil. La historia, también. *El álgebra es tan difícil como la historia.*
2. Esta revista es interesante. Ésa, también. *Esta revista es tan interesante como ésa.*
3. Tú lees muchas novelas. Yo, también.   *Tú lees tantas novela como yo.*
4. Las gemelas García tienen mucho dinero. Ellos, también. *Las gemelas García tienen tanto dinero como ellos.*
5. La maestra sufre mucho. Los alumnos, también. *La maestra sufre tanto como los alumnos.*

6. La máquina de escribir mía es cara. La suya, también. *La máquina de escribir mía es tan cara como la suya.*

7. Ana está triste. Su mamá, también. *Ana está tan triste como su mamá.*

8. Los gemelos nadan muy bien. Su hermano mayor, también. *Los gemelos nadan tan bien como su hermano mayor.*

9. La criada grita exageradamente. La señora, también. *La criada grita tan exageradamente como la señora.*

10. Yo lo siento mucho. Usted, también. *Yo lo siento tanto como usted.*

EXERCISE BOOK: EXERCISES 10 and 11

RECOMBINATION MATERIAL

Dialogs

I

JOSÉ LUIS	¿Cuándo vas a devolverme el libro? Lo necesito.
PATRICIO	Te lo doy mañana por la mañana. Marta lo tiene ahora.
JOSÉ LUIS	Yo se lo pido a ella, entonces. Es de la maestra, y tengo que devolvérselo esta tarde sin falta.
JOSÉ LUIS	Marta, ¿tienes el libro? Se lo tengo que devolver a la maestra.
MARTA	¿Cuál libro? Ah, sí, ése. Dolores lo tiene. Lo necesita para su clase de historia.
JOSÉ LUIS	¡Qué barbaridad! La maestra me mata si no le devuelvo ese libro.
MARTA	Vamos a la casa de Dolores. Ella lo tiene seguramente.
JOSÉ LUIS	¡Si no se lo ha prestado a otra persona!

. . . va . . .←

Se lo doy . . .

. . . tiene . . .

QUESTIONS

1. ¿Qué le pregunta José Luis a Patricio?
2. ¿Quién tiene el libro, según Patricio?
3. ¿De quién es el libro?
4. ¿Cuándo se lo tiene que devolver, sin falta?
5. ¿Tiene el libro Marta?
6. ¿Quién lo tiene, según ella?
7. ¿Para qué lo necesita Dolores?
8. ¿Qué le hace la maestra a José Luis si no le devuelve el libro?
9. ¿Adónde quiere ir Marta?
10. ¿Qué cree José Luis que Marta ha hecho con el libro, probablemente?

VARIATION: The conversation takes place among three people who address each other as *usted*.

II

MÉDICO	A ver, Juan. ¿Qué tiene usted?
JUAN	Me duele mucho la garganta.
MÉDICO	¿Qué más le duele? ¿La cabeza? ¿El estómago?
JUAN	La cabeza. Estoy muy resfriado.
MÉDICO	¿Ha tomado algo?
JUAN	Sí, para la garganta.
MÉDICO	Bueno, usted va a tener que quedarse en casa algunos días. Necesita dormir.
JUAN	¡Ay, no! Tengo un examen importantísimo esta tarde.
MÉDICO	¡Los buenos alumnos se preocupan porque no pueden ir a la escuela y los malos porque tienen que ir!

QUESTIONS

1. ¿Dónde está Juan?
2. ¿Qué le duele?
3. ¿Qué más le duele?
4. ¿Le duele el estómago?
5. ¿Le duelen las piernas?
6. ¿Ha tomado algo?
7. ¿Qué le dice el médico?
8. ¿Quiere Juan quedarse en casa?
9. ¿Por qué no?
10. ¿Qué dice el médico?
11. ¿Es Juan un buen o un mal alumno?
12. ¿Hay muchos alumnos como Juan?

El médico dice "a ver" y le pregunta a Juan qué tiene. Juan le contesta que le duele mucho la garganta. El médico le pregunta a Juan qué más le duele, ¿la cabeza? ¿el estómago? Juan le dice que le duele la cabeza, que él está muy resfriado. El médico le pregunta si ha tomado algo, y Juan dice que sí, para la garganta. El médico dice que bueno, que él va a tener que quedarse en casa algunos días, que necesita dormir. Juan grita "ay no", y le dice al médico que tiene un examen importantísimo esta tarde. El médico dice que los buenos alumnos se preocupan porque no pueden ir a la escuela y los malos porque tienen que ir.

DIALOG VARIATION

Change the dialog to narrative form.

NOTE: DIALOG III IS NOT INCLUDED
IN RECORDED PROGRAM. ⟶ **III**

RAÚL	¡Por fin van a terminar las clases!
PACO	Sí, ¡estamos libres dentro de una semana! El viernes es el último día.
RAÚL	Yo nunca voy a abrir otro libro de álgebra.
PACO	Ni mirar otro libro de historia.
RAÚL	Yo voy a ir a la playa todos los días.
PACO	Yo voy a pasar las vacaciones en el campo, en la hacienda de mi tío.

RAÚL ¡Y no voy a decir ni siquiera una palabra en inglés por
tres meses!

PACO ¡Yo tampoco!

REJOINDERS

¡Por fin estamos libres! *Sí, el viernes es el último día. / ¡Qué brutal! / Yo no voy a decir ni siquiera una palabra en inglés por tres meses. / ¡Por fin! / ¿Dónde vas a pasar las vacaciones?*

¿Con qué palabra empieza esta carta?
Si usted le escribe a una persona que no
conoce bien, ¿empieza la carta con "estimado"
o con "querido"? ¿Y cuando le escribe a un
amigo o a un pariente?

Narrative

¿A usted le gusta recibir cartas largas y llenas
de noticias?
¿Le gusta escribir cartas largas y llenas de
noticias?

Carta de un alumno costarricense*

Queridísimos° viejos[4],

    Estoy contentísimo por la carta que acabo de recibir de
ustedes, larga° y llena° de noticias, como a mí me gustan. Ya la
he leído tres veces y la voy a leer al menos una vez más.

5   Me alegro° mucho de saber que todos están bien y que no
vamos a tener que vender San Fernando. Es la mejor noticia que
he recibido en mi vida. Una hacienda tan bonita y tan grande,
que ha estado en nuestra familia cuatro generaciones*—con ese
clima, ese río° enorme, esa playa que es más bonita que la de
10 Miami—no debemos venderla por nada del mundo.

    Y vieran ustedes qué preocupados han estado, no sólo yo, sino
también todos los compañeros amigos míos. Es que les he hablado
tanto de San Fernando. Muchas veces nos sentamos a conversar
y yo les cuento y les cuento de las cosas que pasan allá y ellos no
15 se cansan de oírme; el que se cansa soy yo. Creen que yo exagero
mucho cuando les digo que hay cantidades* de cocodrilos*,
iguanas*, y monos° allá, pero les encanta escucharme; y cuando
les hablo de las boas* de dos y tres metros*[5] de largo que usted,
viejo, y los peones* han matado en la montaña*, se quedan con
20 la boca abierta.

    Bueno, voy a hablar de otra cosa porque si no, no termino
nunca esta carta, pero quiero decirles antes que me alegra muchísimo la noticia de que este año vamos a pasar todas las vacaciones en la hacienda. Ya tengo hechas las dos maletas y sola-

querido: *dear*

largo: *long*
lleno: *full*
alegrarse: *be glad*
¿Se alegra usted de saber
que las clases van a terminar
pronto?
río: *river*
¿Cómo se llama el río entre
México y Tejas?
¿Como se llama el río más
largo de los Estados Unidos?

mono: *monkey*
¿Hay monos en Costa Rica?
¿Es el mono un animal
tropical?

---

[4] Affectionate way of addressing parents.
[5] The metric system is used throughout Latin America, except in Puerto Rico.

Age-old plowing techniques are used on this farm in Costa Rica.

¿Espera usted a sus amigos después de las clases?

¿Dónde los espera? ¿Delante de la escuela?

25 mente estoy esperando° pasar el último examen, el de álgebra, que es de hoy en ocho, para salir corriendo° directamente* para el aeropuerto.

    A propósito, quiero pedirles permiso para llevar° a dos amigos míos a pasar las vacaciones con nosotros. Son Jack Parducci y
30 Bob O'Brien, de quienes ya les he hablado a ustedes. Son muy buenos muchachos, muy decentes* y simpáticos. Mis dos hermanitas probablemente se van a alegrar mucho de esta noticia. Ya ellos tienen el permiso de la casa y están completamente listos. No hablan de otra cosa más que de montar a caballo° y
35 de entrar a la cueva° para ver si encuentran el famoso tesoro*.

esperar: *wait*

correr: *run*
¿Corre usted muy rápido?

llevar: *take*
¿Cuáles libros va a llevar a casa esta tarde?

¿Va a llevar el libro de español?

¿Sabe usted montar a caballo?

¿Le gusta montar?

montar a caballo:
    horseback ride (mount on horse)

cueva: *cave*
¿Ha estado usted en una cueva?

QUESTIONS

TITLE

1. ¿De dónde es el muchacho que escribe la carta?
2. ¿En cuál país cree usted que está estudiando él?
3. ¿A quiénes les escribe?

    1

4. ¿Cuál palabra usa para referirse* a sus padres?   *1*
5. ¿Por qué está contentísimo?   *2*
6. ¿Es larga la carta que acaba de recibir?   *3*
7. ¿Cuántas veces la ha leído ya?   *4*

8. ¿Va a leerla otra vez? *4*

9. ¿Cuál es la mejor noticia que ha recibido en su vida? *6*

10. ¿Qué es San Fernando? *7*

11. ¿Es una hacienda pequeña? *7*

12. ¿Por cuántas generaciones ha estado San Fernando en esa familia? *8*

13. ¿Es bonita la playa de San Fernando? *9*

14. ¿A quiénes les ha hablado mucho de San Fernando? *12*

15. ¿Ellos se cansan de oírlo? *14*

16. ¿Quién se cansa? *15*

17. ¿Qué creen ellos? *15*

18. ¿Cuáles son algunos de los animales que hay en San Fernando? *16*

19. ¿Qué han matado el padre del autor y los peones? *18*

20. ¿Cómo se quedan los compañeros del autor cuando oyen estas historias? *19*

21. ¿El autor le habla de "tú" o de "usted" a su padre? *18*

22. ¿Ya tiene hechas las maletas el autor? *24*

23. ¿Qué está esperando para salir? *25*

24. ¿Cuál es su último examen? *25*

25. ¿Cuándo es? *26*

26. ¿Qué va a hacer después de pasar ese examen? *26*

27. ¿A quiénes quiere llevar el autor a San Fernando? *28*

28. ¿Cómo se llaman sus dos amigos? *29*

29. ¿Qué dice el autor de ellos? *30*

30. ¿Cree el autor que sus hermanitas se van a alegrar de esta noticia? *32*

31. ¿De qué hablan constantemente Jack y Bob? *34*

32. ¿Qué van a buscar en la cueva? *35*

II ⟵——————— NOTE: PART II OF NARRATIVE IS NOT INCLUDED IN RECORDED PROGRAM.

Mami, usted no debe preocuparse tanto por mí; yo estoy perfectamente bien y voy a estar pasando las vacaciones con ustedes muy pronto. Si no les he escrito en los últimos dos meses, ha sido porque he estado ocupadísimo preparándome para los
40 exámenes finales*. He salido bastante bien de casi todos, pero creo que voy a pasar raspando en el de inglés y en el de historia. No nos han dado las notas todavía, pero no creo que voy a sacar más de una C menos en los dos, si tengo suerte, que es como decir un seis allá. Es que cuando uno tiene que explicar* las
45 cosas en inglés es muy difícil. De todos modos ustedes deben estar muy orgullosos° de mí porque estoy seguro que he sacado mejor nota en estas dos cosas que los otros latinos* de mi grupo; si yo paso raspando, ellos van a pasar "raspandísimo".

Como les digo, todavía tengo un examen más, el de álgebra
50 que es de hoy en ocho, pero no me preocupa. Yo soy, como ustedes saben, bueno para todo lo que es matemáticas, y ni siquiera tengo que estudiar para este examen porque sé que va a

orgulloso: *proud*

¿Están sus padres muy orgullosos de usted?

¿Está usted orgulloso de sus notas?

Much of Costa Rica's tropical coast is unexplored jungle.

ser muy fácil. Pero estoy estudiando de todos modos porque no tengo otra cosa que hacer y estoy aburridísimo.

55   Bueno, por lo menos° tengo tiempo° para comprar algunas de las cosas que ustedes me piden. Ya he comprado dos de los vestidos para tía Matilde; son de minifalda porque falda larga he buscado por todas partes y simplemente no hay. Pero la empleada de la tienda dice que las minifaldas están de última moda° y que

60   en Suramérica hasta° las señoras las usan. Yo no sé si eso es verdad o no. Uno es azul y el otro no recuerdo en este momento*. También tengo ya los zapatos para usted, papá.

Ahora voy a ir de compras porque, qué barbaridad, con la lista que me han dado de cosas que comprar, voy a llegar allá

65   como Papá Noel°. Por favor, no más.

Un beso° y un abrazo° de su hijo que los quiere mucho y espera° verlos muy pronto.

José Rafael

José Rafael

P.D.[6]   Si hay alguna inconveniencia* con la cuestión* de Jack y

70   Bob deben avisarme* inmediatamente por cable*.

---

[6]**P.D. (Postdata)** = *P.S. (Postscript).*

¿Me va a mandar por lo menos una carta este verano?

¿Por cuánto tiempo van a estar ustedes de vacaciones?
por lo menos: *at least*
tiempo: *time* ¿Están las minifaldas de última moda? ¿Qué piensa usted de la última moda? ¿Le gusta?
de última moda: *the latest style (fashion)*
hasta: *even*
Hasta las maestras usan minifalda en esta escuela, ¿verdad?

Papá Noel: *Santa Claus (Papa Christmas)*
beso: *kiss*
abrazo: *hug*
esperar: *hope*
¿Cree usted en el Papá Noel?
¿Le da usted un beso y un abrazo a su mamá antes de salir de la casa?
¿Me da un beso y un abrazo a mí ahora?
¿Espera usted estudiar español el año próximo?
¿Espera volver a esta escuela o piensa ir a otra?

QUESTIONS

1. ¿Quién se preocupa mucho por José Rafael? 36
2. ¿Dónde va a estar él muy pronto? 37
3. ¿Por qué no les ha escrito en los últimos dos meses a sus padres? 38
4. ¿Ha salido muy bien de todos sus exámenes? 40
5. ¿En cuáles cursos* va a pasar raspando? 41
6. ¿Cuál nota piensa que va a sacar en esos cursos? 42
7. ¿Por qué son estos cursos especialmente difíciles para José Rafael? 44
8. ¿Por qué deben estar orgullosos los padres de José Rafael? 46
9. ¿Lo preocupa a José Rafael el examen de álgebra? 50
10. ¿Por qué no? 51
11. ¿Por qué estudia tanto para ese examen, entonces? 53
12. ¿Qué va a poder hacer ahora? 55
13. ¿Qué ha comprado para tía Matilde? 56
14. ¿Cómo son los vestidos? 57
15. ¿Qué está de última moda en Suramérica, según la empleada de la tienda? 59
16. ¿De qué color son los vestidos? 61
17. ¿Qué ha comprado José Rafael para su padre? 62
18. ¿Le han pedido muchas cosas los parientes de José Rafael? 64
19. ¿Cómo quién va a llegar a Costa Rica él? 65
20. ¿Cómo termina la carta? 66
21. ¿Qué les dice en la postdata a sus padres? 69

Conversation Stimulus

Un lugar ideal imaginario (¡o real!)

Use the following questions as a guide:

1. ¿Cuál es el lugar ideal para usted?
2. ¿Es una ciudad? ¿cuál? ¿un pueblo chico? ¿cuál?
3. ¿Dónde está? ¿en el campo? ¿en las montañas? ¿en la costa?
4. ¿Hay playas bonitas allí?
5. ¿La gente se baña todos los días en esas playas?
6. ¿Hace siempre buen tiempo?
7. ¿Hay haciendas inmensas*?
8. ¿Usted puede montar a caballo allí?
9. ¿Hay animales interesantes? ¿cuáles?
10. ¿Tiene que trabajar allí o tiene muchos criados?
11. ¿Hay escuelas y exámenes y maestros furiosos allí?

El lugar ideal para mí es Puerto Rico. Me encanta la ciudad de San Juan, capital de Puerto Rico. San Juan está en la costa, y hay playas lindísimas allí. La gente se baña todos los días, porque nunca hace frío. Siempre hace calor. En el campo hay haciendas bonitas donde uno puede montar a caballo. Yo no tengo muchos criados allí, y tengo que trabajar en la casa. Allí, como aquí, hay escuelas y exámenes y maestros furiosos. Sin embargo, para mí, San Juan es un lugar ideal.

RESPONSE FORMS FOR LISTENING EXERCISES

Do not write in this section. If you do not have the Exercise Book, you will be asked to copy whatever printed material you need for the listening exercises.

EXERCISE 4

	Ex.	1	2	3	4	5	6	7	8
SPANISH	✔								
ENGLISH									

EXERCISE 7

	Ex.	1	2	3	4	5	6	7	8	9	10
SPANISH											
ENGLISH	✔										

EXERCISE 16

	Ex.	1	2	3	4	5	6	7	8	9	10
r											
rr	✔										

EXERCISE 29

	Ex.	1	2	3	4	5	6	7	8	9	10	11	12
SPANISH	✔												
ENGLISH													

EXERCISE 32

	Ex.	1	2	3	4	5	6	7	8	9	10	11	12
A	✔												
B													

EXERCISE 37

Ex.	1	2	3	4	5	6
A	A	A	A	A	A	A
Ⓑ	B	B	B	B	B	B
C	C	C	C	C	C	C

EXERCISE 38

1. ¿Qué escuchas? ¿Unos discos?
2. Quiero practicar con la chica americana.
3. ¿Por qué no practicas conmigo?

1. _____
2. _____
3. _____

EXERCISE 41

Ex.	1	2	3	4	5	6
ⓨⓞ	yo	yo	yo	yo	yo	yo
tú	tú	tú	tú	tú	tú	tú
él	ella	usted	él	ella	usted	él
nosotros	nosotros	nosotros	nosotros	nosotros	nosotros	nosotros
ellos	ellas	ustedes	ellos	ellas	ustedes	ellos

EXERCISE 42

1. Tal vez escuchan una canción.
2. Susana pasa por la escuela.
3. Blanca pronuncia muy bien.

1. _____
2. _____
3. _____

EXERCISE 45

	Ex.	1	2	3	4	5
A	✔					
B						

EXERCISE 46

1. ¿A quién llamas? ¿A ella?
2. ¿Llegan ahora Blanca y Arturo?
3. Yo no sé con quién habla.

1. _____
2. _____
3. _____

EXERCISE 47

1. ¿Con quién habla Pedro?
2. ¿Por qué no quiere Blanca practicar con él?
3. ¿A quién quiere llamar Pedro, entonces?
4. ¿Quiere Blanca llamar a la chica americana?

1. _____
2. _____
3. _____
4. _____

EXERCISE 49

	Ex.	1	2	3	4	5	6	7	8
SPANISH									
ENGLISH	✔								

EXERCISE 52

Ex.	1	2	3
____ *3:00*	____ 1:00	____ 9:00	____ 10:00
____ *6:00*	____ 11:00	____ 3:00	____ 7:00
Ⓐ *1:00*	____ 5:00	____ 12:00	____ 8:00
____ *10:00*	____ 4:00	____ 2:00	____ 3:00

EXERCISE 53

yes	d-yes	diez
yet	k-yet	quieto
yellow	s-yellow	cielo
yet	n-yet	nieto
yen	t-yen	tienda
yet	s-yet	siete

EXERCISE 56

	Ex.	1	2	3	4	5	6	7	8	9	10	11	12
A	✔												
B													

EXERCISE 60

	Ex.	1	2	3	4	5	6	7	8
masculine	✔								
feminine									

EXERCISE 61

1. ¿Vamos a la biblioteca con Pedro?   1. _____
2. El sábado vamos a un baile.   2. _____
3. Blanca habla inglés bastante bien.   3. _____

EXERCISE 65

	Ex.	1	2	3	4	5	6	7	8	9	10	11	12	13	14	15
Statement																
Question	✔															

EXERCISE 66

1. ¿Dónde estudia usted español, señorita?   1. _____
2. ¿Qué día es mañana? Domingo.   2. _____
3. Vamos al mercado y a las tiendas.   3. _____

EXERCISE 67

1. ¿En quién piensa Raúl?   1. _____
2. ¿Qué día llega la chica americana?   2. _____
3. ¿Habla inglés Raúl?   3. _____
4. ¿Cómo habla español la chica americana,   4. _____
   bien o mal?

EXERCISE 73

	Ex.	1	2	3	4	5	6	7	8	9	10	11	12
A	✔												
B													

EXERCISE 75

	Ex.	1	2	3	4	5	6	7	8
d	✔								
r									

EXERCISE 77

	Ex.	1	2	3	4	5	6	7	8	9	10
Ⓐ	A	A	A	A	A	A	A	A	A	A	A
B	B	B	B	B	B	B	B	B	B	B	B
C	C	C	C	C	C	C	C	C	C	C	C

EXERCISE 78

1. Las gemelas García son muy inteligentes.
2. ¿Cuál de las dos es mejor? Ninguna.
3. Miguel llega con alguien.
4. ¿Con Jorge? No, con Guillermo.

1. _____
2. _____
3. _____
4. _____

EXERCISE 79

totter they	tarde	tar day
sweater tay	suerte	swear tay
cotter taw	carta	car taw
cotter nay	carne	car nay
petter though nay	perdone	pear doh nay

EXERCISE 82

	Ex.	1	2	3	4	5	6	7	8	9	10
girl	✔										
boy											
two girls											
mixed group											

EXERCISE 83

1. Quiero comprar un regalo para don Pedro.
2. ¿A qué hora cierran el mercado?
3. La señorita americana no habla ruso.
4. ¡Ah, con razón!

1. _____
2. _____
3. _____
4. _____

EXERCISE 84

todáy say	trece	trace eh
put ówn toe	pronto	prone toe
could Émma	crema	cray ma
good écho	greco	Greco
fit éat oh	frito	free toe
git ón	gran	gran

EXERCISE 87

	Ex.	1	2	3	4	5	6	7	8
A	✔								
B									

EXERCISE 88

1. ¿Son hermanas las dos chicas?
2. ¿Son gemelas?
3. ¿Son idénticas?
4. ¿Cuál de las dos es más alta?

1. _____
2. _____
3. _____
4. _____

EXERCISE 90

	Ex.	1	2	3	4	5	6	7	8	9	10
first	✔										
second											

EXERCISE 92

	Ex.	1	2	3	4	5
A	✔					
B						

EXERCISE 93

1. A propósito, ¿Tomás está aquí?
2. No, está en el café.
3. Ah, con razón. Hoy es sábado.

1. _____
2. _____
3. _____

EXERCISE 96

	Ex.	1	2	3	4	5	6	7	8	9	10
A	✔										
B											

EXERCISE 97

1. ¿Estudias ruso, francés, alemán, o español?
2. ¿Yo? Inglés.
3. José y yo vamos al café.
4. Después vamos al partido de fútbol.

1. _____
2. _____
3. _____
4. _____

EXERCISE 100

	Ex.	1	2	3	4	5	6
A							
B	✔						

EXERCISE 101

1. ¿Cuánto cuestan los boletos? No sé.
2. ¡Cómo gritas, hijo! ¿Qué quieres?
3. ¿Tú estás en tu cuarto?

1. _____
2. _____
3. _____

EXERCISE 102

west	p-west	puesto
wane	b-wane	bueno
wet	f-wet	fuete
we	f-we	fuí
well	m-well	muela
well	n-well	Manuel
web	y-web	llueve

EXERCISE 105

	Ex.	1	2	3	4	5	6	7	8
A	✔								
B									

EXERCISE 106

1. ¿Adónde va Roberto con tanta prisa?
2. ¿De dónde llega tío Arturo?
3. ¿Quiere Eva ir con Roberto?
4. ¿A qué hora llega tío Arturo?

1. _____
2. _____
3. _____
4. _____

EXERCISE 109

Ex.	1	2	3	4	5	6	7	8
(A)	A	A	A	A	A	A	A	A
B	B	B	B	B	B	B	B	B
C	C	C	C	C	C	C	C	C

EXERCISE 112

Ex.	1	2	3	4	5	6	7	8	9	10	11	12	13	14
(es)	es	somos	es	es	es	es	soy	eres	es	son	es	es	son	son
está	está	estamos	está	está	está	está	estoy	estás	está	están	está	está	están	están

EXERCISE 115

	Ex.	1	2	3	4	5	6	7	8
A									
B	✔								

EXERCISE 116

1. ¿Puedo ver la foto de la fiesta?
2. Claro, Felipe.
3. ¿Quién es esa chiquita?
4. Mi prima Beatricita. Es simpatiquísima.

1. _____
2. _____
3. _____
4. _____

EXERCISE 119

Ex.	1	2	3	4	5	6	7	8
A	A	A	A	A	A	A	A	A
B	B	B	B	B	B	B	B	B
Ⓒ	C	C	C	C	C	C	C	C

EXERCISE 120

1. ¿Adónde quiere ir Adela?
2. ¿Quiere ir al cine su hermano?
3. ¿Sabe Adela qué dan?
4. ¿Qué busca ella?
5. ¿Dónde está el periódico?

1. _____
2. _____
3. _____
4. _____
5. _____

EXERCISE 123

Ex.	1	2	3	4
A	A	A	A	A
Ⓑ	B	B	B	B
C	C	C	C	C

EXERCISE 124

Yo

Yo soy Francisco Castro, alumno de la Escuela Americana. Es una escuela muy __1__ y __2__. Me gusta mucho. Mis compañeros son todos muy __3__ y __4__. Aquí tengo dos fotos: una es de la escuela; __5__ ¿no? La otra es de todos los __6__ y __7__ que están en mi __8__, y del maestro, don Pedro. Ése que está __9__ con la chica __10__ soy yo.

1. _____
2. _____
3. _____
4. _____

5. _____
6. _____
7. _____

8. _____
9. _____
10. _____

EXERCISE 128

Ex.	1	2	3	4	5	6	7	8
(A)	A	A	A	A	A	A	A	A
B	B	B	B	B	B	B	B	B
C	C	C	C	C	C	C	C	C

EXERCISE 132

Ex.	1	2	3	4	5	6	7	8	9	10
(A)	A	A	A	A	A	A	A	A	A	A
B	B	B	B	B	B	B	B	B	B	B
C	C	C	C	C	C	C	C	C	C	C

EXERCISE 133

1. María todavía pronuncia muy mal.
2. ¿Qué día es la fiesta? El viernes.
3. ¿Vas al estadio con tu tío?
4. ¿Dónde está el diccionario? En tu cuarto.

1. _____
2. _____
3. _____
4. _____

EXERCISE 136

	Ex.	1	2	3	4	5	6	7	8	9	10
A											
B	✔										

EXERCISE 137

1. ¿Qué quiere hacer Susana esta tarde?
2. ¿Quiere Pedro practicar inglés?
3. ¿Por qué no quiere?
4. ¿Qué quiere hacer Susana, entonces?
5. ¿Quiere Pedro esuchar discos también?
6. ¿Qué tiene él?

1. _____
2. _____
3. _____
4. _____
5. _____
6. _____

EXERCISE 139

	Ex.	1	2	3	4	5	6	7	8
A	✔								
B									

EXERCISE 140

El gordito contesta la carta de Sue
Estimada amiga:

Muchas gracias por __1__ carta tan bonita. __2__ debes ser una chica muy __3__ . Y muy bonita tambien. ¿__4__ años tienes? ¿No tienes una __5__ ?

Yo tengo casi __6__ años. Soy __7__ , y tengo __8__ __9__ . También soy un poco gordo, no muy gordo, un poco __10__ .

1. _____   5. _____   8. _____
2. _____   6. _____   9. _____
3. _____   7. _____   10. _____
4. _____

EXERCISE 143

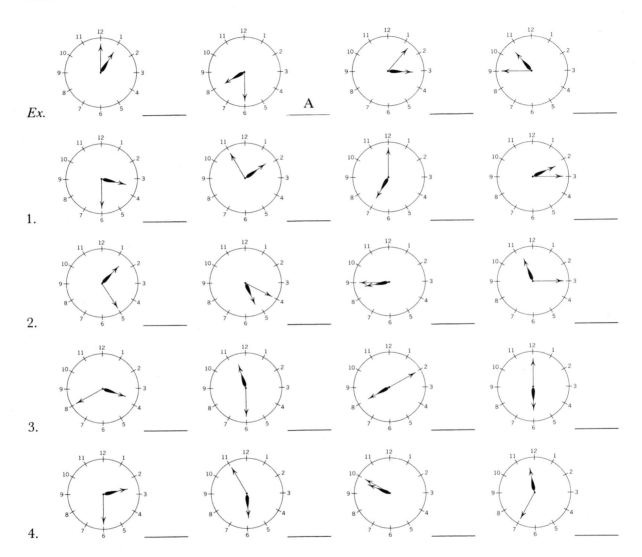

EXERCISE 145

	Ex.	1	2	3	4	5	6	7	8
A	✔								
B									

EXERCISE 148

	Ex.	1	2	3	4	5	6	7	8	9	10
A											
B	✔										

EXERCISE 149

1. ¿Tiene hambre el hijo?
2. ¿Qué hora es?
3. ¿Qué hay de comer?
4. ¿Qué quiere tomar el hijo?

1. _____
2. _____
3. _____
4. _____

EXERCISE 152

Ex. __74__

1. _____
2. _____
3. _____
4. _____
5. _____
6. _____

7. _____
8. _____
9. _____
10. _____
11. _____
12. _____
13. _____

14. _____
15. _____
16. _____
17. _____
18. _____
19. _____
20. _____

EXERCISE 153

Lunes: día feo

¡Imposible! ¡Qué tarde! ¡Lunes! ¡Las siete de la __1__! ¡Escuela! ¡Examen de __2__! ¡Qué __3__! ¡Y no sé nada, absolutamente nada! ¡Examen con don Pedro, el maestro más __4__ del mundo! No, imposible, no puedo ir a la escuela hoy, estoy enfermo, tengo __5__. Yo sé que no sé nada . . . a ver: ¿la capital de __6__? Este . . . este . . . ¡Río de Janeiro! . . . No no no, no es Río de Janeiro, ahora tienen otra nueva, ¿cómo se __7__? . . . no recuerdo. ¿Los productos __8__ de Colombia? No tengo la menor idea.

1. ____
2. ____

3. ____
4. ____

5. ____
6. ____

7. ____
8. ____

EXERCISE 156

	Ex.	1	2	3	4	5	6
A	✔						
B							

EXERCISE 158

	Ex.	1	2	3	4	5	6	7	8	9	10
A	✔										
B											

EXERCISE 161

Ex.	1	2	3	4	5	6	7	8	9	10
A	A	A	A	A	A	A	A	A	A	A
B	B	B	B	B	B	B	B	B	B	B
Ⓒ	C	C	C	C	C	C	C	C	C	C

EXERCISE 162

1. ¿Qué le pasa a la hija?
2. ¿Puede caminar más ella?
3. ¿Adónde quiere ir la hija?
4. ¿Quiere el padre ir al café también?

1. _____
2. _____
3. _____
4. _____

EXERCISE 165

	Ex.	1	2	3	4	5	6
A							
B	✔						

EXERCISE 166

Jeem, Beel, y Beector

Salen de Washington el día 25 de junio y calculan llegar a Laredo, Tejas, cinco días más tarde. El jueves salen de Laredo, pasan el Río Grande y __1__ a México por Nuevo Laredo, donde pasan la noche, para luego continuar su __2__ hasta llegar al Distrito Federal, la __3__, que también se llama México, D.F.

En México van a pasar unos diez días, más o menos, porque quieren __4__ muchos lugares. Quieren ver, por __5__, las famosas __6__ de San Juan Teotihuacán, los __7__ que tienen las __8__ de las grandes __9__ indias de México, los puertos de Acapulco en el Pacífico y Veracruz en el __10__. Y muchas cosas más.

1. _____	5. _____	8. _____
2. _____	6. _____	9. _____
3. _____	7. _____	10. _____
4. _____		

EXERCISE 169

Ex.	1	2	3	4	5	6	7	8	9	10
Ⓐ	A	A	A	A	A	A	A	A	A	A
B	B	B	B	B	B	B	B	B	B	B
C	C	C	C	C	C	C	C	C	C	C

EXERCISE 170

1. Luis ¿cuántas veces has leído este libro? ¡Seis!

2. ¿Qué te han traído? Veinte pesos.

3. Yo no oigo nada. ¿Tú has oído algo?

1. _____

2. _____

3. _____

EXERCISE 173

	Ex.	1	2	3	4	5	6	7	8	9	10	11	12	13	14	15
change																
no change	✔															

EXERCISE 176

	Ex.	1	2	3	4	5	6	7	8
A	✔								
B									

EXERCISE 177

1. ¿Con quién quiere hablar el señor?
2. ¿Por qué no puede hablar con ella?
3. ¿Sabe la criada cuándo vuelve la señorita?
4. ¿Quiere dejar un recado el señor?
5. ¿Qué le dice él a la criada?

1. _____
2. _____
3. _____
4. _____
5. _____

EXERCISE 180

Ex.	1	2	3	4	5	6	7	8	9	10
Ⓐ	A	A	A	A	A	A	A	A	A	A
B	B	B	B	B	B	B	B	B	B	B
C	C	C	C	C	C	C	C	C	C	C
D	D	D	D	D	D	D	D	D	D	D

EXERCISE 181

El teléfono

Ese aparato feo y de color negro, de __1__ poco artística, frío de __2__, ese instrumento que un señor con uniforme de la Compañía Nacional de Electricidad colgó en __3__ __4__ de la cocina de mi casa, ése es nuestro indispensable y sincero amigo, el teléfono.

Si de todos los aparatos __5__ que la técnica moderna ha __6__, alguien me dice que solamente uno puedo tener en mi casa, y me ordena eliminar todos los otros, yo inmediatamente selecciono el teléfono y elimino __6__ __7__, el radio, y todos los otros que tenemos en la casa, inclusive __9__ __10__ en colores que es tan bonita.

1. _____   5. _____   8. _____
2. _____   6. _____   9. _____
3. _____   7. _____   10. _____
4. _____

EXERCISE 184

	Ex.	1	2	3	4	5	6	7	8	9	10
A											
B	✔										

EXERCISE 187

	Ex.	1	2	3	4	5	6	7	8
A	✔								
B									

EXERCISE 190

	Ex.	1	2	3	4	5	6	7	8
A	✔								
B									

EXERCISE 191

1. ¿En qué clase tienen un dictado Pedro y Luisa?
2. ¿Ha estudiado Luisa?
3. ¿Ella siempre sale bien o mal en inglés, según Pedro?
4. ¿Cómo habla la maestra, según Luisa?
5. ¿Qué le contesta Pedro?

1. _____
2. _____
3. _____
4. _____
5. _____

EXERCISE 193

	Ex.	1	2	3	4	5	6	7	8	9	10
[y̶]	✔										
no [y̶]											

EXERCISE 196

	Ex.	1	2	3	4	5	6	7	8
Ⓐ	A	A	A	A	A	A	A	A	
B	B	B	B	B	B	B	B	B	
C	C	C	C	C	C	C	C	C	

EXERCISE 197

América y los americanos

"__1__ Todos los __2__ de este Hemisferio somos americanos, no sólo la __3__ de los Estados Unidos! ¡Porque América es Canadá, es __4__, is todo el Hemisferio Occidental __5__"

Ésta es la eterna protesta de unos pocos extremistas, quienes no están contentos porque los americanos han monopolizado esta palabra y han limitado su __6__ a la nacionalidad de los Estados Unidos. Es una protesta sin mucha __7__. Técnicamente es verdad que todos nosotros somos americanos, pero la realidad de las cosas es que cuando hablamos de "nacionalidad americana" o de "productos americanos", sabemos muy bien que esa nacionalidad y esos productos no __8__ a ningún otro __9__ del Hemisferio sino a los Estados Unidos. Es __10__ una conveniencia, un __11__ que ha sido adaptado por los Estados Unidos y aceptado en todo el mundo, inclusive en el resto de América __12__

1. _____   4. _____   7. _____   10. _____
2. _____   5. _____   8. _____   11. _____
3. _____   6. _____   9. _____   12. _____

EXERCISE 199

	Ex.	1	2	3	4	5	6	7	8	9	10
r	✔										
t											

EXERCISE 201

	Ex.	1	2	3	4	5	6	7	8	9	10
	Ⓐ	A	A	A	A	A	A	A	A	A	A
	B	B	B	B	B	B	B	B	B	B	B
	C	C	C	C	C	C	C	C	C	C	C

EXERCISE 205

	Ex.	1	2	3	4	5	6	7	8
A	✔								
B									

EXERCISE 209

	Ex.	1	2	3	4	5	6	7	8
A	✔								
B									

EXERCISE 210

1. ¿De qué están hablando Roberto y Cristina?
2. ¿Por qué no quiere ir al partido Roberto?
3. ¿Por qué dice eso?
4. ¿Quién va a ir al partido, según Cristina?
5. ¿Qué va a hacer Roberto, de todos modos?

1. _____
2. _____
3. _____
4. _____
5. _____

EXERCISE 213

Ex.	1	2	3	4	5	6	7	8	9	10
A	A	A	A	A	A	A	A	A	A	A
(B)	B	B	B	B	B	B	B	B	B	B
C	C	C	C	C	C	C	C	C	C	C
D	D	D	D	D	D	D	D	D	D	D

EXERCISE 214

El Nuevo Mundo

Si __1__ un mapa del Hemisferio Occidental __2__ podemos observar que el Nuevo Mundo tiene la forma de dos triángulos unidos por una delgada faja de __3__. El triángulo superior contiene tres grandes países __4__ Canadá, Estados Unidos, y México, y llamamos esta parte del continente "__5__". Por esta razón también les decimos "norteamericanos" a los americanos. __6__, nadie les aplica este término a los habitantes de Canadá y México, que por su __7__ geográfica también son norteamericanos. La __8__ de cada una de estas dos __9__ es una palabra tan claramente derivada del nombre del país—canadiense y mexicano—que para no hacer __10__ preferimos reservar "norteamericanos" para los habitantes de los Estados Unidos.

1. _____   5. _____   8. _____
2. _____   6. _____   9. _____
3. _____   7. _____   10. _____
4. _____

EXERCISE 216

	Ex.	1	2	3	4	5	6	7	8
´ – – THIRD-FROM-LAST	✔								
– ´ – NEXT-TO-LAST									
– – ´ LAST									

EXERCISE 218

	Ex.	1	2	3	4	5	6	7	8
A	✔								
B									

EXERCISE 220

	Ex.	1	2	3	4	5	6	7	8
morning	✔								
afternoon									
evening									

EXERCISE 222

	Ex.	1	2	3	4	5	6	7	8
A	✔								
B									

EXERCISE 223

1. ¿Por qué le van a comprar un regalo a Cecilia los dos chicos?
2. ¿Por qué no sabe Carlos qué comprar para Cecilia?
3. Según María, ¿qué le debe comprar Carlos a Cecilia?
4. ¿Carlos le quiere comprar eso?
5. ¿Qué le va a comprar, mejor?

1. _____
2. _____
3. _____
4. _____
5. _____

EXERCISE 227

Ex. **p r i s a**

1. m _ _ _ _
2. a _ _ _ _
3. p _ _ _ _ _ _
4. m _ _ _ _ _ _
5. r _ _ _ _ _ _

6. d _ _ _ _ _ _ _ _ _
7. e _ _ _ _ _ _ _
8. v _ _ _ _
9. b _ _ _ _ _
10. i _ _ _ _ _ _ _ _

EXERCISE 228

Be prepared to write a short paragraph from dictation.

EXERCISE 230

	Ex.	1	2	3	4	5	6	7	8	9	10
A	✔										
B											

EXERCISE 232

Ex. sentarme

1. _____   4. _____   7. _____
2. _____   5. _____   8. _____
3. _____   6. _____   9. _____

EXERCISE 235

Ex.	**1**	**2**	**3**	**4**	**5**	**6**	**7**	**8**	**9**	**10**
Ⓐ	A	A	A	A	A	A	A	A	A	A
B	B	B	B	B	B	B	B	B	B	B
C	C	C	C	C	C	C	C	C	C	C

EXERCISE 236

1. ¿Qué está haciendo la Sra. Ramos?
2. ¿Qué busca ella?
3. ¿Ya ha puesto toda la ropa en la maleta?
4. ¿Qué no ha puesto todavía?
5. ¿La familia Ramos, va a viajar en tren o en avión?

EXERCISE 240

Ex. p i e r n a s

1. h _ _ _ _ _ _ _   6. n _ _ _ _ _
2. p _ _ _ _   7. g _ _ _ _ _ _ _
3. h _ _ _ _ _ _ _   8. c _ _ _ _
4. a _ _ _ _ _ _ _   9. t _ _ _ _ _
5. d _ _ _ _ _   10. t _ _ _ _ _ _

EXERCISE 242

Ex. r

1. ____   5. ____   9. ____
2. ____   6. ____   10. ____
3. ____   7. ____   11. ____
4. ____   8. ____   12. ____

EXERCISE 244

Ex.	1	2	3	4	5	6	7	8	9
A	A	A	A	A	A	A	A	A	A
Ⓑ	B	B	B	B	B	B	B	B	B
C	C	C	C	C	C	C	C	C	C

EXERCISE 245

Be prepared to write a short paragraph from dictation.

EXERCISE 247

Ex. ⓐ   *e*   *o*

1. a   e   o
2. a   e   o
3. a   e   o
4. a   e   i
5. e   i   o

6. e   i   o
7. e   i   o
8. i   o   u
9. i   o   u
10. a   o   i

EXERCISE 249

Ex.	1	2	3	4	5	6	7	8	9	10
A	A	A	A	A	A	A	A	A	A	A
B	B	B	B	B	B	B	B	B	B	B
Ⓒ	C	C	C	C	C	C	C	C	C	C

EXERCISE 251

Ex.	1	2	3	4	5	6
A	A	A	A	A	A	A
Ⓑ	B	B	B	B	B	B
C	C	C	C	C	C	C

EXERCISE 252

Carta de un alumno costarricense

Bueno, voy a hablar de otra cosa porque si no, no __1__ nunca esta carta, pero quiero __2__ antes que me alegra __3__ la noticia de que este año vamos a pasar todas las vacaciones en la hacienda. Ya tengo hechas las dos maletas y solamente estoy __4__ pasar el último examen, el de álgebra, que es de hoy en ocho, para salir __5__ directamente para el aeropuerto.

A propósito, quiero __6__ permiso para llevar a dos amigos míos a pasar las vacaciones con nosotros. Son Jack Parducci y Bob O'Brien, de quienes ya les he hablado a ustedes. Son muy buenos muchachos, muy decentes y simpáticos. Mis dos hermanitas probablemente __7__ van a __8__ mucho de esta noticia. Ya ellos tienen el permiso de la casa y están completamente listos. No hablan de otra cosa más que de montar a __9__ y de entrar a la __10__ para ver si encuentran el famoso tesoro.

1. _____   5. _____   8. _____
2. _____   6. _____   9. _____
3. _____   7. _____   10. _____
4. _____

EXERCISE 253

1. ¿Qué le pregunta la maestra a Carlos?
2. ¿Contesta bien él?
3. ¿Por qué no puede contestar, según él?
4. ¿Y según la maestra?
5. ¿Cuál nota saca Carlos en geografía?
6. ¿Va a pasar este año él?

1. _____
2. _____
3. _____
4. _____
5. _____
6. _____

SPANISH–ENGLISH VOCABULARY

This vocabulary includes the words and phrases which appear in Level One. Not included are names of people and verb forms other than the infinitive, except when another form has been introduced first.

The number or letter-number combination after each definition refers to the unit in which the word or phrase first appears. A number by itself refers to the Basic Dialog of that unit; the letter S refers to the Supplement; G refers to the Grammar section; and N refers to the Narrative.

For adjectives and for nouns that have a masculine and a feminine form, the feminine ending is listed immediately following the masculine form, for example, **barato, –a; tío, –a.**

Alternations in verb stems are given in parentheses after the corresponding verb.

ABBREVIATIONS

abbrev	abbreviation of	*m*	masculine noun
adj	adjective	*pl*	plural
f	feminine noun	*pp*	past participle
fn	footnote		

A

a   to, 1; at, 3
  a fines de   around the end of, 9S; **a la una** at one o'clock, 9S; **al menos** at least, 15; **a propósito** by the way, 5; **¿a qué hora?** at what time?, 3; **a ver** let's see, 6
abajo   down, 14S
abandonar   abandon, 14N
abierto   *pp* **abrir,** 13S
abrazo   hug, 15N
abrigo   coat, 4S
abril   April, 9S
abrir   open, 12S
absolutamente   absolutely, 8N
absoluto   absolute, 13N
absurdo, –a   absurd, 13N
abuelo, –a   grandfather, grandmother, 6S
aburrido, –a   bored, 10S
aburrir   bore, 10S

aburrirse   get bored, 13S
acabar de   have just, 10
  acaba de salir   he has just left, 10
aceptable   acceptable, 11N
aceptar   accept, 11N
acercarse   approach, go towards, 13N
acostar (ue)   put to bed, 13G
  acostarse (ue)   go to bed, lie down, 13
acostumbrado, –a   accustomed, 10N
acostumbrar   accustom, 10N
activo, –a   active, 9N
adaptación *f*   adaptation, 11N
adaptar   adapt, 11N
además   besides, 12S
adicto, –a   addicted, 10N
adiós   good-bye, 4
adivinar   guess, 6
admiración *f*   admiration, 9N
adónde   where, 1
adulto, –a   adult, 13N

aeropuerto   airport, 5S
afecto   affection, 10N
agosto   August, 9
agua (el agua) *f*   water, 8S (*see fn page 133*)
¡ah!   oh! (*exclamation*), 1
ahora   now, 2S
ajá   aha, 5
al (a + el)   to the, 3
álbum *m*   album, 6
alegrar   make happy, 15N
   alegrarse   be glad, 15N
alegre   gay, 15S
alemán *m*   German, 2S
alemán (alemana) *adj*   German, 4
álgebra (el álgebra) *f*   algebra, 15S (*see fn page 291*)
algo   something, 3
alguien   someone, 2S
alguno, –a, –os, –as   some, 10G
   algún   some, 10
almacén *m*   department store, 12S
almorzar (ue)   have lunch, 8
almuerzo   lunch, 6S
aló   hello (*on phone*), 10
alto, –a   tall, 4S
alumno, –a   student, 4S
allá   there, 9 (*see fn page 155*)
allí   there, 8S (*see fn page 155*)
amarillo, –a   yellow, 7S
ambicioso, –a   ambitious, 9N
americano, –a   American, 2
amigo, –a   friend, 1
   tan amiga de él   so friendly with him, 4
amor *m*   love, 12
   mi amor   darling, 12
andar   walk, 11
   Anda tomando agua.   He's out drinking water., 11
animal *m*   animal, 10N
aniversario   anniversary, 13S
anteojos *m pl*   glasses, 14
   anteojos negros   sunglasses, 14
antes   first, beforehand, 3S
   antes de   before, 7G
antipático, –a   unpleasant, 4S
año   year, 7
   ¿Cuántos años tiene?   How old are you?, 7;
   tener ＿＿＿ años   be ＿＿＿ years old, 7
aparato   apparatus, 10N
aparecer (zc)   appear, 13N

aplicación *f*   application, 11N
aplicar   apply, 12N
aprender   learn, 14S
apretar (ie)   squeeze, 3
   Me aprietan mucho los zapatos.   My shoes are too tight., 3
apunte *m*   note, 11S
apurarse   hurry, 13G
apúrate   hurry up, 3G
aquí   here, 5
Argentina   Argentina, 12N
arreglar   fix, clean, 5
arriba   up, 14
artículo   article, 11N
artístico, –a   artistic, 10N
asociado, –a   associated, 12N
asustado, –a   frightened, 10S
asustar   frighten, 10S
   asustarse   get frightened, 13S
atención *f*   attention, 11
Atlántico   Atlantic, 9N
autobús *m*   bus, 9S
aventura   adventure, 9N
avión *m*   plane, 9
avisar   advise, 15N
¡ay!   oh! (*exclamation*), 5
azul   blue, 7

B

bailar   dance, 10S
baile *m*   dance, 3S
bajo, –a   short, 4S
banco   bank, 5S
bañar   bathe, 13G
   bañarse   bathe, 13N
baño   bathroom, 5S
barato, –a   cheap, 5S
barbaridad *f*: **¡Qué barbaridad!**   That's awful!, 11
barco   boat, 9
basar   base, 14N
bastante   pretty, enough, 2S
bata   robe, 14N
baúl *m*   trunk, 14S
belleza   beauty, 10
   salón de belleza   beauty shop, 10
beso   kiss, 15N
biblioteca   library, 2S
bicicleta   bicycle, 9S

bien well, 2S
  bien, gracias fine, thanks, 5S; **muy bien** all right, 4
blanco, –a white, 7S
blusa blouse, 4S
boa boa (*snake*), 15N
boca mouth, 13N
boleto ticket, 5
Bolivia Bolivia, 12N
bolsa bag, 8
bonito, –a pretty, nice, 4 (*see fn page 90*); cute, 6
Brasil Brazil, 12N
brazo arm, 15S
brutal brutal, terrific, 14S
bueno, –a good, 1
  buen good, 10G
buscar look for, 5

C

caballo horse, 15N
  montar a caballo horseback ride, 15N
cabeza head, 15S
cable *m* cable, 15N
cada each, 10N
café *m* café, 5; coffee, 8S
café *adj* brown, 7S (*see fn page 110*)
calcetín *m* sock, 5S
calcular calculate, 9N
caliente hot, 8S (*see fn page 132*)
calor *m* heat, 8S
  tener calor be warm (*for a person*), 8S; **Tengo mucho calor.** I'm very warm., 8S (*see fn page 132*)
calle *f* street, 7S
camarero, –a waiter, waitress, 10S
cambiar change, 13N
caminar walk, 3
camisa shirt, 4S
campeón *m* champion, 5
campo country, 15S
Canadá Canada, 7
canadiense Canadian, 12N
canal *m* canal, 9N; channel, 13N
canción *f* song, 2S
cansado, –a tired, 6S
cansar tire, 13G
  cansarse get tired, 13S
cantar sing, 10S
cantidad *f* quantity, 15N
capital *f* capital, 8N
cara face, 8

¡caramba! darn it! (*exclamation*), 5
carga cargo, 9N
Caribe *m* Caribbean, 12N
carne *f* meat, 8S
caro, –a expensive, 5S
carrera race, 1
  carrera de perros dog races, 1
carro car, 1
carta letter, 7
cartera purse, 14S
cartero mailman, 8
casa house, 1
  en casa at home, 1
casi almost, 3
caso case, 9N
  en todo caso in any case, 12
castaño, –a brown, 7S (*see fn page 110*)
catástrofe *f* catastrophe, 11N
catedral *f* cathedral, 8N
catorce fourteen, 6S
cena supper, dinner, 6S
cenar to have dinner, 8S
centro center, downtown, 3S
Centroamérica Central America, 9N
centroamericano, –a Central American, 12N
cepillo brush, 14S
cero zero, 10
cerrar (ie) close, 3
cien one hundred, 9S
ciento uno one hundred one, 9S
cierto, –a correct, 11N
cinco five, 3S
cincuenta fifty, 9S
cine *m* movies, 3
ciudad *f* city, 14S
civilización *f* civilization, 9N
claramente clearly, 12N
claro of course, 4
clase *f* class, 6N
clasificación *f* classification, 12N
clienta client, 10 (*see fn page 179*)
cliente *m* client, 10 (*see fn page 179*)
clima *m* climate, 9
cocina kitchen, 1
cocodrilo crocodile, 15N
colgar (ue) hang up, 10
colgó he hung up, 10
Colombia Colombia, 6G
colombiano, –a Colombian, 11N
color *m* color, 7
  ¿De qué color es? What color is it?, 7S

coma comma, 11

comedor *m* dining room, 5S

comentador *m* commentator, 13N

comenzar (ie) commence, begin, 10N

comer eat, 7S

 ¿Qué hay de comer? What's there to eat?, 8S

comida dinner, meal, food, 3S

como as, like, 5G; since, 8N

cómo how, 1; **¿cómo?** what?, 1

 ¿Cómo eres tú? What are you like?, 7; **¿Cómo te llamas?** What's your name?, 7S

compañero, –a kid, companion, 4

compañía company, 10N

completo, –a complete, 11N

comprar buy, 3

compras shopping, 12

 ir de compras go shopping, 12

comprender comprehend, be comprised of, 12N

comunicación *f* communication, 10N

con with, 1

 con razón no wonder, 4; **con permiso** excuse me, 8 (*see fn page 131*)

condición *f* condition, 9N

confesar confess, 10N

confortable comfortable, 9N

confusión *f* confusion, 12N

conmigo with me, 2

conocer (zc) know, 8

consiguiente: por consiguiente therefore, 12S

consultar consult, 9N

contacto contact, 10N

contar (ue) tell, 9

contemplar contemplate, 14N

contener (ie) contain, 12N

contento, –a happy, 6S

contestar answer, 2

contigo with you, 7S

continuar (ú) continue, 9N

conveniencia convenience, 11N

conversación *f* conversation, 10N

conversar converse, 10N

convertir (ie) convert, 9N

corbata tie, 4S

correo mail, 8

correr run, 15N

corresponder correspond, 11N

cosa thing, 5

costa coast, 9N

costar (ue) cost, 5

 ¿Cuánto cuestan los boletos? How much are the tickets?, 5; **No saben lo que cuesta el**

dinero. They don't know the value of a dollar., 12

Costa Rica Costa Rica, 12N

costarricense Costa Rican, 15N

cowboy cowboy, 13N

crear create, 10N

creer think, believe, 7

creo I think, I believe, 5

criada maid, 10S

crónico, –a chronic, 10N

cuaderno notebook, 11S

cuál, cuáles which, 4

cualidad *f* quality, 9N

cuando when, 5

cuándo when, 1

cuánto, –a how much, 5

 cuántos, –as how many, 5G

cuarenta forty, 9S

cuarto room, 5; quarter, 8

 Es la una y cuarto. It's a quarter past one., 8S; **Son las dos menos cuarto.** It's a quarter to two., 8S

cuarto, –a *adj* fourth, 10S

cuatro four, 3S

Cuba Cuba, 11N

cubano, –a Cuban, 11N

cuestión *f* question, matter, problem, 15N

cueva cave, 15N

culebra snake, 8

cumpleaños *m* birthday, 13

cumplir fulfill, 13

 cumplir quince be fifteen, 13

cuñado, –a brother-in-law, sister-in-law, 12S

curso course, 15N

CH

charco puddle, 14N

chica girl, 1

chico, –a boy, girl, 2; *adj* small, 14N

Chile Chile, 12N

China China, 11N

chino, –a Chinese, 11N

D

dan they give, 3

 ¿qué dan? what's playing?, 3

dar give, 6G

de of, from, 1
  de nada you're welcome, 14S; **de ojos azules** with blue eyes, 7; **¿De qué color es?** What color is it?, 7S; **de repente** all of a sudden, 14N; **de veras** really, 9
deber must, 7
decente decent, 15N
décimo, –a tenth, 10S
decir (i) (digo) say, tell, 7
dejar leave, 10; let, 12
del (de + el) of the, 5
delante (de) in front (of), 7S
delgado, –a thin, 6S
denominar denominate, name, 11N
dentista *m f* dentist, 10S
dentro (de) within, 15S
departamento apartment, 14S
derecho, –a right, 14
  a la derecha on the right, 14
derivación *f* derivation, 11N
derivar derive, 11N
desayunar have breakfast, 8S
desayuno breakfast, 8S
describir describe, 10N
desear wish, 10
desfile *m* parade, 3S
desgraciadamente unfortunately, 13N
despacio slowly, 11
despertar (ie) awaken, wake up, 13G
  despertarse awaken, wake up, 13S
después later, afterward, 3
  después de after, 7G
detrás (de) behind, in back (of), 7S
devolver (ue) return, 15
día *m* day, 3
  buenos días good morning, 4S; **El Día de la Madre** Mother's Day, 3; **todos los días** every day, 10N
dibujo drawing, 15S
diccionario dictionary, 7
dice he, she says; you say, 7
diciembre December, 9S
dictado dictation, 11
dicho *pp* decir, 13S
diecinueve nineteen, 6S
dieciocho eighteen, 6S
dieciséis sixteen, 6S
diecisiete seventeen, 6S
diez ten, 3S
diferente different, 9N

difícil difficult, 4S
dinero money, 5
dirección *f* direction, 9N; address, 10S
directamente directly, 15N
disco record, 2
distante distant, 9N
distraído, –a absent-minded, 7S
doble *m* double, 13
  el doble de hombres twice as many men, 13
doce twelve, 3S
dólar *m* dollar, 9N
doler (ue) hurt, 15S
doméstico, –a domestic, 10N
domingo Sunday, 3S
don title of respect, 4 (*see fn page 47*)
donde where, 9N
dónde where, 1
doña title of respect, 4 (*see fn page 47*)
dormir (ue) sleep, 9S
  dormirse go to sleep, 13S
dormitorio bedroom, 5S
dos two, 3S
  dos puntos colon, 11S
durante during, 7

E

economizado, –a saved, economized, 9N
economizar save, economize, 9N
Ecuador Ecuador, 14
edición *f* edition, 10
edificio building, 14S
¿eh? eh?, 8N
ejemplo example, 9N
  por ejemplo for example, 9N
el the, 1
él he, 2G, him, 7G
electricidad *f* electricity, 10N
eléctrico, –a electrical, 10N
eliminar eliminate, 10N
El Salvador El Salvador, 12N
ella she, 2G; her, 2
ellas they, 2G; them, 7G
ellos they, 2G; them, 7G
emoción *f* emotion, 14
  ¡qué emocion! how exciting!, 14 (*see fn page 265*)
empezar (ie) start, begin, 3
  Ya casi empieza. It's about to begin., 3
empleado, –a employee, 10

en in, on, at, 1
  en punto exactly, on the dot, 8S
encantar delight, 9
  Me encanta. I love it., 9
encontrar (ue) find, 5
energía energy, 9N
enero January, 9S
enfermo, –a sick, 6S
enojado, –a angry, 10S
enojar anger, make angry, 10S
  enojarse get angry, 13S
enorme enormous, 12N
ensalada salad, 8S
enseñar teach, 14S
entender (ie) understand, 8S
entonces then, 2
entrar enter, 9N
entre between, among, 13N
equipaje *m* baggage, 14S
equivocado, –a mistaken, 10
equivocar mistake, 10
  equivocarse be mistaken, make a mistake, 136
es he, she is; you are, 1
esa that, 8G
ésa that one, 1
escribir write, 7
escrito *pp* **escribir,** 13S
escritorio desk, 11S (*see fn page 200*)
escuchar listen to, 2
escuela school, 2
ese that, 4
ése that one, 6
eso that, 8G
espantoso, –a awful, 14S
España Spain, 9
español *m* Spanish, 2S
español, –a Spaniard, 11
español, –a *adj* Spanish, 4G
especialmente especially, 9N
esperar wait, 15N; hope, 15N
esposo, –a husband, wife, 12S (*see fn page 224*)
esquina corner, 7S
esta this, 4
ésta this one, 14G
está he, she is; you are, 1
estación *f* station, 7S; season, 13S
  ¿En qué estación estamos? What season is this?, 13S
estadio stadium, 5S
estado state, 1

Estados Unidos United States, 1
estadounidense American, from the United States, 11N
están they are, 1
estar be, 6
  ¿Está el Sr. Campos? Is Mr. Campos there?, 10
este this, 6
éste this one, 14G
este . . . uh . . . (*see fn page 69*)
estimado, –a esteemed, dear, (*in letters*), 7N (*see fn page 127*)
esto this, 8
estos, –as these, 8G
éstos, –as these, 14G
estómago stomach, 15S
estricto, –a strict, 8N
estudiar study, 2
estupendo, –a wonderful, 14S
eterno, –a eternal, 11N
exactamente exactly, 9N
exagerar exaggerate, 12
  tan exagerado don't exaggerate, 12
examen *m* exam, 3S
excelente excellent, 11N
excepción *f* exception, 9N
excepto except, 4
exclamación *f* exclamation, 11S
  signo de exclamación exclamation mark, 11S
explicación *f* explanation, 11N
explicar explain, 15N
extensión *f* extension, 12N
extremista *m f* extremist, 11N
extremo, –a extreme, 9N

F

fácil easy, 4S
faja strip, 12N
falda skirt, 4S
falta fault, 15
  sin falta without fail, 15
familia family, 6
famoso, –a famous, 9N
fantástico, –a fantastic, 14N
favor: por favor please, 10
favorito, –a favorite, 13N
febrero February, 9S
fecha date, 9S
  ¿Qué fecha es hoy? What's the date today?, 9S

feo, –a homely, ugly, 6S
fiesta party, 3S
figura figure, 10N
fijarse notice, 13
fíjate just imagine, 13
fin end, 9
  a fines de towards the end of, 9; **por fin** finally, 10
final final, 15N
finalmente finally, 9N
folkórico, –a folk, 14N
foto *f* picture, photograph, 6
francamente frankly, really, 6
francés *m* French, 2S
francés (francesa) *adj* French, 4G
frase *f* sentence, 11
frecuentemente frequently, 10N
frío cold, 8
  tener frío be cold (*for a person*), 8S; **Tengo mucho frío.** I'm very cold., 8
frío, –a *adj* cold, 8
frito, –a fried, 8S
  papas fritas French fries, 8S
furioso, –a furious, 10N
fútbol *m* soccer, 5
  partido de fútbol soccer game, 5; **fútbol americano** football, 5 (*see fn page 69*)

G

ganar earn, win, 12S
ganga bargain, 12S
garganta throat, 15S
gasolina gas, 9N
gastar spend, 12
gemelo, –a twin, 4
generación *f* generation, 15N
gente *f* people, 14N
geografía geography, 8N
geográfico, –a geographic, 12N
gordito, –a little fat boy, girl, 7
gordo, –a fat, 6S
gracias thank you, thanks, 5S
  bien, gracias fine, thanks, 5S
gracioso, –a funny, 6
gran great, 10G
grande big, 4S
gris grey, 7S
gritar shout, scream, 5
guante *m* glove, 5S

guapo, –a handsome, pretty, 6S (*see fn page 90*)
Guatemala Guatemala, 11N
guatemalteco, –a Guatemalan, 11N
gusta it pleases, 4
  A ti te gusta? Do you like it?, 4; **Me gusta mucho.** I like it a lot., 4
gustar please, 4
  Me gusta. I like it., 4

H

haber have (*auxiliary verb*), 10
  hay there is, there are, 8; **¿Qué hay de comer?** What's there to eat?, 8
habitante *m f* inhabitant, 11N
hábito habit, 10N
hablar talk, speak, 2
hacer make, do, 7
  Hace buen tiempo. The weather is nice., 9S; **Hace calor.** It's warm, hot., 9; **Hace frío.** It's cold., 9; **Hace mal tiempo.** The weather is bad., 9S; **hacer las maletas** pack, 14S; **hacer una fiesta** have a party, 13; **hacer un viaje** take a trip, 9
hacienda farm, ranch, 15S
Haití Haiti, 12N
hambre (el hambre) *f* hunger, 8 (*see fn page 132*)
  tener hambre be hungry, 8
hasta until, 4; even, 15N
  hasta luego see you later, 4S; **hasta mañana** see you tomorrow, 4
hay there is, there are, 8
hecho *pp* **hacer**, 13
helado ice cream, 8S
hemisferio hemisphere, 11N
hermano, –a brother, sister, 4S
héroe *m* hero, 13N
hijo, –a son, daughter, 5
Hispanoamérica Spanish America, 12N
hispanoamericano, –a Spanish American, 12N
historia story, 14N; history, 15S
¡hola! hi!, 1
hombre *m* man, 13
Honduras Honduras, 12N
hora hour, 3
  ¿A qué hora? At what time?, 3; **hora de almuerzo** lunch time, 8; **hora del desayuno** breakfast time, 8S; **¿Qué hora es?** What time is it?, 8
horizonte *m* horizon, 14N

horrible   horrible, 8N
hotel *m*   hotel, 9N
hoy   today, 2
   de hoy en ocho días   a week from today, 15S;
   de hoy en quince días   two weeks from today,
   15S (*see fn page 290*)
huevo   egg, 8S

I

idea   idea, 6
ideal   ideal, 9N
idéntico, –a   identical, 4
iguana   iguana, 15N
imaginación   imagination, 14N
imaginario –a   imaginary, 15N
impermeable *m*   raincoat, 14S
importancia   importance, 11N
importante   important, 8N
imposible   impossible, 8N
incluir   include, 12N
inclusive   including, 10N
inconveniencia   inconvenience, 15N
indicar   indicate, 9N
indio, –a   Indian, 9N
indispensable   indispensable, 10N
informar   inform, 10N
inglés *m*   English, 8
inglés (inglesa) *adj*   English, 4G
inicial *f*   initial, 11N
iniciar   initiate, 9N
inmediatamente   immediately, 8N
inmediato, –a   immediate, 10N
inmenso, –a   immense, 15N
instrumento   instrument, 10N
inteligente   intelligent, 4S
intención *f*   intention, 9N
interesante   interesting, 9N
interesar   interest, 13N
intermediario   intermediary, 10N
interrogación *f*   question, 11
   signo de interrogación   question mark, 11S
invierno   winter, 13S
invitar   invite, 13
ir   go, 1
   ir de compras   go shopping, 12; **irse**   go,
   leave, 13; **¡Vamos!**   let's go!, 8; **vamos a ver**
   let's see, 4
italiano, –a   Italian, 3
izquierdo, –a   left, 14
   a la izquierda   on the left, 14

J

Jamaica   Jamaica, 12N
Japón   Japan, 11N
japonés *m*   Japanese, 11N
jardín *m*   garden, 14
jeep *m*   jeep, 9N
jefa   boss, 10S (*see fn page 179*)
jefe *m*   boss, 10S (*see fn page 179*)
joven   young, 14S
jueves *m*   Thursday, 3S
jugar (ue)   play, 5
junio   June, 9S
julio   July, 9S

L

la   the, 2; her, it, you, 12G
lápiz *m* **(lápices** *pl***)**   pencil, 11S
largo, –a   long, 15N
las   the, 2S; them, you, 12G
latino, –a   Latin, 12N; Latin American, 15N
Latinoamérica   Latin America, 12N
latinoamericano, –a   Latin American, 12N
lavar   wash, 13S
   lavarse   wash up, 13S
le   to him, to her, to you, 4S
   A él le gusta mucho.   He likes it a lot., 4S;
   A ella le gusta mucho.   She likes it a lot., 4S;
   A usted le gusta mucho.   You like it a lot., 4S
les   to them, to you, 9G
lección *f*   lesson, 11
leche *f*   milk, 8S
leer   read, 7
lengua   language, tongue, 11N
levantar   lift, 13G
   levantarse   get up, 13
leyenda   legend, 14N
libre   free, 12N
librería   bookstore, 10
libro   book, 6S
Lima   capital of Peru, 9
limitar   limit, 11N
limpiar   clean, 5S
lindo, –a   pretty, nice, 4 (*see fn page 90*)
línea   line, 10
lingüístico, -a   linguistic, 12N
liquidación *f*   sale, 12
lista   list, 13
listo, –a   bright, clever, 7S; ready, 11

lo: lo que what, 11
lo it, 8; him, you, 12G
loco, –a crazy, 11
lógicamente logically, 12N
los the, 1; them, you, 12G
luego then, 4S
 hasta luego see you later, 4S
lugar *m* place, 5
lunes *m* Monday, 3

LL

llamar call, 2
 llamarse be called, named, 7; **¿Cómo te llamas?** What's your name?, 7; **Me llamo Conchita.** My name is Conchita., 7; **se llama** her name is, 7
llave *f* key, 14S
llega he, she arrives; you arrive, 1
llegar arrive, 2
lleno, –a full, 15N
llevar take, 15N
llorar cry, 12
llover (ue) rain, 9

M

madre *f* mother, 3
 El Día de la Madre Mother's Day, 3 (*see fn page 27*)
maestra teacher, 2S
maestro, –a teacher, 3
mal badly, 2
maleta suitcase, 14
malo, –a bad, 10
 mal bad, 10
mamá mom, 3
mami *f* mom, 5
mandar send, 15S
manera manner, 9N
mano *f* hand, 13N
mantequilla butter, 8S
mañana tomorrow, 2S; morning, 12S
 hasta mañana see you tomorrow, 4; **mañana por la mañana** tomorrow morning, 15S
mapa *m* map, 9
máquina de escribir typewriter, 15S
mar *m* sea, 11N
marcar dial, 10S
marido husband, 12 (*see fn page 224*)
marinero sailor, 14N
martes *m* Tuesday, 3S

marzo March, 9S
más more, 2
 más tarde later, 2; **No puedo caminar más.** I can't walk any more., 3; **¿Qué más dice?** What else does she say?, 7
matar kill, 12
matemáticas mathematics, 15S
mayo May, 9S
mayor older, 4
me to me, 3; me 12; myself, 13G
 Me aprietan mucho los zapatos. My shoes are too tight., 3; **Me llamo Conchita.** My name is Conchita., 7S
media stocking, 5; half, 8S
 Es la una y media. It's half past one., 8S
mediados middle, 9S
 a mediados de julio around the middle of July, 9S
mediano medium, 12N
médico doctor, 10S
medio means; 10N
mejor better, instead, 3
mencionar mention, 10N
menor younger, 4S; least, slightest, 6
 No tengo la menor idea. I don't have the slightest idea., 6
menos least, minus, 8S; less, 14G
 al menos at least, 15; **la una menos cinco** five minutes to one, 8S; **por lo menos** at least, 15N
mentira lie, 11
mercado market, 3S
mes *m* month, 9S
 ¿En qué mes estamos? What month is this?, 9S
mesa table, 6S
metro meter, 15N (*see fn page 305*)
mexicano, –a Mexican, 11N
México Mexico, 9N (*see fn page 173*)
mi my, 1
mí me, 4
miércoles *m* Wednesday, 3S
mil thousand, 12
minifalda miniskirt, 15N
minuto minute, 13N
mío, –a my, mine, of mine, 12
mirar look at, 12N
mis my, 5
misterioso, –a mysterious, 14N
mitad *f* half, 13
moda fashion, 15N

de última moda   the latest style, 15N
moderno, –a   modern, 6N
modo   way, 12
   de todos modos   anyway, 12
mojado, –a   wet, 10S
mojar   wet, 10S
   mojarse   get wet, 13G
molestar   bother, fool around, 11
momento   moment, 13N
mono   monkey, 15N
monopolizar   monopolize, 10N
montaña   mountain, 15N
montar   mount, 15N
   montar a caballo   horseback ride, 15N
morir (ue)   die, 14N
muchacho, –a   boy, girl, 13
mucho   much, a lot, 3
mucho, –a   much, 5
   muchos, –as   many 7
muerto *pp*   morir, 14N
mujer *f*   woman, 12
mundo   world, 5
   todo el mundo   everybody, 9
museo   museum, 9N
musical   musical, 13N
muy   very, 2

N

nación *f*   nation, 12N
nacional   national, 10N
nacionalidad *f*   nationality, 10N
nada   nothing, 3
   de nada   you're welcome, 14S
nadar   swim, 10S
nadie   no one, 10N
narración *f*   narrative, 6N
narrador *m*   narrator, 10N
naturalmente   naturally, 11N
necesitar   need, 2
negro, –a   black, 7S
nervioso, –a   nervous, 14N
ni   nor, 11
   ni ... ni ...   neither ... nor, 11
nieto, –a   grandson, granddaughter, 12S
ninguno, –a   neither, none, 4
   ningún   no, 10G
niño, -a   child, 13N
ni siquiera   not even, 11
no   no, 2G; not, 2
noche *f*   night, 4S

Buenas noches.   Good evening., Good night., 4S (*see fn page 48*)
Noel *m*   Christmas 15N
   Papá Noel   Santa Claus
nombre *m*   name, 11N
norte *m*   north, 12N
Norteamérica   North America, 12N
norteamericano   North American, 12N
nos   to us, 9G; us, 12G; ourselves, 13G
nosotras   we, 2G
nosotros   we, 2G
nota   grade, 15; note, 15S
notar   note, notice, 14N
noticias *f pl*   news, 2S
novela   novel, 15S
noveno, –a   ninth, 10S
noventa   ninety, 9S
noviembre   November, 9S
novio, –a   boyfriend, girlfriend, 6S
nuestro, –a   our, 10S; ours, of ours, 12S
nueve   nine, 3S
nuevo, –a   new, 4
número   number, 10
   número de teléfono   telephone number, 10
nunca   never, 9

O

o   or, 1
   o ... o   either ... or, 11
observar   observe, 12N
occidental   occidental, western, 11N
octavo, –a   eighth, 10S
octubre   October, 9S
ocupado, –a   busy, 10
ocurrir   occur, 10N
ochenta   eighty, 9S
ocho   eight, 3S
oficial   official, 12N
oficina   office, 10S
oír (oigo)   hear, 8
ojo   eye, 7
once   eleven, 3S
oportunidad *f*   opportunity, 10N
orden *f*   order, 10
   a sus órdenes   at your service, 10
ordenar   order, 10N
orgulloso, –a   proud, 15N
otoño   autumn, 13S
otro, –a   other, 4

P

paciencia patience, 10N

Pacífico Pacific, 9N

padre *m* father, 6S

  padres *m pl* parents, 12S

país *m* country, 11N

palabra word, 11

pelear fight, 13N

pan *m* bread, 8S

pantalones *m pl* pants, 5S

pañuelo handkerchief, 5S

papa potato, 8S

  papas fritas French fries, 8S

papá *m* papa, dad, 10N

  Papá Noel Santa Claus, 15N

papel *m* paper, 11

papi *m* dad, 9

para for, 3

paraguas *m* umbrella, 14S

Paraguay Paraguay, 12N

parecer (zc) seem, 9

  ¿Qué te parece la idea? What do you think of the idea?, 9

pared *f* wall, 10N

pariente *m f* relative, 12

parque *m* park, 3S

párrafo paragraph, 11S

parte *f* part, 10N

partido game, 5

pasado: pasado mañana the day after tomorrow, 15S

pasaporte *m* passport, 9N

pasar pass, 2

  pasado mañana the day after tomorrow, 15S; **pasar las vacaciones** spend the vacation, 9S; **pasar por** stop by, 2; **¿Qué pasa?** What's the matter?, 2

patio patio, 14N

pedir (i) ask for, 11

peine *m* comb, 14S

pelear fight, 13N

película film, movie, 3

pelirrojo, –a redheaded, 7S

pelo hair, 7S

peluquería barber shop, beauty shop, 10S

peluquero, –a barber, hairdresser, 10S

pensar (ie) think, expect, intend, 13

  pensar en think about, 5

peón *m* peon, 15N

peor worse, 13N

pequeño, –a small, 4S

perder (ie) lose, 10N

perezoso, –a lazy, 7S

perfecto, –a perfect, 9N

periódico newspaper, 6S

permiso permission, 8

  con permiso excuse me, 8

permitir permit, 9N

pero but, 1

perro dog, 1

  carreras de perros dog races, 1

persona person, 10N

personalidad *f* personality, 10N

Perú Peru, 9

peso peso (*Spanish-American monetary unit*), 5

pie *m* foot, 15S

pierna leg, 15S

pintoresco, –a picturesque, 9N

pirámide *f* pyramid, 9N

piscina swimming pool, 15S

pistola pistol, 13N

plan *m* plan, 9N

playa beach, 15S

plaza plaza, square, 7S

pluma pen, 11

población *f* population, 11N

poco little, 7

poco, –a little, 10G

  pocos, –as few, 10G

poder (ue) can, be able, 9G

poner (pongo) put, 8, put on, 13G

  poner atención pay attention, 11; **¿Por qué pones esa cara?** Why are you making that face? 8; **ponerse** put on, 13S

por through, by, 2S

  por consiguiente therefore, 12S; **por ejemplo** for example, 9N; **por favor** please, 10; **por fin** finally, 10; **por lo menos** at least, 15N; **por qué** why, 2

porque because, 2

posición *f* position, 12N

P.D. (postdata) P.S. (postscript), 15N

practicar practice, 2

preferir (ie) prefer, 8S

preguntar ask, 9S

preocupado, –a worried, 10

preocupar worry, 10S

  preocuparse get worried, 13S

preparación *f* preparation, 9N

preparado, –a prepared, 9N

preparar   prepare, 9N
presentar   present, 13G
   presentarse   show up, present oneself, 13
prestar   lend, 11
pretencioso, –a   pretentious, 4
   ¡Qué pretencioso!   What a showoff!, 4
primavera   spring, 13
primero, -a   first, 10S (*see fn page 156*)
   primer   first, 10G
primo, –a   cousin, 6
principal   principal, main, 9N
principio   beginning, 9
   a principios de   around the beginning of, 9
prisa *f*   haste, 5
   ¿Adónde vas con tanta prisa?   Where are you going in such a hurry?, 5; **tener prisa**   be in a hurry, 14
probablemente   probably, 9N
problema *m*   problem, 5
producir (zc)   produce, 11N
producto   product, 8N
programa *m*   program, 13N
prometer   promise, 12
pronto   soon, 11
pronunciación *f*   pronunciation, 11N
pronunciar   pronounce, 2
propósito: a propósito   by the way, 5
protesta   protest, 10N
próximo, -a   next, 15
proyecto   project, 9N
pueblo   village, 14N
puedo   I can, 3
puerta   door, 3S
puerto   port, 9N
puertorriqueño *f*   Puerto Rican, 11N
puesto *pp* **poner**, 13S
punto   dot, 8S; period, 11S
   Es la una en punto.   It's one on the dot., It's exactly one o'clock., 8S; **dos puntos**   colon, 11S; **punto y coma**   semicolon, 11S
pupitre *m*   desk, 11 (*see fn page 200*)

Q

que   that, which, who, 1
qué   what, 1; how, 4
quedarse   stay, 13
querer (ie)   want, 8; love, 12
querido, –a   dear, 15N
quien   who, whom, 10N

quién   who, whom, 2
quiere   he, she wants; you want, 1
quieres   you want, 2
quiero   I want, 2
quince   fifteen, 6S
quinto, –a   fifth, 10S
quitar   take off, 13G
   quitarse   take off, 13S

R

radio   radio, 8N
rápido   fast, rapid, 11
raspar   scrape, 15
   pasar raspando   barely pass, 15
rato   while, 13
razón *f*   reason, 4
   ¡con razón!   no wonder!, 4
reaccionar   react, 10N
realidad *f*   reality, 9N
realmente   really, 10N
recado   message, 10
recibir   receive, 10
reconocer (zc)   recognize, 8S
recordar (ue)   remember, 5
recreo   recess, 7
refrigerador *m*   refrigerator, 10N
regalo   gift, 3
región *f*   region 12N
regresar   return, 14S
regreso   return, 14
reliquia   relic, 9N
reloj *m*   clock, watch, 8
repente: de repente   all of a sudden, 14N
repetido, –a   repeated, 10N
repetir (i)   repeat, 11
república   republic, 9N
República Dominicana   Dominican Republic, 12N
requerir (ie)   require, 9N
reservar   reserve, 12N
resfriado, –a: Está resfriado.   He has a cold., 10S
resfriarse   catch a cold, 10G
respectivamente   respectively, 9N
respecto: con respecto a   with respect to, 9N
restaurante *m*   restaurant, 5S
reunión *f*   meeting, 6S
revista   magazine, 15S
ridículo, –a   ridiculous, 13N
río   river, 15N

rojo, –a red, 7S
romance Romance, 12N
ropa clothes, clothing, 12
rubio, –a blond, 4
Rusia Russia, 11N
ruso Russian, 2S
ruso, –a *adj* Russian, 4G
ruta route, 9N

S

sábado Saturday, 1
sabe he, she knows; you know, 1
saber (sé) know, 7; **quién sabe** I don't know, 12
sacar: sacar un diez en matemáticas get a ten in mathematics, 15S
saco jacket, 12S
  saco sport sport coat, 12S
sala living room, 1
salir (salgo) go out, leave, 8S
salón *m* salon, 10
  salón de belleza beauty shop, 10
saludo greeting, 15N
Santo Saint's day, 13 (*see fn page 246*)
Santos *m:* **El Santos** Brazilian soccer team, 5
satisfacción *f* satisfaction, 11N
satisfactorio, –a satisfactory, 11N
se himself, herself, yourself, itself, themselves, yourselves, 13
  Se llama Sue. Her name is Sue., 7
sé I know, 1
secretaria secretary, 10
sed *f* thirst, 8
  tener sed be thirsty, 8S; **Tengo mucha sed.** I'm very thirsty., 8S
seguir (i) continue, follow, 11G (*see fn page 203*)
  La línea sigue ocupada. The line's still busy., 10
según according to, 8
segundo, –a second, 10S
seguro, –a sure, 12
seis six, 3S
seleccionar select, 10N
semana week, 15
sentado, –a seated, 6
  ése que está sentado the one who's sitting, 6
sentar (ie) seat, 13G
  sentarse (ie) sit down, 13S
sentir (ie) regret, be sorry, 8
  lo siento I'm sorry, 8
señor *m* gentleman, Mr., 2S

señora lady, Mrs., 2S
señorita young lady, Miss, 2S
septiembre September, 9
séptimo, –a seventh, 10S
ser be, 4
  ¿Cómo eres tú? What are you like?, 7; **Es la una.** It's one o'clock., 8S; **Son las dos.** It's two o'clock., 8S
servicio service, 10
servir (i) serve, 11
  No sirve. It's no good., 11
sesenta sixty, 9S
setenta seventy, 9S
sexto, –a sixth, 10S
si if, whether, 1
sí yes, 1
siempre always, 10N
siete seven, 3S
signo de exclamación exclamation mark, 11S
signo de interrogación question mark, 11S
sigue he, she continues; you continue, 10
  sigue molestando he's still fooling around, 11G
sílaba syllable, 11N
silencio silence, quiet, 10N
silla chair, 6S
simpático, –a nice, 4
simplemente simply, 9N
sin without, 7S
sincero, –a sincere, 10N
sin embargo nevertheless, 12N
siquiera: ni siquiera not even, 11
situación *f* situation, 13N
situado, –a situated, 12N
sobrino, –a nephew, niece, 12S
sofá *m* sofa, 1
solamente only, 7
sólo only, 8
solo –a alone, 13S
  Han vuelto solos. They've come back by themselves, 13S
solución *f* solution, 9N
sombrero hat, 4S
sordo, –a deaf, 5
Sr. *abbrev* **señor** (*see fn page 38*)
Sra. *abbrev* **señora** (*see fn page 38*)
Srta. *abbrev* **señorita** (*see fn page 38*)
su its, 1; his, her, your, their, 11G
suelo 'floor, 6

suerte *f* luck, 10
sufrir suffer, 10N
superior superior, upper, 12N
supermercado supermarket, 9N
sur south, 12N
Suramérica South America, 12N
suramericano, –a South American, 12N
suyo, –a (of) his, hers, yours, theirs, 12G
swéater *m* (**swéaters** *pl*) sweater, 12S (*see fn page 224*)

T

tal vez maybe, 2
tamaño size, 12N
también too, also, 3
tampoco either, neither, 3
tan so, so much, 4
tanto, –a so, such, so much, 5
  tantos, –as so many, 10G
tarde late, 2
  más tarde later, 2
tarde *f* afternoon, 4S
  buenas tardes good afternoon, 4S
tarea assignment, 11S
tarjeta card, 15S
te to you, 4; you, 12; yourself, 13
  ¿A ti te gusta? Do you like it?, 4; **¿Cómo te llamas?** What's your name?, 7S
té *m* tea, 8S
técnica technique, technology, 10N
técnicamente technically, 11N
Tejas Texas, 8N
telefónico, –a telephone, 10
"telefonitis" *f* "telephonitis", 10N
teléfono telephone, 1
televisión *f* television, 10N
temperatura temperature, 8N
temprano early, 8
tener (ie) (tengo) have, 8G
  aquí tiene here you are, 8; **tener calor** be warm (*for a person*), 8S; **tener frío** be cold (*for a person*), 8S; **tener hambre** be hungry, 8; **tener prisa** be in a hurry, 14; **tener sed** be thirsty, 8S; **tener __ años** be __ years old, 7
tengo I have, 6
tenis *m* tennis, 7N
teoría theory, 11N
tercero, –a third, 10S

tercer third, 10S
terminar terminate, end, 13N
término term, 11N
territorio territory, 12N
tesoro treasure, 15N
ti you, to you, 4
  ¿A ti te gusta? Do you like it?, 4
tía *f* aunt, 1
tiempo weather, 9S; time, 15N
  Hace buen tiempo. The weather is nice., 9S; **Hace mal tiempo.** The weather is bad., 9S
tienda store, 3
tiene he, she, has; you have, 3
tienes you have, 4
  tienes que you have to, 3
tierra land, 12N
tío, –a uncle, aunt, 1
típico, –a typical, 13N
tocar touch, 14
todavía yet, still, 2
todo everything, 5
todo, –a all, 4
  en todo caso in any case, 12; **todo el mundo** everybody, 9; **todos los días** every day, 10N; **de todos modos** anyway, 12S
tomar drink, take, 8S
  ¿Qué hay de tomar? What's there to drink?, 8S
tópico topic, 10N
total total, 13N
totalmente totally, 9N
trabajar work, 9S
trabajo job, work, 11S
tradición *f* tradition, 14N
traer (traigo) bring, 8
traje *m* suit, 12S
traje de baño *m* bathing suit, 12S
tranquilamente tranquilly, calmly, 14N
tranquilizarse become tranquil, calm down, 14N
transportación *f* transportation, 9N
trece thirteen, 6S
treinta thirty, 9S
  treinta y uno thirty-one, 9S
tren *m* train, 9S
tres three, 3S
triángulo triangle, 12N
trigueño –a brunette, 7S
triste sad, 15S
tú you, 1

tu your, 1
tuyo, –a your, yours, of yours, 12

U

último, –a last, 15
  de última moda the latest style, 15N
un a, an, one, 4
una a 2; one, 3S
  a la una at one o'clock, 3S; **es la una** it's one o'clock, 3S
unas some, 4
uniforme *m* uniform, 10N
unir unite, 12N
uno one, 3S
unos some, 2
Uruguay Uruguay, 12N
usado used, 9N
usar use, 9N
uso use, 11N
usted (*pl* **ustedes**) you, 2G

V

va he, she goes; you go, 5S
vacaciones *f pl* vacation, 9 (*see fn page 155*)
vamos we'll go, 1; let's go, 3
vas you go, 1
veinte twenty, 6S
veinticinco twenty-five, 9S
veinticuatro twenty-four, 9S
veintidós twenty-two, 9S
veintinueve twenty-nine, 9S
veintiocho twenty-eight, 9S
veintiséis twenty-six, 9S
veintisiete twenty-seven, 9S
veintitrés twenty-three, 9S
veintiuno twenty-one, 9S
vela candle, 14N
vender sell, 12S
Venezuela Venezuela, 12N
venir (ie) (vengo) come, 8

ventana window, 3S
ver see, 5
  a ver let's see, 6
verano summer, 13S
veras: de veras really, 9
verdad *f* truth
  ¿verdad? aren't they, isn't it?, 4; **de verdad** really, 13N
verde green, 7S
vestido dress, 4S
vestir (i) dress, 13G
  vestirse get dressed, 13S
vez *f* (**veces** *pl*) time, 10
viajar travel, 9S
viaje *m* trip, 9
viceversa vice versa, 9N
vida life, 10N
viejo, –a old, 13S (*see fn page 305*)
viera you should see, 12
viernes *m* Friday, 3S
visa visa, 9N
visitar visit, 9N
visto *pp* **ver**, 13S
vivir live, 7
volver (ue) return, come back, 9
vosotros, –as you, 2G
voz *f* (**voces** *pl*) voice, 13N
vuelta return, 14
  estar de vuelta be back, 14
vuelto *pp* **volver**, 13S

Y

y and, 1
ya already, 3; now, 8
yo I, 1

Z

zapatería shoe store, 10S
zapatero, –a shoemaker, 10S
zapato shoe, 3

GRAMMATICAL INDEX

353

PHONETIC SYMBOLS

[a]	mamá	[k]	con, qué, quién
[b]	Blanca, vamos	[m]	mamá
[ƀ]	sabe, Eva	[ñ]	señor
[ch]	chica	[o]	cómo
[d]	dos, dónde	[r]	pero, hablar
[đ]	nada	[rr]	perro, ruso
[e]	de, te	[s]	su, cine, tal vez
[f]	foto	[u]	tu
[g]	gordo, alguien	[ú]	continúa, Raúl
[ǥ]	amigo, Miguel	[w]	cuarto, puedo
[h]	mejor, gemela	[y]	piensa
[i]	Lili, y	[ɏ]	yo, llega
[í]	día, traído		

El sistema de enseñanza en Hispanoamérica está basado en general en los modelos de España y de Francia. Por ejemplo, el Ministerio o la Secretaría de Educación del gobierno controla la enseñanza pública en todo el país. Por medio de este control nacional todas las escuelas deben usar los mismos libros de texto, ofrecer los mismos cursos y dar los mismos tipos de exámenes y calificaciones. En esta forma la calidad de enseñanza que reciben los alumnos de las regiones pobres del país es, al menos teóricamente, tan buena como la que ofrecen las escuelas de la capital o de otras ciudades grandes. El sistema de educación esta dividido en tres partes: educación primaria (que puede también incluir el ''kinder''); educación secundaria también llamada colegio o liceo), al terminar la cual los estudiantes se gradúan con el título de bachiller; y finalmente la educación superior o universitaria. Dentro de este sistema general hay, naturalmente, ramificaciones y también diferencias entre la enseñanza de un país y de otro.

La educación pública en Latinoamérica es gratis, pero como la población de estos países crece tan rápidamente, nunca hay suficientes escuelas para todos los niños. Por esta razón, en muchos países las familias que pueden educan a sus hijos en escuelas particulares, la mayoría de las cuales son católicas, religión predominante en toda la América Latina.

Puede decirse que por lo general casi todas las escuelas de América Latina requieren el uso del uniforme. En algunas escuelas, sin embargo, especialmente las escuelas para niños de familias ricas, no es obligatorio. En vez del uniforme usan un guardapolvos sobre su ropa diaria.

Generalmente las clases son de lunes a sábado a mediodía. Pero según la foto de arriba, hoy deber ser domingo. Es día de ir al parque a jugar.

En algunos países, como Costa Rica, por ejemplo, donde el problema de escasez de escuelas públicas no es muy grave, ricos y pobres asisten a ellas. Aquí, sin embargo, el uso del uniforme es absolutamente obligatorio. La razón es muy sencilla: un niño pobre no se siente mal, sentado al lado de un compañero que lleva ropa cara y fina. Todos tienen la misma apariencia.

Haciendo la tarea. Esta algunas veces consiste en pasar en limpio——y luego memorizar——las lecciones de geografía, de historia, etc., que el maestro ha dictado en clase.

Casi todas las escuelas primarias y secundarias todavía mantienen la costumbre de la separación de los sexos. Esta costumbre viene de la actitud tradicional hispánica y católica de evitar un contacto directo entre chicos y chicas. Los tiempos modernos, sin embargo, causan cambios en muchos aspectos de la vida, y ya también en Hispanoamérica comienzan a establecerse los colegios mixtos.

Colegio típico: un edificio antiguo de dos o tres pisos con un patio grande en el centro.

Alumnas del Colegio de Señoritas de San José, Costa Rica, entrando a clases.

Frecuentemente los gobiernos compran mansiones privadas para convertirlas en colegios.

Muchos colegios llevan el nombre de algún país o de un personaje famoso de la historia.

La costumbre del ''blue jean'' para ir a la escuela aun no ha entrado entre las latinas.

En el estudio secundario hay tres ramas: el liceo, la escuela normal y la comercial. Muchas de las materias son las mismas para las tres ramas y no existen los cursos optativos. En el liceo se estudia matemáticas, gramática y literatura española, un idioma extranjero, anatomía, zoología, geografía, historia, química, física, educación cívica y otras materias. Generalmente estos estudios duran cinco años, al cabo de los cuales el estudiante debe presentarse a los exámenes de bachillerato. Si pasa estos exámenes recibe su título de bachiller y con él puede entonces entrar a la universidad. La se-

gunda de las tres ramas de secundaria es la escuela normal. Es una combinación de los estudios secundarios con cursos prácticos y teóricos de pedagogía, y los que se gradúan de esta escuela reciben el título de maestro. En casi todos los países hispanoamericanos, desafortunadamente, hay siempre un exceso de maestros que no encuentran empleo. La causa no es la falta de alumnos sino la falta de dinero para crear nuevas escuelas. En la escuela comercial los alumnos se especializan en contabilidad, taquigrafía e inglés, y reciben el título de perito mercantil.

Miles de hombres, pocas mujeres, llenan los estadios los domingos por la mañana.

El fútbol es indiscutiblemente el deporte de mayor popularidad en todo el mundo. Para dar una idea del enorme entusiasmo que existe hacia este deporte, se calcula que no menos de quinientos millones de espectadores vieron entusiasmados el partido final del campeonato mundial de 1968 entre Brasil e Italia—Brasil ganó 4 a 1— que fue transmitido desde México por television a todas partes del mundo. En casi toda América Latina el fútbol es el deporte número uno de las masas. Es un deporte barato, además, pues lo único que se necesita es una pelota y un campo abierto. Todos los hombres, casi sin excepción lo practican o lo han practicado alguna vez durante su vida. Pero muy pocos son los que llegan a realizar el sueño de ser profesionales algún día y jugar en los grandes estadios y ganar mucho dinero.

El temperamento violento del jugador latino con frecuencia causa la intervención de la policía.

Pelé, el famoso y único Pelé, considerado en el mundo entero como el mejor de todos los tiempos.

El entusiasmo por el fútbol comienza desde muy temprana edad.

Lo más típico español: el toreo. Muchos lo consideran, no un deporte, sino un espectáculo artístico.

La equitación ha producido estrellas de fama mundial en México, Chile, Argentina y España.

A causa de estar más cerca de los Estados Unidos y de una mayor influencia norteamericana, es el béisbol el rey de los deportes en Puerto Rico, República Dominicana, Cuba (todavía), Panamá, Nicaragua y Venezuela. Muchas de las grandes estrellas de las grandes ligas vienen de esos países. Arriba, Roberto Clemente, orgullo de Puerto Rico, quien pereció en trágico accidente.

Jai alai, deporte español de origen vasco. En Estados Unidos lo practican mucho en Florida.

También hay las pequeñas ligas en los países hispanos donde el béisbol es popular.

Recreación y deportes   7

La mayor parte de las familias hispanoamericanas son gente de escasos recursos económicos que no pueden darse el lujo de pertenecer a un "country club", de jugar al golf o al tenis, o de viajar en avión o en carro propio. Buscan entonces (y encuentran siempre) pasatiempos y diversiones más baratas. En los países tropicales, por ejemplo, los hombres sacan una mesa a la acera de sus casas y se sientan por las tardes a jugar dominó o a las damas. Los domingos las familias hacen picnics en las playas o en los parques, y los jóvenes siempre consiguen una pelota y un lugar cualquiera—una calle, un patio grande, un pedazo de playa—donde improvisar un buen partido de fútbol.

La televisión es otra forma barata de entretenimiento para toda la familia. El aparato es caro pero puede comprarse con muy buenas facilidades de pago. Las familias más pobres que no tienen suficiente dinero para comprar un aparato de televisión en ninguna forma, por lo general van a mirarla a la casa de un vecino. O van al cine, que es siempre muy barato.

En los sectores antiguos de muchas ciudades hispanoamericanas se ven hileras de casas de uno o
dos pisos unidas unas con otras por gruesas paredes
y con balcones y ventanas con rejas. Para el hispanoamericano, según su tradición española, la vida
familiar debe ser íntima, sin vista al público. Por
esa razón, en vez de los jardines exteriores, casi
todas tienen un patio interior donde la familia se
reúne a conversar o a jugar.

Las casas modernas de las familias ricas se llaman
"villas" o "chalets". Son casas elegantes en las
cuales ha desaparecido el patio interior y en su
lugar muchas de ellas tienen jardín al frente o a
todo su alrededor. Pero a menos que estos jardines
estén rodeados de altos muros, sirven únicamente
de adorno pues los miembros de la familia rara vez
les dan algún uso práctico.

En las reuniones familiares participan grandes y chicos, tíos, abuelos, primos . . .

Las familias de la clase alta y rica representan una pequeña pero poderosa minoría.

Tanto en la clase alta, como en la clase media o en la clase baja, la familia es considerada como el núcleo principal de las sociedades latinoamericanas. Y el término "familia" define no sólo a los padres con sus hijos, sino que incluye también a los abuelos, a los tíos, primos hermanos, nietos y aun a otros parientes más lejanos, como a los primos segundos y terceros. Entre todos ellos existe un fuerte sentimiento de lealtad hacia todos los que pertenecen a la familia, o como se dice comúnmente, hacia "los suyos".

Madre y abuela quiteña. Las damas de Quito sienten preferencia hacia la ropa oscura.

Los abuelos ocupan un lugar privilegiado en la vida de un hogar hispano. Generalmente viven en la casa de uno de los hijos, donde no es que simplemente "son tolerados" sino más bien respetados, amados y tratados con la mayor consideración por todos sus hijos y nietos. Es "en casa de abuelita" y no "en casa de tío Rodolfo" (que es donde ella vive) donde ocurren las frecuentes y tradicionales reuniones familiares, siendo así los abuelos el lazo que con mayor fuerza mantiene la unidad de la familia.

Una de las comidas básicas de muchos latinoamericanos, especialmente en los países donde predomina la población india o mestiza, es el maíz. Para las clases pobres, especialmente, el maíz representa el pan de cada día, y lo comen de muchas maneras diferentes: como arroz, es decir cocinado en agua caliente; o simplemente tostado, o en forma de tortillas o arepas (la tortilla típica de Colombia); y también en enchiladas, tamales y tacos (comidas típicas de México).

Las fotografías de esta página muestran en parte cómo las mujeres del campo hacen las tortillas. La noche anterior ponen los granos de maíz dentro de un recipiente con agua. Temprano en la mañana siguiente, cuando ya el maíz está suave, lo amasan sobre una piedra plana. Luego toman un poco de esa masa y comienzan a golpearla poco a poco entre las palmas de sus manos hasta dejarla totalmente plana y redonda al mismo tiempo—técnica que requiere mucha práctica. La tortilla, así cruda, se pone luego a cocinarse sobre el fuego en una sartén, al estilo más o menos de los "pancakes" americanos.

Arriba, otros platos criollos (típicos). A la izquierda, el pollo frito que así o cocinado también en otras formas y diversas combinaciones, es tan popular en

Centroamérica y el Caribe. A la derecha, los famosos "bacalaítos" puertorriqueños, hechos a base de bacalao y harina de trigo.

Mujer mexicana haciendo tamales típicos de su país. Aquí la vemos envolviendo la masa y demás ingredientes en cáscaras de maíz.

Las enchiladas son tortillas enrolladas que llevan adentro queso o carne molida con cebolla picada, chile, orégano, sal y otros ingredientes.

Las frutas y verduras que llevan a los mercados son siempre frescas, no tienen colorantes ni aditivos, y son también de una variedad muy grande.

El banano (también llamado banana o plá-tano) que comemos en los Estados Unidos, es importado principalmente del Ecuador, Costa Rica y Honduras. Pero hay otras variedades que aquí son casi desconocidas. El bananito de jardín, por ejemplo, peque-ñito y muy dulce. Otro es un tipo de plátano que se puede comer verde o ma-duro pero que debe ser cocinado antes, como el plátano frito que vemos en la foto a la derecha. Y hay otros.

La reunión de toda la familia a la hora del almuerzo o de la comida es una costumbre heredada de España que aun se mantiene muy fuerte en casi todas partes de América Latina. Excepto en las ciudades muy grandes donde ya las distancias no lo permiten, todos los miembros de la familia van a su casa a almorzar y, naturalmente, lo mismo hacen a la hora de la cena. Son éstos dos eventos sociales en que todos se sientan a comer con tranquilidad y sin prisa, y mientras uno de los criados o criadas va sirviendo los diversos platos que desde la mañana ha estado preparando la cocinera, chicos y grandes conversan, cambian impresiones o cuentan chistes.

La costumbre es casi igual en toda Hispanoamérica; lo único que es diferente de región a región o de país a país son los tipos de comidas, o los nombres. O ambas cosas. En algunos países se acostumbra tomar vino a la hora del almuerzo, en otros limonada, en otros leche, en otros nada. A los frijoles los llaman habichuelas en un país, judías en otro. Al aguacate le dicen palta en Chile y Bolivia. Choclo en Ecuador es el maíz tierno. Y así sigue.

Probablemente la característica más significativa del panorama geográfico de América Latina es su gran diversidad, la cual puede notarse aun en regiones o países que ocupan una extensión de terreno relativamente pequeña. Hay inmensos desiertos, como los del norte de México y de Chile; fértiles y extensas llanuras en Argentina, Colombia, Venezuela; impenetrables selvas tropicales como las del río Amazonas cuyo clima cálido y húmedo, y su exuberante vegetación contrastan con los imponentes picos nevados de los Andes, la gran cordillera que pasa a su lado y se extiende desde Venezuela hasta la Tierra del Fuego. Tales diversidades geográficas constituyen formidables barreras para las comunicaciones por tierra entre las diferentes naciones del hemisferio sur.

Tres cuartas partes de América Latina está situada en la zona tropical. Allí, las condiciones de vida son adversas en comparación con las que ofrece la zona templada donde están situados los Estados Unidos. En esta zona tropical la pesca es uno de los principales medios de vida para la gente de la costa.

Vivir en el trópico no siempre significa tener que padecer de calor. En la zona tropical están situadas también las altas regiones de los Andes, que casi todo el tiempo son frías y ventosas. La gente que vive en estas alturas, especialmente los indios pobres, cubren sus cuerpos con gruesos ponchos y sombreros de fieltro para protegerse del frío.

El volcán Cotopaxi, uno de los picos más altos de los Andes ecuatorianos.

El hombre y su mejor amigo, la llama, que le da leche, lana y transportación.

Ponchos, pieles de alpaca (animal de la familia de la llama) y otros productos indios en una feria de Lima.

Para viajar a las ciudades, la gente del interior depende casi exclusivamente del autobús.

En el interior del continente, donde el escarpado terreno no ha permitido aun la construcción de vías modernas de comunicación, la vida es con frecuencia primitiva y pobre. Para ir, por ejemplo, del puerto de Callao en el Perú a la ciudad de Iquitos, en el mismo país—una distancia aproximada de 1.200 kilómetros—es más fácil quizá tomar un barco hacia el norte, atravesar el Canal de Panamá, bajar luego hacia el sur por la costa del Atlántico y subir por el río Amazonas hasta llegar a Iquitos—una distancia mucho mayor. Este viaje, sin embargo, si alguien lo hace, no es ya necesario, gracias al avión que ha solucionado en parte las comunicaciones trasandinas. Además, hoy en día se han construido ya algunos caminos que permiten efectuar el transporte hacia el interior en autobús. Pero los viajes son peligrosos porque los caminos son angostos y malos, y los vehículos a menudo defectuosos.

El río Amazonas, el más grande del mundo, con una longitud de más de seis mil kilómetros y una anchura de casi siete kilómetros en algunas partes. Es tan caudaloso este río que a trescientos kilómetros de su desembocadura en el Océano Atlántico sus aguas no se han mezclado aún con el agua salada del mar. En su cuenca se encuentra la selva también de mayor extensión en todo el mundo, una selva donde la naturaleza ha triunfado hasta ahora ante los repetidos esfuerzos del hombre por dominarla. Allí, sus únicos habitantes, aparte de unos pocos caseríos y tribus primitivas de indios, son los reptiles y las aves y millones de insectos. Pero los esfuerzos continúan. Ya se están abriendo caminos que penetran más y más hacia el corazón de la selva y están surgiendo nuevos centros de población. Seguramente los nuevos conocimientos tecnológicos del hombre harán posible la conquista total, en menos de cincuenta años, de este vasto territorio.

A la izquierda, una balsa en el lago Titicaca. Este lago, el más "alto" del mundo, ya que se encuentra situado a 3.800 metros sobre el nivel del mar, forma parte de la frontera entre Bolivia y Perú. Su gran profundidad permite la navegación de grandes barcos, los cuales transportan pasajeros y carga entre ambos países.

La pampa argentina, donde la naturaleza es benigna al fin. En estas extensas y fértiles llanuras, las cuales cubren un territorio cinco veces más grande que el área total del estado de Pennsylvania, se cosechan millones de toneladas de trigo, alfalfa y maíz, y se crían tres cuartas partes del ganado vacuno, ovejas y cerdos de la Argentina, país que ocupa uno de los primeros puestos del mundo en la exportación de carne y de lana.

Otro ejemplo de las diversidades geográficas del territorio latinoamericano puede verse en la fotografía a la derecha. Es una fotografía de Portillo, un famoso centro de recreo y para esquiar situado en los Andes chilenos, donde tuvieron lugar los Juegos Olímpicos de Invierno de 1967. La bella laguna que se ve al fondo se llama Laguna del Inca.

La economía de casi todos los países latinoamericanos está basada en el monocomercio, es decir, que depende casi exclusivamente de uno o dos productos. Por ejemplo, en Cuba y la República Dominicana el producto principal es el azúcar; en Colombia es el café, en Costa Rica, el café y el banano, en Venezuela, el petróleo; en Bolivia, el estaño; en Honduras, el banano y la madera; en Argentina, la ganadería; en Chile, es el cobre. El monocomercio no es bueno para la economía de un país, pues si el precio de su producto principal baja unos centavos en el mercado mundial, puede ocurrir una gran crisis en todo el país.

Con la ayuda económica de los Estados Unidos y de otras poderosas naciones, América Latina está haciendo enormes esfuerzos para industrializarse. Pero esto es un proceso lento y sumamente costoso, de tal manera que las industrias latinoamericanas representan apenas una pequeña fracción de la producción total del mundo. Ante esta situación, la América Latina no tiene más recurso que continuar, por muchos años, exportando sus materias primas e importando la mayor parte de los artículos manufacturados producidos en Estados Unidos, Europa y otras naciones avanzadas.

En la mayoría de los países latinoamericanos la industria nacional no ha llegado todavía a un nivel muy alto de desarrollo, y la influencia de las naciones más ricas y avanzadas es, naturalmente, muy notoria aún. ¿Puede usted distinguir, por ejemplo, en estas tres fotografías—San José, Costa Rica, arriba; Buenos Aires, abajo a la izquierda; y Quito, Ecuador, a la derecha abajo—diversas señales de influencia norteamericana o de algún otro país extranjero?

La electricidad y los bananos   23

La vida política, social, económica y cultural de cada uno de los países de América Latina tiende a estar centralizada en una sola ciudad, que naturalmente es en casi todos los casos la capital del país, como Buenos Aires, arriba, la capital de Argentina. En algunos países, como Ecuador, pueden ser dos las ciudades más importantes (Quito y Guayaquil), y sólo en el caso de Colombia encontramos una diversidad mayor (Bogotá, Medellín, Cali, Barranquilla, Cartagena, etc.) Buenos Aires, y otras grandes capitales son ciudades enormes y hermosas que por lo general tienen tres características en común: un sector viejo de los tiempos coloniales, un sector moderno y un sector llamado "las barriadas" donde viven en condiciones miserables los miles de campesinos que cada año vienen a la capital en busca de trabajo y de una vida mejor para sus hijos.

Los problemas económicos de la gran mayoría de los latinoamericanos son muy graves. Para muchos, la única solución es "sacarse el gordo" y por eso la lotería goza de tanta popularidad entre la gente. Muchos son los que prefieren dejar de comer antes que dejar de comprar su billete de lotería, o una fracción del mismo, al menos. Esto le da al más pobre alimento espiritual, esperanza, algo con qué soñar que dentro de algunos días se sacará el gordo y será rico.

Las grandes ciudades de América Latina siguen creciendo y creciendo en forma totalmente desproporcionada a los servicios públicos necesarios en estas metrópolis. La reciente construcción del Metro en México, uno de los sistemas de transporte subterráneo más lujosos y modernos del mundo, vino a solucionar en parte el grave problema de tránsito en esa ciudad.

En Buenos Aires y otras ciudades es necesario esperar hasta cinco años para obtener la instalación de un teléfono privado en una casa de familia. Por eso son tan populares los teléfonos públicos, ante los cuales hay a todas horas gente haciendo cola.

Un limpiabotas en Bolivia. Un medio humilde pero honesto de ganarse la vida.

En Costa Rica un peón gana aproximadamente el equivalente de dos dólares al día.

Varios de los países latinoamericanos, como Brasil, México, Venezuela y otros, han progresado mucho económicamente en los últimos años. Sin embargo, el problema del desempleo, especialmente entre las clases humildes, persiste en toda América Latina. La causa no es únicamente la mala distribución de la riqueza sino también el crecimiento tan rápido de la población, la cual dobla cada veinticinco años. Afortunadamente nadie se muere de hambre pues siempre se encuentran, para quien los busca, medios honestos de ganarse la vida, aunque en la mayoría de los casos no es más que eso, simplemente "ganarse la vida" y nada más. No es ni remotamente una solución ideal, claro está, pero puede decirse al menos que en América Latina hasta el más pobre puede vivir en condiciones menos trágicas que en otras partes de nuestro mundo.

En Puerto Rico el nivel de vida es más alto y los obreros ganan más.

México. Este humilde trabajador es dueño de su propio negocio, una "fábrica" de telas.

Este boliviano se gana la vida remendando zapatos.

También la mujer latinoamericana comienza a "liberarse". Hoy día la vemos no sólo en su tradicional ocupación de maestra, secretaria o enfermera—como la señorita guatemalteca en la foto de arriba—sino que ya también hay, casi en grado de competencia con el número de hombres en algunas profesiones, doctoras, abogadas, arquitectas, y aún policías—como la guarda de tráfico costarricense que vemos en la foto cumpliendo con su deber.

Una chica mexicana ayudando a su madre a vender los productos que han traído a la ciudad.

Explicar cómo es la juventud latinoamericana, cuáles son sus características generales, es prácticamente imposible. Excepto una cosa: no existe el mundo del "teenager" en el sentido en que existe en los Estados Unidos, con su estilo propio, sus modas, su lenguage especial, sus revistas, su música. Aparte de esta característica general inexistente, para hablar del modo de vida de la juventud latinoamericana sería necesario indicar si uno se refiere al joven de la ciudad, al joven del campo, al de la clase baja, al de la clase media, al de la clase alta, al indio, al blanco, y aun quizá, si uno se refiere a los jóvenes de la costa o a los de la sierra, o a los de éste o a los de aquel país. Sería una tarea imposible dentro del poco espacio que tenemos aquí disponible. De las fotografías de estas páginas se pueden extraer, sin embargo, algunas nociones generales.

Un joven argentino trabajando en un mercado. Probablemente ya él ha dejado la escuela.

Dos chicas mexicanas en el oficio de costureras.

Inauguración de unas competencias deportivas intercolegiales en Venezuela. Pero los deportes y otras actividades sociales no ocupan tanto el tiempo de los estudiantes como en las escuelas de los Estados Unidos.

Muchos estudiantes mexicanos se dedican al estudio de las artes plásticas.

En México, particularmente, la guitarra ocupa un lugar prominente en la vida social de los jóvenes.

En sus ratos libres los estudiantes con frecuencia se reúnen en los parques a charlar y a estudiar.

En América Latina también los estudiantes regresan a sus casas a almorzar.

Aun en Puerto Rico el cine sigue siendo la atracción número uno de los niños.

El "chaperón" es cosa del pasado. Pero en vez del "date" solo, las parejas salen en grupos.

Generalmente, dos o tres parejas se ponen de acuerdo para salir a bailar o ir a un picnic.

Si una pareja anda sola, aun de día, la cosa ya es en serio. Y si van de la manita, peor.

Igual que los hispanos de todas partes, a los de Nueva York les encanta salir a pasear y encontrarse y conversar con sus amigos en la calle, en un café, en los parques y en fiestas.

Los puertorriqueños residen en su mayoría en el Noreste, especialmente en Nueva York y Nueva Jersey. Arriba, una familia puertorriqueña paseando por el Parque Central de Nueva York.

La segunda minoría más grande de los Estados Unidos la componen los diez millones de descendientes de España. Racialmente no son todos españoles puros, pues hay entre ellos también gente de color, mulatos, mestizos e indios. Pero en cuanto a la lengua y a la cultura, su origen sí viene de España, y ambas han dejado un claro impacto en el idioma inglés y la cultura de los Estados Unidos. La mayor parte de estos hispanonorteamericanos está formada por los chicanos, los puertorriqueños y los cubanos, pero deben además incluirse a miles de ecuatorianos, dominicanos, colombianos y otros hispanoamericanos.

Los chicanos constituyen una población de siete millones y medio. Residen principalmente en los estados de Texas, Nuevo México, California, Arizona, Nevada, Utah y Colorado, y son los descendientes de los mexicanos que poblaban esa enorme región, la cual perteneció antes a México. Los chicanos descienden también de los muchos inmigrantes que año tras año han llegado y continúan llegando a este país.

La colonia cubana es quizá la más próspera entre toda la población hispana de los Estados Unidos. Los cubanos residen principalmente en Florida y su población creció muy rápidamente con el éxodo de centenares de miles de ellos causado por la revolución de Fidel Castro. A pesar del cambio abrupto que sufrieron al verse obligados a salir de Cuba, y a la falta del conocimiento del inglés, la gran mayoría de ellos pronto se adaptaron a la vida y costumbres de este país. Probablemente hoy día casi todos estos exilados, y sus hijos en particular, preferirán quedarse a vivir en los Estados Unidos aun ante la oportunidad de poder regresar a una Cuba sin Castro.

Hay sectores enteros de Miami donde casi sólo español se oye hablar y donde predomina todo lo cubano.

Como su oficio en Cuba había sido la fabricación de guitarras, este exilado prosperó fácilmente.

Los cubanos se distinguen entre todos los hispanoamericanos por su temperamento alegre y extrovertido.

PICTORIAL SECTION PHOTOGRAPHS: Positions are indicated in abbreviated form as follows: *t*-top, *c*-center, *b*-bottom, *l*-left, *r*-right.
    Pages **1, 2, 3, 4, 5** *all* Harbrace; **6** *tl, tr, cl* Harbrace, *bl* Keystone, *br* Harbrace; **7** *tl* Harbrace, *cl* UPI, *tr, cr, br* Harbrace; **8, 9, 10, 11, 12, 13** *all* Harbrace; **14** *tl, tr* Harbrace, *bl* Gscheidle, Harbrace, *br* Harbrace; **15, 16, 17, 18** *all* Harbrace; **19** *t* Shostal Associates, *bl* Harbrace, *br* Shostal Associates; **20** *t* Harbrace, *c, b* Shostal Associates; **21** *t* Eric Carle, Shostal Associates, *c* Ed Drews, Photo Researchers, *b* Shostal; **22** *tl* T. Hollyman, Photo Researchers, *c* Stephanie Dinkins, Photo Researchers, *bl* Eric Carlye, Shostal Associates, *tr* Jane Lotta, Photo Researchers; **23** *all* Harbrace; **24** *t* Carl Frank, Photo Researchers, *bl, br* Harbrace; **25, 26** *all* Harbrace; **27** *tl* Harbrace, *tr* Shostal Associates, *br* Harbrace; **28, 29, 30** *all* Harbrace; **31** *tl, tr* Eric Carlye, Shostal Associates, *c, b,* Harbrace; **32** *t* M. L. Carlebach, Nancy Palmer Photo Agency, *cl, cr* Peggo Cromer, Nancy Palmer Photo Agency.